ELEGANT COMEDY, TRAGEDY

S0-DSZ-014

A London lothario poses as a eunuch to gain access to other men's willing wives . . .

Anthony and Cleopatra share an immortal moment of love while their world crumbles around them . . .

King Lear triumphs over his daughters' betrayal . . .

In the noble city of Venice the innocence of a beautiful woman is threatened with ravishment . . .

Sophisticated rakes from the city and sturdy gentlemen from the country compete in the lists of love . . .

As cool a pair of lovers as ever played with fire spin a gossamer web of intrigue to satisfy their mutual desire . . .

All these unforgettable players
take center stage in

THE SIGNET CLASSIC BOOK OF RESTORATION DRAMA

RONALD BERMAN is the former Chairman of the National Endowment for the Humanities and is presently teaching English at the University of California at San Diego.

THE SIGNET CLASSIC BOOK OF *RESTORATION DRAMA*

Edited and with an Introduction by
RONALD BERMAN

A SIGNET CLASSIC
NEW AMERICAN LIBRARY
TIMES MIRROR
NEW YORK AND SCARBOROUGH, ONTARIO
THE NEW ENGLISH LIBRARY LIMITED, LONDON

SIGNET, SIGNET CLASSICS, MENTOR, PLUME, MERID-
IAN AND NAL BOOKS are published *in the United States* by
The New American Library, Inc., 1633 Broadway, New York,
New York 10019, *in Canada* by The New American Library of
Canada Limited, 81 Mack Avenue, Scarborough, Ontario M1L
1M8, *in the United Kingdom* by The New English Library
Limited, Barnard's Inn, Holborn, London EC1N 2JR, England.

First Printing, October, 1980

1   2   3   4   5   6   7   8   9

PRINTED IN THE UNITED STATES OF AMERICA

CONTENTS

v

GENERAL INTRODUCTION

History

The phrase *Restoration* refers to May 25, 1660, the day when Puritan rule in England ended and Charles II returned from exile. Historians have used the term to describe his entire reign, which lasted until 1685. Eventually, common use extended it even more, and is now taken to cover not only a historical period but a literary one as well. As such it is now generally used to identify all drama produced in England until the end of the seventeenth century, and even a little beyond.

King James I, the grandfather of Charles II, inherited the crown from his cousin Queen Elizabeth in 1603. Although England was divided by opposing religious and political factions, Elizabeth had managed to keep peace through compromise. The equilibrium she had maintained was broken when James demanded religious conformity and asserted his "divine right" to rule. He alienated the large and powerful community of Puritans, and insisted on the right of the King to dominate Parliament.

Charles I inherited the kingdom in 1625, and from that time until his execution in 1649 he was at odds with many of his subjects. Charles I tried to abridge the powers of Parliament; he raised taxes illegally and misused their proceeds; he tried to force a common worship on dissenters; finally, he appointed advisors like Bishop Laud, who urged him on in the exercise of powers he did not legally or actually possess. The result was the Civil War and the defeat of the royalists. Oliver Cromwell, after some maneuvering, became Lord Protector, and from his accession until 1660 England was a Puritan commonwealth.

Charles II was nothing like his father. During his exile he had evidently thought a good deal about how kings kept their thrones. After his restoration he learned to rule by compromise, much as Elizabeth had, and to exercise a good deal of personal forbearance. We tend to think of him as being personally immoral, which was true enough—he had more mistresses than Henry VIII had wives, and children by many of them. But he ought to be remembered for more than Nell Gwyn, the Duchess of Portsmouth, and the rest of his harem. Charles II was an able diplomat and administrator.

We should recall the things that did *not* happen during the Restoration. England avoided the necessity of a standing army and heavy taxes. Charles maneuvered between the rival demands of Whigs and Tories. He resisted the temptation to make religion yet once more a kind of warfare. Charles tried to ease conflicts rather than aggravate them; as a result he reigned until he died of natural causes, which was not a small accomplishment for a Stuart king.

It was in the realm of culture that Charles II made some of his most impressive achievements. He not only helped found the Royal Society, which event marked the beginning of modern science, but he was also the patron of poets, philosophers, and dramatists. His court was hospitable to men of letters. We may think of him as being mainly the patron of actresses, but he was the chief patron of a new national drama as well. Perhaps chief among the limited virtues of the Restoration was that its tolerance made good drama once more possible in England; a drama whose level has not been approached in the last three hundred years.

The Stage

The theaters had been closed by a Puritan parliament in 1642 for what the Puritans considered their public immorality. With few exceptions, there were no productions in London for most of a generation. With the return of Charles II, theater companies were once again formed. There were two of them, the King's Company and the Duke's Company, sharing a monopoly of dramatic performance, and as their names implied, they were under royal patronage.

The standard reference for scholarship, *The London Stage 1660–1700*, indicates five major accomplishments of the Restoration stage. First among these was the creation of companies themselves. Second was the revolutionary introduction of women in drama. The first actresses—and evidently some of the best ever—appeared only after 1660, breaking the long tradition of female roles being played by subadolescent boys. A third development was the modern playhouse, with its divisions of pit, boxes, and galleries. Fourth was the invention and development of movable scenery. And last was the enlargement of the theatrical program to include music, dance, and other forms of accompaniment.

Although drama had been restored, it was by no means liberated. All plays were subject to censorship both before and after the fact. Certain topics (essentially those dealing with rebellion against monarchy) were prohibited, but censorship did not seriously impede production. There were many things to write about besides politics, and literally hundreds of plays were performed in this period. To attend them was an essential part of social life. Samuel Pepys in his famous *Diary* notes the remark of Thomas Killigrew, manager of the King's Company, who had said in 1667 that not only members of the Court, "but all civil people do think they may come" to the theater. From the King down to his lowest subject, the drama had become an institution.

The Audience

The hundreds of prologues and epilogues to Restoration drama are a valuable source for our knowledge of what authors may have thought about their audience, but they are not especially reliable about the character of that audience. It was a convention for playwrights to complain of the manners and expectations of those who paid for their craft, to include the audience in their satire. *The Country Wife* describes playgoers as fops and bullies; in *All for Love* they are something worse:

> What flocks of critics hover here today,
> As vultures wait on armies for their prey,
> All gaping for the carcass of a play!

In this and other comments we see the Restoration audience constantly described as whores and their keepers; noisy bullies, intolerant and boring critics; as degenerate aristocrats and a stupid middle class; as every possible variety of rake, cully, and coquette. The audience itself became a dramatic character. There was truth in fiction: audiences were noisy and rude. Prostitutes or "vizard-masks" worked the theaters as part of a regular beat, inside and out, during the performance and after. There were sword fights and caterwauling, assaults and antisocial amusements of every kind when the curtain was up as well as when it was down. Pepys' *Diary* informs us that the Duke of Buckingham "did soundly beat" Henry Killigrew at a Saturday performance in 1667, "and take his sword, and make a fool of, till the fellow prayed him to spare his life."

But the best indication we have about the character of the audience is that it mixed license with appreciation and had its moments of silence. Those moments may have been all too brief: Pepys complains that one performance was completely drowned out by the critical observations of Sir Charles Sedley, delivered at full bore over the actors' speeches. Pepys says ruefully that he "lost the pleasure of the play wholly" while he was being edified. Yet the important things to remember are that the audience came in numbers large enough to support the drama for nearly half a century; that it viewed theater attendance as part of the obligation or attraction of social life; and that it was sufficiently knowledgeable to find portraits of character or social class on the stage worth comparison with life as it was actually experienced. The audience may have had an adversary relationship with those who wrote, but it understood and appreciated what it saw.

Drama and Criticism

Modern literary criticism begins in the Restoration and it is only natural to read what the critics said as if that were what the playwrights did. But it would be misleading to suggest that drama can only be interpreted through criticism. Comedy in the Restoration was supposed to correct social behavior: to shame vice, make affectation ridiculous, and introduce moral standards into its art. Many Restoration writers agreed with these stated purposes—in about the same way as a lawyer who insists he respects the law, but continually tries to evade it. Comic writers were not guided by prior rules of criticism, nor did they live up to moral and aesthetic standards. Some Restoration comedies are pornographic and don't pretend to a great deal of redeeming social value. Yet others have far too much farce, mugging, and tomfoolery to please the critics, although they do very well with the audience. The theories of criticism did not provide comedy with the idea that it should be a battle of style or wit. Nor was criticism comprehensive enough to understand that comedy might be interested in ideas as well as in morals. Many of the themes of comedy were developed independently of critical advice. In the case of comedy at least, the drama was far ahead of its critics.

There is somewhat more to say about the relationship of tragedy to the criticism imposed upon it and accepted by it. Like comedy, the definition of tragedy came ultimately from Aristotle, or what the Restoration thought was Aristotle. A certain amount of misinterpretation was involved. By the late seventeenth century the play was supposed to elicit both passionate emotion and moral purgation. The rhetoric of Restoration tragedy is so powerful because of the conception shared by authors and critics alike that terror and pity must be described, staged, and aroused in the audience. Dryden wrote in 1679 in his preface to *Troilus and Cressida* that "Philosophy instructs, but it performs its work by precept; which is not delightful, or not so delightful as example. To purge the passions by example, is therefore the particular instruction which belongs to Tragedy." The effect was to encourage heroic drama, exemplified by Dryden's *All for Love,* and pathetic drama, like Otway's *Venice Preserved.* In the former we see the debate of a great soul torn between love and honor and in the latter the effect of suffering upon sensibility.

Critics and playwrights accepted the canon of probability. Thomas Rymer's essay on Shakespeare's *Othello* is one of the more interesting attempts of the Restoration to impose order upon the drama it had inherited. In this essay Rymer tries to make tragedy *reasonable:* he is driven ultimately to condemn Shakespeare because Othello seems not to have had the dignity of a general and because Desdemona has been careless with her handkerchief! Rymer is indignant because Desdemona dies without a trial, but perhaps what most irritates him is not the failure of human but of poetic justice. Restoration criticism took seriously also the canon of morality. Shakespeare's *King Lear* as "translated" by Nahum Tate is a splendid example of poetic justice: the play ends with the wedding of Cordelia and Edgar and the "Restoration" of the King. As for *Othello,* its moral effect is what matters:

> What can remain with the Audience to carry home with them from this sort of Poetry, for their use and edification? How can it work, unless (instead of settling the mind, and purging our passions) to delude our senses, disorder our thoughts, addle our brain, pervert our affections, hair our imaginations, corrupt our appetite, and

fill our head with vanity, confusion, Tintamarre, and
Jingle-jangle. . . .

From Rymer's point of view, and from that of Restoration
thought, the least satisfying part of Elizabethan drama was
its tragic vision. For Restoration writers, tragedy was a matter
of character and decision, taking place in a universe much
more rational than that perceived by those who came before
them. Tragedy was a social experience—Rymer's anxiety about
unpurged passions indicates that serious drama was thought
to be not only moral but therapeutic.

There was a thriving critical debate during the Restoration
about the opposition of rhyme and blank verse, and over the
so-called unities of time, place, and action. A play was,
supposedly, about a particular action taking place in a single
location within a definite time—within, in fact, a twenty-four-
hour period. But the reader will see that ideas about form were
often ignored by authors. They agreed with critics that the
affective power of a work was important, and perhaps defini-
tive. But they were not conscientious about following the
ground rules of contemporary criticism: for the playwright,
at least, the major aspects of drama were character, language,
and ideas.

Social Themes

The reader of *The Country Wife, The Squire of Alsatia, The
Man of Mode*, and many other Restoration comedies will see
that certain oppositions have been intentionally constructed.
Comedy had for centuries poised the young against the old,
the rich against the poor, and the clever against the merely
moral. Restoration comedy, which was very self-conscious
about its modernity, added some other conflicts. There are
wits against fops; the present against the past; the upper
against the middle class; and libertine against stolid citizen.
One of the more common oppositions of Restoration comedy
is that between country and city, which is to say between
opposing social values.

The country in Restoration comedy is both innocent and
ignorant: like Touchstone in the Forest of Arden, the playwright satirizes pastoral life. He sees it in all its bovine
placidity. In politics, the country is viewed as the home of
outmoded ideas. In *The Squire of Alsatia* those who are
country-bred understand neither education, ideas, nor style.

The country is a prison of moral prejudices. In Congreve's *The Way of the World* country values are hopelessly dull. And in Wycherley's *The Country Wife* existence outside London is made to seem a kind of imprisonment. It is only in the world of London that intelligence and pleasure are to be found.

The Restoration comic dramatist identifies with certain of the values of his audience. His heroes are city-bred, fashionable, and upper-class. They are opposed to *both* Cavalier and Puritan ideals, and frequently satirize both. The moral tradition of Renaissance poetry has its comeuppance in Restoration comedy: all those Horatian poems about the delights of country simplicity are made to seem ridiculous by heroes who loathe quiet, geniality, and the solace of Nature. The protagonist of Restoration comedy is recognizably at one with his audience, and with posterity.

Where the theme of lyric and pastoral poetry (and certain forms of drama-like masque) is innocent love, that of Restoration tragedy and comedy is sexual love. Where pastoral is ideal and mythical, Restoration drama is highly realistic. London symbolizes a new understanding of life. The London wit is not simply clever and opportunistic: he is rational, materialistic, and self-conscious. He often serves as the voice of new social ideas. And, for the wit, London is not only a place but a state of mind.

Restoration comedy in particular is insistently aware of social change. In Shadwell's *The Virtuoso* one of the principal dupes, Snarl, says that he scorns "your filthy, lascivious beasts of this age." He prefers to idealize the age of Cavaliers, with its elegant manners and conventions of heroic passion. But his view is not shared by the two witty heroes of the play, one of whom says of the past, "There was the same wenching then; only they dissembled it. They added hypocrisy to fornication, and so made two sins of what we make but one." Etherege's *The Man of Mode* is a kind of extended joke in five acts on the triumph of modernity. The libertine hero, Dorimant, disguises himself as a gentleman of "forms and ceremonies" because he understands their appeal to the little minds of his adversaries. For himself, he prefers the rather brutal honesty about personal relationships that the Restoration promoted.

Because politics was a forbidden subject, it is difficult to generalize about the social or cultural implications of Restoration tragedies. Some critics have contended that the tragedy of this period was either escapist or entertainment, that is without real social content. Others have remarked that the heroes of this genre represent a new attitude toward the values of the Renaissance. The vast number of humanist writings on morality, responsibility, chastity, duty, and the myriad other social and personal virtues was a more than literary bequest to the late seventeenth century. But the attitude of Restoration drama towards this inheritance was skeptical. In heroic tragedy both protagonist and adversaries share enormous egotism and show crushing self-sufficiency. They are willing slaves to their passions. They can be, almost to the point of parody, self-justifying and self-conscious. If the tragedies do not show a public or political field of activity, they do present a powerful and searching insight into modern individualism.

Drama and Ideas

Many an argument has raged about the "influence" of Hobbes on Dryden and others, or the place that John Locke may have had in the minds of writers and in the speeches of their *personae*. Compromise for its own sake is no solution, but in this case one might conclude that Restoration drama, while artistically independent, maintained a strong and natural interest in a number of ideas. No matter how independent the stage was, it had to exist in a world necessarily alive to doctrines old and new, religious and secular, social and psychological. There seems to be no point in exempting the drama from the influence ideas had during the seventeenth century on other forms of poetry and prose.

In *The Conquest of Granada*, Part I, Dryden makes his hero something of a philosopher:

> I am as free as nature first made man
> 'Ere the base Laws of Servitude began,
> When wild in woods the noble savage ran.

This is more than high-sounding rhetoric, because the intent plainly is to compare human and natural laws, and to suggest (a century before Rousseau) the conflict between them. The psychology of these lines indicates something especially characteristic of modern or post-Renaissance times, the conception of the self as the ultimate judge of values and experience. If we look at *Venice Preserved* we can see that it is full of debates on history, philosophy, marriage, friendship—even politics—and, like Dryden's plays, it is about the role of nature in our lives. When Pierre persuades Jaffeir to join him in a conspiracy against the Senate, he invokes ideas that transcend the business of the stage:

> Nay, it's a cause thou will be fond of *Jaffeir.*
> For it is founded on the noblest basis,
> Our liberties, our natural inheritance;
> There's no religion, no hypocrisy in it.

The point then is not whether Dryden read Hobbes, or Shadwell knew Locke, but the extent to which Restoration drama indicates awareness of ideas circulating almost invisibly through seventeenth-century society. The reader may want to follow closely the invocations of nature in *Venice Preserved,* and to see how far the idea of heroic self-justification is pursued in *All for Love.*

The Theater of Social Life

The Country Wife begins by establishing the place of the theater-house in fashionable life. Sparkish tells Horner that he cannot bear to miss a new play at its first performance and Horner tells Pinchwife that he saw him in the gallery "with a pretty country wench." Margery Pinchwife, the "wench" he has observed, tells Alithea that the play was forgettable, but the actors very handsome. Each of the protagonists tells us something about social expectations and their own: Sparkish is a fop blind to any excellence of performance, wishing only to display *himself* at the theater. Margery is innocent enough to say that she doesn't understand the stage—although she will later put on a different role as a young man, and direct the play to its denouement. As for Horner, he is the greatest "actor" in *The Country Wife,* using the idea of illusion and role-playing to achieve his ends, and reveal some home truths about social life.

Many Restoration plays are about "acting" social roles. *The Man of Mode* begins with a script for a love affair. Dorimant tells us that "the quarrel being thus happily begun, I am to play my part." He is fully aware that his mistress, Loveit, will assume the role of tragic heroine when he tries to break with her, and bring to the performance of that role all of the paraphernalia of tragic passion. Congreve's *The Way of the World* literally sets a stage for that great moment when the aging Lady Wishfort prepares to be seduced. She orders lights, dancers, and music so that her visitor "may be entertained" in more ways than one. She creates a setting identical to the theater itself, in which social life and dramatic illusion are seen to correspond to each other.

Dryden's Cleopatra in *All for Love* is not only a consummate actress who knows how to put on emotions and expressions as required, but a great director as well. We know that because of what Charmion tells her when she returns from attempting to influence Antony's departure:

> I told my message,
> Just as you gave it, broken and disordered;
> I numbered in it all your sighs and tears.

And *Venice Preserved*, in a famous passage, implies the powerful difference between appearance and emotional actuality:

> I never lay by his decrepit side,
> But all that night I pondered on my grave.

"Acting" was used to convey the essential falsity of social relationships. It suggested how individuals might delude others and themselves. It suggested psychological ambiguities. It defined a split between the externals of manner, style, and appearance, and the internal conditions of consciousness and feeling. Shakespeare had said that all the world's a stage, and the Restoration seems to have taken that with renewed seriousness. The stage was one of its great institutions, and the idea of acting one of its great metaphors.

BIBLIOGRAPHY

The eleven volumes of *The London Stage 1660–1800* have a great deal of information on the day-to-day life of the theaters. The first part has been separately published as *The London Stage 1660–1700* (Carbondale, 1968). It is essential for a factual background to criticism. The best historical discussion of Restoration drama is Robert D. Hume's *The Development of English Drama in the Late Seventeenth Century* (Oxford, 1976). For the most comprehensive coverage of Restoration drama in the context of its time see James Sutherland, *English Literature of the Late Seventeenth Century* (Oxford, 1969).

There are a number of excellent historical studies of the Restoration. One of the oldest is also one of the best: Macauley's *History of England from the Accession of James II* (London, 1849). It offers a very detailed account of court life, as well as some highly positive opinions about that life. Some standard interpretations of the period are G. N. Clark's *The Later Stuarts, 1660–1714* (Oxford, 1934) and David Ogg, *England in the Reign of Charles II* (Oxford, 1956).

For the background of ideas there are two important books by Basil Willey: *The Seventeenth-Century Background* (London, 1934) and *The Eighteenth-Century Background* (London, 1940). Two excellent books on literature and ideas are Louis Bredvold's *The Intellectual Milieu of John Dryden* (Ann Arbor, 1934) and Dale Underwood's *Etherege and the Seventeenth-Century Comedy of Manners* (New Haven, 1957).

For collections of critical essays on the plays and their background see John Loftis, *Restoration Drama: Modern Essays in Criticism* (New York, 1966); Bernard Harris and John Russell Brown, *Restoration Theatre* (London, 1965); and Boris Ford, *From Dryden to Johnson* (London, 1957).

The following are good general-purpose books on tragedy, comedy, and the stage: Thomas Fujimura, *The Restoration*

11

Comedy of Wit (Princeton, 1952); Arthur Kirsch, *Dryden's Heroic Dramas* (Princeton, 1965); Allardyce Nicoll, *A History of Restoration Drama, 1660–1700* (Cambridge, 1952); Eric Rothstein, *Restoration Tragedy* (Madison, 1967); John H. Smith, *The Gay Couple in Restoration Comedy* (Cambridge, Mass., 1948); John H. Wilson, *A Preface to Restoration Drama* (Boston, 1965).

The standard collection of criticism by Restoration authors is Joel Spingarn, *Critical Essays of the Seventeenth Century* (Oxford, 1908). The *Essays of John Dryden* have been edited by W. P. Ker (Oxford, 1900). Since Dryden was the central literary figure of the Restoration, much of the study of that period revolves around his work.

The individual authors covered in this volume have been the subject of varying amounts and kinds of criticism. Of the many books written about Dryden, the reader may wish to acquaint himself with Mark Van Doren's *John Dryden* (New York, 1946) and Charles Ward's *The Life of John Dryden* (Chapel Hill, 1961). Two very good collections of essays on Dryden are *Dryden: Twentieth-Century Views,* ed. B. N. Schilling (Englewood Cliffs, N.J., 1963) and *Essential Articles for the Study of John Dryden,* ed. H. T. Swedenberg, Jr. (New York, 1966).

Because so much of the writing devoted to the other authors in this volume is in the form of notes or essays, the reader should consult two sources listing them: the annual volume of *Restoration and Eighteenth-Century Theatre Research* and the bibliography section of James Sutherland's *English Literature of the Late Seventeenth Century* (Oxford, 1969). For Congreve, see Kenneth Muir, "The Comedies of William Congreve," in *Restoration Theatre,* ed. Bernard Harris and John Russell Brown (London, 1965). See also John Loftis, *Comedy and Society from Congreve to Fielding* (Stanford, 1959) and Norman Holland, *The First Modern Comedies* (Cambridge, Mass., 1959).

Robert Hume's *The Development of English Drama in the Late Seventeenth Century* (Oxford, 1976) has a useful review of studies on Thomas Otway. See also Aline Taylor, *Next to Shakespeare* (Durham, 1950), which is a full-length study of Otway's plays on the stage. For Shadwell, see A. S. Borgman's account of his career, *Thomas Shadwell: His Life and Comedies* (New York, 1928). John H. Smith has an important essay, "Shadwell, the Ladies, and the Change in Comedy," *Modern Philology,* xlvi (1948), 22–33.

Nahum Tate's *The History of King Lear* has been edited by James Black (Lincoln, Nebraska, 1975) and contains an up-to-date general introduction on his life and works. There is a worthwhile account of his adaptations in Hazelton Spencer's *Shakespeare Improved* (New York, 1927). The best place to begin study of Wycherley is the excellent edition of *The Complete Plays of William Wycherley* by Gerald Weales (Garden City, New York, 1966). See also the books by Holland and Hume noted above, and Rose Zimbardo's *Wycherley's Drama* (New Haven, 1965).

THE COUNTRY WIFE
⤞ A Comedy ⤝
1675

William Wycherley

INTRODUCTORY NOTE

William Wycherley was born into a Royalist family at Clive, near Shrewsbury, in 1641. He was educated first in France and then spent some time at Oxford. Wycherley's first play, *Love in a Wood,* was very successful at its opening in 1671, winning him the recognition of the audience and the patronage of the Duchess of Cleveland. By the time *The Country Wife* appeared in 1675 Wycherley had an established reputation. Things went badly after 1680, when he married the Countess of Drogheda in opposition to the wishes of the King. After this Wycherley was involved in lawsuits and imprisoned for a time in the Fleet for debt. He was released after four years' imprisonment in 1686, and granted a pension by James II. But, when the Stuart reign ended a few years later, so did Wycherley's new security. He lived on until his seventies, in retirement and in debt. Before his death in 1715 he made the acquaintance of Alexander Pope and passed on to him ideas about poetry and information about his life and times.

The Country Wife, Wycherley's third comedy, was produced in 1675 while he was still in favor. It was very well received and kept its popularity for the rest of Wycherley's lifetime. It has been one of the most frequently produced Restoration plays in the twentieth century, and is generally taken to be one of the best and most representative plays of its age. *The Country Wife* is a comedy of disguise and intrigue. Although it is very much about sex, it might be said to be profane rather than obscene: there is no attempt to make sexuality central to the play. It is witty about the idea of sex rather than pornographic. For a comedy of its reputation, its pleasures are unexpectedly intellectual, a matter of the library rather than the bedroom, inviting comparison with other works of satire upon which it may be based, like Ben Jonson's

Volpone and the poems of Juvenal. If the hero of Wycherley is disguised, he brings other characters into the open.

The play's opposed contexts are the country, with its innocence and naturalness (and a good deal of ignorance), and the city, with its sophistication and moral freedom. Wycherley's hero is a man of the Restoration: aristocratic, not especially moral, amused by intrigue, sex, and power; and more than a little philosophical. He and the other "London" characters sum up a world that is a comic version of Hobbes' *Leviathan*. In this world self-interest if not self-preservation is the greatest good. Horner and Harcourt act the way they do for a number of reasons: because they know what society is like; because physical and intellectual pleasures motivate them; and because their adversaries need punishment.

Horner is himself a powerful satirist. His function is not only the successful pursuit of sex but the dissection of style and ideas. He is poised against "all that force nature, and would be still what she forbids 'em." And he is surprisingly on the side of common sense, as when he says, "Methinks wit is more necessary than beauty, and I think no young woman ugly that has it, and no handsome woman agreeable without it." We ought to be prepared for his assertion of values— which is of course a familiar function of satire—as well as his defiance of moral standards.

The character of Margery Pinchwife brings into the cold and mechanistic London world more than it can really handle. The dogma of London is pleasure, profit, and self-interest, all diminished by her ignorant honesty and more "natural" sense of pleasure. Her husband, who takes pride in being a Machiavellian, is routinely reduced to idiocy by her straightforwardness. Horner's plot is ruined, and the values he lives by made to seem more than a little foolish by this "Damn'd, damn'd loving changeling!" Neither he nor Pinchwife, who live in a world of dismissable pleasures, has ever expected anything so powerfully human. Margery then is truly at the center of this play. Any reasonably good performance will remind us that she is far more than an innocent victim of guile and disguise.

The language of *The Country Wife* generalizes with tremendous power. It is full of aphorisms, epigrams, axioms, arguments, and dialogues on ideas. It tells us what the Restoration thought about love, sex, friendship, honor, reputation, and truth—or at least truthfulness. When Horner says "most men are the contraries to that they would seem," he gives us both a clue to the theme of the play and a verdict that is both psychological and social. If the action of the play is concerned with the pursuit of a beautiful and impossible country girl, its language is concerned with issues that go much farther than that.

The Persons

MR. HORNER
MR. HARCOURT
MR. DORILANT
MR. PINCHWIFE
MR. SPARKISH
SIR JASPAR FIDGET
MRS. MARGERY PINCHWIFE
MRS. ALITHEA
MY LADY FIDGET
MRS. DAINTY FIDGET
MRS. SQUEAMISH
OLD LADY SQUEAMISH

Waiters, Servants, and Attendants
A BOY
A QUACK
LUCY, *Alithea's Maid*

The Scene: London

PROLOGUE

Poets, like cudgelled bullies, never do
At first, or second blow, submit to you;
But will provoke you still, and ne're have done,
Till you are weary first, with laying on:
The late so baffled scribbler[1] of this day,
Though he stands trembling, bids me boldly say,
What we, before most plays are used to do,
For poets out of fear, first draw on you;
In a fierce prologue, the still pit defy,
And e're you speak, like Castril,[2] give the lie;
But though our Bayses[3] battles oft I've fought,
And with bruised knuckles, their dear conquests bought;
Nay, never yet feared odds upon the stage,
In prologue dare not Hector with the age,
But would take quarter from your saving hands,
Though Bays within all yielding countermands,
Says you confederate wits no quarter give,
Therefore his play shan't ask your leave to live:
Well, let the vain rash fop, by huffing so,
Think to obtain the better terms of you;
But we the actors humbly will submit,
Now, and at any time, to a full pit;
Nay, often we anticipate your rage,
And murder poets for you, on our stage:
We set no guards upon our tyring-room;[4]
But when with flying colours, there you come,
We patiently you see, give up to you,
Our poets, virgins, nay our matrons too.

[1] *scribber,* Wycherley himself. His play *The Gentleman Dancing-Master*
(1672) had recently failed.
[2] *Castril,* Comic figure in the popular *Alchemist* (1610) of Ben Jonson.
[3] *Bayses,* poets. Derives from role satirizing Dryden in Buckingham's
The Rehearsal.
[4] *tyring-room,* dressing room.

ACT I

(*Enter* HORNER, *and* QUACK *following him at a distance.*)

HORNER. A quack is as fit for a pimp, as a midwife for a
bawd; they are still but in their way both helpers of
nature.—(*aside*)— Well, my dear doctor, hast thou done
what I desired.

QUACK. I have undone you for ever with the women, and reported you throughout the whole town as bad as a
eunuch, with as much trouble as if I had made you one
in earnest.

HORNER. But have you told all the midwives you know, the
orange wenches at the playhouses, the city husbands, and
old fumbling keepers of this end of the town, for they'll
be the readiest to report it.

QUACK. I have told all the chamber-maids, waiting women,
tyre women, and old women of my acquaintance; nay,
and whispered it as a secret to'em, and to the whisperers
of Whitehall; so that you need not doubt 'twill spread,
and you will be as odious to the handsome young women,
as—

HORNER. As the small pox.—Well—

QUACK. And to the married women of this end of the town,
as—

HORNER. As the great ones; nay, as their own husbands.

QUACK. And to the city dames as anniseed Robin[5] of filthy
and contemptible memory; and they will frighten their
children with your name, especially their females.

HORNER. And cry Horner's coming to carry you away: I am
only afraid 'twill not be believed; you told'em 'twas by

----

[5] *annisseed Robin,* a contemporary hermaphrodite.

an English-French disaster,[6] and an English-French chirurgeon, who has given me at once, not only a cure, but an antidote for the future, against that damn'd malady, and that worse distemper, love, and all other women's evils.

QUACK. Your late journey into France has made it the more credible, and your being here a fortnight before you appeared in public looks as if you apprehended the shame, which I wonder you do not: Well I have been hired by young gallants to belie'em t'other way; but you are the first would be thought a man unfit for women.

HORNER. Dear Mr. Doctor, let vain rogues be contented only to be thought abler men than they are, generally 'tis all the pleasure they have, but mine lies another way.

QUACK. You take, methinks, a very preposterous way to it, and as ridiculous as if we operators in physic should put forth bills to disparage our medicaments, with hopes to gain customers.

HORNER. Doctor, there are quacks in love, as well as physic, who get but the fewer and worse patients, for their boasting; a good name is seldom got by giving it one's self, and women no more than honour are compassed by bragging: Come, come, doctor, the wisest lawyer never discovers[7] the merits of his cause till the trial; the wealthiest man conceals his riches, and the cunning gamester his play; shy husbands and keepers like old rooks[8] are not to be cheated, but by a new unpractised trick; false friendship will pass now no more than false dice upon'em, no, not in the City.

(*Enter* BOY.)

BOY. There are two ladies and a gentleman coming up.

HORNER. A pox, some unbelieving sisters of my former acquaintance, who I am afraid, expect their sense should be satisfied of the falsity of the report.

No—this formal fool and women!

(*Enter* SIR JASPAR FIDGET, LADY FIDGET, *and* MRS. DAINTY FIDGET.)

---

[6] *English-French disaster*, venereal disease.
[7] *discovers*, reveals.
[8] *rooks*, confidence men or crooks.

QUACK. His wife and sister.

SIR JASPAR. My coach breaking just now before your door, sir, I look upon as an occasional reprimand to me, sir, for not kissing your hands, sir, since your coming out of France, sir; and so my disaster, sir, has been my good fortune, sir; and this is my wife, and sister, sir.

HORNER. What then, sir?

SIR JASPAR. My lady, and sister, sir.—Wife, this is Master Horner.

LADY FIDGET. Master Horner, husband!

SIR JASPAR. My lady, my Lady Fidget, sir.

HORNER. So, sir.

SIR JASPAR. Won't you be acquainted with her, sir? So the report is true, I find, by his coldness or aversion to the sex; but I'll play the wag with him.   (*aside*) Pray salute my wife, my Lady, sir.

HORNER. I will kiss no man's wife, sir, for him, sir; I have taken my eternal leave, sir, of the sex already, sir.

SIR JASPAR. Hah, hah, hah; I'll plague him yet.   (*aside*) Not know my wife, sir?

HORNER. I do know your wife, sir, she's a woman, sir, and consequently a monster, sir, a greater monster than a husband, sir.

SIR JASPAR. A husband; how, sir?

HORNER. So, sir; (*makes horns.*)[9] but I make no more cuckolds, sir.

SIR JASPAR. Hah, hah, hah, Mercury, Mercury.[10]

LADY FIDGET. Pray, Sir Jaspar, let us be gone from this rude fellow.

DAINTY. Who, by his breeding, would think, he had ever been in France?

LADY FIDGET. Foh, he's but too much a French fellow, such as hate women of quality and virtue, for their love to their husbands, Sir Jaspar; a woman is hated by'em as much for loving her husband, as for loving their money: But pray, let's be gone.

HORNER. You do well, madam, for I have nothing that you came for: I have brought over not so much as a bawdy

---

[9] *makes horns*, one finger atop each ear: the universal sign of the cuckold.

[10] *Mercury*, used in treatment of venereal disease.

picture, new postures,[11] nor the second part of the *Escole de Filles;*[12] nor—

QUACK. Hold, for shame, sir; what d'ye mean? you'll ruin yourself forever with the sex—   (*apart to* HORNER.)

SIR JASPAR. Hah, hah, hah, hah, he hates women perfectly I find.

DAINTY. What pity 'tis he should.

LADY FIDGET. Ay, he's a base rude fellow for't; but affectation makes not a woman more odious to them than virtue.

HORNER. Because your virtue is your greatest affectation, madam.

LADY FIDGET. How, you saucy fellow, would you wrong my honour?

HORNER. If I could.

LADY FIDGET. How d'ye mean, sir?

SIR JASPAR. Hah, hah, hah, no, he can't wrong your ladyship's honour, upon my honour; he poor man—hark you in your ear—a mere eunuch.

LADY FIDGET. O filthy French beast, foh, foh; why do we stay? let's be gone; I can't endure the sight of him.

SIR JASPAR. Stay but till the chairs come, they'll be here presently.

LADY FIDGET. No, no.

SIR JASPAR. Nor can I stay longer; 'tis—let me see, a quarter and a half quarter of a minute past eleven; the council will be sat, I must away: business must be preferred always before love and ceremony with the wise, Mr. Horner.

HORNER. And the impotent, Sir Jaspar.

SIR JASPAR. Ay, ay, the impotent, Master Horner, hah, ha, ha.

LADY FIDGET. What leave us with a filthy man alone in his lodgings?

SIR JASPAR. He's an innocent man now, you know; pray stay, I'll hasten the chairs to you. —Mr. Horner, your servant, I should be glad to see you at my house; pray, come and dine with me, and play at cards with my wife after dinner, you are fit for women at that game yet; hah, ha— 'Tis as much a husband's prudence to provide innocent diversion for a wife, as to hinder her unlawful pleasures; and he had better employ her than let her employ herself.   (*aside*)
Farewell.   (*Exit* SIR JASPAR.)

---

[11] *postures*, illustrations of sexual acts.
[12] *Escole de Filles*, title of a pornographic book.

HORNER. Your servant, Sir Jaspar.

LADY FIDGET. I will not stay with him, foh—

HORNER. Nay, madam, I beseech you stay, if it be but to see I can be as civil to ladies yet, as they would desire.

LADY FIDGET. No, no, foh, you cannot be civil to ladies.

DAINTY. Not as civil as ladies would desire.

LADY FIDGET. No, no, no, foh, foh, foh.

(*Exeunt* LADY FIDGET *and* DAINTY.)

QUACK. Now I think, I, or you yourself rather, have done your business with the women.

HORNER. Thou art an ass, don't you see already upon the report and my carriage, this grave man of business leaves his wife in my lodgings, invites me to his house and wife, who before would not be acquainted with me out of jealousy.

QUACK. Nay, by this means you may be the more acquainted with the husbands, but the less with the wives.

HORNER. Let me alone, if I can but abuse the husbands, I'll soon disabuse the wives: Stay—I'll reckon you up the advantages I am like to have by my stratagem: First, I shall be rid of all my old acquaintances, the most insatiable sorts of duns, that invade our lodgings in a morning: And next to the pleasure of making a new mistress, is that of being rid of an old one, and of all old debts; love when it comes to be so, is paid the most unwillingly.

QUACK. Well, you may be so rid of your old acquaintances; but how will you get any new ones?

HORNER. Doctor, thou wilt never make a good chemist, thou art so incredulous and impatient; ask but all the young fellows of the town, if they do not lose more time like huntsmen, in starting the game, than in running it down; one knows not where to find'em, who will, or will not; women of quality are so civil, you can hardly distinguish love from good breeding, and a man is often mistaken; but now I can be sure, she that shews an aversion to me loves the sport, as those women that are gone, whom I warrant to be right:[13] And then the next thing is your women of honour, as you call'em, are only chary of their reputations, not their persons, and 'tis scandal they would avoid, not men: Now may I have, by the reputation of a eunuch, the privileges of one; and be seen in a lady's chamber, in a morning as early as her husband;

13 *those women ... right,* i.e., Lady Fidget and Dainty can be had.

kiss virgins before their parents, or lovers; and may be in short the *Pas par tout*[14] of the town. Now, Doctor.

QUACK. Nay, now you shall be the doctor; and your process is so new, that we do not know but it may succeed.

HORNER. Not so new neither, *Probatum est,* Doctor.

QUACK. Well, I wish you luck and many patients whil'st I go to mine. (*Exit* QUACK.)

(*Enter* HARCOURT, *and* DORILANT *to* HORNER.)

HARCOURT. Come, your appearance at the play yesterday, has I hope hardened you for the future against the women's contempt, and the men's raillery; and now you'll abroad as you were wont.

HORNER. Did I not bear it bravely?

DORILANT. With a most theatrical impudence; nay more than the orange-wenches show there, or a drunken vizard mask, or a great-bellied actress; nay, or the most impudent of creatures, an ill poet; or what is yet more impudent, a second-hand critic.

HORNER. But what say the ladies, have they no pity?

HARCOURT. What ladies? the vizard masks[15] you know never pity a man when all's gone, though in their service.

DORILANT. And for the women in the boxes, you'd never pity them, when 'twas in your power.

HARCOURT. They say 'tis pity, but all that deal with common women should be served so.

DORILANT. Nay, I dare swear, they won't admit you to play at cards with them, go to plays with'em, or do the little duties which other shadows of men are wont to do for'em.

HORNER. Who do you call shadows of men?

DORILANT. Half men.

HORNER. What, boys?

DORILANT. Ay your old boys, old *beaux garcons*,[16] who like superannuated stallions are suffered to run, feed, and whinney with the mares as long as they live, though they can do nothing else.

HORNER. Well a pox on love and wenching, women serve but to keep a man from better company; though I can't

---

[14] *Pas par tout,* pass-key.
[15] *vizard masks,* prostitutes often wore masks to attend dramatic performances.
[16] *beaux garcons,* playboys.

enjoy them, I shall you the more: good fellowship and friendship are lasting, rational and manly pleasures.

HARCOURT. For all that give me some of those pleasures you call effeminate too, they help to relish one another.

HORNER. They disturb one another.

HARCOURT. No, mistresses are like books; if you pore upon them too much, they doze you, and make you unfit for company; but if used discreetly, you are the fitter for conversation by'em.

DORILANT. A mistress should be like a little country retreat near the town, not to dwell in constantly, but only for a night and away; to taste the town the better when a man returns.

HORNER. I tell you, 'tis as hard to be a good fellow, a good friend, and a lover of women, as 'tis to be a good fellow, a good friend, and a lover of money: you cannot follow both, then choose your side; wine gives you liberty, love takes it away.

DORILANT. Gad, he's in the right on't.

HORNER. Wine gives you joy, love grief and tortures; besides the chirurgeon's. Wine makes us witty, love only sots: wine makes us sleep, love breaks it.

DORILANT. By the world he has reason, Harcourt.

HORNER. Wine makes—

DORILANT. Ay, wine makes us—makes us princes, love makes us beggars, poor rogues, y gad—and wine—

HORNER. So, there's one converted.— No, no, love and wine, oil and vinegar.

HARCOURT. I grant it; love will still be uppermost.

HORNER. Come, for my part I will have only those glorious, manly pleasures of being very drunk, and very slovenly.

(*Enter* BOY.)

BOY. Mr. Sparkish is below, Sir.

HARCOURT. What, my dear friend! a rogue that is fond of me, only I think for abusing him.

DORILANT. No, he can no more think the men laugh at him, than that women jilt him, his opinion of himself is so good.

HORNER. Well, there's another pleasure by drinking, I thought not of; I shall lose his acquaintance, because he cannot drink; and you know 'tis a very hard thing to be rid of him, for he's one of those nauseous offerers at wit, who like the worst fiddlers run themselves into all companies.

HARCOURT. One, that by being in the company of men of sense would pass for one.

HORNER. And may so to the short-sighted world, as a false jewel amongst true ones, is not discerned at a distance; his company is as troublesome to us, as a cuckold's, when you have a mind to his wife's.

HARCOURT. No, the rogue will not let us enjoy one another, but ravishes our conversation, though he signifies no more to't, than Sir Martin Mar-all's gaping, and awkward thrumming upon the lute, does to his man's voice, and music.[17]

DORILANT. And to pass for a wit in town, shows himself a fool every night to us, that are guilty of the plot.

HORNER. Such wits as he, are, to a company of reasonable men, like rooks to the gamesters, who only fill a room at the table, but are so far from contributing to the play, that they only serve to spoil the fancy of those that do.

DORILANT. Nay, they are used like rooks too, snubbed, checked, and abused; yet the rogues will hang on.

HORNER. A pox on'em, and all that force nature, and would be still what she forbids'em; affectation is her greatest monster.

HARCOURT. Most men are the contraries to that they would seem; your bully, you see, is a coward with a long sword; the little humbly fawning physician with his ebony cane, is he that destroys men.

DORILANT. The usurer, a poor rogue, possessed of moldy bonds, and mortgages; and we they call spendthrifts, are only wealthy, who lay out our money upon daily new purchases of pleasure.

HORNER. Ay, your arrantest cheat is your trustee, or executor; your jealous man, the greatest cuckold; your churchman, the greatest atheist; and your noisy pert rogue of a wit, the greatest fop, dullest ass, and worst company as you shall see: for here he comes.

(*Enter* SPARKISH *to them.*)

SPARKISH. How is't, Sparks, how is't? Well faith, Harry, I must rally thee a little, ha, ha, ha, upon the report in

---

[17] *Sir Martin Mar-all's . . . and music,* fool in a Dryden comedy (1667) who pretended to serenade his mistress while a servant dubbed in voice and music.

town of thee, ha, ha, ha, I can't hold y faith; shall I speak?

HORNER. Yes, but you'll be so bitter then.

SPARKISH. Honest Dick and Frank here shall answer for me, I will not be extreme bitter by the universe.

HARCOURT. We will be bound in ten thousand pound bond, he shall not be bitter at all.

DORILANT. Nor sharp, nor sweet.

HORNER. What, not downright insipid?

SPARKISH. Nay then, since you are so brisk, and provoke me, take what follows; you must know, I was discoursing and rallying with some ladies yesterday, and they happened to talk of the fine new signs in town.

HORNER. Very fine ladies I believe.

SPARKISH. Said I, I know where the best new sign is. Where, says one of the ladies? In Covent Garden, I replied. Said another, In what street? In Russell Street, answered I. Lord says another, I'm sure there was ne're a fine new sign there yesterday. Yes, but there was, said I again, and it came out of France, and has been there a fortnight.

DORILANT. A pox, I can hear no more, prithee.

HORNER. No, hear him out; let him tune his crowd[18] a while.

HARCOURT. The worst music, the greatest preparation.

SPARKISH. Nay faith, I'll make you laugh. It cannot be, says a third lady. Yes, yes, quoth I again. Says a fourth lady,

HORNER. Look to't, we'll have no more ladies.

SPARKISH. No.—then mark, mark, now, said I to the fourth, did you never see Mr. Horner; he lodges in Russell Street, and he's a sign of a man, you know, since he came out of France, heh, hah, he.

HORNER. But the devil take me, if thine be the sign of a jest.

SPARKISH. With that they all fell a laughing, till they bepissed themselves; what, but it does not move you, methinks? well see one had as good go to law without a witness as break a jest without a laughter on one's side.— Come, come, Sparks, but where do we dine, I have left at Whitehall an earl to dine with you.

DORILANT. Why, I thought thou hadst loved a man with a title better than a suit with a French trimming to't.

HARCOURT. Go, to him again.

SPARKISH. No, sir, a wit to me is the greatest title in the world.

18 *crowd*, fiddle.

HORNER. But go dine with your earl, Sir, he may be exceptious;
we are your friends, and will not take it ill to be left,
I do assure you.

HARCOURT. Nay, faith he shall go to him.

SPARKISH. Nay, pray, gentlemen.

DORILANT. We'll thrust you out, if you won't what, disappoint any body for us!

SPARKISH. Nay, dear gentlemen, hear me.

HORNER. No, no, Sir, by no means; pray go, Sir.

SPARKISH. Why, dear rogues.   (*They all thrust him*

DORILANT. No, no.   *out of the room.*)

ALL. Ha, ha, ha.   (SPARKISH *returns.*)

SPARKISH. But, Sparks, pray hear me; what, d'ye think I'll eat
then with gay shallow fops, and silent coxcombs? I think
wit as necessary at dinner as a glass of good wine, and
that's the reason I never have any stomach when I eat
alone.— Come, but where do we dine?

HORNER. Ev'n where you will.

SPARKISH. At Chateline's.

DORILANT. Yes, if you will.

SPARKISH. Or at the Cock.

DORILANT. Yes, if you please.

SPARKISH. Or at the Dog and Partridge.

HORNER. Ay, if you have mind to't, for we shall dine at
neither.

SPARKISH. Pshaw, with your fooling we shall lose the new
play; and I would no more miss seeing a new play the
first day, than I would miss setting in the wit's row;
therefore I'll go fetch my mistress and away.

(*Exit* SPARKISH.)

(*Manent* HORNER, HARCOURT, DORILANT; *Enter to them* MR.
PINCHWIFE.)

HORNER. Who have we here, Pinchwife?

PINCHWIFE. Gentlemen, your humble servant.

HORNER. Well, Jack, by thy long absence from the town, the
grumness[19] of thy countenance, and the slovenliness of
thy habit; I should give thee joy, should I not, of
marriage?

PINCHWIFE. Death does he know I'm married too? I thought
to have concealed it from him at least. (*aside*) My long

---

19 *grumness,* surliness.

stay in the country will excuse my dress, and I have a
suit of law,[20] that brings me up to town, that puts me
out of humour; besides I must give Sparkish tomorrow
five thousand pound to lie with my sister.

HORNER. Nay, you country gentlemen, rather than not purchase, will buy any thing, and he is a cracked title,[21] if we
may quibble: well, but am I to give thee joy, I heard
thou wert married.

PINCHWIFE. What then?

HORNER. Why, the next thing that is to be heard, is thou'rt
a cuckold.

PINCHWIFE. Insupportable name.

HORNER. But I did not expect marriage from such a whoremaster as you, one that knew the town so much, and
women so well.

PINCHWIFE. Why, I have married no London wife.

HORNER. Pshaw, that's all one, that grave circumspection in
marrying a country wife, is like refusing a deceitful
pampered Smithfield jade,[22] to go and be cheated by a
friend in the country.

PINCHWIFE. A pox on him and his simile.   (*aside*)
At least we are a little surer of the breed there, know
what her keeping has been, whether soiled or unsound.

HORNER. Come, come, I have known a clap gotten in Wales,
and there are cousins, justices, clerks, and chaplains in
the country, I won't say coachmen. But she's handsome
and young.

PINCHWIFE. I'll answer as I should do.   (*aside*)
No, no, she has no beauty, but her youth; no attraction,
but her modesty, wholesome, homely, and housewifely,
that's all.

DORILANT. He talks as like a grazier[23] as he looks.

PINCHWIFE. She's too awkward, ill favoured, and silly to
bring to town.

HARCOURT. Then methinks you should bring her, to be taught
breeding.

PINCHWIFE. To be taught; no, sir, I thank you, good wives and

---

20 *suit of law*, lawsuit.
21 *cracked title*, a ruined aristocrat, with a pun intended on his feeble
mind.
22 *Smithfield jade*, Smithfield was a proverbially dishonest horse market.
A jade is either a worthless horse or a whore.
23 *grazier*, cattle feeder.

private soldiers should be ignorant.—I'll keep her from
your instructions, I warrant you.   (aside)

HARCOURT. The rogue is as jealous, as if his wife were not
ignorant.   (aside)

HORNER. Why, if she be ill favoured, there will be less danger
here for you, than by leaving her in the country; we
have such variety of dainties, that we are seldom hungry.

DORILANT. But they have always coarse, constant, swinging
stomachs in the country.

HARCOURT. Foul feeders indeed.

DORILANT. And your hospitality is great there.

HARCOURT. Open house, every man's welcome.

PINCHWIFE. So, so, gentlemen.

HORNER. But prithee, why would'st thou marry her? if she be
ugly, ill-bred, and silly, she must be rich then.

PINCHWIFE. As rich as if she brought me twenty thousand
pound out of this town; for she'll be as sure not to spend
her moderate portion, as a London baggage would be
to spend hers, let it be what it would; so 'tis all one:
then because she's ugly, she's the likelier to be my own;
and being ill-bred, she'll hate conversation; and since
silly and innocent, will not know the difference betwixt a
man of one and twenty, and one of forty.

HORNER. None—to my knowledge; but if she be silly, she'll
expect as much from a man of forty-nine, as from him
of one and twenty: But methinks wit is more necessary
than beauty, and I think no young woman ugly that has
it, and no handsome woman agreeable without it.

PINCHWIFE. 'Tis my maxim, he's a fool that marries, but
he's a greater that does not marry a fool; what is wit
in a wife good for, but to make a man a cuckold?

HORNER. Yes, to keep it from his knowledge.

PINCHWIFE. A fool cannot contrive to make her husband a
cuckold.

HORNER. No, but she'll club with a man that can; and what
is worse, if she cannot make her husband a cuckold,
she'll make him jealous, and pass for one, and then 'tis
all one.

PINCHWIFE. Well, well, I'll take care for one, my wife shall
make me no cuckold, though she had your help, Mr.
Horner; I understand the town, sir.

DORILANT. His help!   (aside)

HARCOURT. He's come newly to town it seems, and has not
heard how things are with him.   (aside)

HORNER. But tell me, has marriage cured thee of whoring, which it seldom does.

HARCOURT. 'Tis more than age can do.

HORNER. No, the word is, I'll marry and live honest; but a marriage vow is like a penitent gamester's oath, and entering into bonds, and penalties to stint himself to such a particular small sum at play for the future, which makes him but the more eager, and not being able to hold out, loses his money again, and his forfeit to boot.

DORILANT. Ay, ay, a gamester will be a gamester, whilst his money lasts; and a whoremaster, whilst his vigour.

HARCOURT. Nay, I have known'em, when they are broke and can lose no more, keep a fumbling with the box in their hands to fool with only, and hinder other gamesters.

DORILANT. That had wherewithal to make lusty stakes.

PINCHWIFE. Well, gentlemen, you may laugh at me, but you shall never lie with my wife, I know the town.

HORNER. But prithee, was not the way you were in better, is not keeping better than marriage?

PINCHWIFE. A pox on't, the jades would jilt me, I could never keep a whore to myself.

HORNER. So then you only married to keep a whore to your self; well, but let me tell you, women, as you say, are like soldiers made constant and loyal by good pay, rather than by oaths and covenants, therefore I'd advise my friends to keep rather than marry; since too I find by your example, it does not serve one's turn, for I saw you yesterday in the eighteen-penny place[24] with a pretty country-wench.

PINCHWIFE. How the devil, did he see my wife then? I sat there that she might not be seen; but she shall never go to a play again.   (*aside*)

HORNER. What, dost thou blush at nine-and-forty, for having been seen with a wench?

DORILANT. No faith, I warrant 'twas his wife, which he seated there out of sight, for he's a cunning rogue, and understands the town.

HARCOURT. He blushes, then 'twas his wife; for men are now more ashamed to be seen with them in public, than with a wench.

---

[24] *eighteen-penny place*, gallery seats in theater usually taken by whores, who did a good deal of business there.

PINCHWIFE. Hell and damnation, I'm undone, since Horner
    has seen her, and they know 'twas she.   (*aside*)
HORNER. But prithee, was it thy wife? she was exceedingly
    pretty; I was in love with her at that distance.
PINCHWIFE. You are like never **to** be nearer to her. Your
    servant, gentlemen.   (*Offers to go.*)
HORNER. Nay, prithee stay.
PINCHWIFE. I cannot, I will not.
HORNER. Come, you shall dine with us.
PINCHWIFE. I have dined already.
HORNER. Come, I know thou hast not; I'll treat thee, dear
    rogue, thou shan't spend none of thy Hampshire money
    today.
PINCHWIFE. Treat me; so, he uses me already like his cuckold.
                                                 (*aside*)
HORNER. Nay, you shall not go.
PINCHWIFE. I must, I have business at home.

                                        (*Exit* PINCHWIFE.)

HARCOURT. To beat his wife, he's as jealous of her, as a
    Cheapside husband of a Covent-garden wife.[25]
HORNER. Why, 'tis as hard to find an old whoremaster without
    jealousy and the gout, as a young one without fear or
    the pox.

        As gout in age, from pox in youth proceeds;
        So wenching past, then jealousy succeeds:
        The worst disease that love and wenching breeds.

ACT II

[SCENE I.]

(MRS. MARGERY PINCHWIFE, *and* ALITHEA: MR. PINCHWIFE
peeping behind at the door.)

MRS. PINCHWIFE. Pray, sister, where are the best fields and
    woods, to walk in in London?
ALITHEA. A pretty question; why, sister! Mulberry Garden,
    and St. James's Park; and for close walks the New
    Exchange.

---

[25] *Cheapside . . . wife,* bourgeois husband of an expensive wife.

MRS. PINCHWIFE. Pray, sister, tell me why my husband looks
    so grum here in town? and keeps me up so close, and
    will not let me go a walking, nor let me wear my best
    gown yesterday?

ALITHEA. O he's jealous, sister.

MRS. PINCHWIFE. Jealous, what's that?

ALITHEA. He's afraid you should love another man.

MRS. PINCHWIFE. How should he be afraid of my loving
    another man, when he will not let me see any but him-
    self.

ALITHEA. Did he not carry you yesterday to a play?

MRS. PINCHWIFE. Ay, but we sat amongst ugly people, he
    would not let me come near the gentry, who sat under
    us, so that I could not see'em: he told me, none but
    naughty women sat there, whom they toused and
    moused;[26] but I would have ventured for all that.

ALITHEA. But how did you like the play?

MRS. PINCHWIFE. Indeed I was aweary of the play, but I
    liked hugeously the actors; they are the goodliest proper-
    est men, sister.

ALITHEA. O but you must not like the actors, sister.

MRS. PINCHWIFE. Ay, how should I help it, sister? pray,
    sister, when my husband comes in, will you ask leave
    for me to go a-walking?

ALITHEA. A-walking, hah, ha; Lord, a country gentlewoman's
    pleasure is the drudgery of a foot-post; and she requires
    as much airing as her husband's horses   (aside)

(*Enter* MR. PINCHWIFE *to them.*)

But here comes your husband; I'll ask, though I'm sure
    he'll not grant it.

MRS. PINCHWIFE. He says he won't let me go abroad, for fear
    of catching the pox.[27]

ALITHEA. Fie, the small pox you should say.

MRS. PINCHWIFE. Oh my dear, dear bud, welcome home; why
    dost thou look so fropish,[28] who has nangered thee?

PINCHWIFE. You're a fool.

(MRS. PINCHWIFE *goes aside, and cries.*)

26 *toused and moused,* handled.
27 *pox,* the great pox was venereal disease.
28 *fropish,* peevish.

ALITHEA. Faith so she is, for crying for no fault, poor tender creature!

PINCHWIFE. What, you would have her as impudent as your self, as errant a jillflirt, a gadder, a magpie, and to say all a mere notorious town-woman?

ALITHEA. Brother, you are my only censurer; and the honour of your family shall sooner suffer in your wife there, than in me, though I take the innocent liberty of the town.

PINCHWIFE. Hark you, mistress, do not talk so before my wife, the innocent liberty of the town!

ALITHEA. Why, pray, who boasts of any intrigue with me? what lampoon has made my name notorious? what ill women frequent my lodgings? I keep no company with any women of scandalous reputations.

PINCHWIFE. No, you keep the men of scandalous reputations company.

ALITHEA. Where? would you not have me civil? answer'em in a box at the plays? in the drawing room at Whitehall? in St. James's Park? Mulberry-garden? or—

PINCHWIFE. Hold, hold, do not teach my wife where the men are to be found; I believe she's the worse for your town documents already; I bid you keep her in ignorance as I do.

MRS. PINCHWIFE. Indeed be not angry with her, bud, she will tell me nothing of the town, though I ask her a thousand times a day.

PINCHWIFE. Then you are very inquisitive to know, I find?

MRS. PINCHWIFE. Not I indeed, dear, I hate London; our place-house in the country is worth a thousand of't, would I were there again.

PINCHWIFE. So you shall I warrant; but were you not talking of plays, and players, when I came in? you are her encourager in such discourses.

MRS. PINCHWIFE. No indeed, dear, she chid me just now for liking the player men.

PINCHWIFE. Nay, if she be so innocent as to own to me her liking them, there is no hurt in't— (aside) Come my poor rogue, but thou lik'st none better than me?

MRS. PINCHWIFE. Yes indeed, but I do, the player men are finer folks.

PINCHWIFE. But you love none better than me?

MRS. PINCHWIFE. You are mine own dear bud, and I know you, I hate a stranger.

PINCHWIFE. Ay, my dear, you must love me only, and like the naughty town women, who only hate their husbands, and love every man else, love plays, visits, fine coaches, fine clothes, fiddles, balls, treats, and so lead a wicked town life.

MRS. PINCHWIFE. Nay, if to enjoy all these things be a town life, London is not so bad a place, dear.

PINCHWIFE. How! if you love me, you must hate London.

ALITHEA. The fool has forbid me discovering to her the pleasures of the town, and he is now setting her a-gog upon them himself.

MRS. PINCHWIFE. But, husband, do the town women love the player men too?

PINCHWIFE. Yes, I warrant you.

MRS. PINCHWIFE. Ay, I warrant you.

PINCHWIFE. Why, you do not, I hope?

MRS. PINCHWIFE. No, no, bud; but why have we no player men in the country?

PINCHWIFE. Ha— Mrs. Minx, ask me no more to go to a play.

MRS. PINCHWIFE. Nay, why, love? I did not care for going; but when you forbid me, you make me as't were desire it.

ALITHEA. So 'twill be in other things, I warrant. (*aside*)

MRS. PINCHWIFE. Pray, let me go to a play, dear.

PINCHWIFE. Hold your peace, I won't.

MRS. PINCHWIFE. Why, love?

PINCHWIFE. Why, I'll tell you.

ALITHEA. Nay if he tell her, she'll give him more cause to forbid her that place. (*aside*)

MRS. PINCHWIFE. Pray, why, dear?

PINCHWIFE. First, you like the actors, and the gallants may like you.

MRS. PINCHWIFE. What, a homely country girl? no bud, nobody will like me.

PINCHWIFE. I tell you, yes, they may.

MRS. PINCHWIFE. No, no, you jest—I won't believe you, I will go.

PINCHWIFE. I tell you then, that one of the lewdest fellows in town, who saw you there, told me he was in love with you.

MRS. PINCHWIFE. Indeed! who, who, pray who wast?

PINCHWIFE. I've gone too far, and slipped before I was aware; how overjoyed she is! (*aside*)

MRS. PINCHWIFE. Was it any Hampshire gallant, any of our neighbours? I promise you, I am beholding to him.

PINCHWIFE. I promise you, you lie; for he would but ruin you, as he has done hundreds: he has no other love for women, but that, such as he, look upon women like basilicks,[29] but to destroy'em.

MRS. PINCHWIFE. Ay, but if he loves me, why should he ruin me? answer me to that: methinks he should not, I would do him no harm.

ALITHEA. Hah, ha, ha.

PINCHWIFE. 'Tis very well; but I'll keep him from doing you any harm, or me either.

(*Enter* SPARKISH *and* HARCOURT.)

But here comes company, get you in, get you in.

MRS. PINCHWIFE. But pray, husband, is he a pretty gentleman, that loves me?

PINCHWIFE. In, baggage, in. (*Thrusts her in: shuts the door.*) What, all the lewd libertines of the town brought to my lodging, by this easy coxcomb! S'death I'll not suffer it.

SPARKISH. Here, Harcourt, do you approve my choice? Dear, little rogue, I told you, I'd bring you acquainted with all my friends, the wits, and— (HARCOURT *salutes*[30] *her.*)

PINCHWIFE. Ay, they shall know her, as well as you yourself will, I warrant you.

SPARKISH. This is one of those, my pretty rogue, that are to dance at your wedding tomorrow; and him you must bid welcome ever, to what you and I have.

PINCHWIFE. Monstrous!— (*aside*)

SPARKISH. Harcourt, how dost thou like her, faith? Nay, dear, do not look down; I should hate to have a wife of mine out of countenance at any thing.

PINCHWIFE. Wonderful!

SPARKISH. Tell me, I say, Harcourt, how dost thou like her? thou hast stared upon her enough to resolve me.

HARCOURT. So infinitely well, that I could wish I had a mistress too, that might differ from her in nothing, but her love and engagement to you.

ALITHEA. Sir, Master Sparkish has often told me, that his acquaintance were all wits and raillieurs, and now I find it.

SPARKISH. No, by the universe, madam, he does not rally now; you may believe him: I do assure you, he is the

---

[29] *basilicks,* mythological serpents (basilisks) whose gaze killed.
[30] *salutes,* kisses. Then a common form of greeting.

honestest, worthiest, true-hearted gentleman—a man of
such perfect honour, he would say nothing to a lady he
does not mean.

PINCHWIFE. Praising another man to his mistress!

HARCOURT. Sir, you are so beyond expectation obliging, that—

SPARKISH. Nay, egad, I am sure you do admire her extremely,
I see't in your eyes.— He does admire you, madam.—
By the world, don't you?

HARCOURT. Yes, above the world, or, the most glorious part
of it, her whole sex; and till now I never thought I
should have envied you, or any man about to marry,
but you have the best excuse for marriage I ever knew.

ALITHEA. Nay, now, sir, I'm satisfied you are of the society
of the wits, and raillieurs, since you cannot spare your
friend, even when he is but too civil to you; but the
surest sign is, since you are an enemy of marriage, for
that I hear you hate as much as business or bad wine.

HARCOURT. Truly, madam, I never was an enemy to marriage,
till now, because marriage was never an enemy to me
before.

ALITHEA. But why, sir, is marriage an enemy to you now?
Because it robs you of your friend here; for you look
upon a friend married, as one gone into a monastery,
that is dead to the world.

HARCOURT. 'Tis indeed, because you marry him; I see, madam,
you can guess my meaning: I do confess heartily and
openly, I wish it were in my power to break the match,
by heavens I would.

SPARKISH. Poor Frank!

ALITHEA. Would you be so unkind to me?

HARCOURT. No, no, 'tis not because I would be unkind to
you.

SPARKISH. Poor Frank, no, gad, 'tis only his kindness to me.

PINCHWIFE. Great kindness to you indeed; insensible fop, let
a man make love to his wife to his face.   (aside)

SPARKISH. Come, dear Frank, for all my wife there that shall
be, thou shalt enjoy me sometimes dear rogue; by my
honour, we men of wit condole for our deceased brother
in marriage, as much as for one dead in earnest: I think
that was prettily said of me, ha Harcourt?—But come
Frank, be not melancholy for me.

HARCOURT. No, I assure you I am not melancholy for you.

SPARKISH. Prithee, Frank, dost think my wife that shall be
there a fine person?

HARCOURT. I could gaze upon her, till I became as blind as you are.

SPARKISH. How, as I am! how!

HARCOURT. Because you are a lover, and true lovers are blind, stockblind.[31]

SPARKISH. True, true; but by the world, she has wit too, as well as beauty: go, go with her into a corner, and try if she has wit, talk to her anything, she's bashful before me.

HARCOURT. Indeed if a woman wants wit in a corner, she has it nowhere.

ALITHEA. Sir, you dispose of me a little before your time.—

(*aside to* SPARKISH)

SPARKISH. Nay, nay, madam let me have an earnest of your obedience, or—go, go, madam—

(HARCOURT *courts* ALITHEA *aside.*)

PINCHWIFE. How, sir, if you are not concerned for the honour of a wife, I am for that of a sister; he shall not debauch her: be a pander to your own wife, bring men to her, let'em make love before your face, thrust'em into a corner together, then leav'em in private! is this your town wit and conduct?

SPARKISH. Hah, ha, ha, a silly wise rogue would make one laugh more than a stark fool, hah, ha: I shall burst. Nay, you shall not disturb'em; I'll vex thee, by the world.

(*Struggles with* PINCHWIFE *to keep him from* HARCOURT *and* ALITHEA.)

ALITHEA. The writings are drawn, sir, settlements made; 'tis too late, sir, and past all revocation.

HARCOURT. Then so is my death.

ALITHEA. I would not be unjust to him.

HARCOURT. Then why to me so?

ALITHEA. I have no obligation to you.

HARCOURT. My love.

ALITHEA. I had his before.

HARCOURT. You never had it; he wants, you see, jealousy, the only infallible sign of it.

ALITHEA. Love proceeds from esteem; he cannot distrust my virtue, besides he loves me, or he would not marry me.

31 *stockblind,* blind as a stock or senseless block of wood.

HARCOURT. Marrying you is no more sign of his love than
bribing your woman, that he may marry you, is a sign
of his generosity: marriage is rather a sign of interest,
than love; and he that marries a fortune, covets a mistress,
not loves her: But if you take marriage for a sign of
love, take it from me immediately.

ALITHEA. No, now you have put a scruple in my head; but in
short, sir, to end our dispute, I must marry him, my
reputation would suffer in the world else.

HARCOURT. No, if you do marry him, with your pardon,
madam, your reputation suffers in the world, and you
would be thought in necessity for a cloak.

ALITHEA. Nay, now you are rude, sir.— Mr. Sparkish, pray
come hither, your friend here is very troublesome, and
very loving.

HARCOURT. Hold, hold—   (*Aside to* ALITHEA)

PINCHWIFE. D'ye hear that?

SPARKISH. Why, d'ye think I'll seem to be jealous, like a
country bumpkin?

PINCHWIFE. No, rather be a cuckold, like a credulous cit.[32]

HARCOURT. Madam, you would not have been so little generous as to have told him.

ALITHEA. Yes, since you could be so little generous, as to
wrong him.

HARCOURT. Wrong him, no man can do't, he's beneath an
injury; a bubble,[33] a coward, a senseless idiot, a wretch
so contemptible to all the world but you, that—

ALITHEA. Hold, do not rail at him, for since he is like to be
my husband, I am resolved to like him: nay, I think I
am obliged to tell him you are not his friend.—Master
Sparkish, Master Sparkish.

SPARKISH. What, what; now dear rogue, has not she wit?

HARCOURT. Not so much as I thought, and hoped she had.

                         (*Speaks surlily.*)

ALITHEA. Mr. Sparkish, do you bring people to rail at you?

HARCOURT. Madam—

SPARKISH. How! no, but if he does rail at me, 'tis but in jest
I warrant; what we wits do for one another, and never
take any notice of it.

---

32 *cit*, citizen or bourgeois.
33 *bubble*, victim.

ALITHEA. He spoke so scurrilously of you, I had no patience to hear him; besides he has been making love to me.

HARCOURT. True, damned tell-tale-woman.   (*aside*)

SPARKISH. Pshaw, to show his parts—we wits rail and make love often, but to show our parts; as we have no affections, so we have no malice, we—

ALITHEA. He said you were a wretch, below an injury.

SPARKISH. Pshaw.

HARCOURT. Damned, senseless, impudent, virtuous jade; well since she won't let me have her, she'll do as good, she'll make me hate her.

ALITHEA. A common bubble.

SPARKISH. Pshaw.

ALITHEA. A coward.

SPARKISH. Pshaw, pshaw.

ALITHEA. A senseless driveling idiot.

SPARKISH. How, did he disparage my parts? Nay, then my honour's concerned, I can't put up that, sir; by the world, brother, help me to kill him;

I may draw now, since we have the odds of him:—'tis a good occasion too before my mistress—   (*aside*)

(*Offers to draw.*)

ALITHEA. Hold, hold.

SPARKISH. What, what.

ALITHEA. I must not let'em kill the gentleman neither, for his kindness to me; I am so far from hating him, that I wish my gallant had his person and understanding:— Nay if my honour—   (*aside*)

SPARKISH. I'll be thy death.

ALITHEA. Hold, hold, indeed to tell the truth, the gentleman said after all, that what he spoke, was but out of friendship to you.

SPARKISH. How! say, I am, I am a fool, that is no wit, out of friendship to me.

ALITHEA. Yes, to try whether I was concerned enough for you, and made love to me only to be satisfied of my virtue, for your sake.

HARCOURT. Kind however—   (*aside*)

SPARKISH. Nay, if it were so, my dear rogue, I ask thee pardon; but why would not you tell me so, faith.

HARCOURT. Because I did not think on't, faith.

SPARKISH. Come, Horner does not come, Harcourt, let's be gone to the new play.— Come, madam.

ALITHEA. I will not go, if you intend to leave me alone in the box, and run into the pit, as you use to do.

SPARKISH. Pshaw, I'll leave Harcourt with you in the box, to entertain you, and that's as good; if I sat in the box, I should be thought no judge, but of trimmings.—Come away, Harcourt, lead her down.

(*Exeunt* SPARKISH, HARCOURT, *and* ALITHEA.)

PINCHWIFE. Well, go thy ways, for the flower of the true town fops, such as spend their estates, before they come to'em, and are cuckolds before they're married. But let me go look to my own free-hold— how—

(*Enter* MY LADY FIDGET, MISTRESS DAINTY FIDGET, *and* MISTRESS SQUEAMISH.)

LADY FIDGET. Your servant, sir, where is your lady? we are come to wait upon her to the new play.

PINCHWIFE. New play!

LADY FIDGET. And my husband will wait upon you presently.

PINCHWIFE. Damn your civility—   (*aside*)
Madam, by no means, I will not see Sir Jaspar here, till I have waited upon him at home; nor shall my wife see you, till she has waited upon your ladyship at your lodgings.

LADY FIDGET. Now we are here, sir—

PINCHWIFE. No, madam.

DAINTY. Pray, let us see her.

SQUEAMISH. We will not stir, till we see her.

PINCHWIFE. A pox on you all—(*aside*) she has locked the door, and is gone abroad. (*Goes to the door, and returns.*)

LADY FIDGET. No, you have locked the door, and she's within.

DAINTY. They told us below, she was here.

PINCHWIFE. Will nothing do?— Well it must out then, to tell you the truth, ladies, which I was afraid to let you know before, lest it might endanger your lives, my wife has just now the small pox come out upon her, do not be frightened; but pray, be gone ladies, you shall not stay here in danger of your lives; pray get you gone ladies.

LADY FIDGET. No, no, we have all had'em.

SQUEAMISH. Alack, alack.

DAINTY. Come, come, we must see how it goes with her, I understand the disease.

LADY FIDGET. Come.

PINCHWIFE. Well, there is no being too hard for women at their own weapon, lying, therefore I'll quit the field. (*aside*)

(*Exit* PINCHWIFE.)

SQUEAMISH. Here's an example of jealousy.

LADY FIDGET. Indeed as the world goes, I wonder there are no more jealous, since wives are so neglected.

DAINTY. Pshaw, as the world goes, to what end should they be jealous.

LADY FIDGET. Foh, 'tis a nasty world.

SQUEAMISH. That men of parts, great acquaintance, and quality should take up with, and spend themselves and fortunes, in keeping little play-house creatures, foh.

LADY FIDGET. Nay, that women of understanding, great acquaintance, and good quality, should fall a keeping too of little creatures, foh.

SQUEAMISH. Why, 'tis the men of quality's fault, they never visit women of honour, and reputation, as they used to do; and have not so much as common civility, for ladies of our rank, but use us with the same indifference, and ill breeding, as if we were all married to'em.

LADY FIDGET. She says true, 'tis an arrant shame women of quality should be so slighted; methinks, birth, birth, should go for something; I have known men admired, courted, and followed for their titles only.

SQUEAMISH. Ay, one would think men of honour should not love no more, than marry out of their own rank.

DAINTY. Fie, fie upon'em, they are come to think cross breeding for themselves best, as well as for their dogs, and horses.

LADY FIDGET. They are dogs and horses for't.

SQUEAMISH. One would think if not for love, for vanity a little.

DAINTY. Nay, they do satisfy their vanity upon us sometimes; and are kind to us in their report, tell all the world they lie with us.

LADY FIDGET. Damned rascals, that we should be only wronged by'em; to report a man has had a person when he has not had a person, is the greatest wrong in the whole world, that can be done to a person.

SQUEAMISH. Well, 'tis an arrant shame noble persons should be so wronged, and neglected.

LADY FIDGET. But still 'tis an arranter shame for a noble person, to neglect her own honour, and defame her own noble person, with little inconsiderable fellows, foh!—

DAINTY. I suppose the crime against our honour, is the same with a man of quality as with another.

LADY FIDGET. How! no, sure the man of quality is likest one's husband, and therefore the fault should be the less.

DAINTY. But then the pleasure should be the less.

LADY FIDGET. Fie, fie, fie, for shame sister, whither shall we ramble? be continent in your discourse, or I shall hate you.

DAINTY. Besides an intrigue is so much the more notorious for the man's quality.

SQUEAMISH. 'Tis true, nobody takes notice of a private man, and therefore with him, 'tis more secret, and the crime's the less, when 'tis not known.

LADY FIDGET. You say true; y faith I think you are in the right on't: 'tis not an injury to a husband, till it be an injury to our honours; so that a woman of honour loses no honour with a private person; and to say truth—

DAINTY. So the little fellow is grown a private person—with her—   (*apart to* SQUEAMISH)

LADY FIDGET. But still my dear, dear honour.

(*Enter* SIR JASPAR, HORNER, DORILANT.)

SIR JASPAR. Ay, my dear, dear of honour, thou hast still so much honour in thy mouth—

HORNER. That she has none elsewhere—   (*aside*)

LADY FIDGET. Oh, what d'ye mean to bring in these upon us?

DAINTY. Foh, these are as bad as wits.

SQUEAMISH. Foh!

LADY FIDGET. Let us leave the room.

SIR JASPAR. Stay, stay, faith to tell you the naked truth.

LADY FIDGET. Fie, Sir Jaspar, do not use that word naked.

SIR JASPAR. Well, well, in short I have business at Whitehall and cannot go to the play with you, therefore would have you go—

LADY FIDGET. With those two to a play?

SIR JASPAR. No, not with t'other, but with Mr. Horner, there can be no more scandal to go with him, than with Mr. Tattle, or Master Limberham.[34]

[34] *Mr. Tattle, or Master Limberham,* stage names for harmless gigolos.

LADY FIDGET. With that nasty fellow! no—no.

SIR JASPAR. Nay, prithee dear, hear me.

(*Whispers to* LADY FIDGET.)

HORNER. Ladies.

DAINTY. Stand off.

(HORNER, DORILANT *drawing near* SQUEAMISH, *and* DAINTY.)

SQUEAMISH. Do not approach us.

DAINTY. You herd with the wits, you are obscenity all over.

SQUEAMISH. And I would as soon look upon a picture of Adam and Eve, without fig leaves, as any of you, if I could help it, therefore keep off, and do not make us sick.

DORILANT. What a devil are these?

HORNER. Why, these are pretenders to honour, as critics to wit, only by censuring others; and as every raw peevish, out-of-humoured, affected, dull, tea-drinking, arithmetical fop sets up for a wit, by railing at men of sense, so these for honour, by railing at the court, and ladies of as great honour, as quality.

SIR JASPAR. Come, Mr. Horner, I must desire you to go with these ladies to the play, sir.

HORNER. I! sir.

SIR JASPAR. Ay, ay, come, sir.

HORNER. I must beg your pardon, sir, and theirs, I will not be seen in women's company in public again for the world.

SIR JASPAR. Ha, ha, strange aversion!

SQUEAMISH. No, he's for women's company in private.

SIR JASPAR. He—poor man—he! hah, ha, ha.

DAINTY. 'Tis a greater shame amongst lewd fellows to be seen in virtuous women's company, than for the women to be seen with them.

HORNER. Indeed, madam, the time was I only hated virtuous women, but now I hate the other too; I beg your pardon, ladies.

LADY FIDGET. You are very obliging, sir, because we would not be troubled with you.

SIR JASPAR. In sober sadness he shall go.

DORILANT. Nay, if he wo'not, I am ready to wait upon the ladies; and I think I am the fitter man.

SIR JASPAR. You, sir, no I thank you for that—master Horner

is a privileged man amongst the virtuous ladies, 'twill be a great while before you are so; heh, he, he, he's my wife's gallant, heh, he, he; no pray withdraw, sir, for as I take it, the virtuous ladies have no business with you.

DORILANT. And I am sure, he can have none with them: 'tis strange a man can't come amongst virtuous women now, but upon the same terms, as men are admitted into the Great Turk's seraglio; but heavens keep me, from being an ombre[35] player with'em: but where is Pinchwife—   (*Exit* DORILANT.)

SIR JASPAR. Come, come, man; what, avoid the sweet society of womankind? that sweet, soft, gentle, tame, noble creature woman, made for man's companion—

HORNER. So is that soft, gentle, tame, and more noble creature a spaniel, and has all their tricks, can fawn, lie down, suffer beating, and fawn the more; barks at your friends, when they come to see you; makes your bed hard, gives you fleas, and the mange sometimes: and all the difference is, the spaniel's the more faithful animal, and fawns but upon one master.

SIR JASPAR. Heh, he, he.

SQUEAMISH. O the rude beast.

DAINTY. Insolent brute.

LADY FIDGET. Brute! stinking, mortified, rotten French wether,[36] to dare—

SIR JASPAR. Hold, an't please your ladyship; for shame Master Horner your mother was a woman—

now shall I never reconcile'em   (*aside*)
Hark you, madam, take my advice in your anger; you know you often want one to make up your drolling pack of ombre players; and you may cheat him easily, for he's an ill gamester, and consequently loves play: Besides you know, you have but two old civil gentlemen (with stinking breaths too) to wait upon you abroad, take in the third, into your service; the other are but crazy:[37] and a lady should have a supernumerary gentleman-usher, as a supernumerary coach horse, lest sometimes you should be forced to stay at home.

---

[35] *ombre*, card game.
[36] *wether*, ram, probably castrated.
[37] *crazy*, rickety.

LADY FIDGET. But are you sure he loves play, and has money?

SIR JASPAR. He loves play as much as you, and has money as much as I.

LADY FIDGET. Then I am contented to make him pay for his scurrility; money makes up in a measure all other wants in men.— Those whom we cannot make hold for gallants, we make fine.[38]   (aside)

SIR JASPAR. So, so; now to mollify, to wheedle him,—   (aside) Master Horner, will you never keep civil company, methinks 'tis time now, since you are only fit for them: Come, come, man, you must e'en fall to visiting our wives, eating at our tables, drinking tea with our virtuous relations after dinner, dealing cards to'em, reading plays and gazettes to'em, picking fleas out of their shocks[39] for'em, collecting receipts, new songs, women, pages, and footmen for'em.

HORNER. I hope they'll afford me better employment, sir.

SIR JASPAR. Heh, he, he, 'tis fit you know your work before you come into your place; and since you are unprovided of a lady to flatter, and a good house to eat at, pray frequent mine, and call my wife mistress, and she shall call you gallant, according to the custom.

HORNER. Who, I?—

SIR JASPAR. Faith, thou sha't for my sake, come for my sake only.

HORNER. For your sake—

SIR JASPAR. Come, come, here's a gamester for you, let him be a little familiar sometimes; nay, what if a little rude; gamesters may be rude with ladies, you know.

LADY FIDGET. Yes, losing gamesters have a privilege with women.

HORNER. I always thought the contrary, that the winning gamester had most privilege with women, for when you have lost your money to a man, you'll lose any thing you have, all you have, they say, and he may use you as he pleases.

SIR JASPAR. Heh, he, he, well, win or lose you shall have your liberty with her.

---

38 *fine*, i.e., if he is sexually inadequate we must accept his money as a penalty or fine.
39 *shocks*, lap dogs.

LADY FIDGET. As he behaves himself; and for your sake I'll give him admittance and freedom.

HORNER. All sorts of freedom, madam?

SIR JASPAR. Ay, ay, ay, all sorts of freedom thou can'st take, and so go to her, begin thy new employment; wheedle her, jest with her, and be better acquainted one with another.

HORNER. I think I know her already, therefore may venter[40] with her, my secret for hers—   (*aside*)

(HORNER *and* LADY FIDGET *whisper.*)

SIR JASPAR. Sister, Cuz, I have provided an innocent playfellow for you there.

DAINTY. Who, he!

SQUEAMISH. There's a playfellow indeed.

SIR JASPAR. Yes sure, what he is good enough to play at cards, blind-man's buff, or the fool with sometimes.

SQUEAMISH. Foh, we'll have no such playfellows.

DAINTY. No, sir, you shan't choose playfellows for us, we thank you.

SIR JASPAR. Nay, pray hear me.   (*Whispering to them.*)

LADY FIDGET. But, poor gentleman, could you be so generous? so truly a man of honour, as for the sakes of us women of honour, to cause yourself to be reported no man? No man! and to suffer yourself the greatest shame that could fall upon a man, that none might fall upon us women by your conversation; but indeed, sir, as perfectly, perfectly, the same man as before your going into France, sir; as perfectly, perfectly, sir?

HORNER. As perfectly, perfectly, madam; nay, I scorn you should take my word; I desire to be tried only, madam.

LADY FIDGET. Well, that's spoken again like a man of honour, all men of honour desire to come to the test: But indeed, generally you men report such things of yourselves, one does not know how, or whom to believe; and it is come to that pass, we dare not take your words, no more than your tailors, without some staid servant of yours be bound with you; but I have so strong a faith in your honour, dear, dear, noble sir, that I'd forfeit mine for yours at any time, dear sir.

---

40 *venter*, bargain.

HORNER. No, madam, you should not need to forfeit it for me, I have given you security already to save you harmless, my late reputation being so well known in the world, madam.

LADY FIDGET. But if upon any future falling out, or upon a suspicion of my taking the trust out of your hands, to employ some other, you yourself should betray your trust, dear sir; I mean, if you'll give me leave to speak obscenely, you might tell, dear sir.

HORNER. If I did, no body would believe me; the reputation of impotency is as hardly recovered again in the world, as that of cowardice, dear madam.

LADY FIDGET. Nay then, as one may say, you may do your worst, dear, dear, sir.

SIR JASPAR. Come, is your ladyship reconciled to him yet? have you agreed on matters? for I must be gone to Whitehall.

LADY FIDGET. Why, indeed, Sir Jaspar, Master Horner is a thousand, thousand times a better man, than I thought him: Cousin Squeamish, Sister Dainty, I can name him now, truly not long ago you know, I thought his very name obscenity, and I would as soon have lain with him, as have named him.

SIR JASPAR. Very likely, poor madam.

DAINTY. I believe it.

SQUEAMISH. No doubt on't.

SIR JASPAR. Well, well—that your ladyship is as virtuous as any she,—I know, and him all the town knows—heh, he, he; therefore now you like him, get you gone to your business together; go, go, to your business, I say, pleasure, whilst I go to my pleasure, business.

LADY FIDGET. Come then, dear gallant.

HORNER. Come away, my dearest mistress.

SIR JASPAR. So, so, why 'tis as I'd have it. (*Exit* SIR JASPAR.)

HORNER. And as I'd have it.

LADY FIDGET.

> Who for his business, from his wife will run;
> Takes the best care, to have her business done.

(*Exeunt omnes.*)

ACT III

[SCENE I.]

(ALITHEA *and* MRS. PINCHWIFE.)

ALITHEA. Sister, what ails you, you are grown melancholy?

MRS. PINCHWIFE. Would it not make any one melancholy to see you go every day fluttering about abroad, whilst I must stay at home like a poor lonely, sullen bird in a cage?

ALITHEA. Ay, sister, but you came young, and just from the nest to your cage, so that I thought you liked it; and could be as cheerful in't, as others that took their flight themselves early, and are hopping abroad in the open air.

MRS. PINCHWIFE. Nay, I confess I was quiet enough, till my husband told me what pure lives the London ladies live abroad, with their dancing, meetings, and junketings, and dressed every day in their best gowns; and I warrant you, play at ninepins every day of the week, so they do.

(*Enter* MR. PINCHWIFE.)

PINCHWIFE. Come, what's here to do? you are putting the town pleasures in her head, and setting her a longing.

ALITHEA. Yes, after ninepins; you suffer none to give her those longings, you mean, but yourself.

PINCHWIFE. I tell her of the vanities of the town like a confessor.

ALITHEA. A confessor! just such a confessor, as he that by forbidding a silly ostler to grease the horses' teeth, taught him to do't.

PINCHWIFE. Come, Mistress flippant, good precepts are lost, when bad examples are still before us; the liberty you take abroad makes her hanker after it; and out of humour at home, poor wretch! she desired not to come to London, I would bring her.

ALITHEA. Very well.

PINCHWIFE. She has been this week in town, and never desired, till this afternoon, to go abroad.

ALITHEA. Was she not at a play yesterday?

PINCHWIFE. Yes, but she ne'er asked me; I was myself the
cause of her going.

ALITHEA. Then if she ask you again, you are the cause of her
asking, and not my example.

PINCHWIFE. Well, tomorrow night I shall be rid of you; and
the next day before 'tis light, she and I'll be rid of the
town, and my dreadful apprehensions: come, be not
melancholy, for thou sha't go into the country after
tomorrow, dearest.

ALITHEA. Great comfort.

MRS. PINCHWIFE. Pish, what d'ye tell me of the country for?

PINCHWIFE. How's this! what, pish at the country?

MRS. PINCHWIFE. Let me alone, I am not well.

PINCHWIFE. O, if that be all—what ails my dearest?

MRS. PINCHWIFE. Truly I don't know; but I have not been
well, since you told me there was a gallant at the play
in love with me.

PINCHWIFE. Ha—

ALITHEA. That's by my example too.

PINCHWIFE. Nay, if you are not well, but are so concerned,
because a lewd fellow chanced to lie, and say he liked
you, you'll make me sick too.

MRS. PINCHWIFE. Of what sickness?

PINCHWIFE. O, of that which is worse than the plague,
jealousy.

MRS. PINCHWIFE. Pish, you jeer, I'm sure there's no such
disease in our receipt-book[41] at home.

PINCHWIFE. No, thou never met'st with it, poor innocent—
well, if thou cuckold me, 'twill be my own fault—for
cuckolds and bastards are generally makers of their own
fortune.   (*aside*)

MRS. PINCHWIFE. Well, but pray, bud, let's go to a play tonight.

PINCHWIFE. 'Tis just done, she comes from it; but why are
you so eager to see a play?

MRS. PINCHWIFE. Faith, dear, not that I care one pin for their
talk there; but I like to look upon the player-men, and
would see, if I could, the gallant you say loves me; that's
all, dear bud.

PINCHWIFE. Is that all, dear bud?

ALITHEA. This proceeds from my example.

MRS. PINCHWIFE. But if the play be done, let's go abroad
however, dear bud.

---

[41] *receipt-book,* book of household remedies.

PINCHWIFE. Come, have a little patience, and thou shalt go into the country on Friday.

MRS. PINCHWIFE. Therefore I would see first some sights, to tell my neighbours of. Nay, I will go abroad, that's once.

ALITHEA. I'm the cause of this desire too.

PINCHWIFE. But now I think on't, who was the cause of Horner's coming to my lodging today? That was you.

ALITHEA. No, you, because you would not let him see your handsome wife out of your lodging.

MRS. PINCHWIFE. Why, o Lord! did the gentleman come hither to see me indeed?

PINCHWIFE. No, no;— You are not cause of that damned question too, Mistress Alithea?—
Well she's in the right of it; he is in love with my wife— and comes after her—'tis so—but I'll nip his love in the bud; lest he should follow us into the country, and break his chariot-wheel near our house, on purpose for an excuse to come to't; but I think I know the town. (*aside*)

MRS. PINCHWIFE. Come, pray bud, let's go abroad before 'tis late; for I will go, that's flat and plain.

PINCHWIFE. So! the obstinacy already of a town-wife, and I must, whilst she's here, humour her like one. (*aside*) Sister, how shall we do, that she may not be seen, or known?

ALITHEA. Let her put on her mask.

PINCHWIFE. Pshaw, a mask makes people but the more inquisitive, and is as ridiculous a disguise, as a stage-beard; her shape, stature, habit will be known: and if we should meet with Horner, he would be sure to take acquaintance with us, must wish her joy, kiss her, talk to her, leer upon her, and the devil and all; no I'll not use her to a mask, 'tis dangerous; for masks have made more cuckolds than the best faces that ever were known.

ALITHEA. How will you do then?

MRS. PINCHWIFE. Nay, shall we go? the Exchange will be shut, and I have a mind to see that.

PINCHWIFE. So—I have it—I'll dress her up in the suit, we are to carry down to her brother, little Sir James; nay, I understand the town tricks: Come let's go dress her; a mask! no—a woman masked, like a covered dish, gives a man curiosity, and appetite, when, it may be, uncovered, 'twould turn his stomach; no, no.

ALITHEA. Indeed your comparison is something a greasy one:

but I had a gentle gallant used to say, a beauty masked,
like the sun in eclipse, gathers together more gazers,
than if it shined out.   (*Exeunt.*)

(*The Scene changes to the new Exchange: Enter* HORNER,
HARCOURT, DORILANT.)

DORILANT. Engaged to women, and not sup with us?

HORNER. Ay, a pox on'em all.

HARCOURT. You were much a more reasonable man in the
morning, and had as noble resolutions against'em, as a
widower of a week's liberty.

DORILANT. Did I ever think to see you keep company with
women in vain.

HORNER. In vain! no—'tis, since I can't love'em, to be revenged on'em.

HARCOURT. Now your sting is gone, you looked in the box
amongst all those women, like a drone in the hive, all
upon you; shoved and ill-used by'em all, and thrust from
one side to t'other.

DORILANT. Yet he must be buzzing amongst'em still, like
other old beetle-headed,[42] lycorish[43] drones; avoid'em,
and hate'em as they hate you.

HORNER. Because I do hate'em, and would hate'em yet more,
I'll frequent'em; you may see my marriage, nothing
makes a man hate a woman more than her constant
conversation: in short, I converse with'em, as you do
with rich fools, to laugh at'em, and use'em ill.

DORILANT. But I would no more sup with women, unless I
could lie with'em, than sup with a rich coxcomb, unless
I could cheat him.

HORNER. Yes, I have known thee sup with a fool, for his
drinking, if he could set out your hand that way only,
you were satisfied; and if he were a wine-swallowing
mouth 'twas enough.

HARCOURT. Yes, a man drinks often with a fool, as he tosses
with a marker, only to keep his hand in ure;[44] but do the
ladies drink?

HORNER. Yes, sir, and I shall have the pleasure at least of
laying'em flat with a bottle; and bring as much scandal
that way upon'em, as formerly t'other.

---

[42] *beetle-headed*, blockheaded.
[43] *lycorish*, lecherous.
[44] *tosses . . . ure*, plays with the scorekeeper to practice or "keep his
hand in."

HARCOURT. Perhaps you may prove as weak a brother amongst-
'em that way, as t'other.

DORILANT. Foh, drinking with women, is as unnatural as
scolding with'em; but 'tis a pleasure of decayed fornica-
tors, and the basest way of quenching love.

HARCOURT. Nay, 'tis drowning love, instead of quenching it;
but leave us for civil women too!

DORILANT. Ay, when he can't be the better for'em; we hardly
pardon a man, that leaves his friend for a wench, and
that's a pretty lawful call.

HORNER. Faith, I would not leave you for'em, if they would
not drink.

DORILANT. Who would disappoint his company at Lewis's, for
a gossiping?

HARCOURT. Foh, wine and women good apart, together as
nauseous as sack and sugar: But hark you, sir, before
you go, a little of your advice, an old maimed general,
when unfit for action is fittest for counsel; I have other
designs upon women, than eating and drinking with them:
I am in love with Sparkish's mistress, whom he is to
marry tomorrow, now how shall I get her?

(*Enter* SPARKISH, *looking about.*)

HORNER. Why, here comes one will help you to her.

HARCOURT. He! He, I tell you, is my rival, and will hinder my
love.

HORNER. No, a foolish rival, and a jealous husband assist their
rival's designs; for they are sure to make their women hate
them, which is the first step to their love for another man.

HARCOURT. But I cannot come near his mistress, but in his
company.

HORNER. Still the better for you, for fools are most easily
cheated, when they themselves are accessories; and he
is to be bubbled of his mistress, as of his money, the
common mistress, by keeping him company.

SPARKISH. Who is that, that is to be bubbled? Faith let me
snack,[45] I han't met with a bubble since Christmas: gad;
I think bubbles are like their brother woodcocks, go out
with the cold weather.

HARCOURT. A pox, he did not hear all I hope.

(*Apart to* HORNER.)

45 *snack*, share.

SPARKISH. Come, you bubbling rogues you, where do we sup— Oh, Harcourt, my mistress tells me you have been making fierce love to her all the play long, hah, ha— but I—

HARCOURT. I make love to her?

SPARKISH. Nay, I forgive thee; for I think I know thee, and I know her, but I am sure I know myself.

HARCOURT. Did she tell you so? see all women are like these of the Exchange, who to enhance the price of their commodities, report to their fond customers offers which were never made'em.

HORNER. Ay, women are as apt to tell before the intrigue, as men after it, and so show themselves the vainer sex; but hast thou a mistress, Sparkish? 'tis as hard for me to believe it, as that thou ever hadst a bubble, as you bragged just now.

SPARKISH. O your servant, sir; are you at your raillery, sir? but we were some of us beforehand with you today at the play: the wits were something bold with you, sir; did you not hear us laugh?

HARCOURT. Yes, but I thought you had gone to plays, to laugh at the poet's wit, not at your own.

SPARKISH. Your servant, sir, no I thank you; gad I go to a play as to a country-treat, I carry my own wine to one, and my own wit to t'other, or else I'm sure I should not be merry at either; and the reason why we are so often louder than the players, is, because we think we speak more wit, and so become the poet's rivals in his audience: for to tell you the truth, we hate the silly rogues; nay, so much that we find fault even with their bawdy upon the stage, whilst we talk nothing else in the pit as loud.

HORNER. But, why should'st thou hate the silly poets, thou hast too much wit to be one, and they like whores are only hated by each other; and thou dost scorn writing, I am sure.

SPARKISH. Yes, I'd have you to know, I scorn writing; but women, women, that make men do all foolish things, make'em write songs too; everybody does it: 'tis even as common with lovers, as playing with fans; and you can no more help rhyming to your Phyllis, than drinking to your Phyllis.

HARCOURT. Nay, poetry in love is no more to be avoided, than jealousy.

DORILANT. But the poets damned your songs, did they?

SPARKISH. Damn the poets, they turned'em into burlesque, as they call it; that burlesque is a hocus-pocus trick, they have got, which by the virtue of hictius doctius, topsey turvey, they make a wise and witty man in the world, a fool upon the stage you know not how; and 'tis therefore I hate'em too, for I know not but it may be my own case; for they'll put a man into a play for looking asquint: Their predecessors were contented to make servingmen only their stage fools, but these rogues must have gentlemen, with a pox to'em, nay knights: and indeed you shall hardly see a fool upon the stage, but he's a knight; and to tell you the truth, they have kept me these six years from being a knight in earnest, for fear of being knighted in a play, and dubbed a fool.

DORILANT. Blame'em not, they must follow their copy, the age.

HARCOURT. But why should'st thou be afraid of being in a play, who expose yourself every day in the playhouses, and as public places.

HORNER. 'Tis but being on the stage, instead of standing on a bench in the pit.

DORILANT. Don't you give money to painters to draw you like? and are you afraid of your pictures, at length in a playhouse, where all your mistresses may see you?

SPARKISH. A pox, painters don't draw the small pox, or pimples in one's face; come damn all your silly authors whatever, all books and booksellers, by the world, and all readers, courteous or uncourteous.

HARCOURT. But, who comes here, Sparkish?

(*Enter* MR. PINCHWIFE, *and his wife in man's clothes,* ALITHEA, LUCY *her maid.*)

SPARKISH. Oh hide me, there's my mistress too.

(SPARKISH *hides himself behind* HARCOURT.)

HARCOURT. She sees you.

SPARKISH. But I will not see her, 'tis time to go to Whitehall, and I must not fail the drawing-room.

HARCOURT. Pray, first carry me, and reconcile me to her.

SPARKISH. Another time, faith the King will have supped.

HARCOURT. Not with the worse stomach for thy absence; thou art one of those fools, that think their attendance at the King's meals, as necessary as his physicians, when you are more troublesome to him, than his doctors, or his dogs.

SPARKISH. Pshaw, I know my interest, sir. Prithee hide me.

HORNER. Your servant, Pinchwife,—what, he knows us not—

PINCHWIFE. Come along. (*To his wife aside.*)

MRS. PINCHWIFE. Pray, have you any ballads, give me six-penny worth?

CLASP. We have no ballads.

MRS. PINCHWIFE. Then give me Covent-Garden Drollery, and a play or two— Oh here's *Tarugo's Wiles*, and *The Slighted Maiden*, I'll have them.

PINCHWIFE. No, plays are not for your reading; come along, will you discover yourself? (*Apart to her.*)

HORNER. Who is that pretty youth with him, Sparkish?

SPARKISH. I believe his wife's brother, because he's some-thing like her, but I never saw her but once.

HORNER. Extremely handsome, I have seen a face like it too; let us follow'em.

(*Exeunt* PINCHWIFE, MISTRESS PINCHWIFE. ALITHEA, LUCY, HORNER, DORILANT *following them.*)

HARCOURT. Come, Sparkish, your mistress saw you, and will be angry you go not to her; besides I would fain be reconciled to her, which none but you can do, dear friend.

SPARKISH. Well that's a better reason, dear friend; I would not go near her now, for hers, or my own sake, but I can deny you nothing; for though I have known thee a great while, never go, if I do not love thee as well as a new acquaintance.

HARCOURT. I am obliged to you indeed, dear friend, I would be well with her only, to be well with thee still; for these ties to wives usually dissolve all ties to friends: I would be contented, she should enjoy you a-nights, but I would have you to myself a-days, as I have had, dear friend.

SPARKISH. And thou shalt enjoy me a-days, dear, dear friend, never stir; and I'll be divorced from her, sooner than from thee; come along—

HARCOURT. So we are hard put to't, when we make our rival our procurer; but neither she, nor her brother, would let me come near her now: when all's done, a rival is the best cloak to steal to a mistress under, without suspicion; and when we have once got to her as we desire, we throw him off like other cloaks. (*aside*)

(*Exit* SPARKISH, *and* HARCOURT *following him.*)

(*Re-enter* MR. PINCHWIFE, MISTRESS PINCHWIFE i*
clothes.*)

PINCHWIFE. Sister, if you will not go, we must leave you—
(*To* ALITHEA.)
The fool her gallant, and she, will muster up all the
young saunterers of this place, and they will leave their
dear seamstresses to follow us; what a swarm of cuckolds, and cuckold-makers are here! (*aside*)
Come, let's be gone, Mistress Margery.

MRS. PINCHWIFE. Don't you believe that, I han't half my
belly full of sights yet.

PINCHWIFE. Then walk this way.

MRS. PINCHWIFE. Lord, what a power of brave signs are
here! stay—the Bull's-head, the Ram's-head, and the
Stag's-head, dear—

PINCHWIFE. Nay, if every husband's proper sign here were
visible, they would be all alike.

MRS. PINCHWIFE. What d'ye mean by that, bud?

PINCHWIFE. 'Tis no matter—no matter, bud.

MRS. PINCHWIFE. Pray tell me; nay, I will know.

PINCHWIFE. They would be all Bull's, Stag's, and Ram's
heads.[46]   (*Exeunt* MR. PINCHWIFE, MRS. PINCHWIFE.)

(*Re-enter* SPARKISH, HARCOURT, ALITHEA, LUCY, *at t'other
door.*)

SPARKISH. Come, dear madam, for my sake you shall be
reconciled to him.

ALITHEA. For your sake I hate him.

HARCOURT. That's something too cruel, madam, to hate me
for his sake.

SPARKISH. Ay indeed, madam, too, too cruel to me, to hate
my friend for my sake.

ALITHEA. I hate him because he is your enemy; and you ought
to hate him too, for making love to me, if you love me.

SPARKISH. That's a good one, I hate a man for loving you; if
he did love you, 'tis but what he can't help, and 'tis your
fault not his, if he admires you: I hate a man for being
of my opinion, I'll ne'er do't, by the world.

ALITHEA. Is it for your honour or mine, to suffer a man to
make love to me, who am to marry you tomorrow?

---

[46] *Bull's, Stag's, and Ram's heads,* i.e., with horns.

SPARKISH. Is it for your honour or mine, to have me jealous? That he makes love to you, is a sign you are handsome; and that I am not jealous, is a sign you are virtuous, that I think is for your honour.

ALITHEA. But 'tis your honour too, I am concerned for.

HARCOURT. But why, dearest madam, will you be more concerned for his honour, than he is himself; let his honour alone for my sake, and his. He! he has no honour—

SPARKISH. How's that?

HARCOURT. But what, my dear friend can guard himself.

SPARKISH. O ho—that's right again.

HARCOURT. Your care of his honour argues his neglect of it, which is no honour to my dear friend here; therefore once more, let his honour go which way it will, dear madam.

SPARKISH. Ay, ay, were it for my honour to marry a woman, whose virtue I suspected, and could not trust her in a friend's hands?

ALITHEA. Are you not afraid to lose me?

HARCOURT. He afraid to lose you, madam! No, no—you may see how the most estimable, and most glorious creature in the world, is valued by him; will you not see it?

SPARKISH. Right, honest Frank, I have that noble value for her, that I cannot be jealous of her.

ALITHEA. You mistake him, he means you care not for me, nor who has me.

SPARKISH. Lord, madam, I see you are jealous; will you wrest a poor man's meaning from his words?

ALITHEA. You astonish me, sir, with your want of jealousy.

SPARKISH. And you make me giddy, madam, with your jealousy, and fears, and virtue, and honour; gad, I see virtue makes a woman as troublesome as a little reading or learning.

ALITHEA. Monstrous!

LUCY. Well, to see what easy husbands these women of quality can meet with, a poor chambermaid can never have such lady-like luck; besides he's thrown away upon her, she'll make no use of her fortune, her blessing, none to a gentleman, for a pure cuckold, for it requires good breeding to be a cuckold. (*behind*)

ALITHEA. I tell you then plainly, he pursues me to marry me.

SPARKISH. Pshaw—

HARCOURT. Come, madam, you see you strive in vain to make

him jealous of me; my dear friend is the kindest creature in the world to me.

SPARKISH. Poor fellow.

HARCOURT. But his kindness only is not enough for me, without your favour; your good opinion, dear madam, 'tis that must perfect my happiness: good gentleman, he believes all I say, would you would do so. Jealous of me! I would not wrong him nor you for the world.

SPARKISH. Look you there; hear him, hear him, and do not walk away so. (ALITHEA walks carelessly, to and fro.)

HARCOURT. I love you, madam, so—

SPARKISH. How's that! Nay—now you begin to go too far indeed.

HARCOURT. So much I confess, I say I love you, that I would not have you miserable, and cast yourself away upon so unworthy, and inconsiderable a thing, as what you see here.

(Clapping his hand on his breast, points at SPARKISH.)

SPARKISH. No faith, I believe thou wouldst not, now his meaning is plain: but I knew before thou wouldst not wrong me nor her.

HARCOURT. No, no, Heavens forbid, the glory of her sex should fall so low as into the embraces of such a contemptible wretch, the last of mankind—my dear friend here—I injure him. *(Embracing* SPARKISH.)

ALITHEA. Very well.

SPARKISH. No, no, dear friend, I knew it, madam, you see he will rather wrong himself than me, in giving himself such names.

ALITHEA. Do not you understand him yet?

SPARKISH. Yes, how modestly he speaks of himself, poor fellow.

ALITHEA. Methinks he speaks impudently of yourself, since— before yourself too, insomuch that I can no longer suffer his scurrilous abusiveness to you, no more than his love to me. *(Offers to go.)*

SPARKISH. Nay, nay, madam, pray stay his love to you: Lord, madam, has he not spoke yet plain enough?

ALITHEA. Yes indeed, I should think so.

SPARKISH. Well then, by the world, a man can't speak civilly to a woman now, but presently she says, he makes love to her: nay, madam, you shall stay, with your pardon, since you have not yet understood him, till he has made an eclaircisment[47] of his love to you, that is what kind of love it is; answer to thy catechism: friend, do you love my mistress here?

HARCOURT. Yes, I wish she would not doubt it.

SPARKISH. But how do you love her?

HARCOURT. With all my soul.

ALITHEA. I thank him, methinks he speaks plain enough now.

SPARKISH. You are out still.   (*To* ALITHEA.)
But with what kind of love, Harcourt?

HARCOURT. With the best, and truest love in the world.

SPARKISH. Look you there then, that is with no matrimonial love, I'm sure.

ALITHEA. How's that, do you say matrimonial love is not best?

SPARKISH. Gad, I went too far e're I was aware: but speak for thyself, Harcourt, you said you would not wrong me, nor her.

HARCOURT. No, no, madam, e'en take him for Heaven's sake.

SPARKISH. Look you there, madam.

HARCOURT. Who should in all justice be yours, he that loves you most.   (*Claps his hand on his breast.*)

ALITHEA. Look you there, Mr. Sparkish, who's that?

SPARKISH. Who should it be? go on, Harcourt.

HARCOURT. Who loves you more than women, titles, or fortune fools.   (*Points at* SPARKISH.)

SPARKISH. Look you there, he means me still, for he points at me.

ALITHEA. Ridiculous!

HARCOURT. Who can only match your faith, and constancy in love.

SPARKISH. Ay.

HARCOURT. Who knows, if it be possible, how to value so much beauty and virtue.

SPARKISH. Ay.

HARCOURT. Whose love can no more be equalled in the world, than that heavenly form of yours.

SPARKISH. No—

HARCOURT. Who could no more suffer a rival, than your absence, and yet could no more suspect your virtue, than his own constancy in his love to you.

SPARKISH. No—

---

[47] *eclaircisment*, explanation.

HARCOURT. Who in fine loves you better than his eyes, that first made him love you.

SPARKISH. Ay—nay, madam, faith you shan't go, till—

ALITHEA. Have a care, lest you make me stay too long—

SPARKISH. But till he has saluted you; that I may be assured you are friends, after his honest advice and declaration: come, pray, madam, be friends with him.

(*Enter* PINCHWIFE, MISTRESS PINCHWIFE.)

ALITHEA. You must pardon me, sir, that I am not yet so obedient to you.

PINCHWIFE. What, invite your wife to kiss men? Monstrous, are you not ashamed? I will never forgive you.

SPARKISH. Are you not ashamed, that I should have more confidence in the chastity of your family, than you have; you must not teach me, I am a man of honour, sir, though I am frank and free; I am frank,[48] sir—

PINCHWIFE. Very frank, sir, to share your wife with your friends.

SPARKISH. He is an humble, menial friend, such as reconciles the differences of the marriage bed; you know man and wife do not always agree, I design him for that use, therefore would have him well with my wife.

PINCHWIFE. A menial friend—you will get a great many menial friends, by showing your wife as you do.

SPARKISH. What then, it may be I have a pleasure in't, as I have to show fine clothes, at a playhouse the first day, and count money before poor rogues.

PINCHWIFE. He that shows his wife or money will be in danger of having them borrowed sometimes.

SPARKISH. I love to be envied, and would not marry a wife, that I alone could love; loving alone is as dull, as eating alone; is it not a frank age, and I am a frank person? and to tell you the truth, it may be I love to have rivals in a wife, they make her seem to a man still but as a kept mistress; and so good night, for I must to Whitehall. Madam, I hope you are now reconciled to my friend; and so I wish you a good night, madam, and sleep if you can, for tomorrow you know I must visit you early with a canonical gentleman. Good night, dear Harcourt.

(*Exit* SPARKISH.)

48 *frank*, generous.

HARCOURT. Madam, I hope you will not refuse my visit to-morrow, if it should be earlier, with a canonical gentleman, than Mr. Sparkish's.

PINCHWIFE. This gentlewoman is yet under my care, therefore you must yet forbear your freedom with her, sir.

(*Coming between* ALITHEA *and* HARCOURT.)

HARCOURT. Must, sir—

PINCHWIFE. Yes, sir, she is my sister.

HARCOURT. 'Tis well she is, sir—for I must be her servant, sir. Madam—

PINCHWIFE. Come away, sister, we had been gone, if it had not been for you, and so avoided these lewd rakehells, who seem to haunt us.

(*Enter* HORNER, DORILANT *to them.*)

HORNER. How now, Pinchwife?

PINCHWIFE. Your servant.

HORNER. What, I see a little time in the country makes a man turn wild and unsociable, and only fit to converse with his horses, dogs, and his herds.

PINCHWIFE. I have business, sir, and must mind it; your business is pleasure, therefore you and I must go different ways.

HORNER. Well, you may go on, but this pretty young gentleman— (*Takes hold of* MRS. PINCHWIFE.)

HARCOURT. The lady—

DORILANT. And the maid—

HORNER. Shall stay with us, for I suppose their business is the same with ours, pleasure.

PINCHWIFE. 'Sdeath he knows her, she carries it so sillily,[49] yet if he does not, I should be more silly to discover it first. (*aside*)

ALITHEA. Pray, let us go, sir.

PINCHWIFE. Come, come—

HORNER. Had you not rather stay with us?

(*To* MRS. PINCHWIFE.)

Prithee, Pinchwife, who is this pretty young gentleman?

PINCHWIFE. One to whom I'm a guardian.

I wish I could keep her out of your hands— (*aside*)

---

[49] *sillily*, innocently.

HORNER. Who is he? I never saw anything so pretty in all my life.

PINCHWIFE. Pshaw, do not look upon him so much, he's a poor bashful youth, you'll put him out of countenance. Come away, brother. *(Offers to take her away.)*

HORNER. O your brother!

PINCHWIFE. Yes, my wife's brother; come, come she'll stay supper for us.

HORNER. I thought so, for he is very like her I saw you at the play with, whom I told you I was in love with.

MRS. PINCHWIFE. O jeminy! is this he that was in love with me, I am glad on't I vow, for he's a curious fine gentleman, and I love him already too. , *(aside)* Is this he, bud? *(To MR. PINCHWIFE.)*

PINCHWIFE. Come away, come away. *(To his wife.)*

HORNER. Why, what haste are you in? why won't you let me talk with him?

PINCHWIFE. Because you'll debauch him, he's yet young and innocent, and I would not have him debauched for any thing in the world.

How she gazes on him! the devil— *(aside)*

HORNER. Harcourt, Dorilant, look you here, this is the likeness of that dowdy he told us of, his wife, did you ever see a lovelier creature? the rogue has reason to be jealous of his wife, since she is like him, for she would make all that see her, in love with her.

HARCOURT. And as I remember now, she is as like him here as can be.

DORILANT. She is indeed very pretty, if she be like him.

HORNER. Very pretty, a very pretty commendation—she is a glorious creature, beautiful beyond all things I ever beheld.

PINCHWIFE. So, so.

HARCOURT. More beautiful than a poet's first mistress of imagination.

HORNER. Or another man's last mistress of flesh and blood.

MRS. PINCHWIFE. Nay, now you jeer, sir; pray don't jeer me—

PINCHWIFE. Come, come.

By Heavens, she'll discover herself. *(aside)*

HORNER. I speak of your sister, sir.

PINCHWIFE. Ay, but saying she was handsome, if like him, made him blush.

I am upon a rack— *(aside)*

HORNER. Methinks he is so handsome, he should not be a man.

PINCHWIFE. O there 'tis out, he has discovered her, I am not able to suffer any longer.

    Come, come away, I say—   (*To his wife.*)

HORNER. Nay, by your leave, sir, he shall not go yet—Harcourt, Dorilant, let us torment this jealous rogue a little.

                                (*To them.*)

HARCOURT.
DORILANT. } How?

HORNER. I'll show you.

PINCHWIFE. Come, pray let him go, I cannot stay fooling any longer; I tell you his sister stays supper for us.

HORNER. Does she, come then we'll all go sup with her and thee.

PINCHWIFE. No, now I think on't, having stayed so long for us, I warrant she's gone to bed—

    I wish she and I were well out of their hands—   (*aside*)
    Come, I must rise early tomorrow, come.

HORNER. Well then, if she be gone to bed, I wish her and you a good night. But pray, young gentleman, present my humble service to her.

MRS. PINCHWIFE. Thank you heartily, sir.

PINCHWIFE. S'death, she will discover herself yet in spite of me.   (*aside*)
    He is something more civil to you, for your kindness to his sister, than I am, it seems.

HORNER. Tell her, dear sweet little gentleman, for all your brother there, that you have revived the love I had for her at first sight in the playhouse.

MRS. PINCHWIFE. But did you love her indeed, and indeed?

PINCHWIFE. So, so.   (*aside*)
    Away, I say.

HORNER. Nay, stay; yes, indeed, and indeed, pray do you tell her so, and give her this kiss from me.   (*Kisses her.*)

PINCHWIFE. O Heavens! what do I suffer; now 'tis too plain he knows her, and yet—   (*aside*)

HORNER. And this, and this—   (*Kisses her again.*)

MRS. PINCHWIFE. What do you kiss me for, I am no woman.

PINCHWIFE. So—there 'tis out.   (*aside*)
    Come, I cannot, nor will stay any longer.

HORNER. Nay, they shall send your lady a kiss too; here Harcourt, Dorilant, will you not?   (*They kiss her.*)

PINCHWIFE. How, do I suffer this? was I not accusing another just now, for this rascally patience, in permitting his

wife to be kissed before his face? ten thousand ulcers
gnaw away their lips.   *(aside)*

Come, come.

HORNER. Good night, dear little gentleman; madam, good night;
farewell, Pinchwife.

Did not I tell you, I would raise his jealous gall.

(Apart to HARCOURT *and* DORILANT.)

(Exeunt HORNER, HARCOURT, *and* DORILANT.)

PINCHWIFE. So they are gone at last; stay, let me see first if
the coach be at this door.   *(Exit.)*

HORNER. What, not gone yet? will you be sure to do as I
desired you, sweet sir?

*(*HORNER, HARCOURT, DORILANT *return.)*

MRS. PINCHWIFE. Sweet sir, but what will you give me then?

HORNER. Anything, come away into the next walk.

(Exit HORNER, *haling away* MRS. PINCHWIFE.)

ALITHEA. Hold, hold,—what d'ye do?

LUCY. Stay, stay, hold—

HARCOURT. Hold, madam, hold, let him present him, he'll
come presently; nay, I will never let you go, till you
answer my question.   *(*ALITHEA, LUCY *struggling*

LUCY. For God's sake, sir, I must   *with* HARCOURT,
follow 'em.   *and* DORILANT.)

DORILANT. No, I have something to present you with too, you
shan't follow them.

*(*PINCHWIFE *returns.)*

PINCHWIFE. Where?—how?—what's become of? gone—
whither?

LUCY. He's only gone with the gentleman, who will give him
something, an't please your worship.

PINCHWIFE. Something—give him something, with a pox—
where are they?

ALITHEA. In the next walk only, brother.

PINCHWIFE. Only, only; where, where?

(Exit PINCHWIFE, *and returns presently, then goes out
again.)*

HARCOURT. What's the matter with him? why so much concerned? but dearest madam—

ALITHEA. Pray, let me go, sir, I have said, and suffered enough already.

HARCOURT. Then you will not look upon, nor pity my sufferings?

ALITHEA. To look upon'em, when I cannot help'em, were cruelty, not pity, therefore I will never see you more.

HARCOURT. Let me then, madam, have my privilege of a banished lover, complaining or railing, and giving you but a farewell reason why, if you cannot condescend to marry me, you should not take that wretch my rival.

ALITHEA. He only, not you, since my honour is engaged so far to him, can give me a reason why I should not marry him; but if he be true, and what I think him to me, I must be so to him; your servant, sir.

HARCOURT. Have women only constancy when 'tis a vice, and like fortune only true to fools?

DORILANT. Thou sha't not stir, thou robust creature, you see I can deal with you, therefore you should stay the rather, and be kind.

(*To* LUCY, *who struggles to get from him.*
Enter PINCHWIFE.)

PINCHWIFE. Gone, gone, not to be found; quite gone, ten thousand plagues go with'em; which way went they?

ALITHEA. But into t'other walk, brother.

LUCY. Their business will be done presently, sure, an't please your worship; it can't be long in doing, I'm sure on't.

ALITHEA. Are they not there?

PINCHWIFE. No, you know where they are, you infamous wretch, eternal shame of your family, which you do not dishonour enough yourself, you think, but you must help her to do it too, thou legion of bawds.

ALITHEA. Good brother.

PINCHWIFE. Damned, damned sister.

ALITHEA. Look you here, she's coming.

(*Enter* MISTRESS PINCHWIFE *in man's clothes, running with her hat under her arm, full of oranges and dried fruit,* HORNER *following.*)

MRS. PINCHWIFE. O dear bud, look you here what I have got, see.

PINCHWIFE. And what I have got here too, which you can't see. (*Aside rubbing his forehead.*)

MRS. PINCHWIFE. The fine gentleman has given me better things yet.

PINCHWIFE. Has he so? Out of breath and colour'd— I must hold yet.   (*aside*)

HORNER. I have only given your little brother an orange, sir.

PINCHWIFE. Thank you, sir.   (*To* HORNER.)
You have only squeezed my orange, I suppose, and given it me again; yet I must have a city-patience.⁵⁰
                                                 (*aside*)
Come, come away—   (*To his wife.*)

MRS. PINCHWIFE. Stay, till I have put up my fine things, bud.

(*Enter* SIR JASPAR FIDGET.)

SIR JASPAR. O Master Horner, come, come, the ladies stay for you; your mistress, my wife, wonders you make not more haste to her.

HORNER. I have stayed this half hour for you here, and 'tis your fault I am not now with your wife.

SIR JASPAR. But pray, don't let her know so much, the truth on't is, I was advancing a certain project to his Majesty, about—I'll tell you.

HORNER. No, let's go, and hear it at your house: good night sweet little gentleman; one kiss more, you'll remember me now I hope.   (*Kisses her.*)

DORILANT. What, Sir Jaspar, will you separate friends? he promised to sup with us; and if you take him to your house, you'll be in danger of our company too.

SIR JASPAR. Alas, gentlemen, my house is not fit for you, there are none but civil women there, which are not for your turn; he, you know, can bear with the society of civil women, now, ha, ha, ha; besides he's one of my family;—he's—heh, heh, heh.

DORILANT. What is he?

SIR JASPAR. Faith, my eunuch, since you'll have it, heh, he, he.

(*Exeunt* SIR JASPAR FIDGET, *and* HORNER.)

DORILANT. I rather wish thou wert his, or my cuckold: Harcourt, what a good cuckold is lost there, for want of a man to make him one; thee and I cannot have Horner's privilege, who can make use of it.

⁵⁰ *city-patience*, middle-class willingness to endure insult.

HARCOURT. Ay, to poor Horner 'tis like coming to an estate at threescore, when a man can't be the better for't.

PINCHWIFE. Come.

MRS. PINCHWIFE. Presently, bud.

DORILANT. Come let us go too: madam, your servant. (*To* ALITHEA.) Good night, strapper.— (*To* LUCY.)

HARCOURT. Madam, though you will not let me have a good day, or night, I wish you one; but dare not name the other half of my wish.

ALITHEA. Good night, sir, for ever.

MRS. PINCHWIFE. I don't know where to put this here, dear bud, you shall eat it; nay, you shall have part of the fine gentleman's good things, or treat as you call it, when we come home.

PINCHWIFE. Indeed I deserve it, since I furnished the best part of it.   (*Strikes away the orange.*)

> The gallant treats, presents, and gives the ball;
> But 'tis the absent cuckold, pays for all.

ACT IV

[SCENE I.] *In* PINCHWIFE'S *house in the morning*

(LUCY, ALITHEA *dressed in new clothes.*)

LUCY. Well—madam, now have I dressed you, and set you out with so many ornaments, and spent upon you ounces of essence, and pulvilio;[51] and all this for no other purpose, but as people adorn, and perfume a corpse, for a stinking second-hand-grave,[52] such or as bad I think Master Sparkish's bed.

ALITHEA. Hold your peace.

LUCY. Nay, madam, I will ask you the reason, why you would banish poor Master Harcourt for ever from your sight? how could you be so hard-hearted?

ALITHEA. 'Twas because I was not hard-hearted.

LUCY. No, no; 'twas stark love and kindness, I warrant.

---

51 *pulvilio*, cosmetic powder.
52 *second-hand-grave*, reopened grave; often used in the seventeenth century for additional burials.

ALITHEA. It was so; I would see him no more, because I love him.

LUCY. Hey day, a very pretty reason.

ALITHEA. You do not understand me.

LUCY. I wish you may yourself.

ALITHEA. I was engaged to marry, you see, another man, whom my justice will not suffer me to deceive, or injure.

LUCY. Can there be a greater cheat or wrong done to a man, than to give him your person, without your heart, I should make a conscience of it.

ALITHEA. I'll retrieve it for him after I am married a while.

LUCY. The woman that marries to love better, will be as much mistaken, as the wencher that marries to live better. No, madam, marrying to increase love, is like gaming to become rich; alas you only lose what little stock you had before.

ALITHEA. I find by your rhetoric you have been bribed to betray me.

LUCY. Only by his merit, that has bribed your heart, you see, against your word, and rigid honour; but what a devil is this honour? 'tis sure a disease in the head, like the megrim,⁵³ or falling-sickness,⁵⁴ that always hurries people away to do themselves mischief; men lose their lives by it: women what's dearer to'em, their love, the life of life.

ALITHEA. Come, pray talk you no more of honour, nor Master Harcourt; I wish the other would come, to secure my fidelity to him, and his right in me.

LUCY. You will marry him then?

ALITHEA. Certainly, I have given him already my word, and will my hand too, to make it good when he comes.

LUCY. Well, I wish I may never stick pin more, if he be not an arrant natural, to t'other fine gentleman.

ALITHEA. I own he wants the wit of Harcourt, which I will dispense withal, for another want he has, which is want of jealousy, which men of wit seldom want.

LUCY. Lord, madam, what should you do with a fool to your husband? You intend to be honest, don't you? then that husbandly virtue, credulity, is thrown away upon you.

ALITHEA. He only that could suspect my virtue, should have cause to do it; 'tis Sparkish's confidence in my truth, that obliges me to be so faithful to him.

---

⁵³ *megrim*, migraine headache.
⁵⁴ *falling-sickness*, epilepsy.

LUCY. You are not sure his opinion may last.

ALITHEA. I am satisfied, 'tis impossible for him to be jealous, after the proofs I have had of him: Jealousy in a husband, Heaven defend me from it, it begets a thousand plagues to a poor woman, the loss of her honour, her quiet, and her—

LUCY. And her pleasure.

ALITHEA. What d'ye mean, impertinent?

LUCY. Liberty is a great pleasure, madam.

ALITHEA. I say loss of her honour, her quiet, nay, her life sometimes; and what's as bad almost, the loss of this town, that is, she is sent into the country, which is the last ill usage of a husband to a wife, I think.

LUCY. O does the wind lie there?   (aside)
Then of necessity, madam, you think a man must carry his wife into the country, if he be wise; the country is as terrible I find to our young English ladies as a monastery to those abroad: and on my virginity, I think they would rather marry a London gaoler, than a high sheriff of a county, since neither can stir from his employment: formerly women of wit married fools, for a great estate, a fine seat, or the like; but now 'tis for a pretty seat only in Lincoln's Inn-fields, St. James's-fields, or the Pall-mall.

(*Enter to them* SPARKISH, *and* HARCOURT *dressed like a parson.*)

SPARKISH. Madam, your humble servant, a happy day to you, and to us all.

HARCOURT. Amen.—

ALITHEA. Who have we here?

SPARKISH. My chaplain faith—O madam, poor Harcourt remembers his humble service to you; and in obedience to your last commands, refrains coming into your sight.

ALITHEA. Is not that he?

SPARKISH. No, fye no; but to show that he ne're intended to hinder our match has sent his brother here to join our hands: when I get me a wife, I must get her a chaplain, according to the custom; this is his brother, and my chaplain.

ALITHEA. His brother?

LUCY. And your chaplain, to preach in your pulpit then—
                                                      (aside)

ALITHEA. His brother!

SPARKISH. Nay, I knew you would not believe it; I told you, sir, she would take you for your brother Frank.

ALITHEA. Believe it!

LUCY. His brother! hah, ha, he, he has a trick left still it seems— *(aside)*

SPARKISH. Come, my dearest, pray let us go to church before the canonical hour is past.

ALITHEA. For shame you are abused still.

SPARKISH. By the world 'tis strange now you are so incredulous.

ALITHEA. 'Tis strange you are so credulous.

SPARKISH. Dearest of my life, hear me, I tell you this is Ned Harcourt of Cambridge, by the world, you see he has a sneaking college look; 'tis true he's something like his brother Frank, and they differ from each other no more than in their age, for they were twins.

LUCY. Hah, ha, he.

ALITHEA. Your servant, sir, I cannot be so deceived, though you are; but come let's hear, how do you know what you affirm so confidently?

SPARKISH. Why, I'll tell you all; Frank Harcourt coming to me this morning, to wish me joy and present his service to you: I asked him, if he could help me to a parson; whereupon he told me, he had a brother in town who was in orders, and he went straight away, and sent him, you see there, to me.

ALITHEA. Yes, Frank goes, and puts on a black coat, then tell's you, he is Ned, that's all you have for't.

SPARKISH. Pshaw, pshaw, I tell you by the same token, the midwife put her garter about Frank's neck, to know'em asunder, they were so like.

ALITHEA. Frank tells you this too?

SPARKISH. Ay, and Ned there too; nay, they are both in a story.

ALITHEA. So, so very foolish.

SPARKISH. Lord, if you won't believe one, you had best try him by your chamber-maid there; for chamber-maids must needs know chaplains from other men, they are so used to'em.

LUCY. Let's see; nay, I'll be sworn he has the canonical smirk, and the filthy, clammy palm of a chaplain.

ALITHEA. Well, most reverend Doctor, pray let us make an end of this fooling.

HARCOURT. With all my soul, divine, heavenly creature, when you please.

ALITHEA. He speaks like a chaplain indeed.

SPARKISH. Why, was there not, soul, divine, heavenly, in what he said.

ALITHEA. Once more, most impertinent black-coat, cease your persecution, and let us have a conclusion of this ridiculous love.

HARCOURT. I had forgot, I must suit my style to my coat, or I wear it in vain. (*aside*)

ALITHEA. I have no more patience left, let us make once an end of this troublesome love, I say.

HARCOURT. So be it, seraphic lady, when your honour shall think it meet, and convenient so to do.

SPARKISH. Gad, I'm sure none but a chaplain could speak so, I think.

ALITHEA. Let me tell you, sir, this dull trick will not serve your turn, though you delay our marriage, you shall not hinder it.

HARCOURT. Far be it from me, munificent patroness, to delay your marriage, I desire nothing more than to marry you presently, which I might do, if you yourself would; for my noble, good-natured and thrice-generous patron here would not hinder it.

SPARKISH. No, poor man, not I faith.

HARCOURT. And now, madam, let me tell you plainly, no body else shall marry you, by heavens! I'll die first, for I'm sure I should die after it.

LUCY. How his love has made him forget his function, as I have seen it in real parsons.

ALITHEA. That was spoken like a chaplain too, now you understand him, I hope.

SPARKISH. Poor man, he takes it heinously to be refused; I can't blame him, 'tis putting an indignity upon him not to be suffered, but you'll pardon me madam, it shan't be, he shall marry us, come away, pray, madam.

LUCY. Hah, ha, he, more ado! 'tis late.

ALITHEA. Invincible stupidity! I tell you he would marry me as your rival, not as your chaplain.

SPARKISH. Come, come, madam. (*Pulling her away.*)

LUCY. I pray, madam, do not refuse this reverend divine, the honour and satisfaction of marrying you; for I dare say, he has set his heart upon't, good doctor.

ALITHEA. What can you hope, or design by this?

HARCOURT. I could answer her, a reprieve for a day only, often revokes a hasty doom; at worst, if she will not take mercy on me, and let me marry her, I have at least the lover's second pleasure, hindering my rival's enjoyment, though but for a time.

SPARKISH. Come, madam, 'tis e'en twelve o'clock, and my mother charged me never to be married out of the canonical hours; come, come, Lord, here's such a deal of modesty, I warrant, the first day.

LUCY. Yes, an't please your worship, married women show all their modesty the first day, because married men show all their love the first day.

(*Exeunt* SPARKISH, ALITHEA, HARCOURT, *and* LUCY.)

(*The scene changes to a bed-chamber, where appear* PINCHWIFE, MRS. PINCHWIFE.)

PINCHWIFE. Come tell me, I say.

MRS. PINCHWIFE. Lord, han't I told it an hundred times over.

PINCHWIFE. I would try, if in the repetition of the ungrateful tale, I could find her altering it in the least circumstance, for if her story be false, she is so too. (*aside*) Come, how was't, baggage?

MRS. PINCHWIFE. Lord, what pleasure you take to hear it sure!

PINCHWIFE. No, you take more in telling it I find, but speak how was't?

MRS. PINCHWIFE. He carried me up into the house, next to the Exchange.

PINCHWIFE. So, and you two were only in the room.

MRS. PINCHWIFE. Yes, for he sent away a youth that was there, for some dried fruit, and China oranges.

PINCHWIFE. Did he so? Damn him for it—and for—

MRS. PINCHWIFE. But presently came up the gentlewoman of the house.

PINCHWIFE. O 'twas well she did, but what did he do whilst the fruit came?

MRS. PINCHWIFE. He kissed me an hundred times, and told me he fancied he kissed my fine sister, meaning me, you know, whom he said he loved with all his soul, and bid me be sure to tell her so, and to desire her to be at her window, by eleven of the clock this morning, and he would walk under it at that time.

PINCHWIFE. And he was as good as his word, very punctual, a pox reward him for't. (*aside*)

MRS. PINCHWIFE. Well, and he said if you were not within, he would come up to her, meaning me you know, bud, still.

PINCHWIFE. So—he knew her certainly, but for this confession, I am obliged to her simplicity. *(aside)* But what, you stood very still when he kissed you?

MRS. PINCHWIFE. Yes I warrant you, would you have had me discover myself?

PINCHWIFE. But you told me, he did some beastliness to you, as you call'd it, what was't?

MRS. PINCHWIFE. Why, he put—

PINCHWIFE. What?

MRS. PINCHWIFE. Why he put the tip of his tongue between my lips, and so musled[55] me—and I said, I'd bite it.

PINCHWIFE. An eternal canker seize it, for a dog.

MRS. PINCHWIFE. Nay, you need not be so angry with him neither, for to say truth, he has the sweetest breath I ever knew.

PINCHWIFE. The devil—you were satisfied with it then, and would do it again.

MRS. PINCHWIFE. Not unless he should force me.

PINCHWIFE. Force you, changeling! I tell you no woman can be forced.

MRS. PINCHWIFE. Yes, but she may sure, by such a one as he, for he's a proper, goodly strong man, 'tis hard, let me tell you, to resist him.

PINCHWIFE. So, 'tis plain she loves him, yet she has not love enough to make her conceal it from me, but the sight of him will increase her aversion for me, and love for him; and that love instruct her how to deceive me, and satisfy him, all idiot as she is: love, 'twas he gave women first their craft, their art of deluding; out of nature's hands, they came plain, open, silly and fit for slaves, as she and Heaven intended 'em; but damned love— Well— I must strangle that little monster, whilst I can deal with him. Go fetch pen, ink and paper out of the next room:

MRS. PINCHWIFE. Yes, bud. *(Exit MRS. PINCHWIFE.)*

PINCHWIFE. Why should women have more invention in love than men? It can only be, because they have more desires, more soliciting passions, more lust, and more of the devil.

---

[55] *musled,* fondled; kissed with open mouth.

(MISTRESS PINCHWIFE *returns*.)

Come, minx, sit down and write.

MRS. PINCHWIFE. Ay, dear bud, but I can't do't very well.

PINCHWIFE. I wish you could not at all.

MRS. PINCHWIFE. But what should I write for?

PINCHWIFE. I'll have you write a letter to your lover.

MRS. PINCHWIFE. O Lord, to the fine gentleman, a letter!

PINCHWIFE. Yes, to the fine gentleman.

MRS. PINCHWIFE. Lord, you do but jeer; sure you jest.

PINCHWIFE. I am not so merry, come write as I bid you.

MRS. PINCHWIFE. What, do you think I am a fool?

PINCHWIFE. She's afraid I would not dictate any love to him, therefore she's unwilling; but you had best begin. (*aside*)

MRS. PINCHWIFE. Indeed, and indeed, but I won't, so I won't.

PINCHWIFE. Why?

MRS. PINCHWIFE. Because he's in town, you may send for him if you will.

PINCHWIFE. Very well, you would have him brought to you; is it come to this? I say take the pen and write, or you'll provoke me.

MRS. PINCHWIFE. Lord, what d'ye make a fool of me for? Don't I know that letters are never writ, but from the country to London, and from London into the country? Now he's in town, and I am in town too; therefore I can't write to him you know.

PINCHWIFE. So I am glad it is no worse, she is innocent enough yet. (*aside*)
Yes you may when your husband bids you write letters to people that are in town.

MRS. PINCHWIFE. O may I so! Then I'm satisfiéd.

PINCHWIFE. Come begin— sir— (*Dictates*.)

MRS. PINCHWIFE. Shan't I say, dear sir? You know one says always something more than bare sir.

PINCHWIFE. Write as I bid you, or I will write whore with this penknife in your face.

MRS. PINCHWIFE. Nay, good bud— sir— (*She writes*.)

PINCHWIFE. Though I suffered last night your nauseous, loathed kisses and embraces— write.

MRS. PINCHWIFE. Nay, why should I say so, you know I told you, he had a sweet breath.

PINCHWIFE. Write.

MRS. PINCHWIFE. Let me but put out, loathed.

PINCHWIFE. Write, I say.

MRS. PINCHWIFE. Well then.   (*Writes.*)

PINCHWIFE. Let's see what have you writ?

Though I suffered last night your kisses and embraces—

(*Takes the paper, and reads.*)

Thou impudent creature, where is nauseous and loathed?

MRS. PINCHWIFE. I can't abide to write such filthy words.

PINCHWIFE. Once more write as I'd have you, and question
it not, or I will spoil thy writing with this. I will stab out
those eyes that cause my mischief.

(*Holds up the penknife.*)

MRS. PINCHWIFE. O Lord, I will.

PINCHWIFE. So—so— Let's see now!   (*Reads.*)
Though I suffered last night your nauseous, loathed
kisses, and embraces. Go on— Yet I would not have you
presume that you shall ever repeat them— So—

(*She writes.*)

MRS. PINCHWIFE. I have writ it.

PINCHWIFE. On then— I then concealed myself from your
knowledge, to avoid your insolencies—   (*She writes.*)

MRS. PINCHWIFE. So—

PINCHWIFE. The same reason now I am out of your hands—

(*She writes.*)

MRS. PINCHWIFE. So—

PINCHWIFE. Makes me own to you my unfortunate, though
innocent frolic, of being in man's clothes.

(*She writes.*)

MRS. PINCHWIFE. So—

PINCHWIFE. That you may for ever more cease to pursue her,
who hates and detests you—   (*She writes on.*)

MRS. PINCHWIFE. So—h—   (*Sighs.*)

PINCHWIFE. What, do you sigh?—detests you—as much as she
loves her husband and her honour—

MRS. PINCHWIFE. I vow, husband, he'll ne'er believe I should
write such a letter.

PINCHWIFE. What, he'd expect a kinder from you? Come now,
your name only.

MRS. PINCHWIFE. What, shan't I say Your most faithful,
humble servant till death?

PINCHWIFE. No, tormenting fiend; her style I find would be
very soft.   (*aside*)

Come wrap it up now, whilst I go fetch wax and a candle; and write on the back side, for Mr. Horner.

(*Exit* PINCHWIFE.)

MRS. PINCHWIFE. For Mr. Horner— So, I am glad he has told me his name; Dear Mr. Horner, but why should I send thee such a letter, that will vex thee, and make thee angry with me?—well, I will not send it— Ay, but then my husband will kill me—for I see plainly, he won't let me love Mr. Horner—but what care I for my husband—I won't, so I won't send poor Mr. Horner such a letter—but then my husband— But oh—what if I writ at bottom, my husband made me write it— Ay but then my husband would see't— Can one have no shift? Ah, a London woman would have had a hundred presently; stay—what if I should write a letter, and wrap it up like this, and write upon't too. Ay, but then my husband would see't— I don't know what to do— But yet y vads[56] I'll try, so I will—for I will not send this letter to poor Mr. Horner, come what will on't.

Dear, Sweet Mr. Horner— So— (*She writes, and repeats what she hath writ.*) my husband would have me send you a base, rude, unmannerly letter—but I won't —*so*—and would have me forbid you loving me—but I wont—*so*—and would have me say to you, I hate you poor Mr. Horner—but I won't tell a lie for him—*there*— for I'm sure if you and I were in the country at cards together,—*so*—I could not help treading on your toe under the table—*so*—or rubbing knees with you, and staring in your face, 'till you saw me—*very well*—and then looking down, and blushing for an hour together —*so*—but I must make haste before my husband come; and now he has taught me to write letters: you shall have longer ones from me, who am

Dear, dear, poor dear Mr. Horner, your most
Humble Friend, and Servant to command
'til death, Margery Pinchwife.

Stay, I must give him a hint at bottom—*so*—now wrap it up just like t'other—*so*—now write for Mr. Horner,— But oh now what shall I do with it? for here comes my husband.

---

[56] *vads*, truly.

(*Enter* PINCHWIFE.)

PINCHWIFE. I have been detained by a sparkish coxcomb,
    who pretended a visit to me; but I fear 'twas to my wife.
                                                          (*aside*)
    What, have you done?

MRS. PINCHWIFE. Ay, ay bud, just now.

PINCHWIFE. Let's see't, what d'ye tremble for; what, you
    would not have it go?

MRS. PINCHWIFE. Here.— No I must not give him that, (*He
    slashes open, and reads the first letter.*) so I had been
    served if I had given him this.   (*aside*)

PINCHWIFE. Come, where's the wax and seal?

MRS. PINCHWIFE. Lord, what shall I do now? Nay then I
    have it—   (*aside*)
    Pray let me see't. Lord, you think me so arrant a fool I
    cannot seal a letter, I will do't, so I will.

(*Snatches the letter from him, changes it for the other, seals
it, and delivers it to him.*)

PINCHWIFE. Nay, I believe you will learn that, and other
    things too, which I would not have you.

MRS. PINCHWIFE. So, han't I done it curiously?
    I think I have, there's my letter going to Mr. Horner;
    since he'll needs have me send letters to folks.   (*aside*)

PINCHWIFE. 'Tis very well, but I warrant, you would not have
    it go now?

MRS. PINCHWIFE. Yes indeed, but I would, bud, now.

PINCHWIFE. Well you are a good girl then, come let me lock
    you up in your chamber, 'till I come back; and be sure
    you come not within three strides of the window, when
    I am gone; for I have a spy in the street.

                                   (*Exit* MRS. PINCHWIFE.)
                                   (PINCHWIFE *locks the door.*)

At least, 'tis fit she think so, if we do not cheat women,
they'll cheat us; and fraud may be justly used with secret
enemies, of which a wife is the most dangerous; and he
that has a handsome one to keep, and a frontier town,
must provide against treachery, rather than open force—
Now I have secured all within, I'll deal with the foe
without with false intelligence.

                                        (*Holds up the letter.*)
                                        (*Exit* PINCHWIFE.)

(*The scene changes to* HORNER's *lodging.*)

(QUACK *and* HORNER.)

QUACK. Well sir, how fadges[57] the new design; have you not the luck of all your brother projectors,[58] to deceive only yourself at last.

HORNER. No, good *Domine* Doctor, I deceive you it seems, and others too; for the grave matrons, and old rigid husbands think me as unfit for love, as they are; but their wives, sisters and daughters, know some of 'em better things already.

QUACK. Already!

HORNER. Already, I say; last night I was drunk with half a dozen of your civil persons, as you call 'em, and people of honour, and so was made free of their society, and dressing rooms for ever hereafter; and am already come to the privileges of sleeping upon their pallats, warming smocks, tying shoes and garters, and the like, Doctor, already, already Doctor.

QUACK. You have made use of your time, sir.

HORNER. I tell thee, I am now no more interruption to 'em, when they sing, or talk bawdy, than a little squab[59] French page, who speaks no English.

QUACK. But do civil persons and women of honour drink and sing bawdy songs?

HORNER. O amongst friends, amongst friends; for your bigots in honour, are just like those in religion; they fear the eye of the world, more than the eye of heaven, and think there is no virtue, but railing at vice; and no sin, but giving scandal: they rail at a poor, little, kept player, and keep themselves some young, modest pulpit comedian to be privy to their sins in their closets, not to tell 'em of them in their chapels.

QUACK. Nay, the truth on't is, priests amongst the women now have quite got the better of us lay confessors, physicians.

HORNER. And they are rather their patients, but—

(*Enter* MY LADY FIDGET, *looking about her.*)

---

57 *fadges*, succeeds.
58 *projectors*, alchemists.
59 *squab*, plump.

Now we talk of women of honour, here comes one. Step
behind the screen there, and but observe; if I have not
particular privileges, with the women of reputation already, Doctor, already.

LADY FIDGET. Well, Horner, am not I a woman of honour?
you see I'm as good as my word.

HORNER. And you shall see, madam, I'll not be behind hand
with you in honour; and I'll be as good as my word too,
if you please but to withdraw into the next room.

LADY FIDGET. But first, my dear sir, you must promise to have
a care of my dear honour.

HORNER. If you talk a word more of your honour, you'll
make me incapable to wrong it; to talk of honour in the
mysteries of love, is like talking of heaven, or the deity
in an operation of witchcraft, just when you are em-
ploying the devil, it makes the charm impotent.

LADY FIDGET. Nay, fie, let us not be smutty; but you talk of
mysteries, and bewitching to me, I don't understand
you.

HORNER. I tell you, madam, the word "money" in a mistress's
mouth, at such a nick of time, is not a more disheart-
ning sound to a younger brother, than that of honour to
an eager lover like myself.

LADY FIDGET. But you can't blame a lady of my reputation
to be chary.

HORNER. Chary—I have been chary of it already, by the
report I have caused of myself.

LADY FIDGET. Ay, but if you should ever let other women
know that dear secret, it would come out; nay, you must
have a great care of your conduct; for my acquaintance
are so censorious—oh 'tis a wicked censorious world,
Mr. Horner—I say, are so censorious, and detracting, that
perhaps they'll talk to the prejudice of my honour,
though you should not let them know the dear secret.

HORNER. Nay, madam, rather than they shall prejudice your
honour, I'll prejudice theirs; and to serve you, I'll lie
with'em all, make the secret their own, and then they'll
keep it: I am a Machiavel in love, madam.

LADY FIDGET. O, no sir, not that way.

HORNER. Nay, the devil take me, if censorious women are to
be silenced any other way.

LADY FIDGET. A secret is better kept I hope, by a single person,
than a multitude; therefore pray do not trust any body
else with it, dear, dear Mr. Horner. (*Embracing him.*)

(*Enter* SIR JASPAR FIDGET.)

SIR JASPAR. How now!

LADY FIDGET. O my husband—prevented—and what's almost
as bad, found with my arms about another man—that
will appear too much—what shall I say?   (*aside*)
Sir Jaspar, come hither, I am trying if Mr. Horner were
ticklish, and he's as ticklish as can be, I love to torment
the confounded toad; let you and I tickle him.

SIR JASPAR. No, your ladyship will tickle him better without
me, I suppose. But is this your buying china? I thought
you had been at the china house?

HORNER. China house, that's my cue, I must take it.   (*aside*)
A pox, can't you keep your impertinent wives at home?
some men are troubled with the husbands, but I with
the wives; but I'd have you to know, since I cannot be
your journeyman by night, I will not be your drudge by
day, to squire your wife about, and be your man of straw,
or scare-crow only to pies and jays; that would be nibbling at your forbidden fruit; I shall be shortly the
hackney gentleman-usher of the town.

SIR JASPAR. Heh, heh, he, poor fellow he's in the right on't;
faith, to squire women about for other folks is as ungrateful an employment, as to tell money for other folks;
(*aside*) heh, he, he, ben't angry Horner—

LADY FIDGET. No, 'tis I have more reason to be angry, who
am left by you, to go abroad indecently alone; or, what
is more indecent, to pin myself upon such ill-bred people
of your acquaintance, as this is.

SIR JASPAR. Nay, prithee what has he done?

LADY FIDGET. Nay, he has done nothing.

SIR JASPAR. But what d'ye take ill, if he has done nothing?

LADY FIDGET. Hah, hah, hah, faith, I can't but laugh however; why d'ye think the unmannerly toad would not
come down to me to the coach? I was fain to come up to
fetch him, or go without him, which I was resolved not
to do; for he knows china very well, and has himself
very good, but will not let me see it, lest I should beg
some; but I will find it out, and have what I came for
yet.   (*Exit* LADY FIDGET, *followed by*
                                       HORNER *to the door.*)

HORNER. Lock the door, madam— (*Apart to* LADY FIDGET *who
                                       locks the door*)
So, she has got into my chamber, and locked me out;

oh the impertinency of woman-kind! Well, Sir Jaspar,
plain dealing is a jewel; if ever you suffer your wife to
trouble me again here, she shall carry you home a pair
of horns, by my Lord Mayor she shall; though I cannot
furnish you myself, you are sure, yet I'll find a way.

SIR JASPAR. Hah, ha, he, at my first coming in, and finding
her arms about him, tickling him it seems, I was half
jealous, but now I see my folly.   (*aside*)
Heh, he, he, poor Horner.

HORNER. Nay, though you laugh now, 'twill be my turn e're
long: Oh women, more impertinent, more cunning, and
more mischievous than their monkeys, and to me almost
as ugly—now is she throwing my things about, and rifling
all I have, but I'll get into her the back way, and so rifle
her for it—

SIR JASPAR. Hah, ha, ha, poor angry Horner.

HORNER. Stay here a little, I'll ferret her out to you presently,
I warrant.   (*Exit* HORNER *at t'other door.*)

SIR JASPAR. Wife, my Lady Fidget, wife, he is coming into
you the back way. (SIR JASPAR *calls through the door
to his wife, she answers from within.*)

LADY FIDGET. Let him come, and welcome, which way he will.

SIR JASPAR. He'll catch you, and use you roughly, and be too
strong for you.

LADY FIDGET. Don't you trouble yourself, let him if he can.

QUACK. (*behind*) This indeed, I could not have believed from
him, nor any but my own eyes.

(*Enter* MISTRESS SQUEAMISH.)

SQUEAMISH. Where's this woman-hater, this toad, this ugly,
greasy, dirty sloven?

SIR JASPAR. So the women all will have him ugly, methinks
he is a comely person; but his wants make his form
contemptible to'em; and 'tis e'en as my wife said yesterday, talking of him, that a proper handsome eunuch,
was as ridiculous a thing as a gigantic coward.

SQUEAMISH. Sir Jaspar, your servant, where is the odious beast?

SIR JASPAR. He's within in his chamber, with my wife; she's
playing the wag with him.

SQUEAMISH. Is she so, and he's a clownish beast, he'll give her
no quarter, he'll play the wag with her again, let me tell
you; come, let's go help her— what, the door's locked?

SIR JASPAR. Ay, my wife locked it—

SQUEAMISH. Did she so, let us break it open then?

SIR JASPAR. No, no, he'll do her no hurt.

SQUEAMISH. No— but is there no other way to get into'em, whither goes this? I will disturb'em. (*aside*)

(*Exit* SQUEAMISH *at another door.*)

(*Enter old* LADY SQUEAMISH.)

LADY SQUEAMISH. Where is this harlotry, this impudent baggage, this rambling tomrigg?[60] O Sir Jaspar, I'm glad to see you here, did you not see my wild grandchild come in hither just now?

SIR JASPAR. Yes.

LADY SQUEAMISH. Ay, but where is she then? where is she? Lord, Sir Jaspar I have e'en rattled myself to pieces in pursuit of her, but can you tell what she makes here, they say below, no woman lodges here.

SIR JASPAR. No.

LADY SQUEAMISH. No— what does she here then? say if it be not a woman's lodging, what makes she here? but are you sure no woman lodges here?

SIR JASPAR. No, nor no man neither, this is Mr. Horner's lodging.

LADY SQUEAMISH. Is it so are you sure?

SIR JASPAR. Yes, yes.

LADY SQUEAMISH. So then there's no hurt in't I hope, but where is he?

SIR JASPAR. He's in the next room with my wife.

LADY SQUEAMISH. Nay if you trust him with your wife, I may with my Biddy; they say he's a merry harmless man now, e'en as harmless a man as ever came out of Italy with a good voice,[61] and as pretty harmless company for a lady as a snake without his teeth.

SIR JASPAR. Ay, ay poor man.

(*Enter* MRS. SQUEAMISH.)

SQUEAMISH. I can't find'em— oh are you here, grandmother, I followed, you must know, my Lady Fidget hither; 'tis the prettiest lodging, and I have been staring on the prettiest pictures.

(*Enter* LADY FIDGET *with a piece of china in her hand, and* HORNER *following.*)

---

60 *tomrigg*, tomboy.
61 *as harmless a man . . . good voice*, i.e., a castrated Italian soprano.

LADY FIDGET. And I have been toiling and moiling, for the prettiest piece of china, my dear.

HORNER. Nay she has been too hard for me, do what I could.

SQUEAMISH. Oh Lord I'll have some china too, good Mr. Horner, don't think to give other people china, and me none, come in with me too.

HORNER. Upon my honour I have none left now.

SQUEAMISH. Nay, nay I have known you deny your china before now, but you shan't put mc off so, come—

HORNER. This lady had the last there.

LADY FIDGET. Yes indeed, madam, to my certain knowledge he has no more left.

SQUEAMISH. O but it may be he may have some you could not find.

LADY FIDGET. What, d'y think if he had had any left, I would not have had it too, for we women of quality never think we have china enough.

HORNER. Do not take it ill, I cannot make china for you all, but I will have a rol-waggon[62] for you too, another time.

SQUEAMISH. Thank you, dear toad.   (*To* HORNER *aside.*)

LADY FIDGET. What do you mean by that promise?

HORNER. Alas she has an innocent, literal understanding.

(*Apart to* LADY FIDGET.)

LADY SQUEAMISH. Poor Mr. Horner, he has enough to do to please you all, I see.

HORNER. Ay madam, you see how they use me.

LADY SQUEAMISH. Poor gentleman, I pity you.

HORNER. I thank you, madam, I could never find pity, but from such reverend ladies as you are, the young ones will never spare a man.

SQUEAMISH. Come come, beast, and go dine with us, for we shall want a man at ombre after dinner.

HORNER. That's all their use of me, madam, you see.

SQUEAMISH. Come, sloven, I'll lead you to be sure of you.

(*Pulls him by the cravatte.*)

LADY SQUEAMISH. Alas poor man, how she tugs him. Kiss, kiss her, that's the way to make such nice women quiet.

HORNER. No madam, that remedy is worse than the torment, they know I dare suffer any thing rather than do it.

---

62 *rol-waggon*, phallic-shaped vase.

LADY SQUEAMISH. Prithee kiss her, and I'll give you her picture
    in little, that you admired so last night, prithee do.

HORNER. Well nothing but that could bribe me, I love a
    woman only in effigy, and good painting as much as I
    hate them— I'll do't, for I could adore the devil well
    painted.   (*Kisses* MRS. SQUEAMISH.)

SQUEAMISH. Foh, you filthy toad, nay now I've done jesting.

LADY SQUEAMISH. Ha, ha, ha, I told you so.

SQUEAMISH. Foh, a kiss of his—

SIR JASPAR. Has no more hurt in't, than one of my spaniel's.

SQUEAMISH. Nor no more good neither.

QUACK. I will now believe any thing he tells me.   (*behind*)

(*Enter* MR. PINCHWIFE.)

LADY FIDGET. O Lord, here's a man! Sir Jaspar, my mask, my
    mask, I would not be seen here for the world.

SIR JASPAR. What, not when I am with you?

LADY FIDGET. No, no, my honour—let's be gone.

SQUEAMISH. Oh grandmother, let us be gone, make haste,
    make haste, I know not how he may censure us.

LADY FIDGET. Be found in the lodging of any thing like a
    man! Away.

(*Exeunt* SIR JASPAR, LADY FIDGET, OLD LADY SQUEAMISH,
    MRS. SQUEAMISH.)

QUACK. What's here, another cuckold—he looks like one, and
    none else sure have any business with him.   (*behind*)

HORNER. Well what brings my dear friend hither?

PINCHWIFE. Your impertinency.

HORNER. My impertinency—why you gentlemen that have got
    handsome wives, think you have a privilege of saying
    any thing to your friends, and are as brutish as if you
    were our creditors.

PINCHWIFE. No sir, I'll ne're trust you any way.

HORNER. But why not, dear Jack. Why diffide in[63] me thou
    know'st so well.

PINCHWIFE. Because I do know you so well.

HORNER. Han't I been always thy friend, honest Jack, always
    ready to serve thee, in love, or battle, before thou wert
    married, and am so still.

PINCHWIFE. I believe so you would be my second now indeed.

HORNER. Well then, dear Jack, why so unkind, so grum, so

---

[63] *diffide in*, distrust.

strange to me, come, prithee kiss me dear rogue; gad, I
was always, I say, and am still as much thy servant as—

PINCHWIFE. As I am yours, sir. What, you would send a kiss
to my wife, is that it?

HORNER. So there 'tis—a man can't show his friendship to a
married man, but presently he talks of his wife to you;
prithee let thy wife alone, and let thee and I be all one,
as we were wont. What, thou art as shy of my kindness
as a Lombard Street alderman of a courtier's civility at
Lockets.

PINCHWIFE. But you are over-kind to me, as kind, as if I
were your cuckold already, yet I must confess you ought
to be kind and civil to me, since I am so kind, so civil
to you, as to bring you this. Look you there, sir.

(*Delivers him a letter.*)

HORNER. What is't?

PINCHWIFE. Only a love letter sir.

HORNER. From whom—how, this is from your wife—hum—
and hum— (*Reads.*)

PINCHWIFE. Even from my wife, sir, am I not wondrous kind
and civil to you, now too?

But you'll not think her so. (*aside*)

HORNER. Ha, is this a trick of his or hers. (*aside*)

PINCHWIFE. The gentleman's surprised I find. What, you expected a kinder letter?

HORNER. No, faith not I, how could I?

PINCHWIFE. Yes yes, I'm sure you did. A man so well made
as you are must needs be disappointed, if the women
declare not their passion at first sight or opportunity.

(*Reads aside.*)

HORNER. But what should this mean? Stay the postscript: Be
sure you love me whatsoever my husband says to the
contrary, and let him not see this, lest he should come
home, and pinch me, or kill my squirrel.

It seems he knows not what the letter contains. (*aside*)

PINCHWIFE. Come, ne're wonder at it so much.

HORNER. Faith I can't help it.

PINCHWIFE. Now I think I have deserved your infinite friendship, and kindness, and have showed myself sufficiently
an obliging kind friend and husband, am I not so, to
bring a letter from my wife to her gallant?

HORNER. Ay, the devil take me, art thou, the most obliging,
kind friend and husband in the world, ha, ha.

PINCHWIFE. Well you may be merry sir, but in short I must tell you sir, my honour will suffer no jesting.

HORNER. What do'st thou mean?

PINCHWIFE. Does the letter want a comment? Then know, sir, though I have been so civil a husband as to bring you a letter from my wife, to let you kiss and court her to my face, I will not be a cuckold, sir, I will not.

HORNER. Thou art mad with jealousy, I never saw thy wife in my life, but at the play yesterday, and I know not if it were she or no. I court her, kiss her!

PINCHWIFE. I will not be a cuckold I say, there will be danger in making me a cuckold.

HORNER. Why, wert thou not well cured of thy last clap?

PINCHWIFE. I wear a sword.

HORNER. It should be taken from thee, lest thou should'st do thyself a mischief with it, thou art mad, man.

PINCHWIFE. As mad as I am, and as merry as you are, I must have more reason from you ere we part, I say again, though you kissed, and courted last night my wife in man's clothes, as she confesses in her letter.

HORNER. Ha—   (aside)

PINCHWIFE. Both she and I say you must not design it again, for you have mistaken your woman, as you have done your man.

HORNER. Oh—I understand something now—   (aside) Was that thy wife? why would'st thou not tell me 'twas she? Faith my freedom with her was your fault, not mine.

PINCHWIFE. Faith so 'twas—   (aside)

HORNER. Fie, I'd never do't to a woman before her husband's face, sure.

PINCHWIFE. But I had rather you should do't to my wife before my face, than behind my back, and that you shall never do.

HORNER. No—you will hinder me.

PINCHWIFE. If I would not hinder you, you see by her letter, she would.

HORNER. Well, I must e'en acquiesce then, and be contented with what she writes.

PINCHWIFE. I'll assure you 'twas voluntarily writ, I had no hand in't, you may believe me.

HORNER. I do believe thee, faith.

PINCHWIFE. And believe her too, for she's an innocent creature, has no dissembling in her, and so fare you well sir.

HORNER. Pray, however, present my humble service to her,

and tell her I will obey her letter to a tittle, and fulfill
her desires be what they will, or with what difficulty
soever I do't, and you shall be no more jealous of me,
I warrant her, and you—

PINCHWIFE. Well then, fare you well, and play with any man's
honour but mine, kiss any man's wife but mine, and
welcome—   (*Exit* MR. PINCHWIFE.)

HORNER. Ha, ha, ha, Doctor.

QUACK. It seems he has not heard the report of you, or does
not believe it.

HORNER. Ha, ha, now, Doctor what think you?

QUACK. Pray let's see the letter—hum—for—dear—love you—

(*Reads the letter.*)

HORNER. I wonder how she could contrive it! what say'st
thou to't, 'tis an original.

QUACK. So are your cuckolds too originals: for they are like
no other common cuckolds, and I will henceforth believe it not impossible for you to cuckold the Grand
Signior amidst his guards of eunuchs, that I say—

HORNER. And I say for the letter, 'tis the first love letter that
ever was without flames, darts, fates, destinies, lying and
dissembling in't.

(*Enter* SPARKISH *pulling in* MR. PINCHWIFE.)

SPARKISH. Come back, you are a pretty brother-in-law, neither
go to church, nor to dinner with your sister bride.

PINCHWIFE. My sister denies her marriage, and you see is
gone away from you dissatisfied.

SPARKISH. Pshaw, upon a foolish scruple, that our parson was
not in lawful orders, and did not say all the common
prayer, but 'tis her modesty only I believe, but let women
be never so modest the first day, they'll be sure to come
to themselves by night, and I shall have enough of her
then; in the mean time, Harry Horner, you must dine
with me, I keep my wedding at my aunt's in the Piazza.

HORNER. Thy wedding, what stale maid has lived to despair of
a husband, or what young one of a gallant?

SPARKISH. O your servant, sir—this gentleman's sister then—
no stale maid.

HORNER. I'm sorry for't.

PINCHWIFE. How comes he so concerned for her—   (*aside*)

SPARKISH. You sorry for't, why, do you know any ill by her?

HORNER. No, I know none but by thee, 'tis for her sake, not yours, and another man's sake that might have hoped, I thought—

SPARKISH. Another man, another man, what is his name?

HORNER. Nay since 'tis past he shall be nameless.

Poor Harcourt! I am sorry thou hast missed her— (*aside*)

PINCHWIFE. He seems to be much troubled at the match— (*aside*)

SPARKISH. Prithee tell me—nay you shan't go, brother.

PINCHWIFE. I must of necessity, but I'll come to you to dinner.

(*Exit* PINCHWIFE.)

SPARKISH. But Harry, what, have I a rival in my wife already? but with all my heart, for he may be of use to me here-after, for though my hunger is now my sauce, and I can fall on heartily without, but the time will come when a rival will be as good sauce for a married man to a wife as an orange to veal.

HORNER. O thou damned rogue, thou hast set my teeth on edge with thy orange.

SPARKISH. Then let's to dinner, there I was with you again. Come.

HORNER. But who dines with thee?

SPARKISH. My friends and relations, my brother Pinchwife, you see, of your acquaintance.

HORNER. And his wife.

SPARKISH. No, gad, he'll ne're let her come amongst us good fellows, your stingy country coxcomb keeps his wife from his friends, as he does his little firkin of ale, for his own drinking, and a gentleman can't get a smack on't, but his servants, when his back is turned broach it at their pleasures, and dust it away,[64] ha, ha, ha, gad I am witty, I think, considering I was married to day, by the world, but come—

HORNER. No, I will not dine with you, unless you can fetch her too.

SPARKISH. Pshaw what pleasure can'st thou have with women now, Harry?

HORNER. My eyes are not gone, I love a good prospect yet, and will not dine with you, unless she does too, go fetch her therefore, but do not tell her husband, 'tis for my sake.

---

[64] *dust it away*, knock it back.

SPARKISH. Well I'll go try what I can do, in the mean time come away to my aunt's lodging, 'tis in the way to Pinchwife's.

HORNER. The poor woman has called for aid, and stretched forth her hand, Doctor, I cannot but help her over the pale out of the briars.

(*Exeunt* SPARKISH, HORNER, QUACK.)

(*The scene changes to* PINCHWIFE'S *house.*)
(MRS. PINCHWIFE *alone leaning on her elbow.*)
(*A table, pen, ink, and paper.*)

MRS. PINCHWIFE. Well 'tis e'en so, I have got the London disease they call love, I am sick of my husband, and for my gallant; I have heard this distemper called a fever, but methinks 'tis liker an ague, for when I think of my husband, I tremble and am in a cold sweat, and have inclinations to vomit, but when I think of my gallant, dear Mr. Horner, my hot fit comes, and I am all in a fever, indeed, and as in other fevers, my own chamber is tedious to me, and I would fain be removed to his, and then methinks I should be well; ah poor Mr. Horner, well I cannot, will not stay here, therefore I'll make an end of my letter to him, which shall be a finer letter than my last, because I have studied it like any thing; O sick, sick!

(*Takes the pen and writes.*)

(*Enter* MR. PINCHWIFE *who, seeing her writing, steals softly behind her, and looking over her shoulder, snatches the paper from her.*)

PINCHWIFE. What, writing more letters?
MRS. PINCHWIFE. O Lord, bud, why d'ye fright me so?

(*She offers to run out: he stops her, and reads.*)

PINCHWIFE. How's this! nay, you shall not stir, madam.
    Dear, dear, dear, Mr. Horner—very well—I have taught you to write letters to good purpose—but let's see't.
    First I am to beg your pardon for my boldness in writing to you, which I'd have you to know, I would not have done, had not you said first you loved me so extremely, which if you do, you will never suffer me to lie in the arms of another man, whom I loath, nauseate, and detest— Now you can write these filthy words but

what follows— Therefore I hope you will speedily find
some way to free me from this unfortunate match, which
was never, I assure you, of my choice, but I'm afraid
'tis already too far gone; however if you love me, as I
do you, you will try what you can do, but you must
help me away before tomorrow, or else, alas, I shall be
for ever out of your reach, for I can defer no longer our
—our— (*The letter concludes.*) what is to follow "our"?
Speak, what? our journey into the country I suppose—
Oh woman, damned woman, and love, damned love,
their old tempter, for this is one of his miracles: in a
moment, he can make those blind that could see, and
those see that were blind, those dumb that could speak,
and those prattle who were dumb before, nay what is
more than all, make these dough baked, senseless, in-
docile animals, women, too hard for us their politic lords
and rulers in a moment; but make an end of your letter,
and then I'll make an end of you thus, and all my
plagues together.   (*Draws his sword.*)

MRS. PINCHWIFE. O Lord, O Lord, you are such a passionate
man, bud.

(*Enter* SPARKISH.)

SPARKISH. How now, what's here to do?

PINCHWIFE. This fool here now!

SPARKISH. What, drawn upon your wife? you should never do
that but at night in the dark when you can't hurt her.
This is my sister-in-law, is it not? (*Pulls aside her handkerchief.*) Ay faith, e'en our country Margery, one may
know her. Come, she and you must go dine with me;
dinner's ready, come. But where's my wife, is she not
come home yet, where is she?

PINCHWIFE. Making you a cuckold, 'tis that they all do, as
soon as they can.

SPARKISH. What, the wedding day? No, a wife that designs to
make a cully[65] of her husband will be sure to let him
win the first stake of love, by the world. But come, they
stay dinner for us, come, I'll lead down our Margery.

PINCHWIFE. No—sir, go, we'll follow you.

SPARKISH. I will not wag without you.

PINCHWIFE. This coxcomb is a sensible torment to me amidst
the greatest in the world.

65 *cully,* dupe.

SPARKISH. Come, come Madam Margery.

PINCHWIFE. No I'll lead her my way, what, would you treat
your friends with mine, for want of your own wife?

(*Leads her to t'other door, and locks her in and returns.*)

I am contented my rage should take breath—

SPARKISH. I told Horner this. (*aside*)

PINCHWIFE. Come now.

SPARKISH. Lord, how shy you are of your wife! But let me tell
you, brother, we men of wit have amongst us a saying,
that cuckolding like the small pox comes with a fear, and
you may keep your wife as much as you will out of
danger of infection, but if her constitution incline her
to't, she'll have it sooner or later by the world, say they.

PINCHWIFE. What a thing is a cuckold, that every fool can
make him ridiculous—   (*aside*)

Well sir— But let me advise you, now you are come to
be concerned, because you suspect the danger, not to
neglect the means to prevent it, especially when the
greatest share of the malady will light upon your own
head, for—

How'so'ere the kind wife's belly comes to swell.
The husband breeds for her, and first is ill.

ACT V

[SCENE I.] MR. PINCHWIFE'S *house*

(*Enter* MR. PINCHWIFE *and* MRS. PINCHWIFE. *A table and
candle.*)

PINCHWIFE. Come take the pen and make an end of the letter,
just as you intended. If you are false in a tittle, I shall
soon perceive it, and punish you with this as you deserve.
(*Lays his hand on his sword.*) Write what was to follow—
let's see—

You must make haste and help me away before tomorrow, or else I shall be for ever out of your reach, for
I can defer no longer our— what follows "our"?—

MRS. PINCHWIFE. Must all out then, bud?—look you there
then.   (MRS. PINCHWIFE *takes the pen and writes.*)

PINCHWIFE. Let's see— for I can defer no longer our— wedding— Your slighted Alithea. What's the meaning of this, my sister's name to't? Speak, unriddle?

MRS. PINCHWIFE. Yes indeed, bud.

PINCHWIFE. But why her name to't? Speak—speak I say.

MRS. PINCHWIFE. Ay but you'll tell her then again. If you would not tell her again.

PINCHWIFE. I will not, I am stunned, my head turns round. Speak.

MRS. PINCHWIFE. Won't you tell her indeed, and indeed?

PINCHWIFE. No, speak I say.

MRS. PINCHWIFE. She'll be angry with me, but I had rather she should be angry with me than you, bud; and to tell you the truth, 'twas she made me write the letter, and taught me what I should write.

PINCHWIFE. Ha—I thought the style was somewhat better than her own (*aside*). But how could she come to you to teach you, since I had locked you up alone?

MRS. PINCHWIFE. O, through the key-hole, bud.

PINCHWIFE. But why should she make you write a letter for her to him, since she can write herself?

MRS. PINCHWIFE. Why she said because—for I was unwilling to do it.

PINCHWIFE. Because what—because?

MRS. PINCHWIFE. Because lest Mr. Horner should be cruel, and refuse her, or vain afterwards, and show the letter, she might disown it, the hand not being hers.

PINCHWIFE. How's this? ha—then I think I shall come to myself again— this changeling could not invent this lie, but if she could, why should she? she might think I should soon discover it—stay—now I think on't too, Horner said he was sorry she had married Sparkish, and her disowning her marriage to me, makes me think she has evaded it, for Horner's sake. Yet why should she take this course? But men in love are fools, women may well be so.— (*aside*)
But hark you, madam, your sister went out in the morning, and I have not seen her within since.

MRS. PINCHWIFE. Alack a day, she has been crying all day above, it seems, in a corner.

PINCHWIFE. Where is she, let me speak with her.

MRS. PINCHWIFE. O Lord then he'll discover all— (*aside*) pray hold, bud, what d'y mean to discover me, she'll know I have told you then. Pray bud, let me talk with her first—

PINCHWIFE. I must speak with her to know whether Horner ever made her any promise; and whether she be married to Sparkish or no.

MRS. PINCHWIFE. Pray, dear bud, don't, till I have spoken with her and told her that I have told you all, for she'll kill me else.

PINCHWIFE. Go then and bid her come out to me.

MRS. PINCHWIFE. Yes, yes bud—

PINCHWIFE. Let me see—

MRS. PINCHWIFE. I'll go, but she is not within to come to him. I have just got time to know of Lucy her maid, who first set me on work, what lie I shall tell next, for I am e'en at my wit's end— (*Exit* MRS. PINCHWIFE.)

PINCHWIFE. Well I resolve it, Horner shall have her. I'd rather give him my sister than lend him my wife, and such an alliance will prevent his pretensions to my wife sure,— I'll make him of kin to her, and then he won't care for her. (MRS. PINCHWIFE *returns*.)

MRS. PINCHWIFE. O Lord, bud, I told you what anger you would make me with my sister.

PINCHWIFE. Won't she come hither?

MRS. PINCHWIFE. No, no, alack a day, she's ashamed to look you in the face, and she says if you go in to her, she'll run away down stairs, and shamefully go herself to Mr. Horner, who has promised her marriage she says, and she will have no other, so she won't—

PINCHWIFE. Did he so—promise her marriage? Then she shall have no other. Go tell her so, and if she will come and discourse with me a little concerning the means, I will about it immediately, go— (*Exit* MRS. PINCHWIFE.) His estate is equal to Sparkish's, and his extraction as much better than his, as his parts are, but my chief reason is, I'd rather be of kin to him by the name of brother-in-law, than that of cuckold—

(*Enter* MRS. PINCHWIFE.)

Well what says she now?

MRS. PINCHWIFE. Why she says she would only have you lead her to Horner's lodging—with whom she first will discourse the matter before she talk with you, which yet she cannot do; for alack, poor creature, she says she can't so much as look you in the face, therefore she'll come to you in a mask, and you must excuse her if she make you no answer to any question of yours, till you have brought her to Mr. Horner, and if you will not chide her, nor question her, she'll come out to you immediately.

PINCHWIFE. Let her come, I will not speak a word to her, nor require a word from her.

MRS. PINCHWIFE. Oh I forgot, besides she says, she cannot look you in the face, though through a mask, therefore would desire you to put out the candle.

PINCHWIFE. I agree to all, let her make haste— (*Exit* MRS. PINCHWIFE, *puts out the candle.*) there 'tis out— my case is something better, I'd rather fight with Horner for not lying with my sister, than for lying with my wife, and of the two I had rather find my sister too forward than my wife; I expected no other from her free education, as she calls it, and her passion for the town— well— wife and sister are names which make us expect love and duty, pleasure and comfort, but we find'em plagues and torments, and are equally, though differently troublesome to their keeper; for we have as much ado to get people to lie with our sisters, as to keep'em from lying with our wives.

(*Enter* MRS. PINCHWIFE *masked, and in hoods and scarves, and a nightgown and petticoat of* ALITHEA'S *in the dark.*)

What, are you come, sister? let us go then—but first let me lock up my wife. Mrs. Margery, where are you?

MRS. PINCHWIFE. Here bud.

PINCHWIFE. Come hither, that I may lock you up, get you in, (*Locks the door.*) Come, sister, where are you now? (MRS. PINCHWIFE *gives her hand, but when he lets her go, she steals softly on t'other side of him, and is lead away by him for his sister* ALITHEA.)

(*The scene changes to* HORNER'S *lodging.*)
(QUACK, HORNER.)

QUACK. What all alone, not so much as one of your cuckolds here, nor one of their wives! they use to take their turns with you, as if they were to watch you.

HORNER. Yes it often happens that a cuckold is but his wife's spy, and is more upon family duty, when he is with her gallant abroad hindering his pleasure, than when he is at home with her playing the gallant, but the hardest duty a married woman imposes upon a lover is, keeping her husband company always.

QUACK. And his fondness wearies you almost as soon as hers.

HORNER. A pox, keeping a cuckold company after you have had his wife, is as tiresome as the company of a country squire to a witty fellow of the town, when he has got all his money.

QUACK. And as at first a man makes a friend of the husband to get the wife, so at last you are fain to fall out with the wife to be rid of the husband.

HORNER. Ay, most cuckold-makers are true courtiers, when once a poor man has cracked his credit for'em, they can't abide to come near him.

QUACK. But at first to draw him in are so sweet, so kind, so dear, just as you are to Pinchwife. But what becomes of that intrigue with his wife?

HORNER. A pox, he's as surly as an alderman that has been bit,[66] and since he's so coy, his wife's kindness is in vain, for she's a silly innocent.

QUACK. Did she not send you a letter by him?

HORNER. Yes, but that's a riddle I have not yet solved—allow the poor creature to be willing, she is silly too, and he keeps her up so close—

QUACK. Yes, so close that he makes her but the more willing, and adds but revenge to her love, which two when met seldom fail of satisfying each other one way or other.

HORNER. What! here's the man we are talking of, I think.

(*Enter* MR. PINCHWIFE *leading in his wife masked, muffled, and in her sister's gown.*)

HORNER. Pshaw.

QUACK. Bringing his wife to you is the next thing to bringing a love letter from her.

HORNER. What means this?

PINCHWIFE. The last time you know sir I brought you a love letter, now you see a mistress, I think you'll say I am a civil man to you.

HORNER. Ay, the devil take me, will I say thou art the civillest man I ever met with, and I have known some; I fancy,

66 *bit,* tricked.

I understand thee now, better than I did the letter, but hark thee in thy ear—

PINCHWIFE. What?

HORNER. Nothing but the usual question, man; is she sound, on thy word?

PINCHWIFE. What, you take her for a wench and me for a pimp?

HORNER. Pshaw, wench and pimp, paw[67] words, I know thou art an honest fellow, and hast a great acquaintance among the ladies, and perhaps hast made love for me rather than let me make love to thy wife—

PINCHWIFE. Come, sir, in short, I am for no fooling.

HORNER. Nor I neither, therefore prithee let's see her face presently, make her show, man, art thou sure I don't know her?

PINCHWIFE. I am sure you do know her.

HORNER. A pox, why dost thou bring her to me then?

PINCHWIFE. Because she's a relation of mine.

HORNER. Is she, faith, man? then thou art still more civil and obliging, dear rogue.

PINCHWIFE. Who desired me to bring her to you.

HORNER. Then she is obliging, dear rogue.

PINCHWIFE. You'll make her welcome for my sake I hope.

HORNER. I hope she is handsome enough to make herself welcome; prithee let her unmask.

PINCHWIFE. Do you speak to her, she would never be ruled by me.

HORNER. Madam— (MRS. PINCHWIFE *whispers to* HORNER.) She says she must speak with me in private; withdraw, prithee.

PINCHWIFE. She's unwilling it seems I should know all her undecent conduct in this business—   (*aside*) Well then I'll leave you together, and hope when I am gone you'll agree, if not you and I shan't agree, sir.—

HORNER. What means the fool?—if she and I agree 'tis no matter what you and I do.

(*Whispers to* MRS. PINCHWIFE, *who makes signs with her hand for him to be gone.*)

PINCHWIFE. In the mean time I'll fetch a parson, and find out Sparkish and disabuse him.

67 *paw*, bad.

You would have me fetch a parson, would you not? Well then— Now I think I am rid of her, and shall have no more trouble with her— Our sisters and daughters, like usurers' money, are safest, when put out; but our wives, like their writings, never safe, but in our closets under lock and key.   (*Exit* MR. PINCHWIFE.)

(*Enter* BOY.)

BOY. Sir Jaspar Fidget, sir, is coming up.
HORNER. Here's the trouble of a cuckold, now we are talking of. A pox on him, has he not enough to do to hinder his wife's sport, but he must other women's too.—Step in here, madam.   (*Exit* MRS. PINCHWIFE.)

(*Enter* SIR JASPAR.)

SIR JASPAR. My best and dearest friend.
HORNER. The old style, Doctor—
          Well be short, for I am busy. (*aside*) What would your impertinent wife have now?
SIR JASPAR. Well guessed y' faith, for I do come from her.
HORNER. To invite me to supper. Tell her I can't come, go.
SIR JASPAR. Nay, now you are out, faith, for my lady and the whole knot of the virtuous gang, as they call themselves, are resolved upon a frolic of coming to you tonight in a masquerade, and are all dressed already.
HORNER. I shan't be at home.
SIR JASPAR. Lord how churlish he is to women—nay prithee don't disappoint 'em, they'll think 'tis my fault, prithee don't; I'll send in the banquet and the fiddles. But make no noise on't, for the poor virtuous rogues would not have it known for the world, that they go a masquerading, and they would come to no man's ball, but yours.
HORNER. Well, well—get you gone, and tell'em if they come, 'twill be at the peril of their honour and yours.
SIR JASPAR. Heh, he, he—we'll trust you for that, farewell—

          (*Exit* SIR JASPAR.)

HORNER. Doctor, anon you too shall be my guest.
          But now I'm going to a private feast.

(*The scene changes to the Piazza of Covent Garden.*)

(SPARKISH, PINCHWIFE.)
(SPARKISH *with the letter in his hand.*)

SPARKISH. But who would have thought a woman could have been false to me, by the world, I could not have thought it.

PINCHWIFE. You were for giving and taking liberty, she has taken it only, sir, now you find in that letter, you are a frank person, and so is she you see there.

SPARKISH. Nay if this be her hand—for I never saw it.

PINCHWIFE. 'Tis no matter whether that be her hand or no, I am sure this hand at her desire lead her to Mr. Horner, with whom I left her just now, to go fetch a parson to'em at their desire too, to deprive you of her for ever, for it seems yours was but a mock marriage.

SPARKISH. Indeed she would needs have it that 'twas Harcourt himself in a parson's habit, that married us, but I'm sure he told me 'twas his brother Ned.

PINCHWIFE. O there 'tis out and you were deceived, not she, for you are such a frank person—but I must be gone— you'll find her at Mr. Horner's. Go and believe your eyes.

(*Exit* MR. PINCHWIFE.)

SPARKISH. Nay I'll to her, and call her as many crocodiles, sirens, harpies, and other heathenish names, as a poet would do a mistress, who had refused to hear his suit, nay, more, his verses on her.

But stay, is not that she following a torch at t'other end of the piazza, and from Horner's certainly—'tis so—

(*Enter* ALITHEA *following a torch, and* LUCY *behind.*)

You are well met, madam, though you don't think so. What, you have made a short visit to Mr. Horner, but I suppose you'll return to him presently, by that time the parson can be with him.

ALITHEA. Mr. Horner, and the parson, sir—

SPARKISH. Come, madam, no more dissembling, no more jilting for I am no more a frank person.

ALITHEA. How's this.

LUCY. So 'twill work I see—   (*aside*)

SPARKISH. Could you find out no easy country fool to abuse? none but me, a gentleman of wit and pleasure about the town? But it was your pride to be too hard for a man of parts, unworthy false woman, false as a friend that lends a man money to lose, false as dice, who undo those that trust all they have to'em.

LUCY. He has been a great bubble by his similes, as they say— *(aside)*

ALITHEA. You have been too merry, sir, at your wedding dinner sure.

SPARKISH. What, d'y mock me too?

ALITHEA. Or you have been deluded.

SPARKISH. By you.

ALITHEA. Let me understand you.

SPARKISH. Have you the confidence, I should call it something else, since you know your guilt, to stand my just reproaches? You did not write an impudent letter to Mr. Horner, who I find now has clubbed with you in deluding me with his aversion for women, that I might not forsooth suspect him for my rival.

LUCY. D'y think the gentleman can be jealous now, madam? *(aside)*

ALITHEA. I write a letter to Mr. Horner!

SPARKISH. Nay madam, do not deny it, your brother showed it me just now, and told me likewise he left you at Horner's lodging to fetch a parson to marry you to him, and I wish you joy madam, joy, joy, and to him too much joy, and to myself more joy for not marrying you.

ALITHEA. So, I find my brother would break off the match, and I can consent to't, since I see this gentleman can be made jealous. *(aside)*

O Lucy, by his rude usage and jealousy, he makes me almost afraid I am married to him; art thou sure 'twas Harcourt himself and no parson that married us?

SPARKISH. No, madam, I thank you. I suppose that was a contrivance too of Mr. Horner's and yours, to make Harcourt play the parson, but I would as little as you have him one now, no, not for the world, for, shall I tell you another truth, I never had any passion for you, 'till now, for now I hate you. 'Tis true I might have married your portion, as other men of parts of the town do sometimes, and so your servant. And to show my unconcernedness, I'll come to your wedding, and resign you with as much joy as I would a stale wench to a new cully, nay with as much joy as I would after the first night, if I had been married to you, there's for you, and so your servant, servant. *(Exit SPARKISH.)*

ALITHEA. How was I deceived in a man!

LUCY. You'll believe then a fool may be made jealous now? for that easiness in him that suffers him to be led by a

wife, will likewise permit him to be persuaded against
her by others.

ALITHEA. But marry Mr. Horner, my brother does not intend
it sure; if I thought he did, I would take thy advice, and
Mr. Harcourt for my husband. And now I wish, that if
there be any over-wise woman of the town, who like me
would marry a fool, for fortune, liberty, or title, first that
her husband may love play, and be a cully to all the town,
but her, and suffer none but fortune to be mistress of his
purse, then if for liberty, that he may send her into the
country under the conduct of some housewifely mother-in
law; and if for title, may the world give'em none but
that of cuckold.

LUCY. And for her greater curse, madam, may he not deserve it.

ALITHEA. Away impertinent is not this my old lady
Lanterlu's?[68]

LUCY. Yes, madam. And here I hope we shall find Mr.
Harcourt—   (*aside*)

(*Exeunt* ALITHEA, LUCY.)

(*The scene changes again to* HORNER'S *lodging.*)

(HORNER, LADY FIDGET, MRS. DAINTY FIDGET, MRS. SQUEAM-
ISH, *a table, banquet, and bottles.*)

HORNER. A pox! they are come too soon—before I have sent
back my new mistress. All I have now to do, is to lock
her in, that they may not see her—   (*aside*)

LADY FIDGET. That we may be sure of our welcome, we have
brought our entertainment with us, and are resolved to
treat thee, dear toad.

DAINTY. And that we may be merry to purpose, have left Sir
Jaspar and my old Lady Squeamish quarrelling at home
at backgammon.

SQUEAMISH. Therefore let us make use of our time, lest they
should chance to interrupt us.

LADY FIDGET. Let us sit then.

HORNER. First that you may be private, let me lock this door,
and that, and I'll wait upon you presently.

LADY FIDGET. No sir, shut'em only and your lips for ever, for
we must trust you as much as our women.

---

68 *Lanterlu,* actually the name of a card game.

HORNER. You know all vanity's killed in me, I have no occa-
　　sion for talking.

LADY FIDGET. Now ladies, supposing we had drunk each of us
　　our two bottles, let us speak the truth of our hearts.

DAINTY and SQUEAMISH. Agreed.

LADY FIDGET. By this brimmer,[69] for truth is nowhere else to
　　be found. Not in thy heart, false man. (*Aside to* HORNER.)

HORNER. You have found me a true man I'm sure.

　　　　　　　　　　　　　　　　(*Aside to* LADY FIDGET.)

LADY FIDGET. Not every way—　　　　(*Aside to* HORNER.)
　　But let us sit and be merry.

LADY FIDGET *sings.*

1.

Why should our damned tyrants oblige us to live.
On the pittance of pleasure which they only give.
　　We must not rejoice,
　　With wine and with noise.
In vain we must wake in a dull bed alone.
Whilst to our warm rival, the bottle, they're gone.
　　Then lay aside charms,
　　And take up these arms.[70]

2.

'Tis wine only gives'em their courage and wit,
Because we live sober, to men we submit.
　　If for beauties you'd pass.
　　Take a lick of the glass.
'Twill mend your complexions, and when they are gone,
The best red we have is the red of the grape.
　　Then sisters lay't on.
　　And damn a good shape.

DAINTY. Dear brimmer! Well, in token of our openness and
　　plain dealing, let us throw our masks over our heads.

HORNER. So 'twill come to the glasses anon.

SQUEAMISH. Lovely brimmer, let me enjoy him first.

LADY FIDGET. No, I never part with a gallant, till I've tried
　　him. Dear brimmer that mak'st our husbands short
　　sighted.

---

[69] *brimmer,* full cup of wine.
[70] *arms,* i.e., wineglasses.

DAINTY. And our bashful gallants bold.

SQUEAMISH. And for want of a gallant, the butler lovely in our eyes; drink, eunuch.

LADY FIDGET. Drink thou representative of a husband, damn a husband.

DAINTY. And as it were a husband, an old keeper.

SQUEAMISH. And an old grandmother.

HORNER. And an English bawd, and a French chirurgeon.

LADY FIDGET. Ay we have all reason to curse'em.

HORNER. For my sake, ladies.

LADY FIDGET. No, for our own, for the first spoils all young gallants' industry.

DAINTY. And the other's art makes'em bold only with common women.

SQUEAMISH. And rather run the hazard of the vile distemper amongst them, than of a denial amongst us.

DAINTY. The filthy toads choose mistresses now, as they do stuffs,[71] for having been fancied and worn by others.

SQUEAMISH. For being common and cheap.

LADY FIDGET. Whilst women of quality, like the richest stuffs, lie untumbled, and unasked for.

HORNER. Ay neat, and cheap, and new, often they think best.

DAINTY. No sir, the beasts will be known by a mistress longer than by a suit.

SQUEAMISH. And 'tis not for cheapness neither.

LADY FIDGET. No, for the vain fops will take up druggets,[72] and embroider'em. But I wonder at the depraved appetites of witty men, they use to be out of the common road, and hate imitation. Pray tell me, beast, when you were a man, why you rather chose to club with a multitude in a common house, for an entertainment, than to be the only guest at a good table.

HORNER. Why faith, ceremony and expectation are unsufferable to those that are sharp bent, people always eat with the best stomach at an ordinary, where every man is snatching for the best bit.

LADY FIDGET. Though he get a cut over the fingers—but I have heard people eat most heartily of another man's meat, that is, what they do not pay for.

HORNER. When they are sure of their welcome and freedom, for ceremony in love and eating, is as ridiculous as in

71 *stuffs*, clothing.
72 *druggets*, cheap cloth.

fighting, falling on briskly is all should be done in those occasions.

LADY FIDGET. Well then let me tell you, sir, there is nowhere more freedom than in our houses, and we take freedom from a young person as a sign of good breeding, and a person may be as free as he pleases with us, as frolic, as gamesome, as wild as he will.

HORNER. Han't I heard you all declaim against wild men.

LADY FIDGET. Yes, but for all that, we think wildness in a man as desirable a quality, as in a duck, or rabbit; a tame man, foh.

HORNER. I know not, but your reputations frightened me, as much as your faces invited me.

LADY FIDGET. Our reputation, Lord! Why should you not think that we women make use of our reputation, as you men of yours, only to deceive the world with less suspicion? Our virtue is like the statesman's religion, the Quaker's word, the gamester's oath, and the great man's honour, but to cheat those that trust us.

SQUEAMISH. And that demureness, coyness, and modesty, that you see in our faces in the boxes at plays, is as much a sign of a kind woman, as a vizard-mask in the pit.[73]

DAINTY. For I assure you, women are least masked, when they have the velvet vizard on.

LADY FIDGET. You would have found us modest women in our denials only.

SQUEAMISH. Our bashfulness is only the reflection of the men's.

DAINTY. We blush, when they are shame-faced.

HORNER. I beg your pardon, ladies, I was deceived in you devilishly, but why that mighty pretence to honour?

LADY FIDGET. We have told you; but sometimes 'twas for the same reason you men pretend business often, to avoid ill company, to enjoy the better, and more privately those you love.

HORNER. But why, would you ne'er give a friend a wink then?

LADY FIDGET. Faith, your reputation frightened us as much, as ours did you, you were so notoriously lewd.

HORNER. And you so seemingly honest.

LADY FIDGET. Was that all that deterred you?

HORNER. And so expensive—you allow freedom, you say?

LADY FIDGET. Ay, ay.

73 *vizard-mask in the pit,* prostitute at the playhouse.

HORNER. That I was afraid of losing my little money, as well as my little time, both which my other pleasures required.

LADY FIDGET. Money, foh—you talk like a little fellow now, do such as we expect money?

HORNER. I beg your pardon, madam, I must confess, I have heard that great ladies, like great merchants, set but the higher prices upon what they have, because they are not in necessity of taking the first offer.

DAINTY. Such as we, make sale of our hearts?

SQUEAMISH. We bribed for our love? Foh.

HORNER. With your pardon, ladies, I know, like great men in offices, you seem to exact flattery and attendance only from your followers, but you have receivers about you, and such fees to pay, a man is afraid to pass your grants.[74] Besides we must let you win at cards, or we lose your hearts; and if you make an assignation, 'tis at a goldsmith's, jeweller's, or china house, where for your honour you deposit to him, he must pawn his to the punctual cit,[75] and so paying for what you take up, pays for what he takes up.

DAINTY. Would you not have us assured of our gallants' love?

SQUEAMISH. For love is better known by liberality, than by jealousy.

LADY FIDGET. For one may be dissembled, the other not—but my jealousy can be no longer dissembled, and they are telling-ripe: (aside)
Come here's to our gallants in waiting, whom we must name, and I'll begin, this is my false rogue.

(Claps him on the back.)

SQUEAMISH. How!

HORNER. So all will out now—

SQUEAMISH. Did you not tell me, 'twas for my sake only, you reported yourself no man?   (Aside to HORNER.)

DAINTY. Oh wretch! did you not swear to me, 'twas for my love, and honour, you passed for that thing you do?

(Aside to HORNER.)

HORNER. So, so.

LADY FIDGET. Come, speak, ladies, this is my false villain.

---

74 *pass your grants,* accept your favors.
75 *to the punctual cit,* to the shopkeeper presenting his bill.

SQUEAMISH. And mine too.

DAINTY. And mine.

HORNER. Well then, you are all three my false rogues too, and there's an end on't.

LADY FIDGET. Well then, there's no remedy, sister sharers, let us not fall out, but have a care of our honour; though we get no presents, no jewels of him, we are savers of our honour, the jewel of most value and use, which shines yet to the world unsuspected, though it be counterfeit.

HORNER. Nay, and is e'en as good, as if it were true, provided the world think so; for honour, like beauty now, only depends on the opinion of others.

LADY FIDGET. Well Harry Common, I hope you can be true to three, swear, but 'tis no purpose, to require your oath; for you are as often forsworn, as you swear to new women.

HORNER. Come, faith, madam, let us e'en pardon one another, for all the difference I find betwixt we men, and you women, we forswear ourselves at the beginning of an amour, you, as long as it lasts.

(*Enter* SIR JASPAR FIDGET, *and old* LADY SQUEAMISH.)

SIR JASPAR. Oh my Lady Fidget, was this your cunning, to come to Mr. Horner without me; but you have been no-where else I hope.

LADY FIDGET. No, Sir Jaspar.

LADY SQUEAMISH. And you came straight hither, Biddy?

SQUEAMISH. Yes indeed, Lady Grandmother.

SIR JASPAR. 'Tis well, 'tis well, I knew when once they were throughly acquainted with poor Horner, they'd ne'er be from him; you may let her masquerade it with my wife, and Horner, and I warrant her reputation safe.

(*Enter* BOY.)

BOY. O sir, here's the gentleman come, whom you bid me not suffer to come up, without giving you notice, with a lady too, and other gentlemen—

HORNER. Do you all go in there, whil'st I send 'em away, and boy, do you desire 'em to stay below 'til I come, which shall be immediately.

(*Exeunt* SIR JASPAR, LADY SQUEAMISH, LADY FIDGET, MISTRESS DAINTY, MRS. SQUEAMISH.)

BOY. Yes Sir.   (*Exit.*)

(*Exit* HORNER *at t'other door, and returns
with* MISTRESS PINCHWIFE.)

HORNER. You would not take my advice to be gone home,
before your husband came back, he'll now discover all.
Yet pray, my dearest, be persuaded to go home, and
leave the rest to my management, I'll let you down the
back way.

MRS. PINCHWIFE. I don't know the way home, so I don't.

HORNER. My man shall wait upon you.

MRS. PINCHWIFE. No, don't you believe, that I'll go at all;
what, are you weary of me already?

HORNER. No my life, 'tis that I may love you long, 'tis to
secure my love, and your reputation with your husband;
he'll never receive you again else.

MRS. PINCHWIFE. What care I, d'ye think to frighten me with
that? I don't intend to go to him again; you shall be my
husband now.

HORNER. I cannot be your husband, dearest, since you are
married to him.

MRS. PINCHWIFE. O would you make me believe that—don't
I see every day at London here, women leave their first
husbands, and go and live with other men as their wives.
Pish, pshaw, you'd make me angry, but that I love you
so mainly.

HORNER. So, they are coming up— In again, in, I hear'em:

(*Exit* MISTRESS PINCHWIFE.)

Well, a silly mistress, is like a weak place, soon got, soon
lost, a man has scarce time for plunder; she betrays her
husband, first to her gallant, and then her gallant, to her
husband.

(*Enter* PINCHWIFE, ALITHEA, HARCOURT, SPARKISH, LUCY,
and a Parson.)

PINCHWIFE. Come, madam, 'tis not the sudden change of your
dress, the confidence of your asseverations, and your
false witness there, shall persuade me I did not bring
you hither just now; here's my witness, who cannot
deny it, since you must be confronted— Mr. Horner,
did not I bring this lady to you just now?

HORNER. Now must I wrong one woman for another's sake,

but that's no new thing with me; for in these cases I am still on the criminal's side, against the innocent. *(aside)*

ALITHEA. Pray, speak, sir.

HORNER. It must be so— I must be impudent, and try my luck, impudence uses to be[76] too hard for truth. *(aside)*

PINCHWIFE. What, you are studying an evasion, or excuse for her! Speak, sir.

HORNER. No, faith, I am something backward only, to speak in women's affairs or disputes.

PINCHWIFE. She bids you speak.

ALITHEA. Ay, pray sir do, pray satisfy him.

HORNER. Then truly, you did bring that lady to me just now.

PINCHWIFE. O ho—

ALITHEA. How, sir—

HARCOURT. How, Horner!

ALITHEA. What mean you, sir, I always took you for a man of honour?

HORNER. Ay, so much a man of honour, that I must save my mistress, I thank you, come what will on't. *(aside)*

SPARKISH. So if I had had her, she'd have made me believe, the moon had been made of a Christmas pie.

LUCY. Now could I speak, if I durst, and solve the riddle, who am the author of it. *(aside)*

ALITHEA. O unfortunate woman! a combination against my honour, which most concerns me now, because you share in my disgrace, sir, and it is your censure which I must now suffer, that troubles me, not theirs.

HARCOURT. Madam, then have no trouble, you shall now see 'tis possible for me to love you, without being jealous, I will not only believe your innocence myself, but make all the world believe it—

Horner, I must now be concerned for this lady's honour.

(Apart to HORNER.)

HORNER. And I must be concerned for a lady's honour too.

HARCOURT. This lady has her honour, and I will protect it.

HORNER. My lady has not her honour, but has given it me to keep, and I will preserve it.

HARCOURT. I understand you not.

HORNER. I would not have you.

MRS. PINCHWIFE. What's the matter with'em all.

(MISTRESS PINCHWIFE peeping in behind.)

76 *uses to be,* is usually.

PINCHWIFE. Come, come, Mr. Horner, no more disputing, here's the parson, I brought him not in vain.

HARCOURT. No sir, I'll employ him, if this lady please.

PINCHWIFE. How, what d'ye mean?

SPARKISH. Ay, what does he mean?

HORNER. Why, I have resigned your sister to him, he has my consent.

PINCHWIFE. But he has not mine sir, a woman's injured honour, no more than a man's, can be repaired or satisfied by any, but him that first wronged it; and you shall marry her presently, or— (*Lays his hand on his sword.*)

(*Enter to them* MISTRESS PINCHWIFE.)

MRS. PINCHWIFE. O Lord, they'll kill poor Mr. Horner! Besides he shan't marry her, whilest I stand by, and look on, I'll not lose my second husband so.

PINCHWIFE. What do I see?

ALITHEA. My sister in my clothes!

SPARKISH. Ha!

MRS. PINCHWIFE. Nay, pray now don't quarrel about finding work for the parson, he shall marry me to Mr. Horner; for now I believe, you have enough of me.

(*To* MR. PINCHWIFE.)

HORNER. Damned, damned loving changeling.

MRS. PINCHWIFE. Pray sister, pardon me for telling so many lies of you.

HARCOURT. I suppose the riddle is plain now.

LUCY. No, that must be my work, good sir, hear me.

(*Kneels to* MR. PINCHWIFE, *who stands doggedly, with his hat over his eyes.*)

PINCHWIFE. I will never hear woman again, but make'em all silent, thus— (*Offers to draw upon his wife.*)

HORNER. No, that must not be.

PINCHWIFE. You then shall go first, 'tis all one to me.

(*Offers to draw on* HORNER, *stopped by* HARCOURT.)

HARCOURT. Hold—

(*Enter* SIR JASPAR FIDGET, LADY FIDGET, LADY SQUEAMISH, MRS. DAINTY FIDGET, MRS. SQUEAMISH.)

SIR JASPAR. What's the matter, what's the matter, pray what's the matter sir, I beseech you communicate sir.

PINCHWIFE. Why my wife has communicated sir, as your wife may have done too sir, if she knows him sir—

SIR JASPAR. Pshaw, with him, ha, ha, he.

PINCHWIFE. D'ye mock me, sir, a cuckold is a kind of a wild beast, have a care, sir—

SIR JASPAR. No sure, you mock me, sir—he cuckold you! it can't be, ha, ha, he, why, I'll tell you, sir.

(Offers to whisper.)

PINCHWIFE. I tell you again, he has whored my wife, and your's too, if he knows her, and all the women he comes near; 'tis not his dissembling, his hypocrisy can wheedle me.

SIR JASPAR. How does he dissemble, is he an hypocrite? nay then—how—wife—sister is he an hypocrite?

LADY SQUEAMISH. An hypocrite, a dissembler, speak, young harlotry, speak how?

SIR JASPAR. Nay then—O my head too—O thou libidinous lady!

LADY SQUEAMISH. O thou harloting harlotry, hast thou done it then?

SIR JASPAR. Speak, good Horner, art thou a dissembler, a rogue? hast thou—

HORNER. Soh—

LUCY. I'll fetch you off, and her too, if she will but hold her tongue. *(Apart to HORNER.)*

HORNER. Canst thou? I'll give thee— *(Apart to LUCY.)*

LUCY to MR. PINCHWIFE. Pray have but patience to hear me, sir, who am the unfortunate cause of all this confusion. Your wife is innocent, I only culpable; for I put her upon telling you all these lies, concerning my mistress, in order to the breaking off the match, between Mr. Sparkish and her, to make way for Mr. Harcourt.

SPARKISH. Did you so, eternal rotten-tooth? Then it seems my mistress was not false to me, I was only deceived by you. Brother that should have been, now man of conduct, who is a frank person now, to bring your wife to her lover—ha—

LUCY. I assure you, sir, she came not to Mr. Horner out of love, for she loves him no more—

MRS. PINCHWIFE. Hold, I told lies for you, but you shall tell none for me, for I do love Mr. Horner with all my soul, and no body shall say me nay; pray don't you go to make poor Mr. Horner believe to the contrary, 'tis spitefully done of you, I'm sure.

HORNER. Peace, dear idiot. (*Aside to* MRS. PINCHWIFE.)

MRS. PINCHWIFE. Nay, I will not peace.

PINCHWIFE. Not 'til I make you.

(*Enter* DORILANT, QUACK.)

DORILANT. Horner, your servant, I am the doctor's guest, he must excuse our intrusion.

QUACK. But what's the matter gentlemen, for Heaven's sake, what's the matter?

HORNER. Oh 'tis well you are come—'tis a censorious world we live in, you may have brought me a reprieve, or else I had died for a crime, I never committed, and these innocent ladies had suffered with me, therefore pray satisfy these worthy, honourable, jealous gentlemen — that— (*Whispers.*)

QUACK. O I understand you, is that all— Sir Jasper, by heavens and upon the word of a physician, sir—

(*Whispers to* SIR JASPAR.)

SIR JASPAR. Nay I do believe you truly—pardon me, my virtuous lady, and dear of honour.

LADY SQUEAMISH. What then, all's right again?

SIR JASPAR. Ay, ay, and now let us satisfy him too.

(*They whisper with* MR. PINCHWIFE.)

PINCHWIFE. A eunuch! pray no fooling with me.

QUACK. I'll bring half the chirurgeons in town to swear it.

PINCHWIFE. They—they'll swear a man that bled to death through his wounds died of an apoplexy.

QUACK. Pray hear me, sir—why all the town has heard the report of him.

PINCHWIFE. But does all the town believe it?

QUACK. Pray inquire a little, and first of all these.

PINCHWIFE. I'm sure when I left the town he was the lewdest fellow in't.

QUACK. I tell you, sir, he has been in France since, pray ask but these ladies and gentlemen, your friend Mr. Dorilant. Gentlemen and ladies, han't you all heard the late sad report of poor Mr. Horner.

ALL LADIES. Ay, ay, ay.

DORILANT. Why thou jealous fool, do'st thou doubt it? he's an arrant French capon.

MRS. PINCHWIFE. 'Tis false, sir, you shall not disparage poor Mr. Horner, for to my certain knowledge—

LUCY. O hold—

SQUEAMISH. Stop her mouth—   (*Aside to* LUCY.)

LADY FIDGET. Upon my honour, sir, 'tis as true.

(*To* PINCHWIFE.)

DAINTY. D'y think we would have been seen in his company—

SQUEAMISH. Trust our unspotted reputations with him!

LADY FIDGET. This you get, and we too, by trusting your secret to a fool—   (*Aside to* HORNER.)

HORNER. Peace, madam,—well, Doctor, is not this a good design that carries a man on unsuspected, and brings him off safe.—   (*Aside to* QUACK.)

PINCHWIFE. Well, if this were true, but my wife—   (*aside*)

(DORILANT *whispers with* MRS. PINCHWIFE.)

ALITHEA. Come, brother, your wife is yet innocent you see, but have a care of too strong an imagination, least like an overconcerned timorous gamester by fancying an unlucky cast it should come; women and fortune are truest still to those that trust 'em.

LUCY. And any wild thing grows but the more fierce and hungry for being kept up, and more dangerous to the keeper.

ALITHEA. There's doctrine for all husbands, Mr. Harcourt.

HARCOURT. I edify madam so much, that I am impatient till I am one.

DORILANT. And I edify so much by example I will never be one.

SPARKISH. And because I will not disparage my parts I'll ne'er be one.

HORNER. And I alas can't be one.

PINCHWIFE. But I must be one—against my will to a country wife, with a country-murrain[77] to me.

MRS. PINCHWIFE. And I must be a country wife still too, I find, for I can't, like a city one, be rid of my musty husband and do what I list.   (*aside*)

HORNER. Now sir, I must pronounce your wife innocent, though I blush whilst I do it, and I am the only man by her now exposed to shame, which I will straight drown

[77] *murrain,* cattle sickness, metaphorically "a curse on me."

in wine, as you shall your suspicion, and the ladies'
troubles we'll divert with a ballet, Doctor, where are your
maskers.

LUCY. Indeed she's innocent, sir, I am her witness, and her
end of coming out was but to see her sister's wedding,
and what she has said to your face of her love to Mr.
Horner was but the usual innocent revenge on a husband's jealousy, was it not, madam, speak—

MRS. PINCHWIFE. Since you'll have me tell more lies—

(*Aside to* LUCY *and* HORNER.)

Yes indeed, bud.

PINCHWIFE. For my own sake fain I would all believe.
　　　Cuckolds like lovers should themselves deceive.
　　　　　But—sighs—
　　　His honour is least safe, (too late I find)
　　　Who trusts it with a foolish wife or friend.

(*A dance of cuckolds.*)

HORNER. Vain fops, but court, and dress, and keep a pother,
　　　To pass for women's men, with one another.
　　　But he who aims by women to be prized,
　　　First by the men, you see, must be despised.

(**F i n i s**)

EPILOGUE

Intended to be spoken by
My Lady Fidget

Now you the vigorous, who daily here
O'er vizard-mask, in public domineer,
And what you'd do to her if in place where;
Nay have the confidence, to cry come out,
Yet when she says lead on, you are not stout;
But to your well-dressed brother straight turn round
And cry, pox on her Ned, she can't be sound:
Then slink away, a fresh one to engage,
With so much seeming heat and loving rage,
You'd frighten listening actress on the stage:
Till she at last has seen you huffing come,
And talk of keeping in the tyring-room,
Yet cannot be provoked to lead her home:
Next you Falstaffs of fifty, who beset
Your buckram maidenheads, which your friends get;
And whilst to them, you of achievements boast,
They share the booty, and laugh at your cost.[78]
In fine, you essenced boys, both old and young,
Who would be thought so eager, brisk, and strong,
Yet do the ladies, not their husbands, wrong:
Whose purses for your manhood make excuse,
And keep your Flanders mares[79] for show, not use;
Encouraged by our woman's man today,
A Horner's[80] part may vainly think to play;

---

[78] *They . . . laugh at your cost*, in Shakespeare's *1 Henry IV*, act II, scene iv, Prince Hal and Poins mock Falstaff's lies about his courage.
[79] *Flanders mares*, mistresses.
[80] *horner's*, lover and cuckold-maker.

And may Intrigues so bashfully disown
That they may doubted be by few or none,
May kiss the cards at picquet, ombre,—Loo,
And so be thought to kiss the lady too;
But gallants, have a care, faith, what you do.
The world, which to no man his due will give,
You by experience know you can deceive,
And men may still believe you vigorous,
But then we women,—there's no cozening[81] us.

(F i n i s)

[81] *Cozening*, deceiving.

1/25/84

1. choral roles
2. Actresses
3. Terms: esp. those useful to Restoration stage.

ALL FOR LOVE
✛ A Tragedy ✛
1678

John Dryden

INTRODUCTORY NOTE

John Dryden was the leading man of letters of the seventeenth century. In addition to writing more than twenty plays he was the greatest critic of his time, the best translator, and a poet who made possible a century of development of the heroic couplet. He ranks near Shakespeare and Milton in the range and importance of his accomplishments. Dryden was born in Northamptonshire in 1731 and attended Westminster School and Trinity College, Cambridge. He published *The Wild Gallant* in 1663 and *The Indian Queen* in 1664 ; thereafter he annually produced comedies and tragedies that influenced every writer of his time.

The high-water marks of his career include the publication of *All for Love* in 1678; *Absalom and Achitophel* in 1681; a translation of *The Works of Vergil* in 1697; and *Fables Ancient and Modern* in 1700, the year of his death. He became Poet Laureate of England under the Stuarts, but, because he was a Catholic, he was deprived of this office after the Revolution of 1688. As both writer and theoretician he participated in most of the great literary debates of the late seventeenth century, and he endowed that age with much of its insight into poetry and ideas.

Charles Ward's *The Life of Dryden* (Chapel Hill, 1961) states that *All for Love* did not have a successful opening. The only two theatrical companies in London were more than usually competitive at the time of the play's production (1678) and not especially well managed. The play seems not to have been well cast, and to have attracted a disappointingly small audience for its run. During the lifetime of its author it was not popular, but during the eighteenth century its reputation steadily gained. It has occasionally been produced

119

in the twentieth century with substantial success: the revival at the Mark Hellinger Theater in New York in 1949 ran for 121 performances.

All for Love was meant to rival Shakespeare as well as to honor him. Dryden's preface to *Troilus and Cressida* states that "we ought not to regard a good imitation as a theft." Instead, great authors "whom we propose to ourselves as patterns of our imitation serve us as a torch, which is lifted up before us to enlighten our passage." Dryden used this play to make an implied statement about the relationship of the great Elizabethan age of drama and his own. And he suggested something of his personal relationship to the greatest of all modern dramatists. It was his intention to "translate" Shakespearean drama into "modern" terms.

All for Love has a famous preface in which Dryden explains his reasons for changing *Antony and Cleopatra* into Restoration form. Some changes are structural: the new version observes the unities of time, place, and action. Because it centers on a single decision the play is, as he suggested, more compact and less diffuse than Shakespeare's. But the changes of character and morality compete less successfully with the original. Dryden's play is very good in its own way, but it runs some danger of being confused with a speech in five acts on the opposition of love and honor.

Antony is "heroic" in the sense that the Restoration understood epical largeness of character: he has feelings and appetites too large to be contained by ordinary social conventions. Ventidius and most others in the cast (with the interesting exception of Alexas, who is not moved) admire his greatness and allow for its being expressed in both good and evil. But Cleopatra does not share in the elevation of character. She has lost her own interesting immorality and become domesticated:

> Nature meant me
> A wife—a silly, harmless, household dove,
> Fond without art, and kind without deceit.

The play has been unified in more than one sense of the term. *Antony and Cleopatra* is complex, full of oppositions between Rome and Egypt, between politics and the self. *All for Love* concentrates on the emotion of love to the exclusion of all other motives. This is a dialogue about how the protagonists love each other, and how they respond to the presence—and to the idea—of each other. The only possible way for this intensification to work is by sheer profundity, which the play does not always demonstrate, and as a result often deviates into self-consciousness; and in fact both hero and heroine are often seen contemplating themselves. At times the play dwindles into sentimentality, as Antony and Cleopatra run out of feelings to express to and about each other.

All for Love is a genuine achievement in its use of language. Dryden, like Shakespeare, knows how to use simplicity of statement. The death scene of Antony is a departure, and a great one, from the overblown rhetoric of much Restoration tragedy:

> 'Tis as with a man
> Removing in a hurry; all pack'd up,
> But one dear jewel that his haste forgot;
> And he, for that, returns upon the spur:
> So I come back for thee.

Wherever the eye goes in this play, from Dolabella's "Men are but children of a large growth" to Cleopatra's "Moderate sorrow/Fits vulgar love" there is the sense of a powerful literary intention dealing with ideas and language that it must condense, clarify, and recast into "modern" idiom.

Dramatis Personae

MARK ANTONY
VENTIDIUS, *his general*
DOLABELLA, *his friend*
ALEXAS, *the queen's eunuch*
SERAPION, *Priest of Isis*
MYRIS, *another priest*
Servants to Antony
CLEOPATRA, *Queen of Egypt*
OCTAVIA, *Antony's wife*
CHARMION ⎫
IRAS ⎭ *Cleopatra's maids*
Antony's two little daughters

Scene: *Alexandria*

[handwritten annotations:]

I points of comparison

1. actresses
2. # of scenes (vs)
3. # of characters (vs)
4. epic vs. dramatic structure: the 3 unities
5. Enobarbus is missing — the barometer
6. Note the introduction of family

PROLOGUE

What flocks of critics hover here today,
As vultures wait on armies for their prey,
All gaping for the carcass of a play!
With croaking notes they bode some dire event,
And follow dying poets by the scent.
Ours gives himself for gone; y'have watched your time!
He fights this day unarmed — without his rhyme —
And brings a tale which often has been told,
As sad as Dido's and almost as old.
His hero, whom you wits his bully call,
Bates of his mettle[1] and scarce rants at all.
He's somewhat lewd, but a well-meaning mind;
Weeps much, fights little, but is wond'rous kind;
In short, a pattern and companion fit
For all the keeping tonies[2] of the pit.
I could name more: a wife, and mistress too,
Both (to be plain) too good for most of you;
The wife well-natured, and the mistress true.
    Now, poets, if your fame has been his care,
Allow him all the candor you can spare.
A brave man scorns to quarrel once a day,
Like Hectors[3] in at every petty fray.
Let those find fault whose wit's so very small,
They've need to show that they can think at all.
Errors, like straws, upon the surface flow;
He who would search for pearls must dive below.
Fops may have leave to level all they can,
As pigmies would be glad to lop a man.
Half-wits are fleas, so little and so light,

---

1 *Bates of his mettle*, is restrained, hence unlike most tragic heroes.
2 *keeping tonies*, fools supporting mistresses.
3 *Hectors*, London bullies.

We scarce could know they live but that they bite.
But as the rich, when tired with daily feasts,
For change become their next poor tenant's guests,
Drink hearty draughts of ale from plain brown bowls,
And snatch the homely rasher from the coals,
So you, retiring from much better cheer,
For once may venture to do penance here.
And since that plenteous autumn now is past,
Whose grapes and peaches have indulged your taste,
Take in good part, from our poor poet's board,
Such rivelled[4] fruits as winter can afford.

4 *rivelled,* shrivelled.

ACT I *action is continuous throughout*

[SCENE I.] *The Temple of Isis*

(*Enter* SERAPION, MYRIS, *Priests of Isis.*)

SERAPION. Portents and prodigies are grown so frequent
    That they have lost their name. Our fruitful Nile
    Flowed ere the wonted season with a torrent
    So unexpected and so wondrous fierce
    That the wild deluge overtook the haste
    Even of the hinds that watched it. Men and beasts
    Were borne above the tops of trees that grew
    On th' utmost margin of the water-mark.
    Then, with so swift an ebb the flood drove backward,
    It slipt from underneath the scaly herd:
    Here monstrous phocae[5] panted on the shore;
    Forsaken dolphins there with their broad tails
    Lay lashing the departing waves; hard by 'em,
    Sea-horses, floundering in the slimy mud,
    Tossed up their heads, and dashed the ooze about them.

(*Enter* ALEXAS *behind them.*)

MYRIS. Avert these omens, Heaven!
SERAPION. Last night, between the hours of twelve and one,
    In a lone aisle of the temple while I walked,
    A whirlwind rose that with a violent blast
    Shook all the dome; the doors around me clapped;
    The iron wicket that defends the vault
    Where the long race of Ptolemics is laid
    Burst open and disclosed the mighty dead.
    From out each monument, in order placed,
    An armèd ghost starts up: the boy-king[6] last

---

5 *phocae*, seals.
6 *boy-king*, Ptolemy XIII (63–47 B.C.) and Ptolemy XIV (59–44 B.C.)
were both married in turn to their sister Cleopatra. Incest was royal
policy for their house.

125

Reared his inglorious head. A peal of groans
Then followed, and a lamentable voice
Cried, "Egypt is no more!" My blood ran back,
My shaking knees against each other knocked;
On the cold pavement down I fell entranced,
And so unfinished left the horrid scene.

ALEXAS. (*Showing himself.*) And dreamed you this? or did
　　invent the story
　　To frighten our Egyptian boys withal,
　　And train them up betimes in fear of priesthood?

SERAPION. My lord, I saw you not,
　　Nor meant my words should reach your ears; but what
　　I uttered was most true.

ALEXAS.

　　　　　　　　　A foolish dream,
　　Bred from the fumes of indigested feasts
　　And holy luxury.

SERAPION.

　　　　　　　　　I know my duty;
　　This goes no farther.

ALEXAS.

　　　　　　　　　'Tis not fit it should,
　　Nor would the times now bear it, were it true.
　　All southern, from yon hills, the Roman camp
　　Hangs o'er us black and threatening like a storm
　　Just breaking on our heads.

SERAPION. Our faint Egyptians pray for Antony;
　　But in their servile hearts they own Octavius.

MYRIS. Why then does Antony dream out his hours,
　　And tempts not fortune for a noble day
　　Which might redeem what Actium lost?[7]

ALEXAS. He thinks 'tis past recovery.

SERAPION.

　　　　　　　　　　　Yet the foe
　　Seems not to press the siege.

ALEXAS.

　　　　　　　　　　Oh, there's the wonder.
　　Maecenas and Agrippa, who can most
　　With Caesar, are his foes. His wife Octavia,
　　Driven from his house, solicits her revenge;

---

[7] *what Actium lost,* i.e., the Roman Empire.

And Dolabella, who was once his friend,
Upon some private grudge now seeks his ruin;
Yet still war seems on either side to sleep.

SERAPION. 'Tis strange that Antony, for some days past,
Has not beheld the face of Cleopatra,
But here in Isis' temple lives retired,
And makes his heart a prey to black despair.

ALEXAS. 'Tis true; and we much fear he hopes by absence
To cure his mind of love.

SERAPION.

                    If he be vanquished
Or make his peace, Egypt is doomed to be
A Roman province, and our plenteous harvests
Must then redeem the scarceness of their soil.
While Antony stood firm, our Alexandria
Rivaled proud Rome (dominion's other seat),
And Fortune, striding like a vast Colossus,
Could fix an equal foot of empire here.

ALEXAS. Had I my wish, these tyrants of all nature
Who lord it o'er mankind, should perish — perish
Each by the other's sword; but, since our will
Is lamely followed by our power, we must
Depend on one, with him to rise or fall.

SERAPION. How stands the queen affected?

ALEXAS.

                        Oh, she dotes,
She dotes, Serapion, on this vanquished man,
And winds herself about his mighty ruins;
Whom would she yet forsake, yet yield him up,
This hunted prey, to his pursuer's hands,
She might preserve us all; but 'tis in vain —
This changes my designs, this blasts my counsels,
And makes me use all means to keep him here,
Whom I could wish divided from her arms
Far as the earth's deep center. Well, you know
The state of things; no more of your ill omens
And black prognostics; labor to confirm
The people's hearts.

(*Enter* VENTIDIUS, *talking aside with a gentleman of*
ANTONY'S.)

SERAPION. These Romans will o'erhear us.
    But who's that stranger? By his warlike port,[8]
    His fierce demeanor, and erected look,
    He's of no vulgar note.
ALEXAS.
                  Oh, 'tis Ventidius,
    Our emperor's great lieutenant in the East,
    Who first showed Rome that Parthia could be conquered.
    When Antony returned from Syria last,
    He left this man to guard the Roman frontiers.
SERAPION. You seem to know him well.
ALEXAS. Too well. I saw him in Cilicia first,
    When Cleopatra there met Antony.
    A mortal foe he was to us and Egypt.
    But — let me witness to the worth I hate —
    A braver Roman never drew a sword;
    Firm to his prince, but as a friend, not slave.
    He ne'er was of his pleasures; but presides
    O'er all his cooler hours and morning counsels;
    In short, the plainness, fierceness, rugged virtue
    Of an old true-stamped Roman lives in him.
    His coming bodes I know not what of ill
    To our affairs. Withdraw, to mark him better;
    And I'll acquaint you why I sought you here,
    And what's our present work.

(*They withdraw to a corner of the stage; and* VENTIDIUS,
with the other, comes forward to the front.)

VENTIDIUS.
                  Not see him, say you?
    I say I must and will.
GENTLEMAN.
             He has commanded,
    On pain of death, none should approach his presence.
VENTIDIUS. I bring him news will raise his drooping spirits,
    Give him new life.
GENTLEMAN.
           He sees not Cleopatra.
VENTIDIUS. Would he had never seen her!
GENTLEMAN. He eats not, drinks not, sleeps not, has no use
    Of anything but thought; or, if he talks,

[8] *port,* bearing, appearance.

'Tis to himself, and then 'tis perfect raving.
Then he defies the world, and bids it pass;
Sometimes he gnaws his lip and curses loud
The boy Octavius; then he draws his mouth
Into a scornful smile and cries, "Take all,
The world's not worth my care."

VENTIDIUS.

Just, just his nature.
Virtue's his path; but sometimes 'tis too narrow
For his vast soul; and then he starts out wide,
And bounds into a vice that bears him far
From his first course and plunges him in ills;
But when his danger makes him find his fault,
Quick to observe, and full of sharp remorse,
He censures eagerly his own misdeeds,
Judging himself with malice to himself,
And not forgiving what as man he did,
Because his other parts are more than man.
He must not thus be lost.

(ALEXAS *and the priests come forward.*)

ALEXAS. You have your full instructions, now advance;
Proclaim your orders loudly.

SERAPION. Romans, Egyptians, hear the queen's command!
Thus Cleopatra bids: Let labor cease;
To pomp and triumphs give this happy day
That gave the world a lord: 'tis Antony's.
Live, Antony; and Cleopatra, live!
Be this the general voice sent up to heaven,
And every public place repeat this echo.

VENTIDIUS. (*aside*) Fine pageantry!

SERAPION.

Set out before your doors
The images of all your sleeping fathers,
With laurels crowned; with laurels wreathe your posts
And strew with flowers the pavement; let the priests
Do present sacrifice; pour out the wine
And call the gods to join with you in gladness.

VENTIDIUS. Curse on the tongue that bids this general joy!
Can they be friends of Antony, who revel
When Antony's in danger? Hide, for shame,
You Romans, your great grandsires' images,

For fear their souls should animate their marbles,[9]
To blush at their degenerate progeny.
ALEXAS. A love which knows no bounds to Antony
Would mark the day with honors when all heaven
Labored for him, when each propitious star
Stood wakeful in his orb to watch that hour
And shed his better influence. Her own birthday
Our queen neglected like a vulgar fate
That passed obscurely by.
VENTIDIUS.

       Would it had slept,
Divided far from his, till some remote
And future age had called it out, to ruin
Some other prince, not him!
ALEXAS.

        Your emperor,
Though grown unkind, would be more gentle than
T' upbraid my queen for loving him too well.
VENTIDIUS. Does the mute sacrifice upbraid the priest?
He knows him not his executioner.
Oh, she has decked his ruin with her love,
Led him in golden bands to gaudy slaughter,[10]
And made perdition pleasing. She has left him
The blank of what he was.
I tell thee, eunuch, she has quite unmanned him. ✓
Can any Roman see and know him now,
Thus altered from the lord of half mankind,
Unbent, unsinewed, made a woman's toy,
Shrunk from the vast extent of all his honors,
And cramped within a corner of the world?
O Antony!
Thou bravest soldier and thou best of friends!
Bounteous as nature; next to nature's God!
Couldst thou but make new worlds, so wouldst thou
  give'em,
As bounty were thy being; rough in battle
As the first Romans when they went to war;
Yet, after victory, more pitiful
Than all their praying virgins left at home!

---

[9] *marbles,* statues.
[10] *Led him . . . slaughter,* in the ancient world it was customary to
dress animal sacrifices in golden decorations.

ALEXAS. Would you could add to those more shining virtues,
    His truth to her who loves him.
VENTIDIUS.

                            Would I could not!
    But wherefore waste I precious hours with thee?
    Thou art her darling mischief, her chief engine,
    Antony's other fate. Go, tell thy queen
    Ventidius is arrived to end her charms.
    Let your Egyptian timbrels[11] play alone,
    Nor mix effeminate sounds with Roman trumpets.
    You dare not fight for Antony; go pray,
    And keep your coward's holiday in temples.

                      (*Exeunt* ALEXAS, SERAPION.)

(*Enter a second gentleman of* MARK ANTONY.)
SECOND GENTLEMAN. The emperor approaches and commands
    On pain of death that none presume to stay.
FIRST GENTLEMAN. I dare not disobey him.

                      (*Going out with the other.*)

VENTIDIUS.

                         Well, I dare.
    But I'll observe him first unseen, and find
    Which way his humor drives. The rest I'll venture.

                        (*Withdraws.*)

(*Enter* ANTONY, *walking with a disturbed motion before he
    speaks.*)
ANTONY. They tell me 'tis my birthday, and I'll keep it
    With double pomp of sadness.
    'Tis what the day deserves which gave me breath.
    Why was I raised the meteor of the world,
    Hung in the skies and blazing as I travelled,
    Till all my fires were spent, and then cast downward
    To be trod out by Caesar?
VENTIDIUS. (*aside*)

                    On my soul,
    'Tis mournful, wondrous mournful!
ANTONY.

                        Count thy gains.

---

11 *timbrels,* tambourines.

Now, Antony, wouldst thou be born for this?
Glutton of fortune, thy devouring youth
Has starved thy wanting age.

VENTIDIUS. (*aside*)

                              How sorrow shakes him!
So now the tempest tears him up by the roots,
And on the ground extends the noble ruin.

ANTONY. (*Having thrown himself down.*) Lie there, thou
            shadow of an emperor;
The place thou pressest on thy mother earth
Is all thy empire now; now it contains thee;
Some few days hence, and then 'twill be too large,
When thou'rt contracted in thy narrow urn,
Shrunk to a few cold ashes. Then Octavia
(For Cleopatra will not live to see it),
Octavia then will have thee all her own,
And bear thee in her widowed hand to Caesar;
Caesar will weep, the crocodile will weep,
To see his rival of the universe
Lie still and peaceful there. I'll think no more on't.
Give me some music; look that it be sad.
I'll soothe my melancholy till I swell
And burst myself with sighing. —   (*Soft music.*)
'Tis somewhat to my humor. Stay, I fancy
I'm now turned wild, a commoner of nature;
Of all forsaken and forsaking all,
Live in a shady forest's sylvan scene,
Stretched at my length beneath some blasted oak,
I lean my head upon the mossy bark
And look just of a piece as I grew from it;
My uncombed locks, matted like mistletoe,
Hang o'er my hoary face; a murm'ring brook
Runs at my foot.

VENTIDIUS. [*aside*] Methinks I fancy
    Myself there, too.

ANTONY.

                  The herd come jumping by me,
And, fearless, quench their thirst while I look on,
And take me for their fellow-citizen.
More of this image, more it lulls my thoughts.

                              (*Soft music again.*)

VENTIDIUS. I must disturb him; I can hold no longer.

                              (*Stands before him.*)

ANTONY. (*Starting up.*) Art thou Ventidius?
VENTIDIUS.

                              Are you Antony?

    I'm liker what I was than you to him
    I left you last.
ANTONY.

             I'm angry.

VENTIDIUS.

             So am I.

ANTONY. I would be private. Leave me.
VENTIDIUS.

             Sir, I love you,

    And therefore will not leave you.
ANTONY.

             Will not leave me!

    Where have you learned that answer? Who am I?
VENTIDIUS. My emperor; the man I love next Heaven;
    If I said more, I think 'twere scarce a sin —
    You're all that's good and good-like.
ANTONY.

             All that's wretched.

    You will not leave me then?
VENTIDIUS.

             'Twas too presuming

    To say I would not; but I dare not leave you,
    And 'tis unkind in you to chide me hence
    So soon, when I so far have come to see you.
ANTONY. Now thou hast seen me, art thou satisfied?
    For, if a friend, thou hast beheld enough;
    And, if a foe, too much.
VENTIDIUS. (*Weeping.*) Look, emperor, this is no common dew.
    I have not wept this forty years; but now
    My mother[12] comes afresh into my eyes;
    I cannot help her softness.
ANTONY. By heaven, he weeps! poor, good old man, he weeps!
    The big round drops course one another down
    The furrows of his cheeks. — Stop 'em, Ventidius,
    Or I shall blush to death; they set my shame,
    That caused 'em, full before me.
VENTIDIUS.

             I'll do my best.

[12] *mother*, feelings or sentiments thought to be inherited from the mother.

ANTONY. Sure, there's contagion in the tears of friends —
          See, I have caught it, too. Believe me, 'tis not
          For my own griefs, but thine. — Nay, father!
VENTIDIUS.

                                                 Emperor!

ANTONY. Emperor! Why, that's the style of victory;
          The conqu'ring soldier, red with unfelt wounds,
          Salutes his general so; but never more
          Shall that sound reach my ears.
VENTIDIUS.

                                        I warrant you.

ANTONY. Actium, Actium! Oh! —
VENTIDIUS.

                                   It sits too near you.

ANTONY. Here, here it lies, a lump of lead by day,
          And, in my short, distracted, nightly slumbers,
          The hag that rides my dreams.
VENTIDIUS. Out with it; give it vent.
ANTONY.

                                Urge not my shame.
          I lost a battle.
VENTIDIUS. So has Julius done.
ANTONY. Thou favor'st me, and speak'st not half thou think'st;
          For Julius fought it out, and lost it fairly,
          But Antony —
VENTIDIUS. Nay, stop not.
ANTONY.

                      •   Antony.
          (Well, thou wilt have it), like a coward fled,
          Fled while his soldiers fought; fled first, Ventidius.
          Thou long'st to curse me, and I give thee leave.
          I know thou cam'st prepared to rail.
VENTIDIUS.

                                            I did.

ANTONY. I'll help thee. — I have been a man, Ventidius.
VENTIDIUS. Yes, and a brave one; but —
ANTONY.

                                  I know thy meaning.
          But I have lost my reason, have disgraced
          The name of soldier with inglorious ease.
          In the full vintage of my flowing honors,
          Sat still, and saw it pressed by other hands.
          Fortune came smiling to my youth, and wooed it,
          And purple greatness met my ripened years.

When first I came to empire, I was borne
On tides of people crowding to my triumphs —
The wish of nations! and the willing world
Received me as its pledge of future peace.
I was so great, so happy, so beloved,
Fate could not ruin me, till I took pains,
And worked against my fortune, chid her from me,
And turned her loose; yet still she came again.
My careless days and my luxurious[13] nights
At length have wearied her, and now she's gone,
Gone, gone, divorced for ever. Help me, soldier,
To curse this madman, this industrious fool,
Who labored to be wretched. Pr'ythee, curse me.

VENTIDIUS. No.

ANTONY.

        Why?

VENTIDIUS.

                You are too sensible already
Of what you've done, too conscious of your failings;
And, like a scorpion, whipped by others first
To fury, sting yourself in mad revenge.
I would bring balm and pour it in your wounds,
Cure your distempered mind and heal your fortunes.

ANTONY. I know thou would'st.

VENTIDIUS.

                I will.

ANTONY.

                  Ha, ha, ha, ha!

VENTIDIUS. You laugh.

ANTONY.

                I do, to see officious love
Give cordials to the dead.

VENTIDIUS. You would be lost, then?

ANTONY.

                I am.

VENTIDIUS. I say you are not. Try your fortune.

ANTONY. I have, to th' utmost. Dost thou think me desperate
Without just cause? No, when I found all lost
Beyond repair, I hid me from the world,
And learned to scorn it here; which now I do
So heartily, I think it is not worth
The cost of keeping.

<hr>

[13] *luxurious,* lustful.

VENTIDIUS.

                              Caesar thinks not so.
    He'll thank you for the gift he could not take.
    You would be killed like Tully,[14] would you? Do,
    Hold out your throat to Caesar, and die tamely.
ANTONY. No, I can kill myself; and so resolve.
VENTIDIUS. I can die with you, too, when time shall serve,
    But fortune calls upon us now to live,
    To fight, to conquer.
ANTONY.

                              Sure, thou dream'st, Ventidius.
VENTIDIUS. No; 'tis you dream. You sleep away your hours
    In desperate sloth, miscalled philosophy.
    Up, up, for honor's sake! Twelve legions wait you
    And long to call you chief. By painful journeys
    I led them, patient both of heat and hunger,
    Down from the Parthian marches[15] to the Nile.
    'Twill do you good to see their sunburnt faces,
    Their scarred cheeks, and chopped[16] hands.
        There's virtue in 'em.
    They'll sell those mangled limbs at dearer rates
    Than yon trim bands can buy.
ANTONY.

                              Where left you them?
VENTIDIUS. I said in Lower Syria.
ANTONY.

                              Bring them hither;
    There may be life in these.
VENTIDIUS.

                              They will not come.
ANTONY. Why didst thou mock my hopes with promised aids,
    To double my despair? They're mutinous.
VENTIDIUS. Most firm and loyal.
ANTONY.

                              Yet they will not march
    To succor. O trifler!
VENTIDIUS.   They petition
    You would make haste to head them.
ANTONY.   I'm besieged.

---

[14] *Tully,* Marcus Tullius Cicero had surrendered to his executioners a
few years before.
[15] *marches,* frontiers.
[16] *chopped,* chapped.

VENTIDIUS. There's but one way shut up.
    How came I hither?
ANTONY. I will not stir.
VENTIDIUS.
                   They would perhaps desire
  A better reason.
ANTONY.
                         I have never used
  My soldiers to demand a reason of
  My actions. Why did they refuse to march?
VENTIDIUS. They said they would not fight for Cleopatra.
ANTONY. What was't they said?
VENTIDIUS. They said they would not fight for Cleopatra.
  Why should they fight, indeed, to make her conquer,
  And make you more a slave? to gain you kingdoms
  Which, for a kiss at your next midnight feast,
  You'll sell to her? Then she new-names her jewels
  And calls this diamond such or such a tax;
  Each pendant in her ear shall be a province.
ANTONY. Ventidius, I allow your tongue free license
  On all my other faults; but, on your life,
  No word of Cleopatra. She deserves
  More worlds than I can lose.
VENTIDIUS.
                    Behold, you powers,
  To whom you have intrusted humankind!
  See Europe, Afric, Asia, put in balance,
  And all weighed down by one light, worthless woman!
  I think the gods are Antonies and give,
  Like prodigals, this nether world away
  To none but wasteful hands.
ANTONY.
                   You grow presumptuous.
VENTIDIUS. I take the privilege of plain love to speak.
ANTONY. Plain love! plain arrogance, plain insolence!
  Thy men are cowards, thou, an envious traitor,
  Who, under seeming honesty, hast vented
  The burden of thy rank, o'erflowing gall.
  O that thou wert my equal, great in arms
  As the first Caesar was, that I might kill thee
  Without a stain to honor!
VENTIDIUS.
                You may kill me;
  You have done more already, — called me traitor.

ANTONY. Art thou not one?
VENTIDIUS.

                   For showing you yourself,
Which none else durst have done? But had I been
That name which I disdain to speak again,
I needed not have sought your abject fortunes,
Come to partake your fate, to die with you.
What hindered me t' have led my conquering eagles
To fill Octavius' bands? I could have been
A traitor then, a glorious, happy traitor,
And not have been so called.
ANTONY.

                      Forgive me, soldier;
I've been too passionate.
VENTIDIUS.   You thought me false;
Thought my old age betrayed you. Kill me, sir,
Pray, kill me. Yet you need not; your unkindness
Has left your sword no work.
ANTONY.

                  I did not think so.
I said it in my rage. Pr'ythee, forgive me.
Why didst thou tempt my anger by discovery
Of what I would not hear?
VENTIDIUS.

                 No prince but you
Could merit that sincerity I used,
Nor durst another man have ventured it;
But you, ere love misled your wandering eyes,
Were sure the chief and best of human race,
Framed in the very pride and boast of nature;
So perfect that the gods who formed you wondered
At their own skill, and cried, "A lucky hit
Has mended our design." Their envy hindered,
Else you had been immortal, and a pattern,
When Heaven would work for ostentation's sake
To copy out again.
ANTONY.

           But Cleopatra —
Go on, for I can bear it now.
VENTIDIUS.

                No more.
ANTONY. Thou dar'st not trust my passion, but thou may'st;
Thou only lov'st, the rest have flattered me.

VENTIDIUS. Heaven's blessing on your heart for that kind word!
    May I believe you love me? Speak again.
ANTONY. Indeed I do. Speak this, and this, and this.

                         (*Hugging him.*)
    Thy praises were unjust, but I'll deserve them,
    And yet mend all. Do with me what thou wilt;
    Lead me to victory! Thou know'st the way.
VENTIDIUS. And will you leave this —
ANTONY.

                   Pr'ythee, do not curse her,
    And I will leave her; though Heaven knows I love
    Beyond life, conquest, empire, all but honor;
    But I will leave her.
VENTIDIUS.

             That's my royal master;
    And shall we fight?
ANTONY.

                 I warrant thee, old soldier
    Thou shalt behold me once again in iron;
    And at the head of our old troops that beat
    The Parthians, cry aloud, "Come, follow me!"
VENTIDIUS. Oh, now I hear my emperor! In that word
    Octavius fell. Gods, let me see that day,
    And, if I have ten years behind, take all;
    I'll thank you for th' exchange.
ANTONY.

             O Cleopatra!
VENTIDIUS. Again?
ANTONY.

         I've done. In that last sigh, she went.
    Caesar shall know what 'tis to force a lover
    From all he holds most dear.
VENTIDIUS.

             Methinks you breathe
    Another soul. Your looks are more divine;
    You speak a hero, and you move a god.
ANTONY. Oh, thou hast fired me! My soul's up in arms,
    And man's each part about me. Once again
    That noble eagerness of fight has seized me,
    That eagerness with which I darted upward
    To Cassius' camp. In vain the steepy hill
    Opposed my way; in vain a war of spears
    Sung round my head and planted all my shield;

I won the trenches while my foremost men
Lagged on the plain below.

VENTIDIUS.

                              Ye gods, ye gods,
For such another hour!

ANTONY.

                              Come on, my soldier!
Our hearts and arms are still the same. I long
Once more to meet our foes, that thou and I,
Like time and death, marching before our troops,
May taste fate[17] to them, mow them out a passage,
And, entering where the foremost squadrons yield,
Begin the noble harvest of the field.   (*Exeunt.*)

ACT II

*action here is
continuous as in
Act I.*

[SCENE I.]

(*Enter* CLEOPATRA, IRAS, *and* ALEXAS.)

CLEOPATRA. What shall I do or whither shall I turn?
      Ventidius has o'ercome, and he will go.

ALEXAS. He goes to fight for you.

CLEOPATRA. Then he would see me ere he went to fight.
      Flatter me not. If once he goes, he's lost,
      And all my hopes destroyed.

ALEXAS.

                              Does this weak passion
Become a mighty queen?

CLEOPATRA.

                              I am no queen.
Is this to be a queen, to be besieged
By yon insulting Roman, and to wait
Each hour the victor's chain? These ills are small;
For Antony is lost, and I can mourn
For nothing else but him. Now come, Octavius,
I have no more to lose! Prepare thy bands;
I'm fit to be a captive; Antony
Has taught my mind the fortune of a slave.

---

[17] *taste fate*, i.e., anticipate victory.

IRAS. Call reason to assist you.
CLEOPATRA.

> I have none,
> And none would have. My love's a noble madness,
> Which shows the cause deserved it. Moderate sorrow
> Fits vulgar love, and for a vulgar man,
> But I have loved with such transcendent passion,
> I soared, at first, quite out of reason's view,
> And now am lost above it. No, I'm proud
> 'Tis thus. Would Antony could see me now!
> Think you he would not sigh? Though he must leave me,
> Sure, he would sigh, for he is noble-natured,
> And bears a tender heart. I know him well.
> Ah, no, I know him not; I knew him once,
> But now 'tis past.

IRAS.

> Let it be past with you.
> Forget him, madam.

CLEOPATRA.

> Never, never, Iras.
> He once was mine; and once, though now 'tis gone,
> Leaves a faint image of possession still.

ALEXAS. Think him unconstant, cruel, and ungrateful.
CLEOPATRA. I cannot. If I could, those thoughts were vain.

> Faithless, ungrateful, cruel though he be,
> I still must love him.

(Enter CHARMION.)

> Now, what news, my Charmion?
> Will he be kind? And will he not forsake me?
> Am I to live, or die? — nay, do I live?
> Or am I dead? For when he gave his answer,
> Fate took the word, and then I lived or died.

CHARMION. I found him, madam —
CLEOPATRA.

> A long speech preparing?
> If thou bring'st comfort, haste, and give it me,
> For never was more need.

IRAS.

> I know he loves you.

CLEOPATRA. Had he been kind, her eyes had told me so

> Before her tongue could speak it. Now she studies
> To soften what he said; but give me death

Just as he sent it, Charmion, undisguised,
And in the words he spoke.

CHARMION.

                              I found him, then,
Encompassed round, I think, with iron statues;
So mute, so motionless his soldiers stood,
While awfully he cast his eyes about
And every leader's hopes or fears surveyed.
Methought he looked resolved, and yet not pleased.
When he beheld me struggling in the crowd,
He blushed, and bade make way.

ALEXAS.

                              There's comfort yet.

CHARMION. Ventidius fixed his eyes upon my passage
Severely, as he meant to frown me back,
And sullenly gave place. I told my message,
Just as you gave it, broken and disordered;
I numbered in it all your sighs and tears,
And while I moved your pitiful request,
That you but only begged a last farewell,
He fetched an inward groan; and every time
I named you, sighed as if his heart were breaking,
But shunned my eyes and guiltily looked down.
He seemed not now that awful Antony
Who shook an armed assembly with his nod;
But, making show as he would rub his eyes,
Disguised and blotted out a falling tear.

CLEOPATRA. Did he then weep? And was I worth a tear?
If what thou hast to say be not as pleasing,
Tell me no more, but let me die contented.

CHARMION. He bid me say, he knew himself so well,
He could deny you nothing if he saw you;
And therefore —

CLEOPATRA. Thou wouldst say, he would not see me?

CHARMION. And therefore begged you not to use a power
Which he could ill resist; yet he should ever
Respect you as he ought.

CLEOPATRA.

                              Is that a word
For Antony to use to Cleopatra?
O that faint word, *respect!* how I disdain it!
Disdain myself for loving, after it!
He should have kept that word for cold Octavia.

Respect is for a wife. Am I that thing,
That dull, insipid lump, without desires,
And without power to give them?

ALEXAS.

You misjudge;
You see through love, and that deludes your sight,
As what is straight seems crooked through the water.
But I, who bear my reason undisturbed,
Can see this Antony, this dreaded man,
A fearful slave who fain would run away,
And shuns his master's eyes. If you pursue him,
My life on't, he still drags a chain along
That needs must clog his flight.

CLEOPATRA.

Could I believe thee! —

ALEXAS. By every circumstance I know he loves,
True, he's hard pressed by int'rest and by honor;
Yet he but doubts and parleys and casts out
Many a long look for succor.

CLEOPATRA.

He sends word
He fears to see my face.

ALEXAS.

And would you more?
He shows his weakness who declines the combat,
And you must urge your fortune. Could he speak
More plainly? To my ears the message sounds —
"Come to my rescue, Cleopatra, come;
Come, free me from Ventidius — from my tyrant;
See me and give me a pretense to leave him!"
I hear his trumpets. This way he must pass.
Please you, retire a while; I'll work him first,
That he may bend more easy.

CLEOPATRA.

You shall rule me;
But all, I fear, in vain.

(*Exit with* CHARMION *and* IRAS.)

ALEXAS.   I fear so, too,
Though I concealed my thoughts, to make her bold,
But 'tis our utmost means, and fate befriend it!

(*Withdraws.*)

(*Enter lictors with fasces*,[18] *one bearing the eagle; then enter* ANTONY *with* VENTIDIUS, *followed by other commanders*.)

ANTONY. Octavius is the minion of blind chance
    But holds from virtue nothing.
VENTIDIUS.

                            Has he courage?
ANTONY. But just enough to season him from coward.
    Oh, 'tis the coldest youth upon a charge,
    The most deliberate fighter! If he ventures
    (As in Illyria once, they say, he did,
    To storm a town), 'tis when he cannot choose;
    When all the world have fixed their eyes upon him,
    And then he lives on that for seven years after;
    But at a close revenge he never fails.
VENTIDIUS. I heard you challenged him.
ANTONY.

                             I did, Ventidius.
    What think'st thou was his answer? 'Twas so tame! —
    He said he had more ways than one to die;
    I had not.
VENTIDIUS. Poor!
ANTONY.

            He has more ways than one,
    But he would choose them all before that one.
VENTIDIUS. He first would choose an ague or a fever.
ANTONY. No; it must be an ague, not a fever;
    He has not warmth enough to die by that.
VENTIDIUS. Or old age and a bed.
ANTONY.

                   Ay, there's his choice,
    He would live like a lamp to the last wink,
    And crawl upon the utmost verge of life.
    O Hercules! Why should a man like this,
    Who dares not trust his fate for one great action,
    Be all the care of Heaven? Why should he lord it
    O'er fourscore thousand men, of whom each one
    Is braver than himself?
VENTIDIUS.

                  You conquered for him.

---

[18] *lictors with fasces*, attendants carrying the rods that symbolized Roman rule.

Philippi[19] knows it; there you shared with him
That empire which your sword made all your own.
ANTONY. Fool that I was, upon my eagle's wings
I bore this wren till I was tired with soaring,
And now he mounts above me.
Good heavens, is this — is this the man who braves me?
Who bids my age make way? Drives me before him
To the world's ridge and sweeps me off like rubbish?
VENTIDIUS. Sir, we lose time; the troops are mounted all.
ANTONY. Then give the word to march.
I long to leave this prison of a town,
To join thy legions, and in open field
Once more to show my face. Lead, my deliverer.

(*Enter* ALEXAS.)

ALEXAS. Great emperor,
In mighty arms renowned above mankind,
But in soft pity to th' oppressed, a god,
This message sends the mournful Cleopatra
To her departing lord.
VENTIDIUS.
                              Smooth sycophant!
ALEXAS. A thousand wishes and ten thousand prayers,
Millions of blessings wait you to the wars;
Millions of sighs and tears she sends you, too,
And would have sent
As many parting kisses to your lips,
But those, she fears, have wearied you already.
VENTIDIUS. (*aside*) False crocodile!
ALEXAS. And yet she begs not now you would not leave her;
That were a wish too mighty for her hopes,
Too presuming
For her low fortune and your ebbing love;
That were a wish for her more prosperous days,
Her blooming beauty and your growing kindness.
ANTONY. (*aside*) Well, I must man it out. — What would the
queen?
ALEXAS. First, to these noble warriors who attend
Your daring courage in the chase of fame, —
Too daring and too dangerous for her quiet, —

19 *Philippi*, battle in which Julius Caesar was avenged by the defeat of
Brutus and Cassius at the hands of Antony and Octavius.

She humbly recommends all she holds dear,
All her own cares and fears, — the care of you.
VENTIDIUS. Yes, witness Actium.
ANTONY.

Let him speak, Ventidius.
ALEXAS. You, when his matchless valor bears him forward
With ardor too heroic, on his foes,
Fall down, as she would do, before his feet;
Lie in his way and stop the paths of death.
Tell him this god is not invulnerable,
That absent Cleopatra bleeds in him,
And, that you may remember her petition,
She begs you wear these trifles as a pawn
Which, at your wished return, she will redeem

(*Gives jewels to the commanders.*)

With all the wealth of Egypt.
This to the great Ventidius she presents,
Whom she can never count her enemy,
Because he loves her lord.
VENTIDIUS.

Tell her, I'll none on't;
I'm not ashamed of honest poverty;
Not all the diamonds of the East can bribe
Ventidius from his faith. I hope to see
These and the rest of all her sparkling store
Where they shall more deservingly be placed.
ANTONY. And who must wear 'em then?
VENTIDIUS.

The wronged Octavia.
ANTONY. You might have spared that word.
VENTIDIUS.

And he, that bribe.
ANTONY. But have I no remembrance?
ALEXAS.

Yes, a dear one;
Your slave the queen —
ANTONY.

My mistress.
ALEXAS.

Then your mistress;
Your mistress would, she says, have sent her soul,
But that you had long since; she humbly begs

This ruby bracelet, set with bleeding hearts,
The emblems of her own, may bind your arm.

(*Presenting a bracelet.*)

VENTIDIUS. Now, my best lord, in honor's name, I ask you,
For manhood's sake and for your own dear safety,
Touch not these poisoned gifts,
Infected by the sender; touch 'em not;
Myriads of bluest[20] plagues lie underneath them,
And more than aconite[21] has dipped the silk.
ANTONY. Nay, now you grow too cynical, Ventidius;
A lady's favors may be worn with honor.
What, to refuse her bracelet! On my soul,
When I lie pensive in my tent alone,
'Twill pass the wakeful hours of winter nights
To tell these pretty beads upon my arm,
To count for every one a soft embrace,
A melting kiss at such a time,
And now and then the fury of her love
When — And what harm's in this?
ALEXAS.
None, none, my lord,
But what's to her, that now 'tis past for ever.
ANTONY. (*Going to tie it.*) We soldiers are so awkward —
help me tie it.
ALEXAS. In faith, my lord, we courtiers, too, are awkward
In these affairs; so are all men indeed,
Even I, who am not one. But shall I speak?
ANTONY. Yes, freely.
ALEXAS.
Then, my lord, fair hands alone
Are fit to tie it; she who sent it can.
VENTIDIUS. Hell! death! this eunuch pander ruins you.
You will not see her?

(ALEXAS *whispers to an attendant, who goes out.*)

ANTONY.
But to take my leave.
VENTIDIUS. Then I have washed an Aethiop.[22] You're undone;

---

20 *bluest*, i.e., the bluish tinge of death.
21 *aconite*, wolfsbane, poison.
22 *washed an Aethiop*, tried to change the color of a Negro, i.e., wasted
my time.

You're in the toils; you're taken; you're destroyed;
Her eyes do Caesar's work.

ANTONY.

                              You fear too soon.
I'm constant to myself; I know my strength;
And yet she shall think me barbarous neither,
Born in the depths of Afric. I'm a Roman,
Bred to the rules of soft humanity.
A guest, and kindly used, should bid farewell.

VENTIDIUS. You do not know
How weak you are to her, how much an infant;
You are not proof against a smile or glance;
A sigh will quite disarm you.

ANTONY.

                              See, she comes!
Now you shall find your error. — Gods, I thank you.
I formed the danger greater than it was,
And now 'tis near, 'tis lessened.

VENTIDIUS.

                              Mark the end yet.

(*Enter* CLEOPATRA, CHARMION, *and* IRAS.)

ANTONY. Well, madam, we are met.

CLEOPATRA.

                              Is this a meeting?
Then, we must part?

ANTONY.

                    We must.

CLEOPATRA.

                              Who says we must?

ANTONY. Our own hard fates.

CLEOPATRA.

                    We make those fates ourselves.

ANTONY. Yes, we have made them; we have loved each other
Into our mutual ruin.

CLEOPATRA. The gods have seen my joys with envious eyes;
I have no friends in heaven, and all the world,
As 'twere the business of mankind to part us,
Is armed against my love. Even you yourself
Join with the rest; you, you are armed against me.

ANTONY. I will be justified in all I do
To late posterity, and therefore hear me.
If I mix a lie

With any truth, reproach me freely with it;
Else, favor me with silence.

CLEOPATRA.

You command me,
And I am dumb.

VENTIDIUS. [*aside*] I like this well; he shows authority.

ANTONY. That I derive my ruin
From you alone —

CLEOPATRA.

O heavens! I ruin you!

ANTONY. You promised me your silence, and you break it
Ere I have scarce begun.

CLEOPATRA.

Well, I obey you.

ANTONY. When I beheld you first, it was in Egypt.
Ere Caesar saw your eyes, you gave me love,
And were too young to know it; that I settled
Your father in his throne was for your sake;
I left th' acknowledgment for time to ripen.
Caesar stepped in and with a greedy hand
Plucked the green fruit ere the first blush of red,
Yet cleaving to the bough. He was my lord,
And was, beside, too great for me to rival.
But I deserved you first, though he enjoyed you.
When, after, I beheld you in Cilicia,
An enemy to Rome, I pardoned you.

CLEOPATRA. I cleared myself —

ANTONY.

Again you break your promise.
I loved you still and took your weak excuses,
Took you into my bosom, stained by Caesar,
And not half mine. I went to Egypt with you,
And hid me from the business of the world,
Shut out inquiring nations from my sight
To give whole years to you.

VENTIDIUS. (*aside*) Yes, to your shame be't spoken.

ANTONY.

How I loved,
Witness, ye days and nights and all your hours
That danced away with down upon your feet,
As all your business were to count my passion!
One day passed by and nothing saw but love;
Another came and still 'twas only love.

The suns were wearied out with looking on,
And I untired with loving.
I saw you every day, and all the day;
And every day was still but as the first,
So eager was I still to see you more.

VENTIDIUS. 'Tis all too true.

ANTONY.

                  Fulvia, my wife, grew jealous,
As she indeed had reason; raised a war
In Italy to call me back.

VENTIDIUS.

              But yet
You went not.

ANTONY.

              While within your arms I lay,
The world fell moldering from my hands each hour,
And left me scarce a grasp — I thank your love for't.

VENTIDIUS. Well pushed: that last was home.

CLEOPATRA.

                    Yet may I speak?

ANTONY. If I have urged a falsehood, yes; else, not.
Your silence says I have not. Fulvia died
(Pardon, you gods, with my unkindness died);
To set the world at peace I took Octavia,
This Caesar's[23] sister; in her pride of youth
And flower of beauty did I wed that lady,
Whom, blushing, I must praise, because I left her.
You called; my love obeyed the fatal summons.
This raised the Roman arms; the cause was yours,
I would have fought by land where I was stronger;
You hindered it; yet, when I fought at sea,
Forsook me fighting; and (O stain to honor!
O lasting shame!) I knew not that I fled,
But fled to follow you.

VENTIDIUS. What haste she made to hoist her purple sails!
And, to appear magnificent in flight,
Drew half our strength away.

ANTONY.

               All this you caused.
And would you multiply more ruins on me?
This honest man, my best, my only friend,

---

[23] *This Caesar's,* after the death of Julius Caesar the word *caesar* was used for each emperor or heir. Octavius is referred to here.

Has gathered up the shipwreck of my fortunes;
Twelve legions I have left, my last recruits,
And you have watched the news, and bring your eyes
To seize them, too. If you have aught to answer,
Now speak, you have free leave.

ALEXAS. (*aside*) She stands confounded.
Despair is in her eyes.

VENTIDIUS. Now lay a sigh i'th' way to stop his passage;
Prepare a tear and bid it for his legions;
'Tis like they shall be sold.

CLEOPATRA. How shall I plead my cause when you, my judge,
Already have condemned me? Shall I bring
The love you bore me for my advocate?
That now is turned against me, that destroys me;
For love, once past, is, at the best, forgotten,
But oft'ner sours to hate. 'Twill please my lord
To ruin me, and therefore I'll be guilty.
But could I once have thought it would have pleased you,
That you would pry, with narrow searching eyes,
Into my faults, severe to my destruction,
And watching all advantages with care
That serve to make me wretched? Speak, my lord,
For I end here. Though I deserve this usage,
Was it like you to give it?

ANTONY.
                            Oh, you wrong me
To think I sought this parting or desired
To accuse you more than what will clear myself
And justify this breach.

CLEOPATRA.
                            Thus low I thank you,
And, since my innocence will not offend,
I shall not blush to own it.

VENTIDIUS. (*aside*)
                            After this,
I think she'll blush at nothing.

CLEOPATRA.
                            You seem grieved
(And therein you are kind) that Caesar first
Enjoyed my love, though you deserved it better.
I grieve for that, my lord, much more than you;
For, had I first been yours, it would have saved
My second choice: I never had been his,
And ne'er had been but yours. But Caesar first,

You say, possessed my love. Not so, my lord.
He first possessed my person; you, my love.
Caesar loved me, but I loved Antony.
If I endured him after, 'twas because
I judged it due to the first name of men,
And, half constrained, I gave as to a tyrant
What he would take by force.

VENTIDIUS.
                              O Siren! Siren!
Yet grant that all the love she boasts were true,
Has she not ruined you? I still urge that,
The fatal consequence.

CLEOPATRA.
                          The consequence, indeed,
For I dare challenge him, my greatest foe,
To say it was designed. 'Tis true I loved you,
And kept you far from an uneasy wife, —
Such Fulvia was.
Yes, but he'll say you left Octavia for me; —
And can you blame me to receive that love
Which quitted such desert for worthless me?
How often have I wished some other Caesar,
Great as the first, and as the second, young,
Would court my love to be refused for you!

VENTIDIUS. Words, words; but Actium, sir; remember Actium.
CLEOPATRA. Even there I dare his malice. True, I counseled
To fight at sea, but I betrayed you not.
I fled, but not to the enemy. 'Twas fear.
Would I had been a man, not to have feared!
For none would then have envied me your friendship,
Who envy me your love.

ANTONY.
                          We're both unhappy.
If nothing else, yet our ill fortune parts us.
Speak; would you have me perish by my stay?

CLEOPATRA. If, as a friend, you ask my judgment, go;
If as a lover, stay. If you must perish —
'Tis a hard word — but stay.

VENTIDIUS. See now th' effects of her so boasted love!
She strives to drag you down to ruin with her;
But could she 'scape without you, oh, how soon
Would she let go her hold and haste to shore
And never look behind!

CLEOPATRA.

Then judge my love by this.

(*Giving* ANTONY *a writing.*)

Could I have borne
A life or death, a happiness or woe
From yours divided, this had given me means.

ANTONY. By Hercules, the writing of Octavius!
I know it well; 'tis that proscribing hand,
Young as it was, that led the way to mine
And left me but the second place in murder. —24
See, see, Ventidius! here he offers Egypt,
And joins all Syria to it as a present,
So, in requital, she forsake my fortunes
And join her arms with his.

CLEOPATRA.

And yet you leave me!
You leave me, Antony; and yet I love you,
Indeed I do. I have refused a kingdom;
That's a trifle;
For I could part with life, with anything,
But only you. Oh, let me die but with you!
Is that a hard request?

ANTONY.

Next living with you,
'Tis all that Heaven can give.

ALEXAS. (*aside*) He melts; we conquer.

CLEOPATRA. No; you shall go. Your interest calls you hence;
Yes, your dear interest pulls too strong for these
Weak arms to hold you here.   (*Takes his hand.*)
Go; leave me, soldier
(For you're no more a lover), leave me dying;
Push me, all pale and panting, from your bosom,
And, when your march begins, let one run after,
Breathless almost for joy, and cry, "She's dead."
The soldiers shout; you then perhaps may sigh
And muster all your Roman gravity.
Ventidius chides; and straight your brow clears up,
As I had never been.

---

24 *that proscribing hand . . . in murder,* when they shared power in
Rome, Octavius and Antony used the power of proscription: making a
list of their enemies, who were then executed.

ANTONY.
                              Gods, 'tis too much —
    Too much for man to bear.
CLEOPATRA.
                              What is't for me, then,
    A weak, forsaken woman and a lover? —
    Here let me breathe my last. Envy me not
    This minute in your arms. I'll die apace,
    As fast as e'er I can, and end your trouble.
ANTONY. Die! Rather let me perish; loosened nature
    Leap from its hinges! Sink the props of heaven,
    And fall the skies to crush the nether world!
    My eyes, my soul, my all!   (*Embraces her.*)
VENTIDIUS.
                              And what's this toy
    In balance with your fortune, honor, fame?
ANTONY. What is't, Ventidius? It outweighs 'em all;
    Why, we have more than conquered Caesar now.
    My queen's not only innocent, but loves me.
    This, this is she who drags me down to ruin!
    "But could she 'scape without me, with what haste
    Would she let slip her hold and make to shore
    And never look behind!"
    Down on thy knees, blasphemer as thou art,
    And ask forgiveness of wronged innocence.
VENTIDIUS. I'll rather die than take it. Will you go?
ANTONY. Go! Whither? Go from all that's excellent!
    Faith, honor, virtue, all good things forbid
    That should go from her who sets my love
    Above the price of kingdoms. Give, you gods,
    Give to your boy, your Caesar,
    This rattle of a globe to play withal,
    This gewgaw world, and put him cheaply off.
    I'll not be pleased with less than Cleopatra.
CLEOPATRA. She's wholly yours. My heart's so full of joy
    That I shall do some wild extravagance
    Of love in public, and the foolish world,
    Which knows not tenderness, will think me mad.
VENTIDIUS. O women! women! women! all the gods
    Have not such power of doing good to man
    As you of doing harm.
ANTONY.
                              Our men are armed.   (*Exit.*)

Unbar the gate that looks to Caesar's camp.
I would revenge the treachery he meant me;
And long security makes conquest easy.
I'm eager to return before I go,
For all the pleasures I have known beat thick
On my remembrance. — How I long for night!
That both the sweets of mutual love may try,
And once triumph o'er Caesar [ere] we die.   (*Exeunt.*)

ACT III

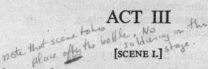

note that scene takes place off the battle. No soldiering on the stage.

[SCENE I.]

(*At one door enter* CLEOPATRA, CHARMION, IRAS, *and* ALEXAS, *a train of Egyptians; at the other,* ANTONY *and Romans. The entrance on both sides is prepared by music; the trumpets first sounding on* ANTONY'S *part, then answered by timbrels, etc., on* CLEOPATRA'S. CHARMION *and* IRAS *hold a laurel wreath betwixt them. A dance of Egyptians. After the ceremony* CLEOPATRA *crowns* ANTONY.)

ANTONY. I thought how those white arms would fold me in,
And strain me close and melt me into love;
So pleased with that sweet image, I sprung forwards,
And added all my strength to every blow.
CLEOPATRA. Come to me, come, my soldier, to my arms!
You've been too long away from my embraces,
But, when I have you fast and all my own,
With broken murmurs and with amorous sighs
I'll say you were unkind, and punish you,
And mark you red with many an eager kiss.
ANTONY. My brighter Venus!
CLEOPATRA.

O my greater Mars!
ANTONY. Thou join'st us well, my love!
Suppose me come from the Phlegraean plains[25]
Where gasping giants lay, cleft by my sword,
And mountain-tops pared off each other blow[26]

---

[25] *Phlegraean plain,* scene of the mythological battle of the gods and Titans.
[26] *pared . . . blow,* i.e., cut off in the heat of battle by random blows.

To bury those I slew. Receive me, goddess!
Let Caesar spread his subtle nets, like Vulcan,[27]
In thy embraces I would be beheld
By heaven and earth at once;
And make their envy what they meant their sport.
Let those who took us blush; I would love on
With awful state, regardless of their frowns,
As their superior god.
There's no satiety of love in thee:
Enjoyed, thou still art new; perpetual spring
Is in thy arms; the ripened fruit but falls,
And blossoms rise to fill its empty place,
And I grow rich by giving.

(*Enter* VENTIDIUS, *and stands apart.*)

ALEXAS. Oh, now the danger's past, your general comes!
He joins not in your joys, nor minds your triumphs;
But with contracted brows looks frowning on,
As envying your success.
ANTONY. Now, on my soul, he loves me; truly loves me;
He never flattered me in any vice,
But awes me with his virtue. Even this minute
Methinks, he has a right of chiding me.—
Lead to the temple—I'll avoid his presence;
It checks too strong upon me.

(*Exeunt the rest.*)
(*As* ANTONY *is going,* VENTIDIUS *pulls him by the robe.*)

VENTIDIUS.

Emperor!
ANTONY. (*Looking back*) 'Tis the old argument. I prithee, spare me.
VENTIDIUS. But this one hearing, emperor.
ANTONY.

Let go
My robe; or, by my father Hercules—
VENTIDIUS. By Hercules his father, that's yet greater,
I bring you somewhat you would wish to know.

[27] Venus, married to Vulcan, was beloved by Mars, god of battle. They were trapped in an iron net *in flagrante* and exhibited to the gods. Mercury saw the joke, but said he would rather be inside the net.

ANTONY. Thou see'st we are observed; attend me here,
    And I'll return.

(*Exit.*)

VENTIDIUS. I'm waning in his favor, yet I love him;
    I love this man who runs to meet his ruin;
    And sure the gods, like me, are fond of him.
    His virtues lie so mingled with his crimes,
    As would confound their choice to punish one
    And not reward the other.

(*Enter* ANTONY.)

ANTONY.

                  We can conquer,
    You see, without your aid.
    We have dislodged their troops;
    They look on us at distance and, like curs
    'Scaped from the lion's paw, they bay *far off,*
    And lick their wounds and faintly threaten war.
    Five thousand Romans with their faces upward
    Lie breathless on the plain.

VENTIDIUS.

                 'Tis well; and he
    Who lost them could have spared ten thousand more.
    Yet if, by this advantage, you could gain
    An easier peace while Caesar doubts the chance
    Of arms—

ANTONY.

          Oh, think not on't, Ventidius!
    The boy pursues my ruin, he'll no peace;
    His malice is considerate in advantage.
    Oh, he's the coolest murderer! so staunch,
    He kills, and keeps his temper.

VENTIDIUS.

               Have you no friend
    In all his army who has power to move him?
    Maecenas, or Agrippa, might do much.

ANTONY. They're both too deep in Caesar's interests.
    We'll work it out by dint of sword, or perish.

VENTIDIUS. Fain I would find some other.

ANTONY.

                Thank thy love.
    Some four or five such victories as this
    Will save thy further pains.

VENTIDIUS. Expect no more—Caesar is on his guard.
    I know, sir, you have conquered against odds,
    But still you draw supplies from one poor town,
    And of Egyptians. He has all the world,
    And at his back nations come pouring in
    To fill the gaps you make. Pray, think again,
ANTONY. Why dost thou drive me from myself, to search
    For foreign aids?—to hunt my memory,
    And range all o'er a waste and barren place
    To find a friend? The wretched have no friends.—
    Yet I had one, the bravest youth of Rome,
    Whom Caesar loves beyond the love of women;
    He could resolve his mind as fire does wax,
    From that hard, rugged image melt him down,
    And mold him in what softer form he pleased.
VENTIDIUS. Him would I see—that man of all the world;
    Just such a one we want.
ANTONY.
                      He loved me, too;
    I was his soul; he lived not but in me.
    We were so closed within each other's breasts,
    The rivets were not found that joined us first.
    That does not reach us yet; we were so mixed
    As meeting streams, both to ourselves were lost;
    We were one mass; we could not give or take
    But from the same, for he was I, I he.
VENTIDIUS. (*aside*) He moves as I would wish him.
ANTONY.
                                    After this
    I need not tell his name.—'Twas Dolabella.
VENTIDIUS. He's now in Caesar's camp.
ANTONY.
                            No matter where,
    Since he's no longer mine. He took unkindly
    That I forbade him Cleopatra's sight,
    Because I feared he loved her. He confessed
    He had a warmth which, for my sake, he stifled,
    For 'twere impossible that two, so one,
    Should not have loved the same. When he departed,
    He took no leave, and that confirmed my thoughts.
VENTIDIUS. It argues that he loved you more than her,
    Else he had stayed. But he perceived you jealous,
    And would not grieve his friend. I know he loves you.
ANTONY. I should have seen him, then, ere now.

VENTIDIUS.

                                                      Perhaps
    He has thus long been laboring for your peace.
ANTONY. Would he were here!
VENTIDIUS.

                                Would you believe he loved you?
    I read your answer in your eyes—you would.
    Not to conceal it longer, he has sent
    A messenger from Caesar's camp with letters.
ANTONY. Let him appear.
VENTIDIUS.

                                I'll bring him instantly.

                    (*Exit* VENTIDIUS, *and re-enters immediately*
                                        with DOLABELLA.)

ANTONY. 'Tis he himself! himself, by holy friendship!

                                (*Runs to embrace him.*)

    Art thou returned at last, my better half?
    Come, give me all myself! Let me not live,
    If the young bridegroom, longing for his night,
    Was ever half so fond!
DOLABELLA. I must be silent, for my soul is busy
    About a nobler work: she's new come home,
    Like a long-absent man, and wanders o'er
    Each room, a stranger to her own, to look
    If all be safe.
ANTONY.

                    Thou hast what's left of me;
    For I am now so sunk from what I was,
    Thou find'st me at my lowest water-mark.
    The rivers that ran in and raised my fortunes
    Are all dried up, or take another course;
    What I have left is from my native spring.
    I've still a heart that swells in scorn of fate
    And lifts me to my banks.
DOLABELLA. Still you are lord of all the world to me.
ANTONY. Why, then I yet am so; for thou art all.
    If I had any joy when thou wert absent,
    I grudged it to myself; methought I robbed
    Thee of thy part. But, O my Dolabella!
    Thou hast beheld me other than I am.
    Hast thou not seen my morning chambers filled
    With sceptred slaves who waited to salute me?

With eastern monarchs who forgot the sun
To worship my uprising?—menial kings
Ran coursing up and down my palace-yard,
Stood silent in my presence, watched my eyes,
And at my least command all started out
Like racers to the goal.

DOLABELLA.
                              Slaves to your fortune.
ANTONY. Fortune is Caesar's now; and what am I?
VENTIDIUS. What you have made yourself I will not flatter.
ANTONY. Is this friendly done?
DOLABELLA. Yes; when his end is so, I must join with him;
    Indeed, I must; and yet you must not chide;
    Why am I else your friend?
ANTONY.
                              Take heed, young man,
    How thou upbraid'st my love. The queen has eyes,
    And thou, too, hast a soul. Canst thou remember
    When, swelled with hatred, thou beheld'st her first,
    As accessory to thy brother's death?
DOLABELLA. Spare my remembrance; 'twas a guilty day,
    And still the blush hangs here.
ANTONY.
                              To clear herself
    For sending him no aid, she came from Egypt.
    Her galley down the silver Cydnos rowed,
    The tackling silk, the streamers waved with gold;
    The gentle winds were lodged in purple sails;
    Her nymphs, like Nereids, round her couch were placed,
    Where she, another sea-born Venus, lay.
DOLABELLA. No more; I would not hear it.
ANTONY.
                              Oh, you must!
    She lay, and leant her cheek upon her hand,
    And cast a look so languishingly sweet
    As if, secure of all beholders' hearts,
    Neglecting, she could take them. Boys like Cupids
    Stood fanning with their painted wings the winds
    That played about her face; but if she smiled,
    A darting glory seemed to blaze abroad,
    That men's desiring eyes were never wearied,
    But hung upon the object. To soft flutes
    The silver oars kept time; and while they played,
    The hearing gave new pleasure to the sight,

And both, to thought. 'Twas heaven or somewhat more;
For she so charmed all hearts, that gazing crowds
Stood panting on the shore, and wanted breath
To give their welcome voice.
Then, Dolabella, where was then thy soul?
Was not thy fury quite disarmed with wonder?
Didst thou not shrink behind me from those eyes
And whisper in my ear "Oh, tell her not
That I accused her of my brother's death?"

DOLABELLA. And should my weakness be a plea for yours?
Mine was an age when love might be excused,
When kindly warmth, and when my springing youth,
Made it a debt to nature. Yours—

VENTIDIUS.

                    Speak boldly.
Yours, he would say, in your declining age,
When no more heat was left but what you forced,
When all the sap was needful for the trunk,
When it went down, then you constrained the course,
And robbed from nature to supply desire;
In you (I would not use so harsh a word)
'Tis but plain dotage.

ANTONY.

                Ha!

DOLABELLA.

                  'Twas urged too home.—
But yet the loss was private that I made;
'Twas but myself I lost. I lost no legions;
I had no world to lose, no people's love.

ANTONY. This from a friend?

DOLABELLA.

               Yes, Antony, a true one;
A friend so tender that each word I speak
Stabs my own heart before it reach your ear.
Oh, judge me not less kind because I chide!
To Caesar I excuse you.

ANTONY.

               O ye gods!
Have I then lived to be excused to Caesar?

DOLABELLA. As to your equal.

ANTONY.

              Well, he's but my equal;
While I wear this, he never shall be more.

DOLABELLA. I bring conditions from him.

ANTONY.

                              Are they noble?
Methinks thou shouldst not bring them else; yet he
Is full of deep dissembling; knows no honor
Divided from his interest. Fate mistook him,
For nature meant him for an usurer;
He's fit indeed to buy, not conquer, kingdoms.

VENTIDIUS. Then, granting this,
    What power was theirs who wrought so hard a temper
    To honorable terms?

ANTONY. It was my Dolabella, or some god.

DOLABELLA. Nor I, nor yet Maecenas, nor Agrippa;
    They were your enemies, and I, a friend,
    Too weak alone; yet 'twas a Roman's deed.

ANTONY. 'Twas like a Roman done; show me that man
    Who has preserved my life, my love, my honor;
    Let me but see his face.

VENTIDIUS.

                      That task is mine,
And, Heaven, thou know'st how pleasing.

                            (*Exit* VENTIDIUS.)

DOLABELLA.

                        You'll remember
To whom you stand obliged?

ANTONY.

                     When I forget it,
Be thou unkind, and that's my greatest curse.
My queen shall thank him, too.

DOLABELLA.

                     I fear she will not.

ANTONY. But she shall do't—the queen, my Dolabella!
    Hast thou not still some grudgings of thy fever?[28]

DOLABELLA. I would not see her lost.

ANTONY.

                  When I forsake her,
Leave me, my better stars! for she has truth
Beyond her beauty. Caesar tempted her,
At no less price than kingdoms, to betray me,
But she resisted all; and yet thou chid'st me
For loving her too well. Could I do so?

---

  28 *grudgings of thy fever,* a touch of your infatuation.

(*Re-enter* VENTIDIUS *with* OCTAVIA, *leading* ANTONY'S *two little daughters.*)

DOLABELLA. Yes; there's my reason.
ANTONY.

                        Where?—Octavia there!

                             (*Starting back.*)

VENTIDIUS. What—is she poison to you?—a disease?
    Look on her, view her well, and those she brings.
    Are they all strangers to your eyes? has nature
    No secret call, no whisper they are yours?
DOLABELLA. For shame, my lord, if not for love, receive them
    With kinder eyes. If you confess a man,
    Meet them, embrace them, bid them welcome to you.
    Your arms should open without your knowledge,
    To clasp them in; your feet should turn to wings,
    To bear you to them; and your eyes dart out
    And aim a kiss ere you could reach the lips.
ANTONY. I stood amazed to think how they came hither.
VENTIDIUS. I sent for 'em; I brought 'em in, unknown
    To Cleopatra's guards.
DOLABELLA.

                  Yet are you cold?
OCTAVIA. Thus long I have attended for my welcome,
    Which, as a stranger, sure I might expect.
    Who am I?
ANTONY.

             Caesar's sister.
OCTAVIA.

                  That's unkind.
    Had I been nothing more than Caesar's sister,
    Know, I had still remained in Caesar's camp.
    But your Octavia, your much injured wife,
    Though banished from your bed, driven from your house,
    In spite of Caesar's sister, still is yours.
    'Tis true, I have a heart disdains your coldness,
    And prompts me not to seek what you should offer;
    But a wife's virtue still surmounts that pride.
    I come to claim you as my own; to show
    My duty first; to ask, nay beg, your kindness.
    Your hand, my lord; 'tis mine, and I will have it.

                      (*Taking his hand.*)

VENTIDIUS. Do, take it; thou deserv'st it.
DOLABELLA.

> On my soul,
> And so she does; she's neither too submissive,
> Nor yet too haughty; but so just a mean
> Shows, as it ought, a wife and Roman too.

ANTONY. I fear, Octavia, you have begged my life.
OCTAVIA. Begged it, my lord?
ANTONY.

> Yes, begged it, my ambassadress;
> Poorly and basely begged it of your brother.

OCTAVIA. Poorly and basely I could never beg.
> Nor could my brother grant.

ANTONY. Shall I, who, to my kneeling slave, could say,
> "Rise up and be a king," shall I fall down
> And cry, "Forgive me, Caesar?" Shall I set
> A man, my equal, in the place of Jove,
> As he could give me being? No—that word
> "Forgive" would choke me up
> And die upon my tongue.

DOLABELLA.

> You shall not need it.

ANTONY. I will not need it. Come, you've all betrayed me—
> My friend too!—to receive some vile conditions.
> My wife has bought me with her prayers and tears,
> And now I must become her branded slave.
> In every peevish mood she will upbraid
> The life she gave; if I but look awry,
> She cries, "I'll tell my brother."

OCTAVIA.

> My hard fortune
> Subjects me still to your unkind mistakes.
> But the conditions I have brought are such
> You need not blush to take; I love your honor,
> Because 'tis mine. It never shall be said
> Octavia's husband was her brother's slave.
> Sir, you are free—free, even from her you loathe;
> For, though my brother bargains for your love,
> Makes me the price and cement of your peace,
> I have a soul like yours; I cannot take
> Your love as alms, nor beg what I deserve.
> I'll tell my brother we are reconciled;
> He shall draw back his troops, and you shall march
> To rule the East. I may be dropped at Athens—

No matter where. I never will complain,
But only keep the barren name of wife,
And rid you of the trouble.

VENTIDIUS. Was ever such a strife of sullen honor!
Both scorn to be obliged.

DOLABELLA. Oh, she has touched him in the tenderest part;
See how he reddens with despite and shame,
To be outdone in generosity!

VENTIDIUS. See how he winks! how he dries up a tear,
That fain would fall!

ANTONY. Octavia, I have heard you, and must praise
The greatness of your soul;
But cannot yield to what you have proposed,
For I can ne'er be conquered but by love,
And you do all for duty. You would free me,
And would be dropped at Athens; was't not so?

OCTAVIA. It was, my lord.

ANTONY.
                 Then I must be obliged
To one who loves me not; who, to herself,
May call me thankless and ungrateful man.—
I'll not endure it—no.

VENTIDIUS. (aside) I am glad it pinches there.

OCTAVIA. Would you triumph o'er poor Octavia's virtue?
That pride was all I had to bear me up;
That you might think you owed me your life,
And owed it to my duty, not my love.
I have been injured, and my haughty soul
Could brook but ill the man who slights my bed.

ANTONY. Therefore you love me not.

OCTAVIA.
                 Therefore, my lord,
I should not love you.

ANTONY. Therefore you would leave me?

OCTAVIA. And therefore I should leave you — if I could.

DOLABELLA. Her soul's too great, after such injuries,
To say she loves; and yet she lets you see it.
Her modesty and silence plead her cause.

ANTONY. O Dolabella, which way shall I turn?
I find a secret yielding in my soul;
But Cleopatra, who would die with me,
Must she be left? Pity pleads for Octavia,
But does it not plead more for Cleopatra?

VENTIDIUS. Justice and pity both plead for Octavia;

For Cleopatra, neither.
One would be ruined with you, but she first
Had ruined you; the other, you have ruined,
And yet she would preserve you.
In everything their merits are unequal.

ANTONY. O my distracted soul!

OCTAVIA. Sweet Heaven, compose it!—
Come, come, my lord, if I can pardon you,
Methinks you should accept it. Look on these—
Are they not yours? or stand they thus neglected
As they are mine? Go to him, children, go;
Kneel to him, take him by the hand, speak to him,
For you may speak and he may own you, too,
Without a blush—and so he cannot all
His children. Go, I say, and pull him to me,
And pull him to yourselves from that bad woman.
You, Agrippina, hang upon his arms,
And you, Antonia, clasp about his waist.
If he will shake you off, if he will dash you
Against the pavement, you must bear it, children,
For you are mine, and I was born to suffer.

(Here the children go to him, etc.)

VENTIDIUS. Was ever sight so moving?—Emperor!

DOLABELLA.

　　　　　　　　　　　　　　　　　Friend!

OCTAVIA. Husband!

BOTH CHILDREN.

　　　　　　　Father!

ANTONY. I am vanquished. Take me,
Octavia—take me, children—share me all.

(Embracing them.)

I've been a thriftless debtor to your loves,
And run out much, in riot, from your stock,
But all shall be amended.

OCTAVIA.

　　　　　　　　　O blest hour!

DOLABELLA. O happy change!

VENTIDIUS.

　　　　　　　　　My joy stops at my tongue,
But it has found two channels here for one,
And bubbles out above.

ANTONY. (*To Octavia*) This is thy triumph. Lead me where thou wilt,
    Even to thy brother's camp.

OCTAVIA.
                        All there are yours.

(*Enter* ALEXAS *hastily.*)

ALEXAS. The queen, my mistress, sir, and yours—

ANTONY. 'Tis past.—
    Octavia, you shall stay this night. Tomorrow
    Caesar and we are one.

                (*Exit, leading* OCTAVIA; DOLABELLA *and*
                           the children follow.)

VENTIDIUS. There's news for you! Run, my officious eunuch,
    Be sure to be the first—haste forward!
    Haste, my dear eunuch, haste!   (*Exit.*)

ALEXAS. This downright fighting fool, this thick-skulled hero,
    This blunt, unthinking instrument of death,
    With plain, dull virtue has outgone my wit.
    Pleasure forsook my earliest infancy;
    The luxury of others robbed my cradle,
    And ravished thence the promise of a man.
    Cast out from nature, disinherited
    Of what her meanest children claim by kind,
    Yet greatness kept me from contempt. That's gone.
    Had Cleopatra followed my advice,
    Then he had been betrayed who now forsakes.
    She dies for love, but she has known its joys.
    Gods, is this just that I, who know no joys,
    Must die because she loves?

(*Enter* CLEOPATRA, CHARMION, IRAS, *and train.*)

    O madam, I have seen what blasts my eyes!
    Octavia's here.

CLEOPATRA. Peace with that raven's note.
    I know it, too, and now am in
    The pangs of death.

ALEXAS.
                You are no more a queen—
    Egypt is lost.

CLEOPATRA. What tell'st thou me of Egypt?
    My life, my soul is lost! Octavia has him!—

O fatal name to Cleopatra's love!
My kisses, my embraces now are hers,
While I—But thou hast seen my rival. Speak—
Does she deserve this blessing? Is she fair?
Bright as a goddess? and is all perfection
Confined to her?—It is. Poor I was made
Of that coarse matter which, when she was finished,
The gods threw by for rubbish.

ALEXAS. She's indeed a very miracle.

CLEOPATRA. Death to my hopes, a miracle!

ALEXAS. (*Bowing.*)

                                  A miracle—
I mean, of goodness; for in beauty, madam,
You make all wonders cease.

CLEOPATRA.

                                I was too rash.
Take this in part of recompense. But, oh! (*Giving a ring.*)
I fear thou flatter'st me.

CHARMION.

                          She comes! She's here!

IRAS. Fly, madam, Caesar's sister!

CLEOPATRA. Were she the sister of the thunderer Jove,
And bore her brother's lightning in her eye,
Thus would I face my rival.

(*Meets* OCTAVIA *with* VENTIDIUS. OCTAVIA *bears up to her.
Their trains come up on either side.*)

OCTAVIA. I need not ask if you are Cleopatra,
Your haughty carriage—

CLEOPATRA.

                        Shows I am a queen.
Nor need I ask you who you are.

OCTAVIA.

                           A Roman;
A name that makes and can unmake a queen.

CLEOPATRA. Your lord, the man who serves me, is a Roman.

OCTAVIA. He was a Roman, till he lost that name
To be a slave in Egypt; but I come
To free him thence.

CLEOPATRA. Peace, peace, my lover's Juno.
When he grew weary of that household clog,
He chose my easier bonds.

OCTAVIA.

                    I wonder not

Your bonds are easy. You have long been practised
In that lascivious art. He's not the first
For whom you spread your snares: let Caesar witness.

CLEOPATRA. I loved not Caesar; 'twas but gratitude
I paid his love. The worst your malice can
Is but to say the greatest of mankind
Has been my slave. The next, but far above him
In my esteem, is he whom law calls yours,
But whom his love made mine.

OCTAVIA. (*Coming up closer to her.*) I would view nearer
That face which has so long usurped my right,
To find the inevitable charms that catch
Mankind so sure, that ruined my dear lord.

CLEOPATRA. Oh, you do well to search, for had you known
But half these charms, you had not lost his heart.

OCTAVIA. Far be their knowledge from a Roman lady —
Far from a modest wife! Shame of our sex,
Dost thou not blush to own those black endearments
That make sin pleasing?

CLEOPATRA.
     You may blush, who want them.
If bounteous nature, if indulgent heaven
Have given me charms to please the bravest man,
Should I not thank them? Should I be ashamed,
And not be proud? I am, that he has loved me.
And when I love not him, heaven change this face
For one like that.

OCTAVIA. Thou lov'st him not so well.

CLEOPATRA. I love him better, and deserve him more.

OCTAVIA. You do not—cannot. You have been his ruin.
Who made him cheap at Rome but Cleopatra?
Who made him scorned abroad but Cleopatra?
At Actium, who betrayed him? Cleopatra!
Who made his children orphans, and poor me
A wretched widow? Only Cleopatra.

CLEOPATRA. Yet she who loves him best is Cleopatra.
If you have suffered, I have suffered more.
You bear the specious title of a wife
To gild your cause and draw the pitying world
To favor it. The world condemns poor me,
For I have lost my honor, lost my fame,
And stained the glory of my royal house,
And all to bear the branded name of mistress.

There wants but life, and that, too, I would lose
For him I love.

OCTAVIA.

Be't so, then; take thy wish.

(*Exit with her train.*)

CLEOPATRA. And 'tis my wish,
Now he is lost for whom alone I lived.
My sight grows dim, and every object dances
And swims before me in the maze of death.
My spirits, while they were opposed, kept up;
They could not sink beneath a rival's scorn,
But now she's gone, they faint.

ALEXAS.

Mine have had leisure
To recollect their strength and furnish counsel
To ruin her, who else must ruin you.

CLEOPATRA.

Vain promiser!
Lead me, my Charmion; nay, your hand, too, Iras.
My grief has weight enough to sink you both.
Conduct me to some solitary chamber,
And draw the curtains round;
Then leave me to myself, to take alone
My fill of grief.
There I till death will his unkindness weep,
As harmless infants moan themselves asleep.

(*Exeunt.*)

ACT IV

[SCENE I.]

(*Enter* ANTONY *and* DOLABELLA.)

DOLABELLA. Why would you shift it from yourself on me?
Can you not tell her you must part?

ANTONY.

I cannot.
I could pull out an eye and bid it go,
And t'other should not weep. O Dolabella,

How many deaths are in this word, *Depart!*
I dare not trust my tongue to tell her so—
One look of hers would thaw me into tears,
And I should melt till I were lost again.

DOLABELLA. Then let Ventidius—
 He's rough by nature.

ANTONY. Oh, he'll speak too harshly;
He'll kill her with the news. Thou, only thou!

DOLABELLA. Nature has cast me in so soft a mould
That but to hear a story feigned for pleasure,
Of some sad lover's death moistens my eyes,
And robs me of my manhood. I should speak
So faintly, with such fear to grieve her heart,
She'd not believe it earnest.

ANTONY.

      Therefore—therefore
Thou, only thou art fit. Think thyself me,
And when thou speak'st (but let it first be long),
Take off the edge from every sharper sound,
And let our parting be as gently made
As other loves begin. Wilt thou do this?

DOLABELLA. What you have said so sinks into my soul
That, if I must speak, I shall speak just so.

ANTONY. I leave you then to your sad task.
 Farewell!
I sent her word to meet you.

     (Goes to the door and comes back.)
        I forgot.
Let her be told I'll make her peace with mine.
Her crown and dignity shall be preserved,
If I have power with Caesar.—Oh, be sure
To think on that!

DOLABELLA.

    Fear not, I will remember.
  (ANTONY goes again to the door and comes back.)

ANTONY. And tell her, too, how much I was constrained;
I did not this but with extremest force.
Desire her not to hate my memory,
For I still cherish hers;—insist on that.

DOLABELLA. Trust me, I'll not forget it.

ANTONY.

      Then that's all.
     (Goes out and returns again.)

Wilt thou forgive my fondness this once more?
Tell her, though we shall never meet again,
If I should hear she took another love,
The news would break my heart.—Now I must go,
For every time I have returned, I feel
My soul more tender, and my next command
Would be to bid her stay, and ruin both.

(*Exit.*)

DOLABELLA. Men are but children of a larger growth;
Our appetites as apt to change as theirs,
And full as craving, too, and full as vain;
And yet the soul, shut up in her dark room,
Viewing so clear abroad, at home sees nothing;
But like a mole in earth, busy and blind,
Works all her folly up and casts it outward
To the world's open view. Thus I discovered,
And blamed, the love of ruined Antony,
Yet wish that I were he, to be so ruined.

(*Enter* VENTIDIUS *above.*)

VENTIDIUS. Alone, and talking to himself? concerned, too?
Perhaps my guess is right; he loved her once,
And may pursue it still.
DOLABELLA.
                          O friendship! friendship!
Ill canst thou answer this; and reason, worse.
Unfaithful in the attempt; hopeless to win;
And, if I win, undone; mere madness all.
And yet the occasion's fair. What injury
To him, to wear the robe which he throws by?
VENTIDIUS. None, none at all. This happens as I wish,
To ruin her yet more with Antony.

(*Enter* CLEOPATRA, *talking with* ALEXAS; CHARMION, IRAS *on the other side.*)

DOLABELLA. She comes! What charms have sorrow on that
        face!
Sorrow seems pleased to dwell with so much sweetness;
Yet, now and then, a melancholy smile
Breaks loose like lightning in a winter's night,
And shows a moment's day.

VENTIDIUS. If she should love him, too— her eunuch there!
That porc'pisce[29] bodes ill weather. Draw, draw nearer,
Sweet devil, that I may hear.

ALEXAS.   Believe me; try
 (DOLABELLA *goes over to* CHARMION *and* IRAS; *seems to
 talk with them.*)
 To make him jealous; jealousy is like
 A polished glass held to the lips when life's in doubt;
 If there be breath, 'twill catch the damp, and show it.

CLEOPATRA. I grant you, jealousy's a proof of love,
But 'tis a weak and unavailing medicine;
It puts out[30] the disease, and makes it show,
But has no power to cure.

ALEXAS. 'Tis your last remedy, and strongest, too.
And then this Dolabella—who so fit
To practise on? He's handsome, valiant, young,
And looks as he were laid for nature's bait
To catch weak women's eyes.
He stands already more than half suspected
Of loving you. The least kind word or glance
You give this youth will kindle him with love;
Then, like a burning vessel set adrift,
You'll send him down amain before the wind
To fire the heart of jealous Antony.

CLEOPATRA. Can I do this? Ah, no. My love's so true
That I can neither hide it where it is,
Nor show it where it is not. Nature meant me
A wife—a silly, harmless, household dove,
Fond without art, and kind without deceit;
But Fortune, that has made a mistress of me,
[Has] thrust me out to the wide world, unfurnished
Of falsehood to be happy.

ALEXAS.   Force yourself.
The event will be, your lover will return
Doubly desirous to possess the good
Which once he feared to lose.

CLEOPATRA.   I must attempt it,

 (*Exit* ALEXAS.)

 But oh, with what regret!
 (*She comes up to* DOLABELLA.)

---

[29] *porc'pisce*, porpoise.
[30] *puts out*, reveals.

VENTIDIUS. So, now the scene draws near; they're in my reach.

CLEOPATRA. (*To* DOLABELLA.) Discoursing with my women!
　　Might not I
　　Share in your entertainment?

CHARMION.　　　　　　　　You have been
　　The subject of it, madam.

CLEOPATRA.　　　　　　　　How! and how?

IRAS. Such praises of your beauty!

CLEOPATRA.　　　　　　　　Mere poetry.
　　Your Roman wits, your Gallus and Tibullus;
　　Have taught you this from Cytheris and Delia.

DOLABELLA. Those Roman wits have never been in Egypt;
　　Cytheris and Delia else had been unsung.
　　I, who have seen—had I been born a poet,
　　Should choose a nobler name.

CLEOPATRA.　　　　　　　　You flatter me.
　　But 'tis your nation's vice. All of your country
　　Are flatterers, and all false. Your friend's like you.
　　I'm sure he sent you not to speak these words.

DOLABELLA. No, madam, yet he sent me —

CLEOPATRA.　　　　　　　　Well, he sent you —

DOLABELLA. Of a less pleasing errand.

CLEOPATRA.　　　　　　　　How less pleasing?
　　Less to yourself, or me?

DOLABELLA.　　　　　　　　Madam, to both.
　　For you must mourn, and I must grieve to cause it.

CLEOPATRA. You, Charmion, and your fellow, stand at dis-
　　tance —
　　(*aside*) Hold up, my spirits.—Well, now your mournful
　　matter,
　　For I'm prepared—perhaps can guess it, too.

DOLABELLA. I wish you would, for 'tis a thankless office
　　To tell ill news; and I, of all your sex,
　　Most fear displeasing you.

CLEOPATRA.　　　　　　　　Of all your sex
　　I soonest could forgive you if you should.

VENTIDIUS. Most delicate advances!
　　Woman! woman!
　　Dear, damned, inconstant sex!

CLEOPATRA.　　　　　　　　In the first place,
　　I am to be forsaken. Is't not so?

DOLABELLA. I wish I could not answer to that question.

CLEOPATRA. Then pass it o'er, because it troubles you;
　　I should have been more grieved another time.

Next, I'm to lose my kingdom—Farewell, Egypt!
Yet, is there any more?

DOLABELLA.   Madam, I fear
Your too deep sense of grief has turned your reason.

CLEOPATRA. No, no, I'm not run mad; I can bear fortune,
And love may be expelled by other love,
As poisons are by poisons.

DOLABELLA.   You o'erjoy me, madam,
To find your griefs so moderately borne.
You've heard the worst; all are not false like him.

CLEOPATRA. No. Heaven forbid they should.

DOLABELLA.   Some men are
constant.

CLEOPATRA. And constancy deserves reward, that's certain.

DOLABELLA. Deserves it not, but give it leave to hope.

VENTIDIUS. I'll swear thou hast my leave. I have enough.—
But how to manage this! Well, I'll consider.   (*Exit.*)

DOLABELLA. I came prepared
To tell you heavy news—news which, I thought,
Would fright the blood from your pale cheeks to hear,
But you have met it with a cheerfulness
That makes my task more easy; and my tongue,
Which on another's message was employed,
Would gladly speak its own.

CLEOPATRA.   The message then
I know was tender, and each accent smooth,
To mollify that rugged word, *Depart.*

DOLABELLA. Oh, you mistake. He chose the harshest words;
With fiery eyes and with contracted brows
He coined his face in the severest stamp;
And fury shook his fabric like an earthquake;
He heaved for vent, and burst like bellowing Aetna.
In sounds scarce human—"Hence, away, for ever,
Let her begone, the blot of my renown,
And bane of all my hopes!

>   (*All the time of this speech* CLEOPATRA *seems more
>   and more concerned till she sinks quite down.*)

Let her be driven as far as men can think
From man's commerce! she'll poison to the center."

CLEOPATRA. Oh, I can bear no more!

DOLABELLA. Help, help!—O wretch! O cursed, cursed wretch!
What have I done!

CHARMION.   Help, chafe her temples, Iras.

IRAS. Bend, bend her forward quickly.
CHARMION.   Heaven be praised,
    She comes again.
CLEOPATRA. Oh, let him not approach me.
    Why have you brought me back to this loathed being,
    The abode of falsehood, violated vows,
    And injured love? For pity, let me go;
    For, if there be a place of long repose,
    I'm sure I want it. My disdainful lord
    Can never break that quiet, nor awake
    The sleeping soul with hollowing in my tomb
    Such words as fright her hence.—Unkind, unkind!
DOLABELLA. (*Kneeling.*) Believe me, 'tis against myself I speak.
    That sure deserves belief—I injured him:
    My friend ne'er spoke those words. Oh, had you seen
    How often he came back, and every time
    With something more obliging and more kind
    To add to what he said; what dear farewells;
    How almost vanquished by his love he parted,
    And leaned to what unwillingly he left!
    I, traitor as I was, for love of you
    (But what can you not do, who made me false?)
    I forged that lie; for whose forgiveness kneels
    This self-accused, self-punished criminal.
CLEOPATRA. With how much ease believe we what we wish!
    Rise, Dolabella; if you have been guilty,
    I have contributed, and too much love
    Has made me guilty too.
    The advance of kindness which I made was feigned
    To call back fleeting love by jealousy,
    But 'twould not last. Oh, rather let me lose
    Than so ignobly trifle with his heart!
DOLABELLA. I find your breast fenced round from human reach,
    Transparent as a rock of solid crystal,
    Seen through, but never pierced. My friend, my friend!
    What endless treasure hast thou thrown away,
    And scattered, like an infant, in the ocean,
    Vain sums of wealth, which none can gather thence!
CLEOPATRA. Could you not beg
    An hour's admittance to his private car?
    Like one who wanders through long barren wilds,
    And yet foreknows no hospitable inn
    Is near to succor hunger, eat his fill
    Before his painful march,

So would I feed a while my famished eyes
Before we part, for I have far to go,
If death be far, and never must return.

(*Enter* VENTIDIUS *with* OCTAVIA, *behind.*)

VENTIDIUS. From whence you may discover — Oh, sweet,
    sweet!
    Would you, indeed? The pretty hand in earnest?
DOLABELLA. I will, for this reward.
    (*Takes her hand.*)

                    Draw it not back,
  'Tis all I e'er will beg.
VENTIDIUS.   They turn upon us.
OCTAVIA. What quick eyes has guilt!
VENTIDIUS. Seem not to have observed them, and go on.

                      (*They enter.*)

DOLABELLA. Saw you the emperor, Ventidius?
VENTIDIUS.   No.
    I sought him, but I heard that he was private,
    None with him but Hipparchus, his freedman.
DOLABELLA. Know you his business?
VENTIDIUS.   Giving him instructions
    And letters to his brother Caesar.
DOLABELLA.   Well,
  He must be found.

(*Exeunt* DOLABELLA *and* CLEOPATRA.)

OCTAVIA.   Most glorious impudence!
VENTIDIUS. She looked, methought,
    As she would say, "Take your old man, Octavia,
    Thank you, I'm better here." Well, but what use
    Make we of this discovery?
OCTAVIA.   Let it die.
VENTIDIUS. I pity Dolabella. But she's dangerous;
    Her eyes have power beyond Thessalian charms
    To draw the moon from heaven; for eloquence,
    The sea-green Syrens taught her voice their flatt'ry;
    And while she speaks, night steals upon the day,
    Unmarked of those that hear. Then she's so charming
    Age buds at sight of her, and swells to youth;
    The holy priests gaze on her when she smiles,
    And with heaved hands, forgetting gravity,
    They bless her wanton eyes. Even I, who hate her,

With a malignant joy behold such beauty,
And while I curse, desire it. Antony
Must needs have some remains of passion still,
Which may ferment into a worse relapse
It now not fully cured. I know, this minute,
With Caesar he's endeavoring her peace.

OCTAVIA. You have prevailed:—But for a further purpose

(*Walks off.*)

I'll prove how he will relish this discovery.
What, make a strumpet's peace! it swells my heart;
It must not, shall not be.

VENTIDIUS.   His guards appear.
Let me begin, and you shall second me.

(*Enter* ANTONY.)

ANTONY. Octavia, I was looking you, my love.
What, are your letters ready? I have given
My last instructions.

OCTAVIA.   Mine, my lord, are written.

ANTONY. Ventidius.   (*Drawing him aside.*)

VENTIDIUS.   My lord?
ANTONY.   A word in private.—
When saw you Dolabella?

VENTIDIUS.   Now, my lord,
He parted hence; and Cleopatra with him.

ANTONY. Speak softly.—'Twas by my command he went
To bear my last farewell.

VENTIDIUS. (*aloud*)   It looked indeed
Like your farewell.

ANTONY.   More softly. —My farewell?
What secret meaning have you in those words
Of "my farewell"? He did it by my order.

VENTIDIUS. (*aloud*) Then he obeyed your order. I suppose
You bid him do it with all gentleness,
All kindness, and all—love.

ANTONY.   How she mourned,
The poor forsaken creature!

VENTIDIUS. She took it as she ought; she bore your parting
As she did Caesar's, as she would another's,
Were a new love to come.

ANTONY. (*aloud*)   Thou dost belie her;
Most basely and maliciously belie her.

VENTIDIUS. I thought not to displease you; I have done.

OCTAVIA. (*Coming up.*) You seem disturbed, my lord.

ANTONY.   A very
    trifle.
    Retire, my love.

VENTIDIUS.   It was indeed a trifle.
    He sent—

ANTONY. (*angrily*) No more. Look how thou disobey'st me;
    Thy life shall answer it.

OCTAVIA.   Then 'tis no trifle.

VENTIDIUS. (*To Octavia.*) 'Tis less—a very nothing. You too
    saw it,
    As well as I, and therefore 'tis no secret.

ANTONY. She saw it!

VENTIDIUS.   Yes. She saw young Dolabella—

ANTONY. Young Dolabella!

VENTIDIUS.   Young, I think him young,
    And handsome too, and so do others think him.
    But what of that? He went by your command,
    Indeed, 'tis probable, with some kind message,
    For she received it graciously; she smiled;
    And then he grew familiar with her hand,
    Squeezed it, and worried it with ravenous kisses;
    She blushed, and sighed, and smiled, and blushed again;
    At last she took occasion to talk softly,
    And brought her cheek up close, and leaned on his;
    At which, he whispered kisses back on hers;
    And then she cried aloud that constancy
    Should be rewarded.

OCTAVIA.   This I saw and heard.
    She blushed, and sighed, and smiled, and blushed again;

VENTIDIUS. I do not lie, my lord.
    Is this so strange? Should mistresses be left,
    And not provide against a time of change?
    You know she's not much used to lonely nights.

ANTONY. I'll think no more on't.
    I know 'tis false, and see the plot betwixt you.—
    You needed not have gone this way, Octavia.
    What harms it you that Cleopatra's just?
    She's mine no more. I see, and I forgive.
    Urge it no further, love.

OCTAVIA.   Are you concerned
    That she's found false?

ANTONY.   I should be, were it so,

For though 'tis past, I would not that the world
Should tax my former choice, that I loved one
Of so light note, but I forgive you both.

VENTIDIUS. What has my age deserved that you should think
I would abuse your ears with perjury?
If Heaven be true, she's false.

ANTONY.   Though Heaven and earth
Should witness it, I'll not believe her tainted.

VENTIDIUS. I'll bring you, then, a witness
From hell to prove her so.—Nay, go not back,

   (*Seeing* ALEXAS *just entering, and starting back.*)

For stay you must and shall.

ALEXAS.   What means my lord?

VENTIDIUS. To make you do what most you hate,—speak truth.
You are of Cleopatra's private counsel,
Of her bed-counsel, her lascivious hours;
Are conscious of each nightly change she makes,
And watch her, as Chaldaeans[31] do the moon,
Can tell what signs she passes through, what day.

ALEXAS. My noble lord!

VENTIDIUS.   My most illustrious pander,[32]
No fine set speech, no cadence, no turned periods,
But a plain homespun truth is what I ask:
I did myself o'erhear your queen make love
To Dolabella. Speak. For I will know
By your confession what more passed betwixt them;
How near the business draws to your employment;
And when the happy hour.

ANTONY. Speak truth, Alexas; whether it offend
Or please Ventidius, care not. Justify
Thy injured queen from malice. Dare his worst.

OCTAVIA. (*aside*) See how he gives him courage! how he fears
To find her false! and shuts his eyes to truth,
Willing to be misled!

ALEXAS. As far as love may plead for woman's frailty,
Urged by desert and greatness of the lover,
So far, divine Octavia, may my queen
Stand even excused to you for loving him
Who is your lord; so far, from brave Ventidius,
May her past actions hope a fair report.

---

[31] *Chaldaeans,* astrologers of Babylon.
[32] *pander,* pimp.

ANTONY. 'Tis well, and truly spoken. Mark, Ventidius.

ALEXAS. To you, most noble emperor, her strong passion
  Stands not excused, but wholly justified.
  Her beauty's charms alone, without her crown,
  From Ind and Meroë[33] drew the distant vows
  Of sighing kings; and at her feet were laid
  The sceptres of the earth exposed on heaps,
  To choose where she would reign.
  She thought a Roman only could deserve her,
  And of all Romans only Antony;
  And, to be less than wife to you, disdained
  Their lawful passion.

ANTONY.   'Tis but truth.

ALEXAS. And yet, though love and your unmatched desert
  Have drawn her from the due regard of honor,
  At last Heaven opened her unwilling eyes
  To see the wrongs she offered fair Octavia,
  Whose holy bed she lawlessly usurped.
  The sad effects of this improsperous war
  Confirmed those pious thoughts.

VENTIDIOUS. (*aside*)   Oh, wheel you there?
  Observe him now; the man begins to mend,
  And talk substantial reason.—Fear not, eunuch,
  The emperor has given thee leave to speak.

ALEXAS. Else had I never dared to offend his ears
  With what the last necessity has urged
  On my forsaken mistress; yet I must not
  Presume to say her heart is wholly altered.

ANTONY. No, dare not for thy life, I charge thee dare not
  Prounounce that fatal word!

OCTAVIA. (*aside*) Must I bear this? Good Heaven, afford me
  patience!

VENTIDIUS. On, sweet eunuch; my dear half-man, proceed.

ALEXAS. Yet Dolabella
  Has loved her long. He, next my god-like lord,
  Deserves her best; and should she meet his passion,
  Rejected as she is by him she loved—

ANTONY. Hence from my sight! for I can bear no more.
  Let furies drag thee quick to hell; let all
  The longer damned have rest; each torturing hand
  Do thou employ till Cleopatra comes;
  Then join thou too, and help to torture her!

---

[33] *Ind and Meroë*, India and upper Egypt.

(*Exit* ALEXAS, *thrust out by* ANTONY.)

OCTAVIA. 'Tis not well,
    Indeed, my lord, 'tis much unkind to me,
    To show this passion, this extreme concernment
    For an abandoned, faithless prostitute.
ANTONY. Octavia, leave me. I am much disordered.
    Leave me, I say.
OCTAVIA.   My lord!
ANTONY.   I bid you leave me.
VENTIDIUS. Obey him, madam. Best withdraw a while,
    And see how this will work.
OCTAVIA. Wherein have I offended you, my lord,
    That I am bid to leave you? Am I false
    Or infamous? Am I a Cleopatra?
    Were I she,
    Base as she is, you would not bid me leave you,
    But hang upon my neck, take slight excuses,
    And fawn upon my falsehood.
ANTONY.   'Tis too much,
    Too much, Octavia. I am pressed with sorrows
    Too heavy to be borne, and you add more.
    I would retire and recollect what's left
    Of man within, to aid me.
OCTAVIA.   You would mourn
    In private for your love, who has betrayed you.
    You did but half return to me; your kindness
    Lingered behind with her. I hear, my lord,
    You make conditions for her,
    And would include her treaty. Wondrous proofs
    Of love to me!
ANTONY.   Are you my friend, Ventidius?
    Or are you turned a Dolabella too,
    And let this Fury loose?
VENTIDIUS.   Oh, be advised,
    Sweet madam, and retire.
OCTAVIA. Yes, I will go, but never to return.
    You shall no more be haunted with his Fury.
    My lord, my lord, love will not always last
    When urged with long unkindness and disdain.
    Take her again whom you prefer to me;
    She stays but to be called. Poor cozened man!
    Let a feigned parting give her back your heart,
    Which a feigned love first got; for injured me,

Though my just sense of wrong forbid my stay,
My duty shall be yours.
To the dear pledges of our former love
My tenderness and care shall be transferred,
And they shall cheer, by turns, my widowed nights.
So, take my last farewell, for I despair
To have you whole, and scorn to take you half.

VENTIDIUS. I combat Heaven, which blasts my best designs;
My last attempt must be to win her back;
But oh! I fear in vain. (*Exit.*)

ANTONY. Why was I framed with this plain, honest heart,
Which knows not to disguise its griefs and weakness,
But bears its workings outward to the world?
I should have kept the mighty anguish in,
And forced a smile at Cleopatra's falsehood.
Octavia had believed it, and had stayed.
But I am made a shallow-forded stream,
Seen to the bottom; all my clearness scorned,
And all my faults exposed.—See where he comes

(*Enter* DOLABELLA.)

Who has profaned the sacred name of friend,
And worn it into vileness!
With how secure a brow, and specious form,
He gilds the secret villain! Sure that face
Was meant for honesty, but Heaven mismatched it,
And furnished treason out with nature's pomp
To make its work more easy.

DOLABELLA. O my friend!

ANTONY. Well, Dolabella, you performed my message?

DOLABELLA. I did, unwillingly.

ANTONY. Unwillingly?
Was it so hard for you to bear our parting?
You should have wished it.

DOLABELLA. Why?

ANTONY. Because you love
me.
And she received my message with as true,
With as unfeigned a sorrow as you brought it?

DOLABELLA. She loves you, even to madness.

ANTONY. Oh, I know it.
You, Dolabella, do not better know
How much she loves me. And should I
Forsake this beauty? This all-perfect creature?

DOLABELLA. I could not, were she mine.

ANTONY.   And yet you first
    Persuaded me. How come you altered since?

DOLABELLA. I said at first I was not fit to go;
    I could not hear her sighs and see her tears,
    But pity must prevail. And so perhaps
    It may again with you, for I have promised
    That she should take her last farewell. And see,
    She comes to claim my word.

    (*Enter* CLEOPATRA.)

ANTONY.   False Dolabella!

DOLABELLA. What's false, my lord?

ANTONY.   Why, Dolabella's false,
    And Cleopatra's false—both false and faithless.
    Draw near, you well-joined wickedness, you serpents
    Whom I have in my kindly bosom warmed,
    Till I am stung to death.

DOLABELLA.   My lord, have I
    Deserved to be thus used?

CLEOPATRA.   Can Heaven prepare
    A newer torment? Can it find a curse
    Beyond our separation?

ANTONY.   Yes, if fate
    Be just, much greater. Heaven should be ingenious
    In punishing such crimes. The rolling stone
    And gnawing vulture[34] were slight pains, invented
    When Jove was young, and no examples known
    Of mighty ills. But you have ripened sin
    To such a monstrous growth 'twill pose the gods
    To find an equal torture. Two, two such!—
    Oh, there's no farther name,—two such! to me,
    To me, who locked my soul within your breasts,
    Had no desires, no joys, no life, but you.
    When half the globe was mine, I gave it you
    In dowry with my heart; I had no use,
    No fruit of all, but you. A friend and mistress
    Was what the world could give. O Cleopatra!
    O Dolabella! how could you betray
    This tender heart which with an infant fondness

---

[34] *The rolling stone and gnawing vulture* may refer to Sisyphus, who
was condemned to roll a huge boulder to the top of a hill, then have
it roll down again all through eternity; and to Prometheus, who stole
fire from the gods and gave it to man: his liver was eaten by an eagle
each day, and grew back for the torture each night.

Lay lulled betwixt your bosoms and there slept,
Secure of injured faith?

DOLABELLA.   If she has wronged you,
Heaven, hell, and you, revenge it.

ANTONY.   If she wronged me!
Thou wouldst evade thy part of guilt. But swear
Thou lov'st not her.

DOLABELLA.   Not so as I love you.

ANTONY. Not so? Swear, swear, I say, thou dost not love her.

DOLABELLA. No more than friendship will allow.

ANTONY.   No more?
Friendship allows thee nothing. Thou art perjured —
And yet thou didst not swear thou lov'd'st her not,
But not so much, no more. O trifling hypocrite,
Who dar'st not own to her, thou dost not love,
Nor own to me, thou dost. Ventidius heard it;
Octavia saw it.

CLEOPATRA.   They are enemies.

ANTONY. Alexas is not so. He, he confessed it;
He, who, next hell, best knew it, he avowed it.
Why do I seek a proof beyond yourself?

                                    (*To* DOLABELLA.)

You, whom I sent to bear my last farewell,
Returned to plead her stay.

DOLABELLA.   What shall I answer?
If to have loved be guilt, then I have sinned;
But if to have repented of that love
Can wash away my crime, I have repented.
Yet, if I have offended past forgiveness,
Let not her suffer. She is innocent.

CLEOPATRA. Ah, what will not a woman do who loves?
What means will she refuse to keep that heart
Where all her joys are placed? 'Twas I encouraged,
'Twas I blew up the fire that scorched his soul,
To make you jealous, and by that regain you.
But all in vain. I could not counterfeit;
In spite of all the dams, my love broke o'er,
And drowned my heart again; fate took the occasion,
And thus one minute's feigning has destroyed
My whole life's truth.

ANTONY.   Thin cobweb arts of falsehood,
Seen, and broke through at first

DOLABELLA.   Forgive your mistress.

CLEOPATRA. Forgive your friend.

ANTONY.   You have convinced[35]
     yourselves.
   You plead each other's cause. What witness have you
   That you but meant to raise my jealousy?

CLEOPATRA. Ourselves, and Heaven.

ANTONY. Guilt witnesses for guilt. Hence, love and friendship!
   You have no longer place in human breasts;
   These two have driven you out. Avoid my sight!
   I would not kill the man whom I have loved,
   And cannot hurt the woman. But avoid me,
   I do not know how long I can be tame,
   For, if I stay one minute more, to think
   How I am wronged, my justice and revenge
   Will cry so loud within me that my pity
   Will not be heard for either.

DOLABELLA.   Heaven has but
   Our sorrow for our sins, and then delights
   To pardon erring man. Sweet mercy seems
   Its darling attribute, which limits justice
   As if there were degrees in infinite,
   And infinite would rather want perfection
   Than punish to extent.

ANTONY.   I can forgive
   A foe, but not a mistress and a friend.
   Treason is there in its most horrid shape
   Where trust is greatest, and the soul, resigned,
   Is stabbed by its own guards. I'll hear no more.—
   Hence from my sight forever!

CLEOPATRA.   How? Forever?
   I cannot go one moment from your sight,
   And must I go forever?
   My joys, my only joys, are centered here.
   What place have I to go to? My own kingdom?
   That I have lost for you. Or to the Romans?
   They hate me for your sake. Or must I wander
   The wide world o'er, a helpless, banished woman,
   Banished for love of you—banished from you?
   Aye, there's the banishment! Oh, hear me, hear me
   With strictest justice, for I beg no favor,
   And if I have offended you, then kill me,
   But do not banish me.

[35] *convinced,* convicted.

ANTONY.   I must not hear you.
  I have a fool within me takes your part,
  But honor stops my ears.

CLEOPATRA.   For pity hear me!
  Would you cast off a slave who followed you?
  Who crouched beneath your spurn?—He has no pity!
  See if he gives one tear to my departure,
  One look, one kind farewell. O iron heart!
  Let all the gods look down and judge betwixt us,
  If he did ever love!

ANTONY.   No more.—Alexas!

DOLABELLA. A perjured villain!

ANTONY. (*To* CLEOPATRA.)   Your Alexas, yours.

CLEOPATRA. Oh, 'twas his plot, his ruinous design,
  T' engage you in my love by jealousy.
  Hear him. Confront him with me. Let him speak.

ANTONY. I have, I have.

CLEOPATRA.   And if he clear me not—

ANTONY. Your creature! one who hangs upon your smiles!
  Watches your eye to say or to unsay
  Whate'er you please! I am not to be moved.

CLEOPATRA. Then must we part? Farewell, my cruel lord!
  Th' appearance is against me, and I go,
  Unjustified, forever from your sight.
  How I have loved, you know; how yet I love,
  My only comfort is, I know myself.
  I love you more, even now you are unkind,
  Than when you loved me most; so well, so truly
  I'll never strive against it but die pleased
  To think you once were mine.

ANTONY. Good Heaven, they weep at parting!
  Must I weep too? That calls them innocent.
  I must not weep. And yet I must, to think
  That I must not forgive.—
  Live, but live wretched; 'tis but just you should,
  Who made me so. Live from each other's sight.
  Let me not hear, you meet. Set all the earth
  And all the seas betwixt your sundered loves;
  View nothing common but the sun and skies.
  Now, all take several ways;
  And each your own sad fate, with mine, deplore;
  That you were false, and I could trust no more.

                        (*Exeunt severally.*)

ACT V

[SCENE I.]

(*Enter* CLEOPATRA, CHARMION, *and* IRAS.)

CHARMION. Be juster, Heaven; such virtue punished thus
    Will make us think that chance rules all above,
    And shuffles with a random hand the lots
    Which man is forced to draw.

CLEOPATRA. I could tear out these eyes that gained his heart,
    And had not power to keep it. O the curse
    Of doting on, even when I find it dotage!
    Bear witness, gods, you heard him bid me go;
    You whom he mocked with imprecating vows
    Of promised faith!—I'll die! I will not bear it.
    You may hold me—

              (*She pulls out her dagger, and they hold her.*)

    But I can keep my breath; I can die inward,
    And choke this love.

(*Enter* ALEXAS.)

IRAS.   Help, O Alexas, help!
    The queen grows desperate; her soul struggles in her
    With all the agonies of love and rage,
    And strive to force its passage.

CLEOPATRA.   Let me go.
    Art thou there, traitor!—Oh,
    Oh, for a little breath, to vent my rage!
    Give, give me away, and let me loose upon him.

ALEXAS. Yes, I deserve it for my ill-timed truth.
    Was it for me to prop
    The ruins of a falling majesty?
    To place myself beneath the mighty flaw,
    Thus to be crushed and pounded into atoms
    By its o'erwhelming weight? 'Tis too presuming
    For subjects to preserve that wilful power
    Which courts its own destruction.

CLEOPATRA.   I would reason
    More calmly with you. Did not you o'errule
    And force my plain, direct, and open love
    Into these crooked paths of jealousy?

Now, what's the event? Octavia is removed,
But Cleopatra's banished. Thou, thou villain,
[Hast] pushed my boat to open sea, to prove
At my sad cost, if thou canst steer it back.
It can not be; I'm lost too far; I'm ruined!—
Hence, thou imposter, traitor, monster, devil!—
I can no more. Thou, and my griefs, have sunk
Me down so low that I want voice to curse thee.

ALEXAS. Suppose some shipwrecked seaman near the shore,
Dropping and faint with climbing up the cliff;
If, from above, some charitable hand
Pull him to safety, hazarding himself
To draw the other's weight, would he look back
And curse him for his pains? The case is yours;
But one step more, and you have gained the height.

CLEOPATRA. Sunk, never more to rise.

ALEXAS. Octavia's gone, and Dolabella banished.
Believe me, madam, Antony is yours.
His heart was never lost, but started off
To jealousy, love's last retreat and covert,
Where it lies hid in shades, watchful in silence,
And listening for the sound that calls it back.
Some other, any man ('tis so advanced)
May perfect this unfinished work, which I
(Unhappy only to myself) have left
So easy to his hand.

CLEOPATRA. Look well thou do't; else—

ALEXAS. Else what your silence threatens.—Anthony
Is mounted up the Pharos,[36] from whose turret
He stands surveying our Egyptian galleys
Engaged with Caesar's fleet. Now death or conquest!
If the first happen, fate acquits my promise;
If we o'ercome, the conqueror is yours.

(*A distant shout within.*)

CHARMION. Have comfort, madam. Did you mark that shout?

(*Second shout nearer.*)

IRAS. Hark! they redouble it.

ALEXAS.   'Tis from the port.
The loudness shows it near. Good news, kind heavens!

---

36 *Pharos,* lighthouse at Alexandria, one of the wonders of the ancient
world.

CLEOPATRA. Osiris make it so!

(*Enter* SERAPION.)

SERAPION. Where, where's the queen?

ALEXAS. How frightfully the holy coward stares
As if not yet recovered of the assault,
When all his gods and, what's more dear to him,
His offerings were at stake!

SERAPION. O horror, horror!
Egypt has been; our latest hour is come;
The queen of nations from her ancient seat
Is sunk forever in the dark abyss;
Time has unrolled her glories to the last,
And now closed up the volume.

CLEOPATRA. Be more plain.
Say whence thou comest, though fate is in thy face,
Which from thy haggard eyes looks wildly out,
And threatens ere thou speakest.

SERAPION. I came from Pharos—
From viewing (spare me, and imagine it)
Our land's last hope, your navy—

CLEOPATRA. Vanquished?

SERAPION. No.
They fought not.

CLEOPATRA. Then they fled!

SERAPION. Nor that. I saw,
With Antony, your well-appointed fleet
Row out; and thrice he waved his hand on high,
And thrice with cheerful cries they shouted back.
'Twas then false Fortune like a fawning strumpet
About to leave the bankrupt prodigal,
With a dissembled smile would kiss at parting,
And flatter to the last; the well-timed oars
Now dipt from every bank, now smoothly run
To meet the foe; and soon indeed they met,
But not as foes. In few, we saw their caps
On either side thrown up. The Egyptian galleys,
Received like friends, passed through and fell behind
The Roman rear. And now they all come forward,
And ride within the port.

CLEOPATRA. Enough, Serapion.
I've heard my doom.—This needed not, you gods:
When I lost Antony, your work was done.

'Tis but superfluous malice.—Where's my lord?
How bears he this last blow?

SERAPION. His fury can not be expressed by words.
Thrice he attempted headlong to have fallen
Full on his foes, and aimed at Caesar's galley;
Withheld, he raves on you; cries he's betrayed.
Should he now find you—

ALEXAS.   Shun him. Seek your safety
Till you can clear your innocence.

CLEOPATRA.   Caesar! No,
I have no business with him.

ALEXAS.   I can work him
To spare your life, and let this madman perish.

CLEOPATRA. Base, fawning wretch! wouldst thou betray him
too?
Hence from my sight! I will not hear a traitor.
'Twas thy design brought all this ruin on us.—
Serapion, thou art honest. Counsel me—
But haste, each moment's precious.

SERAPION. Retire. You must not yet see Antony.
He who began this mischief,
'Tis just he tempt the danger. Let him clear you;
And, since he offered you his service tongue,
To gain a poor precarious life from Caesar
Let him expose that fawning eloquence,
And speak to Antony.

ALEXAS.   O Heaven! I dare not;
I meet my certain death.

CLEOPATRA.   Slave, thou deservest it.—
Not that I fear my lord, will I avoid him;
I know him noble. When he banished me,
And thought me false, he scorned to take my life:
But I'll be justified, and then die with him.

ALEXAS. O pity me, and let me follow you!

CLEOPATRA. To death, if thou stir hence. Speak if thou canst
Now for thy life which basely thou wouldst save,
While mine I prize at—this. Come, good Serapion.

(*Exeunt* CLEOPATRA, SERAPION, CHARMION, *and* IRAS.)

ALEXAS. O that I less could fear to lose this being,
Which, like a snowball in my coward hand,
The more 'tis grasped, the faster melts away.
Poor reason! what a wretched aid art thou!

For still, in spite of thee,
These two long lovers, soul and body, dread
Their final separation. Let me think;
What can I say to save myself from death,
No matter what becomes of Cleopatra?

ANTONY. (*within*) Which way? where?

VENTIDIUS. (*within*) This leads to the monument.

ALEXAS. Ah me! I hear him; yet I'm unprepared,
My gift of lying's gone;
And this court-devil, which I so oft have raised,
Forsakes me at my need. I dare not stay,
Yet can not far go hence.   (*Exit.*)

(*Enter* ANTONY *and* VENTIDIUS.)

ANTONY. O happy Caesar! thou hast men to lead!
Think not 'tis thou hast conquered Antony,
But Rome has conquered Egypt. I'm betrayed.

VENTIDIUS. Curse on this treacherous train!
Their soil and heaven infect them all with baseness,
And their young souls come tainted to the world
With the first breath they draw.

ANTONY. The original villain sure no god created;
He was a bastard of the sun by Nile,[37]
Aped into man;[38] with all his mother's mud
Crusted about his soul.

VENTIDIUS.   The nation is
One universal traitor, and their queen
The very spirit and extract of them all.

ANTONY. Is there yet left
A possibility of aid from valor?
Is there one god unsworn to my destruction?
The least unmortgaged hope? for, if there be,
Methinks I can not fall beneath the fate
Of such a boy as Caesar.
The world's one half is yet in Antony,
And from each limb of it that's hewed away,
The soul comes back to me.

VENTIDIUS.   There yet remain
Three legions in the town. The last assault
Lopt off the rest. If death be your design—
As I must wish it now—these are sufficient

---

[37] *Nile,* i.e., created by spontaneous generation, from mud and sunlight.
[38] *Aped into man,* a corrupt imitation of humanity.

> To make a heap about us of dead foes,
> An honest pile for burial.

ANTONY.   They're enough.
> We'll not divide our stars, but, side by side,
> Fight emulous, and with malicious eyes
> Survey each other's acts, so every death
> Thou giv'st, I'll take on me as a just debt,
> And pay thee back a soul.

VENTIDIUS. Now you shall see I love you. Not a word
> Of chiding more. By my few hours of life,
> I am so pleased with this brave Roman fate
> That I would not be Caesar to outlive you.
> When we put off this flesh and mount together,
> I shall be shown to all the ethereal crowd,—
> "Lo, this is he who died with Antony!"

ANTONY. Who knows but we may pierce through all their
>   troops,
> And reach my veterans yet? 'tis worth the 'tempting
> To o'erleap this gulf of fate,
> And leave our wondering destinies behind.

(Enter ALEXAS, trembling.)

VENTIDIUS. See, see, that villain!
> See Cleopatra stamped upon that face
> With all her cunning, all her arts of falsehood!
> How she looks out through those dissembling eyes!
> How he has set his count'nance for deceit,
> And promises a lie before he speaks!
> *(Drawing.)* Let me dispatch him first.

ALEXAS.   O spare me, spare
>   me!

ANTONY. Hold. He's not worth your killing.—On thy life,
> Which thou may'st keep because I scorn to take it,
> No syllable to justify thy queen.
> Save thy base tongue its office.

ALEXAS.   Sir, she's gone
> Where she shall never be molested more
> By love, or you.

ANTONY.   Fled to her Dolabella!
> Die, traitor! I revoke my promise! die!

(Going to kill him.)

ALEXAS. O hold! she is not fled.
ANTONY.   She is. My eyes

Are open to her falsehood; my whole life
Has been a golden dream of love and friendship;
But, now I wake, I'm like a merchant roused
From soft repose to see his vessel sinking,
And all his wealth cast o'er. Ingrateful woman!
Who followed me but as the swallow summer,
Hatching her young ones in my kindly beams,
Singing her flatteries to my morning wake;
But now my winter comes, she spreads her wings,
And seeks the spring of Caesar.

ALEXAS.   Think not so:
Her fortunes have in all things mixed with yours.
Had she betrayed her naval force to Rome,
How easily might she have gone to Caesar,
Secure by such a bribe.

VENTIDIUS.   She sent it first,
To be more welcome after.

ANTONY.   'Tis too plain,
Else would she have appeared to clear herself.

ALEXAS. Too fatally she has. She could not bear
To be accused by you, but shut herself
Within her monument, looked down and sighed,
While from her unchanged face the silent tears
Dropped, as they had not leave, but stole their parting.
Some undistinguished words she inly murmured;
At last she raised her eyes, and, with such looks
As dying Lucrece cast—

ANTONY.   My heart forebodes—

VENTIDIUS. All for the best;—go on.

ALEXAS.   She snatched her
    poniard,
And, ere we could prevent the fatal blow,
Plunged it within her breast, then turned to me:
"Go, bear my lord," said she, "my last farewell,
And ask him if he yet suspect my faith."
More she was saying, but death rushed betwixt.
She half pronounced your name with her last breath,
And buried half within her.

VENTIDIUS.   Heaven be praised!

ANTONY. Then art thou innocent, my poor dear love?
And art thou dead?
O those two words! their sound should be divided;
Hadst thou been false, and died; or hadst thou lived,
And hadst been true—But innocence and death!

This shows not well above. Then what am I,
The murderer of this truth, this innocence!
Thoughts can not form themselves in words so horrid
As can express my guilt!

VENTIDIUS. Is't come to this? The gods have been too gracious,
And thus you thank 'em for't!

ANTONY. (*To* ALEXAS.)   Why stayest thou here?
Is it for thee to spy upon my soul
And see its inward mourning? Get thee hence.
Thou art not worthy to behold what now
Becomes a Roman emperor to perform.

ALEXAS. (*aside*) He loves her still:
His grief betrays it. Good! the joy to find
She's yet alive completes the reconcilement.
I've saved myself and her. But, oh! the Romans!
Fate comes too fast upon my wit,
Hunts me too hard, and meets me at each double.[39]

                                                    (*Exit.*)

VENTIDIUS. Would she had died a little sooner, though,
Before Octavia went; you might have treated;
Now 'twill look tame, and would not be received.
Come, rouse yourself, and let's die warm together.

ANTONY. I will not fight: there's no more work for war.
The business of my angry hours is done.

VENTIDIUS. Caesar is at your gates.

ANTONY.   Why, let him enter;
He's welcome now.

VENTIDIUS. What lethargy has crept into your soul?

ANTONY. 'Tis but a scorn of life, and just desire
To free myself from bondage.

VENTIDIUS.   Do it bravely.

ANTONY. I will; but not by fighting. O Ventidius!
What should I fight for now?—my queen is dead.
I was but great for her; my power, my empire,
Were but my merchandise to buy her love,
And conquered kings, my factors. Now she's dead,
Let Caesar take the world,—
An empty circle since the jewel's gone
Which made it worth my strife; my being's nauseous;
For all the bribes of life are gone away.

VENTIDIUS. Would you be taken?

[39] *each double,* doubling back on the trail like a hunted fox.

ANTONY.   Yes, I would be taken,
But as a Roman ought,—dead, by Ventidius.
For I'll convey my soul from Caesar's reach,
And lay down life myself. 'Tis time the world
Should have a lord, and know whom to obey.
We two have kept its homage in suspense,
And bent the globe, on whose each side we trod,
Till it was dinted inwards. Let him walk
Alone upon't; I'm weary of my part.
My torch is out; and the world stands before me
Like a black desert at th' approach of night.
I'll lay me down and stray no farther on.

VENTIDIUS. I could be grieved,
But that I'll not outlive you. Choose your death,
For I have seen him in such various shapes,
I care not which I take—I'm only troubled,
The life I bear is worn to such a rag,
'Tis scarce worth giving. I could wish, indeed,
We threw it from us with a better grace;
That, like two lions taken in the toils,
We might at least thrust out our paws and wound
The hunters that inclose us.

ANTONY.   I have thought on it.
Ventidius, you must live.

VENTIDIUS.   I must not, sir.

ANTONY. Wilt thou not live to speak some good of me?
To stand by my fair fame and guard the approaches
From the ill tongues of men?

VENTIDIUS.   Who shall guard mine
For living after you?

ANTONY.   Say I command it.

VENTIDIUS. If we die well, our deaths will speak themselves,
And need no living witness.

ANTONY.   Thou hast loved me,
And fain I would reward thee. I must die.
Kill me, and take the merit of my death
To make thee friends with Caesar.

VENTIDIUS.   Thank your kindness.
You said I loved you; and in recompense
You bid me turn a traitor.—Did I think
You would have used me thus?—that I should die
With a hard thought of you?

ANTONY.   Forgive me, Roman.
Since I have heard of Cleopatra's death,

My reason bears no rule upon my tongue,
But lets my thoughts break all at random out.
I've thought better; do not deny me twice.

VENTIDIUS. By Heaven, I will not.
Let it not be to outlive you.

ANTONY.   Kill me first,
And then die thou; for 'tis but just thou serve
Thy friend before thyself.

VENTIDIUS.   Give me your hand.
We soon shall meet again. Now farewell, emperor!—

(*Embrace.*)

Methinks that word's too cold to be my last:
Since death sweeps all distinctions, farewell, friend!
That's all—
I will not make a business of a trifle;
And yet I can not look on you and kill you;
Pray turn your face.

ANTONY.   I do. Strike home, be sure.

VENTIDIUS. Home as my sword will reach.   (*Kills himself.*)

ANTONY. Oh, thou mistak'st;
That wound was none of thine; give it me back;
Thou robb'st me of my death.

VENTIDIUS.   I do, indeed;
But think 'tis the first time I e'er deceived you,
If that may plead my pardon.—And you, gods,
Forgive me if you will; for I die perjured
Rather than kill my friend.   (*Dies.*)

ANTONY. Farewell! Ever my leader, even in death!
My queen and thou have got the start of me,
And I'm the lag of honor.—Gone so soon?
Is death no more? he used him carelessly,
With a familiar kindness; ere he knocked,
Ran to the door and took him in his arms,
As who should say, "You're welcome at all hours,
A friend need give no warning." Books had spoiled him,
For all the learn'd are cowards by profession.
'Tis not worth
My farther thought; for death, for aught I know,
Is but to think no more. Here's to be satisfied.

(*Falls on his sword.*)

I've missed my heart. O unperforming hand!
Thou never couldst have erred in a worse time.

My fortune jades me to the last; and death,
Like a great man, takes state, and makes me wait
For my admittance—

> > > > (*Trampling within.*)
> > > > Some, perhaps, from Caesar

> > If he should find me living, and suspect
> > That I played booty with[40] my life! I'll mend
> > My work ere they can reach me. (*Rises upon his knees.*)

(*Enter* CLEOPATRA, CHARMION, *and* IRAS.)

CLEOPATRA. Where is my lord? where is he?
CHARMION.   There he lies,
And dead Ventidius by him.
CLEOPATRA. My fear were prophets; I am come too late.

> > > > (*Runs to him.*)

O that accursed Alexas!
ANTONY.   Art thou living?
Or am I dead before I knew, and thou
The first kind ghost that meets me?
CLEOPATRA.   Help me seat him.
Send quickly, send for help!

> > > (*They place him in a chair.*)
ANTONY.   I am answered.
We live both. Sit thee down, my Cleopatra;
I'll make the most I can of life, to stay
A moment more with thee.
CLEOPATRA.   How is it with you?
ANTONY. 'Tis as with a man
Removing in a hurry; all packed up,
But one dear jewel that his haste forgot;
And he, for that, returns upon the spur;
So I came back for thee.
CLEOPATRA. Too long, you heavens, you have been cruel to me;
Now show your mended faith, and give me back
His fleeting life!
ANTONY.   It will not be, my love;
I keep my soul by force.
Say but, thou are not false.
CLEOPATRA.   'Tis now too late
To say I'm true: I'll prove it, and die with you.

40 *played booty with,* pretended to lose.

Unknown to me, Alexas feigned my death,
Which, when I knew, I hasted to prevent
This fatal consequence. My fleet betrayed
Both you and me.

ANTONY.   And Dolabella—

CLEOPATRA   Scarce
Esteemed before he loved; but hated now.

ANTONY. Enough. My life's not long enough for more.
Thou say'st thou wilt come after: I believe thee,
For I can now believe whate'er thou sayest,
That we may part more kindly.

CLEOPATRA.   I will come.
Doubt not, my life, I'll come, and quickly too;
Caesar shall triumph o'er no part of thee.

ANTONY. But grieve not, while thou stay'st,
My last disastrous times.
Think we have had a clear and glorious day,
And Heaven did kindly to delay the storm
Just till our close of evening. Ten years' love,
And not a moment lost, but all improved
To the utmost joys,—what ages have we lived!
And now to die each other's; and, so dying,
While hand in hand we walk in groves below,
Whole troops of lovers' ghosts shall flock about us,
And all the train be ours.

CLEOPATRA. Your words are like the notes of dying swans,
Too sweet to last. Were there so many hours
For your unkindness, and not one for love?

ANTONY. No, not a minute.—This one kiss—worth more
Than all I leave to Caesar.   (Dies.)

CLEOPATRA.   O tell me so again,
And take ten thousand kisses for that word.
My lord, my lord! Speak, if you yet have being;
Sign to me, if you can not speak; or cast
One look! Do anything that shows you live.

IRAS. He's gone too far to hear you,
And this you see, a lump of senseless clay,
The leavings of a soul.

CHARMION.   Remember, madam,
He charged you not to grieve.

CLEOPATRA.   And I'll obey him.
I have not loved a Roman not to know
What should become his wife—his wife, my Charmion!
For 'tis to that high title I aspire,

And now I'll not die less. Let dull Octavia
Survive to mourn him, dead. My nobler fate
Shall knit our spousals with a tie too strong
For Roman laws to break.

IRAS.   Will you then die?

CLEOPATRA. Why shouldst thou make that question?

IRAS. Caesar is merciful.

CLEOPATRA.   Let him be so
To those that want his mercy. My poor lord
Made no such covenant with him to spare me
When he was dead. Yield me to Caesar's pride?
What! to be led in triumph through the streets,
A spectacle to base plebian eyes,
While some dejected friend of Antony's
Close in a corner, shakes his head, and mutters
A secret curse on her who ruined him?
I'll none of that.

CHARMION.   Whatever you resolve,
I'll follow, even to death.

IRAS.   I only feared
For you, but more should fear to live without you.

CLEOPATRA. Why, now, 'tis as it should be. Quick, my friends,
Dispatch. Ere this, the town's in Caesar's hands.
My lord looks down concerned, and fears my stay,
Lest I should be surprised.
Keep him not waiting for his love too long.
You, Charmion, bring my crown and richest jewels;
With them, the wreath of victory I made
(Vain augury!) for him who now lies dead.
You, Iras, bring the cure of all our ills.

IRAS. The aspics,[41] madam?

CLEOPATRA.   Must I bid you twice?

(*Exeunt* CHARMION *and* IRAS.)

'Tis sweet to die when they would force life on me,
To rush into the dark abode of death,
And seize him first. If he be like my love,
He is not frightful, sure.
We're now alone in secrecy and silence;
And is not this like lovers? I may kiss
These pale, cold lips; Octavia does not see me.

[41] *aspics,* asps, poisonous snakes.

And oh! 'tis better far to have him thus
Than see him in her arms.—Oh, welcome, welcome!

(*Enter* CHARMION *and* IRAS.)

CHARMION. What must be done?
CLEOPATRA.   Short ceremony, friends,
But yet it must be decent. First, this laurel
Shall crown my hero's head; he fell not basely,
Nor left his shield behind him.—Only thou
Couldst triumph o'er thyself; and thou alone
Wert worthy so to triumph.
CHARMION.   To what end
These ensigns of your pomp and royalty?
CLEOPATRA. Dull that thou art! why, 'tis to meet my love
As when I saw him first on Cydnos' bank,
All sparkling, like a goddess; so adorned,
I'll find him once again. My second spousals
Shall match my first in glory. Haste, haste, both.
And dress the bride of Antony.
CHARMION.   —'Tis done.
CLEOPATRA. Now seat me by my lord. I claim this place,
For I must conquer Caesar, too, like him,
And win my share o' th' world.—Hail, you dear relics
Of my immortal love!
O let no impious hand remove you hence,
But rest for ever here! Let Egypt give
His death that peace which it denied his life.—
Reach me the casket.
IRAS.   Underneath the fruit
The aspic lies.
CLEOPATRA. Welcome, thou kind deceiver!

(*Putting aside the leaves.*)

Thou best of thieves, who, with an easy key,
Dost open life and, unperceived by us,
Even steal us from ourselves, discharging so
Death's dreadful office better than himself,
Touching our limbs so gently into slumber
That Death stands by, deceived by his own image,
And thinks himself but sleep.
SERAPION. (*within*)   The queen, where is she?
The town is yielded, Caesar's at the gates.

CLEOPATRA. He comes too late to invade the rights of death.
    Haste, bare my arm, and rouse the serpent's fury.

                (*Holds out her arm, and draws it back.*)

    Coward flesh,
    Wouldst thou conspire with Caesar to betray me
    As thou wert none of mine? I'll force thee to 't,
    And not be sent by him,
    But bring, myself, my soul to Antony.

         (*Turns aside, and then shows her arm bloody.*)

    Take hence. The work is done.
SERAPION. (*within*)   Break ope the door
    And guard the traitor well.
CHARMION.   The next is ours.
IRAS. Now, Charmion, to be worthy
    Of our great queen and mistress.

                  (*They apply the aspics.*)

CLEOPATRA. Already, death, I feel thee in my veins.
    I go with such a will to find my lord
    That we shall quickly meet.
    A heavy numbness creeps through every limb,
    And now 'tis at my head. My eyelids fall,
    And my dear love is vanished in a mist.——
    Where shall I find him—where? O turn me to him,
    And lay me on his breast!—Caesar, thy worst.
    Now part us, if thou canst.

                        (*Dies.*)
           (IRAS *sinks down at her feet, and dies;*
           CHARMION *stands behind her chair, as*
                dressing her head.)

    (*Enter* SERAPION, *two priests,* ALEXAS, *bound, Egyptians.*)
PRIEST.   Behold, Serapion,
    What havoc death has made!
SERAPION.   'Twas what I feared.——
    Charmion, is this well done?
CHARMION. Yes, 'tis well done, and like a queen, the last
    Of her great race. I follow her.   (*Sinks down and dies.*)
ALEXAS.   'Tis true,
    She has done well. Much better thus to die
    Than live to make a holiday in Rome.

SERAPION. See, see how the lovers sit in state together,
As they were giving laws to half mankind!
Th' impression of a smile, left in her face,
Shows she died pleased with him for whom she lived,
And went to charm him in another world.
Caesar's just entering; grief has now no leisure.
Secure that villain as our pledge of safety
To grace the imperial triumph.—Sleep, blest pair,
Secure from human chance, long ages out,
While all the storms of fate fly o'er your tomb;
And fame to late posterity shall tell,
No lovers lived so great or died so well.

(*Exeunt.*)

Curtain

EPILOGUE

Poets, like disputants when reasons fail,
Have one sure refuge left—and that's to rail.
Fop, coxcomb, fool, are thundered through the pit;
And this is all their equipage of wit.
We wonder how the devil this difference grows
Betwixt our fools in verse, and yours in prose;
For, 'faith, the quarrel rightly understood,
'Tis civil war with their own flesh and blood.
The threadbare author hates the gaudy coat;
And swears at the gilt coach, but swears afoot;
For 'tis observed of every scribbling man,
He grows a fop as fast as e'er he can;
Prunes up,[42] and asks his oracle, the glass,
If pink or purple best become his face.
For our poor wretch, he neither rails nor prays;
Nor likes your wit just as you like his plays;
He has not yet so much of Mr. Bayes.[43]
He does his best; and if he can not please,
Would quickly sue out his *writ of ease*.[44]
Yet, if he might his own grand jury call,
By the fair sex he begs to stand or fall.
Let Caesar's power the men's ambition move,
But grace you him who lost the world for love!
Yet if some antiquated lady say,
The last age is not copied in his play;
Heaven help the man who for that face must drudge,

[42] *Prunes up*, primps, preens, dresses up.
[43] *Bayes*, i.e., Dryden was satirized as Mr. Bayes, a foolish poet, in Buckingham's *The Rehearsal* (1671).
[44] *writ of ease*, discharge.

Which only has the wrinkles of a judge.
Let not the young and beauteous join with those;
For should you raise such numerous hosts of foes,
Young wits and sparks he to his aid must call;
'Tis more than one man's work to please you all.

THE HISTORY OF KING LEAR
∽≫ A Tragedy ≪∼
1681

Nahum Tate

INTRODUCTORY NOTE

Nahum Tate was born in 1652 and educated at Trinity College, Dublin. He was a good journeyman man of letters, for in addition to "translating" *King Lear* for a Restoration audience, he collaborated on the libretto for Purcell's *Dido and Aeneas* and published a famous version of the Psalms in 1696. He was, in fact, appointed Poet Laureate of England, a position that he held for more than twenty years.

Tate's version of Shakespeare's *King Lear* held the stage for more than a century. One reason for its popularity was given by Dr. Johnson, who said that the happy ending, with its marriage of Cordelia and Edgar, might well be an improvement. In a famous passage from his "Notes on the Plays" he describes the intensity of his own reaction to the change:

> In the present case the public has decided. Cordelia, from the time of Tate, has always retired with victory and felicity. And, if my sensations could add anything to the general suffrage, I might relate, I was many years ago so shocked by Cordelia's death that I know not whether I ever endured to read again the last scenes of the play till I undertook to revise them as an editor.

There are a number of reasons for our becoming acquainted with *The History of King Lear*. It was a kind of historical phenomenon, lasting well into the Romantic period. When we read about people responding to performances of *King Lear* between Dryden's time and Wordsworth's, we are to understand that they refer not only to Shakespeare but also to Nahum Tate. A second reason is that the Tate version accorded with a new literary belief in poetic justice. Many writers and critics of drama agreed with Dr. Johnson's observation that "all reasonable beings naturally love justice." They wished to see it observed in drama because all literature was supposed to have a moral effect. Shakespeare was "improved" or "made fit" to reinterpret Elizabethan tragedy for a new and different audience. That audience evidently wished to see human experience depicted in terms more rational, more intelligible, and more ethical than before.

Tate's version shows how men make their own destiny. The gods are mentioned a good deal in this play, but the action proceeds neither by their will nor by the random operations of chance. Edmund is moved by lust and power, Cordelia and Edgar by law and justice. There are no hidden motives, no sense of the moral neutrality of the universe. The play's events take place among those who have very little doubt about the nature of things.

In almost every respect Tate tries to clarify motivations. He adds a great deal of politics, for example, in an interesting attempt to avoid the normal controls of censorship. In dealing with such an ancient subject he evidently felt himself free to state some political ideas. For example, Regan and Gonerill rule badly when their turn comes, and they provoke a revolution. We can see that the play centers in the Tate version on the love match between Cordelia and Edgar; but it may not be quite as obvious that they represent also the civilized virtues of loyalty and good government. The most interesting figure in the play is Edmund, no less wicked than in the original story, but here a summary of Restoration fears about uncontrolled egotism, sexuality, and social pathology.

Tate's *Lear* gives us some sense not only of a change in the conception of tragedy but also of a new language of feeling. The new style is to luxuriate in feeling, to imagine indescribable pleasure, and to make pity and love the center of imagination. The evil Edmund frankly sums up love in its most sensate—and sentimental—form:

> Charming queen,
> Take all my blooming youth, forever fold me
> In those soft arms, lull me in endless sleep,
> That I may dream of pleasures too transporting
> for life to bear.

As for Edgar, when he contemplates Cordelia it is in the language of worship and allegory: "such amazing piety, such tenderness."

There is of course a major problem with Tate's style: when we hear of Edmund's "ecstasies of love" they are described from outside, after the event, and in a language not capable of doing very much with them. Tate does not really write love poetry, he tells us about the way his characters feel about being in love. But there is a positive and useful side to his method. Tate's *Lear* is of course not the original, yet it is a play, separate in itself, that manages to convey Restoration sensibility. It translates emotion into sentiment and sexuality; and in that respect is both less than its original and superbly accurate as a historical indication.

The Persons

1. The enormous change is of course the loss of the Fool: not neoclassical.

KING LEAR
GLOSTER
KENT
EDGAR
BASTARD
CORNWALL
ALBANY
BURGUNDY
GENTLEMAN-USHER
AN OLD MAN
PHYSICIAN
GONERILL
REGAN
CORDELIA
ARANTE

Guards, Officers, Messengers, Ruffians, Attendants

PROLOGUE

Since by mistakes your best delights are made
(For even your wives can please in masquerade),
'Twere worth our while t'have drawn you in this day
By a new name to our old honest play;
But he that did this evening's treat prepare
Bluntly resolved before-hand to declare
Your entertainment should be most old fare;
Yet hopes, since in rich Shakespeare's soil it grew,
'Twill relish yet with those whose tastes are true,
And his Ambition is to please a few.
If then this heap of flowers shall chance to wear
Fresh beauty in the order they now bear,
Even this[1] Shakespeare's praise, each rustic knows
'Mongst plenteous flowers a garland to compose,
Which strung by his coarse hand may fairer show,
But 'twas a power divine first made 'em grow.
Why should these scenes lie hid, in which we find
What may at once divert and teach the mind?
Morals were always proper for the stage,
But are even necessary in this age.
Poets must take the churches' teaching trade,
Since priests their province of intrigue invade;
But we the worst in this exchange have got,
In vain our poets preach, whilst church-men plot.[2]

[1] *this*, this is.
[2] *whilst church-men plot*, the Primate of Ireland had in 1680 been accused of conspiring to rebel; he was later executed.

ACT I

[SCENE I.] *Palace of King Lear*

(*Enter* BASTARD *solus.*)

BASTARD. Thou, Nature, art my goddess; to thy law
 My services are bound. Why am I then
 Deprived of a son's right because I came not
 In the dull road that custom has prescribed?
 Why bastard, wherefore base, when I can boast
 A mind as generous and a shape as true
 As honest madam's issue? Why are we
 Held base, who in the lusty stealth of nature
 Take fiercer qualities than what compound
 The scanted[3] births of the stale marriage-bed?
 Well then, legitimate Edgar, to thy right
 Of law I will oppose a bastard's cunning.
 Our father's love is to the bastard Edmund
 As to legitimate Edgar. With success
 I've practiced yet on[4] both their easy[5] natures.
 Here comes the old man chafed with th'information
 Which last I forged against my brother Edgar;
 A tale so plausible, so boldly uttered,
 And heightened by such lucky accidents,
 That now the slightest circumstance confirms him,
 That base-born Edmund spite of law inherits.

(*Enter* KENT *and* GLOSTER.)

GLOSTER. Nay, good my lord, your charity
 O'ershoots itself to plead in his behalf;
 You are yourself a father, and may feel

---

3 *scanted,* lesser.
4 *practiced yet on,* deceived.
5 *easy,* gullible.

The sting of disobedience from a son
First-born and best beloved. Oh, villain Edgar!

KENT. Be not too rash, all may be forgery,
And time yet clear the duty of your son.

GLOSTER. Plead with the seas, and reason down the winds,
Yet shalt thou ne'er convince me. I have seen
His foul designs through all a father's fondness.
But be this light and thou my witnesses
That I discard him here from my possessions,
Divorce him from my heart, my blood and name.

BASTARD. It works as I could wish; I'll show myself.

GLOSTER. Ha, Edmund! Welcome, boy. O Kent, see here
Inverted nature, Gloster's shame and glory.
This by-born,[6] the wild sally[7] of my youth,
Pursues me with all filial offices,
Whilst Edgar, begged of Heaven and born in honour,
Draws plagues on my white head that urge me still
To curse in age the pleasure of my youth.
Nay weep not, Edmund, for thy brother's crimes;
O generous boy, thou sharest but half his blood,
Yet lovest beyond the kindness of a brother.
But I'll reward thy virtue. Follow me.
My lord, you wait the king, who comes resolved
To quit the toils of empire, and divide
His realms amongst his daughters. Heaven succeed it,
But much I fear the change.

KENT. I grieve to see him
With such wild starts of passion hourly seized,
As renders majesty beneath itself.

GLOSTER. Alas! 'tis the infirmity of his age.
Yet has his temper ever been unfixed,
Choleric[8] and sudden. Hark, they approach.

(*Exeunt* GLOSTER *and* BASTARD.)

(*Flourish. Enter* LEAR, CORNWALL, ALBANY, BURGUNDY,
EDGAR, GONERILL, REGAN, CORDELIA: EDGAR *speaking to*
CORDELIA *at entrance.*)

EDGAR. Cordelia, royal fair, turn yet once more,
And ere successful Burgundy receive
The treasure of thy beauties from the king,

[6] *by-born*, bastard.
[7] *sally*, outburst.
[8] *Choleric*, prone to anger.

Ere happy Burgundy for ever fold thee,
Cast back one pitying look on <u>wretched Edgar</u>.

the romantic interest

CORDELIA. Alas, what would the wretched Edgar with
The more unfortunate Cordelia
Who in obedience to a father's will
Flies from her Edgar's arms to Burgundy's?

LEAR. Attend my lords of Albany and Cornwall
With princely Burgundy.

ALBANY. We do, my liege.

LEAR. Give me the map. Know, lords, we have divided
In three our kingdom, having now resolved
To disengage from our long toil of state,
Conferring all upon your younger years.
You, Burgundy, Cornwall and Albany,
Long in our court have made your amorous sojourn
And now are to be answered. —Tell me, my daughters,
Which of you loves us most, that we may place
Our largest bounty with the largest merit.
Gonerill, our eldest-born, speak first.

GONERILL. Sir, I do love you more than words can utter,
Beyond what can be valued, rich or rare;
Nor liberty, nor sight, health, fame, or beauty
Are half so dear, my life for you were vile;[9]
As much as child can love the best of fathers.

LEAR. Of all these bounds, even from this line to this,
With shady forests and wide-skirted meads,
We make thee lady; to thine and Albany's issue.
Be this perpetual. —What says our second daughter?

REGAN. My sister, sir, in part expressed my love,
For such as hers is mine, though more extended;
Sense has no other joy that I can relish,
I have my all in my dear liege's love!

LEAR. Therefore to thee and thine hereditary
Remain this ample third of our fair kingdom.

CORDELIA (*aside*). Now comes my trial. How am I distressed,
That must with cold speech tempt the choleric king
Rather to leave me dowerless, than condemn me
To <u>loathed embraces!</u>

note the redefinition: not integrity but sex now motivates.

LEAR. Speak now our last, not least in our dear love;
So ends my task of state. —Cordelia, speak:

---

[9] *my life for you were vile,* unclear. Possibly "for" should be replaced by "without."

What can'st thou say to win a richer third
Than what thy sisters gained?

CORDELIA. Now must my love in words fall short of theirs
As much as it exceeds in truth. —Nothing, my lord.

LEAR. Nothing can come of nothing; speak again.

CORDELIA. Unhappy am I that I can't dissemble.
Sir, as I ought, I love Your Majesty;
No more nor less.

LEAR. Take heed, Cordelia,
Thy fortunes are at stake; think better on't
And mend thy speech a little.

CORDELIA. O my liege,
You gave me being, bred me, dearly love me,
And I return my duty as I ought,
Obey you, love you, and most honour you!
Why have my sisters husbands, if they love you all?
Happ'ly when I shall wed, the lord whose hand
Shall take my plight[10] will carry half my love;
For I shall never marry, like my sisters,
To love my father all.

LEAR. And goes thy heart with this?
'Tis said that I am choleric. Judge me, gods,
Is there not cause? Now, minion,[11] I perceive
The truth of what has been suggested to us:
Thy fondness for the rebel son of Gloster,
False to his father, as thou art to my hopes.
And oh take heed, rash girl, lest we comply
With thy fond[12] wishes, which thou wilt too late
Repent; for know our nature cannot brook
A child so young and so ungentle.

CORDELIA. So young, my lord, and true.

LEAR. Thy truth then be thy dower.
For by the sacred sun and solemn night
I here disclaim all my paternal care,
And from this minute hold thee as a stranger
Both to my blood and favour.

KENT. This is frenzy.
Consider, good my liege—

LEAR. Peace, Kent.
Come not between a dragon and his rage.

---

10 *plight*, pledge.
11 *minion*, one whose value depends solely on the power of another.
12 *fond*, foolish.

I loved her most, and in her tender trust
Designed to have bestowed my age at ease!
So be my grave my peace as here I give
My heart from her, and with it all my wealth.
My lords of Cornwall and of Albany,
I do invest you jointly with full right
In this fair third, Cordelia's forfeit dower.
Mark me, my lords, observe our last resolve:
Ourself, attended with an hundred knights,
Will make abode with you in monthly course;
The name alone of King remain with me;
Yours be the execution and revenues.
This is our final will, and to confirm it
This coronet part between you.

KENT. Royal Lear,
    Whom I have ever honoured as my king,
    Loved as my father, as my master followed,
    And as my patron thought on in my prayers—

LEAR. Away, the bow is bent, make from[13] the shaft.

KENT. No, let it fall and drench[14] within my heart,
    Be Kent unmannerly when Lear is mad:
    Thy youngest daughter—

LEAR. On thy life, no more!

KENT. What wilt thou do, old man?

LEAR. Out of my sight!

KENT. See better first.

LEAR. Now, by the gods,—

KENT. Now by the gods, rash king, thou swearest in vain.

LEAR. Ha, traitor—

KENT. Do, kill thy physician, Lear.
    Strike through my throat, yet with my latest breath
    I'll thunder in thine ear my just complaint,
    And tell thee to thy face that thou dost ill.

LEAR. Hear me, rash man, on thy allegiance hear me:
    Since thou hast striven to make us break our vow
    And pressed between our sentence and our power,
    Which nor our nature nor our place can bear,
    We banish thee forever from our sight
    And kingdom; if when three days are expired
    Thy hated trunk be found in our dominions,
    That moment is thy death; away!

13 *make from*, avoid.
14 *drench*, plunge.

KENT. Why, fare thee well, king. Since thou art resolved
 I take thee at thy word, and will not stay
 To see thy fall: the gods protect the maid
 That truly thinks, and has most justly said.
 Thus to new climates my old truth I bear,
 Friendship lives hence, and banishment is here. (*Exit.*)

LEAR. Now, Burgundy, you see her price is fallen,
 Yet if the fondness of your passion still
 Affects[15] her as she stands, dowerless, and lost
 In our esteem, she's yours; take her or leave her.

BURGUNDY. Pardon me, royal Lear, I but demand
 The dower yourself proposed, and here I take
 Cordelia by the hand, Duchess of Burgundy.

LEAR. Then leave her, sir, for by a father's rage
 I tell you all her wealth. Away!

BURGUNDY. Then sir be pleased to charge the breach
 Of our alliance on your own will,
 Not my inconstancy.

    (*Exeunt. Manent* EDGAR *and* CORDELIA.)

EDGAR. Has Heaven then weighed the merit of my love,
 Or is't the raving of my sickly thought?
 Could Burgundy forgo so rich a prize
 And leave her to despairing Edgar's arms?
 Have I thy hand, Cordelia, do I clasp it,
 The hand that was this minute to have joined
 My hated rival's? Do I kneel before thee
 And offer at they feet my panting heart?
 Smile, Princess, and convince me, for as yet
 I doubt, and dare not trust the dazzling joy.

CORDELIA. Some comfort yet that 'twas no vicious blot
 That has deprived me of a father's grace,
 But merely want of that that makes me rich
 In wanting it, a smooth professing tongue:
 O sisters, I am loth to call your fault
 As it deserves; but use our father well,
 And wronged Cordelia never shall repine.

EDGAR. O heavenly maid that art thyself thy dower,
 Richer in virtue than the stars in light,
 If Edgar's humble fortunes may be graced
 With thy acceptance, at thy feet he lays 'em.

---

15 *Affects*, values.

Ha, my Cordelia! Dost thou turn away?
What have I done t'offend thee?

CORDELIA. Talked of love.

EDGAR. Then I've offended oft, Cordelia too
Has oft permitted me so to offend.

CORDELIA. When, Edgar, I permitted your addresses,
I was the darling daughter of a king;
Nor can I now forget my royal birth,
And live dependent on my lover's fortune.
I cannot to so low a fate submit;
And therefore study to forget your passion,
And trouble me upon this theme no more.

EDGAR. Thus majesty takes most state in distress!
How are we tossed on Fortune's fickle flood!
The wave that with surprising kindness brought
The dear wreck to my arms, has snatched it back,
And left me mourning on the barren shore.

CORDELIA. This baseness of th'ignoble Burgundy   (*aside*)
Draws just suspicion on the race of men.
His love was interest,[16] so may Edgar's be.
And he but with more compliment dissemble.
If so, I shall oblige him by denying:
But if his love be fixt, such constant flame
As warms our breasts, if such I find his passion,
My heart as grateful to his truth shall be,
And cold Cordelia prove as kind as he.   (*Exit.*)

(*Enter* BASTARD *hastily.*)

BASTARD. Brother, I've found you in a lucky minute;
Fly and be safe, some villain has incensed
Our father against your life.

EDGAR. Distressed Cordelia! but oh! more cruel!

BASTARD. Hear me sir, your life, your life's in danger.

EDGAR. A resolve so sudden
And of such black importance!

BASTARD. 'Twas not sudden,
Some villain has of long time laid the train.[17]

EDGAR. And yet perhaps 'twas but pretended coldness,
To try how far my passion would pursue.

BASTARD. He hears me not; wake, wake, sir.

16 *interest,* self-interest.
17 *laid the train,* i.e., as in setting a charge of gunpowder.

EDGAR. Say ye, brother?—
    No tears, good Edmund, if thou bring'st me tidings
    To strike me dead, for charity delay not.
    That present will befit so kind a hand.
BASTARD. Your danger, sir, comes on so fast
    That I want time t'inform you, but retire
    Whilst I take care to turn the pressing stream.
    O gods! for Heavens sake, sir.
EDGAR. Pardon me sir, a serious thought
    Had seized me, but I think you talked of danger
    And wished me to retire. Must all our vows
    End thus!—Friend, I obey you—O Cordelia!   (*Exit.*)
BASTARD. Ha! ha! Fond man, such credulous honesty
    Lessens the glory of my artifice;
    His nature is so far from doing wrongs
    That he suspects none. If this letter speed
    And pass for Edgar's, as himself would own
    The counterfeit but for the foul contents,
    Then my designs are perfect.—Here comes Gloster.

(Enter GLOSTER.)

GLOSTER. Stay, Edmund, turn, what paper were your reading?
BASTARD. A trifle, sir.
GLOSTER. What needed then that terrible dispatch of it
    Into your pocket? Come, produce it, sir.
BASTARD. A letter from my brother, sir; I had
    Just broke the seal but knew not the contents.
    Yet, fearing they might prove to blame,
    Endeavoured to conceal it from your sight.
GLOSTER. 'Tis Edgar's character.[18]   (*Reads.*)
    "This policy of fathers is intolerable, that keeps our
    fortunes from us till age will not suffer us to enjoy
    'em. I am weary of the tyranny: come to me that of
    this I may speak more. If our father would sleep till
    I waked him, you should enjoy half his possessions,
    and lived beloved of your brother
                         Edgar."
    "Would sleep till I waked him, you should enjoy
    Half his possessions"—Edgar to write this
    'Gainst his indulgent father! Death and hell!
    Fly, Edmund; seek him out, wind me into him

18 *character,* handwriting.

That I may bite the traitor's heart, and fold
    His bleeding entrails on my vengeful arm.

BASTARD. Perhaps 'twas writ, my lord, to prove[19] my virtue.

GLOSTER. These late eclipses of the sun and moon
    Can bode no less: love cools, and friendship fails,
    In cities mutiny, in countries discord,
    The bond of nature crack't 'twixt son and father.
    Find out the villain, do it carefully
    And it shall lose thee nothing.   *(Exit.)*

BASTARD. So, now my project's firm, but to make sure
    I'll throw in one proof more and that a bold one:
    I'll place old Gloster where he shall o'er-hear us
    Confer of this design, whilst to his thinking,
    Deluded Edgar shall accuse himself.
    Be honesty my interest and I can
    Be honest too, and what saint so divine
    That will successful villainy decline!   *(Exit.)*

[SCENE II.] ALBANY's *palace*

(Enter KENT *disguised.)*

KENT. Now banished, Kent, if thou canst pay thy duty
    In this disguise where thou dost stand condemned,
    Thy master Lear shall find thee full of labours.

(Enter LEAR *attended.)*

LEAR. In there, and tell our daughter we are here
    Now, what art thou?

KENT. A man, sir.

LEAR. What dost thou profess, or wouldst with us?

KENT. I do profess to be no less than I seem, to serve him
    truly that puts me in trust, to love him that's honest, to
    converse with him that's wise and speaks little, to fight
    when I can't choose; and to eat no fish.

LEAR. I say, what art thou?

KENT. A very honest-hearted fellow, and as poor as the king.

LEAR. Then art thou poor indeed—what can'st thou do?

KENT. I can keep honest counsel, mar a curious tale in the
    telling, deliver a plain message bluntly. That which
    ordinary men are fit for I am qualified in, and the best
    of me is diligence.

LEAR. Follow me, thou shalt serve me

19 *prove*, test.

(*Enter one of* GONERILL's GENTLEMEN.)

Now sir?

GENTLEMAN. Sir—

(*Exit;* KENT *runs after him.*)

LEAR. What says the fellow? Call the clatpole[20] back.

ATTENDANT. My lord I know not, but methinks Your Highness
is entertained with slender ceremony.

SERVANT. He says, my lord, your daughter is not well.

LEAR. Why came not the slave back when I called him?

SERVANT. My lord, he answered me i'the surliest manner
That he would not.

(*Re-enter* GENTLEMAN, *brought in by* KENT.)

LEAR. I hope our daughter did not so instruct him:
Now, who am I sir?

GENTLEMAN. My lady's father.

LEAR. My lord's knave—   (*Strikes him.*)
    (GONERILL *at the Entrance.*)

GENTLEMAN. I'll not be struck, my lord.

KENT. Nor tripped neither, thou vile civet-box.[21]

(*Strikes up his heels.*)

GONERILL. By day and night, this is insufferable;
I will not bear it.

LEAR. Now, daughter, why that frontlet[22] on?
Speak, does that frown become our presence?

GONERILL. Sir, this licentious insolence of your servants
Is most unseemly; hourly they break out
In quarrels bred by their unbounded riots.
I had fair hope by making this known to you
T'have had a quick redress, but find too late
That you protect and countenance their outrage;
And therefore, sir, I take this freedom, which
Necessity makes discreet.

LEAR. Are you our daughter?

GONERILL. Come, sir, let me entreat you to make use
Of your discretion, and put off betimes
This disposition that of late transforms you
From what you rightly are.

[20] *clatpole*, blockhead.
[21] *civet-box*, perfume bottle.
[22] *frontlet*, forehead, i.e., expression.

LEAR. Does any here know me? Why, this is not Lear.
    Does Lear walk thus? Speak thus? Where are his eyes?
    Who is it that can tell me who I am?
GONERILL. Come, sir, this admiration's much o'the savour
    Of other your new humours. I beseech you
    To understand my purposes aright.
    As you are old, you should be staid and wise.
    Here do you keep an hundred knights and squires,
    Men so debauched and bold that this our palace
    Shows like a riotous inn, a tavern, brothel.
    Be then advised by her that else will take
    The thing she begs, to lessen your attendance.
    Take half a way, and see that the remainder
    Be such as may befit your age, and know
    Themselves and you.
LEAR. Darkness and devils!
    Saddle my horses, call my train together.
    Degenerate viper, I'll not stay with thee;
    I yet have left a daughter—serpent, monster,
    Lessen my train, and call 'em riotous?
    All men approved of choice and rarest parts,
    That each particular of duty know—
    How small, Cordelia, was thy fault! O Lear,
    Beat at this gate that let thy folly in,
    And thy dear judgment out. Go, go, my people.

                (*Going off meets* ALBANY *entering.*)

    Ingrateful duke, was this your will?
ALBANY. What, sir?
LEAR. Death! fifty of my followers at a clap!
ALBANY. The matter, madam?
GONERILL. Never afflict yourself to know the cause,
    But give his dotage way.
LEAR. Blasts upon thee,
    Th' untented[23] woundings of a father's curse
    Pierce every sense about thee. Old fond eyes,
    Lament this cause again, I'll pluck ye out
    And cast ye with the waters that ye lose
    To temper clay—no, gorgon, thou shalt find
    That I'll resume the shape which thou dost think
    I have cast off forever.
GONERILL. Mark ye that.

23 *untented,* too deep to be probed.

LEAR. Hear, Nature!
    Dear goddess, hear, and if thou dost intend
    To make that creature fruitful, change thy purpose;
    Pronounce upon her womb the barren curse,
    That from her blasted[24] body never spring
    A babe to honour her—but if she must bring forth,
    Defeat her joy with some distorted birth
    Or monstrous form, the prodigy o'the time,
    And so perverse of spirit, that it may live
    Her torment as 'twas born, to fret her cheeks
    With constant tears, and wrinkle her young brow.
    Turn all her mother's pains to shame and scorn
    That she may curse her crime too late, and feel
    How sharper than a serpent's tooth it is
    To have a thankless child! Away, away.   *Exit cum suis.*
GONERILL. Presuming thus upon his numerous train
    He thinks to play the tyrant here, and hold
    Our lives at will.
ALBANY. Well, you may bear too far.   (*Exit.*)

                                        (*End of the First Act*)

ACT II

[SCENE I.] GLOSTER's *house*

(*Enter* BASTARD.)

BASTARD. The duke comes here tonight; I'll take advantage
    Of his arrival to complete my project.
    Brother, a word. Come forth; 'tis I, your friend

(*Enter* EDGAR.)

    My father watches for you, fly this place,
    Intelligence[25] is given where you are hid.
    Take the advantage of the night: bethink ye,
    Have you not spoke against the Duke of Cornwall
    Something might show you a favourer of
    Duke Albany's party?

---

[24] *blasted*, blighted.
[25] *Intelligence*, news, secret information.

EDGAR. Nothing, why ask you?

BASTARD. Because he's coming here to night in haste
    And Regan with him—hark! the guards, away.

EDGAR. Let 'em come on, I'll stay and clear myself.

BASTARD. Your innocence at leisure may be heard,
    But Gloster's storming rage as yet is deaf,
    And you may perish ere allowed the hearing.

                               (*Exit* EDGAR.)

    Gloster comes yonder: now to my feigned scuffle—
    Yield, come before my father! Lights here, lights!
    Some blood drawn on me would beget opinion
                             (*Stabs his arm.*)
    Of our more fierce encounter—I have seen
    Drunkards do more than this in sport.

  (*Enter* GLOSTER *and Servants.*)

GLOSTER. Now, Edmund, where's the traitor?

BASTARD. That name, sir,
    Strikes horror through me; but my brother, sir,
    Stood here i'the dark.

GLOSTER. Thou bleed'st. Pursue the villain
    And bring him piece-meal to me.

BASTARD. Sir, he's fled.

GLOSTER. Let him fly far, this kingdom shall not hide him.
    The noble duke, my patron, comes tonight;
    By his authority I will proclaim
    Rewards for him that brings him to the stake,
    And death for the concealer.
    Then of my lands, loyal and natural boy,
    I'll work the means to make thee capable.[26]   (*Exeunt.*)

[SCENE II] *Outside* GLOSTER's *house*

  (*Enter* KENT [*disguised still*] *and* GONERILL's GENTLEMAN,
  severally.)

GENTLEMAN. Good morrow friend, belong'st thou to this
    house?

KENT. Ask them will answer thee.

GENTLEMAN. Where may we set our horses?

KENT. I'the mire.

---

[26] *capable*, legal heir.

GENTLEMAN. I am in haste. Prithee an'thou lov'st me, tell me.

KENT. I love thee not.

GENTLEMAN. Why then, I care not for thee.

KENT. An I had thee in Lipsbury Pinfold,[27] I'd make thee care for me.

GENTLEMAN. What dost thou mean? I know thee not.

KENT. But, minion,[28] I know thee.

GENTLEMAN. What dost thou know me for?

KENT. For a base, proud, beggarly, white-livered, glass-gazing, superserviceable finical rogue; one that would be a pimp in way of good service, and art nothing but a composition of knave, beggar, coward, pandar—

GENTLEMAN. What a monstrous fellow art thou to rail at one that is neither known of thee nor knows thee!

KENT. Impudent slave, not know me, who but two days since tripped up they heels before the king! Draw, miscreant,[29] or I'll make the moon shine through thee.

GENTLEMAN. What means the fellow? Why prithee, prithee; I tell thee I have nothing to do with thee.

KENT. I know your rogueship's office. You come with letters against the king, taking my young Lady Vanity's part against her royal father. Draw, rascal.

GENTLEMAN. Murther! murther! help, ho!

KENT. Dost thou scream, peacock? Strike, puppet, stand, dapper slave.

GENTLEMAN. Help help! Murther, help! (*Exit.* KENT *after him.*)

[SCENE III.] *Outside* GLOSTER'S *house*

(*Flourish. Enter* DUKE OF CORNWALL, REGAN, *attended,* GLOSTER, BASTARD.)

GLOSTER. All welcome to Your Graces. You do me honour.

DUKE. Gloster, w'have heard with sorrow that your life
    Has been attempted by your impious son,
    But Edmund here has paid you strictest duty.

GLOSTER. He did betray his practice,[30] and received
    The hurt you see, striving to apprehend him.

DUKE. Is he pursued?

GLOSTER. He is, my lord.

---

27 *in Lipsbury Pinfold,* between my teeth.
28 *minion,* parasite (see note 11).
29 *miscreant,* without honor.
30 *practice,* treachery.

REGAN. Use our authority to apprehend
    The traitor and do justice on his head.
    For you, Edmund, that have so signalized
    Your virtue, you from henceforth shall be ours;
    Natures of such firm trust we much shall need.
    (*aside*.) A charming youth, and worth my further thought.
DUKE. Lay comforts, noble Gloster, to your breast
    As we to ours. This night be spent in revels.
    We choose you, Gloster, for our host to night,
    A troublesome expression[31] of our love.
    On, to the sports before us—Who are these?

    (*Enter the* GENTLEMAN *pursued by* KENT.)

GLOSTER. Now, what's the matter?
DUKE. Keep peace upon your lives; he dies that strikes.
    Whence and what are ye?
ATTENDANT. Sir, they are messengers, the one from your
    sister,[32] the other from the king.
DUKE. Your difference? Speak.
GENTLEMAN. I'm scarce in breath, my lord.
KENT. No marvel, you have so bestirred your valor.
    Nature disclaims the dastard,[33] a tailor made him.
DUKE. Speak yet, how grew your quarrel?
GENTLEMAN. Sir, this old ruffian here, whose life I spared
    In pity to his beard—
KENT. Thou essence[34] bottle!
    In pity to my beard?—Your leave, my lord,
    And I will tread the muss-cat[35] into mortar.
DUKE. Know'st thou our presence?
KENT. Yes, sir, but anger has a privilege.
DUKE. Why art thou angry?
KENT. That such a slave as this should wear a sword
    And have no courage; office and no honesty.
    Not frost and fire hold more antipathy
    Than I and such a knave.
GLOSTER. Why dost thou call him knave?
KENT. His countenance likes me not.
DUKE. No more perhaps does mine, nor his or hers.

---

[31] *troublesome expression,* imposition.
[32] *sister,* sister-in-law.
[33] *dastard,* coward.
[34] *essence,* perfume.
[35] *muss-cat,* civet, from whose glands musk is extracted to make perfume.

KENT. Plain-dealing is my trade, and to be plain, sir,
  I have seen better faces in my time
  Than stands on any shoulders now before me.
REGAN. This is some fellow that having once been praised
  For bluntness, since affects a saucy rudeness;
  But I have known one of these surly knaves
  That in his plainness harboured more design
  Than twenty cringing complimenting minions.
DUKE. What's the offence you gave him?
GENTLEMAN. Never any, sir.
  It pleased the king his master lately
  To strike me on a slender misconstruction:
  Whilst watching his advantage this old lurcher[36]
  Tripped me behind, for which the king extolled him;
  And, flushed with th'honour of this bold exploit,
  Drew on me here agen.
DUKE. Bring forth the stocks. We'll teach you.
KENT. Sir, I'm too old to learn;
  Call not the stocks for me. I serve the king.
  On whose employment I was sent to you.
  You'll show too small respect, and too bold malice
  Against the person of my royal master,
  Stocking his messenger.
DUKE. Bring forth the stocks; as I have life and honour
  There shall he sit till noon.
REGAN. Till noon, my lord? till night, and all night too.
KENT. Why, madam, if I were your father's dog
  You would not use me so.
REGAN. Sir, being his knave, I will.
GLOSTER. Let me beseech Your Graces to forbear him;
  His fault is much, and the good king his master
  Will check him for't, but needs must take it ill
  To be thus slighted in his messenger.
DUKE. We'll answer that;
  Our sister may receive it worse to have
  Her gentleman assaulted. To our business lead. (*Exit.*)
GLOSTER. I am sorry for thee, friend, 'tis the duke's pleasure,
  Whose disposition will not be controlled;
  But I'll entreat for thee.
KENT. Pray do not, sir—
  I have watched and travelled hard,
  Some time I shall sleep out, the rest I'll whistle:

---

36 *lurcher*, rogue.

Farewell t'ye, sir.   *Exit* GLOSTER.
All weary and o'er-watched,
I feel the drowsy guest steal on me. Take
Advantage, heavy eyes, of this kind slumber,
Not to behold this vile and shameful lodging.   (*Sleeps.*)

[SCENE IV.] *A heath*

(*Enter* EDGAR.)

EDGAR. I heard myself proclaimed,
    And by the friendly hollow of a tree
    Escaped the hunt. No port is free, no place
    Where guards and most unusual vigilance
    Do not attend to take me. How easy now
    'Twere to defeat the malice of my trail,
    And leave my griefs on my sword's reeking point.
 ✓ But love detains me from death's peaceful cell,
    Still whispering me Cordelia's in distress.
    Unkind as she is I cannot see her wretched,
    But must be near to wait upon her fortune.
    Who knows but the white minute yet may come
    When Edgar may do service to Cordelia;
    That charming hope still ties me to the oar
    Of painful life, and makes me, too, submit
    To the humblest shifts to keep that life afoot.
 ✓ My face I will besmear and knit my locks;
    The country gives me proof and precedent
    Of bedlam beggars, who with roaring voices
    Strike in their numbed and mortified bare arms
    Pins, iron spikes, thorns, sprigs of rosemary,
    And thus from sheep-cotes, villages and mills,
    Sometimes with prayers, sometimes with lunatic bans[37]
    Enforce their charity. Poor Tyrligod! poor Tom!
    That's something yet: Edgar, I am no more.   (*Exit.*)

traveling incognito

[SCENE V.] *Outside* GLOSTER'*s house*

(KENT *in the stocks still; enter* LEAR *attended.*)

LEAR. 'Tis strange that they should so depart from home
    And not send back our messenger.
KENT. Hail, noble master.

---

[37] *bans,* curses.

LEAR. How? Mak'st thou this shame thy pastime?
　　　What's he that has so much mistook thy place
　　　To set thee here?
KENT. It is both he and she, sir, your son and daughter.
LEAR. No.
KENT. Yes.
LEAR. No I say.
KENT. I say yea.
LEAR. By Jupiter, I swear no.
KENT. By Juno I swear, I swear ay.
LEAR. They durst not do't.
　　　They could not, would not do't; 'tis worse than murder
　　　To do upon respect such violent outrage.
　　　Resolve me with all modest haste which way
　　　Thou mayst deserve, or they impose this usage.
KENT. My lord, when at their home
　　　I did commend Your Highness' letters to them,
　　　Ere I was risen arrived another post
　　　Steered[38] in his haste, breathless and panting forth
　　　From Gonerill his mistress salutations.
　　　Whosè message being delivered, they took horse,
　　　Commanding me to follow and attend
　　　The leisure of their answer, which I did.
　　　But meeting that other messenger
　　　Whose welcome I perceived has poisoned mine,
　　　Being the very fellow that of late
　　　Had shown such rudeness to Your Highness, I,
　　　Having more man than wit about me, drew,
　　　On which he raised the house with coward cries.
　　　This was the trespass which your son and daughter
　　　Thought worth the shame you see it suffer here.
LEAR. Oh! how this spleen swells upward to my heart
　　　And heaves for passage—down thou climbing rage!
　　　Thy element's below.[39] Where is this daughter?
KENT. Within, sir, at a masque.

(*Enter* GLOSTER.)

LEAR. Now Gloster?—　　　　　　　　(*Subdued conversation.*)
　　　Ha!
　　　Deny to speak with me? Th'are sick, th'are weary,

---

[38] *Steered,* agitated.
[39] Passion (in the original *King Lear* known as "mother" or "hysterica passio") was thought to arise from the spleen.

They have travelled hard to night—mere fetches![40]
Bring me a better answer.

GLOSTER. My dear lord,
You know the fiery quality of the duke—

LEAR. Vengeance! Death, plague, confusion!
Fiery? what quality? Why, Gloster, Gloster,
I'd speak with the Duke of Cornwall and his wife.

GLOSTER. I have informed 'em so.

LEAR. Informed 'em! Dost thou understand me, man?
I tell thee, Gloster—

GLOSTER. Ay, my good lord.

LEAR. The king would speak with Cornwall, the dear father
Would with his daughter speak, commands her service.
Are they informed of this? My breath and blood!
Fiery! the fiery duke! Tell the hot duke—
No, but not yet, may be he is not well:
Infirmity does still neglect all office.
I beg his pardon, and I'll chide my rashness
That took the indisposed and sickly fit
For the sound man—but wherefore sits he there?
Death on my state! This act convinces me
That this retiredness of the duke and her
Is plain contempt; give me my servant forth,
Go tell the duke and's wife I'd speak with 'em.
Now, instantly, bid 'em come forth and hear me,
Or at their chamber door I'll beat the drum
Till it cry sleep to death—

(*Enter* CORNWALL *and* REGAN.)

Oh! are ye come?

DUKE. Health to the king.

REGAN. I am glad to see Your Highness.

LEAR. Regan, I think you are; I know what cause
I have to think so; shoud'st thou not be glad
I would divorce me from thy mother's tomb.
Beloved Regan, thou wilt shake to hear
What I shall utter: thou couldst ne'r ha'thought it.

(KENT *here set at liberty.*)

Thy sister's naught, O Regan, she has tied
Ingratitude, like a keen vulture, here. (*Points to his heart.*)
I scarce can speak to thee.

---

[40] *fetches,* excuses.

REGAN. I pray you, sir, take patience; I have hope
    That you know less to value her desert
    Then she to slack her duty.
LEAR. Ha! how's that?
REGAN. I cannot think my sister in the least
    Would fail in her respects, but if perchance
    She has restrain'd the riots of your followers,
    'Tis on such grounds, and to such wholesome ends
    As clears her from all blame.
LEAR. My curses on her.
REGAN. O sir, you are old
    And should content you to be ruled and led
    By some discretion that discerns your state
    Better than you yourself. Therefore, sir,
    Return to our sister, and say you have wronged her.
LEAR. Ha! ask her forgiveness?
    No, no, 'twas my mistake; thou didst not mean so.
    Dear daughter, I confess that I am old;
    Age is unnecessary, but thou art good,
    And wilt dispense with my infirmity.
REGAN. Good sir, no more of these unsightly passions.
    Return back to our sister.
LEAR. Never, Regan,
    She has abated me of half my train,
    Looked black upon me, stabbed me with her tongue;
    All the stored vengeances of Heaven fall
    On her ingrateful head! Strike her young bones
    Ye taking airs, with lameness.
REGAN. O the blessed gods! Thus will you wish on me
    When the rash mood—
LEAR. No, Regan, thou shalt never have my curse;
    Thy tender nature cannot give thee o'er
    To such impiety. Thou better know'st
    The offices of nature, bond of childhood,
    And dues of gratitude. Thou bearest in mind
    The half o'the kingdom which our love conferred
    On thee and thine.
REGAN. Good sir, to the purpose.
LEAR. Who put my man i'the stocks?   (*Trumpet.*)
DUKE. What trumpet's that?
REGAN. I know't, my sister's, this confirms her letters.

    (*Enter* GONERILL'S GENTLEMAN.)

    Sir, is your lady come?

LEAR. More torture still?
    This is a slave whose easy borrowed pride
    Dwells in the fickle grace of her he follows;
    A fashion-fop that spends the day in dressing,
    And all to bear his lady's flattering message;
    That can deliver with a grace her lie,
    And with as bold a face bring back a greater.
    Out, varlet, from my sight.
DUKE. What means your grace?
LEAR. Who stocked my servant? Regan, I have hope
    Thou didst not know it.

    (*Enter* GONERILL.)

    Who comes here? Oh Heavens!
    If you do love old men, if your sweet sway
    Allow obedience, if yourselves are old,
    Make it your cause, send down and take my part.
    Why, gorgon, dost thou come to haunt me here?
    Art not ashamed to look upon this beard?
    Darkness upon my eyes, they play me false;
    O Regan, wilt thou take her by the hand?
GONERILL. Why not by the hand, sir? How have I offended?
    All's not offense that indiscretion finds,
    And dotage terms so.
LEAR. Heart, thou art too tough.
REGAN. I pray you, sir, being old, confess you are so.
    If till the expiration of your month
    You will return and sojourn with our sister,
    Dismissing half your train, come then to me.
    I am now from home, and out of that provision
    That shall be needful for your entertainment.
LEAR. Return with her and fifty knights dismissed?
    No, rather I'll forswear all roofs, and choose
    To be companion to the midnight wolf,
    My naked head exposed to the merciless air,
    Then have my smallest wants supplied by her.
GONERILL. At your choice, sir.
LEAR. Now I prithee, daughter, do not make me mad.
    I will not trouble thee, my child, farewell,
    We'll meet no more, no more see one another.
    Let shame come when it will, I do not call it.
    I do not bid the thunder-bearer strike,
    Nor tell tales of thee to avenging Heaven.
    Mend when thou canst, be better at thy leisure.

I can be patient, I can stay with Regan,
    I, and my hundred knights.
REGAN. Your pardon, sir,
    I looked not for you yet, nor am provided
    For your fit welcome.
LEAR. Is this well spoken now?
REGAN. My sister treats you fair; what! fifty followers?
    Is it not well? What should you need of more?
GONERILL. Why might not you, my lord, receive attendance
    From those whom she calls servants, or from mine?
REGAN. Why not, my lord? If then they chance to slack you
    We could control 'em. If you come to me—
    For now I see the danger—I entreat you
    To bring but five and twenty; to no more
    Will I give place.
LEAR. Hold now my temper, stand this bolt unmoved
    And I am thunder-proof.
    The wicked when compared with the more wicked
    Seem beautiful, and not to be the worst
    Stands in some rank of praise. Now, Gonerill,
    Thou art innocent again, I'll go with thee.
    Thy fifty yet does double five and twenty,
    And thou art twice her love.
GONERILL. Hear me, my lord,
    What need you five and twenty, ten, or five,
    To follow in a house where twice so many
    Have a command t'attend you?
REGAN. What need one?
LEAR. Blood, fire! hear—Leprosies and bluest[41] plagues!
    Room, room for hell to belch her horrors up
    And drench the Circes in a stream of fire!
    Hark how th'infernals[42] echo to my rage
    Their whips and snakes—
REGAN. How lewd[43] a thing is passion!
GONERILL. So old and stomachful[44] (*Lightning and Thunder.*)
LEAR. Heavens drop your patience down;
    You see me here, ye Gods, a poor old man
    As full of griefs as age, wretched in both—
    I'll bear no more! No, you unnatural hags,

---

[41] *bluest,* i.e., the apparent color of corpses.
[42] *th'infernals,* the furies of Hell.
[43] *lewd,* vile.
[44] *stomachful,* wilfull.

I will have such revenges on you both,
That all the world shall—I will do such things
What they are yet I know not, but they shall be
The terrors of the earth. You think I'll weep

(Thunder again.)

This heart shall break into a thousand pieces
Before I'll weep—O gods! I shall go mad.   *(Exit.)*
DUKE. 'Tis a wild night, come out o'the storm.   *(Exeunt.)*

(End of the Second Act)

ACT III

[SCENE I.] *A desert heath*

(Enter LEAR *and* KENT *in the storm.)*

LEAR. Blow, winds, and burst your cheeks; rage louder yet.
    Fantastic lightning singe, singe my white head.
    Spout cataracts, and hurricanes fall
    Till you have drowned the towns and palaces
    Of proud, ingrateful man.
KENT. Not all my best entreaties can persuade him
    Into some needful shelter, or to 'bide
    This poor slight covering on his aged head,
    Exposed to this wild war of earth and Heaven.
LEAR. Rumble thy fill, fight whirlwind, rain, and fire:
    Not fire, wind, rain or thunder are my daughters.
    I tax not you, ye elements, with unkindness.
    I never gave you kingdoms, called you children,
    You owe me no obedience. Then let fall
    Your horrible pleasure; here I stand your slave,
    A poor, infirm, weak and despised old man.
    Yet I will call you servile ministers,
    That have with two pernicious daughters joined
    Their high-engendered[45] battle against a head
    So old and white as mine. Oh! oh! 'tis foul.
KENT. Hard by, sir, is a hovel that will lend
    Some shelter from this tempest.

---

[45] *high-engendered,* created in the sky.

LEAR. I will forget my nature. What? So kind a father.
    Ay, there's the point.
KENT. Consider, good my liege, things that love night
    Love not such nights as this, these wrathful skies
    Frighten the very wanderers o'the dark,
    And make 'em keep their caves. Such drenching rain,
    Such sheets of fire, such claps of horrid thunder,
    Such groans of roaring winds have ne'er been known.
LEAR. Let the great gods,
    That keep this dreadful pudder[46] o'er our heads
    Find out their enemies now. Tremble thou wretch,
    That hast within thee undiscovered crimes.
    Hide, thou bloody hand,
    Thou perjured villain, holy, holy hypocrite,
    That drink'st the widow's tears, sigh now and cry
    These dreadful summoners grace. I am a man
    More sinned against than sinning.
KENT. Good sir, to th'hovel.
LEAR. My wit begins to burn.
    Come on my boy, how dost my boy? Art cold?
    I'm cold myself. Show me this straw, my fellow.
    The art of our necessity is strange
    And can make vile things precious. My poor knave,
    Cold as I am at heart, I've one place there (*Loud Storm.*)
    That's sorry yet for thee.   (*Exit.*)

[SCENE II.] GLOSTER's *palace*

(*Enter* BASTARD.)

BASTARD. The storm is in our louder rev'lings drowned.
    Thus would I reign could I but mount a throne.
    The riots of these proud imperial sisters
    Already have imposed the galling yoke
    Of taxes and hard impositions on
    The drudging peasants' neck, who bellow out
    Their loud complaints in vain. Triumphant queens!
    With what assurance do they tread the crowd.
    O for a taste of such majestic beauty,
    Which none but my hot veins are fit t'engage!
    Nor are my wishes desperate, for even now

---

[46] *pudder,* turmoil.

During the banquet I observed their glances
Shot thick at me, and as they left the room
Each cast by stealth a kind inviting smile,
The happy earnest[47]—ha!

(*Two servants from several entrances deliver him each a
letter, and exeunt.*)

"Where merit is so transparent, not to behold it (*Reads.*)
Were blindness, and not to reward it ingratitude.

                                        Gonerill."

Enough! blind and ingrateful should I be
Not to obey the summons of this oracle.
Now for a second letter.   (*Opens the other.*)
"If modesty be not your enemy, doubt not to find me
your friend.

                                        Regan."

Excellent sybil![48] O my glowing blood!
I am already sick of expectation,
And pant for the possession—Here Gloster comes
With business on his brow; be hushed, my joys.

GLOSTER. I come to seek thee, Edmund, to impart a business of
    importance; I know thy loyal heart is touched to see the
    cruelty of these ingrateful daughters against our royal
    master.

BASTARD. Most savage and unnatural.

GLOSTER. This change in the state sits uneasy. The commons
    repine aloud at their female tyrants. Already they cry
    out for the re-installment of their good old king, whose
    injuries I fear will inflame 'em into mutiny.

BASTARD. 'Tis to be hoped, not feared.

GLOSTER. Thou has it boy, 'tis to be hoped indeed.
    On me they cast their eyes, and hourly court me
    To lead 'em on, and whilst this head is mine
    I am theirs. A little covert craft, my boy,
    And then for open action; 'twill be employment
    Worthy such honest daring souls as thine.
    Thou, Edmund, art my trusty emissary;
    Haste on the spur at the first break of day
    With these dispatches to the Duke of Cambrai.

                                        (*Gives him letters.*)

47 *earnest*, down-payment.
48 *sybil*, prophet.

You know what mortal feuds have always flamed
Between this Duke of Cornwall's family and his.
Full twenty thousand mountaineers
Th'inveterate[49] prince will send to our assistance.
Dispatch; commend us to His Grace, and prosper
BASTARD (*aside*). Yes, credulous old man,
I will commend you to His Grace,
His Grace the Duke of Cornwall—instantly
To show him these contents in thy own character,
And sealed him these contents in thy own character,
And sealed with thy own signet. Then forthwith
The choleric duke gives sentence on thy life;
And to my hand thy vast revenues fall
To glut my pleasure that till now has starved.

(GLOSTER *going off is met by* CORDELIA *entering,* BASTARD *observing at a distance.*)

CORDELIA. Turn, Gloster, turn, by all the sacred powers
I do conjure you give my griefs a hearing.
You must, you shall, nay I am sure you will
For you were always styled the just and good.
GLOSTER. What wouldst thou, princess? Rise and speak thy
griefs.
CORDELIA. Nay, you shall promise to redress 'em too,
Or here I'll kneel for ever. I entreat
Thy succour for a father and a king,
An injured father and an injured king.
BASTARD. O charming sorrow! how her tears adorn her
Like dew on flowers. But she is virtuous,
And I must quench this hopeless fire i'the kindling.
GLOSTER. Consider, princess,
For whom thou begg'st, 'tis for the king that wronged
thee.
CORDELIA. O name not that; he did not, could not wrong me.
Nay muse not, Gloster, for it is too likely
This injured king ere this is past your aid,
And gone distracted with his savage wrongs.
BASTARD. I'll gaze no more—and yet my eyes are charmed.
CORDELIA. Or what if it be worse? Can there be worse?
As 'tis too probable this furious night
Has pierced his tender body, the bleak winds
And cold rain chilled, or lightning struck him dead.

49 *inveterate*, forever hostile.

If it be so, your promise is discharged,
And I have only one poor boon to beg,
That you convey me to his breathless trunk:
With my torn robes to wrap his hoary head,
With my torn hair to bind his hands and feet,
Then, with a shower of tears,
To wash his clay-smeared cheeks, and die beside him.

GLOSTER. Rise, fair Cordelia, thou has piety
Enough t'at one for both thy sister's crimes.
I have already plotted to restore
My injured master, and thy virtue tells me
We shall succeed, and suddenly.   (*Exit.*)

CORDELIA. Dispatch, Arante,
Provide me a disguise. We'll instantly
Go seek the king, and bring him some relief.

ARANTE. How, madam? are you ignorant
Of what your impious sisters have decreed?
Immediate death for any that relieve him.

CORDELIA. I cannot dread the furies in this case.

ARANTE. In such a night as this? Consider, madam,
For many miles about there's scarce a bush
To shelter in.

CORDELIA. Therefore no shelter for the king,
And more our charity to find him out.
What have not women dared for vicious love?
And we'll be shining proofs that they can dare
For piety as much. Blow winds, and lightnings fall:
Bold in my virgin innocence, I'll fly
My royal father to relieve, or die.   (*Exit.*)

BASTARD. "Provide me a disguise, we'll instantly
Go seek the king"—ha! ha! a lucky change.
That virtue which I feared would be my hindrance
Has proved the bond to my design.
I'll bribe two ruffians that shall at a distance follow,
And seize 'em in some desert place; and there
Whilst one retains her t'other shall return
T'inform me where she's lodged; I'll be disguised too.
Whilst they are poaching for me I'll to the duke
With these dispatches. Then to the field,
This Semele[50] in a storm. 'Twill deaf her cries

[50] *Semele*, one of the many loves of Jove, destroyed when the god revealed himself in all his powers.

Like drums in battle, lest her groans should pierce
My pitying ear, and make the amorous fight less fierce.

              (*Exit.*)

[SCENE III.] *The field*

(*Storm still. Enter* LEAR *and* KENT.)

KENT. Here is the place, my lord; good my lord, enter.
      The tyranny of this open night's too rough
      For nature to endure.
LEAR. Let me alone.
KENT. Good my lord, enter.
LEAR. Wilt break my heart?
KENT. Beseech you, sir.
LEAR. Thou think'st 'tis much that this contentious storm
      Invades us to the skin; so 'tis to thee:
      But where the greater malady is fixed
      The lesser is scarce felt: the tempest in my mind
      Does from my senses take all feeling else
      Save what beats there. Filial ingratitude!
      Is it not as this mouth should tear this hand
      For lifting food to't? But I'll punish home.
      No, I will weep no more; in such a night
      To shut me out—pour on, I will endure
      In such a night as this. O Regan, Gonerill,
      Your old kind father whose frank heart gave all—
      Oh, that way madness lies, let me shun that,
      No more of that.
KENT. See, my lord, here's the entrance.
LEAR. Well, I'll go in
      And pass it all. I'll pray, and then I'll sleep:
      Poor naked wretches, wheresoe'er you are,
      That 'bide the pelting of this pitiless storm,
      How shall your houseless heads and unfed sides
      Sustain this shock? your raggedness defend you
      From seasons such as these?
      O, I have ta'en too little care of this.
      Take physic, Pomp,
      Expose thyself to feel what wretches feel,
      That thou mayst cast the superflux[51] to them
      And show the heavens more just.

the famous plu law; compassion & sympathy

---

[51] *superflux*, unneeded wealth.

(EDGAR *in the hovel, disguised.*)

EDGAR. Five fathom and a half! poor Tom!

KENT. What art thou that dost grumble there i'the straw?
Come forth.

EDGAR. Away! The foul fiend follows me—through the sharp
hawthorn blows the cold wind. Mum! go to thy bed and
warm thee.
(*aside*) Ha! what do I see?
By all my griefs, the poor old king bareheaded,
And drenched in this foul storm. Professing siren,
Are all your protestations come to this?

LEAR. Tell me, fellow, didst thou give all to thy daughters?

EDGAR. Who gives anything to poor Tom? whom the foul fiend
has led through fire and through flame, through bushes
and bogs, that has laid knives under his pillow, and halters
in his pew,[52] that has made him proud of heart to ride
on a bay-trotting horse over four inched bridges, to
course[53] his own shadow for a traitor.—Bless thy five
wits, Tom's a cold. (*Shivers.*) Bless thee from whirlwinds,
star-blasting[54] and taking.[55] Do poor Tom some charity,
whom the foul fiend vexes.—Sa, sa, there I could have
him now, and there, and there again.

LEAR. Have his daughters brought him to this pass?
Couldst thou save nothing? Didst thou give 'em all?

KENT. He has no daughters, sir.

LEAR. Death, traitor, nothing could have subdued nature
To such a lowness but his unkind daughters.

EDGAR. Pillicock sat upon Pillicock Hill; hallo, hallo, hallo.

LEAR. Is it the fashion that discarded fathers
Should have such little mercy on their flesh?
Judicious punishment, 'twas this flesh begot
Those pelican[56] daughters.

EDGAR. Take heed of the foul fiend, obey thy parents, keep thy
word justly, swear not, commit not with man's sworn
spouse, set not thy sweet heart on proud array. Tom's a
cold.

LEAR. What hast thou been?

EDGAR. A serving-man proud of heart, that curled my hair,

---

52 *knives . . . pew*, inducements to suicide and damnation.
53 *course*, hunt.
54 *star-blasting*, the evils of astrology.
55 *taking*, enchantment.
56 *pelican*, thought to feed its young with its own blood.

used perfume and washes; that served the lust of my mistress's heart, and did the act of darkness with her. Swore as many oaths as I spoke words, and broke 'em all in the sweet face of Heaven. Let not the paint, nor the patch,[57] nor the rushing of silks betray thy poor heart to woman. Keep thy foot out of brothels, thy hand out of plackets,[58] thy pen from creditors' books, and defy the foul fiend—still through the hawthorn blows the cold wind—sess, suum, mun, nonny. Dolphin my boy—hist! the boy, sesey! soft, let him trot by.

LEAR. Death! thou wert better in thy grave than thus to answer with thy uncovered body this extremity of the sky. And yet consider him well, and man's no more than this. Thou art indebted to the worm for no silk, to the beast for no hide, to the cat for no perfume—ha! here's two of us are sophisticated.[59] Thou art the thing itself; unaccommodated man is no more than such a poor bare forked animal as thou art.

Off, off ye vain disguises, empty lendings.

I'll be my original self, quick, quick, uncase me.

KENT. Defend his wits, good Heaven!

LEAR. One point I had forgot; what's your name?

EDGAR. Poor Tom, that eats the swimming frog, the walnut, and the water-nut; that in the fury of his heart when the foul fiend rages eats cow dung for sallets,[60] swallows the old rat and the ditch-dog; that drinks the green mantle of the standing pool; that's whipped from tithing to tithing;[61] that has three suits to his back, six shirts to his body.

> Horse to ride, and weapon to wear,
> But rats and mice, and such small deer[62]
> Have been Tom's food for seven long year.

Beware, my follower; peace, Smulkin; peace, thou foul fiend.

LEAR. One word more, but be sure true council; tell me, is a madman a gentleman, or a yeoman?

KENT. I feared 'twould come to this; his wits are gone.

---

57 *patch*, artificial beauty mark.
58 *plackets*, slit of petticoats.
59 *sophisticated*, corrupted.
60 *sallets*, salads.
61 *tithing*, parish.
62 *deer*, animals.

EDGAR. Fraterreto calls me, and tells me Nero is an angler in the lake of darkness. Pray, innocent, and beware the foul fiend.

LEAR. Right, ha! ha! was it not pleasant to have a thousand with red hot spits come hizzing in upon 'em?

EDGAR (*aside*). My tears begin to take his part so much { empathy
They mar my counterfeiting.

LEAR. The little dogs and all, Trey, Blanch and Sweet-heart, see they bark at me.

EDGAR. Tom will throw his head at 'em; avaunt ye curs.

> Be thy mouth or black or white,
> Tooth that poisons if it bite,
> Mastiff, grey hound, mungrill grim
> Hound or spaniel, brach or hym,[63]
> Bob-tail, tight,[64] or trundle-tail,[65]
> Tom will make 'em weep and wail.
> For with throwing thus my head
> Dogs leap the hatch and all are fled.

Ud, de, de, de. Se, se, se. Come march to wakes, and fairs, and market-towns—poor Tom, thy horn is dry.

LEAR. You sir, I entertain you for one of my hundred, only I do not like the fashion of your garments. You'll say they're Persian, but no matter, let 'em be changed.

(*Enter* GLOSTER.)

EDGAR. This is the foul Flibertigibet. He begins at curfew and walks at first cock; he gives the web and the pin,[66] knits the elf-lock, squints the eye, and makes the hair-lip, mildews the white wheat, and hurts the poor creature of the earth;

> Swithin footed thrice the cold,
> He met the night-mare and her nine-fold,
>   'Twas there he did appoint her;
> He bid her alight and her troth plight,
>   And arroynt[67] the witch, arroynt her.

---

[63] *brach or hym*, bitch or (lym) bloodhound.
[64] *Bob-tail, tight*, should probably read *bobtail tike*, a mongrel with its tail cut off.
[65] *trundle-tail*, long-tailed.
[66] *web and the pin*, cataract.
[67] *arroynt*, avoid.

GLOSTER. What, has Your Grace no better company?

EDGAR. The Prince of Darkness is a gentleman; Modo he is call'd, and Mahu.

GLOSTER. Go with me, sir, hard by I have a tenant. My duty cannot suffer me to obey in all your daughters' hard commands, who have enjoined me to make fast my doors and let this tyrannous night take hold upon you. Yet have I ventured to come seek you out, and bring you where both fire and food is ready.

KENT. Good my lord, take his offer.

LEAR. First let me talk with this philosopher.
Say, Stagirite,[68] what is the cause of thunder?

GLOSTER. Beseech you, sir, go with me.

LEAR. I'll talk a word with this same learned Theban.[69]
What is your study?

EDGAR. How to prevent the fiend, and to kill vermin.

LEAR. Let me ask you a word in private.

KENT. His wits are quite unsettled; good sir, let's force him hence.

GLOSTER. Canst blame him? his daughters seek his death. This bedlam but disturbs him more. Fellow, be gone.

EDGAR. Child Roland to the dark tower came,
His word was still, "Fie, fo, and fum,
I smell the blood of a British man."—Oh, torture! (*Exit.*)

GLOSTER. Now, I prithee, friend, let's take him in our arms, and carry him where he shall meet both welcome and protection.
Good sir, along with us.

LEAR. You say right, let 'em anatomize Regan, see what breeds about her heart; is there any cause in nature for these hard hearts?

KENT. Beseech Your Grace.

LEAR. Hist!—make no noise, make no noise—so, so; we'll to supper i'the morning.   (*Exeunt.*)

[SCENE IV.] *The field*

(*Enter* CORDELIA *and* ARANTE.)

ARANTE. Dear madam, rest ye here, our search is vain.
Look, here's a shed; beseech ye, enter here.

---

68 *Stagirite,* Aristotle, born at Stagira, was often known by that term.
69 *Theban,* i.e., scholar.

CORDELIA. Prithee go in thyself, seek thy own ease;
 Where the mind's free, the body's delicate.
 This tempest but diverts me from the thought
 Of what would hurt me more.

(*Enter* TWO RUFFIANS.)

1 RUFFIAN. We have dogged 'em far enough, this place is
  private.
 I'll keep 'em prisoners here within this hovel
 Whilst you return and bring Lord Edmund hither.
 But help me first to house 'em.
2 RUFFIAN. Nothing but this dear devil (*Shows gold.*)
 Should have drawn me through all this tempest;
 But to our work.

(*They seize* CORDELIA *and* ARANTE, *who shriek out.*)

 Soft, madam, we are friends; dispatch, I say!
CORDELIA. Help, murder, help! gods! some kind thunderbolt
 To strike me dead.

(*Enter* EDGAR.)

EDGAR. What cry was that? Ha, women seized by ruffians?
 Is this a place and time for villainy?
 Avaunt ye bloodhounds.

      (Drives 'em with his quarter-staff.) [70]

BOTH. The devil, the devil!   (*Run off.*)
EDGAR. O speak, what are ye that appear to be
 O'the tender sex, and yet unguarded wander
 Through the dead mazes of this dreadful night,
 Where (tho' at full) the clouded moon scarce darts
 Imperfect glimmerings.
CORDELIA. First say what art thou,
 Our guardian angel, that were pleased t'assume
 That horrid shape to fright the ravishers?
 We'll kneel to thee.
EDGAR. O my tumultuous blood!
 By all my trembling veins, Cordelia's voice!
 'Tis she herself!—My senses sure conform
 To my wild garb, and I am mad indeed.

---

70 *quarter-staff*, stout pole up to eight feet long, tipped with iron. In
common use as a weapon.

CORDELIA. Whate'er thou art, befriend a wretched virgin,
    And if thou canst, direct our weary search.
EDGAR. Who relieves poor Tom, that sleeps on the nettle, with
    the hedge-pig for his pillow?

> Whilst Smug plyed the bellows
> She trucked[71] with her fellows
> The freckled-faced Mab
> Was a blouze[72] and a drab,[73]

Yet Swithin made Oberon jealous.——Oh! torture.
ARANTE. Alack, madam, a poor wandering lunatic.
CORDELIA. And yet his language seemed but now well-
    tempered.
    Speak, friend, to one more wretched than thyself,
    And if thou hast one interval of sense,
    Inform us if thou canst where we may find
    A poor old man, who through this heath has strayed
    The tedious night.——Speak, sawest thou such a one?
EDGAR (aside). The king, her father, whom she's come to seek
    Through all the terrors of this night. O gods!
    That such amazing piety, such tenderness,
    Shou'd yet to me be cruel!——
    Yes, fair one, such a one was lately here,
    And is conveyed by some that came to seek him
    T' a neighboring cottage; but distinctly where,
    I know not.
CORDELIA. Blessings on 'em.
    Let's find him out, Arante, for thou see'st
    We are in Heaven's protection.   (Going off.)
EDGAR. O Cordelia!
CORDELIA. Ha!——Thou knowst my name.
EDGAR. As you did once know Edgar's.
CORDELIA. Edgar!
EDGAR. The poor remains of Edgar: what your scorn
    Has left him.
CORDELIA. Do we wake, Arante?
EDGAR. My father seeks my life, which I preserved
    In hopes of some blessed minute to oblige
    Distressed Cordelia, and the gods have given it;
    That thought alone prevailed with me to take

---

71 *trucked,* bartered, perhaps fornicated.
72 *blouze,* wench.
73 *drab,* whore.

This frantic dress, to make the earth my bed,
With these bare limbs all change of seasons bide,
Noon's scorching heat, and midnight's piercing cold;
To feed on offals, and to drink with herds,
To combat with the winds, and be the sport
Of clowns,[74] or what's more wretched yet, their pity.

ARANTE. Was ever tale so full of misery!

EDGAR. But such a fall as this I grant was due
To my aspiring love, for 'twas presumptuous,
Though not presumptuously pursued;
For well you know I wore my flames concealed,
And silent as the lamps that burn in tombs,
'Till you perceived my grief, with modest grace
Drew for the secret, and then sealed my pardon.

CORDELIA. You had your pardon, nor can you challenge more.

EDGAR. What do I challenge more?
Such vanity agrees not with these rags.
When in my prosperous state, rich Gloster's heir,
You silenced my pretences, and enjoined me
To trouble you upon that theme no more.
Then what reception must love's language find
From these bare limbs and beggar's humble weeds?

CORDELIA. Such as the voice of pardon to a wretch
condemned;
Such as the shouts
Of succouring forces to a town besieged.

EDGAR. Ah! what new method now of cruelty?

CORDELIA. Come to my arms, thou dearest, best of men,
And take the kindest vows that e'er were spoke
By a protesting maid.

EDGAR. Is't possible?

CORDELIA. By the dear vital stream that bathes my heart,
These hallowed rags of thine, and naked virtue,
These abject tassels, these fantastic shreds
(Ridiculous ev'n to the meanest[75] clown)
To me are dearer than the richest pomp
Of purple monarchs.

EDGAR. Generous charming maid,
The gods alone that made, can rate they worth!
This most amazing excellence shall be
Fame's triumph, in succeeding ages, when

74 *clowns*, yokels.
75 *meanest*, poorest.

Thy bright example shall adorn the scene,
    And teach the world perfection.
CORDELIA. Cold and weary,
    We'll rest a while, Arante, on that straw,
    Then forward to find out the poor old king.
EDGAR. Look, I have flint and steel, the implements
    Of wandering lunatics. I'll strike a light,
    And make a fire beneath this shed to dry
    Thy storm-drenched garments, e'er thou lie to rest thee.
    Then fierce and wakeful as th'Hesperian dragon,[76]
    I'll watch beside thee to protect thy sleep;
    Meanwhile, the stars shall dart their kindest beams,
    And angels visit my Cordelia's dreams.   (*Exeunt.*)

[SCENE V.] GLOSTER's *palace*

(*Enter* CORNWALL, REGAN, BASTARD, *Servants.* CORNWALL
with GLOSTER's *letters.*)

DUKE. I will have my revenge ere I depart his house.
    Regan, see here, a plot upon our state;
    'Tis Gloster's character, that has betrayed
    His double trust of subject and of host.
REGAN. Then double be our vengeance; this confirms
    The intelligence that we have now received,
    That he has been this night to seek the king.
    But who, sir, was the kind discoverer?
DUKE. Our eagle, quick to spy, and fierce to seize,
    Our trusty Edmund.
REGAN. 'Twas a noble service.
    O Cornwall, take him to thy deepest trust,
    And wear him as a jewel at thy heart.
BASTARD. Think, sir, how hard a fortune I sustain,
    That makes me thus repent of serving you!   (*Weeps.*)
    O that this treason had not been, or I
    Not the discoverer.
DUKE. Edmund, thou shalt find
    A father in our love, and from this minute
    We call thee Earl of Gloster. But there yet
    Remains another justice to be done,
    And that's to punish this discarded traitor.

---

[76] *Hesperian dragon,* guardian of the golden apples of the Hesperides.

But lest thy tender nature should relent
At his just sufferings, nor brook the sight,
We wish thee to withdraw.

REGAN. The grotto, sir, within the lower grove,

(*To* EDMUND *aside.*)

Has privacy to suit a mourner's thought.

BASTARD. And there I may expect a comforter,
Ha, madam?

REGAN. What may happen, sir, I know not,
But 'twas a friend's advice.   (*Exit* BASTARD.)

DUKE. Bring in the traitor.
   (GLOSTER *brought in.*)
   Bind fast his arms.

GLOSTER. What mean Your Graces?
   You are my guests, pray do me no foul play.

DUKE. Bind him, I say, hard, harder yet.

REGAN. Now, traitor, thou shalt find—

DUKE. Speak, rebel, where hast thou sent the king?
   Whom spite of our decree thou saw'st last night.

GLOSTER. I'm tied to the stake, and I must stand the course.[77]

REGAN. Say where, and why thou hast concealed him.

GLOSTER. Because I would not see thy cruel hands
   Tear out his poor old eyes, nor thy fierce sister
   Carve his anointed flesh; but I shall see
   The swift winged vengeance overtake such children.

DUKE. See't shalt thou never. Slaves, perform your work.
   Out with those treacherous eyes. Dispatch, I say.
   If thou seest vengeance—

GLOSTER. He that will think to live till he be old,
   Give me some help—Oh, cruel, oh! ye gods!

(*They put out his eyes.*)

SERVANT. Hold, hold, my lord, I bar your cruelty.
   I cannot love your safety and give way
   To such a barbarous practice.

DUKE. Ha, my villain.[78]

SERVANT. I have been your servant from my infancy,
   But better service have I never done you
   Than with this boldness—

---

[77] *tied . . . course,* like a bear baited by dogs.
[78] *villain,* serf.

DUKE. Take thy death, slave.
SERVANT. Nay, then revenge whilst yet my blood is warm.

(*Fight.*)

REGAN. Help here—are you not hurt, my lord?
GLOSTER. Edmund, enkindle all the sparks of nature
    To quit[79] this horrid act.
REGAN. Out, treacherous villain,
    Thou call'st on him that hates thee. It was he
    That broached thy treason, showed us thy dispatches;
    There—read, and save the Cambrian[80] prince a labour;
    If thy eyes fail thee call for spectacles.
GLOSTER. O my folly!
    Then Edgar was abused; kind gods, forgive me that.
REGAN. How is't my lord?
DUKE. Turn out that eyeless villain, let him smell
    His way to Cambrai. Throw this slave upon a dunghill.
    Regan, I bleed apace, give me your arm.   (*Exeunt.*)
GLOSTER. All dark and comfortless!
    Where are those various objects that but now
    Employ'd my busy eyes? Where those eyes?
    Dead are their piercing rays that lately shot
    O'er flowery vales to distant sunny hills,
    And drew with joy the vast horizon in.
    These groping hands are now my only guides,
    And feeling all my sight.
    O misery! what words can sound my grief?
    Shut from the living whilst among the living;
    Dark as the grave amidst the bustling world.
    At one from business and from pleasure barred;
    No more to view the beauty of the spring,
    Nor see the face of kindred, or of friend.
    Yet still one way the extremest fate affords,
    And ev'n the blind can find the way to death.
    Must I then tamely die, and unrevenged?
    So Lear may fall: no, with these bleeding rings
    I will present me to the pitying crowd,
    And with the rhetoric of these dropping veins
    Enflame 'em to revenge their king and me.
    Then when the glorious mischief is on wing,

---

[79] *quit*, revenge.
[80] *Cambrian*, i.e., Duke of Cambrai or Wales.

This lumber[81] from some precipice I'll throw,
And dash it on the ragged flint below;
Whence my freed soul to her bright sphere shall fly,
Through boundless orbs, eternal regions spy,
And like the sun, be all one glorious eye.

(*End of the Third Act*)

ACT IV

[SCENE I.] *A grotto*

(EDMUND *and* REGAN *amorously seated, listening to music.*)

BASTARD. Why were those beauties made another's right,
 Which none can prize like me? Charming queen,
 Take all my blooming youth, for ever fold me
 In those soft arms, lull me in endless sleep,
 That I may dream of pleasures too transporting
 For life to bear.
REGAN. Live, live, my Gloster,
 And feel no death but that of swooning joy.
 I yield thee blisses on no harder terms
 Than that thou continue to be happy.
BASTARD. This jealousy is yet more kind, is't possible
 That I should wander from a paradise
 To feed on sickly weeds? Such sweets live here
 That constancy will be no virtue in me.
 And yet must I forthwith go meet her sister,   (*aside.*)
 To whom I must protest as much—
 Suppose it be the same; why, best of all,
 And I have then my lesson ready conned.
REGAN. Wear this remembrance of me—I dare now

(*Gives him a ring.*)

 Absent myself no longer from the duke.
 Whose wound grows dangerous—I hope mortal.
BASTARD. And let this happy image of your Gloster

---

81 *lumber*, i.e., his body.

—lives unnoticed

(*Pulling out a picture* drops *a note.*)

Lodge in that breast where all his treasure lies.   (*Exit.*)

REGAN. To this brave youth a woman's blooming beauties
　　Are due; my fool usurps my bed. What's here?
　　Confusion on my eyes.   (*Reads.*)
　　"Where merit is so transparent, not to behold it were
　　blindness, and not to reward it, ingratitude.

　　　　　　　　　　　　　　　　　　　　Gonerill."

plot turn — Regan learns that she's being two-timed

　　Vexatious accident! Yet fortunate too,
　　My jealousy confirmed, and I am taught
　　To cast[82] for my defence—   (*Enter an* OFFICER.)
　　Now, what mean those shouts? and what thy hasty
　　　　entrance?

OFFICER. A most surprizing and a sudden change.
　　The peasants are all up in mutiny,
　　And only want a chief to lead 'em on
　　To storm your palace.

REGAN. On what provocation?

OFFICER. At last day's[83] public festival, to which
　　The yeomen from all quarters had repaired,
　　Old Gloster, whom you late deprived of sight,
　　(His veins yet streaming fresh) presents himself,
　　Proclaims your cruelty, and their oppression,
　　With the king's injuries; which so enraged 'em
　　That now that mutiny which long had crept
　　Takes wing, and threatens your best powers.

REGAN. White-livered slave!
　　Our forces raised and led by valiant Edmund
　　Shall drive this monster of rebellion back
　　To her dark cell. Young Gloster's arm allays
　　The storm his father's feeble breath did raise.   (*Exit.*)

[SCENE II.] *The field*

(*Enter* EDGAR.)

EDGAR. The lowest and most abject thing of fortune
　　Stands still in hope, and is secure from fear.
　　The lamentable change is from the best,
　　The worst returns to better—who comes here?

(*Enter* GLOSTER, *led by an* OLD MAN.)

---

82 *cast*, scheme.
83 *last day's*, yesterday's.

My father poorly led! deprived of sight!
The precious stones torn from their bleeding rings!
Something I heard of this inhumane deed
But disbelieved it, as an act too horrid
For the hot hell of a cursed woman's fury.
When will the measure of my woes be full?

GLOSTER. Revenge, thou art afoot; success attend thee.
    Well have I sold my eyes, if the event
    proves happy for the injured king.

OLD MAN. O, my good lord, I have been your tenant and your
    father's tenant these fourscore years.

GLOSTER. Away, get thee away, good friend be gone;
    Thy comforts can do me no good at all.
    Thee they may hurt.

OLD MAN. You cannot see your way.

GLOSTER. I have no way, and therefore want no eyes; *Again the*
    I stumbled when I saw. O dear son Edgar, *paradox: see with*
    The food of thy abused father's wrath, *blinding sight.*
    Might I but live to see thee in my touch
    I'd say I had eyes again.

EDGAR. Alas, he's sensible that I was wronged;
    And should I own myself, his tender heart
    Would break betwixt th'extremes of grief and joy.

OLD MAN. How now, who's there?

EDGAR. A charity for poor Tom. Play fair, and defy the foul
    fiend.
    O Gods! and must I still pursue this trade,   *(aside.)*
    Trifling beneath such loads of misery?

OLD MAN. 'Tis poor mad Tom.

GLOSTER. In the late storm I such a fellow saw,
    Which made me think a man a worm.
    Where is the lunatic?

OLD MAN. Here, my lord.

GLOSTER. Get thee now away, if for my sake,
    Thou wilt o'er take us hence a mile or two
    I'the way toward Dover, do't for ancient love,
    And bring some covering for this naked wretch
    Whom I'll entreat to lead me.

OLD MAN. Alack, my lord, he's mad.

GLOSTER. 'Tis the time's plague when madmen lead the blind.
    Do as I bid thee.

OLD MAN. I'll bring him the best 'parrel that I have
    Come on't what will.   *(Exit.)*

GLOSTER. Sirrah, naked fellow.

EDGAR. Poor Tom's a-cold—I cannot fool it longer,
    And yet I must—bless thy sweet eyes, they bleed;
    Believe't poor Tom ev'n weeps his blind to see 'em.

GLOSTER. Know'st thou the way to Dover?

EDGAR. Both stile and gate, horse-way and foot-path, poor Tom
    has been feared out of his good wits; bless every true
    man's son from the foul fiend.

GLOSTER. Here, take this purse; that I am wretched
    Makes thee the happier: Heaven deal so still.
    Thus let the griping usurer's hoard be scattered.
    So distribution shall undo excess.
    And each man have enough. Dost thou know Dover?

EDGAR. Aye, master.

GLOSTER. There is a cliff, whose high and bending head
    Looks dreadfully down on the roaring deep.
    Bring me but to the very brink of it,
    And I'll repair the poverty thou bear'st
    With something rich about me. From that place
    I shall no leading need.

EDGAR. Give me thy arm: poor Tom shall guide thee.

GLOSTER. Soft, for I hear the tread of passengers.

(*Enter* KENT *and* CORDELIA.)

CORDELIA. Ah me! your fear's too true, it was the king.
    I spoke but now with some that met him
    As made as the vexed sea, singing aloud,
    Crowned with rank fumiter and furrow weeds,
    With berries, burdocks, violets, daisies, poppies,
    And all the idle flowers that grow
    In our sustaining corn.[84] Conduct me to him
    To prove[85] my last endeavours to restore him,
    And Heaven so prosper thee.

KENT. I will, good lady.
    Ha, Gloster here! Turn, poor dark man, and hear
    A friend's condolement, who at sight of thine
    Forgets his own distress, thy old true Kent.

GLOSTER. How, Kent? From whence return'd?

KENT. I have not since my banishment been absent,
    But in disguise followed the abandoned king;
    'Twas me thou saw'st with him in the late storm.

[84] *corn*, wheat.
[85] *prove*, test.

GLOSTER. Let me embrace thee. Had I eyes I now
    Should weep for joy, but let this trickling blood
    Suffice instead of tears.

CORDELIA. O misery!
    To whom shall I complain, or in what language?
    Forgive, O wretched man, the piety
    That brought thee to this pass, 'twas I that caused it.
    I cast me at thy feet, and beg of thee
    To crush these weeping eyes to equal darkness,
    If that will give thee any recompence.

EDGAR. Was ever season so distressed as this?   (*aside.*)

GLOSTER. I think Cordelia's voice! Rise, pious princess,
    And take a dark man's blessing.

CORDELIA. O, my Edgar,
    My virtue's now grown guilty, works the bane
    Of those that do befriend me. Heaven forsakes me,
    And when you look that way, it is but just
    That you should hate me too.

EDGAR. O waive this cutting speech, and spare to wound
    A heart that's on the rack.

GLOSTER. No longer cloud thee, Kent, in that disguise.
    There's business for thee and of noblest weight.
    Our injured country is at length in arms,
    Urged by the King's inhuman wrongs and mine,
    And only want a chief to lead 'em on.
    That task be thine.

EDGAR. Brave Britons, then there's life in't yet.   (*aside.*)

KENT. Then have we one cast for our fortune yet.
    Come, princess, I'll bestow you with the king,
    Then on the spur to head these forces.
    Farewell, good Gloster, to our conduct trust.

GLOSTER. And be your cause as prosperous as 'tis just.

                       (*Exeunt.*)

[SCENE III.] GONERILL's *palace*

(*Enter* GONERILL, GENTLEMAN, *Attendants.*)

GONERILL. It was great ignorance Gloster's eyes being out,
    To let him live; where he arrives he moves
    All hearts against us. Edmund I think is gone
    In pity to his misery to dispatch him.

GENTLEMAN. No, madam, he's returned on speedy summons
    Back to your sister.

GONERILL. Ha! I like not that,
    Such speed must have the wings of love. Where's Albany?
GENTLEMAN. Madam, within, but never man so chang'd;
    I told him of the uproar of the peasants,
    He smiled at it; when I informed him
    Of Gloster's treason—
GONERILL. Trouble him no further.
    It is his coward spirit. Back to our sister,
    Hasten her musters, and let her know
    I have given the distaff[86] into my husband's hands.
    That done, with special care deliver these dispatches
    In private to young Gloster.

(*Enter a* MESSENGER.)

MESSENGER. O madam, most unseasonable news,
    The Duke of Cornwall's dead of his late wound
    Whose loss your sister has in part supplied
    Making brave Edmund general of her forces.
GONERILL. One way I like this well;   (*aside.*)
    But being widow, and my Gloster with her,
    May blast the promised harvest of our love.
    A word more, sir: add speed to your journey,
    And if you chance to meet with that blind traitor,
    Preferment falls on him that cuts him off.   (*Exeunt.*)

[SCENE IV.] *The field*

(GLOSTER *and* EDGAR.)

GLOSTER. When shall we come to the top of that same hill?
EDGAR. We climb it now, mark how we labour.
GLOSTER. Methinks the ground is even.
EDGAR. Horrible steep; hark, do you hear the sea?
GLOSTER. No, truly.
EDGAR. Why then your other senses grow imperfect
    By your eyes' anguish.
GLOSTER. So may it be indeed.
    Methinks thy voice is altered, and thou speak'st
    In better phrase and matter than thou did'st.
EDGAR. You are much deceived; in nothing am I altered
    But in my garments.
GLOSTER. Methinks y'are better spoken.

---

[86] *distaff,* staff for spinning flax; women's work.

EDGAR. Come on, sir, here's the place: how fearful
    And dizzy 'tis to cast one's eyes so low.
    The crows and choughs[87] that wing the mid-way air
    Show scarce so big as beetles. Half-way down
    Hangs one that gathers samphire,[88] dreadful trade!
    The fishermen that walk upon the beach
    Appear like mice, and yon tall anchoring barque
    Seems lessened to her cock,[89] her cock a buoy
    Almost too small for sight; the murmuring surge
    Cannot be heard so high. I'll look no more,
    Lest my brain turn, and the disorder make me
    Tumble down headlong.
GLOSTER. Set me where you stand.
EDGAR. You are now within a foot of th'extreme verge.
    For all beneath the moon I would not now
    Leap forward.
GLOSTER. Let go my hand.
    Here, friend, is another purse, in it a jewel
    Well worth a poor man's taking; get thee further,
    Bid me farewell, and let me hear thee going.
EDGAR. Fare you well, sir.—That I do trifle thus
    With this his despair is with design to cure it.
GLOSTER. Thus, mighty Gods, this world I do renounce,
    And in your sight shake my afflictions off;
    If I could bear 'em longer and not fall
    To quarrel with your great opposeless wills,
    My snuff[90] and feebler part of nature should
    Burn itself out. If Edgar live, oh bless him.
    Now, fellow, fare thee well.
EDGAR. Gone, sir! Farewell.
    And yet I know not how conceit[91] may rob
    The treasury of life; had he been where he thought.
    By this had thought been past.—Alive, or dead?
    Hoa sir, friend; hear you, sir, speak—
    Thus might he pass indeed—yet he revives.
    What are you, sir?
GLOSTER. Away, and let me die.
EDGAR. Hadst thou been aught but gosmore,[92] feathers, air,

---

87 *choughs,* jackdaws.
88 *samphire,* aromatic plant used for pickling.
89 *cock,* cockboat or dinghy.
90 *snuff,* used up candle wick.
91 *conceit,* imagination.
92 *gosmore,* gossamer or floating cobwebs.

    Falling so many fathom down
    Thou hadst shivered like an egg; but thou dost breathe,
    Hast heavy substance, bleedst not, speak'st, art sound;
    Thy life's a miracle.
GLOSTER. But have I fallen or no?
EDGAR. From the dread summit of this chalky bourn:[93]
    Look up an height, the shrill-tuned lark so high
    Cannot be seen, or heard. Do but look up.
GLOSTER. Alack, I have no eyes.
    Is wretchedness deprived that benefit
    To end itself by death?
EDGAR. Give me your arm.
    Up so, how is't? Feel you your legs? you stand.
GLOSTER. Too well, too well.
EDGAR. Upon the crown o'the cliff, what thing was that
    Which parted from you?
GLOSTER. A poor unfortunate beggar.
EDGAR. As I stood here below, methought his eyes
    Were two full moons, wide nostrils breathing fire.
    It was some fiend. Therefore thou happy father,
    Think that the all-powerful gods who make them honours
    Of men's impossibilities,[94] have preserved thee.
GLOSTER. 'Tis wonderful; henceforth I'll bear affliction
    Till it expire. The goblin which you speak of,
    I took it for a man: oft-times 'twould say,
    "The fiend, the fiend": he led me to that place.
EDGAR. Bear free and patient thoughts: but who comes here?

(*Enter* LEAR, *a coronet of flowers on his head. Wreaths and garlands about him.*)

LEAR. No, no, they cannot touch me for coining. I am the king himself.
EDGAR. O piercing sight!
LEAR. Nature's above art in that respect. There's your press-money.[95] That fellow handles his bow like a cow-keeper —draw me a clothier's yard.[96] A mouse! a mouse! peace, hoa—there's my gauntlet, I'll prove it on a giant—

93 *this chalky bourn,* i.e., the white cliffs of Dover.
94 *Think that . . . impossibilities,* i.e., the gods compel reverence by miracles.
95 *press-money,* cash paid to a military recruit.
96 *clothier's yard,* length of an arrow.

bring up the brown bills[97]—O well-flown bird—i'the
white, i'the white—hewgh! give the word.

EDGAR. Sweet marjoram.[98]

LEAR. Pass.

GLOSTER. I know that voice.

LEAR. Ha! Gonerill with a white beard! They flattered me
like a dog, and told me I had white hairs on my chin
before the black ones were there; to say "Aye" and
"No" to everything that I said; "Aye" and "No" too was
no good divinity.[99] When the rain came once to wet me,
and the winds to make me chatter; when the thunder
would not peace at my bidding. There I found 'em,
there I smelt 'em out. Go to, they are not men of their
words. They told me I was a king, 'tis a lie. I am not
ague-proof.

GLOSTER. That voice I well remember, is't not the king's?

LEAR. Aye, every inch a king. When I do stare
See how the subject quakes.
I pardon that man's life; what was the cause?
Adultery? Thou shalt not die. Die for adultery!
The wren goes to't, and the small gilded fly
Engenders in my sight: let copulation thrive,
For Gloster's bastard son was kinder to his father
Than were my daughters got i'the lawful bed.
To't luxury,[100] pell-mell, for I lack soldiers.

GLOSTER. Not all my sorrows past so deep have touched me,
As these sad accents: sight were now a torment—

LEAR. Behold that simpering lady, she that starts
At pleasure's name, and thinks her ear profaned
With the least wanton word; would you believe it.
The fitchew[101] nor the pampered steed goes to't
With such a riotous appetite: down from the waist they
are centaurs, tho women all above; but to the girdle do
the Gods inherit, beneath all is the fiends; there's Hell,
there's darkness, the sulphorous unfathomed—fie! fie!
pah!—an ounce of civet, good apothecary, to sweeten my
imagination—there's money for thee.

---

97 *brown bills*, pikes or edged weapons set on the end of long staffs.
98 *Sweet marjoram*, Edgar invokes the herb used to treat madness.
99 *to say . . . good divinity*, i.e., he was constantly humored. But the
Bible (James 5:12) says, "Let your yea be yea, and your nay, nay."
100 *luxury*, lust.
101 *fitchew*, polecat.

GLOSTER. Let me kiss that hand.

LEAR. Let me wipe it first; it smells of mortality.

GLOSTER. Speak, sir; do you know me?

LEAR. I remember thy eyes well enough; nay, do thy worst,
blind Cupid, I'll not love—read me this challenge, mark
but the penning of it.

GLOSTER. Were all the letters suns, I could not see.

EDGAR. I would not take this from report. Wretched Cordelia,
    What will thy virtue do when thou shalt find
    This fresh affliction added to the tale
    Of thy unparalleled griefs.

LEAR. Read.

GLOSTER. What? with this case of eyes?

LEAR. O ho! are you there with me? No eyes in your head,
and no money in your purse? Yet you see how this
world goes.

GLOSTER. I see it feelingly.

LEAR. What? art mad? A man may see how this world goes
with no eyes. Look with thy ears, see how yon justice
rails on that simple thief; shake 'em together, and the
first that drops, be it thief or justice, is a villain.—Thou
has seen a farmer's dog bark at a beggar.

GLOSTER. Aye, sir.

LEAR. And the man ran from the cur; there thou mightst
behold the great image of authority. A dog's obeyed
in office. Thou rascal, beadle, hold thy bloody hand.
Why dost thou lash that strumpet? Thou hotly lust'st
to enjoy her in that kind for which thou whip'st her;
do, do, the judge that sentenced her has been beforehand with thee.

GLOSTER. How stiff is my vile sense that yields not yet!

LEAR. I tell thee the usurer hangs the cozener;[102] through
tattered robes small vices do appear, robes and fur gowns
hide all. Place sins with gold—why there 'tis for thee, my
friend, make much of it, it has the power to seal the
accuser's lips. Get thee glass eyes, and like a scurvy
politician, seem to see the things thou dost not. Pull, pull
off my boots; hard, harder, so, so.

GLOSTER. O matter and impertinency[103] mixed!
    Reason in madness.

---

[102] *cozener*, cheat.
[103] *matter and impertinency*, substance and incoherence.

LEAR. If thou wilt weep my fortunes, take my eyes,
I know thee well enough, thy name is Gloster.
Thou must be patient, we came crying hither—
Thou knowest, the first time that we taste the air
We wail and cry—I'll preach to thee. Mark.

EDGAR. Break, laboring heart.

LEAR. When we are born we cry that we are come
To this great stage of fools.—

(*Enter two or three* GENTLEMEN.)

GENTLEMEN. O, here he is; lay hand upon him, sir,
Your dearest daughter sends—

LEAR. No rescue? what, a prisoner? I am even the natural fool
of Fortune; use me well, you shall have ransom. Let me
have surgeons; oh, I am cut to the brains.

GENTLEMAN. You shall have anything.

LEAR. No seconds? All myself? I will die bravely like a smug
bridegroom, flushed and pampered as a priest's whore.
I am a king, my masters, know ye that?

GENTLEMAN. You are a royal one, and we obey you.

LEAR. It were an excellent stratagem to shoe a troop of horse
with felt. I'll put in proof[104]—no noise, no noise—now
will we steal upon these sons-in-law, and then—kill, kill,
kill!   (*Exit running.*)

GLOSTER. A sight more moving in the meanest wretch,
Past speaking in a king. Now, good sir, what are you?

EDGAR. A most poor man made tame to Fortune's strokes,
And prone to pity by experienced sorrows;
Give me your hand.

GLOSTER. You ever-gentle gods, take my breath from me,
And let not my ill genius tempt me more
To die before you please.

(*Enter* GONERILL's GENTLEMAN-USHER.)

GENTLEMAN. A proclaimed prize! O most happily met,
That eyeless head of thine was first framed flesh
To raise my fortunes. Thou old unhappy traitor,
The sword is out that must destroy thee.

GLOSTER. Now let thy friendly hand put strength enough to't.

GENTLEMAN. Wherefore, bold peasant,
Dar'st thou support a published traitor? Hence,
Lest I destroy thee too. Let go his arm.

[104] *put in proof*, test it.

EDGAR. Chill not let go, zir, without vurther 'casion.

GENTLEMAN. Let go, slave, or thou diest!

EDGAR. Good gentleman, go your gait, and let poor volk pass; and 'chu'd ha' bin zwagger'd out of my life it wou'd not a bin zo long as 'tis by a vortnight—Nay, an'thou com'st near th'old man, I'ce try whether your costard[105] or my ballow[106] be the harder.

GENTLEMAN. Out, dunghill.

EDGAR. Chill pick your teeth, zir; come, no matter vor your voines.[107]   *(Fight.)*

GENTLEMAN. Slave, thou hast slain me; oh untimely death.

EDGAR. I know thee well, a serviceable villain,
    As duteous to the vices of thy mistress
    As lust could wish.

GLOSTER. What, is he dead?

EDGAR. Sit you, sir, and rest you.
    This is a letter carrier, and may have
    Some papers of intelligence that may stand
    Our party in good stead to know—what's here?
        (Takes a letter out of his pocket, opens, and reads.)
    "To Edmund, Earl of Gloster.
    Let our mutual loves be remembered. You have many opportunities to cut him off. If he return the conqueror then I am still a prisoner, and his bed my jail, from the loathed warmth of which deliver me, and supply the place for your labour.

                        Gonerill."

    A plot upon her husband's life,
    And the exchange my brother! Here i'the sands
    I'll rake thee up, thou messenger of lust.
    Grieved only that thou hadst no other deathsman.
    In time and place convenient I'll produce
    These letters to the sight of the injured duke.
    As best shall serve our purpose. Come, your hand.
    Far off methinks I hear the beaten drum,
    Come, sir, I will bestow you with a friend   *(Exeunt.)*

[SCENE V.] *A chamber*

(LEAR asleep on a couch; CORDELIA, PHYSICIAN, Gentlemen and Attendants standing by him.)

---

[105] *costard,* head.
[106] *ballow,* cudgel.
[107] *voines,* sword-thrusts.

CORDELIA. His sleep is sound, and may have good effect
　　To cure his jarring senses, and repair
　　This breach of nature.

PHYSICIAN. We have employed the utmost power of art,
　　And this deep rest will perfect our design.

CORDELIA. O Regan, Gonerill, inhuman sisters,
　　Had he not been your father, these white hairs
　　Had challenged sure some pity. Was this a face
　　To be exposed against the jarring winds?
　　My enemy's dog, though he had bit me, should
　　Have stood that night against my fire.—He wakes,
　　Speak to him.

GENTLEMAN. Madam, do you, 'tis fittest.

CORDELIA. How does my royal lord? How fares Your Majesty?

LEAR. You do me wrong to take me out o'the grave.
　　Ha! is this too a world of cruelty?
　　I know my privilege, think not that I will
　　Be used still like a wretched mortal; no,
　　No more of that.

CORDELIA. Speak to me, sir, who am I?

LEAR. You are a soul in bliss, but I am bound
　　Upon a wheel of fire, which my own tears
　　Do scald like molten lead.

CORDELIA. Sir, do you know me?

LEAR. You are a spirit, I know; where did you die?

CORDELIA. Still, still, far wide.

PHYSICIAN. Madam, he's scarce awake; he'll soon grow more
　　composed.

LEAR. Where have I been? Where am I? Fair daylight!
　　I am mightily abused, I should even die with pity
　　To see another thus. I will not swear
　　These are my hands.

CORDELIA. O look upon me, sir,
　　And hold your hands in blessing o'er me; nay,
　　You must not kneel.

LEAR. Pray do not mock me.
　　I am a very foolish, fond old man,
　　Fourscore and upward, and to deal plainly with you,
　　I fear I am not in my perfect mind.

CORDELIA. Nay then, farewell to patience; witness for me
　　Ye mighty powers, I ne'er complained till now!

LEAR. Methinks I should know you, and know this man,
　　Yet I am doubtful, for I am mainly ignorant
　　What place this is, and all the skill I have

Remembers not these garments, nor do I know
Where I did sleep last night—pray do not mock me—
For, as I am a man, I think that lady
To be my child Cordelia.

CORDELIA. O my dear, dear father!

LEAR. Be your tears wet? Yes, faith; pray do not weep.
I know I have given thee cause, and am so humbled
With crosses[108] since, that I could ask
Forgiveness of thee were it possible
That thou couldst grant it, but I'm well assur'd
Thou canst not; therefore I do stand thy justice.
If thou hast poison for me I will drink it,
Bless thee and die.

CORDELIA. O pity, sir, a bleeding heart, and cease
This killing language.

LEAR. Tell me, friends, where am I?

GENTLEMAN. In your own kingdom, sir.

LEAR. Do not abuse me.

GENTLEMAN. Be comforted, good madam, for the violence
Of his distemper's past. We'll lead him in,
Nor trouble him, till he is better setled.
Wilt please you sir, walk into freer air?

LEAR. You must bear with me, I am old and foolish

They lead him off.

CORDELIA. The gods restore you—hark, I hear afar
The beaten drum, old Kent's a man of's word.
O for an arm
Like the fierce thunderer's, when the earth-born sons
Stormed Heaven,[109] to fight this injured father's battle.
That I could shift my sex, and dye me deep
In his opposer's blood. But as I may
With women's weapons, piety and prayers,
I'll aid his cause—you never-erring Gods
Fight on his side, and thunder on his foes
Such tempest as his poor aged head sustained;
Your image suffers when a monarch bleeds;
'Tis your own cause, for that your succours bring,
Revenge your selves, and right an injured king.

(*End of the Fourth Act*)

---

[108] *crosses*, afflictions.
[109] *Like . . . Heaven*, like the revolt of the Titans against the gods in
Greek mythology.

ACT V

[SCENE I.] *A camp*

(*Enter* GONERILL *and Attendants.*)

GONERILL. Our sister's powers already are arrived,
And she herself has promised to prevent[110]
The night with her approach. Have you provided
The banquet I bespoke for her reception
At my tent?
ATTENDANT. So please Your Grace, we have.
GONERILL. But thou, my poisoner, must prepare the bowl
That crowns this banquet. When our mirth is high,
The trumpets sounding and the flutes replying,
Then is the time to give this fatal draught
To this imperious sister. If then our arms succeed,
Edmund, more dear than victory, is mine.
But if defeat or death itself attend me,
'Twill charm my ghost to think I've left behind me
No happy rival. (*Trumpet.*) Hark, she comes. (*Exeunt.*)

[SCENE II.] *The camp*

(*Enter* BASTARD *in his tent.*)

BASTARD. To both these sisters have I sworn my love,
Each jealous of the other, as the stung
Are of the adder. Neither can be held
If both remain alive. Where shall I fix?
Cornwall is dead, and Regan's empty bed
Seems cast by fortune for me, but already
I have enjoyed her, and bright Gonerill
With equal charms brings dear variety,
And yet untasted beauty. I will use
Her husband's countenance[111] for the battle, then
Usurp at once his bed and throne.

(*Enter* OFFICERS.)

My trusty scouts, y'are well returned; have ye descried
The strength and posture of the enemy?

---

110 *prevent,* anticipate.
111 *countenance,* recognition, possibly trust.

OFFICERS. We have, and were surprised to find
    The banished Kent returned, and at their head;
    Your brother Edgar on the rear; old Gloster
    (A moving spectacle) led through their ranks,
    Whose powerful tongue, and more prevailing wrongs,
    Have so enraged their rustic spirits that with
    The approaching dawn we must expect their battle.
BASTARD. You bring a welcome hearing. Each to his charge.
    Line well your ranks and stand on your award.[112]
    Tonight repose you, and i'the morn we'll give
    The sun a sight that shall be worth his rising. (*Exeunt.*)

       [SCENE III.] *A valley near the camp*

  (*Enter* EDGAR *and* GLOSTER.)

EDGAR. Here, sir, take you the shadow of this tree
    For your good host: pray that the right may thrive.
    If ever I return to you again
    I'll bring you comfort. | (*Exit.*)
GLOSTER. Thanks, friendly sir;
    The fortune your good cause deserves betide you.

    (*An alarum, after which* Gloster *speaks.*)

    The fight grows hot; the whole war's now at work,
    And the gored battle bleeds in every vein
    Whilst drums and trumpets drown loud slaughter's roar.
    Where's Gloster now, that used to head the fray,
    And scour the ranks where deadliest danger lay?
    Here like a shepherd in a lonely shade,
    Idle, unarmed, and listening to the fight.
    Yet the disabled courser, maimed and blind,
    When to his stall he hears the rattling war,
    Foaming with rage tears up the battered ground,
    And tugs for liberty.
    No more of shelter, thou blind worm, but forth
    To the open field: the war may come this way
    And crush thee into rest. Here lay thee down
    And tear the earth, that work befits a mole.
    O dark despair! When, Edgar, wilt thou come
    To pardon and dismiss me to the grave!

                (*A retreat sounded.*)

    Hark! a retreat. The king has lost or won.

            (*Re-enter* EDGAR, *bloody.*)

[112] *stand on your award,* follow your orders.

EDGAR. Away, old man, give me your hand, away!
    King Lear has lost, he and his daughter ta'en.
    And this, ye gods, is all that I can save
    Of this most precious wreck! Give me your hand.
GLOSTER. No farther, sir, a man may rot even here.
EDGAR. What? In ill thoughts again? Men must endure
    Their going hence ev'n as their coming hither.
GLOSTER. And that's true too.   (*Exeunt.*)

[SCENE IV.] *The battlefield*

(*Flourish. Enter in conquest,* ALBANY, GONERILL, REGAN, BASTARD. LEAR, KENT *and* CORDELIA *as prisoners.*)

ALBANY. It is enough to have conquered; cruelty
    Should ne'er survive the fight. Captain o'the guards,
    Treat well our royal prisoners till you have
    Our further orders, as you hold our pleasure.
GONERILL (*to the* CAPTAIN, *aside*). Hark, sir, not as you hold
      our husband's pleasure
    But as you hold your life, dispatch your prisoners.
    Our empire can have no sure settlement
    But in their death; the earth that covers them
    Binds fast our throne. Let me hear they are dead.
CAPTAIN. I shall obey your orders.
BASTARD. Sir, I approve it safest to pronounce
    Sentence of death upon this wretched king,
    Whose age has charms in it, his title more,
    To draw the commons once more to his side.
    'Twere best prevent—
ALBANY. Sir, by your favour,
    I hold you but a subject of this war,
    Not as a brother.
REGAN. That's as we list to grace him.
    Have you forgot that he did lead our powers?
    Bore the commission of our place and person?
    And that authority may well stand up
    And call itself your brother.
GONERILL. Not so hot,
    In his own merits he exalts himself
    More than in your addition.[113]

(*Enter* EDGAR, *disguised.*)

[113] *addition*, summary of accomplishments.

ALBANY. What art thou?

EDGAR. Pardon me, sir, that I presume to stop
 A prince and conqueror. Yet ere you triumph,
 Give ear to what a stranger can deliver
 Of what concerns you more than triumph can.
 I do impeach your general there of treason,
 Lord Edmund, that usurps the name of Gloster.
 Of foulest practice 'gainst your life and honour;
 This charge is true, and wretched though I seem
 I can produce a champion that will prove
 In single combat what I do avouch,[114]
 If Edmund dares but trust his cause and sword.

BASTARD. What will not Edmund dare! My lord, I beg
 The favour that you'd instantly appoint
 The place where I may meet this challenger,
 Whom I will sacrifice to my wronged fame.
 Remember, sir, that injured honour's nice[115]
 And cannot brook delay.

ALBANY. Anon, before our tent, i' the army's view,
 There let the herald cry.

EDGAR. I thank Your Highness in my champion's name,
 He'll wait your trumpet's call.

ALBANY. Lead.   (*Exeunt.*)

(*Manent,* LEAR, KENT, CORDELIA *guarded*)

LEAR. O Kent, Cordelia!
 You are the only pair that I e'er wronged,
 And the just gods have made you witnesses
 Of my disgrace, the very shame of Fortune;
 To see me chained and shackled at these years!
 Yet were you but spectators of my woes,
 Not fellow-sufferers, all were well!

CORDELIA. This language, sir, adds yet to our affliction.

LEAR. Thou, Kent, didst head the troops that fought my battle,
 Exposed thy life and fortunes for a master
 That had (as I remember) banished thee.

KENT. Pardon me, sir, that once I broke your orders:
 Banished by you, I kept me here disguised
 To watch your fortunes, and protect your person.
 You know you entertained a rough blunt fellow,
 One Cajus, and you thought he did you service.

---

[114] *avouch,* avow.
[115] *nice,* sensitive.

LEAR. My trusty Cajus, I have lost him too!   *Weeps.*
    'Twas a rough honesty.
KENT. I was that Cajus,
    Disguised in that coarse dress to follow yōu.
LEAR. My Cajus too! wert thou my trusty Cajus?
    Enough, enough—
CORDELIA. Ah me, he faints! his blood forsakes his cheek,
    Help, Kent—
LEAR. No, no they shall not see us weep.
    We'll see them rot first—guards, lead away to prison!
    Come, Kent; Cordelia come
    We two will sit alone, like birds i'the cage.
    When thou dost ask me blessing, I'll kneel down
    And ask of thee forgiveness. Thus we'll live,
    And pray, and sing, and tell old tales, and laugh
    At gilded butterflies; hear sycophants
    Talk of court news, and we'll talk with them too:
    Who loses, and who wins, who's in, who's out.
    And take upon us the mystery of things
    As if we were Heaven's spies.
CORDELIA. Upon such sacrifices
    The gods themselves throw incense.
LEAR. Have I caught ye?
    He that parts us must bring a brand from Heaven.
    Together we'll out-toil the spite of Hell,
    And die the wonders of the world. Away.

                           (*Exeunt, guarded.*)

[SCENE V.] *The camp*

(*Flourish: Enter before the tents,* ALBANY, GONERILL, REGAN, BASTARD, *Guards and Attendants;* GONERILL *speaking apart to the* CAPTAIN OF THE GUARDS *entering.*)

GONERILL. Here's gold for thee. Thou knowest our late
    command
    Upon your prisoners' lives; about it straight, and at
    Our ev'ning banquet let it raise our mirth
    To hear that they are dead.
CAPTAIN. I shall not fail your order   (*Exit.*)
           (ALBANY, GONERILL, REGAN *take their seats.*)
ALBANY. Now, Gloster, trust to thy single virtue, for thy
    soldiers,

All levied in my name, have in my name
Took their discharge. Now let our trumpets speak.
And, herald, read out this.

HERALD. "If any man of quality, within the lists of the army
will maintain upon Edmund, supposed Earl of Gloster,
that he is a manifold traitour, let him appear by the third
sound of the trumpet. He is bold in his defence. (*First
trumpet.*) Again. (*Second trumpet.*) Again." (*Third
trumpet. Trumpet answers from within. Enter* EDGAR,
armed.)

ALBANY. Lord Edgar!

BASTARD. Ha! my brother!
This is the only combatant that I could fear,
For in my breast guilt duels on his side.
But, Conscience, what have I to do with thee?
Awe thou thy dull legitimate slaves, but I
Was born a libertine,[116] and so I keep me.

EDGAR. My noble prince, a word—e'er we engage
Into Your Highness's hands I give this paper.
It will the truth of my impeachment prove
Whatever be my fortune in the fight.

ALBANY. We shall peruse it.

EDGAR. Now, Edmund, draw thy sword,
That if my speech has wrong'd a noble heart,
Thy arm may do thee justice. Here i'the presence
Of this high prince, these queens, and this crowned list,
I brand thee with the spotted name of traitor,
False to thy gods, thy father and thy brother,
And what is more, thy friend; false to this prince.
If then thou shar'st a spark of Gloster's virtue,
Acquit thyself, or if thou shar'st his courage,
Meet this defiance bravely.

BASTARD. And dares Edgar,
The beaten, routed Edgar, brave his conqueror?
From all thy troops and thee I forced the field.
Thou has lost the general stake; and art thou now
Come with thy petty single stock to play
This after-game?

EDGAR. Half-blooded man,
Thy father's sin first, then his punishment;
The dark and vicious place where he begot thee

---

[116] *libertine,* without moral values.

Cost him his eyes. From thy licentious mother
Thou draw'st thy villainy; but for thy part
Of Gloster's blood, I hold thee worth my sword.

BASTARD. Thou bear'st thee on thy mother's piety,
Which I despise. Thy mother being chaste
Thou art assur'd thou art but Gloster's son.
But mine, disdaining constancy, leaves me
To hope that I am sprung from nobler blood,
And possibly a king might be my sire.
But be my birth's uncertain chance as 'twill,
Who 'twas that had the hit to father me
I know not; 'tis enough that I am I.
Of this one thing I'm certain—that I have
A daring soul, and so have at thy heart.
Sound, trumpet.   (*Fight,* BASTARD *falls.*)

GONERILL and REGAN. Save him, save him.

GONERILL. This was practice,[117] Gloster.
Thou won'st the field, and wast not bound to fight
A vanquished enemy. Thou are not conquered
But cozened and betrayed.

ALBANY. Shut your mouth, lady,
Or with this paper I shall stop it—hold, sir.
Thou worse than any name, read thy own evil:
No tearing, lady, I perceive you know it.

GONERILL. Say if I do, who shall arraign me for't?
The laws are mine, not thine.

ALBANY. Most monstrous! Ha, thou know'st it too?

BASTARD. Ask me not what I know,
I have not breath to answer idle questions.

ALBANY. I have resolved—your right, brave sir, has conquer'd

(*To* EDGAR.)

Along with me, I must consult your father.

(*Exeunt* ALBANY *and* EDGAR.)

REGAN. Help every hand to save a noble life;
My half o'the kingdom for a man of skill
To stop this precious stream.

BASTARD. Away ye empirics,[118]
Torment me not with your vain offices;

117 *practice,* deceit.
118 *empirics,* quack doctors.

The sword has pierced too far. Legitimacy
At last has got it.

REGAN. The pride of nature dies.

GONERILL. Away, the minutes are too precious,
Disturb us not with thy impertinent sorrow.

REGAN. Art thou my rival then professed?

GONERILL. Why, was our love a secret? Could there be
Beauty like mine, and gallantry like his
And not a mutual love? Just Nature then
Had erred. Behold that copy of perfection,
That youth whose story will have no foul page
But where it says he stooped to Regan's arms,
Which yet was but compliance, not affection;
A charity to begging, ruined beauty!

REGAN. Who begged when Gonerill writ that? Expose it.

(Throws her a letter.)

And let it be your army's mirth, as 'twas
This charming youth's and mine, when in the bower
He breathed the warmest ecstasies of love,
Then, panting on my breast, cry'd "Matchless Regan!
That Gonerill and thou should e'er be kin!"

GONERILL. Die, Circe, for thy charms are at an end!
Expire before my face, and let me see
How well that boasted beauty will become
Congealing blood and death's convulsive pangs.
Die and be hushed, for at my tent last night
Thou drank'st thy bane, amidst thy reveling bowls.
Ha! dost thou smile? Is then thy death thy sport?
Or has the trusty potion made thee mad?

REGAN. Thou com'st as short of me in thy revenge
As in my Gloster's love. My jealousie
Inspir'd me to prevent thy feeble malice
And poison thee at thy own banquet.

GONERILL. Ha!

BASTARD. No more, my queens, of this untimely strife.
You both deserved my love and both possessed it.
Come soldiers, bear me in; and let
Your royal presence grace my last minutes.
Now, Edgar, thy proud conquest I forgive.
Who would not choose, like me, to yield his breath
T'have rival queens contend for him in death?   *(Exeunt.)*

[SCENE VI.] *A prison*

(LEAR *asleep, with his head on* CORDELIA's *lap.*)

CORDELIA. What toils, thou wretched king, hast thou endured
    To make thee draw, in chains, a sleep so sound?
    Thy better angel charm thy ravished mind
    With fancied freedom. Peace is used to lodge
    On cottage straw; thou hast the beggar's bed,
    Therefore shou'dst have the beggar's careless thought.
    And now, my Edgar, I remember thee.
    What fate has seized thee in this general wreck
    I know not, but I know thou must be wretched
    Because Cordelia holds thee dear.
    O gods! a suddain gloom o'erwhelms me, and the image
    Of death o'erspreads the place. Ha! who are these?

(*Enter* CAPTAIN *and* OFFICERS *with cords.*)

CAPTAIN. Now, sir, dispatch, already you are paid
    In part, the best of your reward's to come.

LEAR. Charge, charge upon their flank, their last wing halts;
    Push, push the battle, and the day's our own.
    Their ranks are broke, down, down with Albany.
    Who holds my hands? O thou deceiving sleep,
    I was this very minute on the chase;
    And now a prisoner here. What mean the slaves?
    You will not murder me?

CORDELIA. Help earth and Heaven!
    For your souls' sakes, dear sirs, and for the gods!

OFFICER. No tears, good lady, no pleading against gold and
    preferment. Come, sirs, make ready your cords.

CORDELIA. You, sir, I'll seize,
    You have a human form, and if no prayers
    Can touch your soul to spare a poor king's life,
    If there be anything that you hold dear,
    By that I beg you to dispatch me first.

CAPTAIN. Comply with her request, dispatch her first.

LEAR. Off, Hell-hounds, by the Gods I charge you spare her!
    Tis my Cordelia, my true pious daughter.
    No pity? Nay then, take an old man's vengeance.

(*Snatches a partizan,*[119] *and strikes down two of them; the
rest quit* CORDELIA, *and turn upon him. Enter* EDGAR *and*
ALBANY.)

[119] *partizan,* spear.

EDGAR. Death! Hell! Ye vultures, hold your impious hands,
    Or take a speedier death than you would give.
CAPTAIN. By whose command?
EDGAR. Behold the duke, your lord.
ALBANY. Guards, seize those instruments of cruelty.
CORDELIA. My Edgar, oh!
EDGAR. My dear Cordelia! Lucky was the minute
    Of our approach. The gods have weighed our sufferings;
    We're past the fire, and now must shine to ages.
GENTLEMAN. Look here, my lord, see where the generous[120]
    king
    Has slain two of 'em.
LEAR. Did I not, fellow?
    I've seen the day, with my good biting falchion[121]
    I could have made 'em skip. I am old now,
    And these vile crosses spoil me. Out of breath!
    Fie, oh! Quite out of breath and spent.
ALBANY. Bring in old Kent; and Edgar, guide you hither
    Your father, whom you said was near.   (*Exit* EDGAR.)
    He may be an ear-witness at the least
    Of our proceedings.
  (KENT *brought in here.*)
LEAR. Who are you?
    My eyes are none o' the best, I'll tell you straight.
    Oh, Albany! Well, sir, we are your captives,
    And you are come to see death pass upon us.
    Why this delay? Or is't Your Highness' pleasure
    To give us first the torture? Say ye so?
    Why here's old Kent and I, as tough a pair
    As e'er bore tyrant's stroke. But my Cordelia,
    My poor Cordelia here, O pity!
ALBANY. Take off their chains. Thou injured majesty,
    The wheel of Fortune now has made her circle,
    And blessings yet stand 'twixt thy grave and thee.
LEAR. Comest thou, inhuman lord, to sooth us back
    To a fool's paradise of hope, to make
    Our doom more wretched? Go to, we are too well
    Acquainted with misfortune to be gulled
    With lying hope. No, we will hope no more.
ALBANY. I have a tale t'unfold so full of wonder

[120] *generous*, courageous.
[121] *falchion*, sword.

As cannot meet an easy faith;
But by that royal injured head 'tis true.

KENT. What would Your Highness?

ALBANY. Know, the noble Edgar
Impeached Lord Edmund since the fight, of treason,
And dared him for the proof to single combat,
In which the gods confirmed his charge by conquest.
I left ev'n now the traitor wounded mortally.

LEAR. And whither tends this story?

ALBANY. Ere they fought
Lord Edgar gave into my hands this paper,
A blacker scroll of treason, and of lust,
Than can be found in the records of Hell.
There, sacred sir, behold the character
Of Gonerill, the worst of daughters, but
More vicious wife.

CORDELIA. Could there be yet addition to their guilt?
What will not they that wrong a father do?

ALBANY. Since then my injuries, Lear, fall in with thine;
I have resolved the same redress for both.

KENT. What says my lord?

CORDELIA. Speak, for methought I heard
The charming voice of a descending god.

ALBANY. The troops by Edmund raised, I have disbanded.
Those that remain are under my command.
What comfort may be brought to cheer your age
And heal your savage wrongs, shall be applied;
For to your majesty we do resign
Your kingdom, save what part yourself conferred
On us in marriage.

KENT. Hear you that, my liege?

CORDELIA. Then there are gods, and virtue is their care. *important statement*

LEAR. Is't possible?
Let the spheres stop their course, the sun make halt,
The winds be hushed, the seas and fountains rest;
All nature pause, and listen to the change.
Where is my Kent, my Cajus?

KENT. Here, my liege.

LEAR. Why I have news that will recall thy youth.
Ha! didst thou hear't, or did the inspiring gods
Whisper to me alone? Old Lear shall be
A king again.

KENT. The prince, that like a god has power, has said it.
LEAR. Cordelia then shall be a queen, mark that:
    Cordelia shall be queen. Winds, catch the sound
    And bear it on your rosy wings to Heaven.
    Cordelia is a queen.
    (*Re-enter* EDGAR *with* GLOSTER.)
ALBANY. Look, sir, where pious Edgar comes
    Leading his eyeless father. O my liege!
    His wondrous story will deserve your leisure:
    What he has done and suffered for your sake,
    What for the fair Cordelia's.
GLOSTER. Where is my liege? Conduct me to his knees to hail
    His second birth of empire. My dear Edgar
    Has, with himself, revealed the king's blest restoration.
LEAR. My poor dark Gloster.
GLOSTER. O let me kiss that once-more sceptered hand!
LEAR. Hold, thou mistakest the majesty, kneel here.
    Cordelia has our power, Cordelia's queen.
    Speak, is not that the noble suffering Edgar?
GLOSTER. My pious son, more dear than my lost eyes.
LEAR. I wronged him too, but here's the fair amends.
EDGAR. Your leave, my liege, for an unwelcome message:
    Edmund (but that's a trifle) is expired.
    What more will touch you, your imperious daughters
    Gonerill and haughty Regan, both are dead.
    Each by the other poisoned at a banquet.
    This, dying, they confessed.
CORDELIA. O fatal period of ill-governed life!
LEAR. Ingrateful as they were, my heart feels yet
    A pang of nature for their wretched fall.
    But, Edgar, I defer thy joys too long.
    Thou servedst distressed Cordelia; take her crowned,
    Th'imperial grace fresh blooming on her brow.
    Nay, Gloster, thou hast here a father's right,
    Thy helping hand t'heap blessings on their heads.
KENT. Old Kent throws in his hearty wishes too.
EDGAR. The gods and you too largely recompense
    What I have done; the sight strikes merit dumb.
CORDELIA. Nor do I blush to own myself o'erpaid
    For all my sufferings past.
GLOSTER. Now, gentle gods, give Gloster his discharge.
LEAR. No, Gloster, thou hast business yet for life.
    Thou, Kent and I, retired to some cool cell,

Will gently pass our short reserves of time
In calm reflections on our fortunes past.
Cheered with relation of the prosperous reign
Of this celestial pair. Thus our remains[122]
Shall in an even course of thought be past,
Enjoy the present hour, nor fear the last.

EDGAR. Our drooping country now erects her head,
Peace spreads her balmy wings, and Plenty blooms.
Divine Cordelia, all the gods can witness
How much thy love to empire I prefer!
Thy bright example shall convince the world
(Whatever storms of Fortune are decreed)
That truth and virtue shall at last succeed.

Edgar rejects Empire for Love.   (*Exeunt omnes.*)

(Finis)

---

[122] *remains,* last days.

EPILOGUE

Inconstancy, the reigning sin o'th' age,
Will scarce endure true lovers on the stage;
You hardly ev'n in plays with such dispense,
And poets kill 'em in their own defence.
Yet one bold proof I was resolved to give,
That I could three hours constancy out-live.
You fear, perhaps, whilst on the stage w'are made
Such saints, we shall indeed take up the trade;
Sometimes we threaten—but our virtue may
For truth I fear with your pit-valor[123] weigh:
For (not to flatter either) I much doubt
When we are off the stage, and you are out,
We are not quite so coy, nor you so stout.
We talk of nunneries—but to be sincere
Whoever lives to see us cloistered there,
May hope to meet our critics at Tangier.
For shame give over this inglorious trade
Of worrying poets, and go maul the Alcade.[124]
Well—since y'are all for blustering in the pit
This play's reviver humbly does admit
Your absolute power to damn his part of it;
But still so many master-touches shine
Of that vast hand that first laid this design,
That in great Shakespeare's right, he's bold to say
If you like nothing you have seen today
The play your judgment damns, not you the play.

[123] *pit-valor*, false courage of critics in the audience.
[124] *Alcade*, Alcalde or Mayor (Spanish).

VENICE PRESERVED
⌇ A Tragedy ⌇
1682

Thomas Otway

INTRODUCTORY NOTE

Thomas Otway's life was short and unhappy. Born in 1652, he attended Oxford briefly and then, by his own account, "stray'd" to London to try his hand at acting. He did poorly on the stage, and even worse in the pursuit of his one great passion in life, the beautiful Elizabeth Barry. Mrs. Barry was the mistress of the Earl of Rochester while Otway was very much on the fringes of society. Money seems not to have stuck to his hands in spite of the success of his plays: bitterly resentful of his poverty, he lived—as one scholar says—"in destitution" until his death of a fever in 1685.

Venice Preserved was a great success when produced in 1682. Mrs. Barry, for whom the role of Belvidera was probably designed, was triumphant in her performance. She was surrounded by a brilliant cast, which included the great Betterton as Jaffeir. The play has never really gone out of production, remaining for over two centuries one of the most popular Restoration tragedies. Modern opinion rates Otway nearly as high as that of his contemporaries, which was expressed by a poem entitled "The Death of Dryden" (1703):

> Otway! who more than any of his age
> Did charm the audience and adorn the stage.

Venice Preserved shares with other tragedies of the Restoration an exotic scene, high-flown rhetoric, and a passionate debate between the rival claims of love and honor. But it may be more memorable for what it does not share with other plays, most of which retain far less appeal for a modern audience. Other playwrights had taken for their scene Granada, Rome, or Alexandria in order to distance their action. They managed in that way to escape censorship of what might appear to be current political allusions, and to remove tragedy completely from everyday life. Otway's Venice is much closer to England than most authors cared to go: there are even recognizable political figures like the Earl of Shaftesbury (as Antonio) in the cast of characters. And while Otway's language is full of rant and bombast (much more satisfying to the contemporary audience than it is now), it has also a vein of hard, precise, and compact imagery. When Pierre asks whether Renault used any violence towards Belvidera, Jaffeir replies:

> No, no! out on't, violence!
> Played with her neck, brushed her with his gray beard,
> Struggled and tousled, tickled her till she squeaked a little,
> Maybe, or so—but not a jot of violence.

His rage is no less for being suppressed, and for being expressed with demonic precision.

As for honor and love, they were the stock dilemmas of many a Restoration tragedy, but here they receive psychological and sexual delineation as well. Antonio's politics are suggested by his masochism. As for his qualities as a lover, Aquilina says ruefully,

> I never lay by his decrepit side
> But all that night I pondered on my grave.

The frantic sensuality of Jaffeir and Belvidera is powerfully realized, and connotes far more than the sexual sensibility of the age. It is sentimental, morbidly self-conscious and self-aggrandizing; in short the equivalent in emotional terms of much larger cultural views. It is as if Otway were consciously ending a tradition three centuries long of Petrarchan love, of a set of conventions that failed to express what he saw to be the nature of modern character and feeling. The modern world, he implied, has no use for heroic passions, whether in the private or in the public sphere.

While much of the play is operatic, set against a scene of vast passions and betrayals, expressed in long bursts of lyrics, its language is also capable of great clarity and compression. After the most fulsome expressions of loyalty and love Renault says simply, "I never loved these huggers." After a dissertation on freedom Pierre thinks of the morbid beauty of the city aflame, hissing down to its foundations:

> How lovely the Adriatic whore,
> Dressed in her flames, will shine!

In lines such as these Otway condenses seventeenth-century language, simplifying and removing adjectives and epithets, and making it direct and expressive. It is perhaps in that respect most of all that *Venice Preserved* differs from those many tragedies that it has outlived.

Personae Dramatis

DUKE OF VENICE
PRIULI, *father to* BELVIDERA, *a Senator*
ANTONIO, *a fine speaker in the senate*
JAFFEIR
PIERRE
RENAULT
BEDAMAR
SPINOSA
THEODORE
ELIOT
REVILLIDO
DURAND } *conspirators*
MEZZANA
BRAINVEIL
TERNON
BRABE
RETROSI
BELVIDERA
AQUILINA
Two Women, attendants on BELVIDERA
Two Women, servants to AQUILINA
The Council of Ten
Officer
Guard
Friar
Executioner and Rabble

PROLOGUE

In these distracted times,[1] when each man dreads
The bloody stratagems of busy heads;
When we have feared three years we know not what,
Till witnesses begin to die o' the rot,
What made our poet meddle with a plot?[2]
Was't that he fancied, for the very sake
And name of plot, his trifling play might take?
For there's not in't one inch-board evidence,[3]
But 'tis, he says, to reason plain and sense,
And that he thinks a plausible defence.
Were truth by sense and reason to be tried,
Sure all our swearers might be laid aside:
No, of such tools our author has no need,
To make his plot or make his play succeed;
He, of black bills,[4] has no prodigious tales,
Or Spanish pilgrims[5] cast ashore in Wales;
Here's not one murthered magistrate[6] at least,
Kept rank like venison for a city feast,
Grown four days stiff, the better to prepare
And fit his pliant limbs to ride in chair:
Yet here's an army raised, though under ground,
But no man seen, nor one commission found;

[1] *In these distracted times,* for several years England had been the scene of violent religious and political oppositions.
[2] *plot,* the "Popish Plot" of 1678 was supposedly an attempt by Catholics to seize the government.
[3] *inch-board evidence,* swearing hard enough to penetrate a block of wood.
[4] *bills,* halberds or blades mounted on spear shafts.
[5] *Spanish pilgrims,* disguised Irish soldiers.
[6] *magistrate,* the "Popish Plot" began with the murder of Sir Edmund Berry Godfrey, a justice of the peace supposedly murdered by Catholic traitors.

Here is a traitor too, that's very old,
Turbulent, subtle, mischievous and bold,
Bloody, revengeful, and to crown his part,
Loves fumbling with a wench, with all his heart;
Till after having many changes passed,
In spite of age (thanks Heaven) is hanged at last:
Next is a senator that keeps a whore,
In Venice none a higher office bore;
To lewdness every night the lecher ran,
Show me, all London, such another man,
Match him at Mother Creswold's[7] if you can.
Oh Poland, Poland! had it been thy lot,
T' have heard in time of this Venetian plot,
Thou surely chosen hadst one king from thence,[8]
And honoured them as thou hast England since.

---

[7] *Mother Creswold's,* Mother Cresswell was a notorious go-between for whores.
[8] *one king from thence,* The Earl of Shaftesbury, supposedly satirized by this play, aspired to the elective monarchy of Poland.

ACT I

[SCENE I.]

(*Enter* PRIULI *and* JAFFEIR.)

PRIULI. No more! I'll hear no more; begone and leave.
JAFFEIR. Not hear me! by my sufferings but you shall!
    My lord, my lord; I'm not that abject wretch
    You think me: Patience! where's the distance throws
    Me back so far, but I may boldly speak
    In right, though proud oppression will not hear me!
PRIULI. Have you not wronged me?
JAFFEIR.
                        Could my nature e'er
    Have brooked injustice or the doing wrongs,
    I need not now thus low have bent myself,
    To gain a hearing from a cruel father!
    Wronged you?
PRIULI.
               Yes! wronged me, in the nicest point:
    The honour of my house; you have done me wrong;
    You may remember: (for I now will speak,
    And urge its baseness) when you first came home
    From travel, with such hopes, as made you looked on
    By all men's eyes, a youth of expectation;
    Pleased with your growing virtue, I received you;
    Courted, and sought to raise you to your merits:
    My house, my table, nay my fortune too,
    My very self, was yours; you might have used me
    To your best service; like an open friend,
    I treated, trusted you, and thought you mine;
    When in requital of my best endeavours,
    You treacherously practised[9] to undo me,
    Seduced the weakness of my age's darling,

---

[9] *practised*, schemed.

My only child, and stole her from my bosom:
Oh Belvidera!

JAFFEIR.

              'Tis to me you owe her,
Childless you had been else, and in the grave,
Your name extinct, nor no more Priuli heard of.
You may remember, scarce five years are past,
Since in your brigandine you sailed to see
The Adriatic wedded by our Duke,[10]
And I was with you: Your unskilful pilot
Dashed us upon a rock; when to your boat
You made for safety; entered first yourself;
The affrighted Belvidera following next,
As she stood trembling on the vessel side,
Was by a wave washed off into the deep,
When instantly I plunged into the sea,
And buffeting the billows to her rescue,
Redeemed her life with half the loss of mine;
Like a rich conquest in one hand I bore her,
And with the other dashed the saucy waves,
That thronged and pressed to rob me of my prize:
I brought her, gave her to your despairing arms:
Indeed you thanked me; but a nobler gratitude
Rose in her soul: for from that hour she loved me,
Till for her life she paid me with herself.

PRIULI. You stole her from me, like a thief you stole her,
At dead of night; that cursed hour you chose
To rifle me of all my heart held dear.
May all your joys in her prove false like mine;
A sterile fortune, and a barren bed,
Attend you both: continual discord make
Your days and nights bitter and grievous: still
May the hard hand of a vexatious need
Oppress, and grind you; till at last you find
The curse of disobedience all your portion.

JAFFEIR. Half of your curse you have bestowed in vain,
Heaven has already crowned our faithful loves
With a young boy, sweet as his mother's beauty:
May he live to prove more gentle than his grandsire,
And happier than his father!

---

[10] *The Adriatic wedded by our Duke,* annual Venetian ritual of praising
the sea that protected the city and gave it commerce.

PRIULI.
                                        Rather live
      To bait thee for his bread, and din your ears
      With hungry cries: whilst his unhappy mother
      Sits down and weeps in bitterness of want.
JAFFEIR. You talk as if it would please you.
PRIULI.
                                        'Twould by Heaven.
      Once she was dear indeed; the drops that fell
      From my sad heart, when she forgot her duty,
      The fountain of my life was not so precious:
      But she is gone, and if I am a man
      I will forget her.
JAFFEIR. Would I were in my grave.
PRIULI.
                              And she too with thee;
      For, living here, you're but my cursed remembrancers
      I once was happy.
JAFFEIR. You use me thus, because you know my soul
      Is fond of Belvidera: you perceive
      My life feeds on her, therefore thus you treat me;
      Oh! could my soul ever have known satiety:
      Were I that thief, the doer of such wrongs
      As you upbraid me with, what hinders me,
      But I might send her back to you with contumely,
      And court my fortune where she would be kinder!
PRIULI. You dare not do't.—
JAFFEIR.
                              Indeed, my lord, I dare not.
      My heart that awes me is too much my master:
      Three years are past since first our vows were plighted,
      During which time, the world must bear me witness,
      I have treated Belvidera like your daughter,
      The daughter of a senator of Venice;
      Distinction, place, attendance and observance,
      Due to her birth, she always has commanded;
      Out of my little fortune I have done this;
      Because (though hopeless e'er to win your nature)
      The world might see, I loved her for herself,
      Not as the heiress of the great Priuli.—
PRIULI. No more!

JAFFEIR.

> Yes! all, and then adieu for ever.
> There's not a wretch that lives on common charity
> But's happier than me: for I have known
> The luscious sweets of plenty; every night
> Have slept with soft content about my head,
> And never waked but to a joyful morning,
> Yet now must fall like a full ear of corn,[11]
> Whose blossom scaped, yet's withered in the ripening.

PRIULI. Home and be humble, study to retrench;
> Discharge the lazy vermin of thy hall,
> Those pageants of thy folly,
> Reduce the glittering trappings of thy wife
> To humble weeds,[12] fit for thy little state;
> Then to some suburb[13] cottage both retire;
> Drudge, to feed loathsome life: get brats, and starve—
> Home, home, I say.—   (*Exit* PRIULI.)

JAFFEIR.

> Yes, if my heart would let me—
> This proud, this swelling heart: home I would go,
> But that my doors are hateful to my eyes,
> Filled and damned up with gaping creditors,
> Watchful as fowlers when their game will spring;
> I have now not fifty ducats in the world,
> Yet still I am in love, and pleased with ruin.
> Oh Belvidera! oh she's my wife—
> And we will bear our wayward fate together,
> But ne'er know comfort more.

(*Enter* PIERRE.)

PIERRE.

> My friend good morrow!
> How fares the honest partner of my heart?
> What, melancholy! not a word to spare me?

JAFFEIR. I'm thinking, Pierre, how that damned starving quality
> Called honesty, got footing in the world.

PIERRE. Why, powerful villainy first set it up,
> For its own ease and safety: honest men
> Are the soft easy cushions on which knaves

---

[11] *corn*, wheat.
[12] *weeds*, clothing.
[13] *suburb*, part of the city devoted to prostitution.

Repose and fatten: were all mankind villains,
They'd starve each other; lawyers would want practice,
Cutthroats rewards: each man would kill his brother
Himself, none would be paid or hanged for murder:
Honesty was a cheat invented first
To bind the hands of bold deserving rogues,
That fools and cowards might sit safe in power,
And lord it uncontrolled above their betters.

JAFFEIR. Then honesty is but a notion.

PIERRE.

Nothing else,
Like wit, much talked of, not to be defined:
He that pretends to most too, has least share in't;
'Tis a ragged virtue: honesty! no more on't.

JAFFEIR. Sure thou art honest?

PIERRE.

So indeed men think me,
But they're mistaken, Jaffeir: I am a rogue
As well as they;
A fine gay bold-faced villain, as thou seest me;
'Tis true, I pay my debts when they're contracted;
I steal from no man; would not cut a throat
To gain admission to a great man's purse,
Or a whore's bed; I'd not betray my friend,
To get his place or fortune: I scorn to flatter
A blown-up fool above me, or crush the wretch beneath
    me,
Yet, Jaffeir, for all this, I am a villain!

JAFFEIR. A villain—

PIERRE.

Yes a most notorious villain:
To see the sufferings of my fellow creatures,
And own myself a man: To see our senators
Cheat the deluded people with a show
Of liberty, which yet they ne'er must taste of;
They say, by them our hands are free from fetters,
Yet whom they please they lay in basest bonds;
Bring whom they please to infamy and sorrow;
Drive us like wrecks down the rough tide of power,
Whilst no hold's left to save us from destruction;
All that bear this are villains; and I one,
Not to rouse up at the great call of Nature,
And check the growth of these domestic spoilers,
That make us slaves and tell us 'tis our charter.

JAFFEIR. Oh Aquilina! Friend, to lose such beauty,
    The dearest purchase of thy noble labours;
    She was thy right by conquest, as by love.
PIERRE. Oh Jaffeir! I'd so fixed my heart upon her,
    That wheresoe'er I framed a scheme of life
    For time to come, she was my only joy
    With which I wished to sweeten future cares;
    I fancied pleasures, none but one that loves
    And dotes as I did can imagine like 'em:
    When in the extremity of all these hopes,
    In the most charming hour of expectation,
    Then when our eager wishes soar the highest,
    Ready to stoop and grasp the lovely game,
    A haggard[14] owl, a worthless kite[15] of prey,
    With his foul wings sailed in and spoiled my quarry.
JAFFEIR. I know the wretch, and scorn him as thou hat'st him
PIERRE. Curse on the common good that's so protected,
    Where every slave that heaps up wealth enough
    To do much wrong, becomes a lord of right:
    I, who believed no ill could e'er come near me,
    Found in the embraces of my Aquilina
    A wretched old but itching senator;
    A wealthy fool, that had bought out my title,
    A rogue, that uses beauty like a lambskin,
    Barely to keep him warm: that filthy cuckoo too
    Was in my absence crept into my nest,
    And spoiling all my brood of noble pleasure.
JAFFEIR. Didst thou not chase him thence?
PIERRE.

                        I did, and drove
    The rank old bearded hirco[16] stinking home:
    The matter was complained of in the Senate,
    I, summoned to appear, and censured basely,
    For violating something they call privilege—
    This was the recompence of my service:
    Would I'd been rather beaten by a coward!
    A soldier's mistress Jaffeir, his religion,
    When that's profaned, all other ties are broken,
    That even dissolves all former bonds of service,
    And from that hour I think myself as free

---

[14] *haggard*, wild.
[15] *kite*, bird of prey, crook.
[16] *hirco*, goat, lecher.

To be the foe as e'er the friend of Venice—
Nay, dear revenge, when e'er thou call'st I am ready.
JAFFEIR. I think no safety can be here for virtue,
And grieve, my friend, as much as thou to live
In such a wretched state as this of Venice;
Where all agree to spoil the public good,
And villains fatten with the brave man's labours.
PIERRE. We have neither safety, unity, nor peace,
For the foundation's lost of common good;
Justice is lame as well as blind amongst us;
The laws (corrupted to their ends that make 'em)
Serve but for instruments of some new tyranny,
That every day starts up to enslave us deeper:
Now could this glorious cause but find out friends
To do it right! oh Jaffeir! then might'st thou
Not wear these seals of woe upon thy face,
The proud Priuli should be taught humanity,
And learn to value such a son as thou art.
I dare not speak! But my heart bleeds this moment!
JAFFEIR. Curst be the cause, though I thy friend be part on't:
Let me partake the troubles of thy bosom,
For I am used to misery, and perhaps
May find a way to sweeten't to thy spirit.
PIERRE. Too soon it will reach thy knowledge—
JAFFEIR.
                                        Then from thee
Let it proceed. There's virtue in thy friendship
Would make the saddest tale of sorrow pleasing,
Strengthen my constancy, and welcome ruin.
PIERRE. Then thou are ruined!
JAFFEIR.
                            That I long since knew,
I and ill fortune have been long acquaintance.
PIERRE. I past this very moment by thy doors,
And found them guarded by a troop of villains;
The sons of public rapine were destroying:
They told me, by the sentence of the law
They had commission to seize all thy fortune,
Nay more, Priuli's cruel hand hath signed it.
Here stood a ruffian with a horrid face
Lording it o'er a pile of massy plate,
Tumbled into a heap for public sale:
There was another making villainous jests
At thy undoing; he had ta'en possession

Of all thy ancient most domestic ornaments,
Rich hangings, intermixed and wrought with gold;
The very bed, which on thy wedding night
Received thee to the arms of Belvidera,
The scene of all thy joys, was violated
By the course hands of filthy dungeon villains,
And thrown amongst the common lumber.

JAFFEIR. Now thanks Heaven—

PIERRE. Thank Heaven! for what?

JAFFEIR.
                                  That I am not worth a ducat.

PIERRE. Curse thy dull stars, and the worse fate of Venice,
Where brothers, friends, and fathers, all are false;
Where there's no trust, no truth; where innocence
Stoops under vile oppression; and vice lords it:
Had'st thou but seen, as I did, how at last
Thy beauteous Belvidera, like a wretch
That's doomed to banishment, came weeping forth,
Shining through tears, like April suns in showers
That labour to o'ercome the cloud that loads 'em,
Whilst two young virgins, on whose arms she leaned,
Kindly looked up, and at her grief grew sad,
As if they catched the sorrows that fell from her:
Even the lewd rabble that were gathered round
To see the sight, stood mute when they beheld her;
Governed their roaring throats and grumbled pity:
I could have hugged the greasy rogues: they pleased me.

JAFFEIR. I thank thee for this story from my soul,
Since now I know the worst that can befall me:
Ah Pierre! I have a heart, that could have born
The roughest wrong my fortune could have done me:
But when I think what Belvidera feels,
The bitterness her tender spirit tastes of,
I own myself a coward: bear my weakness,
If throwing thus my arms about thy neck,
I play the boy, and blubber in thy bosom.
Oh! I shall drown thee with my sorrows!

PIERRE.   Burn!
First burn, and level Venice to thy ruin!
What! Starve like beggar's brats in frosty weather,
Under a hedge, and whine ourselves to death!
Thou, or thy cause, shall never want assistance,
Whilst I have blood or fortune fit to serve thee;
Command my heart: Thou are every way its master.

JAFFEIR. No: there's a secret pride in bravely dying.
PIERRE. Rats die in holes and corners, dogs run mad;
    Man knows a braver remedy for sorrow:
    Revenge! the attribute of Gods, they stamped it
    With their great image on our natures; die!
    Consider well the cause that calls upon thee:
    And if thou art base enough, die then: Remember
    Thy Belvidera suffers: Belvidera!
    Die—damn first—what, be decently interred
    In a church-yard, and mingle thy brave dust
    With stinking rogues that rot in dirty winding sheets,
    Surfeit-slain fools, the common dung o'the soil!
JAFFEIR. Oh!
PIERRE.
          Well said, out with't, swear a little—
JAFFEIR.
                          Swear!
    By sea and air! by earth, by Heaven and Hell,
    I will revenge my Belvidera's tears!
    Hark thee my friend—Priuli—is—a senator!
PIERRE. A dog!
JAFFEIR.
       Agreed.
PIERRE.
          Shoot him.
JAFFEIR.
               With all my heart.
    No more: Where shall we meet at night?
PIERRE.
                     I'll tell thee;
    On the Rialto every night at twelve
    I take my evening's walk of meditation,
    There we two will meet, and talk of precious
    Mischief—
JAFFEIR. Farewell.
PIERRE.
        At twelve.
JAFFEIR.
             At any hour, my plagues
    Will keep me waking.   (*Exit* PIERRE.)
    Tell me why, good Heaven,
    Thou mad'st me what I am, with all the spirit,
    Aspiring thoughts and elegant desires

That fill the happiest man? Ah! rather why
Did'st thou not form me sordid as my fate,
Base minded, dull, and fit to carry burdens?
Why have I sense to know the curse that's on me?
Is this just dealing, Nature? Belvidera!

(*Enter* BELVIDERA, ATTENDANTS)

    Poor Belvidera!

BELVIDERA.
                Lead me, lead me my virgins!
To that kind voice. My lord, my love, my refuge!
Happy my eyes, when they behold thy face:
My heavy heart will leave its doleful beating
At sight of thee, and bound with sprightful joys.
Oh smile, as when our loves were in their spring,
And cheer my fainting soul.

JAFFEIR.
                      As when our loves
Were in their spring? has then my fortune changed?
Art thou not Belvidera, still the same,
Kind, good, and tender, as my arms first found thee?
If thou art altered, where shall I have harbour?
Where ease my loaded heart? Oh! where complain?

BELVIDERA. Does this appear like change, or love decaying,
When thus I throw myself into thy bosom,
With all the resolution of a strong truth?
Beats not my heart, as 'twould alarm thine
To a new charge of bliss? I joy more in thee,
Than did thy mother when she hugged thee first,
And blessed the gods for all her travel[17] past

JAFFEIR. Can there in woman be such glorious faith?
Sure all ill stories of thy sex are false;
Oh woman! lovely woman! Nature made thee
To temper man: We had been brutes without you;
Angels are painted fair, to look like you;
There's in you all that we believe of Heaven,
Amazing brightness, purity and truth,
Eternal joy, and everlasting love.

BELVIDERA. If love be treasure, we'll be wondrous rich:
I have so much, my heart will surely break with't;
Vows cannot express it, when I would declare
How great's my joy, I am dumb with the big thought;

[17] *travel*, travail.

I swell, and sigh, and labour with my longing.
Oh lead me to some desert wide and wild,
Barren as our misfortunes, where my soul
May have its vent: Where I may tell aloud
To the high heavens, and every listening planet,
With what a boundless stock my bosom's fraught;
Where I may throw my eager arms about thee,
Give loose to love with kisses, kindling joy,
And let off all the fire that's in my heart.

JAFFEIR. Oh Belvidera! double I am a beggar,
Undone by fortune, and in debt to thee;
Want! worldly want! that hungry meager fiend
Is at my heels, and chases me in view;
Can'st thou bear cold and hunger? Can these limbs,
Framed for the tender offices of love,
Endure the bitter grip of smarting poverty?
When banished by our miseries abroad,
(As suddenly we shall be) to seek out
(In some far climate where our names are strangers)
For charitable succour; wilt thou then,
When in a bed of straw we shrink together,
And the bleak winds shall whistle round our heads;
Wilt thou then talk thus to me? Wilt thou then
Hush my cares thus, and shelter me with love?

BELVIDERA. Oh I will love thee, even in madness love thee:
Tho my distracted senses should forsake me,
I'd find some intervals, when my poor heart
Should swage[18] itself and be let loose to thine.
Though the bare earth be all our resting-place,
Its roots our food, some clift our habitation,
I'll make this arm a pillow for thy head;
As thou sighing liest, and swelled with sorrow,
Creep to thy bosom, pour the balm of love
Into thy soul, and kiss thee to thy rest;
Then praise our god, and watch thee 'till the morning.

JAFFEIR. Hear this you Heavens, and wonder how you made
her!
Reign, reign ye monarchs that divide the world,
Busy rebellion ne'er will let you know
Tranquility and happiness like mine;
Like gaudy ships, the obsequious billows fall
And rise again, to lift you in your pride;

18 *swage*, assuage.

They wait but for a storm and then devour you:
I, in my private bark, already wrecked,
Like a poor merchant driven on unknown land,
That had by chance packed up his choicest treasure
In one dear casket, and saved only that:
Since I must wander further on the shore,
Thus hug my little, but my precious store;
Resolved to scorn, and trust my fate no more. (*Exeunt.*)

ACT II

[SCENE I.]

(*Enter* PIERRE *and* AQUILINA.)

AQUILINA. By all thy wrongs, thou art dearer to my arms
Than all the wealth of Venice: prithee stay,
And let us love tonight.
PIERRE.
                              No: there's fool,
There's fool about thee: when a woman sells
Her flesh to fools, her beauty's lost to me;
They leave a taint, a sully where th'ave past;
There's such a baneful quality about 'em,
Even spoils complexions with their own nauseousness;
They infect all they touch; I cannot think
Of tasting anything a fool has palled.
AQUILINA. I loath and scorn that fool thou mean'st, as much
Or more than thou can'st; but the beast has gold
That makes him necessary: power too,
To qualify my character, and poise me
Equal with peevish virtue, that beholds
My liberty with envy: in their hearts
Are loose as I am; but an ugly power
Sits in their faces, and frights pleasures from 'em.
PIERRE. Much good may't do you, madam, with your senator.
AQUILINA. My senator! why, can'st thou think that wretch
E'er filled thy Aquilina's arms with pleasure?
Think'st thou, because I sometimes give him leave
To foil himself at what he is unfit for;
Because I force myself to endure and suffer him,

Think'st thou I love him? No, by all the joys
Thou ever gavest me, his presence is my penance;
The worst thing an old man can be's a lover,
A mere *memento mori* to poor woman.
I never lay by his decrepit side,
But all that night I pondered on my grave.

PIERRE. Would he were well sent thither.

AQUILINA.

                       That's my wish too:
For then, my Pierre, I might have cause with pleasure
To play the hypocrite: Oh! how I could weep
Over the dying dotard, and kiss him too,
In hopes to smother him quite; then, when the time
Was come to pay my sorrows at his funeral,
For he has already made me heir to treasures,
Would make me out-act a real widow's whining:
How could I frame my face to fit my mourning!
With wringing hands attend him to his grave,
Fall swooning on his hearse: take mad possession,
Even of the dismal vault, where he lay buried,
There like the Ephesian matron[19] dwell, till thou,
My lovely soldier, comest to my deliverance;
Then throwing up my veil, with open arms
And laughing eyes, run to new dawning joy.

PIERRE. No more! I have friends to meet me here tonight,
And must be private. As you prize my friendship,
Keep up your coxcomb: Let him not pry nor listen,
Nor fisk[20] about the house as I have seen him,
Like a tame mumping[21] squirrel with a bell on;
Curs will be abroad to bite him, if you do.

AQUILINA. What friends to meet? may I not be of your council?

PIERRE. How! a woman ask questions out of bed?
Go to your senator, ask him what passes
Amongst his brethren, he'll hide nothing from you;
But pump not me for politics. No more!
Give order that whoever in my name
Comes here, receive admittance: so good night.

---

[19] *Ephesian matron*, much-repeated allusion in the Renaissance to the story of a widow who was easily consoled. An early version is in the *Satyricon* of Petronius.
[20] *fisk*, run.
[21] *mumping*, nibbling.

AQUILINA. Must we ne'er meet again! Embrace no more!
    Is love so soon and utterly forgotten!
PIERRE. As you henceforward treat your fool, I'll think on't.
AQUILINA. Cursed be all fools, and doubly cursed myself,
    The worst of fools—I die if he forsakes me;
    And how to keep him, Heaven or Hell instruct me.

                            (*Exeunt.*)

[SCENE II.] *The Rialto*

(*Enter* JAFFEIR.)

JAFFEIR. I am here, and thus, the shades of night around me,
    I look as if all Hell were in my heart,
    And I in Hell. Nay, surely 'tis so with me;—
    For every step I tread, methinks some fiend
    Knocks at my breast, and bids it not be quiet:
    I've heard, how desperate wretches, like myself,
    Have wandered out at this dead time of night
    To meet the foe of mankind in his walk:
    Sure I am so cursed, that, tho' of Heaven forsaken,
    No minister of darkness cares to tempt me.
    Hell! Hell! why sleepest thou?

(*Enter* PIERRE.)

PIERRE. Sure I have stayed too long:
    The clock has struck, and I may lose my proselyte.
    Speak, who goes there?
JAFFEIR.
                 A dog, that comes to howl
    At yonder moon: What's he that asks the question?
PIERRE. A friend to dogs, for they are honest creatures,
    And ne'er betray their masters; never fawn
    On any that they love not: Well met, friend:
JAFFEIR.   The same. Oh Pierre! Thou art come in season,
    I was just going to pray.
PIERRE.
              Ah that's mechanic.[22]
    Priests make a trade on't, and yet starve by it too:
    No praying, it spoils business, and time's precious;
    Where's Belvidera?

---

[22] *mechanic,* plebian.

JAFFEIR.

> For a day or two
> I've lodged her privately, 'till I see farther
> What Fortune will do with me. Prithee, friend,
> If thou would'st have me fit to hear good council,
> Speak not of Belvidera—

PIERRE.

> Speak not of her.

JAFFEIR. Oh no!

PIERRE.

> Nor name her. May be I wish her well.

JAFFEIR. Who well?

PIERRE.

> Thy wife, thy lovely Belvidera,
> I hope a man may wish his friend's wife well,
> And no harm done!

JAFFEIR.

> Y'are merry, Pierre!

PIERRE.

> I am so:
> Thou shalt smile too, and Belvidera smile;
> We'll all rejoice, here's something to buy pins,
> Marriage is chargeable.[23]

JAFFEIR.

> I but half wished
> To see the Devil, and he's here already.
> Well!
> What must this buy, rebellion, murder, treason?
> Tell me which way I must be damned for this.

PIERRE. When last we parted, we had no qualms like these,
> But entertained each other's thoughts like men,
> Whose souls were well acquainted. Is the world
> Reformed since our last meeting? What new miracles
> Have happened? Has Priuli's heart relented?
> Can he be honest?

JAFFEIR.

> Kind Heaven! let heavy curses
> Gall his old age; cramps, aches, rack his bones;
> And bitterest disquiet wring his heart;
> Oh let him live 'till life become his burden!
> Let him groan under't long, linger an age
> In the worst agonies and pangs of death,
> And find its ease, but late.

23 *chargeable*, expensive.

PIERRE.

                              Nay, could'st thou not
As well, my friend, have stretched the curse to all
The senate round, as to one single villain?

JAFFEIR. But curses stick not: could I kill with cursing,
By Heaven I know not thirty heads in Venice
Should not be blasted; senators should rot
Like dogs on dunghills; but their wives and daughters
Die of their own diseases. Oh for a curse
To kill with!

PIERRE.

                  Daggers, daggers, are much better!

JAFFEIR. Ha!

PIERRE. Daggers

JAFFEIR.

              But where are they?

PIERRE.

                              Oh, a thousand
May be disposed in honest hands in Venice.

JAFFEIR. Thou talk'st in clouds.

PIERRE.

                              But yet a heart half wronged
As thine has been, would find the meaning, Jaffeir.

JAFFEIR. A thousand daggers, all in honest hands;
And have not I a friend will stick one here?

PIERRE. Yes, if I thought thou wert not to be cherished
To a nobler purpose, I'd be that friend.
But thou hast better friends, friends whom thy wrongs
Have made thy friends; friends worthy to be called so;
I'll trust thee with a secret: there are spirits
This hour at work. But as thou art a man,
Whom I have picked and chosen from the world,
Swear, that thou wilt be true to what I utter,
And when I have told thee, that which only gods
And men like gods are privy to, then swear,
No chance or change shall wrest it from thy bosom.

JAFFEIR. When thou would'st bind me, is there need of oaths?
Green-sickness[24] girls lose maidenheads with such
    counters.[25]

---

[24] *Green-sickness,* anemic, possibly adolescent.
[25] *counters,* money.

For thou art so near my heart, that thou may'st see
Its bottom, sound its strength, and firmness to thee:
A coward, fool, or villain, in my face?
If I seem none of these, I dare believe
Thou would'st not use me in a little cause,
For I am fit for honour's toughest task;
Nor ever yet found fooling was my province;
And for a villainous inglorious enterprise,
I know thy heart so well, I dare lay mine
Before thee, set it to what point thou wilt.

PIERRE. Nay, it's a cause thou wilt be fond of, Jaffeir.
For it is founded on the noblest basis,
Our liberties, our natural inheritance;
There's no religion, no hypocrisy in't;
We'll do the business, and ne'er fast and pray for't:
Openly act a deed, the world shall gaze
With wonder at, and envy when it is done.

JAFFEIR. For liberty!

PIERRE.

         For liberty, my friend,
Thou shalt be freed from base Priuli's tyranny,
And thy sequestered fortunes healed again.
I shall be freed from opprobrious wrongs,
That press me now, and bend my spirit downward:
All Venice free, and every growing merit
Succeed to its just right: fools shall be pulled
From wisdom's seat; those baleful unclean birds,
Those lazy owls, who (perched near Fortune's top)
Sit only watchful with their heavy wings
To cuff down new fledged virtues, that would rise
To nobler heights, and make the grove harmonious.

JAFFEIR. What can I do?

PIERRE.

         Cans't thou not kill a senator?

JAFFEIR. Were there one wise or honest, I could kill him
For herding with that nest of fools and knaves;
By all my wrongs, thou talk'st as if revenge
Were to be had, and the brave story warms me.

PIERRE. Swear then!

JAFFEIR.

         I do, by all those glittering stars,
And yond great ruling planet of the night!
By all good powers above, and ill below!

By love and friendship, dearer than my life!
No power or death shall make me false to thee.
PIERRE. Here we embrace, and I'll unlock my heart.
A council's held hard by, where the destruction
Of this great empire's hatching: There I'll lead thee!
But be a man, for thou art to mix with men
Fit to disturb the peace of all the world,
And rule it when it's widest—
JAFFEIR.
                              I give thee thanks
For this kind warning: Yes, I will be a man,
And charge thee, Pierre, when e'er thou see'st my fears
Betray me less, to rip this heart of mine
Out of my breast, and show it for a coward's.
Come let's begone, for from this hour I chase
All little thoughts, all tender human follies
Out of my bosom: vengeance shall have room:
Revenge!
PIERRE. And liberty!
JAFFEIR.
                    Revenge! Revenge—   (*Exeunt.*)

[SCENE III.] *The scene changes to* AQUILINA's *house, the Greek
courtesan*

(*Enter* RENAULT.)

RENAULT. Why was my choice ambition, the worst ground
A wretch can build on? it's indeed at distance
A good prospect, tempting to the view,
The height delights us, and the mountain top
Looks beautiful, because it's nigh to Heaven,
But we ne'er think how sandy's the foundation,
What storm will batter, and what tempest shake us!
Who's there?

(*Enter* SPINOSA.)

SPINOSA.
                    Renault, good morrow! for by this time
I think the scale of night has turned the balance,
And weighs up morning: has the clock struck twelve?
RENAULT. Yes, clocks will go as they are set: but man,
Irregular man's ne'er constant, never certain:
I've spent at least three precious hours of darkness

In waiting dull attendance; 'tis the curse
Of diligent virtue to be mixed like mine, .
With giddy tempers, souls but half resolved.

SPINOSA. Hell seize that soul amongst us, it can frighten.

RENAULT. What's then the cause that I am here alone?
Why are we not together?

(*Enter* ELIOT.)

O sir, welcome!
You are an Englishman. When treason's hatching
One might have thought you'd not have been behind-
hand.
In what whore's lap have you been lolling?
Give but an Englishman his whore and ease,
Beef and a sea-coal fire, he's yours for ever.

ELIOT. Frenchman, you are saucy.

RENAULT.

How!

(*Enter* BEDAMAR *the ambassador*, THEODORE, BRAINVEIL,
DURAND, BRABE, REVELLIDO, MEZZANA, TERNON, RETROSI,
Conspirators.)

BEDAMAR.   At difference? Fy!
Is this a time for quarrels? Thieves and rogues
Fall out and brawl: Should men of your high calling,
Men separated by the choice of providence,
From the gross heap of mankind, and set here
In this great assembly as in one great jewel,
T'adorn the bravest purpose it e'er smiled on;
Should you like boys wrangle for trifles?

RENAULT.

Boys!

BEDAMAR. Renault, thy hand!

RENAULT.

I thought I'd given my heart
Long since to every man that mingles here;
But grieve to find it trusted with such tempers,
That can't forgive my froward age its weakness.

BEDAMAR. Eliot, thou once had'st virtue, I have seen
Thy stubborn temper bend with godlike goodness,
Not half thus courted: 'Tis thy nation's glory,
To hug the foe that offers brave alliance.
Once more embrace, my friends—we'll all embrace—

United thus, we are the mighty engine
Must twist this rooted empire from its basis!
Totters it not already?

ELIOT.

Would it were tumbling.

BEDAMAR. Nay it shall down: this night we seal its ruin.

(*Enter* PIERRE.)

Oh Pierre! thou art welcome!
Come to my breast, for by its hopes thou look'st
Lovelily dreadful, and the fate of Venice
Seems on thy sword already. Oh my Mars!
The poets that first feigned a god of war
Sure prophesied of thee.

PIERRE.

Friends! was not Brutus,
(I mean that Brutus, who in open senate
Stabbed the first Caesar that usurped the world)
A gallant man?

RENAULT.

Yes, and Catiline too;
Tho' story wrong his fame: for he conspired
To prop the reeling glory of his country:
His cause was good.

BEDAMAR.

And ours as much above it,
As, Renault, thou are superior to Cethegus,[26]
Or Pierre to Cassius.[27]

PIERRE.

Then to what we aim at
When do we start? or must we talk for ever?

BEDAMAR. No Pierre, the deed's near birth: fate seems to have
set
The business up, and given it to our care:
I hope there's not a heart nor hand amongst us
But is firm and ready.

ALL. All! We'll die with Bedamar.

BEDAMAR.

Oh men,
Matchless, as will your glory be hereafter.
The game is for a matchless prize, if won;
If lost, disgraceful ruin.

[26] *Cethegus*, a conspirator with Catiline against the Roman republic.
[27] *Cassius*, conspirator with Brutus against Julius Caesar.

RENAULT.

                                  What can lose it?
  The public stock's a beggar; one Venetian
  Trusts not another: look into their stores
  Of general safety; empty magazines,
  A tattered fleet, a murmuring unpaid army,
  Bankrupt nobility, a harassed commonalty,
  A factious, giddy, and divided senate,
  Is all the strength of Venice. Let's destroy it;
  Let's fill their magazines with arms to awe them,
  Man out their fleet, and make their trade maintain it;
  Let loose the murmuring army on their masters,
  To pay themselves with plunder; lop their nobles
  To the base roots, whence most of 'em first sprung;
  Enslave the rout,[28] whom smarting will make humble,
  Turn out their droning senate, and possess
  That seat of empire which our souls were framed for.
PIERRE. Ten thousand men are armed at your nod,
  Commanded all by leaders fit to guide
  A battle for the freedom of the world;
  This wretched state has starved them in its service,
  And by your bounty quickened, they're resolved
  To serve your glory, and revenge their own!
  Th' have all their different quarters in this city,
  Watch for th' alarm, and grumble 'tis so tardy.
BEDAMAR. I doubt not, friend, but thy unwearied diligence
  Has still kept waking, and it shall have ease;
  After this night it is resolved we meet
  No more, till Venice own us for her lords.
PIERRE. How lovely the Adriatic whore,
  Dressed in her flames, will shine! devouring flames!
  Such as shall burn her to the watery bottom
  And hiss in her foundation.
BEDAMAR.

                              Now if any
  Amongst us that owns this glorious cause,
  Have friends or interest, he'd wish to save,
  Let it be told, the general doom is sealed;
  But I'd forgo the hopes of a world's empire,
  Rather than wound the bowels[29] of my friend.
PIERRE. I must confess you there have touched my weakness,

28 *rout*, mob.
29 *bowels*, compassion.

I have a friend; hear it, such a friend!
My heart was ne'er shut to him: nay, I'll tell you,
He knows the very business of this hour;
But he rejoices the cause, and loves it,
We have changed a vow to live and die together,
And he's at hand to ratify it here.

RENAULT. How! all betrayed?

PIERRE.

      No—I've dealt nobly with you;
I've brought my all into the public stock;
I had but one friend, and him I'll share amongst you!
Receive and cherish him: Or if, when seen
And searched, you find him worthless, as my tongue
Has lodged this secret in his faithful breast,
To ease your fears I wear a dagger here
Shall rip it out again, and give you rest.
Come forth, thou only good I e'er could boast of.

(Enter JAFFEIR *with a dagger.)*

BEDAMAR. His presence bears the show of manly virtue.

JAFFEIR. I know you'll wonder all, that thus uncalled,
I dare approach this place of fatal councils;
But I am amongst you, and by heaven it glads me.
To see so many virtues thus united,
To restore justice and dethrone oppression.
Command this sword, if you would have it quiet,
Into this breast; but if you think it worthy
To cut the throats of reverend rogues in robes,
Send me into the cursed assembled senate;
It shrinks not, tho' I meet a father there;
Would you behold this city flaming? Here's
A hand shall bear a lighted torch at noon
To the arsenal, and set its gates on fire.

RENAULT. You talk this well, sir.

JAFFEIR.

      Nay—by Heaven I'll do this.
Come, come, I read distrust in all your faces,
You fear me a villain, and indeed it's odd
To hear a stranger talk thus at first meeting,
Of matters, that have been so well debated;
But I come ripe with wrongs as you with councils;
I hate this senate, am a foe to Venice;
A friend to none, but men resolved like me,

To push on mischief: Oh did you but know me,
I need not talk thus!

BEDAMAR.

Pierre! I must embrace him,
My heart beats to this man as if it knew him.

RENAULT. I never loved these huggers. (*aside*)

JAFFEIR.

Still I see
The cause delights me not. Your friends survey me,
As I were dangerous—but I come armed
Against all doubts, and to your trust will give
A pledge, worth more than all the world can pay for.
My Belvidera! Ho! my Belvidera!

BEDAMAR. What wonder next?

JAFFEIR.

Let me entreat you,
As I have henceforth hopes to call ye friends,
That all but the ambassador, this
Grave guide of councils, with my friend that owns me,
Withdraw a while to spare a woman's blushes.

(*Exeunt all but* BEDAMAR, RENAULT, JAFFEIR, PIERRE.)

BEDAMAR. Pierre, whither will this ceremony lead us?
JAFFEIR. My Belvidera! Belvidera!

(*Enter* BELVIDERA.)

BELVIDERA.

Who?
Who calls so loud at this late peaceful hour?
That voice was wont to come in gentler whispers,
And fill my ears with the soft breath of love:
Thou hourly image of my thoughts, where art thou?

JAFFEIR. Indeed 'tis late.

BELVIDERA.

Oh! I have slept, and dreamt,
And dreamt again: Where hast thou been thou loiterer?
Tho' my eyes closed, my arms have still been opened;
Stretched every way betwixt my broken slumbers,
To search if thou wert come to crown my rest;
There's no repose without thee: Oh the day
Too soon will break, and wake us to our sorrow;
Come, come to bed, and bid thy cares good night.

JAFFEIR. Oh Belvidera! we must change the scene

In which the past delights of life were tasted:
The poor sleep little, we must learn to watch
Our labours late, and early every morning,
Mid'st winter frosts, thin clad and fed with sparing,
Rise to our toils, and drudge away the day.

BELVIDERA. Alas! where am I! whither is't you lead me!
Methinks I read distraction in your face,
Something less gentle than the fate you tell me:
You shake and tremble too! your blood runs cold!
Heaven guard my love, and bless his heart with patience.

JAFFEIR. That I have patience, let our fate bear witness,
Who has ordained it so, that thou and I
(Thou the divinest good man e'er possesed,
And I the wretchedest of the race of man)
This very hour, without one tear, must part.

BELVIDERA. Part! must we part? Oh! am I then forsaken?
Will my love cast me off? have my misfortunes
Offended him so highly, that he'll leave me?
Why drag you from me? whither are you going?
My dear! my life! my love!

JAFFEIR.
                                   Oh friends!

BELVIDERA.
                                              Speak to me.

JAFFEIR. Take her from my heart,
She'll gain such hold else, I shall ne'er get loose.
I charge thee take her, but with tenderest care,
Relieve her troubles and assuage her sorrows.

RENAULT. Rise, madam! and command amongst your servants!

JAFFEIR. To you, sirs, and your honours, I bequeath her,
And with her this, when I prove unworthy—

                                   (*Gives a dagger.*)

You know the rest:—then strike it to her heart;
And tell her, he, who three whole happy years
Lay in her arms, and each kind night repeated
The passionate vows of still increasing love,
Sent that reward for all her truth and sufferings.

BELVIDERA. Nay, take my life, since he has sold it cheaply;
Or send me to some distant clime your slave,
But let it be far off, least my complainings
Should reach his guilty ears, and shake his peace.

JAFFEIR. No Belvidera, I've contrived thy honour;
Trust to my faith, and be but fortune kind

To me, as I'll preserve that faith unbroken,
When next we meet, I'll lift thee to a height,
Shall gather all the gazing world about thee,
To wonder what strange virtue placed thee there.
But if we ne'er meet more—

BELVIDERA.

                    Oh thou unkind one,
Never meet more! have I deserved this from you?
Look on me, tell me, tell me, speak thou dear deceiver,
Why am I separated from thy love?
If I am false, accuse me; but if true,
Don't, prithee don't in poverty forsake me.
But pity the sad heart, that's torn with parting.
Yet hear me! yet recall me—

        (*Exeunt* RENAULT, BEDAMAR *and* BELVIDERA.)

JAFFEIR.

                    Oh my eyes!
Look not that way, but turn yourselves awhile
Into my heart, and be weaned all together.
My friend, where art thou?

PIERRE.

                Here, my honour's brother.

JAFFEIR. Is Belvidera gone?

PIERRE.

                Renault has led her
Back to her own apartment: but, by Heaven!
Thou must not see her more till our work's over.

JAFFEIR. No:

PIERRE.

        Not for your life.

JAFFEIR.

                Oh Pierre, wert thou but she,
How I could pull thee down into my heart,
Gaze on thee till my eye-strings cracked with love,
Till all my sinews with its fire extended,
Fixt me upon the rack of ardent longing;
Then swelling, sighing, raging to be blessed,
Come like a panting turtle[30] to thy breast,
On thy soft bosom, hovering, bill and play,
Confess the cause why last I fled away;
    Own 'twas a fault, but swear to give it o'er,
    And never follow false ambition more. (*Exeunt ambo.*)

30 *turtle*, dove.

ACT III

[SCENE I.] AQUILINA's *house*

(*Enter* AQUILINA *and her* MAID.)

AQUILINA. Tell him I am gone to bed: tell him I am not at
home; tell him I've better company with me, or any
thing; tell him in short I will not see him, the eternal
troublesome vexatious fool: He's worse company than an
ignorant physician—I'll not be disturbed at these unseasonable hours.

MAID. But madam! He's here already, just entered the doors.

AQUILINA. Turn him out again, you unnecessary, useless, giddy-
brained ass! if he will not begone, set the house a fire
and burn us both: I had rather meet a toad in my dish
than that old hideous animal in my chamber tonight.

(*Enter* ANTONIO.)

ANTONIO. Nacky, Nacky, Nacky—how dost do, Nacky? Hurry
durry. I am come little Nacky; past eleven-a-clock, a late
hour; time in all conscience to go to bed, Nacky—Nacky
did I say? Ay Nacky; Aquilina, lina, lina, quilina, quilina,
quilina, Aquilina, Naquilina, Naquilina, Acky, Acky,
Nacky, Nacky, Queen Nacky—come let's to bed—you
fubbs, you pug you—you little puss—purree tuzzey—I
am a senator.

AQUILINA. You are a fool, I am sure.

ANTONIO. May be so too sweet-heart. Never the worse senator
for all that. Come, Nacky, Nacky, let's have a game at
rump, Nacky.

AQUILINA. You would do well, signior, to be troublesome here
no longer, but leave me to myself, be sober and go home,
sir.

ANTONIO. Home, Madonna!

AQUILINA. Ay home, sir. Who am I?

ANTONIO. Madonna, as I take it you are my—you are—thou
art my little Nicky Nacky—that's all!

AQUILINA. I find you are resolved to be troublesome, and so
to make short of the matter in few words, I hate you,
detest you, loathe you. I am weary of you, sick of you—
hang you, you are an old, silly, impertinent, impotent,

solicitous coxcomb, crazy in your head, and lazy in your body, love to be meddling with everything, and if you had not money, you are good for nothing.

ANTONIO. Good for nothing! Hurry durry, I'll try that presently. Sixty-one years old, and good for nothing; that's brave. (*To the Maid*) Come, come, come, Mistress Fiddlefaddle, turn you out for a season; go, turn out, I say, it is our will and pleasure to be private some moments—out, out when you are bid to—(*Puts her out and locks the door.*) Good for nothing, you say?

AQUILINA. Why what are you good for?

ANTONIO. In the first place, madam, I am old, and consequently very wise, very wise, Madonna, d'e mark that? in the second place take notice, if you please, that I am a senator, and when I think fit can make speeches, Madonna. Hurry durry, I can make a speech in the senate-house now and then—would make your hair stand on end, Madonna.

AQUILINA. What care I for your speeches in the senate-house? if you would be silent here, I should thank you.

ANTONIO. Why, I can make speeches to thee too, my lovely Madonna; for example—
My cruel fair one,

(*Takes out a purse of gold, and at every pause shakes it.*)

Since it is my fate, that you should with
Your servant angry prove; tho late at night—
I hope 'tis not too late with this to gain
Reception for my love—
There's for thee, my little Nicky Nacky—take it, here take it—I say take it, or I'll throw it at your head—how now, rebel!

AQUILINA. Truly, my illustrious senator, I must confess your honour is at present most profoundly eloquent indeed.

ANTONIO. Very well: Come, now let's sit down and think upon't a little—come sit I say—sit down by me a little, my Nicky Nacky, hah—(*Sits down*) hurry durry—good for nothing—

AQUILINA. No sir, if you please I can know my distance and stand.

ANTONIO. Stand: how? Nacky up and I down! Nay then let me exclaim with the poet:
    Shew me a case more pitiful who can,
    A standing woman, and a falling man.

Hurry durry—not sit down—See this ye gods—you won't
sit down?

AQUILINA. No sir.

ANTONIO. Then look you now, suppose me a bull, a Basan[31]
bull, the bull of bulls, or any bull. Thus up I get and
with my brows thus bent—I broo, I say I broo, I broo,
I broo. You won't sit down will you?—I broo—

(*Bellows like a bull, and drives her about.*)

AQUILINA. Well, Sir, I must endure this. (*She sits down.*)
Now your honour has been a bull, pray what beast will
your worship please to be next?

ANTONIO. Now I'll be a senator again, and thy lover, little
Nicky Nacky! (*He sits by her.*) Ah toad, toad, toad, toad!
spit in my face a little, Nacky—spit in my face prithee,
spit in my face, never so little: spit but a little bit—spit,
spit, spit, spit when you are bid I say; do, prithee spit—
now, now, now, spit: what you won't spit, will you? Then
I'll be a dog.

AQUILINA. A dog, my lord?

ANTONIO. Ay a dog—and I'll give thee this to'ther purse to
let me be a dog—and to use me like a dog a little. Hurry
durry—I will—here 'tis.—   (*Gives the purse.*)

AQUILINA. Well, with all my heart. But let me beseech your
dogship to play your trick's over as fast as you can, that
you may come to stinking the sooner, and be turned out
of doors as you deserve.

ANTONIO. Ay, ay—no matter for that—that (*He gets under
the table*) shan't move me—Now, bough waugh waugh,
bough waugh—   (*Barks like a dog.*)

AQUILINA. Hold, hold, hold sir, I beseech you: what is't you
do? If curs bite, they must be kicked, sir. Do you see,
kicked thus.

ANTONIO. Ay with all my heart: do kick, kick on, now I am
under the table, kick again—kick harder—harder yet,
bough waugh waugh, waugh, bough—'odd, I'll have a
snap at thy shins—bough waugh wough, waugh, bough—
'odd she kicks bravely—

AQUILINA. Nay then I'll go another way to work with you: and
I think here's an instrument fit for the purpose. (*Fetches
a whip and bell.*) What, bite your mistress, sirrah! out,

---

[31] *Basan*, the bulls of Bashan (Psalm XXII) were a by-word for
ferocity.

out of doors, you dog, to kennel and be hanged—bite your mistress by the legs, you rogue?— (*She whips him.*)

ANTONIO. Nay prithee, Nacky, now thou art too loving: Hurry durry, 'odd I'll be a dog no longer.

AQUILINA. Nay none of your fawning and grinning: But be gone, or here's the discipline: what, bite your mistress by the legs, you mungril? out of doors—hout hout, to kennel, sirra! go.

ANTONIO. This is very barbarous usage, Nacky, very barbarous: look you, I will not go—I will not stir from the door, that I resolve—hurry durry, what shut me out?

(*She whips him out.*)

AQUILINA. Ay, and if you come here any more tonight I'll have my footmen lug you,[32] you cur: what, bite your poor mistress Nacky, sirrah!

(*Enter* MAID.)

MAID. Heavens, madam! What's the matter?

(*He howls at the door like a dog.*)

AQUILINA. Call my footmen hither presently.

(*Enter two footmen.*)

MAID. They are here already, madam, the house is all alarmed with a strange noise, that nobody knows what to make of.

AQUILINA. Go all of you and turn that troublesome beast in the next room out of my house—If I ever see him within these walls again, without my leave for his admittance, you sneaking rogues—I'll have you poisoned all, poisoned, like rats: every corner of the house shall stink of one of you: go and learn hereafter to know my pleasure. So now for my Pierre:

Thus when Godlike lover was displeased;
We sacrifice our fool and he's appeased. (*Exeunt.*)

[SCENE II.]

(*Enter* BELVIDERA.)

BELVIDERA. I'm sacrificed! I am sold! betrayed to shame!
Inevitable ruin has enclosed me!
No sooner was I to my bed repaired,

32 *lug* you, drag you away.

To weigh, and (weeping) ponder my condition,
But the old hoary wretch, to whose false care
My peace and honour was intrusted, came
(Like Tarquin) ghastly with infernal lust.
Oh thou Roman Lucrece!
Thou could'st find friends to vindicate thy wrong;
I never had but one, and he's proved false;
He that should guard my virtue, has betrayed it;
Left me! undone me! Oh that I could hate him!
Where shall I go! Oh whither, whither wander?

(*Enter* JAFFEIR.)

JAFFEIR. Can Belvidera want a resting place
When these poor arms are open to receive her?
Oh 'tis in vain to struggle with desires
Strong as my love to thee; for every moment
I am from thy sight, the heart within my bosom
Moans like a tender infant in its cradle
Whose nurse had left it: come, and with the songs
Of gentle love persuade it to its peace.
BELVIDERA. I fear the stubborn wanderer will not own me,
'Tis grown a rebel to be ruled no longer,
Scorns the indulgent bosom that first lulled it,
And like a disobedient child disdains
The soft authority of Belvidera.
JAFFEIR. There was a time—
BELVIDERA.

                        Yes, yes, there was a time,
When Belvidera's tears, her cries, and sorrows,
Were not despised; when if she chanced to sigh,
Or look but sad;—there was indeed a time
When Jaffeir would have ta'en her in his arms,
Eased her declining head upon his breast,
And never left her 'till he found the cause.
But let her now weep seas,
Cry, 'till she rend the earth; sigh 'till she burst
Her heart asunder; still he bears it all;
Deaf as the wind, and as the rocks unshaken.
JAFFEIR. Have I been deaf? am I that rock unmoved,
Against whose root, tears beat and sighs are sent
In vain? have I beheld thy sorrows calmly?
Witness against me Heavens, have I done this?

Then bear me in a whirlwind back again,
And let that angry dear one ne'er forgive me!
Oh thou too rashly censur'st of my love!
Could'st thou but think how I have spent this night,
Dark and alone, no pillow to my head,
Rest in my eyes, nor quiet in my heart,
Thou would'st not, Belvidera, sure thou would'st not
Talk to me thus, but like a pitying angel
Spreading thy wings come settle on my breast,
And hatch warm comfort there ere sorrows freeze it.

BELVIDERA. Why, then, poor mourner, is what baleful corner
Hast thou been talking with that witch the night?
On what cold stone hast thou been stretched along,
Gathering the grumbling winds about thy head,
To mix with theirs the accents of thy woes?
Oh now I find the cause my love forsakes me!
I am no longer fit to bear a share
In his concernments: my weak female virtue
Must not be trusted; 'tis too frail and tender.

JAFFEIR. Oh Portia! Portia! What a soul was thine?

BELVIDERA. That Portia was a woman, and when Brutus,
Big with the fate of Rome, (Heaven guard thy safety!)
Concealed from her the labours of his mind,
She let him see, her blood was great as his,
Flowed from a spring as noble, and a heart
Fit to partake his troubles, as his love:
Fetch, fetch that dagger back, the dreadful dower
Thou gavest last night in parting with me; strike it
Here to my heart; and as the blood flows from it,
Judge if it run not pure as Cato's daughter's.

JAFFEIR. Thou art too good, and I indeed unworthy,
Unworthy so much virtue: teach me how
I may deserve such matchless love as thine,
And see with what attention I'll obey thee.

BELVIDERA. Do not despise me: that's the all I ask.

JAFFEIR. Despise thee! Hear me—

BELVIDERA.

                              Oh thy charming tongue
Is but too well acquainted with my weakness,
Knows, let it name but love, my melting heart
Dissolves within my breast; 'till with closed eyes
I reel into thy arms, and all's forgotten.

JAFFEIR. What shall I do?
BELVIDERA.

                   Tell me! be just, and tell me
Why dwells that busy cloud upon thy face?
Why am I made a stranger? why that sigh,
And I not know the cause? Why when the world
Is wrapt in rest, why chooses then my love
To wander up and down in horrid darkness,
Loathing his bed, and these desiring arms?
Why are these eyes bloodshot, with tedious watching?
Why starts he now? and looks as if he wished
His fate were finished? Tell me, ease my fears;
Least when we next time meet, I want the power
To search into the sickness of thy mind,
But talk as wildly then as thou look'st now.
JAFFEIR. Oh Belvidera!
BELVIDERA. Why was I last night delivered to a villain?
JAFFEIR. Hah, a villain!
BELVIDERA. Yes! to a villain! Why at such an hour
Meets that assembly all made up of wretches
That look as Hell had drawn 'em into league?
Why, I in this hand, and in that a dagger,
Was I delivered with such dreadful ceremonies?
"To you, Sirs, and to your Honour I bequeath her,
And with her this: When e'er I prove unworthy,
You know the rest, then strike it to her heart."
Oh! why's that rest concealed from me? must I
Be made the hostage of a hellish trust?
For such I know I am; that's all my value!
But by the love and loyalty I owe thee,
I'll free thee from the bondage of these slaves;
Straight to the senate, tell 'em all I know,
All that I think, all that my fears inform me!
JAFFEIR. Is this the Roman virtue! this the blood
That boasts its purity with Cato's Daughter!
Would she have e'er betray'd her Brutūs?
BELVIDERA.

                           No:
For Brutus trusted her: Wer't thou so kind,
What would not Belvidera suffer for thee?
JAFFEIR. I shall undo myself, and tell thee all.

BELVIDERA. Look not upon me as I am, a woman,
    But as a bone,[33] thy wife, thy friend; who long
    Has had admission to thy heart, and there
    Studied the virtues of thy gallant nature;
    Thy constancy, thy courage and thy truth,
    Have been my daily lesson: I have learnt them,
    Am bold as thou, can suffer or despise
    The worst of fates for thee; and with thee share them.

JAFFEIR. Oh you divinest powers! look down and hear
    My prayers! instruct me to reward this virtue!
    Yet think a little, ere thou tempt me further:
    Think I have a tale to tell, will shake thy nature,
    Melt all this boasted constancy thou talk'st of
    Into vile tears and despicable sorrows:
    Then if thou should'st betray me!

BELVIDERA.
                             Shall I swear?

JAFFEIR. No: do not swear: I would not violate
    Thy tender nature with so rude a bond:
    But as thou hop'st to see me live my days,
    And love thee long, lock this within thy breast;
    I've bound myself by all the strictest sacraments,
    Divine and human—

BELVIDERA.
                          Speak!—

JAFFEIR.
                          To kill thy father—

BELVIDERA. My father!

JAFFEIR.
              Nay the throats of the whole Senate
    Shall bleed, my Belvidera: he amongst us
    That spares his father, brother, or his friend,
    Is damned: how rich and beauteous will the face
    Of ruin look, when these wide streets run blood;
    I and the glorious partners of my fortune
    Shouting, and striding o'er the prostrate dead;
    Still to new waste; whilst thou, far off in safety
    Smiling, shalt see the wonders of our daring;
    And when night comes, with praise and love receive me.

BELVIDERA. Oh!

---

[33] *Bone,* i.e., Eve was created from Adam's rib.

JAFFEIR.
                    Have a care, and shrink not even in thought!
For if thou do'st—
BELVIDERA.
                              I know it, thou wilt kill me,
Do, strike thy sword into this bosom: lay me
Dead on the earth, and then thou wilt be safe:
Murder my father! tho his cruel nature
Has persecuted me to my undoing,
Driven me to basest wants; can I behold him
With smiles of vengeance, butchered in his age?
The sacred fountain of my life destroyed?
And canst thou shed the blood that gave me being?
Nay, be a traitor too, and sell thy country?
Can thy great heart descend so vilely low,
Mix with hired slaves, bravoes, and common stabbers,
Nose-slitters,[34] ally-lurking villains! join
With such a crew, and take a ruffian's wages,
To cut the throats of wretches as they sleep?
JAFFEIR. Thou wrong'st me, Belvidera! I've engaged
With men of souls: fit to reform the ills
Of all mankind: There's not a heart amongst them,
But's as stout as death, yet honest as the nature
Of man first made, e'er fraud and vice were fashions.
BELVIDERA. What's he, to whose cursed hands last night thou
        gavest me?
Was that well done? Oh! I could tell a story
Would rouse thy lion heart out of its den,
And make it rage with terrifying fury.
JAFFEIR. Speak on, I charge thee!
BELVIDERA.
                              Oh my love! if e'er
Thy Belvidera's peace deserved thy care,
Remove me from this place: Last night, last night!
JAFFEIR. Distract me not, but give me all the truth.
BELVIDERA. No sooner wer't thou gone, and I alone,
Left in the power of that old son of mischief;
No sooner was I lain on my sad bed,
But that vile wretch approached me; loose, unbuttoned,
Ready for violation: Then my heart

---

[34] *Nose-slitters,* Restoration aristocrats sometimes hired thugs to beat or maim their enemies. The Coventry Act was named after one of their victims.

Throbbed with its fears: Oh how I wept and sighed,
And shrunk and trembled; wished in vain for him
That should protect me. Thou alas! wert gone!

JAFFEIR. Patience, sweet Heaven! 'till I make vengeance sure.

BELVIDERA. He drew the hideous dagger forth thou gavest him,
And with upbraiding smiles he said, "behold it;
This is the pledge of a false husband's love:"
And in my arms then pressed, and would have clasped me;
But with my cries I scared his coward heart,
'Till he withdrew, and muttered vows to Hell.
These are thy friends! with these thy life, thy honour,
Thy love, all's staked, and all will go to ruin.

JAFFEIR. No more: I charge thee keep this secret close;
Clear up thy sorrows, look as if thy wrongs
Were all forgot, and treat him like a friend,
As no complaint were made. No more, retire,
Retire my life, and doubt not of my honour;
I'll heal its failings, and deserve thy love.

BELVIDERA. Oh should I part with thee, I fear thou wilt
In anger leave me, and return no more.

JAFFEIR. Return no more! I would not live without thee
Another night to purchase the creation.

BELVIDERA. When shall we meet again?

JAFFEIR.
                          Anon at twelve!
I'll steal myself to thy expecting arms,
Come like a travelled dove and bring thee peace.

BELVIDERA. Indeed?

JAFFEIR.
              By all our loves!

BELVIDERA.
                      'Tis hard to part:
But sure no falsehood e'er looked so fairly.
Farewell—remember twelve.   (*Exit* BELVIDERA.)

JAFFEIR.
                      Let Heaven forget me
When I remember not thy truth, thy love.
How cursed is my condition, tossed and jostled,
From every corner; Fortune's common fool,
The jest of rogues, an instrumental ass
For villains to lay loads of shame upon,
And drive about just for their ease and scorn.

(*Enter* PIERRE.)

PIERRE. Jaffeir!
JAFFEIR.

>   Who calls!

PIERRE.

>   A friend, that could have wished
> T'have found thee otherwise employed: what, hunt
> A wife on the dull foil![35] sure a staunch husband
> Of all hounds is the dullest? wilt thou never,
> Never be weaned from caudles[36] and confections?
> What feminine tale hast thou been listening to,
> Of unair'd shirts; catharhs and tooth ache got
> By thin-soled shoes? damnation! that a fellow
> Chosen to be a sharer in the destruction
> Of a whole people, should sneak thus in corners
> To ease his fulsome lusts, and fool his mind.

JAFFEIR. May not a man then trifle out an hour
> With a kind woman and not wrong his calling?

PIERRE. Not in a cause like ours.

JAFFEIR.

>   Then friend our cause
> Is in a damned condition: for I'll tell thee,
> That canker-worm called Lechery has touched it,
> 'Tis tainted vilely: would'st thou think it, Renault,
> (That mortified old withered winter rogue)
> Loves simple fornication like a priest,
> I found him out for watering at my wife:
> He visited her last night like a kind guardian:
> Faith she has some temptations, that's the truth on't.

PIERRE. He durst not wrong his trust!

JAFFEIR.

>   'Twas something late tho
> To take the freedom of a lady's chamber.

PIERRE. Was she in bed?

JAFFEIR.

>   Yes faith in virgin sheets
> White as her bosom, Pierre, dished neatly up,
> Might tempt a weaker appetite to taste.
> Oh how the old fox stunk I warrant thee
> When the rank fit was on him.

---

[35] *hunt . . . dull foil,* trail a wife.
[36] *caudles,* sick-bed drinks.

PIERRE.

                                   Patience guide me!
      He used no violence?

JAFFEIR.

                          No, no! out on't, violence!
      Played with her neck; brushed her with his gray beard,
      Struggled and tousled,[37] tickled her 'till she squeaked a
          little
      Maybe, or so—but not a jot of violence—

PIERRE. Damn him.

JAFFEIR.

                          Ay, so say I: but hush, no more on't;
      All hitherto is well, and I believe
      Myself no monster[38] yet: Tho no man knows
      What fate he's born to: sure 'tis near the hour
      We all should meet for our concluding orders:
      Will the ambassador be here in person?

PIERRE. No: he has sent commission to that villain, Renault,
      To give the executing charge;
      I'd have thee be a man if possible
      And keep thy temper; for a brave revenge
      Ne'er comes too late.

JAFFEIR.

                          Fear not, I am cool as Patience:
      Had he completed my dishonour, rather
      Than hazard the success our hopes are ripe for,
      I'd bear it all with mortifying virtue.

PIERRE. He's yonder coming this way through the hall;
      His thoughts seem full.

JAFFEIR.

                          Prithee retire, and leave me
      With him alone: I'll put him to some trial,
      See how his rotten part will bear the touching.

PIERRE. Be careful then.   (*Exit* PIERRE.)

JAFFEIR.

                          Nay never doubt, but trust me.
      What, be a Devil! take a damning oath
      For shedding native blood! can there be a sin
      In merciful repentance? Oh this villain.

      (*Enter* RENAULT.)

[37] *tousled,* handled.
[38] *monster,* i.e., horned cuckold.

RENAULT. Perverse! and peevish! what a slave is man!
    To let his itching flesh thus get the better of him!
    Dispatch the tool her husband—that were well.
    Who's there?

JAFFEIR.

            A man.

RENAULT.

                 My friend, my near ally!
    The hostage of your faith, my beauteous charge,
    Is very well.

JAFFEIR.

            Sir, are you sure of that?
    Stands she in perfect health? beats her pulse even?
    Neither too hot nor cold?

RENAULT.

                What means that question?

JAFFEIR. Oh women have fantastic constitutions,
    Inconstant as their wishes, always wavering,
    And ne'er fixt; was it not boldly done
    Even at first sight to trust the thing I loved
    (A tempting treasure too!) with youth so fierce
    And vigorous as thine? but thou art honest.

RENAULT. Who dares accuse me?

JAFFEIR.

                Cursed be him that doubts
    Thy virtue, I have tried it, and declare,
    Were I to choose a guardian of my honour
    I'd put it into thy keeping: for I know thee.

RENAULT. Know me!

JAFFEIR.

          Ay know thee: there's no falsehood in thee.
    Thou look'st just as thou art: Let us embrace.
    Now would'st thou cut my throat or I cut thine?

RENAULT. You dare not do't.

JAFFEIR.

             You lie sir.

RENAULT.   How!

JAFFEIR.

                 No more.
  'Tis a base world, and must reform, that's all.

(*Enter* SPINOSA, THEODORE, ELIOT, REVELLIDO, DURAND,
BRAINVEIL, *and the rest of the Conspirators.*)

RENAULT. Spinosa! Theodore!

SPINOSA.

The same.

RENAULT.

You are welcome!

SPINOSA. You are trembling, sir.

RENAULT.

'Tis a cold night indeed, I am aged,
Full of decay and natural infirmities;

(PIERRE *re-enters*.)

We shall be warm, my friend, I hope tomorrow.

PIERRE. 'Twas not well done, thou shou'd'st have stroked him
And not have galled him.

JAFFEIR.

Damn him, let him chew on't.
Heaven! where am I? beset with cursed fiends,
That wait to damn me: what a devil's man,
When he forgets his nature—hush, my heart.

RENAULT. My friends, 'tis late: are we assembled all?
Where's Theodore?

THEODORE.

At hand.

RENAULT.

Spinosa.

SPINOSA.

Here.

RENAULT. Brainveil.

BRAINVEIL.

I am ready.

RENAULT.

Durand and Brabe.

DURAND.

Command us,
We are both prepared!

RENAULT.

Mezzana, Revellido,
Ternon, Retrosi; Oh you are men I find
Fit to behold your fate, and meet her summons;
Tomorrow's rising sun must see you all
Decked in your honours! are the soldiers ready?

OMNES. All, all.

RENAULT. You, Durand, with your thousand must possess
    St. Mark's; You, Captain, know your charge already;
    'Tis to secure the Ducal Palace: you
    Brabe with a hundred more must gain the Secque.
    With the like number Brainveil to the Procuralle.
    Be all this done with the least tumult possible,
    'Till in each place you post sufficient guards:
    Then sheath your swords in every breast you meet.
JAFFEIR. Oh reverend cruelty: Damned bloody villain!
RENAULT. During this execution, Durand, you
    Must in the mid'st keep your battalia fast,
    And Theodore be sure to plant the cannon
    That may command the streets; whilst Revellido,
    Mezzana, Ternon and Retrosi guard you.
    This done, we'll give the general alarm,
    Apply petards,[39] and force the Arsenal gates;
    Then fire the city round in several places,
    Or with our cannon (if it dare resist)
    Batter't to ruin. But above all I charge you,
    Shed blood enough, spare neither sex nor age,
    Name nor condition; if there live a senator
    After tomorrow, tho the dullest rogue
    That e'er said nothing, we have lost our ends;
    If possible, let's kill the very name
    Of senator, and bury it in blood.
JAFFEIR. Merciless, horrid slave!—Ay, blood enough!
    Shed blood enough, old Renault: how thou charm'st me!
RENAULT. But one thing more, and then farewell till fate
    Join us again, or separate us ever:
    First, let's embrace, Heaven knows who next shall thus
    Wing ye together: but let's all remember
    We wear no common cause upon our swords,
    Let each man think that on his single virtue
    Depends the good and fame of all the rest;
    Eternal honour or perpetual infamy.
    Let's remember, through what dreadful hazards
    Propitious fortune hitherto has led us,
    How often on the brink of some discovery
    Have we stood tottering, and yet still kept our ground
    So well, the busiest searchers ne'er could follow
    Those subtle tracks which puzzled all suspicion:
    You droop, sir.

[39] *petards,* explosives.

JAFFEIR.
No: with a most profound attention
I've heard it all, and wonder at thy virtue.

RENAULT. Though there be yet few hours 'twixt them and ruin,
Are not the senate lulled in full security,
Quiet and satisfied, as fools are always!
Never did so profound repose forerun
Calamity so great: Nay our good fortune
Has blinded the most piercing of mankind:
Strengthened the fearful'st, charmed the most suspectful,
Confounded the most subtle: for we live,
We live my friends, and quickly shall our life
Prove fatal to these tyrants: let's consider
That we destroy oppression, avarice,
A people nursed up equally with vices
And loathsome lusts, which nature most abhors,
And such as without shame she cannot suffer.

JAFFEIR. Oh Belvidera, take me to thy arms
And show me where's my peace, for I've lost it.

(*Exit* JAFFEIR.)

RENAULT. Without the least remorse then let's resolve
With fire and sword t'exterminate these tyrants;
And when we shall behold those cursed tribunals,
Stained by the tears and sufferings of the innocent,
Burning with flames rather from Heaven than ours,
The raging, furious and unpitying soldier
Pulling his reeking dagger from the bosoms
Of gasping wretches; death in every quarter,
With all that sad disorder can produce,
To make a spectacle of horror: then,
Then let's call to mind, my dearest friends,
That there's nothing pure upon the earth,
That the most valued things have most allays,[40]
And that in change of all those vile enormities,
Under whose weight this wretched country labours,
The means are only in our hands to crown them.

PIERRE. And may those powers above that are propitious
To gallant minds record this cause, and bless it.

RENAULT. Thus happy, thus secure of all we wish for,
Should there my friends be found amongst us one

[40] *allays*, alloys or mixtures.

False to this glorious enterprise, what fate,
What vengeance were enough for such a villain?
ELIOT. Death here without repentance, Hell hereafter.
RENAULT. Let that be my lot, if as here I stand
    Lifted by fate amongst her darling sons,
    Tho I had one only brother, dear by all
    The strictest ties of Nature; tho one hour
    Had given us birth, one fortune fed our wants,
    One only love, and that but of each other,
    Still filled our minds: could I have such a friend
    Joined in this cause, and had but ground to fear
    Meant foul play; may this right hand drop from me,
    If I'd not hazard all my future peace,
    And stab him to the heart before you: who
    Would do less? Would'st not thou, Pierre, the same?
PIERRE. You have singled me, sir, out for this hard question,
    As if 'twere started only for my sake!
    Am I the thing you fear? Here, here's my bosom,
    Search it with all your swords! am I a traitor?
RENAULT. No: but I fear your late commended friend
    Is little less: Come, sirs, 'tis now no time
    To trifle with our safety. Where's this Jaffeir?
SPINOSA. He left the room just now in strange disorder.
RENAULT. Nay, there is danger in him: I observed him,
    During the time I took for explanation,
    He was transported from most deep attention
    To a confusion which he could not smother.
    His looks grew full of sadness and surprise,
    All which betray'd a wavering spirit in him,
    That laboured with reluctancy and sorrow;
    What's requisite for safety must be done
    With speedy execution: he remains
    Yet in our power: I for my own part wear
    A dagger.
PIERRE.
        Well.
RENAULT.
            And I could wish it—
PIERRE.
                  Where?
RENAULT. Buried in his heart.
PIERRE.   Away! w'are yet all friends;
    No more of this, 'twill breed ill blood amongst us.

SPINOSA. Let us all draw our swords, and search the house,
    Pull him from the dark hole where he sits brooding
    O'er his cold fears, and each man kill his share of him.
PIERRE. Who talks of killing? who's he'll shed the blood
    That's dear to me? is't you? or you? or you sir?
    What not one speak? how you stand gaping all
    On your grave oracle, your wooden god there;
    Yet not a word: Then sir, I'll tell you a secret:
    Suspicion's but at best a coward's virtue! (*To* RENAULT.)
RENAULT. A coward—   *Handles his sword.*
PIERRE.

             Put, put up thy sword, old man,
    Thy hand shakes at it; come let's heal this breach,
    I am too hot: we yet may live friends.
SPINOSA. 'Till we are safe, our friendship cannot be so.
PIERRE. Again: who's that?
SPINOSA.

                    'Twas I.
THEODORE.

                And I.
REVELLIDO.

                  And I.
ELIOT. And all.
RENAULT. Who are on my side?
SPINOSA.

             Every honest sword:
    Let's die like men and not be sold like slaves.
PIERRE. One such word more, by Heaven I'll to the senate
    And hang ye all, like dogs in clusters.
    Why peep your coward swords half out their shells?
    Why do you not all brandish them like mine?
    You fear to die, and yet dare talk of killing?
RENAULT. Go to the Senate and betray us, hasten,
    Secure thy wretched life, we fear to die
    Less than thou dar'st be honest.
PIERRE.

             That's rank falsehood,
    Fear'st not thou death? fye there's a knavish itch
    In that salt blood, an utter foe to smarting.
    Had Jaffeir's wife prov'd kind, he had still been true.
    Foh—how that stinks?
    Thou die! thou kill my friend! or thou, or thou,
    Or thou, with that lean withered wretched face!

Away! disperse all to your several charges,
And meet tomorrow where your honour calls you,
I'll bring that man, whose blood you so much thirst for,
And you shall see him venture for you fairly—
Hence, hence, I say.   (*Exit* RENAULT *angrily*.)

SPINOSA.

                    I fear we have been too blame,
And done too much.

THEODORE. 'Twas too far urged against the man you loved.

REVELLIDO. Here, take our swords and crush 'em with your
      feet.

SPINOSA. Forgive us, gallant friend.

PIERRE.

                              Nay, now y' have found
The way to melt and cast me as you will:
I'll fetch this friend and give him to your mercy:
Nay he shall die if you will take him from me,
For your repose I'll quit my heart's jewel;
But would not have him torn away by villains
And spiteful villainy.

SPINOSA.

                    No; may you both
For ever live and fill the world with fame!

PIERRE. Now you are too kind. Whence rose all this discord?
Oh what a dangerous precipice have we scaped!
How near a fall was all we had long been building!
What an eternal blot had stained our glories,
If one the bravest and the best of men
Had fallen a sacrifice to rash suspicion,
Butchered by those whose cause he came to cherish:
Oh could you know him all as I have known him,
How good he is, how just, how true, how brave,
You would not leave this place till you had seen him;
Humbled yourselves before him, kissed his feet,
And gained remission for the worst of follies;
Come but tomorrow all your doubts shall end,
And to your loves me better recommend,
That I've preserved your fame, and saved my friend.

                              (*Exeunt omnes.*)

ACT IV

[SCENE I.]

(*Enter* JAFFEIR *and* BELVIDERA.)

JAFFEIR. Where dost thou lead me? Every step I move,
Methinks I tread upon some mangled limb
Of a racked friend: Oh my dear charming ruin!
Where are we wandering?

BELVIDERA.

To eternal honour;
To do a deed shall chronicle thy name,
Among the glorious legends of those few
That have saved sinking nations: thy renown
Shall be the future song of all the virgins,
Who by thy piety have been preserved
From horrid violation: every street
Shall be adorned with statues to thy honour,
And at thy feet this great inscription written,
"Remember him that propped the fall of Venice."

JAFFEIR. Rather, remember him, who after all
The sacred bonds of oaths and holier friendship,
In fond compassion to a woman's tears
Forgot his manhood, virtue, truth and honour,
To sacrifice the bosom that relieved him.
Why wilt thou damn me?

BELVIDERA.

Oh inconstant man!
How will you promise? how will you deceive?
Do, return back, replace me in my bondage,
Tell all thy friends how dangerously thou lovst me;
And let thy dagger do its bloody office.
Oh that kind dagger, Jaffeir, how t'will look
Stuck through my heart, drenched in my blood to the
    hilts!
Whilst these poor dying eyes shall with their tears
No more torment thee, then thou wilt be free:
Or if thou think'st it nobler, let me live
Till I am a victim to the hateful lust
Of that infernal devil, that old fiend
That's damned himself and would undo mankind:
Last night, my love!

JAFFEIR.
                              Name, name it not again.
It shows a beastly image to my fancy,
Will wake me into madness. Oh the villain!
That durst approach such purity as thine
On terms so vile: destruction, swift destruction
Fall on my coward head, and make my name
The common scorn of fools if I forgive him;
If I forgive him, if I not revenge
With utmost rage, and most unstaying fury,
Thy sufferings thou dear darling of my life, love.

BELVIDERA. Delay no longer then, but to the Senate;
And tell the dismal'st story e'er was uttered,
Tell 'em what bloodshed, rapines, desolations,
Have been prepared, how near's the fatal hour!
Save thy poor country, save the reverend blood
Of all its nobles, which tomorrow's dawn
Must else see shed: save the poor tender lives
Of all those little infants which the swords
Of murtherers are whetting for this moment;
Think thou already hearst their dying screams,
Think that thou seest their sad distracted mothers
Kneeling before thy feet, and begging pity
With torn disheveled hair and streaming eyes,
Their naked mangled breasts besmeared with blood,
And even the milk with which their fondled babes
Softly they hushed, dropping in anguish from 'em.
Think thou seest this, and then consult thy heart.

JAFFEIR. Oh!
BELVIDERA.
                    Think too, if thou lose this present minute,
What miseries the next day brings upon thee.
Imagine all the horrors of that night,
Murther and rapine, waste and desolation,
Confusedly ranging. Think what then may prove
My lot! the ravisher may then come safe,
And midst the terror of the public ruin
Do a damned deed; perhaps to lay a train
May catch thy life; then where will be revenge,
The dear revenge that's due to such a wrong?

JAFFEIR. By all Heaven's powers, prophetic truth dwells in thee,
For every word thou speak'st strikes through my heart
Like a new light, and shows it how 't was wandered;

Just what th' hast made me, take me, Belvidera,
And lead me to the place where I'm to say
This bitter lesson, where I must betray
My truth, my virtue, constancy and friends:
Must I betray my friends? Ah take me quickly,
Secure me well before that thought's renewed;
If I relapse once more, all's lost for ever.

BELVIDERA. Hast thou a friend more dear than Belvidera?

JAFFEIR. No, th'art my soul itself; wealth, friendship, honour,
All present joys, and earnest of all future,
Are summed in thee: methinks when in thy arms
Thus leaning on thy breast, one minute's more
Than a long thousand years of vulgar hours.
Why was such happiness not given me pure?
Why dashed with cruel wrongs, and bitter wantings?
Come, lead me forward now like a tame lamb
To sacrifice: thus in his fatal garlands,
Decked fine and pleased, the wanton skips and plays,
Trots by the enticing flattering priestess' side,
And much transported with his little pride,
Forgets his dear companions of the plain,
Till by her, bound, he's on the altar lain;
Yet then too hardly bleats, such pleasure's in the pain.

(*Enter* OFFICER *and six* GUARDS.)

OFFICER. Stand: who goes there?

BELVIDERA. Friends.

JAFFEIR. Friends, Belvidera! hide me from my friends,
By Heaven I'd rather see the face of Hell,
Than meet the man I love.

OFFICER.

                    But what friends are you?

BELVIDERA. Friends to the Senate and the state of Venice.

OFFICER. My orders are to seize on all I find
At this late hour, and bring 'em to the council,
Who now are sitting.

JAFFEIR.

            Sir, you shall be obeyed.
Hold, brutes, stand off, none of your paws upon me.
Now the lot's cast, and Fate do what thou wilt.

                       (*Exeunt guarded.*)

[SCENE II.] *The senate-house*

(*Where appear sitting, the* DUKE OF VENICE, PRIULI,
ANTONIO, *and eight other senators.*)

DUKE. Antony, Priuli, senators of Venice,
    Speak; why are we assembled here this night?
    What have you to inform us of, concerns
    The state of Venice, honour, or its safety?
PRIULI. Could words express the story I have to tell you,
    Fathers, these tears were useless, these sad tears
    That fall from my old eyes; but there is cause
    We all should weep; tear off these purple robes,
    And wrap ourselves in sack-cloth, sitting down
    On the sad earth, and cry aloud to Heaven.
    Heaven knows if yet there be an hour to come
    Ere Venice be no more!
ALL SENATORS.

                How!

PRIULI.

                Nay we stand
    Upon the very brink of gaping ruin,
    Within this city's formed a dark conspiracy,
    To massacre us all, our wives and children,
    Kindred and friends, our palaces and temples
    To lay in ashes: nay the hour too, fixed;
    The swords, for ought I know, drawn even this moment,
    And the wild waste begun: from unknown hands
    I had this warning: but if we are men
    Let's not be tamely butchered, but do something
    That may inform the world in after ages,
    Our virtue was not ruined though we were.
    A noise without. Room, room, make room for some
        prisoners—
2 SENATORS. Let's raise the city.

(*Enter* OFFICER *and* GUARD.)

PRIULI.

             Speak there, what disturbance?
OFFICER. Two prisoners have the guard seized in the streets,
    Who say they come to inform this reverend senate
    About the present danger.

(*Enter* JAFFEIR *and* BELVIDERA *guarded.*)

ALL.

                Give 'em entrance—

  Well, who are you?

JAFFEIR.

              A villain.

ANTONIO.

                 Short and pithy.

  The man speaks well.

JAFFEIR.

                Would every man that hears me
Would deal so honestly, and own his title.

DUKE. 'Tis rumoured that a plot has been contrived
    Against this state; that you have a share in't too.
    If you are a villain, to redeem your honour,
    Unfold the truth and be restored with mercy.

JAFFEIR. Think not that I to save my life come hither,
    I know its value better; but in pity
    To all those wretches whose unhappy dooms
    Are fixed and sealed. You see me here before you,
    The sworn and covenanted foe of Venice.
    But use me as my dealings may deserve
    And I may prove a friend.

DUKE.

              The slave capitulates,
  Give him the tortures.

JAFFEIR.

               That you dare not do,
    Your fears won't let you, nor the longing itch
    To hear a story which you dread the truth of:
    Truth which the fear of smart shall ne'er get from me.
    Cowards are scared with threatnings. Boys are whipped
    Into confessions: but a steady mind
    Acts of itself, ne'er asks the body counsel.
    Give him the tortures! Name but such a thing
    Again; by Heaven I'll shut these lips for ever,
    Not all your racks, your engines or your wheels
    Shall force a groan away—that you may guess at.

ANTONIO. A bloody-minded fellow I'll warrant;
    A damned bloody-minded fellow.

DUKE. Name your conditions.

JAFFEIR.

              For myself full pardon,
  Besides the lives of two and twenty friends
                     (Displays a list.)

Whose names are here enrolled: nay, let their crimes
Be ne'er so monstrous, I must have the oaths
And sacred promise of this reverend council,
That in a full assembly of the Senate
The thing I ask be ratified. Swear this,
And I'll unfold the secrets of your danger.

ALL. We'll swear.

DUKE.

Propose the oath.

JAFFEIR.

By all the hopes
Ye have of peace and happiness hereafter,
Swear.

ALL. We all swear.

JAFFEIR.

To grant me what I've asked,
Ye swear.

ALL.

We swear.

JAFFEIR.

And as ye keep the oath,
May you and your posterity be blest
Or cursed for ever.

ALL.

Else be cursed for ever.

JAFFEIR. Then here's the list, and with't the full disclose
Of all that threatens you.   (*Delivers the list.*)
Now Fate thou hast caught me.

ANTONIO. Why what a dreadful catalogue of cut-throats is
here! I'll warrant you not one of these fellows but has a
face like a lion. I dare not so much as read their names
over.

DUKE. Give orders that all diligent search be made
To seize these men, their characters are public,
The paper intimates their rendevous
To be at the house of a famed Grecian courtesan
Called Aquilina; see that place secured.

ANTONIO. What, my Nicky Nacky, Hurry Durry, Nicky Nacky
in the plot!—I'll make a speech. Most noble senators,
What headlong apprehension drives you on,
Right noble, wise and truly solid senators,
To violate the laws and right of nations?
The lady is a lady of renown.

'Tis true, she holds a house of fair reception,
And though I say't myself, as many more
Can say as well as I—

2 SENATORS.

My lord, long speeches
Are frivolous here, when dangers are so near us;
We all well know your interest in that lady,
The world talks loud on't.

ANTONIO.

Verily I have done,
I say no more.

DUKE.

But since he has declared
Himself concerned, pray, Captain, take great caution
To treat the fair one as becomes her character,
And let her bed-chamber be searched with decency.
You, Jaffeir, must with patience bear till morning,
To be our prisoner.

JAFFEIR.

Would the chains of death
Had bound me fast e'er I had known this minute!
I've done a deed will make my story hereafter
Quoted in competition with all ill ones:
The history of my wickedness shall run
Down through the low traditions of the vulgar,
And boys be taught to tell the tale of Jaffeir.

DUKE. Captain, withdraw your prisoner.

JAFFEIR.

Sir, if possible,
Lead me where my own thoughts themselves may lose me,
Where I may doze out what I've left of life,
Forget myself and this day's guilt and falsehood.
Cruel remembrance how shall I appease thee!

(*Exit guarded.*)

(*Noise without.*) More traitors; room, room, make room
there.

DUKE. How's this, guards?
Where are our guards? shut up the gates, the treason's
Already at our doors.

(*Enter* OFFICER.)

OFFICER.

My lords, more traitors:
Seized in the very act of consultation;
Furnished with arms and instruments of mischief.
Bring in the prisoners.

(*Enter* PIERRE, RENAULT, THEODORE, ELIOT, REVILLIDO *and
other Conspirators, in fetters, guarded.*)

PIERRE.

You, my lords and fathers,
(As you are pleased to call yourselves) of Venice;
If you sit here to guide the course of justice,
Why these disgraceful chains upon the limbs
That have so often laboured in your service?
Are these the wreaths of triumphs ye bestow
On those that bring you conquests home and honours?

DUKE. Go on, you shall be heard, sir.

ANTONIO. And be hanged too, I hope.

PIERRE. Are these the trophies I've deserved for fighting
Your battles with confederated powers,
When winds and seas conspired to overthrow you,
And brought the fleets of Spain to your own harbours?
When you, great Duke, shrunk trembling in your palace,
And saw your wife, th'Adriatic, ploughed
Like a lewd whore by bolder prows than yours,
Stepped not I forth, and taught your loose Venetians
The task of honour and the way to greatness,
Raised you from your capitulating fears
To stipulate the terms of sued-for peace,
And this my recompence? If I am a traitor,
Produce my charge; or show the wretch that's base enough
And brave enough to tell me I am a traitor.

DUKE. Know you one Jaffeir? (*All the Conspirators murmur.*)

PIERRE.

Yes, and know his virtue.
His justice, truth, his general worth, and sufferings
From a hard father taught me first to love him.

DUKE. See him brought forth.

(*Enter* JAFFEIR *guarded.*)

PIERRE.

My friend, too, bound? nay then
Our fate has conquer'd us, and we must fall.
Why droops the man whose welfare's so much mine

They're but one thing? these reverend tyrants, Jaffeir,
Call us all traitors, art thou one, my brother?

JAFFEIR. To thee I am the falsest, veriest slave
That e'er betrayed a generous trusting friend,
And gave up honour to be sure of ruin.
All our fair hopes which morning was to have crowned
Has this cursed tongue o'erthrown.

PIERRE.
                                        So, then all's over:
Venice has lost her freedom; I my life;
No more, farewell.

DUKE.
                        Say; will you make confession
Of your vile deeds and trust the Senate's mercy?

PIERRE. Cursed be your Senate: cursed your constitution:
The curse of growing factions and division
Still vex your councils, shake your public safety,
And make the robes of government, you wear,
Hateful to you, as these base chains to me.

DUKE. Pardon or death?

PIERRE.
                        Death, honourable death.

RENAULT. Death's the best thing we ask or you can give.

ALL CONSPIRATORS. No shameful bonds, but honourable death.

DUKE. Break up the council: Captain, guard your prisoners.
Jaffeir, y'are free, but these must wait for judgment.

(*Exit all the Senators and* BELVIDERA.)

PIERRE. Come, where's my dungeon? lead me to my straw:
It will not be the first time I've lodged hard
To do your Senate service.

JAFFEIR.
                        Hold one moment.

PIERRE. Who's he disputes the judgment of the Senate?
Presumptuous rebel—on—   (*Strikes* JAFFEIR.)

JAFFEIR.
                        By Heaven you stir not.
I must be heard, I must have leave to speak:
Thou hast disgraced me, Pierre, by a vile blow:
Had not a dagger done thee nobler justice?
But use me as thou wilt, thou canst not wrong me,
For I am fallen beneath the basest injuries;
Yet look upon me with an eye of mercy,
With pity and with charity behold me;

Shut not thy heart against a friend's repentance,
But as there dwells a god-like nature in thee,
Listen with mildness to my supplications.

PIERRE. What whining monk art thou? what holy cheat
That wouldst encroach upon my credulous ears
And cant'st thus vilely? Hence! I know thee not.
Dissemble and be nasty: leave me, hypocrite.

JAFFEIR. Not know me Pierre?

PIERRE.
No, know thee not: what art thou?

JAFFEIR. Jaffeir, thy friend, thy once loved, valued friend,
Though now deservedly scorned, and used most hardly.

PIERRE. Thou Jaffeir! Thou my once loved, valued friend!
By Heavens thou liest; the man so called, my friend,
Was generous, honest, faithful, just and valiant,
Noble in mind, and in his person lovely,
Dear to my eyes and tender to my heart:
But thou a wretched, base, false, worthless coward,
Poor even in soul, and loathsome in thy aspect,
All eyes must shun thee, and all hearts detest thee.
Prithee avoid, nor longer cling thus round me,
Like something baneful, that my nature's chilled at.

JAFFEIR. I have not wronged thee, by these tears I have not.
But still am honest, true, and hope, too, valiant;
My mind still full of thee: therefore still noble.
Let not thy eyes then shun me, nor thy heart
Detest me utterly: oh look upon me,
Look back and see my sad sincere submission!
How my heart swells, as even 'twould burst my bosom;
Fond of its gaol, and labouring to be at thee!
What shall I do? what say to make thee hear me?

PIERRE. Hast thou not wronged me? dar'st thou call thyself
Jaffeir, that once loved, valued friend of mine,
And swear thou hast not wronged me? Whence these
chains?
Whence the vile death, which I may meet this moment?
Whence this dishonour, but from thee, thou false one?

JAFFEIR. All's true, yet grant one thing, and I've done asking.

PIERRE. What's that?

JAFFEIR.
To take thy life on such conditions
The council have proposed: thou and thy friends
May yet live long, and to be better treated.

PIERRE. Life! ask my life! confess! record myself
 A villain for the privilege to breathe,
 And carry up and down this cursed city
 A discontented and repining spirit,
 Burthensome to itself, a few years longer,
 To lose, it may be, at last in a lewd quarrel
 For some new friend, treacherous and false as thou art!
 No, this vile world and I have long been jangling,
 And cannot part on better terms than now,
 When only men like thee are fit to live in't.

JAFFEIR. By all that's just—

PIERRE.
       Swear by some other powers,
 For thou hast broke that sacred oath too lately.

JAFFEIR. Then by that hell I merit, I'll not leave thee,
 Till to thyself at least, thou'rt reconciled,
 However thy resentments deal with me.

PIERRE. Not leave me!

JAFFEIR.
     No, thou shalt not force me from thee.
 Use me reproachfully, and like a slave,
 Tread on me, buffet me, heap wrongs on wrongs
 On my poor head; I'll bear it all with patience,
 Shall weary out thy most unfriendly cruelty,
 Lie at thy feet and kiss 'em though they spurn me,
 Till, wounded by my sufferings, thou relent,
 And raise me to thy arms with dear forgiveness.

PIERRE. Art thou not—

JAFFEIR.
    What?

PIERRE.
     A traitor?

JAFFEIR.
      Yes.

PIERRE.
       A villain?

JAFFEIR. Granted.

PIERRE.
   A coward, a most scandalous coward,
 Spiritless, void of honour, one who has sold
 Thy everlasting fame, for shameless life?

JAFFEIR. All, all, and more, much more: my faults are
 numberless.

PIERRE. And wouldst thou have me live on terms like thine?
Base as thou art false?

JAFFEIR.

No, 'tis to me that's granted
The safety of thy life was all I aimed at,
In recompence for faith, and trust so broken.

PIERRE. I scorn it more because preserved by thee.
And as when first my foolish heart took pity
On thy misfortunes, sought thee in thy miseries,
Relieved thy wants, and raised thee from thy state
Of wretchedness in which thy fate had plunged thee,
To rank thee in my list of noble friends;
All I received in surety for thy truth,
Were unregarded oaths; and this, this dagger,
Given with a worthless pledge, thou since hast stolen:
So I restore it back to thee again,
Swearing by all those powers which thou hast violated,
Never from this cursed hour to hold communion,
Friendship or interest with thee, though our years
Were to exceed those limited the world.
Take it—farewell—for now I owe thee nothing.

JAFFEIR. Say thou wilt live then.

PIERRE.

For my life, dispose it
Just as thou wilt, because 'tis what I'm tired with.

JAFFEIR. Oh, Pierre!

PIERRE.

No more.

JAFFEIR.

My eyes won't lose the sight of thee,
But languish after thine, and ache with gazing.

PIERRE. Leave me—nay, then thūs, thus, I throw thee from me.
And curses, great as is thy falsehood, catch thee. (*Exit.*)

JAFFEIR. Amen.
He's gone, my father, friend, preserver,
And here's the portion he has left me.

(*Holds the dagger up.*)

This dagger, well remembered, with this dagger
I gave a solemn vow of dire importance,
Parted with this and Belvidera together;
Have a care, memory, drive that thought no farther;
No, I'll esteem it as a friend's last legacy,
Treasure it up in this wretched bosom,

Where it may grow acquainted with my heart,
That when they meet, they start not from each other;
So; now for thinking: a blow, call'd traitor, villain,
Coward, dishonourable coward, fogh!
Oh for a long sound sleep, and so forget it!
Down, busy devil.—

(*Enter* BELVIDERA.)

BELVIDERA.
                Whither shall I fly?
Where hide me and my miseries together?
Where's now the Roman constancy I boasted?
Sunk into trembling fears and desperation!
Not daring now to look up to that dear face
Which used to smile even on my faults, but down
Bending these miserable eyes to earth,
Must move in penance, and implore much mercy.

JAFFEIR. Mercy! kind Heaven has surely endless stores
Hoarded for thee of blessings yet untasted;
Let wretches loaded hard with guilt as I am,
Bow with the weight and groan beneath the burthen,
Creep with a remnant of that strength th' have left,
Before the footstool of that Heaven th' have injured.
Oh Belvidera! I'm the wretched'st creature
E'er crawl'd on earth; now if thou hast virtue, help me,
Take me into thy arms, and speak the words of peace
To my divided soul, that wars within me,
And raises every sense to my confusion;
By Heaven I am tottering on the very brink
Of peace; and thou art all the hold I've left.

BELVIDERA. Alas! I know thy sorrows are most mighty;
I know th'hast cause to mourn; to mourn, my Jaffeir,
With endless cries, and never ceasing wailings;
Th'hast lost—

JAFFEIR.
          Oh I have lost what can't be counted;
My friend too, Belvidera, that dear friend,
Who, next to thee, was all my health rejoiced in,
Has used me like a slave; shamefully used me;
'Twould break thy pitying heart to hear the story.
What shall I do? resentment, indignation,
Love, pity, fear, and memory how I've wronged him,
Distract my quiet with the very thought on't,
And tear my heart to pieces in my bosom.

BELVIDERA. What has he done?
JAFFEIR.
                              Thou'dst hate me, should I tell thee.
BELVIDERA. Why?
JAFFEIR.   Oh he has used me—yet by Heaven I bear it—
He has used me, Belvidera,—but first swear
That when I've told thee, thou'lt not loath me utterly,
Though vilest blots and stains appear upon me;
But still at least with charitable goodness,
Be near me in the pangs of my affliction,
Not scorn me, Belvidera, as he has done.
BELVIDERA. Have I then e'er been false that now I am doubted?
Speak, what's the cause I am grown into distrust,
Why thought unfit to hear my love's complainings?
JAFFEIR. Oh!
BELVIDERA.
              Tell me.
JAFFEIR.
                          Bear my failings, for they are many,
Oh my dear angel! in that friend I've lost
All my soul's peace; for every thought of him
Strikes my sense hard, and deads it in my brains;
Wouldst thou believe it—
BELVIDERA.
                              Speak.
JAFFEIR.
                              Before we parted,
Ere yet his guards had led him to his prison,
Full of severest sorrows for his sufferings,
With eyes o'erflowing and a bleeding heart,
Humbling myself almost beneath my nature,
As at his feet I kneeled, and sued for mercy,
Forgetting all our friendship, all the dearness,
In which w' have lived so many years together,
With a reproachful hand, he dashed a blow,
He struck me, Belvidera, by Heaven, he struck me,
Buffeted, call'd me traitor, villain, coward;
Am I a coward? am I a villain? tell me:
Th'art the best judge, and mad'st me, if I am so.
Damnation; coward!
BELVIDERA.
                          Oh! forgive him, Jaffeir.
And if his sufferings wound thy heart already,
What will they do tomorrow?

JAFFEIR.

Hah!

BELVIDERA.

Tomorrow,
When thou shalt see him stretched in all the agonies
Of a tormenting and a shameful death,
His bleeding bowels, and his broken limbs,
Insulted o'er by a vile, butchering villain;
What will thy heart do then? Oh sure 'twill stream
Like my eyes now.

JAFFEIR.

What means thy dreadful story?
Death, and tomorrow? broken limbs and bowels?
Insulted o'er by a vile, butchering villain?
By all my fears I shall start out to madness,
With barely guessing, if the truth's hid longer.

BELVIDERA. The faithless senators, 'tis they've decreed it:
They say according to our friend's request,
They shall have death, and not ignoble bondage:
Declare their promised mercy all as forfeited;
False to their oaths, and deaf to intercession;
Warrants are passed for public death tomorrow.

JAFFEIR. Death! doomed to die! condemned unheard! un-
pleaded!

BELVIDERA. Nay, cruelest racks and torments are preparing,
To force confessions from their dying pangs;
Oh do not look so terribly upon me,
How your lips shake, and all your face disordered!
What means my love?

JAFFEIR. Leave me, I charge thee, leave me—strong tempta-
tions
Wake in my heart.

BELVIDERA.

For what?

JAFFEIR.

No more, but leave me.

BELVIDERA. Why?

JAFFEIR.

Oh! by Heaven I love thee with that fondness
I would not have thee stay a moment longer,
Near these curst hands: are they not cold upon thee?

(*Pulls the dagger half out of his bosom and puts it back again.*)

BELVIDERA. No, everlasting comfort's in thy arms,
    To lean thus on thy breast is softer ease
    Than downy pillows decked with leaves of roses.
JAFFEIR. Alas, thou thinkest not of the thorns 'tis filled with,
    Fly ere they gall thee: there's a lurking serpent
    Ready to leap and sting thee to thy heart:
    Art thou not terrified?
BELVIDERA.

               No.

JAFFEIR.

               Call to mind
What thou hast done, and whither thou hast brought me.
BELVIDERA. Hah!
JAFFEIR.

         Where's my friend? my friend, thou smiling
    mischief?
    Nay, shrink not, now 'tis too late, thou shouldst have fled
    When thy guilt first had cause, for dire revenge
    Is up and raging for my friend. He groans,
    Hark how he groans, his screams are in my ears
    Already; see, th' have fixed him on the wheel,
    And now they tear him—Murther! perjured Senate!
    Murther—Oh!—hark thee, traitress, thou hast done this;
    Thanks to thy tears and false persuading love.

               (Fumbling for his dagger.)

    How her eyes speak! Oh thou bewitching creature!
    Madness cannot hurt thee: Come, thou little trembler,
    Creep, even into my heart, and there lie safe;
    'Tis thy own citadel—hah—yet stand off,
    Heaven must have justice, and my broken vows
    Will sink me else beneath its reaching mercy;
    I'll wink and then 'tis done—

               (Draws the dagger, offers to stab her.)

BELVIDERA.

               What means the lord
Of me, my life and love, what's in thy bosom,
Thou grasp'st at so? nay, why am I thus treated?
What wilt thou do? Ah, do not kill me, Jaffeir,
Pity these panting breasts, and trembling limbs,
That used to clasp thee when thy looks were milder,

That yet hang heavy on my unpurged soul,
And plunge it not into eternal darkness.
JAFFEIR. No, Belvidera, when we parted last
I gave this dagger with thee as in trust
To be thy portion, If I e'er proved false.
On such condition was my truth believed:
But now 'tis forfeited and must be paid for.

(Offers to stab her again.)

BELVIDERA. Oh, mercy!   *(Kneeling.)*
JAFFEIR.
    Nay, no struggling.
BELVIDERA.
        Now then kill me

(Leaps upon his neck and kisses him.)

While thus I cling about thy cruel neck,
Kiss thy revengeful lips and die in joys
Greater than any I can guess hereafter.
JAFFEIR. I am, I am a coward; witness't, Heaven,
Witness it, earth, and every being witness;
'Tis but one blow yet: by immortal love,
I cannot longer bear a thought to harm thee,

(He throws away the dagger and embraces her.)

The seal of providence is sure upon thee.
And thou wert born for yet unheard-of wonders:
Oh thou wert either born to save or damn me!
By all the power that's given thee o'er my soul,
By thy resistless tears and conquering smiles,
By the victorious love that still waits on thee;
Fly to thy cruel father: save my friend,
Or all our future quiet's lost forever:
Fall at his feet, cling round his reverend knees;
Speak to him with thy eyes, and with thy tears
Melt the hard heart, and wake dead nature in him;
Crush him in th'arms, and torture him with thy softness:
  Nor, till thy prayers are granted, set him free,
  But conquer him, as thou hast vanquished me.

(Exeunt ambo.)

ACT V

[SCENE I.] *A street*

(*Enter* PRIULI *solus.*)

PRIULI. Why, cruel Heaven, have my unhappy days
    Been lengthened to this sad one? Oh! dishonour
    And deathless infamy is fallen upon me.
    Was it my fault? Am I a traitor? No.
    But then, my only child, my daughter, wedded;
    There my best blood runs foul, and a disease
    Incurable has seized upon my memory,
    To make it rot and stink to after ages.
    Curst be the fatal minute when I got her;
    Or would that I'd been anything but man,
    And raised an issue which would ne'er have wronged me.
    The miserablest creatures (man excepted)
    Are not the less esteemed, though their posterity
    Degenerate from the virtues of their fathers;
    The vilest beasts are happy in their offsprings,
    While only man gets traitors, whores and villains.
    Curst be the name, and some swift blow from fate
    Lay his head deep, where mine may be forgotten.

(*Enter* BELVIDERA *in a long mourning veil.*)

BELVIDERA. He's there, my father, my inhuman father,
    That, for three years, has left an only child
    Exposed to all the outrages of fate,
    And cruel ruin—oh!—
PRIULI.   What child of sorrow
    Art thou that com'st thus wrapt in weeds of sadness,
    And mov'st as if thy steps were towards a grave?
BELVIDERA. A wretch, who from the very top of happiness
    Am fallen into the lowest depths of misery,
    And want your pitying hand to raise me up again.
PRIULI. Indeed thou talk'st as thou hadst tasted sorrows;
    Would I could help thee.
BELVIDERA.   'Tis greatly in your power,
    The world too, speaks you charitable, and I,
    Who ne'er ask'd alms before, in that dear hope
    Am come a begging to you, sir.

PRIULI. For what?

BELVIDERA. Oh, well regard me, is this voice a strange one?
Consider too, when beggars once pretend
A case like mine, no little will content 'em.

PRIULI. What wouldst thou beg for?

BELVIDERA. Pity and forgiveness;

(*Throws up her veil.*)

By the kind tender names of child and father,
Hear my complaints and take me to your love.

PRIULI. My daughter?

BELVIDERA. Yes, your daughter, by a mother
Virtuous and noble, faithful to your honour,
Obedient to your will, kind to your wishes,
Dear to your arms; by all the joys she gave you,
When in her blooming years she was your treasure,
Look kindly on me; in my face behold
The lineaments of hers y'have kissed so often,
Pleading the cause of your poor cast-off child.

PRIULI. Thou art my daughter.

BELVIDERA. Yes—And y'have oft told me
With smiles of love and chaste paternal kisses,
I'd much resemblance of my mother.

PRIULI. Oh!
Hadst thou inherited her matchless virtues
I'd been too blessed.

BELVIDERA. Nay, do not call to memory
My disobedience, but let pity enter
Into your heart, and quite deface the impression;
For could you think how mine's perplexed, what sadness,
Fears and despairs distract the peace within me,
Oh, you would take me in your dear, dear arms,
Hover with strong compassion o'er your young one,
To shelter me with a protecting wing,
From the black gathered storm, that's just, just breaking.

PRIULI. Don't talk thus.

BELVIDERA. Yes, I must, and you must hear too.
I have a husband.

PRIULI. Damn him.

BELVIDERA. Oh, do not curse him!
He would not speak so hard a word towards you
On any terms, how e'er he deal with me.

PRIULI. Hah! what means my child?

BELVIDERA.   Oh there's but this short moment
'Twixt me and fate, yet send me not with curses
Down to my grave, afford me one kind blessing
Before we part: just take me in your arms
And recommend me with a prayer to Heaven,
That I may die in peace; and when I'm dead—

PRIULI. How my soul's catched!

BELVIDERA.   Lay me, I beg you, lay me
By the dear ashes of my tender mother.
She would have pitied me, had fate yet spared her.

PRIULI. By Heaven, my aching heart forebodes much mischief,
Tell me thy story, for I'm still thy father.

BELVIDERA. No, I'm contented.

PRIULI.   Speak.

BELVIDERA.   No matter.

PRIULI.   Tell me.
By yon blest Heaven, my heart runs o'er with fondness.

BELVIDERA. Oh!

PRIULI.   Utter't.

BELVIDERA.   Oh my husband, my dear husband
Carries a dagger in his once kind bosom
To pierce the heart of your poor Belvidera.

PRIULI. Kill thee?

BELVIDERA.   Yes, kill me; when he passed his faith
And covenant against your state and Senate,
He gave me up as hostage for his truth,
With me a dagger and a dire commission,
When e'er he failed, to plunge it through this bosom;
I learnt the danger, chose the hour of love
T'attempt his heart, and bring it back to honour;
Great love prevailed and blessed me with success,
He came, confessed, betrayed his dearest friends
For promised mercy; now they're doomed to suffer,
Galled with remembrance of what then was sworn,
If they are lost, he vows t'appease the gods
With this poor life, and make my blood th' atonement.

PRIULI. Heavens!

BELVIDERA. Think you saw what passed at our last parting;
Think you beheld him like a raging lion,
Pacing the earth and tearing up his steps,
Fate in his eyes, and roaring with the pain
Of burning fury; think you saw his one hand
Fixed on my throat, while the extended other

Grasped a keen, threatening dagger; oh 'twas thus
We last embraced, when, trembling with revenge,
He dragged me to the ground, and at my bosom
Presented horrid death, cried out, "My friends,
Where are my friends?" swore, wept, raged, threatened,
  loved,
For he yet loved, and that dear love preserved me,
To this last trial of a father's pity.
I fear not death, but cannot bear a thought
That that dear hand should do th' unfriendly office;
If I was ever then your care, now hear me;
Fly to the Senate, save the promised lives
Of his dear friends, e're mine be made the sacrifice.

PRIULI. Oh, my heart's comfort!

BELVIDERA.   Will you not, my father?
Weep not but answer me.

PRIULI.   By Heaven, I will.
Not one of 'em but what shall be immortal.
Canst thou forgive me all my follies past?
I'll henceforth be indeed a father; never,
Never more thus expose, but cherish thee,
Dear as the vital warmth that feeds my life,
Dear as these eyes that weep in fondness o'er thee.
Peace to thy heart. Farewell.

BELVIDERA.   Go, and remember,
'Tis Belvidera's life her father pleads for.

                            (*Exeunt severally.*)

(*Enter* ANTONIO.)

ANTONIO. Hum, hum, hah. Seignior Priuli, my lord Priuli, my
  lord, my lord, my lord: now, we lords love to call one
  another by our titles. My lord, my lord, my lord—pox on
  him, I am a lord as well as he, and so let him fiddle—I'll
  warrant him he's gone to the Senate-house, and I'll be
  there too, soon enough for somebody. Odd—here's a
  tickling speech about the plot, I'll prove there's a plot
  with a vengeance—would I had it without book; let me
  see—
      "Most reverend senators,
  that there is a plot, surely by this time, no man that hath
  eyes or understanding in his head will presume to doubt,
  'tis as plain as the light in the cowcumber"—no—hold
  there—"cowcumber" does not come in yet— 'tis as plain

as the light in the sun, or as the man in the moon, even at
noon day; It is indeed a pumpkin-plot, which, just as it
was mellow, we have gathered, and now we have gathered
it, prepared and dressed it, shall we throw it like a pickled
cowcumber out at the window? no: that it is not only a
bloody, horrid, execrable, damnable and audacious plot,
but it is, as I may so say, a saucy plot: and we all know,
most reverend fathers, that what is sauce for a goose is
sauce for a gander: Therefore, I say, as those blood-
thirsty ganders of the conspiracy would have destroyed
us geese of the Senate, let us make haste to destroy them;
so I humbly move for hanging"—hah, hurry, durry—I
think this will do, tho' I was something out, at first, about
the sun and the cowcumber.

(*Enter* AQUILINA.)

AQUILINA. Good morrow, Senator.

ANTONIO. Nacky, my dear Nacky, morrow, Nacky, odd I am
very brisk, very merry, very pert, very jovial—h-a-a-a-a-a
—kiss me, Nacky; how dost thou do, my little tory rory
strumpet, kiss me, I say, hussy, kiss me.

AQUILINA. "Kiss me, Nacky!" hang you, sir coxcomb, hang
you, sir.

ANTONIO. Hayty tayty, is it so indeed, with all my heart, faith
—*Hey then up go we,* faith—*hey then up go we,* dum
dum derum dump.   (*Sings.*)

AQUILINA. Seignior.

ANTONIO. Madonna.

AQUILINA. Do you intend to die in your bed?—

ANTONIO. About threescore years hence, much may be done,
my dear.

AQUILINA. You'll be hanged, seignior.

ANTONIO. Hanged, sweetheart! prithee be quiet, hanged
quoth-a, that's a merry conceit, with all my heart; why
thou jok'st, Nacky, thou art given to joking, I'll swear;
well, I protest, Nacky, nay, I must protest, and will
protest that I love joking dearly, man. And I love thee for
joking, and I'll kiss thee for joking, and touse thee for
joking, and odd, I have a devilish mind to take thee aside
about that business for joking too, odd I have, and *Hey
then up go we,* dum dum derum dump.   (*Sings.*)

AQUILINA. See you this, Sir?   . (*Draws a dagger.*)

ANTONIO. O laud, a dagger! Oh laud! it is naturally my aversion, I cannot endure the sight on't, hide it, for Heaven's

sake, I cannot look that way till it be gone—hide it, hide it, oh, oh, hide it!

AQUILINA. Yes, in your heart, I'll hide it.

ANTONIO. My heart! what, hide a dagger in my heart's blood!

AQUILINA. Yes, in thy heart, thy throat, thou pampered devil;
> Thou hast helped to spoil my peace, and I'll have vengeance
> On thy cursed life, for all the bloody Senate,
> The perjured faithless Senate: Where's my lord,
> My happiness, my love, my god, my hero,
> Doomed by thy accursed tongue, amongst the rest,
> T' a shameful wrack? By all the rage that's in me
> I'll be whole years in murthering thee.

ANTONIO. Why, Nacky, wherefore so passionate? what have I done? what's the matter, my dear Nacky? am not I thy love, thy happiness, thy lord, thy hero, thy senator, and everything in the world, Nacky?

AQUILINA. Thou! thinkst thou, thou art fit to meet my joys;
> To bear the eager clasps of my embraces?
> Give me my Pierre, or—

ANTONIO. Why, he's to be hanged, little Nacky, trussed up for treason, and so forth, child.

AQUILINA. Thou liest, stop down thy throat that hellish sentence,
> Or 'tis thy last: swear that my love shall live,
> Or thou art dead.

ANTONIO.   Ah-h-h-h.

AQUILINA.   Swear to recall his doom,
> Swear at my feet, and tremble at my fury.

ANTONIO. I do; now if she would but kick a little bit, one kick now Ah-h-h-h.   (*Aside*)

AQUILINA. Swear, or—

ANTONIO. I do, by these dear fragrant foots and little toes, sweet as, e-e-e-e my Nacky, Nacky, Nacky.

AQUILINA. How!

ANTONIO. Nothing but untie thy shoe-string a little faith and troth, that's all, that's all, as I hope to live, Nacky, that's all.

AQUILINA. Nay, then—

ANTONIO.   Hold, hold, thy love, thy lord, thy hero
> Shall be preserved and safe.

AQUILINA.   Or may this poniard
> Rust in thy heart.

ANTONIO. With all my soul.

AQUILINA. Farewell—(*Exit* AQUILINA.)

ANTONIO. Adieu. Why what a bloody-minded, inveterate, termagant strumpet have I been plagued with! oh-h-h yet
more! nay then I die, I die—I am dead already.

(*Stretches himself out.*)

[SCENE II.] *A street*

(*Enter* JAFFEIR.)

JAFFEIR. Final destruction seize on all the world:
Bend down, ye Heavens, and shutting round this earth,
Crush the vile globe into its first confusion;
Scorch it, with elemental flames, to one cursed cinder,
And all us little creepers in't, call'd men,
Burn, burn to nothing: but let Venice burn
Hotter than all the rest: Here kindle Hell
Ne'er to extinguish, and let souls hereafter
Groan here, in all those pains which mine feels now.

(*Enter* BELVIDERA.)

BELVIDERA. My life— (*Meeting him.*)

JAFFEIR. My plague— (*Turning from her.*)

BELVIDERA. Nay then I see my ruin,
If I must die!

JAFFEIR. No, Death's this day too busy,
Thy father's ill timed mercy came too late,
I thank thee for thy labours tho and him too,
But all my poor betrayed unhappy friends
Have summons to prepare for fate's black hour;
And yet I live.

BELVIDERA. Then be the next my doom.
I see thou hast passed my sentence in thy heart,
And I'll no longer weep or plead against it,
But with the humblest, most obedient patience
Meet thy dear hands, and kiss 'em when they wound me;
Indeed I am willing, but I beg thee do it
With some remorse, and where thou giv'st the blow,
View me with eyes of a relenting love,
And show me pity, for 'twill sweeten justice.

JAFFEIR. Show pity to thee?

BELVIDERA.   Yes, and when thy hands,
    Charged with my fate, come trembling to the deed,
    As thou hast done a thousand thousand dear times,
    To this poor breast, when kinder rage has brought thee,
    When our stinged hearts have leaped to meet each other,
    And melting kisses sealed our lips together,
    When joys have left me gasping in thy arms,
    So let my death come now, and I'll not shrink from't.

JAFFEIR. Nay, Belvidera, do not fear my cruelty,
    Nor let the thoughts of death perplex thy fancy,
    But answer me to what I shall demand,
    With a firm temper and unshaken spirit.

BELVIDERA. I will when I've done weeping—

JAFFEIR.   Fie, no more on't—
    How long is't since the miserable day
    We wedded first—

BELVIDERA.   Oh-h-h.

JAFFEIR.   Nay, keep in thy tears,
    Lest they unman me too.

BELVIDERA.   Heaven knows I cannot;
    The words you utter sound so very sadly,
    These streams will follow—

JAFFEIR.   Come, I'll kiss 'em dry then.

BELVIDERA. But, was't a miserable day?

JAFFEIR.   A cursed one.

BELVIDERA. I thought it otherwise, and you've oft sworn,
    In the transporting hours of warmest love
    When sure you spoke the truth, you've sworn you blessed
    it.

JAFFEIR. Twas a rash oath.

BELVIDERA.   Then why am I not cursed too?

JAFFEIR. No, Belvidera; by th' eternal truth,
    I doat with too much fondness.

BELVIDERA.   Still so kind?
    Still then do you love me?

JAFFEIR.   Nature, in her workings,
    Inclines not with more ardour to creation,
    Than I do now towards thee; man ne'er was bless'd,
    Since the first pair first met, as I have been.

BELVIDERA. Then sure you will not curse me.

JAFFEIR.   No, I'll bless thee.
    I came on purpose, Belvidera, to bless thee.
    'Tis now, I think, three years w'have lived together.

BELVIDERA. And may no fatal minute ever part us,
    Till, reverend grown, for age and love, we go
    Down to one grave, as our last bed, together,
    There sleep in peace till an eternal morning.

JAFFEIR. When will that be?   (*Sighing.*)

BELVIDERA.   I hope long ages hence.

JAFFEIR. Have I not hitherto (I beg thee tell me
    Thy very fears) used thee with tender'st love?
    Did e'er my soul rise up in wrath against thee?
    Did I e'er frown when Belvidera smiled,
    Or, by the least unfriendly word, betray
    Abating passion? have I ever wronged thee?

BELVIDERA. No.

JAFFEIR.   Has my heart, or have my eyes e'er wandered
    To any other woman?

BELVIDERA.   Never, never—
    I were the worst of false ones should I accuse thee.
    I own I've been too happy, blessed above
    My sex's charter.

JAFFEIR.   Did I not say I came
    To bless thee?

BELVIDERA.   Yes.

JAFFEIR.   Then hear me, bounteous Heaven,
    Pour down your blessings on this beauteous head,
    Where everlasting sweets are always springing.
    With a continual giving hand, let peace,
    Honour and safety always hover round her,
    Feed her with plenty, let her eyes ne'er see
    A sight of sorrow, nor her heart know mourning,
    Crown all her days with joy, her nights with rest,
    Harmless as her own thoughts, and prop her virtue,
    To bear the loss of one that too much loved,
    And comfort her with patience in our parting.

BELVIDERA. How, parting, parting!

JAFFEIR.   Yes, for ever parting,
    I have sworn, Belvidera; by yon Heaven,
    That best can tell how much I lose to leave thee,
    We part this hour for ever.

BELVIDERA.   Oh, call back
    Your cruel blessings, stay with me and curse me!

JAFFEIR. No, 'tis resolved.

BELVIDERA.   Then hear me too, just Heaven,
    Pour down your curses on this wretched head

With never-ceasing vengeance, let despair,
Danger or infamy, nay all surround me;
Starve me with wantings, let my eyes ne'er see
A sight of comfort, nor my heart know peace,
But dash my days with sorrow, nights with horrours
Wild as my own thoughts now, and let loose fury
To make me mad enough for what I lose,
If I must lose him; If I must! I will not.
Oh turn and hear me!

JAFFEIR.   Now hold, heart, or never.

BELVIDERA. By all the tender days we have lived together,
By all our charming nights, and joys that crowned 'em,
Pity my sad condition, speak, but speak.

JAFFEIR. Oh-h-h.

BELVIDERA.   By these arms that now cling round thy neck,
By this dear kiss and by ten thousand more,
By these poor streaming eyes—

JAFFEIR.   Murther! unhold me:
By th'immortal destiny that doomed me

                        (*Draws his dagger.*)

To this cursed minute, I'll not live one longer.
Resolve to let me go or see me fall—

BELVIDERA. Hold, sir, be patient.   (*Passing-bell tolls.*)

JAFFEIR.   Hark, the dismal bell
Tolls out for death, I must attend its call too,
For my poor friend, my dying Pierre expects me,
He sent a message to require I'd see him
Before he died, and take his last forgiveness.
Farewell forever.   (*Going out looks back at her.*)

BELVIDERA.   Leave thy dagger with me.
Bequeath me something—Not one kiss at parting?
Oh my poor heart, when wilt thou break?

JAFFEIR.   Yet stay,
We have a child, as yet a tender infant.
Be a kind mother to him when I am gone,
Breed him in virtue and the paths of honour,
But let him never know his father's story;
I charge thee guard him from the wrongs my fate
May do his future fortune or his name.
Now—nearer yet—   (*Approaching each other.*)
Oh that my arms were riveted
Thus round thee ever! But my friends, my oath!

This and no more. *(Kisses her.)*

BELVIDERA. Another, sure another,
For that poor little one you've ta'en care of,
I'll give't him truly.

JAFFEIR. So, now farewell.

BELVIDERA. Forever?

JAFFEIR. Heaven knows, forever; all good angels guard thee.

(Exit.)

BELVIDERA. All ill ones sure had charge of me this moment.
Cursed be my days, and doubly cursed my nights,
Which I must now mourn out in widowed tears;
Blasted be every herb and fruit and tree,
Cursed be the rain that falls upon the earth,
And may the general curse reach man and beast;
Oh give me daggers, fire or water,
How I could bleed, how burn, how drown the waves
Huzzing and booming round my sinking head,
Till I descended to the peaceful bottom!
Oh there's all quiet, here all rage and fury,
The air's too thin, and pierces my weak brain,
I long for thick substantial sleep: Hell, Hell,
Burst from the center, rage and roar aloud,
If thou art half so hot, so mad as I am.

(Enter PRIULI and Servants.)

Who's there?

PRIULI. Run, seize and bring her safely home,

(They seize her.)

Guard her as you would life: Alas poor creature!

BELVIDERA. What? to my husband then conduct me quickly,
Are all things ready? shall we die most gloriously?
Say not a word of this to my old father,
Murmuring streams, soft shades, and springing flowers,
Lutes, laurels, seas of milk, and ships of amber. *(Exit.)*

[SCENE III.]

(Scene opening discovers a scaffold and a wheel prepared for the executing of PIERRE, then enter Officers, PIERRE and Guards, a Friar, Executioner and a great Rabble.)

OFFICERS. Room, room there—stand all by, make room for the prisoner.

PIERRE. My friend not come yet?

FRIAR.
                                    Why are you so obstinate?
PIERRE. Why you so troublesome, that a poor wretch
    Cannot die in peace?
    But you, like ravens will be croaking round him—
FRIAR. Yet, Heaven—
PIERRE.
                        I tell thee, Heaven and I are friends,
    I ne'er broke peace with't yet, by cruel murthers,
    Rapine, or perjury, or vile deceiving,
    But lived in moral justice towards all men,
    Nor am a foe to the most strong believers:
    How e'er my own short-sighted faith confine me.
FRIAR. But an all-seeing judge—
PIERRE.
                            You say my conscience
    Must be mine accuser: I have searched that conscience,
    And find no records there of crimes that scare me.
FRIAR. 'Tis strange you should want faith.
PIERRE.
                            You want to lead
    My reason blindfold, like a hampered lion,
    Checked of its nobler vigour; then, when baited
    Down to obedient tameness, make it couch,
    And show strange tricks which you call signs of faith.
    So silly souls are gulled and you get money.
    Away, no more: Captain, I would hereafter
    This fellow write no lies of my conversion,
    Because he has crept upon my troubled hours.

(*Enter* JAFFEIR.)

JAFFEIR. Hold: eyes, be dry;
    Heart, strengthen me to bear
    This hideous sight, and humble me to take
    The last forgiveness of a dying friend,
    Betrayed by my vile falsehood, to his ruin.
    Oh Pierre!
PIERRE.
                Yet nearer.
JAFFEIR.
                        Crawling on my knees,
    And prostrate on the earth, let me approach thee:
    How shall I look up to thy injured face,
    That always used to smile, with friendship, on me?

It darts an air of so much manly virtue,
That I, methinks, look little in thy sight,
And stripes are fitter for me than embraces.

PIERRE. Dear to my arms, though thou hast undone my fame,
I cannot forget to love thee: prithee, Jaffeir,
Forgive that filthy blow my passion dealt thee;
I am now preparing for the land of peace,
And fain would have the charitable wishes
Of all good men, like thee, to bless my journey.

JAFFEIR. Good! I am the vilest creature, worse then e'er
Suffered the shameful fate thou art going to taste of.
Why was I sent for to be used thus kindly?
Call, call me villain, as I am, describe
The foul complexion of my hateful deeds,
Lead me to the rack, and stretch me in thy stead,
I've crimes enough to give it its full load,
And do it credit: thou wilt but spoil the use on't,
And honest men hereafter bear its figure
About 'em, as a charm from treacherous friendship.

OFFICER. The time grows short, your friends are dead already.

JAFFEIR. Dead!

PIERRE. Yes, dead, Jaffeir, they've all died like men too,
Worthy their character.

JAFFEIR.
                    And what must I do?

PIERRE. Oh, Jaffeir!

JAFFEIR.
                    Speak aloud thy burthened soul,
And tell thy troubles to thy tortured friend.

PIERRE. Friend! Could'st thou yet be a friend, a generous
    friend,
I might hope comfort from thy noble sorrows.
Heaven knows I want a friend.

JAFFEIR.
                    And I a kind one,
That would not thus scorn my repenting virtue,
Or think, when he is to die, my thoughts are idle.

PIERRE. No! live, I charge thee, Jaffeir.

JAFFEIR.
                    Yes, I will live,
But it shall be to see thy fall revenged
At such a rate, as Venice long shall groan for.

PIERRE. Wilt thou?

JAFFEIR.

           I will, by Heaven.

PIERRE.

                    Then still thou'rt noble,
And I forgive thee, oh—yet—shall I trust thee?

JAFFEIR. No: I've been false already.

PIERRE.

                    Dost thou love me?

JAFFEIR. Rip up my heart, and satisfy thy doubtings.

PIERRE. Curse on this weakness.   (*He weeps.*)

JAFFEIR.

               Tears! Amazement! Tears!
I never saw thee melted thus before;
And know there's something laboring in thy bosom
That must have vent: Though I'm a villain, tell me.

PIERRE. Seest thou that engine?   (*Pointing to the wheel.*)

JAFFEIR. Why?

PIERRE. Is't fit a soldier, who has lived with honour,
    Fought nation's quarrels, and been crowned with
        conquest,
    Be exposed a common carcass on a wheel?

JAFFEIR. Hah!

PIERRE.

        Speak! is't fitting?

JAFFEIR.

                Fitting?

PIERRE.

                    Yes, is't fitting?

JAFFEIR. What's to be done?

PIERRE.

               I'd have thee undertake
Something that's noble, to preserve my memory
From the disgrace that's ready to attaint it.

OFFICER. The day grows late, sir.

PIERRE.

               I'll make haste! oh Jaffeir,
Though thou'st betrayed me, do me some way justice.

JAFFEIR. No more of that: Thy wishes shall be satisfied,
I have a wife, and she shall bleed, my child too
Yield up his little throat, and all t'appease thee—
        (*Going away,* PIERRE *holds him.*)

PIERRE. No—this—no more!　　　(*He whispers* JAFFEIR.)
JAFFEIR.　　　　　　　Hah! is't then so?
PIERRE.　　　　　　　　　　　Most certainly.
JAFFEIR. I'll do't.
PIERRE.　　　Remember.
OFFICER.　　　　　　Sir.
PIERRE.　　　　　　　　Come, now I'm ready.

　　　　　(*He and* JAFFEIR *ascend the scaffold.*)

Captain, you should be a gentleman of honour,
Keep off the rabble, that I may have room
To entertain my fate, and die with decency.
Come!

(*Takes off his gown. Executioner prepares to bind him.*)

FRIAR. Son!
PIERRE.　　Hence, tempter.
OFFICER.　　　　　　Stand off, priest.
PIERRE.　　　　　　　　　I thank you, sir.
You'll think on't?　　　　　　(*To* JAFFEIR.)
JAFFEIR.　　　　'Twon't grow stale before tomorrow.
PIERRE. Now, Jaffeir! now I am going. Now;—

　　　　　(*Executioner having bound him.*)

JAFFEIR.　　　　　　　　Have at thee,
Thou honest heart, then—here—　　(*Stabs him.*)
And this is well too.　　(*Then stabs himself.*)
FRIAR. Damnable deed!
PIERRE.　　　　Now thou hast indeed been faithful.
This was done nobly—we have deceived the Senate.
JAFFEIR. Bravely.
PIERRE.　　　Ha ha ha—oh oh—　　　(*Dies.*)
JAFFEIR.　　　　　　　Now, ye cursed rulers,
Thus of the blood y'have shed I make libation,
And sprinkle't mingling: may it rest upon you,
And all your race: be henceforth peace a stranger
Within your walls; let plagues and famine waste
Your generations—oh poor Belvidera!
Sir, I have a wife, bear this in safety to her,
A token that with my dying breath I blessed her,
And the dear little infant left behind me.
I am sick—I'm quiet—　　　　(JAFFEIR *dies.*)

OFFICER.   Bear this news to the Senate,
And guard their bodies till there's farther order:
Heav'n grant I die so well—   (*Scene shuts upon them.*)

[SCENE IV.]

(*Soft music. Enter* BELVIDERA *distracted, led by two of her Women,* PRIULI *and Servants.*)

PRIULI. Strengthen her heart with patience, pitying Heaven.
BELVIDERA. Come come come come come. Nay, come to bed!
Prithee my love. The winds! hark how they whistle!
And the rain beats: oh how the weather shrinks me!
You are angry now, who cares? pish, no indeed.
Choose then, I say you shall not go, you shall not;
Whip your ill nature; get you gone then! oh,

(JAFFEIR'*s ghost rises.*)

Are you returned? See, Father, here he's come again,
Am I to blame to love him! oh thou dear one.

(*Ghost sinks.*)

Why do you fly me? are you angry still then?
Jaffeir! where art thou? Father, why do you do thus?
Stand off, don't hide him from me. He's here somewhere.
Stand off I say! what gone? remember't, tyrant!
I may revenge myself for this trick one day.

(*Enter Officer and Others.*)

I'll do't—I'll do't. Renault's a nasty fellow.
Hang him, hang him, hang him.
PRIULI.   News, what news? (OFFICER *whispers* PRIULI.)
OFFICER.

                    Most sad, sir.
Jaffeir, upon the scaffold, to prevent
A shameful death, stab'd Pierre, and next himself:
Both fell together.
PRIULI.   Daughter.
BELVIDERA.   Hah, look there!

(*The ghosts of* JAFFEIR *and* PIERRE *rise together, both bloody.*)

My husband bloody, and his friend too! Murther!
Who has done this? speak to me thou sad vision,

(*Ghosts sink.*)

On these poor trembling knees I beg it. Vanished—
Here they went down; Oh I'll dig, dig the den up.
You shan't delude me thus. Hoa, Jaffeir, Jaffeir,
Peep up and give me but a look. I have him!
I've got him, father: Oh now how I'll smuggle him!
My love! my dear! my blessing! help me, help me!
They have hold on me, and drag me to the bottom.
Nay—now they pull so hard—farewell—   (*She dies.*)

MAID. Breathless and dead.   She's dead.

PRIULI.

                          Then guard me from the sight on't:
Lead me into some place that's fit for mourning;
Where the free air, light and the cheerful sun
May never enter: hang it round with black;
Set up one taper that may last a day
As long as I've to live: and there all leave me.
        Sparing no tears when you this tale relate,
        But bid all cruel fathers dread my fate.

                    (*Exeunt omnes. curtain falls.*)

Finis

EPILOGUE

The text is done, and now for application,
And when that's ended, pass your approbation.
Though the conspiracy's prevented here,
Methinks I see another hatching there;
And there's a certain faction fain would sway,
If they had strength enough, and damn this play,
But this the author bade me boldly say:
If any take his plainness in ill part,
He's glad on't from the bottom of his heart;
Poets in honour of the truth should write,
With the same spirit brave men for it fight;
And though against him causeless hatreds rise,
And daily where he goes of late, he spies
The scowls of sullen and revengeful eyes;
'Tis what he knows with much contempt to bear,
And serves a cause too good to let him fear:
He fears no poison from an incensed drab,[41]
No ruffian's five-foot-sword, nor rascal's stab;
Nor any other snares of mischief laid,
Not a Rose-alley cudgel-ambuscade,[42]
From any private cause where malice reigns,
Or general pique all blockheads have to brains:
Nothing shall daunt his pen when truth does call,
No, not the picture-mangler at Guild-hall.[43]
The rebel-tribe, of which that vermin's one,
Have now set forward and their course begun;

[41] *drab*, whore.
[42] *Rose-alley cudgel-ambuscade,* i.e., John Dryden, one of the most famous writers of his age, was beaten in Rose Alley in 1679.
[43] *picture-mangler at Guild-Hall,* unknown defacer of a portrait of the Duke of York.

And while that prince's figure they deface,
    As they before had massacred his name,
Durst their base fears but look him in the face,
    They'd use his person as they've used his fame;
A face, in which such lineaments they read
Of that great martyr's[44] whose rich blood they shed,
That their rebellious hate they still retain,
And in his son would murther him again;
With indignation then, let each brave heart
Rouse and unite to take his injured part;
Till royal love and goodness call him home,
And songs of triumph meet him as he come;
Till Heaven his honour and our peace restore,
And villains never wrong his virtue more.

[44] that great martyr's, Charles I.

THE SQUIRE OF ALSATIA
ᵗᶻᵉ A Comedy ᵉᵗ
1688

Thomas Shadwell

INTRODUCTORY NOTE

Thomas Shadwell was born in 1642, the year in which the Civil War began and the theaters were closed by Parliament. After his education at Cambridge he became associated with the stage in London, marrying Ann Gibbs, a member of the Duke's Company, and becoming a dramatist, poet, and controversialist. Shadwell is best known to us because John Dryden lampooned him in the famous satires "The Medal" and "Mac Flecknoe," in which political and cultural differences between the two were mercilessly exaggerated. As for personality and appearance, Shadwell has become immortal as the drunken Og in the second part of Dryden's "Absalom and Achitophel": "Round as a globe, and liquor'd every chink."

Shadwell did well in the Restoration and was in fact thought to be its leading writer of comedies. *The Virtuoso* and *The Squire of Alsatia* were highly successful, and the critics as well as the audience praised the inventiveness of his characters and the range of their "humours." Shadwell replaced Dryden as Poet Laureate in 1689 because his politics and religion were more acceptable. He died in 1692, probably from an overdose of opium.

Although we tend to think of him principally as the butt of Dryden's satire, we may find that the Restoration audience was pretty much right: Shadwell was a first-rate talent in comedy.

The Squire of Alsatia is an adaptation of the Roman play *Adelphoe*, by Terence. In taking it for a model Shadwell kept its characters but very much changed its ideas. There are still two older brothers and two younger brothers, with an assortment of various women to be pursued. One pair (father and son) still hail from the country, the other is still city bred. But the old story is now packed full of arguments about life, society, and politics.

Sir William Belfond and his son are described by Shadwell in terms that leave nothing either to doubt or suspense: one is "rigid, morose, most sordidly covetous, clownish, obstinate, positive, and froward." The other is "lewd, abominably vicious, stubborn, and obstinate." They are not only socially but politically intolerable, at least to the Poet Laureate of the Revolution of 1688. Sir William is the very image—perhaps one should say caricature—of a confirmed Tory. He lives in the country not only because he lacks urbanity but because that is where, secure in possession of his property, he is able to tyrannize his family and community. He is not only ignorant but an admirer of ignorance. On almost every subject on which he thinks himself an authority—patriotism, education, human nature—he comes out on the losing end of the dialogue. What was for Terence a comedy of age and passion has become for Shadwell one of character and idea.

The play reveals the strange mixture of materialism and sentimentality that marked its period. It is simply accepted that gentlemen pursue pleasure—most often in the shape of wine and women—as either a natural right or a natural inclination. The assumption is that after enough pleasure there is a voluntary turn towards good sense. At the same time, it is assumed by author and hero that pleasure has no real hold on either body or mind. If rightly educated we can do pretty much what we want, then mature into the attitude expressed by Belfond Junior in the finale:

> There is no peace but in a virtuous life,
> Nor lasting joy but in a tender wife.

It may be that the idealism so often expressed by the city father and his (adopted) son are no less suspect than the brutal materialism of their counterparts.

Of all Restoration plays this has the richest resources of low comedy language. It takes a substantial dictionary to follow the whoring and boozing of Alsatia, the thieves' hideaway, and to understand its argot and customs. Shadwell had a keen eye for life as it was lived past the boundaries of the middle class; his description of the world below it is a triumph of comic exaggeration and psychological realism.

Dramatis Personae.

SIR WILLIAM BELFOND
A gentleman of above £3,000 per annum, who in his youth had been a spark of the town, but married and retired into the country, where he turned to the other extreme, rigid, morose, most sordidly covetous, clownish, obstinate, positive, and froward[1]

SIR EDWARD BELFOND
His brother, a merchant who by lucky hits had gotten a great estate, lives single with ease and pleasure, reasonably and virtuously. A man of great humanity and gentleness and compassion towards mankind; well read in good books, possessed with all gentleman-like qualities

BELFOND SENIOR
Eldest son to Sir William, bred after his father's rustic, swinish manner, with great rigor and severity, upon whom his father's estate is entailed, the confidence of which makes him break out into open rebellion to his father, and become lewd, abominably vicious, stubborn, and obstinate

BELFOND JUNIOR
Second son to Sir William, adopted by Sir Edward, and bred from his childhood by him with all the tenderness and familiarity and bounty and liberty that can be; instructed in all the liberal sciences, and in all gentleman-like education; somewhat given to women, and now and then to good fellowship, but an ingenious, well-accomplished gentleman, a man of honor and of excellent disposition and temper

TRUMAN
His friend, a man of honor and fortune

CHEATLY
A rascal who, by reason of debts, dares not stir out of

---

1 *froward*, perverse.

Whitefriars, but there inveigles young heirs in tail,[2] and help 'em to goods and money upon great disadvantages; is bound for them, and shares with them till he undoes them. A lewd, impudent, debauched fellow, very expert in the cant about the town

SHAMWELL
Cousin to the Belfonds, an heir who, being ruined by Cheatly, is made a decoy duck for others, not daring to stir out of Alsatia, where he lives; is bound with Cheatly for heirs, and lives upon them, a dissolute, debauched life

CAPTAIN HACKUM
A block-headed bully of Alsatia, a cowardly, impudent, blustering fellow, formerly a sergeant in Flanders, run from his colors, retreating into Whitefriars for a very small debt, where, by the Alsatians, he is dubbed a captain, marries one that lets lodgings, sells cherry brandy, and is a bawd

SCRAPEALL
A hypocritical, repeating, praying, psalm-singing, precise[3] fellow, pretending to great piety; a godly knave who joins with Cheatly and supplies young heirs with goods and money

ATTORNEY TO SIR WILLIAM BELFOND
Who solicits his business and receives all his packets

LOLPOOP
A North-country fellow, servant to Belfond Senior, much displeased at his master's proceedings

TERMAGANT
A sharper, brother to Mrs. Termagant

LA MAR
French valet de chambre

ROGER
Servant to Belfond, Junior

PARSON
An indebted Alsatian divine

RUTH
A precise governess to Teresia and Isabella

TERESIA
Daughter to Scrapeall, in love with, and beloved by, Truman

ISABELLA
His niece, in love with, and beloved by, Belfond Junior

---

[2] *in tail*, legal beneficiaries.
[3] *precise*, puritanical.

LUCIA

    The Attorney's daughter, a young, beautiful girl, of a mild and tender disposition, debauched by Belfond Junior

MRS. TERMAGANT

    A neglected mistress of Belfond Junior, by whom he has had a child; a furious, malicious, and revengeful woman, perpetually plaguing him and crossing him in all designs, pursuing him continually with her malice, even to the attempting of his life

MRS. HACKUM

    Wife to Captain Hackum

MRS. BETTY

    Lolpoop's whore

MRS. MARGARET

    His master's whore

    Fiddlers, Constables, Tipstaff, Watch, Sergeant, Musketeers, Rabble, &c.

PROLOGUE

How have we in the space of one poor age
Beheld the rise and downfall of the stage!
When, with our king restored, it first arose,
They did each day some good old play expose,
And then it flourished, till, with manna tired,
For wholesome food ye nauseous trash desired.
Then rose the whiffling[4] scribblers of those days
Who since have lived to bury all their plays,
And had their issue full as num'rous been
As Priam's,[5] they the fate of all had seen.
  With what prodigious scarcity of wit
Did the new authors starve the hungry pit!
Infected by the French, you must have rhyme,
Which long to please the ladies' ears did chime.
Soon after this came ranting fustian in,
And none but plays upon the fret[6] were seen:
Such roaring bombast stuff, which fops would praise,
Tore our best actors' lungs, cut short their days.
Some in small time did this distemper kill,
And had the savage authors gone on still,
Fustian had been a new disease i'th' bill.[7]
When Time, which all things tries, had laid rhyme dead,
The vile usurper, Farce, reigned in its stead.
Then came machines, brought from a neighbor nation:[8]
Oh, how we suffered under decoration!

---

[4] *whiffling*, frivolous.
[5] *Priam's*, i.e., King Priam had a hundred children, at least as described by Homer in the *Iliad*.
[6] *upon the fret*, high-pitched.
[7] *bill*, bills or lists of mortality published in London that indicated among other things the numbers dead each week from plague.
[8] *machines, brought from a neighbor nation*, French stage settings.

If all this stuff has not quite spoiled your taste,
Pray let a comedy once more be graced,
Which does not monsters represent, but men,
Conforming to the rules of Master Ben.[9]
Our author, ever having him in view,
At humble distance would his steps pursue.
He to correct, and to inform did write.
If poets aim at nought but to delight,
Fiddlers have to the bays an equal right.

    Our poet found your gentle fathers kind,
And now some of his works your favor find.
He'll treat you still with somewhat that is new,
But whether good or bad, he leaves to you.
Bawdy the nicest[10] ladies need not fear,
The quickest fancy shall extract none here.
We will not make 'em blush, by which is shown
How much their bought red differs from their own.
No fop, no beau shall just exceptions make,
None but abandoned knaves offense shall take:
Such knaves as he industriously offends,
And should be very loth to have his friends.
For you who bring good humor to the play,
We'll do our best to make you laugh today.

9 *Master Ben*, Ben Jonson.
10 *nicest*, most refined.

ACT I

[SCENE I.] *A street in Whitefriars*

(*Enter* BELFOND SENIOR, *meeting* SHAMWELL.)

BELFOND SENIOR. Cousin Shamwell, well met. Good morrow to
you.

SHAMWELL. Cousin Belfond, your humble servant. What
makes you abroad so early? 'Tis not much past seven.

BELFOND SENIOR. You know we were boozy last night. I am
a little hot-headed this morning, and come to take the
fresh air here in the Temple Walks.

SHAMWELL. Well, and what do you think of our way of living
here? Is not rich, generous wine better than your poor
hedge-wine, stummed,[11] or dull March beer? Are not
delicate well-bred, well-dressed women better than dairy-
maids, tenants' daughters, or barefoot strumpets? Streets
full of fine coaches better than a yard full of dung-carts?
A magnificent tavern than a thatched ale-house? Or the
society of brave, honest, witty, merry fellows than the
conversation of unthinking, hunting, hawking blockheads,
or high-shoed peasants and their wiser cattle?

BELFOND SENIOR. O yes, a world, adad! Ne'er stir, I could
never have thought there had been such a gallant place as
London. Here I can be drunk over night, and well next
morning; can ride in a coach for a shilling as good as a
Deputy-Lieutenant's; and such merry wags and ingenious
companions—! Well, I vow and swear, I am mightily
beholding to you, dear cousin Shamwell. Then for the
women! Mercy upon us! so civil and well bred. And I'll
swear upon a Bible, finer all of them than knight-
baronets' wives with us.

---

[11] *poor hedge-wine, stummed,* countryside wine, twice-fermented.

SHAMWELL. And so kind and pleasant!

BELFOND SENIOR. Ay, I vow, pretty rogues! No pride in them
in the world, but so courteous and familiar, as I am an
honest man, they'll do whatever one would have them
presently. Ah, sweet rogues! While in the country, a
pize[12] take them! There's such a stir with "pish, fy, nay,
Mr. Timothy, what do you do? I vow I'll squeak, never
stir, I'll call out," ah hah—

SHAMWELL. And if one of them happened to be with child,
there's straight an uproar in the country as if the hundred[13] were sued for a robbery.

BELFOND SENIOR. Ay, so there is. And I am in that fear of my
father besides, adad, he'd knock me i'th' head, if he
should hear of such a thing. To say truth, he's so terrible
to me, I can never enjoy myself for him. Lord! What
will he say when he comes to know I am at London?
Which he in all his life-time would never suffer me to see,
for fear I should be debauched, forsooth; and allows me
little or no money at home neither.

SHAMWELL. What matter what he says? Is not every foot of
the estate entailed upon you?

BELFOND SENIOR. Well, I'll endur't no longer! If I can but
raise money, I'll teach him to use his son like a dog, I'll
warrant him.

SHAMWELL. You can ne'er want that. Take up on the reversion,
'tis a lusty one; and Cheatly will help you to the ready[14]
and thou shalt shine and be as gay as any spruce prig[15]
that ever walked the street.

BELFOND SENIOR. Well, adad, you are pleasant men, and have
the neatest sayings with you: "ready" and "spruce prig,"
and abundance of the prettiest witty words.—But sure
that Mr. Cheatly is as fine a gentleman as any wears a
head, and as ingenious, ne'er stir, I believe he would run
down the best scholar in Oxford, and put 'em in a mouse-
hole with his wit.

SHAMWELL. In Oxford! Ay, and in London, too.

BELFOND SENIOR. Goodsookers, cousin! I always thought they
had been wittiest in the universities.

SHAMWELL. O, fie, cousin. A company of puts,[16] mere puts.

---

12 *pize*, pox.
13 *hundred*, community.
14 *the ready*, cash.
15 *spruce prig*, man about town.
16 *puts*, innocents.

BELFOND SENIOR. "Puts, mere puts!" Very good, I'll swear. Ha, ha, ha!

SHAMWELL. They are all scholar-boys, and nothing else as long as they live there; and yet there are as confident as if they knew everything, when they understand no more beyond Magdalen Bridge than mere Indians. But Cheatly is a rare fellow. I'll speak a bold word: he shall cut a sham or banter with the best wit or poet of 'em all.

BELFOND SENIOR. Good again: "cut a sham[17] or banter!" I shall remember all these quaint words in time. But Mr. Cheatly's a prodigy, that's certain.

SHAMWELL. He is so, and a worthy brave fellow, and the best friend where he takes, and the most sincere of any man breathing.

BELFOND SENIOR. Nay, I must needs say I have found him very frank, and very much a gentleman, and am most extremely obliged to him and you for your great kindness.

SHAMWELL. This morning your clothes and liveries will come home, and thou shalt appear rich and splendid like thyself, and the mobile[18] shall worship thee.

BELFOND SENIOR. The "mobile!" That's pretty.

(*Enter* CHEATLY.)

Sweet Mr. Cheatly, my best friend, let me embrace thee.

CHEATLY. My sprightly son of timber and of acres! My noble heir, I salute thee! The cole is coming, and shall be brought this morning.

BELFOND SENIOR. Coal? Why, 'tis summer, I need no firing now. Besides, I intend to burn billets.

CHEATLY. My lusty rustic, learn, and be instructed. "Cole" is in the language of the witty, money; the ready, the rhino. Thou shalt be rhinocerical my lad, thou shalt.

BELFOND SENIOR. Admirable, I swear! "Cole, ready, rhino, rhinocerical!" Lord, how long may a man live in ignorance in the country!

SHAMWELL. Ay, but what asses you'll make of the country gentlemen when you go amongst them! 'Tis a providence you are fallen into so good hands.

BELFOND SENIOR. 'Tis a mercy, indeed! How much cole, ready, and rhino shall I have?

17 *cut a sham*, lie.
18 *mobile*, mob.

CHEATLY. Enough to set thee up to spark it in thy brother's face; and ere thou shalt want the ready, the darby, thou shalt make thy fruitful acres in reversion fly, and all thy sturdy oaks to bend like switches! But thou must squeeze, my lad; squeeze hard, and seal, my bully. Shamwell and I are to be bound with thee.

BELFOND SENIOR. I am mightily beholding to you both, I vow and swear. My uncle, Sir Edward, took my brother when he was a child, and adopted him. Would it had been my lot!

SHAMWELL. He is a noble gentleman, and maintains him in coach and equipage fit for him.

CHEATLY. Thou shalt not see the prig, thy brother, till thou shalt out-jingle him in ready, outshine him in thy ornaments of body, out-spark him in thy coach and liveries; and shalt be so equipped that thou shalt dazzle the whole town with thy outrageous splendor.

BELFOND SENIOR. I vow his tongue is rarely hung!

CHEATLY. Thy brother's heart shall break with envy at thy gallantry; the fops and beaux shall be astonished at thy brightness. What ogling there will be between thee and the blowings![19] Old[20] staring at thy equipage! And every buttock shall fall down before thee!

BELFOND SENIOR. Ha, ha, ha! I vow, you are the pleasantest man I ever met with, and I'll swear, the best friend I ever had in my life; that I must needs say. I was resolved not to let my brother see me till I was in circumstances, d'ye see? And for my father, he is in Holland. My mother's brother died, and left him sole executor. He'll not be here these six weeks.

SHAMWELL. Well, when you see your brother, he'll envy you, and rail at those who made you flourish so. We shall be cast off.

BELFOND SENIOR. Gudsookers, cousin! I take it very unkindly that you should say so. I'll cast off all the relations in the world before I'll part with such true, such loving friends, adad.

(*Enter* CAPTAIN HACKUM.)

O noble Captain Hackum, your servant; servant, Captain.

---

[19] *blowings*, whores.
[20] *Old*, what.

HACKUM. Your humble trout[21] good noble squire. You were brave and boozy last night, i'faith, you were.

BELFOND SENIOR. Yes, really, I was clear[22] for I do not remember what I did, or where I was. Clear, clear—is not that right?

SHAMWELL. Ay, ay. Why, you broke windows, scoured[23] broke open a house in Dorset Court, and took a pretty wench, a gentleman's natural,[24] away by force.

CHEATLY. Very true. And this magnanimous spark, this thunderbolt of war, Captain Hackum, laid about him like a hero, as did some other of your friends, or else the watch had mauled us. But we made them scour.

BELFOND SENIOR. Nay, o' my conscience, the captain's mighty valiant; there's terror in that countenance and whiskers. He's a very Scanderbeg[25] incarnate. And now you put me in mind, I recollect somewhat of this matter. My shoulders are plaguy sore, and my arms black and blue. But where's the wench, the natural—ha, Captain?

HACKUM. Ah, squire, I led her off. I have her safe for you.

BELFOND SENIOR. But does not the gallant thunder and roar for her?

HACKUM. The scoundrel dares not. He knows me, who never knew fear in my life. For my part, I love magnanimity and honor, and those things, and fighting is one of my recreations.

He that wears a brave soul, and dares honestly do,
Is a herald to himself, and a godfather, too.

BELFOND SENIOR. O brave captain!

CHEATLY. The prigster[26] lugged out[27] in defence of his natural, the captain whipped his porker[28] out, and away rubbed prigster, and called the watch.

BELFOND SENIOR. "Prigster, lugged out, natural, porker, rubbed"—admirable! This is very ingenious conversation! Y'are the purest company! Who would not keep company with the wits? Pox o' the country, I say!

---

21 *trout,* pal.
22 *clear,* dead drunk.
23 *scoured,* ran away.
24 *natural,* mistress.
25 *Scanderbeg,* Balkan general who defeated the Turks; a byword in the Renaissance for heroism.
26 *prigster,* rascal.
27 *lugged out,* drew.
28 *porker,* sword.

HACKUM. But, squire, I had damned ill luck afterwards: I went up to the gaming ordinary[29] and lost all my ready, they left me not a rag or sock. Pox o' the tatts[30] for me! I believe they put the doctor[31] upon me.

BELFOND SENIOR. "Tatts," and "doctor!" What's that?

SHAMWELL. The tools of sharpers—false dice.

HACKUM. Hark you. Prithee, noble squire, equip me with a couple of megs, or two couple of smelts.

BELFOND SENIOR. "Smelts?" What, shall we bespeak another dish of fish for our dinner?

SHAMWELL. No, no, megs are guineas, smelts are half-guineas. He would borrow a couple of guineas.

BELFOND SENIOR. "Megs, smelts!" Ha, ha, ha! Very pretty, by my troth. And so thou shalt, dear Captain. There are two megs, and I vow and swear I am glad to have 'em to pleasure you, adad, I am.

HACKUM. You are so honest a gentleman, quarrel every day, and I'll be your second; once a day, at least. And I'll say this for you, there's not a finer gentleman this day walks the Friars—no dispraise to any man, let him be what he will.

BELFOND SENIOR. Adad, you make me proud, sir.

(*Enter* LOLPOOP.)

Oh, Lolpoop, where have you been all this morning, sirrah?

LOLPOOP. Why, 'tis but rear.[32] Marry, 'tis meet a bit past eight. By'r lady, yeow were so sow drunken last neeght I had thoughten yeow wouden ha leen a bed aw th' morn. Well, mine eyne ake a-gazing up and down on aw the fine sights; but for aw that, send me north to my own county again.

BELFOND SENIOR. Oh, silly rogue! you are only fit for cattle. Gentlemen, you must excuse him, he knows no better.

LOLPOOP. Marry, better, quotha! By th' mess, this is a life for the deel.[33] To be drunken each night, break windows, roar, sing, and swear i'th' streets; go to loggerheads with the constable and the watch, han harlots in gold and silver lace! Hea'n bless us! and send me a whome again.

---

29 *ordinary*, tavern.
30 *tatts*, dice.
31 *doctors*, loaded dice.
32 *rear*, early.
33 *deel*, devil.

BELFOND SENIOR. Peace, you saucy scoundrel, or I'll cudgel you to pap. Sirrah, do not provoke me, I say, do not.

LOLPOOP. Ods-flesh, where's money for aw this? Yeowst be run agraunt soon, and you takken this caurse, Ise tell a that.

BELFOND SENIOR. Take that, sirrah! (*beats him*) I'll teach you to mutter. What, my man become my master?

LOLPOOP. Waunds! Give me ten times more, and send me a whome agen at after. What will awd maaster say to this? I mun ne'er see the face of him, I wot.

SHAMWELL. Hang him, rogue! Toss him in a blanket.

CHEATLY. Let me talk with him a little. Come on, fellow.

LOLPOOP. Talk! Well, what sen you?

CHEATLY. (*Bantering*) Your master being in this matter, to deport his count'nance somewhat obliquely to some principles which others but out of a mature gravity may have weighed, and think too heavy to be undertaken; what does it avail you if you shall precipitate or plunge yourself into affairs as unsuitable to your phys'nomy as they are to your complexion?

LOLPOOP. Hah, what sen yeow? Yeow mistaken me: I am not book-learned. I understand a not.

CHEATLY. No, 'tis the strangest thing! Why, put the case you are indebted to me £20 upon a *scire facias*:[34] I extend this up to an outlawry, upon affidavit upon the *nisi prius*;[35] I plead to all this matter, *non est inventus*[36] upon the panel. What is there to be done more in this case as it lies before the bench but to award out execution upon the *posse comitatus*,[37] who are presently to issue out a *certiorari*?[38]

LOLPOOP. I understand a little of sizes, nisi prizes, affidavi, sussurari! But by the mess, I can not tell what to mack of aw this together, not I.

BELFOND SENIOR. Ha, ha! Puppy! Owl! Loggerhead! O silly country put! Here's a prig, indeed! He'll ne'er find out what 'tis to cut a sham or banter. Well, I swear, sir, you do it the best of any man in the world.

CHEATLY. No, no, I swear, not I.

BELFOND SENIOR. I protest you do it incomparably.

---

34 *scire facias*, court order.
35 *nisi prius*, order to call a jury.
36 *non est inventus*, the defendent cannot be found.
37 *posse comitatus*, constables.
38 *certiorari*, court order.

CHEATLY. Nay, now you compliment. Faith, you make me blush.

LOLPOOP. Sham and banter are heathen Greek to me. But yeow have cut out fine wark for yoursel last neeght. I went to see the hause yeow had brocken. Aw the windows are pood dawn. I asked what was the matter, and by the mass, they haw learnt your nam, too; they saiden Squire Belfond had done it, and ravished a wench, and that they hadden gotten the lord chief justice' warren for you, and wodden bring a pawr of actions against yeow.

BELFOND SENIOR. Is this true?

LOLPOOP. Ay, by th' mass.

CHEATLY. No matter. We'll bring you off with a wet finger;[39] trust me for that.

BELFOND SENIOR. Dear friend, I rely upon you for every thing.

SHAMWELL. We value not twenty such things of a rush.

HACKUM. If any of their officers dare invade our privileges, we'll send 'em to hell without bail or mainprize.[40]

LOLPOOP. But I can tella a wor' news than aw this: I ne'er saw flesh alive, and I saw not your father's man, Roger, come out o'th' Temple-yate e'en now. Your father's in town, that's certain.

BELFOND SENIOR. How! my father, say you? 'Tis impossible.

CHEATLY. Courage, my heir in tail:[41] thy father's a poor sneaking tenant for life; thou shalt live better than he can. And if we do contract a debt upon the dirty acres in the north, I have designed for you a fine young lady with a swinging fortune to redeem all. And 'tis impossible, my lad, to miss her.

BELFOND SENIOR. Sir, let me embrace you, and love you. Never man embraced a better friend! *Amicus certus in re incerta cernitur,*[42] as the saying is.

LOLPOOP. Sir, sir, let me speak one word with yeow. Odsflesh, I'll die the death of a dog and aw these yeow seen here be not rogues, cheats, and pickpockets.

BELFOND SENIOR. Peace, you rascal! Adad, I would not have any of 'em here for five hundred pounds. You were a dead man.

LOLPOOP. What is the reason they dare not stir out of this privileged place but on Sabbath days?

---

[39] *with a wet finger,* with no harm.
[40] *mainprize,* bond.
[41] *in tail,* sole legal.
[42] *Amicus . . . cernitur,* from Cicero: a friend in need.

BELFOND SENIOR. You blockhead, Mr. Cheatly had an alderman's young wife run away with him, is sued for't, and is in fear of a substantial jury of city cuckolds. Shamwell's unnatural father lays wait for him, to apprehend him, and run into the country. The brave and valiant gentleman, Captain Hackum, who is as stout as a lion, beat a judge's son t'other day. And now your questions are fully answered, you put, you.

CHEATLY. Honest Shamwell, thou art a rare fellow. Thy cousin here is the wealthiest caravan we have met with a long; time; the hopefullest sealer[43] that ever yet touched wax among us. But we must take off that evil counsellor of his.

(*Enter* Tailor *with a bundle, a* Periwig-maker, Hatter, Shoe-maker.)

SHAMWELL. I warrant you.—Oh, cousin, here's your tailor with your clothes and liveries, hatter, shoe-maker, periwig-maker.

CHEATLY. All your moveables together. Go into your lodging and fit them. Your new footmen, and your French *valet de chambre* are there. I'll wait on you there presently.

LOLPOOP. Ods-flesh, here's whaint wark![44] By'r lady, this is fine! Whaw, whaw!

BELFOND SENIOR. Get you in, you rogue! An you mutter one word more, adad, I'll mince you, sirrah!—Well, go in, all of you. Gentlemen, I shall see you presently. (*Exeunt.*)

CHEATLY. Immediately.—Let us hug ourselves, my dear rascal, in this adventure. You have done very well to engage him last night in an outrage; and we must take care to put him upon all the expense we can. We must reduce him to have as much need of us as possible.

SHAMWELL. Thou art i'th' right. But, Captain, where's the convenient, the natural?

HACKUM. Why, at my house. My wife has wrought her into a good humor. She is very pretty, and is now pleased to think the Squire will be a better keeper than her former, for he was but a sharper, a tatmonger,[45] and when he wanted money, would kick and beat her most immoderately.

SHAMWELL. Well. I'll say that for the Captain's wife, she's as

---

[43] *sealer,* one who pawns.
[44] *whaint wark,* queer work.
[45] *tatmonger,* cheat.

good an able, discreet woman to carry on an intrigue as
ere a woman in the Friars. Nay, better.

HACKUM. Your servant, good Mr. Shamwell. She's a very good
woman, thanks be to heaven. I have great comfort in
her; she has a cup of the best cherry brandy in the Friars.

SHAMWELL. (*aside*) And commonly a good whore, to boot.—
But prithee, Captain, go home, and let her and the young
girl prepare to dine with us. We must have a great dinner,
and fiddlers at the George, to season the Squire in his
new equipage.

HACKUM. Well, well, it shall be done.   (*Exit.*)

SHAMWELL. You'll find this fellow a necessary tool in consort
with his wife, who is, indeed, a bawd of parts. He is a
good ruffian enough, for, though he be not stout, he's
impudent, and will roar and keep a filthy pother, which is
enough to make fools believe he's stout.

CHEATLY. Let him, and the small fry, pick up the Squire's
loose crumbs, while we share in the lusty sums.

(*Enter* SCRAPEALL)

Oh, here comes Mr. Scrapeall, with all his zeal—our
godly accomplice in all designs. Leave him to me.

                              (*Exit* SHAMWELL.)

Oh, Mr. Scrapeall! Have you brought the money for the
Squire?

SCRAPEALL. I come to tell you that my man approacheth with
the money and the goods for your Squire.

CHEATLY. I hope you have not burdened him with too many
goods at first.

SCRAPEALL. No; but a fourth part. 'Tis true, the goods are
somewhat stale, but I will take them off at small under
rates. You know I am not seen in furnishing of the goods
and money, but only in the buying of the goods. My
lawyer accompanieth my man to testify the writings.

CHEATLY. 'Tis as it should be. He is a fat squire; the estate
in tail is full £3000 a year. He will yield well.

SCRAPEALL. (*aside*) This squire is to take to wife a niece I
have in charge. His father is to give me £5000 out of
her fortune, and the squire's lewdness and prodigality will
soon let me deep into his reversion. Besides, his lighting
into these hands will make his father, when he finds it,
hasten to agree with me for his redemption. I like the
business well.—I am going to the man you call Crump,

who helpeth solicitors to affidavitmen,[46] and swearers, and bail.

CHEATLY. His office is next door his wardrobe for bail and witnesses. Here he comes. Let's meet him.   (*Exeunt.*)

(*Enter* SIR WILLIAM BELFOND *and an* Attorney.)

SIR WILLIAM. Sure I should know the face of that fellow that's going there into Whitefriars.

ATTORNEY. 'Tis a most notorious one. You have seen him often, this, that most audacious rogue, Cheatly, who has drawn so many young heirs, and undone so many sealers. He's a bolter of[47] Whitefriars.

SIR WILLIAM. It is that villain!

ATTORNEY. I am very glad, sir, you have dispatched your business so soon in Holland.

SIR WILLIAM. I had great success and finished all six weeks, at least, ere I expected; and had time to come by the way of Flanders and see that country, which I desired. And from Newport I came to Dover, and, riding posts from thence, I took a boat to Southwark; and landed just now here at the Temple. But I am troubled you had sent my packet to Holland ere I came.

ATTORNEY. I received none from you of late. No packet has arrived this fortnight from Holland.

SIR WILLIAM. Have you heard no news from my son, nor my steward in the country?

ATTORNEY. None this ten or twelve days.

SIR WILLIAM. That son is all the joy of my life. For him I hurry up and down, take pains, spare, and live hard to raise his fortune.

ATTORNEY. Indeed, I hear he's a fine gentleman, and understands his country affairs as well as e'er a farmer of them all.

SIR WILLIAM. I must confess he proves after my own heart. He's a solid young man, a dutiful child as ever man had, and I think I have done well for him in providing him a wife with such a fortune, which he yet knows nothing of. But will not this godly man, this Mr. Scrapeall, take a farthing less, say you, for his niece?

ATTORNEY. Not a sou I have higgled[48] with him as if I were

---

46 *affidavit-men*, bought witnesses.
47 *bolter of*, runaway to.
48 *higgled*, bargained.

to buy of a horse-courser, and he will not take a farthing less than £5000 for his niece.

SIR WILLIAM. He's a strange mixture, a perpetual sermon-hunter, repeats and sings psalms continually, and prays so loud and vehemently that he is a disturbance to his neighbors; he is so heavenward pious, and seems a very saint of a scrivener.

ATTORNEY. He finds the sweet of that; it gets him many a good trust and executorship.

SIR WILLIAM. Pox on him for a damned godly knave, forsooth! Can not he be contented to sell her whom his own brother committed to his charge, but he must extort so much for her? Well, I must agree with him. I know she has full £20,000 left her, and has been brought up as strictly as my son. Get writings ready. I'll send post for my son Timothy today.

ATTORNEY. They are ready. You may seal in the afternoon, if you please.

SIR WILLIAM. And I will then. I'll detain you no longer. Get my writings ready: I am resolved to settle my other boy well. But my town son afflicts me whene'er I hear him named.

ATTORNEY. Your humble servant, Sir William Belfond.

(*Exit* Attorney.)

(*Enter* Servant *to* SIR WILLIAM.)

SERVANT. Sir, I have been at your brother's house, and they say he is come to some lawyer's chamber in the King's Bench Buildings.

SIR WILLIAM. That's lucky enough. I'll walk here then, and do you watch.

(*Enter* HACKUM *and another* Bully.)

Who are these? Some inhabitants of Whitefriars; some bullies of Alsatia.

HACKUM. I was plaguy boozy last night with Squire Belfond. We had fiddles, whores, scoured, broke windows, beat watches, and roared like thunder.

BULLY. Ah, I heard you.

SIR WILLIAM. (*aside*) What says he?

HACKUM. He drinks, whores, swears, sings, roars, rants, and scours with the best of us.

SIR WILLIAM. Sir, with your favor, are you acquainted with young Belfond?

HACKUM. Yes, that I am. (*aside*) What country put's this?

SIR WILLIAM. What countryman is he, sir?

HACKUM. Prithee, old prigster, why dost ask? He is a northern
man. He has a damned, rustic, miserable rascal to his
father, who lives a nasty, brutal life in the country, like
a swine. But the Squire will be even with him, I warrant
him.

SIR WILLIAM. I have something to say to him, if I could see
him.

HACKUM. You, you old prig! You damned country put! You
have something to say to him! I am ready to give you
satisfaction. Lug out—come, you put! I'll make you
scamper!

SIR WILLIAM. D'ye hear, bully rascal? Put up and walk your
way, or, by heaven! I'll beat you as long as you're able
to be beaten. (*draws his sword*)

BULLY. I'll stand by you. You may easily beat this old fellow.

HACKUM. No man e'er gave me such words, but forfeited his
life. I could whip thee through the lungs immediately,
but I'll desist at present.—Who the devil would have
thought this put durst have drawn a sword?—Well, sir,
we shall take a time, sir, another time, sir.

SIR WILLIAM. You lie, you rascal, you will take no time. Here's
a fine companion of my son's!

(*Exeunt* HACKUM *and* Bully.)

(*Enter* SIR EDWARD BELFOND.)

SIR EDWARD. Who's this I see? My brother? Sir William
Belfond! Your humble servant. You are welcome into
England. I looked not for you these six weeks.

SIR WILLIAM. I landed at the Temple Stairs even now. My man
has been at your house, and he heard there you were here.

SIR EDWARD. I hope you have done your business.

SIR WILLIAM. Beyond my expectation.

SIR EDWARD. Has your wife's brother done by you in his will as
you would have had him?

SIR WILLIAM. Truly, yes. He has made me sole executor, and
left my two sons, £5000 to be paid at each of their days
of marriage, or at my death.

SIR EDWARD. Well, brother, you are a happy man, for wealth
flows up upon you on every side, and riches you account
the greatest happiness.

SIR WILLIAM. I find that wealth alone will not make me happy.
Ah, brother, I must confess it was a kindness in you,

when heaven had blessed you with a great estate by
merchandise, to adopt my younger son, and take him and
breed him from his childhood. But you have been so
gentle to him, he is run into all manner of vice and riot;
no bounds can hold him, no shame can stop him, no
laws nor customs can restrain him.

SIR EDWARD. I am confident you are mistaken. He has as fair
a reputation as any gentleman about London. 'Tis true,
he's a good fellow, but no sot; he loves mirth and society,
without drunkenness; he is, as all young fellows, I believe,
are, given to women, but it is in private; and in short
keeps as good company as any man in England.

SIR WILLIAM. Your over-weening makes you look through a
false glass upon him. Company! Why, he keeps company
for the devil! Had you come a minute sooner, you might
have seen two of his companions; they were praising him
for roaring, swearing, ranting, scouring, whoring, beating
watches, breaking windows. I but asked one of 'em if he
knew him, and said I had somewhat to say to him; the
rogue, the most seeming terrible of the two, told me, if
I had anything to say to Squire Belfond, he would give
me satisfaction.

SIR EDWARD. What kind of fellow?

SIR WILLIAM. He came out of Whitefriars. He's some Alsatian
bully.

SIR EDWARD. 'Tis impossible; he never keeps such company.

SIR WILLIAM. The rogue drew upon me, bid me "Lug out,"
called me "old prig," "country put," and spoke a particular language which such rogues have made to themselves called canting, as beggars, gipsies, thieves, and
jail-birds do; but I made his bullies go away very tamely
at the sight of my drawn sword.

SIR EDWARD. I am sure he keeps no such company; it must be
some other of his name.

SIR WILLIAM. You make me mad to excuse him thus. The
town rings of him. You have ruined him by your in-
dulgence; besides, he throws away money like dirt; his
infamy is notorious.

SIR EDWARD. Infamy! Nay, there you wrong him. He does no
ungentlemanlike things. Prithee, consider youth a little.
What if he does wench a little, and now and then is
somewhat extravagant in wine? Where is the great crime?
All young fellows that have mettle in them will do the

first; and if they have wit and good humor in them, in this drinking country, they will sometimes be forced upon the latter; and he must be a very dull phlegmatic lump whom wine will not elevate to some extravagance now and then.

SIR WILLIAM. Will you distract me? What, are drinking and whoring no faults? His courses will break my heart, they bring tears into my eyes so often.

SIR EDWARD. One would think you had been drinking and were maudlin. Think what we ourselves did when we were young fellows. You were a spark, would drink, scour, and wench with the best o'th' town.

SIR WILLIAM. Ay, but I soon repented, married, and settled.

SIR EDWARD. And turned as much to the other extreme; and perhaps I mislike these faults, caused by his heat of youth. But how do you know he may not be reclaimed suddenly?

SIR WILLIAM. Reclaimed? How can he be reclaimed without severity? You should cudgel him and allow him no money; make him not dare to offend you thus. Well, I have a son whom by my strictness I have formed according to my heart. He never puts on his hat in my presence; rises at second course, takes away his plate, says grace, and saves me the charge of a chaplain. Whenever he committed a fault, I mauled him with correction. I'd fain see him once dare to be extravagant! No, he's a good youth, the comfort of my age. I weep for joy to think of him. Good sir, learn to be a father of him that is one; I have a natural care of him you have adopted.

SIR EDWARD. You are his father by nature. I by choice; I took him when he was a child, and bred him with gentleness and that kind of conversation that has made him my friend. He conceals nothing from me, or denies nothing to me. Rigor makes nothing but hypocrites.

SIR WILLIAM. Perhaps, when you begin late; but you should have been severe to him in his childhood, abridged him of liberty and money, and have had him soundly whipped often; he would have blessed you for it afterwards.

SIR EDWARD. Too much straitness to the minds of youth, like too much lacing to the body, will make them grow crooked.

SIR WILLIAM. But no lacing at all will make them swell and grow monsters.

SIR EDWARD. I must govern by love. I had as leave govern a

dog as a man, if it must be by fear; this I take to be the difference between a good father to children, and a harsh master over slaves.

SIR WILLIAM. Yes, and see what your government is come to: his vice and prodigality will distract me.

SIR EDWARD. Why should you be so concerned? He is mine, is he not?

SIR WILLIAM. Yes, by adoption, but he is mine by nature.

SIR EDWARD. 'Tis all but custom.

SIR WILLIAM. Mine is a tender care.

SIR EDWARD. Your passion blinds you. I have as tender care as you can have; I have been ever delighted with him from his childhood; he is endeared to me by long custom and familiarity. I have had all the pleasure of a father without the drudgery of getting a son upon a damned wife, whom perhaps I should wish hanged.

SIR WILLIAM. And will you let him run on in his lewdness and prodigality?

SIR EDWARD. He is mine. If he offends, 'tis me; if he squanders away money, 'tis mine; and what need you care? Pray take care of your own; if you will take care of this, too, what do you do but take him from me?

SIR WILLIAM. This you come to always! I take him from you? No, I'd not be troubled with him. Well, let him run on and be ruined, hanged, and damned. I'll never speak a word more about him. Let him go on.

SIR EDWARD. This heat of you will be allayed ere long, I warrant you.

SIR WILLIAM. No, no, let him go on, let him go on. I'll take care of my own at home; and happy were this rake-hell, if he would take example by his brother. But I say no more; I have done—let him go.

SIR EDWARD. Now you are angry, your passion runs away with you.

SIR WILLIAM. No, no, I have done. What would you have more?

SIR EDWARD. Let us go and see him. I'll lay my life you'll find him perusing some good author. He spends his whole morning in study.

SIR WILLIAM. I must into the city, the first thing I do, and get my bills accepted; and then, if you will, we'll see him; and no doubt but we shall find him perusing of some whore or other, instead of a book.

SIR EDWARD. I am not of your opinion. But I'll carry you in my coach into the city, and then bring you back to him. He is of so good a disposition, so much a gentleman, and has such worth and honor, that if you knew him as well as I, you'd love him as well as I do.

SIR WILLIAM. Well, well, I hear you, sir. I must send for my son post—I'll show you a son! Well, heaven bless him, I should be weary of this wicked world but for the comforts I find in him. Come along, I'll show you a son.

(*Exeunt ambo.*)

ACT II

[SCENE I.] BELFOND JUNIOR's *chambers*

(*Enter* BELFOND JUNIOR *and* LUCIA.)

BELFOND JUNIOR. Why dost thou sigh, and show such sadness in thy looks, my pretty miss?

LUCIA. Have I not reason?

BELFOND JUNIOR. Dost thou mislike thy entertainment?

LUCIA. Ah, cruel Belfond, thou hast undone me.

BELFOND JUNIOR. My pretty little rogue, I sooner would undo myself a thousand times.

LUCIA. How I tremble to think what I ha' done! I have made myself forever miserable.

BELFOND JUNIOR. Oh, say not so, dear child! I'll kiss those tears from off thy beauteous eyes. But I shall wrong thy cheeks, on which they fall like precious drops of dew on flowers.

LUCIA. Heaven! What have I done?

BELFOND JUNIOR. No more than what thy mother did before thee; no more than thy whole sex is born to do.

LUCIA. Oh, had I thought you would have been so cruel, I never would have seen your face—I swear I would not.

BELFOND JUNIOR. I swear thou would'st, I know thou would'st. Cruel! No billing turtle e'er was kinder to his tender mate. In billing, cooing, and in gentle murmurs we expressed our kindness; and coo'd and murmured and loved on.

LUCIA. The more unhappy fool was I. Go, go, I hate you now.

BELFOND JUNIOR. O my sweet little one! Thou canst not be so unkind. Those pretty tell-tales of thy heart, thy eyes, say better things.

LUCIA. Do they so? I'll be revenged on 'em for't, for they shall never see you more.

BELFOND JUNIOR. Ah, say not so. I had rather much the sun should never shine on me than thou be hidden from my sight. Thou art not sure in earnest?

LUCIA. Yes, sure, I think I am.

BELFOND JUNIOR. No, sweet love, I think thou art not.

LUCIA. Oh, Lord, how shall I look! How shall I bear myself! If any of my friends shall fix their eyes upon me, I shall look down, and blush, and think they know all.

BELFOND JUNIOR. How many fair ones daily do the same, and look demurely as any saints?

LUCIA. They are confident things, I warrant 'em.

BELFOND JUNIOR. Let love be made familiar to thee, and thou wilt bear it better. Thou must see me every day. Canst thou be so hard-hearted to forbear the sight of me?

LUCIA. Perhaps I may desire now and then a look, a sight of thee at some distance. But I will never venture to come near thee more, I vow.

BELFOND JUNIOR. Let me kiss that vow from off thy lips while 'tis warm there. I have it here. 'Tis gone. Thou wilt not kill me, sure? Didst thou not say thou loved'st me?

LUCIA. Yes, I loved too much, or this had never happened. I could not else have been undone.

BELFOND JUNIOR. Undone? Thou art made. Woman is but half a creature till she be joined to man. Now thou art whole and perfect.

LUCIA. Wicked man! Can I be so confident once to come near thee more?

BELFOND JUNIOR. Shouldst thou but fail one day, I never should survive it; and then my ghost will haunt thee. Canst thou look on me, pretty creature, and talk thus?

LUCIA. Well, go thy ways, thou flattering tongue, and those bewitching eyes were made to ruin womankind.

BELFOND JUNIOR. Could I but think thou wert in earnest, these arms should clasp thee ever here. I'd never part with thee.

LUCIA. No, no, now I must be gone; I shall be missed. How shall I get home, and not be known? Sure, everybody will discover me.

BELFOND JUNIOR. Thy mask will cover all. There is a chair[49] below in the entry to carry thee and set thee down where thou wilt.

LUCIA. Farewell, dear, cruel man! And must I come tomorrow morning, say you? No, no.

BELFOND JUNIOR. Yes, yes; tomorrow and tomorrow, and every morning of our lives; I die else.

(*Enter* Footboy.)

FOOTBOY. Sir, your singing master is coming.

BELFOND JUNIOR. My singing master, Mr. Solfa, is coming.

LUCIA. O Lord, hide me! He is my master, he'll know me! I shall not be able to go by him for trembling.

BELFOND JUNIOR. Pretty miss, into the closet. I'll dispatch him soon.   (LUCIA *goes in.*)

(*Enter* Singing Master *and his daughter.*)

Come, Master, let your daughter sing the song you promised me.

SOLFA. Come, Betty. Please to put in a flute, sir.

BELFOND JUNIOR. Come on.

(*Song with two flutes and a thorough bass.*)

THE EXPOSTULATION

Still wilt thou sigh, and still in vain
    A cold neglectful nymph adore;
No longer fruitlessly complain,
    But to thyself thyself restore.
In youth thou caught'st this fond disease
    And shouldst abandon it in age;
Some other nymph as well may please,
    Absence or bus'ness disengage.

On tender hearts the wounds of love,
    Like those imprinted on young trees,
Or kill at first, or else they prove
    Larger b'insensible degrees.
Business I tried, she filled my mind;
    On other lips my dear I kissed;
But never solid joy could find,
    Where I my charming Sylvia missed.

49 *chair,* sedan chair, carried by two servants.

Long absence, like a Greenland night,
    Made me but wish for sun the more;
And that inimitable light
    She, none but she, could e'er restore.
She never once regards thy fire,
    Nor ever vents one sigh for thee.
I must the glorious sun admire,
    Though he can never look on me.

Look well, you'll find she's not so rare,
    Much of her former beauty's gone;
My love her shadow larger far
    Is made by her declining sun.
What if her glories faded be,
    My former wounds I must endure:
For should the bow unbended be,
    Yet that can ever help the cure.

BELFOND JUNIOR. 'Tis very easy and natural: your daughter sings delicately.

(*Enter* TRUMAN.)

TRUMAN. Belfond, good morrow to thee. I see thou still tak'st care to melt away thy hours in soft delights.

BELFOND JUNIOR. Honest Truman! All the pleasures and diversions we can invent are little enough to make the farce of life go down.

TRUMAN. And yet what a coil they keep! How busy and industrious are those who are reckoned grave and wise, about this life, as if there were something in it.

BELFOND JUNIOR. Those fools are in earnest, and very solid; they think there's something in't, while wise men know there's nothing to be done here but to make the best of a bad market.

TRUMAN. You are mighty philosophical this morning. But shall I not hear one song as well as you?

BELFOND JUNIOR. Have you set that ode in Horace?

SOLFA. I have.

BELFOND JUNIOR. Then I hope you will be encouraged to set more of them; we then shall be sure of wit and music together, while you great musicians do often take most pains about the silliest words. Prithee, Truman, sing it.

(TRUMAN *sings Integer vitae sceler isque purus &c.*—Hor., Ode 22, I)

BELFOND JUNIOR. Very well. You have obliged me. Please to accept of this. And, madam, you shall give me leave to show my gratitude by a small present.

SOLFA AND DAUGHTER. Your servant, sir.   (*Exeunt.*)

TRUMAN. You are so immoderately given to music, methinks it should jostle love out of your thoughts.

BELFOND JUNIOR. Oh, no! Remember Shakespeare: if music be the food of love, play on.[50] There's nothing nourishes that soft passion like it, it imps[51] his wings, and makes him fly a higher pitch. But, prithee, tell me what news of our dear mistresses? I was never yet so sincerely in love as with my pretty hypocrite. There is a fire in those eyes that strikes like lightning. What a constant churchman she has made of me!

TRUMAN. And mine has made an entire conquest of me! 'Tis the most charming pretty creature that e'er my eyes beheld.

BELFOND JUNIOR. Let us not fall out, like the heroes in *The Rehearsal*,[52] for not being in love with the same woman.

TRUMAN. Nothing could be so fortunate as our difference in this case,—the only one we disagree in.

BELFOND JUNIOR. Thou art in the right. Mine hath so charmed me, I am content to abandon all other pleasures, and live alone for her. She has subdued me even to marriage.

TRUMAN. Mine has no less vanquished me. I'll surrender upon discretion. Ah, rogue Belfond, I see by your bed, for all your constant love, you have had a wench this night.

BELFOND JUNIOR. Peace, peace, man. 'Tis dangerous to fast too long, for fear of losing an appetite quite.

TRUMAN. You are a sincere, honest lover, indeed.

BELFOND JUNIOR. Faith, Truman, we may talk of mighty matters; of our honesty and morality; but a young fellow carries that about him that will make him a knave now and then, in spite of his teeth. Besides, I am afraid 'tis impossible for us profane fellows to succeed into that sanctified family.

TRUMAN. You will not say so when you know what progress I have made in our affairs already.

---

50 See Shakespeare's *Twelfth Night*, I, i.

51 *imps*, strengthens.

52 In *The Rehearsal*, a satire by the Duke of Buckingham, two male leads quarrel because they are *not* in love with the same woman.

BELFOND JUNIOR. Thou reviv'st my drooping hopes! Tell me,
are we like to succeed? Oh, if I can but prevail upon my
pretty little churchwoman, I am resolved to conform to
her forever!

TRUMAN. Look under my coat! Am I not well habited? with a
plain band, bob peruke,[53] and no cuffs.

BELFOND JUNIOR. Verily, like one of the pure ones.

TRUMAN. Yea. And our frequenting of sermons and lectures
(which, heaven knows, we did out of no good, but for
the sake of the little ones) has used me to their style.
Thus qualified, I got access into the house; having found
that their governante is sister to a weaver in the west
whom I know, I pretended to be her cousin, and to bring
a token sent to her by her brother, and was very welcome
to her.

BELFOND JUNIOR. Most fortunate! Why does he keep 'em so
strictly? Never to see the face of man?

TRUMAN. Be not troubled at that, 'twill forward our design;
they'll be the more earnest to be delivered. But no Italian
women are so closely confined; the pure knave intends to
sell them, even his daughter, who has a good fortune left
her by a widow that was her aunt; and for his niece, he
has as good as agreed already with your father for £5000
to marry her to your brother in the country. Her uncle
gave her £20,000, and this is the reason for confining
'em, for fear of losing the money.

BELFOND JUNIOR. With my father, say you?

TRUMAN. Most certain. This I learned out of Madam Governante at the first interview.

BELFOND JUNIOR. This is a very odd accident; 'twill make my
difficulty greater.

TRUMAN. Not at all. As liars are always readiest to believe lies,
I never knew an hypocrite but might easily be cozened by
another hypocrite. I have made my way, and I warrant
thee a good event. I intend to grow great with the father.

BELFOND JUNIOR. Thy sanguine temper makes thee always
hope in every enterprise.

TRUMAN. You might observe, whenever he stared upon them,
they would steal a look at us; and by stealth have often
twisted eyebeams with us.

BELFOND JUNIOR. The sour and devout look, indeed, seems
but put on. There is a pretty warmth and tenderness in

53 peruke, wig.

their eyes that now and then glides o'er the godly look;
like the sun's light, when breaking through a cloud, it
swiftly glides upon a field of corn.

TRUMAN. The air of their faces plainly shows they have wit
that must despise these trifling forms; their precise looks
most surely are constrained.

(*Enter* MRS. TERMAGANT.)

BELFOND JUNIOR. How. Madam Termagant here! Then we
shall have fine work.—What wind blows you hither?

TERMAGANT. How dare you think that I of all womenkind
should be used thus?

BELFOND JUNIOR. You mean, not used—that's your grievance.

TERMAGANT. Good Mr. Disdain, I shall spoil your scoffing.
Has my love deserved to be thus slighted? I that have
refused princes for your sake? Did not all the town court
me? And must I choose such an ungrateful wretch?

BELFOND JUNIOR. When you were first in season, you were a
little courted by some of quality. Mistresses, like green
peas, at first coming, are only had by the rich, but afterwards they come to everybody.

TERMAGANT. Curse on your saucy similes! Was I not yours,
and only yours?

BELFOND JUNIOR. I had not faith enough for that; but if you
were, I never had any that was mine, and only mine, but
I made 'em all mankind's before I had done.

TERMAGANT. Ah, traitor! And you must pick me out to make
this base example of. Must I be left?

BELFOND JUNIOR. Left? Yes, sure, left! Why, you were not
married to me; I took no lease of your frail tenement; I
was but tenant at my own will.

TERMAGANT. Insolent! How dare you thus provoke my fury?
Was ever woman's love like mine to thee? Perfidious man!
(*Weeps*)

BELFOND JUNIOR. So: after the thunder, thus the heat-drops
fall.

TERMAGANT. No; I scorn that thou shouldst bring tears into
my eyes.

BELFOND JUNIOR. Why do you come to trouble me?

TERMAGANT. Since I can please no longer, I'll come to plague
thee, and if I die before thee, my ghost shall haunt thee.

BELFOND JUNIOR. Indeed, your love was most particular with
spitting and scratching, like caterwauling. And in the
best of humors you were ever murmuring and complain-

ing: Oh, my head aches, I am so sick; and jealous to madness, too.

TERMAGANT. Oh, devil incarnate!

TRUMAN. Belfond, thou art the most ungentle knight alive.

TERMAGANT. Methinks the pretty child I have had by you should make you less inhumane.

BELFOND JUNIOR. Let me have it; I'll breed it up.

TERMAGANT. No, thou shalt never have it while thou livest. I'll pull it limb from limb ere thou shalt have it.

BELFOND JUNIOR. This is so unnatural that you will make me so far from thinking it mine, that I shall not believe it yours, but that you have put a false child upon me.

TERMAGANT. Unworthy wretch!

BELFOND JUNIOR. When thou art old enough, thy malice and ill humor will qualify thee for a witch, but thou hadst never douceurs[54] enough in thy youth to fit thee for a mistress.

TERMAGANT. How dare you provoke me thus? For what little dirty wench am I thus used? If she be above ground, I'll find her, and tear her eyes out. Hah—by the bed, I see the devil has been here tonight.—Oh, oh, I can not bear it!

(Falls into a fit.)

TRUMAN. Belfond, help the lady, for shame. Lay hold on her.

BELFOND JUNIOR. No, no, let her alone; she will not hurt herself, I warrant thee. She is a rare actor. She acts a fit of the mother[55] the best of any one in England. Ha, ha, ha!

TRUMAN. How canst thou be so cruel?

BELFOND JUNIOR. What a devil should I do? If a man lies once with a woman, is he bound to do it forever?

TERMAGANT. Oh, oh!

BELFOND JUNIOR. Very well, faith; admirably well acted.

TERMAGANT. Is it so? Devil, devil, I'll spoil your *point de Venise*[56] for you. *(Flies at him.)*

BELFOND JUNIOR. Will you force me to make my footman turn you out?

(Enter Footman.)

FOOTMAN. Sir, your father and your uncle are coming hither.

---

[54] *douceurs,* grace.
[55] *mother,* hysteria.
[56] *point de Venise,* Venetian lace.

BELFOND JUNIOR. 'Sdeath! My father! 'Tis impossible.

FOOTMAN. By heaven, 'tis true. They are coming up by this time.

BELFOND JUNIOR. Look you, madam, you may, if you will, ruin me, and put me out of all means of doing for you or your child. Try me once more, and get into the bed and cover yourself with the quilt, or I am undone.

TERMAGANT. Villain, you deserve to be ruined. But I love my child too well.

TRUMAN. For heaven's sake, hide yourself in the bed quickly.

TERMAGANT. No, no, I'll run into the closet.

BELFOND JUNIOR. Death and hell! I am ruined! There's a young girl there; she'll make yet a worse uproar.

TRUMAN. Peace, let me alone.—Madam, whatever happens, ruin not yourself and child inevitably.

(*Enter* SIR WILLIAM BELFOND, SIR EDWARD, *and* Servants.)

SIR EDWARD. Ned, good morrow to thee.

BELFOND JUNIOR. Your blessing, sir.

SIR EDWARD. Heaven bless thee. Here's one unexpected.

BELFOND JUNIOR. My father! I beg your blessing, sir.

SIR WILLIAM. Heaven mend you; it can never bless you in the lewd course you are in.

BELFOND JUNIOR. You are misinformed, sir; my courses are not so lewd as you imagine.

SIR WILLIAM. Do you see? I am misinformed; he'll give me the lie.

BELFOND JUNIOR. I would first bite my tongue in pieces, and spit it at you. Whatever little heats of youth I have been guilty of, I doubt not but in short time to please you fully.

SIR EDWARD. Well said, Ned. I dare swear thou wilt.

SIR WILLIAM. Good brother Credulous, I thank heaven I am not so. You were not drunk last night with bullies, and roared and ranted, scoured, broke windows, beat the watch, broke open a house, and forced away a wench in Salisbury Court! This is a fine life! This he calls heats of youth.

BELFOND JUNIOR. I was at home by eight o'clock last night, and supped at home; and never keep such company.

SIR WILLIAM. No, no? You are not called Squire Belfond by the scoundrels, your companions? 'Twas not you no, no!

BELFOND JUNIOR. Not I, upon my faith. I never keep such company, or do such actions. If any one should call me squire, I'd break his head. Some rascal has usurped my name.

SIR EDWARD. Look you, brother, what would you have? This must be some mistake.

SIR WILLIAM. What a devil! You believe this too? Ounds! You make me mad! Is there any of our name in England but ourselves? Does he think to flam[57] me with a lie?

BELFOND JUNIOR. I scorn a lie. 'Tis the basest thing a gentleman can be guilty of. All my servants can testify I stirred not out last night.

TRUMAN. I assure you, sir, he was not abroad last night.

SIR WILLIAM. You assure me! Who are you—one of his hopeful companions? No, your clothes are not good enough; you may be his pimp.

TRUMAN. You are the father of my friend, an old gentleman, and a little mad.

SIR WILLIAM. Old! Walk down—I'll try your youth; I'll fight with the bravest ruffian he keeps company with.

SIR EDWARD. Brother, are you mad? Has the country robbed you of all good manners and common sense?

SIR WILLIAM. I had a bout with two of your bullies in the Temple walks.

BELFOND JUNIOR. Whom does he mean? This is a gentleman of estate and quality; he has above £2,000 a year.

SIR EDWARD. You are a mad man. I am ashamed of you.—Sir, I beseech you pardon my brother's passion, which transports him beyond civility.

BELFOND JUNIOR. I know you will for my sake.

TRUMAN. He is the father of my dearest friend. I shall be glad to serve him.

SIR EDWARD. Will you never be of age of discretion? For shame! Use me, your son, and everybody better.

SIR WILLIAM. Well, I must be run down like a tame puppy.

LUCIA. (*Within*) Murder, murder! Help, help! Ah, ah!

(TERMAGANT *pulls* LUCIA *out by the hair; they part them.*)

BELFOND JUNIOR. Oh, this damned she-devil!

TERMAGANT. I'll make you an example. Will you see him, whether I will or not, you young whore!

SIR WILLIAM. Here's a son! Here's a fine son! Here's your breeding! Here's a pretty son! Here's a delicate son! Here's a dainty son!

[57] *flam*, deceive.

SIR EDWARD. If he be mad, will you be madder?

BELFOND JUNIOR. Turn out this she-bear; turn her out to the rabble.

TERMAGANT. Revenge, you villain, revenge!

(*Exeunt* TERMAGANT *and* Footman.)

BELFOND JUNIOR. Dear friend, prithee see this innocent girl safe in the chair, from that outrageous strumpet's fury.

(*Exeunt* TRUMAN *and* LUCIA.)

SIR WILLIAM. Here's a son! Here's a son! Very well, make much of him! Here's the effect of whoring!

BELFOND JUNIOR. No, sir, 'tis the effect of not whoring; this rage is because I have cast her off.

SIR WILLIAM. Yes, yes, for a younger—a sweet reformation! Let me not see your face, nor hear you speak; you will break my heart.

BELFOND JUNIOR. Sir, the young girl was never here before; she brought me linen from the Exchange.

SIR WILLIAM. A fine bawd, her mistress, in the meantime.

BELFOND JUNIOR. This furious wench coming in to rail at me for my leaving her, I was forced to put the other into that closet; and at your coming up, against my will, this run into the same closet.

SIR WILLIAM. Sirrah, most audacious rogue, do you sham me? Do you think you have your uncle to deal with? Avoid my presence, sirrah. Get you out, sirrah.

BELFOND JUNIOR. I am sorry I offended; I obey.

(*Exit* BELFOND JUNIOR.)

SIR WILLIAM. I could have found in my heart to have cudgelled him.

SIR EDWARD. Shame of our family! You behave yourself so like a madman and a fool, you will be begged: these fits are more extravagant than anything he can be guilty of. Do you give your son the words of command you use to dogs?

SIR WILLIAM. Justify him, do! He's an excellent son! a very pretty son! a delicate son! a discreet son! he is.

SIR EDWARD. Pray use me better, or I'll assure you, we must never see one another. Besides, I shall entail my estate for want of issue by this son here, upon another's family, if you will treat me thus.

SIR WILLIAM. (*aside*) What says he?—Well, brother, I ha'

done: his lewdness distracted me! Oh, my poor boy in
the country! I long to see him, the great support of my
declining age.

SIR EDWARD. Let us calmly reason: what has your breeding
made of him (with your patience) but a blockhead?

SIR WILLIAM. A blockhead! When he comes, the world shall
judge which of us has been the wiser in the education of
a son. A blockhead? Why, he knows a sample of any
grain as well as e'er a fellow in the north; can handle a
sheep or bullock as well as any one; knows his seasons of
plowing, sowing, harrowing, laying fallow; understands
all sorts of manure; and ne'er a one that wears a head
can wrong him in a bargain.

SIR EDWARD. A very pretty fellow for a gentleman's baily.[58]

SIR WILLIAM. For his own baily, and to be a rich—

SIR EDWARD. Swine, and live as nastily, and keep worse company than beasts in a forest.

SIR WILLIAM. He knows no vice, poor boy.

SIR EDWARD. He will have his turn to know it, then, as sure as
he will have the small pox; and then he'll be fond on't
when his brother has left it.

SIR WILLIAM. I defy the omen; he never whores, nor drinks
hard but upon design, as driving a bargain or so; and that
I allow him.

SIR EDWARD. Knavish and designing drunkenness you allow;
but not good fellowship for mirth and conversation.

SIR WILLIAM. Now, brother, pray what have you made your
son good for, with your breeding you so much boast of?
Let's hear that now. Come on, let's hear.

SIR EDWARD. First, I bred him at Westminster School till he
was master of the Greek and Latin tongues; then I kept
him at the university where I instructed him to read the
noble Greek and Roman authors.

SIR WILLIAM. Well, and what use can he make of the noble
Greek and Latin but to prate like a pedant, and show his
parts over a bottle?

SIR EDWARD. To make a man fit for the conversation of learned
gentlemen is one noble end of study. But those authors
make him wiser and honester, sir, to boot.

SIR WILLIAM. Wiser! Will he ever get sixpence, or improve, or
keep his estate by 'em?

SIR EDWARD. Mean notions. I made him well versed in history.

---

[58] *baily,* bailliff or farm manager.

SIR WILLIAM. That's a pretty study, indeed! How can there be a true history when we see no man living is able to write truly the history of the last week?

SIR EDWARD. He, by the way, read natural philosophy, and had insight enough in the mathematics.

SIR WILLIAM. Natural philosophy knows nothing! Nor would I give a fart for any mathematician but a carpenter, bricklayer, or measurer of land, or sailor.

SIR EDWARD. Some moderate skill in it will use a man to reason closely.

SIR WILLIAM. Very pretty. Reason! Can he reason himself into six shillings by all this?

SIR EDWARD. He needs it not. But to go on: after three years I removed him from the university (lest he should have too strong a tincture of it) to the Temple,[59] there I got a modest learned lawyer, of little practice, for want of impudence—and there are several such that want, while empty impudent fellows thrive and swagger at the bar; this man I got to instruct my son in some old common law books, the statutes, and the best pleas of the crown, and the constitution of the old true English government.

SIR WILLIAM. Does he get a shilling by all this? But what a devil made you send him into France, to make an arrant, vain coxcomb of him?

SIR EDWARD. There he did all his manly exercises; saw two campaigns; studied history, civil laws, and laws of commerce; the language he spoke well ere he went. He made the tour of Italy, and saw Germany and the Low Countries, and returned well skilled in foreign affairs, and a complete accomplished English gentleman.

SIR WILLIAM. And to know nothing of his own estate but how to spend it. My poor boy has travelled to better purpose, for he has travelled all about my lands, and knows every acre and nook, and the value of it. There's travel for you! Poor boy!

SIR EDWARD. And he enjoys so little of that estate he sees as to be impatient for your death. I dare swear mine wishes my life, next to his own. I have made him a complete gentleman, fit to serve his country in any capacity.

SIR WILLIAM. Serve his country! Pox on his country! 'Tis a country of such knaves 'tis not worth the serving. All those who pretend to serve it, mean nothing but them-

59 the Temple, seventeenth-century equivalent of law school.

selves. But among all things, how came you to make him
a fiddler, always fluting or scraping? I had as lief hear a
jew's-harp.

SIR EDWARD. I love music. Besides, I would have young gentlemen have as many helps to spend their time alone as can
be. Most of our youth are ruined by having time lie
heavy on their hands, which makes them run into base
company to shun themselves.

SIR WILLIAM. And all this gentleman's education is come to
drinking, whoring, and debauchery.

(*Enter* Servant *to* SIR WILLIAM.)

SERVANT. Sir, Mr. Scrapeall is at your attorney's chamber in
the Temple, and desires to discourse you.

SIR WILLIAM. Brother, I must go, I shall tell you when I see
you next, what is my business with him.

SIR EDWARD. Be sure to dine with me.

SIR WILLIAM. I will.   (*Exeunt.*)

[SCENE II.]

(*Enter* BELFOND SENIOR, SHAMWELL, CHEATLY, HACKUM,
LOLPOOP, French Valet, *two* Footmen *at the* "George" *in
Whitefriars.*)

CHEATLY. Now thou look'st like an heir indeed, my lad. When
thou cam'st up, thou hadst the scurvy phiz[60] of a mere
country put. He did thee a kindness that took thee for a
chief constable.

SHAMWELL. Now thou shinest, cousin, like a true Belfond!
What! £3,000 a year, entailed, and live like a butcher or
a grazier, in the country?

HACKUM. Give you joy, noble sir, now you look like a true
gallant squire.

LOLPOOP. Like a squire? Like a puppy, by th' mass. Ods-flesh,
what will the awd man say? He'll be stark wood.[61]

BELFOND SENIOR. Well, I was the fortunat'st man to light upon
such true, such real friends. I had never known any
breeding or gentility without you.

SHAMWELL. You buried all your good parts in a sordid, swinish
life in the north.

---

[60] *phiz,* physiognomy or face.
[61] *wood,* mad.

BELFOND SENIOR. My father kept me in ignorance, and would have made a very silly blockheadly put of me. Why, I never heard a gentleman banter, or cut a sham in my life before I saw you, nor ever heard such ingenious discourse.

HACKUM. Nay, the world knows Mr. Cheatly and Mr. Shamwell are as complete gentlemen as ever came within the Friars. And yet we have as fine gentlemen as any in England; we have those here who have broke for £10,000.

BELFOND SENIOR. Well, I protest and vow I am so very fine, I do not know where to look upon myself first; I don't think my lord mayor's son is finer.

CHEATLY. He is a scoundrel compared to thee. There's not a prig at court out-shines thee. Thou shalt strut in the Park, where countesses shall be enamored on thee.

BELFOND SENIOR. I am overjoyed. I can stand no ground! My dear friend Cheatly! My sweet cousin Shamwell! Let me embrace such dear, such loving friends! I could grow to you, methinks, and stick here forever.   (*They embrace.*)

LOLPOOP. Ah! Dear, loving dogs! They love him, by'r lady, as a cat loves a mause.

BELFOND SENIOR. What's that you mutter, sirrah? Come hither, sirrah! You are finer than any squire in the country.

LOLPOOP. Pox of finery, I say! Yeow maken a meer ass, an owl o' me. Here are sleeves fit for nought but a miller to steal with when he takes toll; and damned cuffs here, one can not dip one's meat i'th' sauce for them. Ods-flesh, give me my awd clothes again. Would I were a whome in my frock, dressing of my geldings. Poor tits,[62] they wanten me dearly, I warrant a.

BELFOND SENIOR. Well, there's no making a whistle of a pig's tail. This puppy will never learn any breeding. Sirrah, behold me: here's a rigging[63] for you. Here's a nab.[64] You never saw such a one in your life.

CHEATLY. A rum[65] nab. It is a beaver of £5.

BELFOND SENIOR. Look you there, blockhead.

LOLPOOP. (*aside*) Look yeow there, blockhead, I say.

---

[62] *tits*, nags.
[63] *a rigging*, clothes.
[64] *nab*, beaver hat.
[65] *rum*, fine.

HACKUM. Let me see your porker. Here's a porker! Here's a titler![66] Ha, ha! Oh, how I could whop a prigster through the lungs! Ha, ha!   (*Thrusts at* LOLPOOP.)

CHEATLY. It cost sixteen louis d'ors in Paris.

HACKUM. Ha, ha!   (*He pushes towards* LOLPOOP.)

LOLPOOP. Hawd you, hawd you! And I take kibbo[67] I'st raddle the bones o' thee, I'se tell a that, for aw th'art a captain mun.

BELFOND SENIOR. Look, sirrah, here's a show, you rogue. Here's a sight of cole, darby, the ready, and the rhino. You rascal, you understand me not! You loggerhead, you silly put, you understand me not! Here are megs and smelts. I ne'er had such a sight of my own in my life. Here are more megs and smelts, you rogue; you understand me not.

LOLPOOP. By'r lady, not I. I understand not this south-country speech, not I.

BELFOND SENIOR. Ah, methinks I could tumble in 'em. But d'ee hear, put, put, put, sirrah. Here's a scout.[68] What's o'clock? What's o'clock, sirrah? Here's a tatler[69], gold, gold, you rogue. Look on my finger, sirrah, look here: here's a famble,[70] put, put. You don't know what a famble, a scout, or a tatler is, you put.

LOLPOOP. Fine sights for my awd master. Marry, would I were sent from constable to constable, and whipped home again, by'r lady!

BELFOND SENIOR. Let's whet. Bring some wine. Come on, I love a whet. Pray let's huzza; I love huzzaing mightily. But where's your lady, Captain, and the blowen that is to be my natural, my convenient, my pure?

(*Enter* Servants *with bottles*.)

HACKUM. They're just coming in. Come, Betty.

(*Enter* MRS. HACKUM *and* MRS. MARGARET.)

MRS. HACKUM. Come in, Mrs. Margaret, come.

MARGARET. I am so ashamed.

BELFOND SENIOR. Madam, your servant. I am very much obliged to your favors.

---

[66] *titler*, sword.
[67] *kibbo*, a cudgel.
[68] *scout*, watch.
[69] *tatler*, alarm watch.
[70] *famble*, ring.

MRS. HACKUM. I shall be proud to do a gentleman like you any service that lies in my power as a gentlewoman.

BELFOND SENIOR. O Lord, madam, your most humble servant to command. My pretty blowen, let me kiss thee. Thou shalt be my natural. I must rummage thee. She is a pure blowen. My pretty rogue—how happy shall I be? Pox o' the country, I say. Madam Hackum, to testify my gratitude, I make bold to equip you with some megs, smelts, decus's, and Georges.[71]

MRS. HACKUM. I am your faithful servant, and I shall be glad of any occasion whereby to express how ready I am to serve any gentleman or person of quality as becomes a gentlewoman; and upon honor, sir, you shall never find me tardy.

CHEATLY. Come on, sirrah, fill up all the glasses; a health to this pretty lady.

BELFOND SENIOR. Ay, and, i'faith, I'll drink it, pretty rogue.

SHAMWELL. Let them be facers.

BELFOND SENIOR. Facers! What are those? Nay, give the lady and the Captain's lady, too.

MARGARET. No, I can not drink, I am not dry.

MRS. HACKUM. Give it me.

SHAMWELL. There's a facer for you.

(*Drinks the glass clear off, and puts it to his face. All do the like.*)

BELFOND SENIOR. Excellent, adad! Come to our facers. It is the prettiest way of drinking! Fill again, we'll have more facers.

(*Fiddles flourish without.*)

Ha, boys! The musicians are come. Ha, boys, we'll sing, dance, roar, fling the house out of the windows; and I will manage my pretty natural, my pure blowen here. Huzza! My dear friends Shamwell and Cheatly, I am transported! My pretty natural, kiss me, kiss me! Huzza!

MARGARET. Nay, pooh, you do so ruffle one's things.

BELFOND SENIOR. I'll ruffle thee more, my little rogue, before I have done with thee. Well, I shall never make you amends, my dear friends. Sirrah, Lolpoop, is not this better than the country, sirrah? Give the rogue a facer to my mistress. Come, fill about the facers. Come on, my

71 *decus's, and Georges,* coins.

lads, stand to't. Huzza! I vow 'tis the prettiest way of drinking, never stir.

(*Enter four* Servants *with four dishes of meat, who cross the stage.*)

CHEATLY. So here's the prog, here's the dinner coming up. The cloth's laid in the next room. Here's a noble dinner!

BELFOND SENIOR. Ha, boys, we'll sing and roar and huzza like devils.

(*Enter* SIR WILLIAM BELFOND *at the door.*)

Ounds! Who's here? My father! Lolpoop, Lolpoop, hide me! Give me my Joseph.[72] Let's sneak into the next room.

SHAMWELL. Death! What shall we do? This is the bully's father.

CHEATLY. Let me alone: I warrant you.

HACKUM. This is the old fellow I had like to have had a rubbers[73] with in the morning.

SIR WILLIAM. Is he fallen into these hands? Nay, then, he's utterly lost; his estate is spent before he has it.

CHEATLY. How now, prig, what makes you come into our room?

SIR WILLIAM. I would speak with Squire Belfond.

CHEATLY. Here's no such man.

SIR WILLIAM. Oh, bully, are you there, and my ungracious kinsman, too? Would you bring my son to the gallows! you most notorious seducer of young heirs, I know you, too. I warrant you I'll keep my dear boy in the country far enough from your clutches. In short, I would speak with my rebellious town-son, who is here, and bespoke this great dinner.

CHEATLY. (*Bantering*) Why, look you, sir, according to your assertion of things, doubtful in themselves, you must be forced to grant that whatsoever may be, may also as well not be, in their own essential differences and degrees.

SIR WILLIAM. What stuff's this? Where's my son?

CHEATLY. Your question consists of two terms: the one, *ubi*, where; but of that I shall say nothing, because here is no son nor any thing belonging to you, to be the subject of debate at this time; forasmuch as—

---

[72] *Joseph*, cloak.
[73] *a rubbers*, trouble.

SIR WILLIAM. Do you hear me, sir, let me see my son; and offer to banter me, or sham me once more, and I will cut your throat, and cudgel your brace of cowards.

CHEATLY. Nay, then, 'tis time to take a course with you. Help, help! An arrest, an arrest—a baily,[74] a baily!

HACKUM AND SHAMWELL. An arrest, an arrest!

SIR WILLIAM. You dogs! Am I a baily?

CHEATLY. You shall be used like one, you old prig. An arrest!

SIR WILLIAM. Impudent dogs! I must run, or I shall be pulled in pieces. Help, help, an arrest! An arrest!

(All cry out, An arrest! Drawers[75] and some of the rabble come in and join with the cry, which gets into the street; there they cry out, too. He joins the cry, and runs away. CHEATLY, SHAMWELL, HACKUM, Drawers follow him, and cry out: Stop, stop, a baily!)

CHEATLY, SHAMWELL, HACKUM. (*In the street.*) Stop, stop, a baily, a baily!

(SIR WILLIAM *runs; the rabble pursue him across the stage.*)

ACT III

[SCENE I.] *Street in front of* SIR EDWARD's *house*
(*Enter* MRS. TERMAGANT *and her* Brother.)

TERMAGANT. As I told you, I have had a child by him; he is my husband by contract, and casts me off; has dishonored me, and made me infamous. Shall you think to game and bully about the town, and not vindicate the honor of your family?

BROTHER. No man shall dare to dishonor our family.

(*Enter* BELFOND JUNIOR.)

TERMAGANT. If you do not cut his throat, you'll be kicked up and down for a damned coward; and besides, you shall never see a penny of mine more.

---

74 *baily*, officer of the law.
75 *Drawers*, bartenders.

BROTHER. I'll fight him, as he be above ground.

TERMAGANT. There, there's the traitor walking before his uncle's door. Be sure, dispatch him; on, I'll withdraw.

(*Exit.*)

BROTHER. Do you hear, sir, do you know Mrs. Termagant?

BELFOND JUNIOR. What makes you ask such a familiar question, sir?

BROTHER. I am her brother.

BELFOND JUNIOR. Perhaps so. Well, I do. What then, sir?

BROTHER. Ours is an ancient family as any in England, tho' perhaps unfortunate at present. The Termagants came in with the Conqueror.

BELFOND JUNIOR. It may be so; I am no herald.

BROTHER. And do you think you shall dishonor this family, and debauch my sister, unchastized? You are contracted to her, and have lain with her.

BELFOND JUNIOR. Look you, sir, I see what you would be at; she's mad, and puts you upon this. Let me advise you, 'tis a foolish quarrel.

BROTHER. You debauched her, and have ruined her.

BELFOND JUNIOR. 'Tis false; the silliest coxcombly beau in town had the first of her.

BROTHER. You had a child by her.

BELFOND JUNIOR. Then I have added one to your ancient family that came in with the Normans. Prithee, do not provoke me to take away one from it.

BROTHER. You are contracted to her, and if you will marry her, I will save your life.

BELFOND JUNIOR. 'Tis a lie. I am not contracted to her. Begone, urge me no more.

BROTHER. Draw.

BELFOND JUNIOR. Have at you.

(*Enter* SIR EDWARD BELFOND.)

SIR EDWARD. Hold! Hold! (BELFOND *strikes up the Brother's heels and disarms him.*) Oh, my son, my son! What's the matter? My dear son, art thou not hurt? Let me see.

BELFOND JUNIOR. No, sir, not at all, dear sir. Here, take your sword and begone. Next time you come to trouble me, I'll cut your throat. (*Exit* BROTHER.)

SIR EDWARD. What's the matter, dear Ned? This is about some wench, I warrant.

BELFOND JUNIOR. 'Tis a brother of that furious wench you saw, sir; her violent love is converted into hatred.

SIR EDWARD. You young fellows will never get knowledge but at your own cost. The precepts of the old weigh nothing with you.

BELFOND JUNIOR. Your precepts have ever been sacred to me; and so shall your example be henceforward. You are the best of men, the best of fathers. I have as much honor for you as I can have for human nature, and I love you ten thousand times above my life.

SIR EDWARD. Dear Ned, thou art the greatest joy I have. And believe thy father and thy friend, there's nothing but anxiety in vice. I am not straight-laced, but when I was young, I ne'er knew anything gotten by wenching but duels, claps, and bastards; and every drunken fit is a short madness that cuts off a good part of life.

BELFOND JUNIOR. You have reason, sir, and shall ever be my oracle hereafter.

SIR EDWARD. 'Tis time now to take up, and think of being something in the world. See then, my son, tho' thou shouldst not be over busy to side with parties and with factions, yet that thou takest a care to make some figure in the world, and to sustain that part thy fortune, nature, and education fit thee for.

BELFOND JUNIOR. Your wise advice I'll strive to follow. But I must confess, I am most passionately in love, and am, with your consent, resolved to marry, tho' I will perish ere I do without it.

SIR EDWARD. Be sure to know the humor of the woman; you run a mighty hazard. But if you be valiant enough to venture (which, I must confess, I never was), I'll leave it to your own choice. I know you have so much honor, you will do nothing below your self.

BELFOND JUNIOR. I doubt not of your approbation, but till I can be sure of obtaining her, pardon me if I conceal her name.

(*Enter* SIR WILLIAM BELFOND.)

SIR EDWARD. Your father comes. Retire a little within hearing till I soften him somewhat. He is much moved, as he always is, I think.   (BELFOND JUNIOR *retires.*)

SIR WILLIAM. Now, brother, as I was saying, I can convince

you, your son, your darling whom you long have fostered in his wickedness, is become the most profligate of all rascals.

SIR EDWARD. Still upon this subject.

SIR WILLIAM. 'Tis very well. My mouth must be stopped, and your ears. 'Tis wondrous well. But I have had much ado to escape with life from him and his notorious fellow rogues. As I told you, when I had found that the rogue was with his wicked associates at the "George" in White-friars, when they saw I was resolved to see my son, and was rough with 'em, Cheatly and his rogues set up a cry against me: "An arrest! a baily, an arrest!" The mobile and all the rakehells in the house and thereabout the streets assembled; I run, and they had a fair course after me into Fleet Street. Thanks to the vigor I have left, my heels have saved my life. Your infamous rogue would have suffered me to have been sacrificed to the rabble.

SIR EDWARD. Ha, ha, ha, very pretty, i' faith! It runs very well. Can you tell it over again, think you?

SIR WILLIAM. Ounds! Am I become your scorn? Your laughter?

(BELFOND JUNIOR *appears*.)

SIR EDWARD. Ned, you hear all this?

BELFOND JUNIOR. Yes, and am distracted to know the meaning of it.

SIR WILLIAM. Vile parricide! Are you gotten here before me? You are monstrous nimble, sir.

BELFOND JUNIOR. By all the powers of heaven! I never was at the "George" in my life.

SIR WILLIAM. Oh, then they stay for you, you have not yet been there. You'll lose your dinner, 'tis served up—vile wretch!

BELFOND JUNIOR. All this is cross purposes to me. I came to my uncle's house from my own lodgings immediately, when you were pleased to banish me your presence, and here have been ever since.

SIR WILLIAM. Nay, he that will be a thorough villain must be a complete liar. Were not you even now with your associates—rascals at the "George"?

BELFOND JUNIOR. No, by heaven! Nor was I ever in the company of any of that gang. I know their infamy too well to be acquainted with their persons.

SIR WILLIAM. I am not drunk, nor mad; but you will make me one of them.

BELFOND JUNIOR. These rascals have gotten somebody to personate me, and are undoubtedly carrying on some cheat in my name.

SIR EDWARD. Brother, it must be.

SIR WILLIAM. Yes, yes, no doubt it must be so; and I must be in a dream all this while, I must.

SIR EDWARD. You say yourself and you did not see my son there.

SIR WILLIAM. No, he was too nimble for me, and got out some back way, to be here before me, so to face down the truth.

BELFOND JUNIOR. I'll instantly go thither and discover this imposture that I may suffer no longer for the faults of others.

SIR EDWARD. Dine first. My dinner's ready.

BELFOND JUNIOR. Your pardon, sir, I will go instantly. I can not rest till I have done my self right.

SIR EDWARD. Let's in and discourse of this matter. Brother, I must say this, I never took him in a lie since he could speak.

SIR WILLIAM. Took him! no, nor never will take him in anything.

SIR EDWARD. Let's in—and send your own man with him.

SIR WILLIAM. It shall be so, though I am convinced already. Is there any of thy name but you, and I, and my two sons, in England?

BELFOND JUNIOR. Be pleased to send my footmen out to me, sir.

SIR EDWARD. Have a care of a quarrel, and bringing the Alsatians about your ears. Come, brother.

(*Exeunt* SIR EDWARD *and* SIR WILLIAM.)

(*Enter* LUCIA *running,* TERMAGANT *pursuing her.*)

LUCIA. Help, help, help!

TERMAGANT. Now I have found you, you little whore, I'll make you an example!

LUCIA. Oh, Lord! are you here! Save me, save me! This barbarous woman threatens to murder me for your sake.

BELFOND JUNIOR. Save thee, dear miss! That I would at the peril of my life. No danger should make me quit thee, cannons, nor bombs.

TERMAGANT. Damned false fellow! I'll take a time to slit her nose.

LUCIA. Oh, heaven! she'll kill me.

BELFOND JUNIOR. Thou devil, in thy properest shape of furious and malicious woman! Resolve to leave off this course this moment, or, by heaven! I'll lay thee fast in Bedlam.[76] Had'st thou fifty brothers, I'd fight with them all, in defence of this dear, pretty miss.

LUCIA. Dear, kind creature! This sweet love of thine, methinks, does make me valiant, and I fear her not so much.

(*Enter* ROGER *and his two* Footmen.)

BELFOND JUNIOR. Dear, pretty miss, I'll be thy safeguard.

TERMAGANT. Thou falsest, basest of thy sex, look to see thy child sent thee in pieces, baked in a pie,[77] for so I will.

BELFOND JUNIOR. Though thou hat'st every thing besides thyself, yet thou has too much tenderness for thy own person to bring it to the gallows. Offer to follow us one step, and I'll set the rabble upon thee. Come, my dear child.

(*Exeunt all but* TERMAGANT.)

TERMAGANT. Thou shalt be dogged, and I'll know who she is. Oh, revenge, revenge! If thou dost not exceed, thou equall'st al the ecstasies of love!   (*Exit* TERMAGANT.)

[SCENE II.] *Room in the "George" Tavern*

(*Enter* CHEATLY *and* SHAMWELL.)

CHEATLY. Thus far our matters go swimmingly. Our squire is debauched and prodigal as we can wish.

SHAMWELL. I told you all England could not afford an heir like this for our purpose, but we must keep him always hot.

CHEATLY. That will be easy. We made him so devilish drunk the first two or three days, the least bumper will warm his addle head afresh at any time. He paid a great fine, and may sit at a little rent. I must be gone for a moment. Our Suffolk heir is nabbed for a small business, and I must find him some sham bail. See the Captain performs his charge.   (*Exit.*)

(*Enter* HACKUM.)

76 *Bedlam*, Bethlehem Hospital for the insane.
77 The crime of Atreus in Greek tragedy.

SHAMWELL. Here he comes. See, Captain, you make that blockhead drunk, and do as we directed.

HACKUM. He's almost drunk, and we are in readiness for him. The squire is retired with his natural, so fond.

SHAMWELL. 'Tis well. About your business—I'll be with you soon. (*Exit* SHAMWELL.)

(*Enter* LOLPOOP.)

HACKUM. Come on, Mr. Lolpoop. You and I'll be merry by ourselves.

LOLPOOP. I must needs say, Captain, yeow are a civil gentleman, but yeow han given me so many bumpers, I am meet[78] drunken already.

HACKUM. Come on, I warrant you. Here's a bumper to the squire's lady.

LOLPOOP. With all my heart.

(*Enter* BETTY.)

HACKUM. Oh, Mrs. Betty, art thou come? I sent for this pretty rogue to keep you company. She's as pretty a company-keeper as any in the Friars.

LOLPOOP. Odsflesh, what should I do in company with gentlewoman? 'Tis not for such fellees as I.

HACKUM. Have courage, man. You shall have her, and never want such a one while I am your friend.

LOLPOOP. O Lord, I? Do yeow know what yeow saen?

BETTY. A proper, handsome gentleman, I swear.

LOLPOOP. Who, I? No, no. What done yeow mean, forsooth?

BETTY. I vow I have not seen a handsomer. So proper! So well shaped!

LOLPOOP. Oh, Lord, I? I! Yeow jeern me naw.

HACKUM. Why don't you salute her, man?

LOLPOOP. Who—I? By the mass, I dare not be so bold. What! I kiss such a fine gentlewoman!

HACKUM. Kiss—kiss her, man! This town affords us such everywhere! You'll hate the country when you see a little more. Kiss her, I say.

LOLPOOP. I am so hala.[79] I am ashamed.

BETTY. What! Must I do it to you, then?

---

[78] *meet drunken,* drunk enough.
[79] *so hala,* such an unattractive fellow.

LOLPOOP. Oh, rare! By th' mass! Whoo kisses daintily? And
    whoo has a breath like a caw?

HACKUM. Come, t'other bumper. To her health let his be.
    Here's to you!

LOLPOOP. Thanks, forsooth, and yeow pleasen.

(Drinks to her.)

BETTY. Yes, anything that you do will please me.

(HACKUM *steals out and leaves them together.*)

LOLPOOP. Captain! Captain! What, done yeow leave me?

BETTY. What! Are you afraid of me?

LOLPOOP. Nay, by'r lady. I am ashamed, who's farinely[80] a
    pratty lass! Marry!

BETTY. A handsome man, and ashamed!

(She edges nearer to him.)

LOLPOOP. Who, I? A handsome man? Nay, nay!

BETTY. A lovely man, I vow. I can not forbear kissing you.

LOLPOOP. O dear! 'Tis your goodness. Odsflesh, whoo loves
    me! who'll make me stark wood e'en naw! And yeow
    kissen me, by'r lady, I's kiss yeow.

BETTY. What care I?

LOLPOOP. Looka there naw. Waunds, whoo's a dainty lass,
    pure white and red? And most of the London lasses are
    pure white and red. Welly aw like; and I had her in
    some nook—. Odsflesh, I say no more.

BETTY. I'll stay no longer. Farewell.   *(She retires.)*

LOLPOOP. Nay, I's not leave a soo. Marry, whoo's a gallant
    lass!   *(Exit, following her.)*

(*Enter* HACKUM.)

HACKUM. So, he's caught. This will take him off from teasing
    his master with his damned good counsel.

(*Enter* CHEATLY *and* SHAMWELL.)

CHEATLY. I have seen our Alsatian attorney, and as substantial
    bail as can be wished for the redemption of our Suffolk
    caravan. He's ripe for another judgment; he begins to
    want the ready much.

SHAMWELL. Scrapeall is provided for him. How now, Captain,
    what's become of your blockhead?

---

[80] *farinely,* such.

HACKUM. He's nibbling at the bait; he'll swallow presently.

CHEATLY. But hark you, Shamwell. I have chosen the subtlest and handsomest wench about this town for the great fortune I intend to bestow this hopeful kinsman of yours upon. 'Tis Mrs. Termagant, his brother's cast mistress, who resents her being left to that degree that, tho' she meditates all the revenge besides that woman's nature is capable of against him, yet her heart leapt for joy at this design of marrying his elder brother. If it were for nothing but to plague the younger, and take place of his wife.

SHAMWELL. I have seen her. She will personate a town lady of quality admirably, and be as haughty and impertinent as the best of 'em. Is the lodging, and plate, and things ready for her?

CHEATLY. It is. She comes there this afternoon. She has set her hand to a good, swinging judgment; and thou and I will divide, my lad. And now all we have to do is to preserve him to ourselves from any other correspondence, and at downright enmity with his father and brother; and we must keep him continually hot, as they do in a glass-house, or our work will go backward.

(*Enter* BELFOND SENIOR, MRS. MARGARET, MRS. HACKUM, *and his* Servants.)

BELFOND SENIOR. Oh, my dear friend and cousin, tread upon my neck; make me your footstool! You have made me a happy man to know plenty and pleasure, good company, good wine, music, fine women. Mrs. Hackum and I have been at bumpers, hand to fist. Here's my pretty natural, my dear, pretty rogue! Adad, she's a rare creature, a delicious creature! And between you and I, dear friend, she has all her goings as well as e'er a blowen in Christendom. Dear Madam Hackum, I am infinitely obliged to you.

MRS. HACKUM. I am glad, sir, she gives your worship content, sir.

BELFOND SENIOR. Content! Ah, my pretty rogue! Pox o' the country, I say, Captain. Captain—here, let me equip you with a quid.[81]

HACKUM. Noble squire, I am your spaniel dog.

81 *a quid,* a guinea, cash.

BELFOND SENIOR. Pox o' the country, I say! The best team of horses my father has shall not draw me thither again.

SHAMWELL. Be firm to your resolution, and thou'lt be happy.

CHEATLY. If you meet either your father or brother or any from those prigsters, stick up thy countenance, or thou art ruined, my son of promise, my brisk lad in remainders.[82] When one of 'em approaches thee, we'll all pull down our hats and cry bow wow.

BELFOND SENIOR. I warrant you, I am hardened. I knew my brother in the country, but they shan't sham me; they shall find me a smokey[83] thief. I vow 'twill be a very pretty way. "Bow wow"—I warrant thee, I'll do it.

(*Enter* BELFOND JUNIOR, *two* Footmen, *and* ROGER.)

SHAMWELL. Who the devil's here? Your brother! Courage!

CHEATLY. Courage! Be rough and haughty, my bumpkin.

BELFOND SENIOR. Hey, where are all my servants? Call 'em in.   (Captain *calls them.*)

BELFOND JUNIOR. Who is that in this house here who usurps my name, and is called Squire Belfond?

BELFOND SENIOR. One who is called so without usurping. Bow wow!

BELFOND JUNIOR. Brother! Death! Do I dream? Can I trust my senses? Is this my brother?

BELFOND SENIOR. Ay, ay, I know I am transmogrified, but I am your very brother, Ned.

BELFOND JUNIOR. Could you be so unkind to come to town and not see your nearest kindred, your uncle, and myself?

BELFOND SENIOR. I would not come to disgrace you, till my equipage was all ready. Hey, La Mar, is my coach at the gate next to the "Green Dragon"?

VALET. *Oui, Monsieur.*

BELFOND SENIOR. But I was resolved to give you a visit tomorrow morning.

BELFOND JUNIOR. I should have been glad to have seen you anywhere but here.

BELFOND SENIOR. But here! Why, 'tis as good a tavern as any's in town. Sirrah, fill some bumpers. Here, brother, here's a facer to you. We'll huzza. Call in the fiddlers.

BELFOND JUNIOR. I am struck with astonishment. Not all Ovid's *Metamorphosis* can show such a one as this.

---

[82] *in remainders,* inheritor.
[83] *smokey,* knowing.

BELFOND SENIOR. I see you wonder at my change. What, would you never have a man learn breeding, adad? Should I always be kept a country bubble,[84] a caravan, a mere put? I am brave and boozy.

BELFOND JUNIOR. 'Slife! He has gotten the cant, too.

BELFOND SENIOR. I shall be clear by and by. T'other bumper, brother.

BELFOND JUNIOR. No, I'll drink no more. I hate drinking between meals.

BELFOND SENIOR. Oh, Lord! Oh, Lord! hate drinking between meals! What company do you keep? But 'tis all one. Here, brother, pray salute this pretty rogue. I manage her, she is my natural, my pure blowen. I am resolved to be like a gentleman, and keep, brother.

DELFOND JUNIOR. (*aside*) A thorough-paced Whitefriars man! —I never refuse to kiss a pretty woman. (*Salutes*[85] *her.*)

BELFOND SENIOR. This is Mrs. Hackum. I am obliged to her. Pray salute her.

BELFOND JUNIOR. What a pox! Will he make me kiss the bawd, too?

BELFOND SENIOR. Brother, now pray know these gentlemen here; they are the prettiest wits that are in the town, and between you and I, brother, brave, gallant fellows, and the best friends I ever had in my life. This is Mr. Cheatly, and this is my cousin Shamwell.

BELFOND JUNIOR. I know 'em, and am acquainted with their worth.

CHEATLY. Your humble servant, sweet sir.

SHAMWELL. Your servant, cousin.

BELFOND SENIOR. And this is my dear friend, Captain Hackum. There is not a braver fellow under the sun.

BELFOND JUNIOR. By heaven, a downright Alsatian.

BELFOND SENIOR. Come, musicians, strike up; and sing the catch the Captain gave you, and we'll all join, i'faith. We can be merry, brother, and can roar!

HACKUM. 'Tis a very pretty, magnanimous military business upon the victory in Hungary.

> Hark, how the Duke of Lorraine comes,
>   The brave, victorious soul of war,
> With trumpets and with kettle drums
>   Like thunder rolling from afar.

[84] *bubble,* victim.
[85] *Salutes,* kisses.

On the left wing the conquering horse
    The brave Bavarian Duke does lead;
These heroes with united force
    Fill all the Turkish host with dread.

Their bright caparisons behold;
    Rich habits, streamers, shining arms,
The glittering steel and burnished gold,
    The pomp of war with all its charms.

With solemn march and fatal pace
    They bravely on the foe press on;
The cannons roar, the shot takes place,
    Whilst smoke and dust obscure the sun.

The horses neigh, the soldiers shout,
    And now the furious bodies join,
The slaughter rages all about,
    And men in groans their blood resign.

The weapons clash, the roaring drum,
    With clangor of the trumpets sound,
The howls and yells of men o'ercome,
    And from the neighboring hills rebound.

Now, now the infidels give place,
    Then all in routs they headlong fly,
Heroes in dust pursue the chase,
    While deaf'ning clamors rend the sky.

BELFOND SENIOR. You see, brother, what company I keep. What's the matter, you are melancholy?

BELFOND JUNIOR. I am not a little troubled, brother, to find you in such cursed company.

BELFOND SENIOR. Hold, brother, if you love your life. They are all stout; but that same Captain has killed his five men.

BELFOND JUNIOR. Stout, say you? This fellow Cheatly is the most notorious rascal and cheat that ever was out of a dungeon; this kinsman, a most silly bubble first, and afterwards, a betrayer of young heirs, of which they have not ruined less than two hundred, and made them run out their estates before they came to them.

BELFOND SENIOR. Brother, do you love your life? The Captain's a lion!

BELFOND JUNIOR. An ass, is he not? He is a ruffian, and cock-bawd to that hen. (*points to* MRS. HACKUM)

CHEATLY. If you were not the brother to my dearest friend, I know what my honor would prompt me to.

Walks in a huff

SHAMWELL. My dear cousin, thou shalt now find how entirely I am thine. My honor will not let me strike thy brother.

HACKUM. But that the punctilios of honor are sacred to me, which tell me nothing can provoke me against the brother of my noble friend, I had whipped him through the lungs ere this.

BELFOND SENIOR. Well, never man met with such true, such loving friends.

BELFOND JUNIOR. Look you, brother, will this convince you that you are fallen into the hands of fools, knaves, scoundrels, and cowards?

BELFOND SENIOR. Fools! Nay, there I am sure you are out. They are all deep, they are very deep and sharp; sharp as needles, adad; the wittiest men in England. Here's Mr. Cheatly, in the first place, shall sham and banter with you or any one you shall bring for £500 of my money.

BELFOND JUNIOR. Rascally stuff, fit for no places but Ram Alley or Pie Corner.

BELFOND SENIOR. Persuade me to that! They are the merriest companions, and the truest friends to me. 'Tis well for you, adad, that they are so, for they are all of them as stout as Hector.

BELFOND JUNIOR. This is most amazing.

SHAMWELL. Did I not tell you he would envy your condition, and be very angry with us that put you into't?

CHEATLY. He must needs be a kind brother. We prove ourselves your true friends, and have that respect for your blood that we will let none of it out, where'er we meet it upon any cause.

BELFOND SENIOR. You see, brother, how their love prevails over their valor.

BELFOND JUNIOR. Their valor! Look you, brother, here's valor.

(*Kicks* CHEATLY *and* SHAMWELL.)

CHEATLY. I understand honor and breeding; besides, I have been let blood today.

SHAMWELL. Nothing shall make me transgress the rules of honor, I say.

BELFOND JUNIOR. Here! Where are you, sirrah kill-cow?

(*Takes* HACKUM *by the nose and leads him.*)

HACKUM. 'Tis no matter; I know honor; I know punctilios to a hair. You owe your life to your brother. Besides, I am to be second to a dear friend, and preserve my vigor for his service; but for all that, were he not your brother—

BELFOND JUNIOR. Will not this convince you, brother, of their cowardice?

BELFOND SENIOR. No, I think not, for I am sure they are valiant. This convinces me of their respect and friendship to me. My best friends, let me embrace you. A thousand thanks to you.

BELFOND JUNIOR. (*aside*) I will redeem him yet from these rascals, if I can.—You are upon the brink of ruin if you go not off with me, and reconcile yourself to my father. I'll undertake it upon good terms.

BELFOND SENIOR. No, I thank you. I'll see no father; he shall use me no more like a dog; he shall put upon me no longer. Look you, sir, I have ready, rhino, cole, darby— look here, sir.

BELFOND JUNIOR. Dear brother, let me persuade you to go along with me.

BELFOND SENIOR. You love me! and use my best friends thus? Ne'er stir, I desire none of your company. I'll stick to my friends. I look upon what you have done as an affront to me.

HACKUM. No doubt it is so.

SHAMWELL. That's most certain. You are in the right, cousin.

CHEATLY. We love you but too well—that angers him.

BELFOND JUNIOR. Well, I shall take my leave. You are in your cups. You will wish you had heard me. Rogues, I shall take a course with you.

BELFOND SENIOR. Rogues! They scorn your words.

BELFOND JUNIOR. Fare you well.

BELFOND SENIOR. Fare you well, sir, and you be at that sport.

BELFOND JUNIOR. Roger, do not discover him to my father yet; I'll talk with him cool in a morning first. Perhaps I may redeem him.

ROGER. I'll do it as you would have me.

(*Exeunt* BELFOND JUNIOR, ROGER, *and two* Footmen.)

BELFOND SENIOR. So now we are free. Dear friends, I never can be grateful enough. But 'tis late; I must show my new coach. Come, ladies.   (*Exeunt.*)

[SCENE III.] *A street*

(*Enter* Attorney *and* LUCIA.)

ATTORNEY. How now, daughter Lucia! Where hast thou been?

LUCIA. I have been at evening prayers at St. Bride's, and am going home through the Temple.

ATTORNEY. Thou art my good girl.

(*Enter* MRS. TERMAGANT.)

LUCIA. Oh, heaven! Who's here!

ATTORNEY. What's the matter?

LUCIA. I am taken ill on a sudden. I'll run home.

TERMAGANT. Stay, stay, thou wicked author of my misfortunte.

ATTORNEY. How's this? Stay, Lucia! What mean you, madam? The girl's strangely disordered.

LUCIA. Oh, heaven! I am utterly ruined—beyond redemption.

TERMAGANT. Is she your daughter, sir?

ATTORNEY. She is.

TERMAGANT. Then hear my story. I am contracted with all the solemnity that can be, to Mr. Belfond, the merchant's son; and for this wicked girl he has lately cast me off. And this morning I went to his lodging to inquire a reason for his late carriage to me. I found there in his closet this young, shameless creature, who has been in bed with him.

ATTORNEY. Oh, heaven and earth! Is this true, huswife?

LUCIA. Oh, Lord I—I never saw the gentleman nor her in my life. Oh, she's a confident thing!

TERMAGANT. May all the judgments due to perjury fall on me, if this be not true! I tore her by the hair, and pomelled her to some tune,[86] till that inhuman wretch, Belfond, turned me out of doors, and set her away in a chair.

LUCIA. O wicked creature! Are you not afraid the earth should open and swallow you up? As I hope to be saved. I never saw her!

TERMAGANT. Though young in years, yet old in impudence! Did I not pursue thee since, in the street, till you run into Belfond's arms just before his father's house? Or I had marked thee for a young whore.

LUCIA. As I hope to live, sir, 'tis all false, every word and tittle of it. I know not what she means.

86 *to some tune,* soundly.

ATTORNEY. Have I bestowed so much, and taken so much care in thy education, to have no other fruit but this?

LUCIA. Oh, Lord, sir! Why will you believe this wicked woman?

ATTORNEY. No, young impudence! I believe you? What made you ready to swoon at the sight of this lady, but your guilt?

LUCIA. She mistakes me for some other, as she did today, when she pursued me to have killed me, which made me tremble at the sight of her now.

ATTORNEY. And yet you never saw her before! I am convinced. Go, wicked wretch go home. This news will kill thy mother. I'll to my chamber, and follow thee.

LUCIA. But if I ever see her, or you either, to be locked from my dear Belfond,[87] I shall deserve whatever you can do to me.   (*Exit.*)

ATTORNEY. Madam, I beseech you, make as few words as you can of this.

TERMAGANT. I had much rather for my own honor have concealed it. But I shall say no more, provided you will keep her from him.

ATTORNEY. I warrant you, madam, I'll take a course with her. Your servant.   (*Exit.*)

(*Enter* CHEATLY.)

CHEATLY. Madam, your most humble servant. You see I am punctual to my word.

TERMAGANT. You are, sir.

CHEATLY. Come, madam, your lodging, furniture, and everything, are ready. Let's lose no time. I'll wait on you thither, where we will consult about our affairs.

TERMAGANT. Come on. It is a rare design, and if it succeeds, I shall sufficiently be revenged on my ungrateful devil.

CHEATLY. I warrant the success.   (*Exeunt.*)

[SCENE IV.] *A room in* SCRAPEALL'*s house*

(*Enter* ISABELLA *and* TERESIA.)

ISABELLA. We must be very careful of this book. My uncle, or our dame governante, will burn it if they find it.

---

87 *But if . . . Belfond,* meaning unclear. Probably means, If I ever allow anyone to keep me from Belfond.

TERESIA. We can not have a pleasant or a witty book, but they serve it so. My father loads us with books such as *The Trial of Man in the Isle of Man, or Manshire; A Treatise on Sabbath-breakers;* and *Health out-drinking, or Life out-healthing Wretches; A Caustick, or Corrosive, for a Scared Conscience.*

ISABELLA. *A Sovereign Ointment for a Wounded Soul; A Cordial for a Sick Sinner; The Nothingness of Good Works; Waxed Boot-Grace for the Sussex Ways of Affliction;* and deal of such stuff. But all novels, romances, or poetry except Quarles and Withers[88] are an abomination. Well, this is a jewel if we can keep it.

(*Enter* RUTH *behind them.*)

> Anger, in hasty words or blows
> Itself discharges on our foes;
> And sorrow too finds some relief
> In tears which wait upon our grief:
> Thus every passion but fond love
> Unto its own redress does move.

TERESIA. 'Tis sweet poetry. There is a pleasing charm in all he writes.

RUTH. (*She snatches the book.*) Yea, there is a charm of Satan's in it. 'Tis vanity and darkness. This book hateth and is contrary to the light; and ye hate the light.

ISABELLA. That's much; and this evening, a little before night, thou blamed'st us for looking out of the window, and threatened to shut the painted sashes.

TERESIA. Now, if thou shut'st those, thou hat'st the light, and not we.

RUTH. Look thee, Teresia, thou art wanton, and so is thy cousin Isabella. Ye seek temptation; you look out of the casement to pick and cull young men, whereby to feed the lust of the eye. Ye may not do it. And look thee, Isbel, and Theresia, if you open the casements once more, I will place ye in the back rooms, and lock the fore rooms up.

TERESIA. We will obey thee, Ruth.

ISABELLA. We will not resist thy power, but prithee, leave us that book.

---

88 *Quarles and Wither*, religious poets.

RUTH. No, it is wanton, and treateth of love. I will instantly
  commit it to the flames.   (*Exit.*)

ISABELLA. Shame on this old wall-eyed hypocrite! She is the
  strictest sort of jailor.

TERESIA. We are as narrowly looked to as if we had been
  clapped up for treason. We are kept from books, pen,
  ink, and paper.

ISABELLA. Well, it is a most painful life, to dissemble constantly.

TERESIA. 'Tis well we are often alone, to unbend to one
  another; one had as good be a player, and act continually,
  else.

ISABELLA. I can never persuade myself that religion can con-
  sist in scurvy, out-of-fashion clothes, stiff constrained behavior, and sour countenances.

TERESIA. A tristful aspect, looking always upon one's nose,
  with a face full of spiritual pride.

ISABELLA. And when one walks abroad, not to turn one's head
  to the right or left, but hold it straight forward, like an
  old, blind mare.

TERESIA. True religion must make one cheerful, and effect one
  with the most ravishing joy—which must appear in the
  face, too.

ISABELLA. My good mother had the government and brought
  me up to better things, as thy good aunt did thee.

TERESIA. But we can make no use of our education under this
  tyranny.

ISABELLA. If we should sing or dance, 'twere worse than
  murder.

TERESIA. But of all things, why do they keep such a stir to
  keep us from the conversation of mankind? Sure, there
  must be more in it than we can imagine; and that makes
  one have a mind to try.

ISABELLA. Thou hast been so unquiet in thy sleep of late, and
  so given to sigh and get alone when thou art awake, I
  fancy thou dost imagine somewhat of it.

TERESIA. Ah, rogue, and I have observed the same in thee.
  Canst thou not guess at love? Come, confess, and I'll tell
  thee all.

ISABELLA. Sometimes in my dreams, methinks I am in love.
  Then a certain youth comes to me, and I grow chill, and
  pant, and feel a little pain. But 'tis the prettiest thing,
  methinks! And then I awake and blush, and am afraid.

TERESIA. Very pretty. And when I am awake, when I see one
gentleman, methinks I could look through him, and my
heart beats like the drums in the camp.

ISABELLA. I dare not ask who 'tis for fear it should be my
man, for there are two come often to our church that
stare at us continually, and one of them is he.

TERESIA. I have observed them; one who sat by us at church
knew them by their names. I am for one of them, too.

ISABELLA. I well remember it.

TERESIA. If it be my man thou lik'st, I'll kill thee.

ISABELLA. And if thou lov'st my man, we must not live together.

TERESIA. Name him.

ISABELLA. Do thou name first.

TERESIA. Let's write their names.

ISABELLA. Agreed. We each have a black-lead pen.

*(They write their papers and give them to one another, at
which they both speak together, and start.)*

TERESIA. Truman! Mercy on me! }
ISABELLA. Belfond! Oh, heavens! }

TERESIA. What's this I see? Would I were blind.

ISABELLA. Oh, my Teresia!

TERESIA. Get thee from me.

ISABELLA. 'Tis as it should be. I wrote the wrong name on
purpose to discover who was your man more clearly; the
other's my beloved; Belfond's my heart's delight.

TERESIA. Say'st thou so, my girl? Good wits jump. I had the
same thought with thee. Now 'tis out, Truman for me;
and methinks they keep such a staring at us, if we contrive to meet them, we need not despair.

ISABELLA. Nay, they come not for devotion, that's certain; I
see that in their eyes. Oh, that they were ordained to
free us from this odious jail.

(Enter RUTH and TRUMAN, disguised.)

RUTH. Go into your chamber. Here is a man cometh about
business; ye may not see him.

TERESIA. We go. Come, cousin.

RUTH. Come, friend. Let us retire also.   *(Exeunt.)*

ACT IV

[SCENE I.] BELFOND JUNIOR'S *chambers*

(*Enter* BELFOND JUNIOR *and* LUCIA.)

LUCIA. I never more must see the face of a relation.

BELFOND JUNIOR. I warrant thee, my pretty rogue, I'll put thee into that condition, the best of all thy kindred shall visit thee and make their court to thee; thou shalt spark it in the boxes, shine at the Park, and make all the young fellows in the town run mad for thee. Thou shalt never want while I have anything.

LUCIA. I could abandon all the world for thee, if I could think that thou wouldst love me always.

BELFOND JUNIOR. Thou hast so kindly obliged me, I shall never cease to love thee.

LUCIA. Pray heaven I do not repent of it. You were kind to Mrs. Termagant, and sure it must be some barbarous usage which thus provokes her now to all this malice.

BELFOND JUNIOR. She was debauched by the most nauseous coxcomb, the most silly beau and shape about the town; and had cuckolded him with several before I had her. She was, indeed, handsome, but the most froward, ill-natured creature, always murmuring or scolding, perpetually jealous and exceptious, ever thinking to work her ends by hectoring and daring.

LUCIA. Indeed! Was she such a one? I am sure you were the first that ever had my heart, and you shall be the last.

BELFOND JUNIOR. My dear, I know I had thy virgin heart and I'll preserve it. But for her, her most diverting minutes were unpleasant. Yet for all her malice, which you see, I still maintain her.

LUCIA. Ungrateful creature! She is, indeed, a fury. Should'st thou once take thy love from me, I never should use such ways; silently should mourn and pine away; but never think of once offending thee.

BELFOND JUNIOR. Thou art the prettiest, sweetest, softest creature! And all the tenderest joys that wait on love are ever with thee.

LUCIA. Oh, this is charming kindness! May all the joys on earth be still with thee.

BELFOND JUNIOR. (*aside*) Now here's a mischief on the other side: for how can a good-natured man think of ever quitting so tender and so kind a mistress, whom no respect but love has thrown into my arms? And yet I must. But I will better her condition.——Oh, how does my friend?

(*Enter* TRUMAN.)

LUCIA. Oh, Lord! Who's here?

BELFOND JUNIOR. My dear, go to the lodging I have prepared for thee; thou wilt be safe, and I'll wait on thee soon. Who's there?

(*Enter* Servants.)

Do you wait on this lady's chair, you know whither.

(*Exeunt* LUCIA *and* Servants.)

TRUMAN. Thou art a pretty fellow, Belfond, to take thy pleasure thus, and put thy friend upon the damned'st drudgery.

BELFOND JUNIOR. What drudgery? A little dissembling?

TRUMAN. Why, that were bad enough, to dissemble myself an ass; but to dissemble love, nay, lust, is the more irksome task a man can undergo.

BELFOND JUNIOR. But prithee come to the point. In short, have we any hopes?

TRUMAN. 'Tis done; the business is done. Whip on your habit; make no words.

BELFOND JUNIOR. I'll put it on in my dressing-room. This news transports me.

TRUMAN. If you had undergone what I have done, 'twould have humbled you. I have enjoyed a lady; but I had as lief have had a Lancashire witch just after she had alighted from a broom-staff. I have been uncivil, and enjoyed the governante in most lewd dalliance.

BELFOND JUNIOR. Thou art a brave fellow, and makest nothing of it.

TRUMAN. Nothing? 'Sdeath, I had rather have stormed a half-moon,[89] I had more pleasure at the battle of Mons.

BELFOND JUNIOR. But hast thou done our work, as well as hers?

[89] *half-moon*, crescent-shaped gun platform.

TRUMAN. I have. For after the enjoyment of her person had led me into some familiarity with her, I proposed, she accepted, for she is covetous as well as amorous; and she has so far wrought for us that we shall have an interview with our mistresses, whom she says, we shall find very inclinable; and she has promised this night to deliver 'em into our hands.

BELFOND JUNIOR. Thou art a rare friend to me and to thyself. Now farewell, all the vanity of this lewd town. At once I quit it all. Dear rogue, let's in.

TRUMAN. Come in, in, and dress in your habit.   (*Exeunt.*)

[SCENE II.] *Street*

(*Enter* SIR WILLIAM, SIR EDWARD, *and* SCRAPEALL.)

SCRAPEALL. Look you, Sir William, I am glad you like my niece; and I hope also that she may look lovely in your son's eyes.

SIR EDWARD. No doubt but he will be extremely taken with her. Indeed, both she and your daughter are very beautiful.

SIR WILLIAM. He like her! What's matter whether he like her, or no? Is it not enough for him that I do? Is a son, a boy, a jackanapes, to have a will of his own? That were to have him be the father, and me the son. But, indeed, they are both very handsome.

SCRAPEALL. Let me tell you both, Sir William, and Sir Edward, beauty is but vanity, a mere nothing; but they have that which will not fade: they have grace.

SIR EDWARD. (*aside*) They look like pretty spirited, witty girls.

SCRAPEALL. I am sorry I must leave ye so soon; I thought to have bidden ye to dinner. But I am to pay down a sum of money upon a mortgage this afternoon. Farewell.

SIR WILLIAM. Farewell, Mr. Scrapeall.

SIR EDWARD. Pray meet my brother at my house at dinner.

SCRAPEALL. Thank you, Sir Edward, I know not but I may.

(*Exit* SCRAPEALL.)

SIR EDWARD. The person of this girl is well chosen for your son, if she were not so precise[90] and pure.

SIR WILLIAM. Prithee, what matter what she is; has she not fifteen thousand pounds clear?

90 *precise*, puritanically religious.

SIR EDWARD. For a husband to differ in religion from a wife—

SIR WILLIAM. What, with fifteen thousand pound?

SIR EDWARD. A precise wife will think herself so pure, she will be apt to condemn her husband.

SIR WILLIAM. Ay, but fifteen thousand pound, brother.

SIR EDWARD. You know how intractable misguided zeal and spiritual pride are.

SIR WILLIAM. What, with fifteen thousand pound!

SIR EDWARD. I would not willingly my son should have her.

SIR WILLIAM. Not with fifteen thousand pound?

SIR EDWARD. I see there's no answer to be given to fifteen thousand pound.

SIR WILLIAM. A pox o' this godly knave! It should have been twenty.

SIR EDWARD. Nor would I buy a wife for my son.

SIR WILLIAM. Not if you could have her a good pennyworth? Your son, quoth ye! He is like to make a fine husband. For all your precious son—

SIR EDWARD. Again, brother?

SIR WILLIAM. Look you, brother, you fly out so. Pray, brother, be not passionate; passion drowns one's parts; let us calmly reason; I have fresh matter; have but patience, and hear me speak.

SIR EDWARD. Well, brother, go on, for I see I might as soon stop a tide.

SIR WILLIAM. To be calm and patient; your jewel, though he denied that outrage in Dorset Court, yet he committed it, and was last night hurried before the Lord Chief Justice for it.

SIR EDWARD. It can not be, on my certain knowledge. (*aside*) I could convince him, but it is not time.

SIR WILLIAM. What a devil! Are all the world mistaken but you?

SIR EDWARD. He was with me all the evening.

SIR WILLIAM. Why, he got bail immediately, and came to you. Ounds, I never saw such a man in my life!

SIR EDWARD. I am assured of the contrary.

SIR WILLIAM. Death and hell! You make me stark mad! You will send me to Bedlam—you will not believe your own senses! I'll hold you a thousand pound.

SIR EDWARD. Brother, remember passion drowns one's parts.

SIR WILLIAM. Well, I am tame, I am cool.

SIR EDWARD. I'll hold you a hundred, which is enough for one brother to win of another.

(*Enter* ATTORNEY.)

And here's your own attorney comes opportunely enough
to hold stakes. I'll bind it with ten.

SIR WILLIAM. Done.

SIR EDWARD. Why, I saw your man Roger, and he says your
son found there a rascal that went by his name.

ATTORNEY. Oh, Sir William, I am undone, ruined, made a
miserable man!

SIR WILLIAM. What's the matter, man?

ATTORNEY. Though you have been an exceeding good client
to me, I have reason to curse one of your family that has
ruined mine.

SIR WILLIAM. Pray explain yourself.

ATTORNEY. Oh, sir, your wicked son, your most libidinous
son!—

SIR WILLIAM. Look you, brother, d'ye hear? D'ye hear? Do
you answer?

ATTORNEY. —has corrupted, debauched my only daughter,
whom I had brought up with all the care and charge I
could, who was the hopes, the joy of all our family.

SIR WILLIAM. Here's a son! Here's a rare son! Here's a hopeful
son! And he were mine, I'd lash him with a dog-whip;
I'd cool his courage.

SIR EDWARD. How do you know it is he?

ATTORNEY. I have a witness for it that saw her rise from his
bed the other day morning, and last night she ran away
to him, and they have lain at a private lodging.

SIR EDWARD. Be well assured ere you conclude, for there is a
rascal that has taken my son's name, and has swaggered
in and about Whitefriars with Cheatly and that gang of
rogues, whom my son will take a course with.

ATTORNEY. Oh, sir, I am too well assured. My wife tears her
hair, and I, for my part, shall run distracted.

SIR WILLIAM. Oh, wicked rascal! Oh, my poor Tim! my dear
boy Tim! I think each day a year till I see thee.

SIR EDWARD. Sir, I am extremely sorry for this, if it be so; but
let me beg of you, play the part of a wise man; blaze not
this dishonor abroad, and you shall have all the reparation the case is capable of.

SIR WILLIAM. Reparation for making his daughter a whore?
What a pox, can he give her her maidenhead again?

SIR EDWARD. Money shall not be wanting will stop that witness's mouth; and I will give your daughter such a

fortune that, were what you believe true and publicly
known, she should live above contempt as the world
goes now.

ATTORNEY. You speak like the worthy gentleman the world
thinks you, but there can be no salve for this sore.

SIR WILLIAM. Why, you are enough to damn forty sons, if you
had them: you encourage them to whore. You are fit to
breed up youth!

SIR EDWARD. You are mad.—But pray, sir, let me entreat you
to go home, and I will wait upon you, and we will consult how to make the best of this misfortune, in which,
I assure you, I have a great share.

ATTORNEY. I will submit to your wise advice, sir. My grief has
made me forget: here is a letter comes out of the country
for you.   (*Exit* ATTORNEY.)

SIR WILLIAM. For me? 'Tis welcome. Now for news from my
dear boy! Now you shall hear, brother. He is a son
indeed.

SIR EDWARD. (*aside*) Yes, a very hopeful one. I will not undeceive him till Ned has tried once more to recover him.

SIR WILLIAM. (*Reads*) "On the tenth of this month your son,
my young master, about two of the clock in the morning,
rode out with his man, Lolpoop, and notwithstanding all
the search and enquiry we can make"—Oh, heaven!—
"he can not be found or heard of."

(*He drops the letter, not able to hold it.*)

SIR EDWARD. How's this?

SIR WILLIAM. Oh, my poor boy! He is robbed and murdered,
and buried in some ditch, or flung into some pond. Oh,
I shall never see thee more, dear Tim! The joy and the
support of all my life! The only comfort which I had on
earth.

SIR EDWARD. Have patience, brother, 'tis nothing but a little
ramble in your absence.

SIR WILLIAM. Oh, no. He durst not ramble; he was the duti-
fullest child! I shall never see his face again. Look you,
he goes on: "We have searched and made inquiry in
three adjacent counties, and no tidings can be heard of
him." What have I done that heaven should thus afflict
me?

SIR EDWARD. What if, after all, this son should be he that has made all this noise in Whitefriars, for which mine has been so blamed?

SIR WILLIAM. My son—my son play such pranks? That's likely! One so strictly, so soberly educated? One that's educated your way can not do otherwise.

(*Enter* ROGER.)

ROGER. Sir, sir, mercy upon me, here's my young master's man, Lolpoop, coming along the streets with a wench.

(*Enter* LOLPOOP, *leading* BETTY *under the arm.*)

SIR WILLIAM. Oh, heaven! What say you?
SIR EDWARD. (*To himself*) Now it works. Ha, ha, ha!

(SIR WILLIAM *lays hold on* LOLPOOP *ere he or she sees him.*)

BETTY. How now! What have you to say to my friend, my dear?

(SIR WILLIAM *and* LOLPOOP *start, and stand amazed at one another; and, after a great pause,* SIR WILLIAM *falls upon* LOLPOOP, *beats the whore, beats* ROGER, *strikes at his brother, and lays about him like a madman; the rabble get all about him.*)

SIR WILLIAM. Sirrah, rogue, dog, villain! Whore! And you rogue, rogue! Confound the world! Oh, that the world were all on fire!
SIR EDWARD. Brother, for shame, be more temperate. Are you a madman?
SIR WILLIAM. Plague o' your dull philosophy!
SIR EDWARD. The rabble are gathered together about you.
SIR WILLIAM. Villain, rogue, dog, toad, serpent! Where's my son? Sirrah, you have robbed him and murdered him.

(*He beats* LOLPOOP, *who roars out murder.*)

LOLPOOP. Hold, hold, your son is alive, and alive like. He's in London.
SIR WILLIAM. What say you, sirrah? In London? And is he well? Thanks be to heaven for that. Where is he, sirrah?
LOLPOOP. He is in Whitefriars with Mr. Cheatly, his cousin Shamwell, and Captain Hackum.

(SIR WILLIAM *pauses, as amazed; then beats him again.*)

SIR WILLIAM. And, you rogue, you damned dog, would you suffer him to keep such company, and commit such villainous actions?

LOLPOOP. Hold, hold, hold, I pray you, sir. I am but a servant. How could I help it, marry?

SIR WILLIAM. You could not help being with a whore yourself, sirrah, sirrah, sirrah! Here, honest mob, course[91] this whore to some purpose. A whore, a whore, a whore!

(*She runs out, the rabble run after and tear her, crying, "A whore! a whore!"*)

SIR EDWARD. This is wisely done! If they murder her, you'll be hanged. I am in commission[92] for Middlesex; I must seek to appease them.

SIR WILLIAM. Sirrah, rogue, bring me to my son instantly, or I'll cut your throat. (*Exeunt.*)

[SCENE III.] *A room in* SCRAPEALL'*s house*

(*Enter* ISABELLA, TERESIA, RUTH.)

ISABELLA. Dear Ruth, thou dost forever oblige us.

TERESIA. And so much that none but our own mothers could ever do it more.

RUTH. Oblige yourselves, and be not silly, coy, and nice. Strike me when the iron's hot, I say. They have great estates, and are both friends. I know both their families and conditions.

(*Enter* BELFOND JUNIOR *and* TRUMAN.)

Here they are. Welcome, friends.

TRUMAN. How dost thou?

RUTH. These are the damsels. I will retire and watch, lest the old man surprise us. (*Exit* RUTH.)

BELFOND JUNIOR. Look thee, Isabella, I come to confer with thee in a matter which concerneth us both, if thou be'st free.

ISABELLA. Friend, 'tis like I am.

TRUMAN. And mine with thee is of the same nature.

91 *course,* hunt.
92 *in commission,* justice of the peace for.

TERESIA. Proceed.

BELFOND JUNIOR. Something within me whispereth that we were made as helps for one another.

TERESIA. They act very well, cousin.

ISABELLA. For young beginners. Come, leave off your Canaanitish dialect and talk like the inhabiters of this world.

TERESIA. We are as arrant hypocrites as the best of you.

ISABELLA. We were bred otherwise than you see, and are able to hear you talk like gentlemen.

TERESIA. You come to our meeting like sparks and beaux, and I never could perceive much devotion in you.

ISABELLA. 'Tis such a pain to dissemble that I am resolved I'll never do it when I must.

BELFOND JUNIOR. Dear madam, I could wish all forms were laid aside betwixt us. But in short I am most infinitely in love with you, and must be forever miserable if I go without you.

ISABELLA. A frank and hearty declaration, which you make with so much confidence I warrant you have been used to it.

TRUMAN. There is not a difficulty in the world which I would stop at to obtain your love, the only thing on earth could make me happy.

TERESIA. And you are as much in earnest now as you were when you came first to us—even now.

ISABELLA. That's well urged. Can not you gentlemen counterfeit love as well as religion?

BELFOND JUNIOR. Love is so natural it can not be affected.

TRUMAN. To show mine is so, take me at my word; I am ready to surrender on discretion.

TERESIA. And was this the reason you frequented our parish church?

BELFOND JUNIOR. Could you think our business was to hear your teacher spin out an hour over a velvet cushion?

ISABELLA. Profane men! I warrant they came to ogle.

TRUMAN. Even so. Our eyes might tell you what we came for.

BELFOND JUNIOR. In short, dear madam, our opportunities are like to be so few, your confinement being so close, that 'tis fit to make use of this. 'Tis not your fortune which I aim at—my uncle will make a settlement equal to it, were it more—but 'tis your charming person.

ISABELLA. And you would have me a fine forward lady, to love *extempore*.

BELFOND JUNIOR. Madam, you have but a few minutes to make use of, and therefore should improve those few. Your uncle has sold you for £5,000 and, for aught I know, you have not this night good for your deliverance.

TRUMAN. Consider, ladies, if you had not better trust a couple of honest gentlemen than an old man that makes his market of you; for I can tell you, you, though his own daughter, are to be sold, too.

TERESIA. But for all that, our consents are to be had.

BELFOND JUNIOR. You can look for nothing but a more strict confinement, which must follow your refusal. Now, if you have the courage to venture an escape, we are the knights that will relieve you.

TRUMAN. I have an estate, madam, equal to your fortune, but I have nothing can deserve your love. But I'll procure your freedom; then use it as you please.

BELFOND JUNIOR. If you are unwilling to trust us, you can trust your governess, whom you shall have with you.

ISABELLA. And what would you and the world say of us for this?

BELFOND JUNIOR. We should adore you; and I am apt to think the world would not condemn your choice.

TRUMAN. But I am sure all the world will condemn your delay, in the condition you are in.

(*Enter* RUTH.)

RUTH. I see Mr. Scrapeall coming at the end of the street. Begone. I'll bring them to your chamber in the Temple this evening. Haste, haste out at the back door.

BELFOND JUNIOR. This is most unfortunate.

TRUMAN. Dear madam, let me seal my vows.

RUTH. Go, go; begone, begone, friends. (*Exeunt.*)

[SCENE IV.] *Street outside* SCRAPEALL'*s house*

(*Enter* SCRAPEALL, *crosses the stage; enter* MRS. TERMAGANT *and her* Brother.)

TERMAGANT. You see, brother, we have dogged Belfond till we saw him enter the house of this scrivener with his friend Truman, both in disguises; which, with what we have heard even now at the neighboring ale-house, convinces me that 'tis he is to marry the rich niece.

BROTHER. They say she is to be married to the son of Sir
William Belfond, and that Sir William gives a great sum
of money to her uncle for her. By this it should seem to
be the elder son, and not our enemy, who is designed
for her.

TERMAGANT. If so, the villain would not at full day go thither.

BROTHER. But 'tis in disguise.

TERMAGANT. With that, I suppose the son pretends to be a
Puritan, too, or she would not have him; it must be he.
And if you will do as I direct you, I warrant I'll break
off this match, and by that, work an exquisite piece of
revenge.

BROTHER. I am wholly at your dispose.

TERMAGANT. Now is the time—the door opens. Pursue me
with a drawn dagger, with all the seeming fury imaginable, now as the old man comes out.

(SCRAPEALL *passes over the stage.* Brother *thereupon*
pursues TERMAGANT *with a drawn dagger; she runs, and*
gets into the house, and claps the door after her.)

BROTHER. Where is the jade? Deliver her to me, I'll cut her in
piecemeal. Deliver her, I say! Well, you will not deliver
her? I shall watch her.|

[SCENE V.] *Room in* SCRAPEALL'*s house*

(*Enter within* RUTH, TERESIA, ISABELLA, MRS. TERMAGANT.)

TERMAGANT. Oh, oh! Where is the murderer? Where is he? I
die with fear, I die!

RUTH. Prithee, woman, comfort thyself. No man shall hurt
thee here. Take a sup of this bottle.

(*She pulls out a silver strong-water*[93] *bottle.*)

TERMAGANT. Thou art safe?

ISABELLA. We will defend thee here, as in a castle. But what
is the occasion of this man's fury?

TERMAGANT. You are so generous in giving me this succor,
and promising my defence, that I am resolved not to
conceal it from you, though I must confess I have no
reason to boast of it; but I hope your charity will interpret
it as well as you can, on my side.

---

[93] *strong-water,* brandy.

RUTH. Go one; thou need'st not fear.

TERMAGANT. Know, then, I am a gentlewoman whose parents, dying when I was sixteen, left me a moderate fortune, yet able to maintain me like their daughter. I chose an aunt to be my guardian; one of those jolly widows who loves gaming and have great resort in the evenings, at their houses.

RUTH. Good; proceed.

TERMAGANT. There it was my misfortune to be acquainted with a young gentleman whose face, aid, mien, wit, and breeding, not I alone, but the whole town admires.

RUTH. Very good.

TERMAGANT. By all his looks, his gestures and addresses he seemed in love with me. The joy that I conceived at this I wanted cunning to conceal; but he must needs perceive it flash in my eyes and kindle in my face; he soon began to court me in such sweet, such charming words as would betray a more experienced heart than mine.

RUTH. Humph. Very well—she speaks notably.

TERMAGANT. There was but little left for him to do, for I had done it all before for him. He had a friend within, too ready to give up the fort; yet I held out as long as I could make defence.

RUTH. Good lackaday! Some men have strange charms, it is confessed.

TERMAGANT. Yet I was safe by solemn mutual oaths, in private contracted. He would have it private because he feared to offend an uncle from whom he had great expectance. But now came all my misery.

RUTH. Alack, alack, I warrant he was false.

TERMAGANT. False as a crocodile. He watched the fatal minute, and he found it and greedily seized upon me, when I trusted to his honor and his oaths; he still swore on that he would marry me, and I sinned on. In short, I had a daughter by him, now three years old, as true a copy of e'er nature drew, beauteous, and witty to a miracle.

RUTH. Nay, men are faithless; I can speak it.

TERESIA. Poor lady! I am strangely concerned for her.

ISABELLA. She was a fool to be catched in so common a snare.

TERMAGANT. From time to time he swore he would marry me, though I must think I am his wife as much as any priest can make me; but still he found excuses about his uncle.

I would have patiently waited till his uncle's death, had
he been true, but he has thrown me off, abandoned me
without so much as a pretended crime.

RUTH. Alack, and well-a-day! It makes me weep.

TERMAGANT. But 'tis for an attorney's daughter, whom he
keeps and now is fond of, while he treats me with all contempt and hatred.

ISABELLA. Though she was a fool, yet he's a base, inhuman
fellow.

TERESIA. To scorn and hate her for her love to him!

TERMAGANT. By this means my dishonor, which had been
yet concealed, became so public my brother, coming from
the wars of Hungary, has heard all, has this day fought
with the author of my misery, but was disarmed; and
how by accident he spied me by your house, I having fled
the place where I had lodged, for fear of him; and here
the bloody man would have killed me for the dishonor
done to his family, which never yet was blemished.

RUTH. Get the chief justice's warrant, and bind him to the
peace.

TERESIA. She tells her story well.

ISABELLA. 'Tis a very odd one, but she expresses it so sensible,
I can not but believe her.

TERMAGANT. (aside) If they do not ask me who this is, I have
told my tale in vain.—Now, ladies, I hope you have
charity enough to pardon the weakness of a poor young
woman who suffers shame enough within.

TERESIA. We shall be glad to do you what kindness we can.

TERMAGANT. Oh, had you seen this most bewitching person,
so beautiful, witty, and well-bred, and full of most
gentleman-like qualities, you would be the readier to have
compassion on me.

ISABELLA. Pray, who is it?

TERMAGANT. Alas, 'tis no secret; it is Belfond, who calls Sir
Edward Belfond father, but is his nephew.

ISABELLA. What do I hear? Was ever woman so unfortunate
as I in her first love!

TERESIA. 'Tis most unlucky.

TERMAGANT. (aside) That is the niece; I see 'twas he who
was to marry her.

ISABELLA. But I am glad I have thus early heard it; I'll never
see his face more.

RUTH (*aside*) All this is false: he is a pious man, and true professor. This vile woman will break the match off, and undo my hopes.

TERMAGANT. 'Tis as I thought. He is a ranting blade, a roysterer of the town.

RUTH. Come, you are an idle woman, and belie him. Begone out of the doors—there's the back way, you need not pretend fear of your brother.

TERMAGANT. I am obliged enough in the present defence you gave me. I intended not to trouble you long. But heaven can witness what I say is true.

ISABELLA. Do you hear, cousin? 'Tis most certain, I'll never see him.

RUTH. Go, wicked woman, go. What evil spirit sent thee hither? I say, begone.

TERMAGANT. I go.—(*aside*) I care not what she says; It works where I would have it.—Your servant, ladies. (*Exit.*)

RUTH. Go, go, thou wicked slanderer.

TERESIA. See him but once, to hear what he can say in his defence.

ISABELLA. Yes, to hear him lie as all the sex will. Persuade me not; I am fixed.

RUTH. Look thee, Isabella—

ISABELLA. I am resolved. (*Exit* ISABELLA *hastily.*)

TERESIA. Dear Ruth, thou dearest friend, whom once we took for our most cruel jailor, let's follow, and help me to convince her of her error; but I am resolved, if she be stubborn to undo herself, she shall not ruin me: I will escape.

RUTH. Let us persuade her. (*Exeunt.*)

[SCENE VI.] *A room in the "George" Tavern*

(*Enter* BELFOND SENIOR *and* HACKUM.)

BELFOND SENIOR. Captain, call all my servants. Why don't they wait?

(*Enter* MARGARET *and* MRS. HACKUM *with a caudle.*[94])

Oh, my pure blowen, my convenient, my tackle!

MARGARET. How dost thou, my dear?

---

[94] *caudle,* warm drink or gruel for the sick.

MRS. HACKUM. I have brought you a caudle here. There's ambergris[95] in it. 'Tis a rare, refreshing, strengthening thing.

BELFOND SENIOR. What, adad, you take me for a bridegroom? I scorn a caudle; give me some cherry brandy, I'll drink her health in a bumper. Do thee eat this, child.

MRS. HACKUM. I have that at hand—here, sir.

(*She fetches the brandy.*)

(*Enter* CAPTAIN HACKUM *and* Servants.)

BELFOND SENIOR. Come, my dear natural, here's a bumper of cherry brandy to thy health; but first let me kiss thee, my dear rogue.

(*Enter* SIR WILLIAM.)

SIR WILLIAM. Some thunderbolt light on my head! What's this I see?

BELFOND SENIOR. My father!

(*Enter* CHEATLY *and* SHAMWELL.)

SIR WILLIAM. Hey, here's the whole kennel of hell-hounds!

CHEATLY. Beat up to him—bow, wow!

SHAMWELL. Do not flinch—bow, wow!

BELFOND SENIOR. Bow, wow! Bow, wow!

SIR WILLIAM. Most impudent, abandoned rascal! Let me go, let me come at him! Audacious varlet, how durst thou look on me?

(*He endeavors to fly at his son; footmen hold him.*)

BELFOND SENIOR. Go strike your dogs, and call them names; you have nothing to do with me. I am of full age; and I thank heaven, am gotten loose from your yoke. Don't think to put upon me, I'll be kept no longer like a prigster, a silly country put, fit for nothing but to be a bubble, a caravan, or so.

SIR WILLIAM. A most perfect, downright, canting rogue! Am I not your father, sirrah? Sirrah, am I not.

BELFOND SENIOR. Yes, and tenant for life to my estate in tail, and I'll look to you that you commit no waste. What a pox, did you think to nose[96] me forever, as the saying is?

95 *ambergris,* whale by-product; thought to have invigorating powers.
96 *nose,* overawe.

I am not so dark, neither, I am sharp, sharp as a needle. I can smoke now as soon as another.

SIR WILLIAM. Let me come at him!

CHEATLY. So long as you forbear all violence you are safe; but if you strike here, we command the Friars, and we will raise the posse.

SIR WILLIAM. O villain! thou notorious undoer of young heirs! And thou pernicious wretch, thou art no part of me; have I [not] from thy first swaddling nourished thee and bred thee up with care?

BELFOND SENIOR. Yes, with care to keep your money from me, and bred me in the greatest ignorance, fit for your slave, and not your son. I had been finely dark if I had stayed at home.

SIR WILLIAM. Were you not educated like a gentleman?

BELFOND SENIOR. No, like a grazier or a butcher. If I had stayed in the country, I had never seen such a nab, such a rum nab, such a modish porker, such spruce and neat accoutrements: here is a tattle, here's a famble, and here's the cole, the ready, the rhino, the darby. I have a lusty cod,[97] old prig. I'd have thee know, and am very rhinocerical: here are megs and smelts, good store, decus's and Georges. The land is entailed, and I will have my snack of it while I am young, adad, I will. Hah!

SIR WILLIAM. Some mountain cover me and hide my shame forever from the world! Did I not beget thee, rogue?

BELFOND SENIOR. What know I whether you did or not? But 'twas not to use me like a slave. But I am sharp and smoky; I had been purely bred, had I been ruled by you, I should never have known these worthy, ingenious gentlemen, my dear friends. All this fine language had been heathen Greek to me, and I had ne'er been able to have cut a sham or banter while I had lived, adad. Odsookers, I know myself, and will have nothing to do with you.

SIR WILLIAM. I am astonished!

BELFOND SENIOR. Shall my younger brother keep his coach and equipage, and shine like a spruce prig, and I be your baily in the country? Hie, La Mar, bid my coach be ready at the door; I'll make him know I am elder brother, and I will have the better liveries; and I am resolved to manage my natural, my pure blowen, my convenient, my

[97] *cod*, the male organ.

peculiar, my tackle, my purest pure as the rest of the
young gentlemen of the town do.

SIR WILLIAM. (*aside*) A most confirmed Alsatian rogue!—
Thou most ungracious wretch to break off from me at
such a time when I had provided a wife for you, a pretty
young lady with fifteen thousand pound down, have
settled a great jointure upon her, and a large estate in
present on you, the writings all sealed, and nothing
wanting but you, whom I had sent for, post, out of the
country to marry her!

BELFOND SENIOR. Very likely, that you, who have cudgelled
me from my cradle, and made me your slave, and
grudged me a crown in my pocket, should do all this.

CHEATLY. Believe him not—there's not one work of truth
in't.

SHAMWELL. This is a trick to get you in his power.

SIR WILLIAM. The writings are all at my attorney's in the
Temple; you may go with me and see 'em all; and if you
will comply, I'll pardon what is past, and marry you.

BELFOND SENIOR. No, no, I am sharp, as I told you, and
smokey; you shall not put upon me, I understand your
shams; but to talk fairly, in all occurrences of this
nature, which either may, or may not be, according to
the different accidents which often intervene upon several
opportunities, from whence we may collect either good or
bad according to the nature of the things themselves; and
forasmuch as whether they be good or bad concerns
themselves; and forasmuch as whether they be good or
bad concerns only the understanding so far forth as it
employs its faculties; now since all this is premised, let
us come to the matter in hand.

SIR WILLIAM. Prodigious impudence! O devil! I'll to my lord
chief justice, and with his tipstaff[98] I'll do your business
—rogues, dogs, and villains, I will!   (*Exit in a fury.*)

CHEATLY. That was bravely carried on.

SHAMWELL. Most admirably.

BELFOND SENIOR. Ay, was't not? Don't I begin to banter
pretty well? Ha?

CHEATLY. Rarely. But a word in private, my resplendent prig.
You see your father resolves to put some trick upon you.
Be beforehand with him, and marry this fortune I have

---

[98] *tipstaff*, constable.

prepared. Lose no time but see her, and treat with her, if you like her, as soon as you can.

BELFOND SENIOR. You are in the right. Let not my blowen hear a word. I'll to her instantly.

CHEATLY. Shamwell and I'll go and prepare her for a visit. You know the place.

BELFOND SENIOR. I do. Come along— (*Exeunt.*)

[SCENE VII.]

(*Enter* CHEATLY, SHAMWELL, *and* MRS. TERMAGANT, *in her fine lodgings.*)

CHEATLY. Madam, you must carry yourself somewhat stately, but courteously, to the bubble.

SHAMWELL. Somewhat reservedly, and yet so as to give him hopes.

TERMAGANT. I warrant you, let me alone; and if I effect this business, you are the best friends; such friends as I could never yet expect. 'Twill be an exquisite revenge.

CHEATLY. He comes!—Come, noble esquire.

(*Enter* BELFOND SENIOR.)

Madam, this is the gentleman whom I would recommend to your ladyship's favor, who is ambitious of kissing your hand.

BELFOND SENIOR. Yes, madam, as Mr. Cheatly says, I am ambitious of kissing your hand, and your lip, too, madam; for I vow to gad, madam, there is not a person in the world, madam, has a greater honor for your person. And, madam, I assure you I am a person.

TERMAGANT. My good friend Mr. Cheatly, with whom I trust the management of my small fortune—

CHEATLY. Small fortune! Nay, it is a large one—

TERMAGANT. He's told me of your family and character. To your name I am no stranger, nor to your estate, though this is the first time I have had the honor to see your person.

BELFOND SENIOR. Hold, good madam, the honor lies on my side.—(*aside*) She's a rare lady, ten times handsomer than my blowens, and here's a lodging and furniture for a queen!—Madam, if your ladyship please to accept of my affection in an honorable way, you shall find I am no

put, no country prigster, nor shall ever want the megs,
the melts, decus's, and Georges, the ready, and the
rhino: I am rhinocerical.

TERMAGANT. I want nothing, sir, heaven be thanked.

SHAMWELL. Her worst servants eat in plate, and her maids
have all silver chamber-pots.

BELFOND SENIOR. Madam, I beg your pardon. I am somewhat
boozy. I have been drinking bumpers and facers till I
am almost clear; I have £1,000 a year, and £20,000
worth of wood, which I can turn into cole and ready, and
my estate ne'er the worse; there's only the incumbrance
of an old fellow upon it, and I shall break his heart
suddenly.

TERMAGANT. This is a weighty matter and requires advice, nor
is it a sudden work to persuade my heart to love. I have
my choice of fortunes.

BELFOND SENIOR. Very like, madam. But Mr. Cheatly and my
cousin Shamwell can tell you that my occasions require
haste, d'ee see? And therefore I desire you to resolve
as soon as conveniently you can.

(*A noise of a tumult without, and blowing of a horn.*)

CHEATLY. What's this I hear?

SHAMWELL. They are up in the Friars. Pray heaven, the sheriff's
officers be not come.

CHEATLY. 'Slide, 'tis so. Shift for yourselves!—Squire, let me
conduct you—This is your wicked father with officers.

(*Exeunt.*)

(*Cry without:* The tipstaff! An arrest! An arrest! *and the
horn blows.*)

[SCENE VIII.] *Street in Whitefriars*

(*Enter* SIR WILLIAM BELFOND *and a* Tipstaff, *with the*
Constable *and his* Watchmen; *and against them the posse
of the* Friars *drawn up,* Bankrupts *hurrying to escape.*)

SIR WILLIAM. Are you mad to resist the tipstaff, the king's
authority?

(*They cry out:* An arrest! *Several flock to 'em with all
sorts of weapons. Women with fire-forks, spits, paring-
shovels, &c.*)

(*Enter* CHEATLY, SHAMWELL, BELFOND SENIOR, *and* HACKUM.)

CHEATLY. We are too strong for 'em. Stand your ground.

SIR WILLIAM. We demand that same squire, Cheatly, Shamwell, and Bully Hackum. Deliver them up, an all the rest of you are safe.

HACKUM. Not a man.

SIR WILLIAM. Nay, then, have at you.

TIPSTAFF. I charge you in the king's name, all to assist me.

RABBLE. Fall on!

(*Rabble beat the* Constable *and the rest into the Temple.* Tipstaff *runs away. They take* SIR WILLIAM *prisoner.*)

CHEATLY. Come on, thou wicked author of this broil! You are our prisoner.

SIR WILLIAM. Let me go, rogue.

SHAMWELL. Now we have you in the Temple, we'll show you the pump first.

SIR WILLIAM. Dogs, rogues, villains!

SHAMWELL. To the pump! To the pump!

HACKUM. Pump him, pump him!

BELFOND SENIOR. Ah, pump him, pump him, old prig!

RABBLE. Pump, pump, to the pump! Huzza!

(*Enter* BELFOND JUNIOR. TRUMAN, *and several* Gentlemen, Porter *of the Temple, and* BELFOND's Footmen.)

BELFOND JUNIOR. What's the matter here?

TRUMAN. The rabble have catched a bailiff.

BELFOND JUNIOR. Death and hell! 'tis my father—'tis a gentleman, my father. Gentlemen, I beseech you lend me your hands to his rescue.

TRUMAN. Come on, rascals. Have we caught you? We'll make an example.

(*All draw and fall upon the rabble.* BELFOND SENIOR *runs first away. The* Templers *beat 'em, and take* CHEATLY, SHAMWELL, *and* HACKUM *prisoners.*)

BELFOND JUNIOR. Here! Where are the officers of the Temple? Porter, do you shut the gates into Whitefriars.

PORTER. I will, sir.

BELFOND JUNIOR. Here's a guinea among ye. See these three rogues well pumped, and let 'em go through the whole course.

CHEATLY. Hold, hold,—I am a gentleman!

SHAMWELL. I am your cousin!

HACKUM. Hold, hold, scoundrels, I am a captain!

BELFOND JUNIOR. Away with 'em.

SIR WILLIAM. Away with 'em. Dear son, I am infinitely obliged to you. I ask your pardon for all that I have said against you. I have wronged you.

BELFOND JUNIOR. Good sir, reflect not on that. I am resolved, e'er I have done, to deserve your good word.

SIR WILLIAM. 'Twas ill fortune we have missed my most ungracious rebel, that monster of villainy.

BELFOND JUNIOR. Let me alone with him, sir. Upon my honor I will deliver him safe this night. But now let us see the execution.

SIR WILLIAM. Dear Ned, you bring tears into my eyes. Let me embrace thee, my only comfort now.

BELFOND JUNIOR. Good sir, let's on and see the justice of this place.   (*Exeunt.*)

ACT V

[SCENE I.] *Room at the "George" Tavern*

(*Enter* CHEATLY, SHAMWELL, HACKUM.)

CHEATLY. O merciful dogs! Were ever gentlemen used thus before? I am drenched into a quartan ague.[99]

SHAMWELL. My limbs are stiff and numbed all over, but where I am beaten and bruised, there I have some sense left.

HACKUM. Dry blows I could have borne magnanimously; but to be made such a sop of—! Besides, I have had the worst of it by wearing my own hair. To be shaved all on one side, and with a lather made of channel dirt instead of a wash-ball![100] I have lost half the best head of hair in the Friars, and a whisker worthy fifty pound in its intrinsic value to a commander.

CHEATLY. Indeed, your magnanimous phiz is somewhat disfigured by it, Captain.

SHAMWELL. Your military countenance has lost much of its ornament.

---

99 *quartan ague,* intermittent fever.
100 *wash-ball,* soap.

HACKUM. I am as disconsolate as a bee that has lost his sting. The other moiety of whisker must follow, then all the terror of my face is gone; that face that used to fright young prigs into submission. I shall now look like an ordinary man.

CHEATLY. We'll swinge[101] these rogues with an indictment for a riot and with actions *sans nombre*.[102]

SHAMWELL. What reparation will that be? I am a gentleman, and can never show my face among my kindred more.

CHEATLY. We that can show our faces after what we have done, may well show 'em after what we have suffered. Great souls are above ordinances, and never can be slaves to fame.

HACKUM. My honor is tender, and this one affront will cost me at least five murders.

CHEATLY. Let's not prate and shiver in cold fits here; but call your wife with the cherry brandy, and let's ask after the squire. If they have taken him, 'tis the worst part of the story.

HACKUM. No, I saw the squire run into the Friars at first. But I'll go fetch some cherry brandy, and that will comfort us. (*Steps in for brandy.*)

Here's the bottle. Let's drink by word of mouth.

(*Drinks.*)

CHEATLY. Your cherry brandy is most sovereign and edifying.

(CHEATLY *drinks.*)

SHAMWELL. Most exceeding comfortable after our Temple-pickling. (*Drinks.*)

CHEATLY. A fish has a damned life on't. I shall have that aversion to water after this that I shall scarce ever be cleanly enough to wash my face again.

HACKUM. Well! I'll to the barber's and get myself shaved; then go to the squire, and be new accoutred.

(*Exit* HACKUM.)

CHEATLY. Dear Shamwell, we must not for a little affliction forget our main business. Our caravan must be well managed. He is now drunk, and when he wakes, will be

---

101 *swinge*, punish.
102 *sans nombre*, infinite.

very fit to be married. Mrs. Termagant has given us a judgment of £2,000 upon that condition.

SHAMWELL. The sooner we dispose of him the better; for all his kindred are bent to retrieve him, and the Temple joining in the war against us, will be too hard for us, so that we must make what we can of him immediately.

CHEATLY. If he should be once cool or irresolute, we have lost him and all our hopes; but when we have sufficiently dipped[103] him, as we shall by this marriage and her judgment, he is our own forever.

SHAMWELL. But what shall we do for our Whitefriars chaplain, our Alsatia divine? I was in search of him before our late misfortune, and the rogue is holed somewhere. I could not find him, and we are undone without him.

CHEATLY. 'Tis true. Pray go instantly and find him out. He dares not stir out of this covert. Beat it well all over for him; you'll find him tappes'd[104] in some ale-house, bawdy-house, or brandy-shop.

SHAMWELL. He's a brave, swinging orthodox, and will marry any couple at any time; he defies licence and canonical hours and all those foolish ceremonies.

CHEATLY. Prithee look after him while I go to prepare the lady.

SHAMWELL. You rogue Cheatly, you have a loving design upon her, you will go to twelve[105] with the squire. If you do, I will have my snack.

CHEATLY. Go, go, you are a wag.   (*Exeunt severally.*)

[SCENE II.]

(*Enter* RUTH, BELFOND JUNIOR, *and* TRUMAN *at* SCRAPEALL'S *house.*)

RUTH. She told her tale so passionately that Isabella believes every word of it; and is resolved, as she says, never to see thee more.

BELFOND JUNIOR. Oh, this most malicious and most infamous of her sex! There is not the least truth in her accusation.

TRUMAN. That to my knowledge. He is not a man of those principles.

---

103 *dipped*, indebted.
104 *tappes'd*, lying low.
105 *go to twelve*, share.

RUTH. I will send them to you if I can; and in the meantime, be upon the watch.

TRUMAN. Take this writing with thee, which is a bond from us to make good our agreement with thee.

RUTH. 'Tis well, and still I doubt not to perform my part.

BELFOND JUNIOR. Was ever a man plagued with a wench like me? Well, say what they will, the life of a whoremaster is a foolish, restless, anxious life, and there's an end on't. What can be done with this malicious devil? A man can not offer violence to a woman.

TRUMAN. Steal away her child, and then you may awe her.

BELFOND JUNIOR. I have emissaries abroad to find out the child; but she'll sacrifice that and all the world, to her revenge.

TRUMAN. You must arrest her upon a swinging action, which she can not get bail for, and keep her till she is humbled.

(*Enter* TERESIA.)

Madam, I kiss your hands.

TERESIA. You have done well, Mr. Belfond. Here has been a lady whom you have had a child by, were contracted to, and have deserted for an attorney's daughter which you keep. My cousin says she will never see you more.

BELFOND JUNIOR. If this be true, madam, I deserve never to see her more, which would be worse than death to me.

TERESIA. I have prevailed with her once more to see you, and hear what you can say to this. Come, come, cousin.

(*She leads in* ISABELLA.)

Look you, cousin, Mr. Belfond denies all this matter.

ISABELLA. I never doubted that. But certainly it is impossible to counterfeit so lively as she did.

BELFOND JUNIOR. Heaven is my witness that her accusation is false. I never was yet contracted to any woman, nor made the least promise, or gave any one the least hope of it; and if I do not demonstrate my innocence to you, I will be content forever to be debarred the sight of you, more prized by me than liberty or life.

ISABELLA. And yet perhaps these very words were said to her.

TRUMAN. Madam, you have not time, if you value your own liberty, to argue any longer. We will carry you to Sir Edward Belfond's; his sister is his housekeeper; and there you may be entertained with safety of your honor.

TERESIA. He is esteemed a worthy gentleman, nor could we choose a better guardian.

ISABELLA. At least, how could you use a woman ill you had a child by?

BELFOND JUNIOR. Not all the malice of mankind can equal hers. I have been frail, I must confess, as others; and though I have provided for her and her child, yet every day she does me all the most outrageous mischief she can possibly conceive. But this has touched me in the tender'st point.

ISABELLA. 'Twould be much for my honor, to put myself into the hands of a known wencher.

BELFOND JUNIOR. Into the hands of one who has abandoned all thoughts of vice and folly, for you.

TRUMAN. Madam, you neither of you trust us. Your governness is with you, and yet we are ready to make good our words by the assistance of the parson.

TERESIA. That's another point. But I'm sure, cousin, there is no dallying about our liberty. If you be in love with your jail, stay; I, for my part, am resolved to go.

BELFOND JUNIOR. My uncle's a virtuous, honorable man; my aunt, his sister, a lady of great piety. Think if you will not be safer there than with your uncle, by whom you are sold for £5,000—to my knowledge to one who is the most debauched, dissolute fellow this day in London.

TERESIA. Liberty, liberty, I say. I'll trust myself and my governess.

(*Enter* RUTH.)

RUTH. Haste and agree: your father has sent to have supper ready in less than half an hour.

TERESIA. Away, away! I am ready. Cousin, farewell.

BELFOND JUNIOR. For heaven's sake, madam, on my knees I beg you to make use of this occasion, or you have lost yourself; and I, too, shall forever lose you for marriage, which alone can keep me from being the most miserable. You may advise, and all things shall be cleared up to your wish.

TERESIA. Farewell, dear cousin. Let's kiss at parting.

ISABELLA. Sure thou hast not the conscience. Thou wilt not leave me?

TERESIA. By my troth, but I will.

ISABELLA. By my troth, but you shall not, for I'll go with thee.

BELFOND JUNIOR. May all the joys of life forever wait on you.
RUTH. Haste! Haste! Begone—   (*Exeunt.*)

[SCENE III.] *Room at* SIR EDWARD'*s house*

(*Enter* SIR WILLIAM BELFOND.)

SIR WILLIAM. That I should live to this unhappy age! To see
    the fruit of all my hopes thus blasted! How long like
    chemists[106] have I watched and toiled? And in the minute
    when I expected to have seen the projection,[107] all is
    blown up *in fumo.*[108]

(*Enter* SIR EDWARD.)

    Brother! I am ashamed to look on you, my disappoint-
    ment is so great. Oh, this most wicked recreant! This
    perverse and infamous son!

SIR EDWARD. Brother, a wise man is never disappointed. Man's
    life is like a game at tables;[109] if at any time the cast[110]
    you most shall need does not come up, let that which
    comes instead of it be mended by your play.

SIR WILLIAM. How different have been our fates! I left the
    pleasures of the town to marry, which was no small
    bondage, had children, which brought more care upon
    me. For their sakes I lived a rustic, painful, hard, severe,
    and melancholy life: morose, inhospitable, sparing even
    necessaries; tenacious, even to griping, for their good.
    My neighbors shunned me, my friends neglected me, my
    children hate me and wish my death. Nay, this wicked
    son in whom I have set up my rest and principally for
    whose good I thus had lived, has now defeated all my
    hopes.

SIR EDWARD. 'Twas your own choice. You would not learn
    from others.

SIR WILLIAM. You have lived ever at ease, indulged all
    pleasures, and melted down your time in daily feasts
    and in continual revels; gentle, complaisant, affable and
    liberal, and at great expense. The world speaks well of
    you; mankind embrace you; your son loves you and

106 *chemists,* alchemists.
107 *projection,* transmutation of base metal to gold.
108 *in fumo,* in smoke.
109 *tables,* backgammon.
110 *cast,* throw of dice.

wishes your life as much as he can do his own. But I'll
perplex myself no more. I look upon this rascal as an
excrement, a wen, a gangrened limb lopped off.

SIR EDWARD. Rather look upon him as a dislocated one, and
get him set again. By this time, you see, severity will do
nothing. Entice him back to you by love. In short, give
him liberty and a good allowance. There now remains
no other way to reclaim him; for, like a stone-horse[111]
broke in among the mares, no fence hereafter will con-
tain him.

SIR WILLIAM. Brother, I look upon you as a true friend that
would not insult upon my folly and presumption; and
confess you are nearer to the right than I. Your son, I
hope, will be a comfort to me.

SIR EDWARD. I doubt it not. But consider, if you do not reconcile yourself and reclaim yours as I tell you, you lop off
the paternal estate, which is all entailed forever upon
your family. For, in the course he is, the reversion will
be gone in your lifetime.

(*Enter* BELFOND JUNIOR, TRUMAN, ISABELLA, TERESIA, *and*
RUTH.)

BELFOND JUNIOR. Here are my father and my uncle. Mask
yourselves, ladies, you must not yet discover who you are.

SIR EDWARD. Yonder's Ned and his friend, with ladies masked.
Who should they be?

SIR WILLIAM. Whores, whores, what should they be else?
Here's a comfortable sight again! He is incorrigible.

SIR EDWARD. 'Tis you that are incorrigible. How ready are you
with your censures!

BELFOND JUNIOR. Sir, pardon the freedom I use with you. I
humbly desire protection for these ladies in your house.
They are women of honor, I do assure you, and desire
to be concealed for some small time. An hour hence I
will discover all to you, and you will then approve of
what I do.

SIR EDWARD. Dear Ned, I will trust thy honor, and, without
any examination, do as you would have me.

SIR WILLIAM. Why, brother, what a pox! will you pimp for
your son? What a devil, will you make your house a
bawdy-house?

---

[111] *stone-horse,* stallion.

SIR EDWARD. What, will the must[112] never be gotten out of your old vessel? Ladies; be pleased to honor my house, and be assured that while you are there, 'tis yours.

(*He waits on the ladies and* RUTH.)

BELFOND JUNIOR. Sir, my friend and I are just now going to do you a service. I'll pawn my life to you, sir, I will retrieve your rebel son and immediately restore him to you, and bring him, as he ought to come, on's knees with a full submission.

SIR WILLIAM. You will oblige me. Thus gain'st upon me hourly, and I begin to love thee more and more.

BELFOND JUNIOR. There's nothing in the world I aim at now but your love; and I will be bold to say, I shortly will deserve it. But this business requires haste, for I have laid everything ready. 'Tis almost bed-time. Come, friend.

(*Exit with* TRUMAN.)

SIR WILLIAM. Well, I'll say that for him—he is a good-natured boy; it makes me weep to think how harsh I have been with him. I'll in to my brother and expect the event.

[SCENE IV.] *Street in front of* MRS. TERMAGANT'*s lodgings*

(*Enter* BELFOND SENIOR, CHEATLY, SHAMWELL, *and* HACKUM.)

CHEATLY. I value you not misfortune so long as I have my dear friend still within my arms.

SHAMWELL. My dear, dear cousin! I will hug thee close to me. I feared to have lost thee.

BELFOND SENIOR. How happy am I in the truest, the dearest friends that ever man enjoyed! Well, I was so afflicted for you I was forced to make myself devilish boozy to comfort me.

CHEATLY. Your brother has heard of this great match you are towards. She has to my knowledge (for I do all her law business for her) £1500 a year jointure, and ten thousand pound in plate, money, and jewels; and this damned, envious brother of yours will break it off, if you make not haste and prevent him.

112 *must*, pulp.

BELFOND SENIOR. My dear friends, you are in the right. Never man met with such before. I'll disappoint the rogue, my brother, and the old prig, my father, and I'll do it instantly.   (*Exeunt.*)

[SCENE V.] *Scene changes to* MRS. TERMAGANT'*s fine lodgings*

(*Enter* BELFOND SENIOR, CHEATLY, SHAMWELL, HACKUM, Parson, MRS. TERMAGANT, *and her* Servants.)

CHEATLY. Madam, the time permits of no longer deliberation. If you take not this opportunity, my friend here will be ravished from us.

BELFOND SENIOR. Ay, madam, if you take me not now, you will lose me, madam. You will consider what to do.

TERMAGANT. Well, Mr. Cheatly, you dispose of me as you please. I have ever been guided by your wise advice.

SHAMWELL. Come, parson, do your office. Have you your book about ye?

PARSON. What, do you think I am without the tools of my trade?

CHEATLY. Can't you come presently to the joining of hands and leave out the rest of the formalities?

PARSON. Ay, ay. Come, stand forth.

(BELFOND SENIOR *and* MRS. TERMAGANT *stand forth.*)

(*Enter* BELFOND JUNIOR, TRUMAN, Constable, Sergeant, Musketeers.)

BELFOND JUNIOR. Here they are—seize them all!

CHEATLY. Hell and damnation! We are all undone.

BELFOND SENIOR. Hands off! Let me alone. I am going to be married. You envious rascal, to come just in the nick!

BELFOND JUNIOR. Brother, be satisfied there's nothing but honor meant to you; 'tis for your service.

TERMAGANT. Oh, this accursed wretch, to come in this unlucky minute and ruin all my fortune!

BELFOND SENIOR. She has fifteen hundred a year jointure, and ten thousand pounds in money, &c., and I had been married to her in three minutes.

BELFOND JUNIOR. You have 'scaped the worst of ruins. Resist not; if you do, you shall be carried by head and heels. Your father will receive you, and be kind and give you as good an allowance as ever I had.

SHAMWELL. Where's your warrant?

CONSTABLE. 'Tis here, from my lord chief justice.

BELFOND JUNIOR. Let me see your bride that was to be. Oh, Mrs. Termagant! Oh, horror! horror! What a ruin you have 'scaped! This was my mistress, and still maintained by me. I have a child by her three years old.

TERMAGANT. Impudent villain! how dare you lie so basely!

BELFOND JUNIOR. By heaven, 'tis true.

TERMAGANT. I never saw him in my life before.

BELFOND JUNIOR. Yes, often, to my plague. Brother, if I do not prove this to you, believe me not in aught I e'er shall say.

(TERMAGANT *goes to stab at* BELFOND JUNIOR. TRUMAN *lays hold on her.*)

TRUMAN. Belfond, look to yourself!

BELFOND JUNIOR. Ha! Disarm her. This is another show of her good nature. Brother, give me your hand, I'll wait on you, and you will thank me for your deliverance.

TRUMAN. I am assured you will. You are delivered from the most infamous and destructive villains that ever took sanctuary here.

BELFOND JUNIOR. And from two mischiefs you must have forever sunk under, incest and beggary. Those three are only in the warrant with my brother. Him I'll wait upon; bring you the rest. Hey! the cry is up! But we are provided.

(*A great noise in the streets, and the horn blowing:* An arrest! An arrest!)

CHEATLY. Undone, undone, all's lost!

SHAMWELL. Ruined! Forever lost!

HACKUM. I am surprised, and can not fight my way through.

BELFOND SENIOR. What! are all these rogues? and that a whore? and am I cheated?

BELFOND JUNIOR. Even so. Come along. Make ready, musketeers. Do you take care of my brother and conduct him with the rest to my uncle's house. I must go before and carry my little mistress, to make up the business with her father.

TRUMAN. I'll do it, I warrant you.

SERGEANT. We are ready.

(*Exeunt all but* MRS. TERMAGANT.)

TERMAGANT. Oh, vile misfortune! had he but stayed six
minutes, I had crowned all my revenge with one brave
act in marrying of his brother. Well, I have one piece
of vengeance which I will execute or perish. Besides, I'll
have his blood, and then I'll die contented.   (*Exit.*)

[SCENE VI.] *The street*

(*Enter* BELFOND JUNIOR, CHEATLY, SHAMWELL, HACKUM,
TRUMAN, Constable, Sergeant, Guards.)

TRUMAN. What do all these rabble here?
CONSTABLE. Fire amongst 'em.
SERGEANT. Present—!

(*The debtors run up and down, some without their
breeches, others without their coats; some out of balconies;
some crying out,* Oars, oars! Sculler, five pound for a boat!
Ten pound for a boat! Twenty pound for a boat! *The inhabitants all come out armed as before, but as soon as they
see the* Musketeers, *they run, and everyone shifts for
himself.*)

TRUMAN. Hey, how they run!   (*Exeunt.*)

[SCENE VII.]

(*Enter in* SIR EDWARD'*s house,* SIR EDWARD BELFOND *and*
Attorney.)

SIR EDWARD. This is the time I appointed my son to bring your
daughter hither. The witness is a most malicious, lying
wench, and can never have credit. Besides, you know an
action will sufficiently stop her mouth; for, were it true,
she can never prove what she says.
ATTORNEY. You are right, sir. Next to her being innocent is
the concealing of her shame.

(*Enter* BELFOND JUNIOR *and* LUCIA.)

LUCIA. And can I live to hear my fatal sentence of parting
with you? Hold, heart, a little.
BELFOND JUNIOR. It is with some convulsions I am torn from
you, but I must marry—I can not help it.
LUCIA. And must I never see you more?
BELFOND JUNIOR. As a lover, never; but your friend I'll be
while I have breath.

LUCIA. (*To herself*) Heart, do not swell so. This has awakened me and made me see my crime. Oh, that it had been sooner!

BELFOND JUNIOR. Sir, I beg a thousand pardons that I should attempt to injure your family, for it has gone no farther yet. For any fact, she's innocent, but 'twas no thanks to me—I am not so.—(*aside*) If a lie be ever lawful, 'tis in this case.

SIR EDWARD. Come, pretty lady, let me present you to your father. Though, as my son says, she's innocent, yet, because his love had gone so far, I present her with £1,500. My son and you shall be trustees for her. Tomorrow you shall have the money.

BELFOND JUNIOR. You are the best of all mankind.

ATTORNEY. All the world speaks your praises justly.

LUCIA. A thousand thanks, sir, for your bounty. And if my father please to pardon me this slip, in which I was so far from fact that I had scarce intention, I will hereafter outlive the strictest nun.

ATTORNEY. Rise; I do pardon you.

SIR EDWARD. That's well. And if they be not kind to you, appeal to me. It will be fit for you to go from hence with the least notice that can be. Tomorrow I'll bring the money.

(*Exeunt* Attorney *and* LUCIA.)

Who are the ladies you have entrusted me with, Ned?

BELFOND JUNIOR. Scrapeall's niece and daughter. The niece my father was to give £5,000 for, for his son. If you will give me leave, I shall marry her for nothing; and the other will take my friend—

SIR EDWARD. How, Ned! She's a Puritan!

BELFOND JUNIOR. No more than you, sir. She was bred otherwise, but was fain to comply for peace. She is beautiful and witty to a miracle, and I beg your consent, for I will die before I marry without it.

SIR EDWARD. Dear Ned, thou hast it; but what hast thou done with the Alsatians?

BELFOND JUNIOR. I have the rogues in custody, and my brother, too, whom I rescued in the very minute he was going to be married to a whore—to my whore, who plagues me continually. I see my father coming; pray prepare him while I prepare my brother for meeting with him. He shall not see me. (*Exit.*)

(*Enter* SIR WILLIAM BELFOND.)

SIR WILLIAM. Your servant, brother. No news of Ned yet?

SIR EDWARD. Oh, yes; he has your son and the three rogues in custody, and will bring them hither. Brother, pray resolve not to lose a son, but use him kindly, and forgive him.

SIR WILLIAM. I will, brother; and let him spend what he will, I'll come up to London, feast and revel, and never take a minute's care while I breathe, again.

(*Enter a* Servant *to* SIR EDWARD.)

SERVANT. Sir, a young gentleman would speak with you.

SIR EDWARD. Bid him come in.

(*Enter* MRS. TERMAGANT *in man's clothes.*)

TERMAGANT. If you be Sir Edward Belfond, I come to tell you what concerns your honor and my love.

SIR EDWARD. I am he.

TERMAGANT. Know then, sir, I am informed your brother Sir William Belfond's son is to marry Isabella, the niece of Mr. Scrapeall.

SIR EDWARD. What then, sir?

TERMAGANT. Then he invades my right. I have been many months contracted to her, and as you are a man of honor, I must tell you we have sealed that contract with mutual enjoyments.

SIR WILLIAM. How! What, was my son to marry a whore? I'll to this damned fellow instantly, and make him give up my articles.

SIR EDWARD. Have patience. Be not too rash.

SIR WILLIAM. Patience! What, to have my son marry a whore?

SIR EDWARD. Look you, brother, you must stay a moment.

(*Enter* BELFOND JUNIOR.)

SIR WILLIAM. Oh, Ned, your brother has 'scraped a fine match. This same Isabella is contracted to, and has been enjoyed by, this gentleman, as he calls it. He had liked to have married a whore.

BELFOND JUNIOR. Yes, that he had; but I will cut the throat of him that affirms that of Isabella.

TERMAGANT. Sir, I demand the protection of your house.

SIR EDWARD. Hold, son.

TERMAGANT. (*aside*) What devil sent him hither at this time?

BELFOND JUNIOR. I'll bring them to confront this rogue. What a devil's this? Have we another brother of that devil Termagant's here? *(Exit.)*

SIR EDWARD. This is a very odd story.

SIR WILLIAM. Let me go, brother; 'tis true enough. But what makes Ned concerned?

SIR EDWARD. Let us examine yet farther.

(Enter BELFOND JUNIOR with ISABELLA, TERESIA, and RUTH, and TRUMAN.)

SIR WILLIAM. Look, here they are all! How the devil comes this about?

TERMAGANT. O madam, are you here? I claim your contract, which I suppose will not offend you.

ISABELLA. What means this impudent fellow? I ne'er saw his face before.

TERMAGANT. Yes, madam, you have seen, and more than seen me often, since we were contracted.

ISABELLA. What instrument of villainy is this?

TERMAGANT. Nay, if you deny—! Friends, come in.

(Enter two Alsatian affidavit men.)

Friends, do you know this gentlewoman?

FIRST WITNESS. Yes, she is Mrs. Scrapeall's niece.

SECOND WITNESS. We were both witness to a contract of marriage between you two.

ISABELLA. Oh, impious wretches! What conspiracy is this?

SIR WILLIAM. Can anything be more plain? They seem civil, grave, substantial men.

BELFOND JUNIOR. Hold, hold, have I found ye? 'Tis she, it could be no other devil but herself.

(He pulls off her peruke.)

SIR WILLIAM. A woman!

SIR EDWARD. Secure those witnesses!

BELFOND JUNIOR. A woman! No. She has out-sinned her sex, and is a devil. Oh, devil, most complete devil! This is the lady I have been so much of late obliged to.

ISABELLA. This is she that told us the fine story today.

TERESIA. I know her face again, most infamous, lying creature!

TERMAGANT. I am become desperate! Have at thee!

(She snaps a pistol at BELFOND, which only flashes in the pan. The ladies shriek.)

BELFOND JUNIOR. Thank you, madam. Are you not a devil?
'Twas loaden, 'twas well meant, truly.

(*Takes the pistol from her.*)

SIR EDWARD. Lay hold on her. I'll send her to a place where
she shall be tamed. I never yet heard of such malice.

SIR WILLIAM. Dear Ned, thou hast so obliged me, thou melt'st
my heart. That thou shouldst steal away those ladies, and
save me £5,000! Now I hope, madam, my son Tim shall
be your husband without bargain and sale.

ISABELLA. No, I can assure you, sir, I would never have performed that bargain of my uncle's. We had determined
to dispose of ourselves before that, and now are more
resolved.

TERESIA. We have broken prison by the help of these gentlemen, and I think we must e'en take the authors of our
liberty.

ISABELLA. Will not that be a little hard, cousin, to take their
liberty from them who have given it to us?

SIR WILLIAM. Well, I am disappointed; but I can not blame
thee, Ned.

(TRUMAN *goes to* TERESIA.)

(*Enter* BELFOND SENIOR.)

SIR EDWARD. Your son. Pray use him kindly.

BELFOND SENIOR. I have been betrayed, cheated, and abused.
Upon my knees I beg your pardon and never will offend
you more; adad. I will not. I thought they had been the
honestest, the finest gentlemen in England, and it seems
they are rogues, cheats, and blockheads.

SIR WILLIAM. Rise, Tim. I profess thou makest me weep; thou
hast subdued me. I forgive thee. I see all human care is
vain. I will allow thee £500 a year, and come and live
with ease and pleasure here. I'll feast and revel, and wear
myself with pain and care no more.

BELFOND SENIOR. A thousand thanks. I'll ne'er displease you
while I live, again; adad, I won't. (*aside*) Here's an
alteration! I ne'er had good word from him before.

SIR WILLIAM. I would have married you to that pretty lady,
but your brother has been too hard for you.

BELFOND SENIOR. She's very pretty. But 'tis no matter; I am
in no such haste but I can stay and see the world first.

SIR EDWARD. Welcome, dear nephew, to my house and me. And now, my dear son, be free, and before all this company, let me know all the encumbrances you have upon you.

BELFOND JUNIOR. That good-natured lady is the only one that's heavy upon me. I have her child in my possession, which she says is mine.

TERMAGANT. Has he my child? Then I am undone forever. Oh, cursed misfortune!

SIR EDWARD. Look you, madam, I will settle an annuity of £100 a year upon you so long as you shall not disturb my son; and for your child, I'll breed her up and provide for her like a gentlewoman. But if you are not quiet, you shall never see her more.

TERMAGANT. You speak like a noble gentleman. I'll strive to compose myself. I am at last subdued, but will not stay to see the triumphs.— (*Exits hastily.*)

SIR EDWARD. Well, dear Ned, dost owe any money?

BELFOND JUNIOR. No, my dear father, no. You have been too bountiful for that. I have five hundred guineas in my cabinet.

SIR EDWARD. Now, madam, if you please to accept him for a husband, I will settle fifteen hundred pounds a year on him in present, which shall be your jointure. Besides that, your own money shall be laid out in land and settled on you, too. And at my death the rest of my estate.

ISABELLA. You do me too much honor; you much out-bid my value.

BELFOND JUNIOR. You best of fathers and of all mankind, I throw myself thus at your feet. Let me embrace your knees and kiss those hands.

SIR EDWARD. Come, rise and kiss these hands.

BELFOND JUNIOR. A long farewell to all the vanity and lewdness of youth. I offer myself at your feet as a sacrifice without a blemish now.

ISABELLA. Rise, I beseech you, rise.

TERESIA. (*To* TRUMAN) Your offers, sir, are better much than I could expect or can deserve.

TRUMAN. That's impossible. The wealth of both the Indies could not buy you from me, I am sure.

RUTH. Come, come, I have been governess, I know their minds. Come, give me your hands where you have given your hearts. Here, friend Truman, first take this.

TERESIA. My governess will have it so.

SIR EDWARD. Joy, sir, be ever with you. Please to make my house your own.

ISABELLA. How can I be secure you will not fall to your old courses again?

BELFOND JUNIOR. I have been so sincere in my confessions you can trust me; but I call heaven to witness I will hereafter be entirely yours. I look on marriage as the most solemn vow a man can make; and 'tis by consequence the basest perjury to break it.

RUTH. Come, come, I know your mind, too; take him, take him.

ISABELLA. If fate will have it so.

BELFOND JUNIOR. Let me receive this blessing on my knee.

ISABELLA. You are very devout of late.

SIR EDWARD. A thousand blessings on you both.

SIR WILLIAM. Perpetual happiness attend you both.

BELFOND SENIOR. Brother and madam, I wish you joy from my heart, adad, I do. (*aside to* BELFOND JUNIOR) Though between you and I, brother, I intend to have my swing at whoring and drinking as you had, before I come to it, though.

SIR EDWARD. Here! Bring in these rogues.

(*The* Constable *brings in* CHEATLY, SHAMWELL, *and* HACKUM.)

Come, rascals, I shall take a care to see examples made of you.

CHEATLY. We have substantial bail.

SIR EDWARD. I'll see it shall be substantial bail; it is my lord chief justice's warrant, returnable to none but him. But I will prosecute you, I assure you.

CHEATLY. Squire, dear squire!

HACKUM. Good, noble squire, speak for us.

SHAMWELL. Dear cousin!

BELFOND SENIOR. Oh, rogues! Cousin, you have cozened me; you made a put, a caravan, a bubble of me. I gave a judgment for £1,600 and had but 250, but there's some goods they talk of. But if e'er I be catched again, I'll be hanged.

SIR WILLIAM. Unconscionable villains! the chancery shall relieve us.

SIR EDWARD. I'll rout this knot of most pernicious knaves, for all the privilege of your place. Was ever such impudence suffered in a government? Ireland's conquered; Wales subdued; Scotland united; but there are some few spots of ground in London, just in the face of the government, unconquered yet, that hold in rebellion still. Methinks 'tis strange that places so near the king's palace should be no part of his dominions. 'Tis a shame to the societies of the law to countenance such practices. Should any place be shut against the king's writ, or *posse comitatus?* Take them away, and those two witnesses.

(*The* Constable *and* Watch *hales 'em away.*)

BELFOND SENIOR. Away with 'em, rogues, rascals, damned prigs!

SIR EDWARD. Come, ladies, I have sent for some neighbors to rejoice with us. We have fiddles. Let's dance a brisk round or two, and then we'll make a collation.

(*In the flourish before the dance enter* SCRAPEALL.)

SCRAPEALL. Oh, Sir William, I am undone, ruined! The birds are flown. Read the note they left behind 'em.

SIR WILLIAM. Peace, they are dancing. They have disposed of themselves.

SCRAPEALL. Oh, seed of serpents! Am I cheated then? I'll try a trick of law, you frogs of the bottomless pit, I will, and instantly—What, dancing too? Then they are fallen, indeed!

(*They dance. Exit* SCRAPEALL *hastily.*)

SIR EDWARD. Come, brother, now who has been in the right, you or I?

SIR WILLIAM. You have. Prithee, do not triumph.

BELFOND JUNIOR. Farewell forever, all the vices of the age!
　　　There is no peace but in a virtuous life,
　　　Nor lasting joy but in a tender wife.

SIR EDWARD. You that would breed your children well, by kindness and liberality endear 'em to you, and teach 'em by example.
　　　Severity spoils ten for one it mends:
　　　If you'd not have your sons desire your ends,
　　　By gentleness and bounty make those
　　　　sons your friends.

(*Exeunt omnes.*)

EPILOGUE

Ye mighty scourers of the narrow seas,
Who suffer not a bark to sail in peace,
But with your tire of culverins[113] ye roar,
Bring 'em by th' lee, and rummage all their store;
Our poet ducked and looked as if half dead
At every shot that whistled o'er his head.
Frequent engagements ne'er could make him bold.
He sneaked into a corner of the hold.
Since he submits, pray ease him of his fear,
And with a joint applause bid him appear;
Good critics don't insult and domineer.
He fears not sparks, who with brisk dress and mien
Come not to hear or see, but to be seen.
Each prunes himself, and with a languishing eye
Designs to kill a lady by the by
Let each fantastic ugly beau and shape,
Little of man, and very much of ape,
Admire himself, and let the poet 'scape.

Ladies, your anger most he apprehends,
And is grown past the age of making friends
Of any of the sex whom he offends.
No princess frowns, no hero roars and whines,
Nor his weak sense embroidered with strong lines;
No battles, trumpets, drums; not any die;
No mortal wounds to please your cruelty,
Who like not anything but tragedy,
With fond, unnatural extravagances
Stolen from the silly authors of romances.
Let such the chamber-maid's diversions be;
Pray be you reconciled to comedy.

113 *tire of culverins,* row of cannon.

For when we make you merry, you must own
You are much prettier than when you frown.
With charming smiles you use to conquer still,
The melancholy look's not apt to kill.
Our poet begs you who adorn this sphere,
This shining circle will not be severe.
Here no chit chat, here no tea tables are.
The cant he hopes will not be long unknown,
'Tis almost grown the language of the town.
For fops, who feel a wretched want of wit,
Still set up something that may pass for it.
He begs that you will often grace his play,
And lets you know Monday's[114] his visiting day.

---

[114] *Monday's*, i.e., the third day of production, when box-office receipts went to the author. That was why it was important to have at least a three-day run.

THE WAY OF THE WORLD
A Comedy
1700

William Congreve

INTRODUCTORY NOTE

William Congreve wrote less than most of his contemporaries but achieved in his own lifetime a reputation as the greatest of all authors of the comedy of manners, which continues to the present.

Congreve was born in 1670 near Leeds in Yorkshire. He went to Trinity College, Dublin, where he was a fellow student of Jonathan Swift. Congreve began to study law at the Middle Temple, but gave it up to write drama and poetry. His first play, *The Old Bachelor,* was produced in 1693. His two great plays, *Love for Love* and *The Way of the World,* were produced respectively in 1695 and 1700. From the performance of his first play to his last Congreve was acknowledged to be one of the masters of the London stage.

The first three of Congreve's plays met with resounding acclaim from audience and critics. Although *The Way of the World* was less popular it was by no means a failure. To its original reception the next two centuries added their own verdict: it is generally thought to be the best comedy written after Shakespeare. Millamant was played by Anne Bracegirdle, who was probably Congreve's mistress; and the role has been played by dozens of the leading ladies of following generations. The play has become a part of our own repertory, and appears in new versions regularly.

A contemporary critic noted that *The Way of the World* may have been "too Keen a Satyr" on the world it represented. Congreve evidently wanted to get away from the farce and sex that were by 1700 main staples of comedy. His play was intended to appeal to a wider audience than those who went to the theater for the peripheral pleasures of music, farce, and interludes which had begun to invade the stage. It may

well be that he had in mind the standards of Jonathan Swift
and Alexander Pope, friends who in their own prose and
poetry took up serious issues in the guise of comic situations.
The hero and heroine of *The Way of the World* are the
wittiest "gay couple" of their time; its fops and fools are
characters of real interest; and its villains more complex,
more human, and more understandable than the usual adversaries of satire. Far from being a display of "manners" or
style the play has human interest that is broad, deep, and
consistent.

The Way of the World is one of the few Restoration
comedies—or comedies of any kind or period—to develop a
sense of character and psychological depth. Mirabell and
Millamant are pictured as being radically different from their
early Restoration counterparts. Their wit is not so much directed at the usual butts of comedy as at larger objectives of
satire. They deal with the nature of the world and of themselves. It might be suggested that the most powerful and
significant difference between *The Way of the World* and
other comedies of sex and money is that the issues are taken
seriously here. What in other plays is simply a dance of the
bedsheets is in Congreve a powerful study of the growth and
ending of desire. He has worked out a psychology of manners
for the comedy of manners:

> One's cruelty is one's power, and when one parts with
> one's cruelty, one parts with one's power; and when one
> has parted with that, I fancy one's old and ugly.

The run of Restoration comedies are libertine, and look forward to nothing more than the enjoyment of love and the
conquest of money. This play has more to say: the action
takes place in a context of the decline of love and pleasure,
and with a highly modern sense of character divided against
itself.

The wit of this comedy is not free-floating; not, as in so
many other plays, a shower of sparks thrown off at random.
Mirabell and Millamant have to contend with most of the
"blocking characters" of comedy—but their central struggle
or *agon* is between their own desires.

They succeed in evading various provisos of the law, in
outwitting their adversaries, and in achieving finally the great
goods of their age, love and money. Yet the play insists on
the complexity of human nature, and implies that both
Mirabell and Millamant will have divided hearts.

Perhaps the best way to approach the language is through the play's theme. A context of human limitations surrounds character and action: Mrs. Fainall finds that "Men are ever in Extremes; either doting or averse," while Mrs. Marwood finds even less to hope for in women, for " 'tis not in our Natures long to persevere." Mirabell thinks of love in images of a shifting compass and a whirling windmill; Millamant knows that it is as temporary as youth and as hard to maintain. There is a deep vein of metaphor and image suggesting social and psychological delusion: Lady Wishfort gazing passionately into her mirror and seeing Art where Nature ought to be; Fainall weaving a tangled web that catches only himself at the end. It is a vein intensely realistic. Millamant knows that she will have to "dwindle into a wife" and Mirabell that even a witty lover becomes "enlarged into a husband." In language as well as theme, *The Way of the World* shows that what is serious is the province of what is comic.

Dramatis Personae

MEN

FAINALL, *in love with Mrs. Marwood*

MIRABELL, *in love with Mrs. Millamant*

WITWOUD,
PETULANT, } *followers of Mrs. Millamant*

SIR WILFULL WITWOUD, *half brother to Witwoud, and nephew
    to Lady Wishfort*

WAITWELL, *servant to Mirabell*

WOMEN

LADY WISHFORT, *enemy to Mirabell, for having falsely
    pretended love to her*

MRS. MILLAMANT, *A fine lady, niece to Lady Wishfort, and
    loves Mirabell*

MRS. MARWOOD, *friend to Mr. Fainall, and likes Mirabell*

MRS. FAINALL, *daughter to Lady Wishfort, and wife to Fainall,
    formerly friend to Mirabell*

FOIBLE, *woman to Lady Wishfort*

MINCING, *woman to Mrs. Millamant*

Dancers, Footmen, and Attendants

Scene: London

The time equal to that of the presentation

PROLOGUE

Of those few fools, who with ill stars are cursed,
Sure scribbling fools, called poets, fare the worst.
For they're a sort of fools which Fortune makes,
And after she has made 'em fools, forsakes.
With Nature's oafs 'tis quite a different case,
For Fortune favours all her idiot-race:
In her own nest the cuckoo-eggs we find,
O'er which she broods to hatch the changeling-kind.[1]
No portion for her own she has to spare,
So much she dotes on her adopted care.

   Poets are bubbles,[2] by the town drawn in,
Suffered at first some trifling stakes to win:
But what unequal hazards do they run!
Each time they write, they venture all they've won: }
The squire that's buttered[3] still, is sure to be undone. }
This author, heretofore, has found your favour,
But pleads no merit from his past behaviour.
To build on that might prove a vain presumption,
Should grants to poets made, admit resumption:
And in Parnassus he must lose his seat,
If that be found a forfeited estate.

   He owns, with toil, he wrought the following scenes,
But if they're naught ne'er spare him for his pains:
Damn him the more; have no commiseration
For dullness on mature deliberation.
He swears he'll not resent one hissed-off scene,
Nor, like those peevish wits, his play maintain,
Who, to assert their sense, your taste arraign.

---

1 *the changeling-kind*, one child substituted for another.
2 *bubbles*, victims.
3 *buttered*, cheated into letting all his bets ride.

Some plot we think he has, and some new thought;
Some humour too, no farce; but that's a fault.
Satire, he thinks, you ought not to expect,
For so reformed a town, who dares correct?
To please, this time, has been his sole pretence,
He'll not instruct, lest it should give offence.
Should he by chance a knave or fool expose,
That hurts none here, sure here are none of those.
In short, our play, shall (with your leave to show it)
Give you one instance of a passive poet.
Who to your judgments yields all resignation;
So save or damn, after your own discretion.

ACT I

(MIRABELL *and* FAINALL *rising from cards.* BETTY *waiting.*)

MIRABELL. You are a fortunate man, Mr. Fainall.

FAINALL. Have we done?

MIRABELL. What you please. I'll play on to entertain you.

FAINALL. No, I'll give you your revenge another time, when
you are not so indifferent; you are thinking of something
else now, and play too negligently; the coldness of a
losing gamester lessens the pleasure of the winner: I'd no
more play with a man that slighted his ill fortune, than
I'd make love to a woman who undervalued the loss of
her reputation.

MIRABELL. You have a taste extremely delicate, and are for
refining on your pleasures.

FAINALL. Prithee, why so reserved? Something has put you out
of humour.

MIRABELL. Not at all: I happen to be grave today; and you are
gay; that's all.

FAINALL. Confess, Millamant and you quarrelled last night,
after I left you; my fair cousin has some humours, that
would tempt the patience of a stoic. What, some coxcomb came in, and was well received by her, while you
were by.

MIRABELL. Witwoud and Petulant; and what was worse, her
aunt, your wife's mother, my evil genius; or to sum up
all in her own name, my old Lady Wishfort came in.

FAINALL. O there it is then—She has a lasting passion for
you and with reason.—What, then my wife was there?

MIRABELL. Yes, and Mrs. Marwood and three or four more,
whom I never saw before; seeing me, they all put on their
grave faces, whispered one another; then complained

aloud of the vapours,[4] and after fell into a profound silence.

FAINALL. They had a mind to be rid of you.

MIRABELL. For which reason I resolved not to stir. At last the good old lady broke thro' her painful taciturnity, with an invective against long visits. I would not have understood her, but Millamant joining in the argument, I rose and with a constrained smile told her, I thought nothing was so easy as to know when a visit began to be troublesome; she reddened and I withdrew, without expecting her reply.

FAINALL. You were to blame to resent what she spoke only in compliance with her aunt.

MIRABELL. She is more mistress of herself, than to be under the necessity of such a resignation.

FAINALL. What? tho' half her fortune depends upon her marrying with my lady's approbation?

MIRABELL. I was then in such a humour, that I should have been better pleased if she had been less discreet.

FAINALL. Now I remember, I wonder not they were weary of you; last night was one of their cabal[5]-nights; they have 'em three times a week, and meet by turns, at one another's apartments, where they come together like the coroner's inquest, to sit upon the murdered reputations of the week. You and I are excluded; and it was once proposed that all the male sex should be excepted; but somebody moved that to avoid scandal there might be one man of the community; upon which motion Witwoud and Petulant were enrolled members.

MIRABELL. And who may have been the foundress of this sect? My Lady Wishfort, I warrant, who publishes her detestation of mankind; and full of the vigour of fifty-five, declares for a friend and ratifia;[6] and let posterity shift for itself, she'll breed no more.

FAINALL. The discovery of your sham addresses to her, to conceal your love to her niece, has provoked this separation: had you dissembled better things might have continued in the state of nature.

MIRABELL. I did as much as man could, with any reasonable conscience; I proceeded to the very last act of flattery with her, and was guilty of a song in her commendation:

---

[4] *the vapours,* depression, the blues.
[5] *cabal,* political conspiracy.
[6] *ratifia,* fruit brandy.

nay, I got a friend to put her into a lampoon, and compliment her with the imputation of an affair with a young fellow, which I carried so far, that I told her the malicious town took notice that she was grown fat of a sudden; and when she lay in of a dropsy,[7] persuaded her she was reported to be in labour. The Devil's in't, if an old woman is to be flattered further, unless a man should endeavour downright personally to debauch her; and that my virtue forbade me. But for the discovery of that amour, I am indebted to your friend, or your wife's friend, Mrs. Marwood.

FAINALL. What should provoke her to be your enemy, without she has made you advances, which you have slighted? Women do not easily forgive omissions of that nature.

MIRABELL. She was always civil to me, till of late; I confess I am not one of those coxcombs who are apt to interpret a woman's good manners to her prejudice; and think that she who does not refuse 'em everything, can refuse 'em nothing.

FAINALL. You are a gallant man, Mirabell; and tho' you may have cruelty enough, not to satisfy a lady's longing; you have too much generosity, not to be tender of her honour. Yet you speak with an indifference which seems to be affected; and confesses you are conscious of a negligence.

MIRABELL. You pursue the argument with a distrust that seems to be unaffected, and confesses you are conscious of a concern for which the lady is more indebted to you, than your wife.

FAINALL. Fie, fie friend, if you grow censorious I must leave you; —I'll look upon the gamesters in the next room.

MIRABELL. Who are they?

FAINALL. Petulant and Witwoud. (*To Betty.*) Bring me some chocolate.

(*Exit.*)

MIRABELL. Betty, what says your clock?

BETTY. Turned of the last canonical hour,[8] sir.

(*Exit.*)

MIRABELL. How pertinently the jade answers me! Ha? almost one a'clock (*Looking at his watch.*) O, y'are come—

---

[7] *dropsy*, watery swelling.
[8] *canonical hour*, last legal hour of the day for marriage ceremony.

(Enter a Servant.)

Well, is the grand affair over? You have been something tedious.

SERVANT. Sir, there's such coupling at Pancras,[9] that they stand behind one another, as 'twere in a country dance. Ours was the last couple to lead up; and no hopes appearing of dispatch, besides, the parson growing hoarse, we were afraid his lungs would have failed before it came to our turn; so we drove round to Duke's Place;[10] and there they were riveted in a trice.

MIRABELL. So, so, you are sure they are married.

SERVANT. Married and bedded, sir; I am witness.

MIRABELL. Have you the certificate?

SERVANT. Here it is, sir.

MIRABELL. Has the tailor brought Waitwell's clothes home, and the new liveries?

SERVANT. Yes, sir.

MIRABELL. That's well. Do you go home again, d'ye hear, and adjourn the consummation till farther order; bid Waitwell shake his ears, and Dame Partlet[11] rustle up her feathers, and meet me at one a'clock by Rosamond's Pond. That I may see her before she returns to her lady; and as you tender[12] your ears be secret.

(Exit Servant.)

(Re-enter FAINALL.)

FAINALL. Joy of your success, Mirabell; you look pleased.

MIRABELL. Aye; I have been engaged in a matter of some sort of mirth, which is not yet ripe for discovery. I am glad this is not a cabal-night. I wonder, Fainall, that you who are married, and of consequence should be discreet, will suffer your wife to be of such a party.

FAINALL. Faith, I am not jealous. Besides, most who are engaged are women and relations; and for the men, they are of a kind too contemptible to give scandal.

MIRABELL. I am of another opinion. The greater the coxcomb, always the more the scandal: for a woman who is not a

9 *Pancras*, St. Pancras Church, exempt from license rules.
10 *Duke's Place*, location of St. James Church.
11 *Dame Partlet*, wife of Chanticleer in the fable of the cock and the fox; byword for housewife.
12 *tender*, value.

fool, can have but one reason for associating with a
man that is.

FAINALL. Are you jealous as often as you see Witwoud entertained by Millamant?

MIRABELL. Of her understanding I am, if not of her person.

FAINALL. You do her wrong; for to give her her due, she has
wit.

MIRABELL. She has beauty enough to make any man think so;
and complaisance enough not to contradict him who shall
tell her so.

FAINALL. For a passionate lover, methinks you are a man
somewhat too discerning in the failings of your mistress.

MIRABELL. And for a discerning man, somewhat too passionate
a lover; for I like her with all her faults; nay, like her for
her faults. Her follies are so natural, or so artful, that they
become her; and those affectations which in another
woman would be odious, serve but to make her more
agreeable. I'll tell thee, Fainall, she once used me with
that insolence, that in revenge I took her to pieces; sifted
her and separated her failings; I studied 'em, and got 'em
by rote. The catalogue was so large, that I was not without hopes, one day or other to hate her heartily: to which
end I so used myself to think of 'em, that at length, contrary to my design and expectation, they gave me every
hour less and less disturbance; 'till in a few days it became
habitual to me, to remember 'em without being displeased. They are now grown as familiar to me as my
own frailties; and in all probability in a little time longer
I shall like 'em as well.

FAINALL. Marry her, marry her; be half as well acquainted
with her charms, as you are with her defects, and my
life on't, you are your own man again.

MIRABELL. Say you so?

FAINALL. Aye, aye, I have experience:

(Enter Messenger.)

MESSENGER. Is one Squire Witwoud here?

BETTY. Yes; what's your business?

MESSENGER. I have a letter for him, from his brother Sir
Wilfull, which I am charged to deliver into his own hands.

BETTY. He's in the next room, friend—that way.

(Exit Messenger.)

MIRABELL. What, is the chief of that noble family in Town,
      Sir Wilfull Witwoud?

FAINALL. He is expected today. Do you know him?

MIRABELL. I have seen him, he promises to be an extraordinary
      person; I think you have the honour to be related to him.

FAINALL. Yes; he is half-brother to this Witwoud by a former
      wife, who was sister to my Lady Wishfort, my wife's
      mother. If you marry Millamant you must call cousins
      too.

MIRABELL. I had rather be his relation than his acquaintance.

FAINALL. He comes to town in order to equip himself for
      travel.

MIRABELL. For travel! Why the man that I mean is above forty.

FAINALL. No matter for that; 'tis for the honour of England,
      that all Europe should know we have blockheads of all
      ages.

MIRABELL. I wonder there is not an act of parliament to save
      the credit of the nation, and prohibit the exportation of
      fools.

FAINALL. By no means, 'tis better as 'tis; 'tis better to trade
      with a little loss, than to be quite eaten up, with being
      overstocked.

MIRABELL. Pray, are the follies of this knight-errant, and those
      of the squire his brother, anything related?

FAINALL. Not at all; Witwoud grows by the knight, like a
      medlar grafted on a crab. One will melt in your mouth,
      and t'other set your teeth on edge; one is all pulp, and
      the other all core.

MIRABELL. So one will be rotten before he be ripe, and the
      other will be rotten without ever being ripe at all.

FAINALL. Sir Wilfull is an odd mixture of bashfulness and
      obstinacy—But when he's drunk, he's as loving as the
      monster in *The Tempest;*[13] and much after the same man-
      ner. To give t'other his due; he has something of good
      nature, and does not always want wit.

MIRABELL. Not always; but as often as his memory fails him,
      and his commonplace of comparisons. He is a fool with
      a good memory, and some few scraps of other folks' wit.
      He is one whose conversation can never be approved, yet
      it is now and then to be endured. He has indeed one good

13 *the Monster in The Tempest,* Caliban, a popular role in a Restoration
opera based on Shakespeare's play.

quality, he is not exceptious; for he so passionately affects the reputation of understanding raillery; that he will construe an affront into a jest; and call downright rudeness and ill language, satire and fire.

FAINALL. If you have a mind to finish his picture, you have an opportunity to do it at full length. Behold the original.

(*Enter* WITWOUD.)

WITWOUD. Afford me your compassion, my dears; pity me, Fainall, Mirabell, pity me.

MIRABELL. I do from my soul.

FAINALL. Why, what's the matter?

WITWOUD. No letters for me, Betty?

BETTY. Did not the messenger bring you one but now, sir?

WITWOUD. Ay, but no other?

BETTY. No, Sir.

WITWOUD. That's hard, that's very hard;—A messenger, a mule, a beast of burden, he has brought me a letter from the fool my brother, as heavy as a panegyric in a funeral sermon, or a copy of commendatory verses from one poet to another. And what's worse, 'tis as sure a forerunner of the author, as an epistle dedicatory.

MIRABELL. A fool, and your brother, Witwoud!

WITWOUD. Ay, ay, my half-brother. My half-brother he is, no nearer, upon honour.

MIRABELL. Then 'tis possible he may be but half a fool.

WITWOUD. Good, good Mirabell, *le drôle!* Good, good, hang him, don't let's talk of him;—Fainall, how does your lady? Gad, I say anything in the world to get this fellow out of my head. I beg pardon that I should ask a man of pleasure, and the town, a question at once so foreign and domestic. But I talk like an old maid at a marriage, I don't know what I say: but she's the best woman in the world.

FAINALL. 'Tis well you don't know what you say, or else your Commendation would go near to make me either vain or jealous.

WITWOUD. No man in town lives well with a wife but Fainall: Your judgment, Mirabell?

MIRABELL. You had better step and ask his wife; if you would be credibly inform'd.

WITWOUD. Mirabell.

MIRABELL. Aye.

WITWOUD. My dear, I ask ten thousand pardons;—gad, I have forgot what I was going to say to you.

MIRABELL. I thank you heartily, heartily.

WITWOUD. No, but prithee excuse me,—my memory is such a memory.

MIRABELL. Have a care of such apologies, Witwoud;—for I never knew a fool but he affected to complain, either of the spleen[14] or his memory.

FAINALL. What have you done with Petulant?

WITWOUD. He's reckoning his money,—my money it was,— I have no luck today.

FAINALL. You may allow him to win of you at play;—for you are sure to be too hard for him at repartee: since you monopolize the wit that is between you, the fortune must be his, of course.

MIRABELL. I don't find that Petulant confesses the superiority of wit to be your talent, Witwoud.

WITWOUD. Come, come, you are malicious now, and would breed debates.—Petulant's my friend, and a very honest fellow, and a very pretty fellow, and has a smattering— faith and troth a pretty deal of an odd sort of a small wit: nay, I'll do him justice. I'm his friend, I won't wrong him neither.—And if he had but any judgment in the world,—he would not be altogether contemptible. Come, come, don't detract from the merits of my friend.

FAINALL. You don't take your friend to be overnicely bred.

WITWOUD. No, no, hang him, the rogue has no manners at all, that I must own—no more breeding than a bum-baily,[15] that I grant you,—'tis pity, faith; the fellow has fire and life.

MIRABELL. What, courage?

WITWOUD. Hum, faith I don't know as to that,—I can't say as to that.—Yes, faith, in a controversy he'll contradict anybody.

MIRABELL. Tho' 'twere a man whom he feared, or a woman whom he loved?

WITWOUD. Well, well, he does not always think before he speaks;—We have all our failings; you're too hard upon him, you are, faith. Let me excuse him;—I can defend most of his faults, except one or two; one he has, that's

14 *the spleen*, thought to be the organ or of sensibility; associated with wit and artistry.
15 *bum-baily*, hired by the court to arrest debtors. As Dr. Johnson said, an official "of the meanest kind."

the truth on't, if he were my brother, I could not acquit him—that indeed I could wish were otherwise.

MIRABELL. Ay marry, what's that, Witwoud?

WITWOUD. O pardon me—expose the infirmities of my friend. —No, my dear, excuse me there.

FAINALL. What I warrant he's unsincere, or 'tis some such trifle.

WITWOUD. No, no, what if he be? 'Tis no matter for that, his wit will excuse that: a wit should no more be sincere, than a woman constant; one argues a decay of parts, as t'other of beauty.

MIRABELL. May be you think him too positive?

WITWOUD. No, no, his being positive is an incentive to argument, and keeps up conversation.

FAINALL. Too illiterate?

WITWOUD. That! that's his happiness—his want of learning, gives him the more opportunities to show his natural parts.

MIRABELL. He wants words?

WITWOUD. Ay; but I like him for that now; for his want of words gives me the pleasure very often to explain his meaning.

FAINALL. He's impudent?

WITWOUD. No; that's not it.

MIRABELL. Vain?

WITWOUD. No.

MIRABELL. What, he speaks unseasonable truths sometimes, because he has no wit enough to invent an evasion?

WITWOUD. Truths! Ha, ha, ha! No, no, since you will have it, —I mean he never speaks truth at all,—that's all. He will lie like a chambermaid, or a woman of quality's porter. Now that is a fault.

(*Enter Coachman.*)

COACHMAN. Is Master Petulant here, mistress?

BETTY. Yes.

COACHMAN. Three gentlewomen in the coach would speak with him.

FAINALL. O brave Petulant, three!

BETTY. I'll tell him.

COACHMAN. You must bring two dishes of chocolate and a glass of cinnamon-water.

(*Exit* Betty, *and Coachman.*)

WITWOUD. That should be for two fasting strumpets, and a bawd troubl'd with wind. Now you may know what the three are.

MIRABELL. You are very free with your friend's acquaintance.

WITWOUD. Ay, ay, friendship without freedom is as dull as love without enjoyment, or wine without toasting; but to tell you a secret, these are trulls that he allows coach-hire, and something more by the week, to call on him once a day at public places.

MIRABELL. How!

WITWOUD. You shall see he won't go to 'em because there's no more company here to take notice of him—why this is nothing to what he used to do;—before he found out this way, I have known him call for himself—

FAINALL. Call for himself? What dost thou mean?

WITWOUD. Mean, why he would slip you out of this chocolate-house, just when you had been talking to him—as soon as your back was turned—whip, he was gone;—then trip to his lodging, clap on a hood and scarf, and mask, slap into a hackney-coach, and drive hither to the door again in a trice; where he would send in for himself, that I mean, call for himself, wait for himself, nay and what's more, not finding himself, sometimes leave a letter for himself.

MIRABELL. I confess this is something extraordinary—I believe he waits for himself now, he is so long a-coming; Oh, I ask his pardon.

(*Enter* PETULANT.)

BETTY. Sir, the coach stays.

PETULANT. Well, well; I come.—'Sbud, a man had as good be a professed midwife as a professed whoremaster, at this rate; to be knocked up and raised at all hours and in all places. Pox on 'em, I won't come.—D'ye hear, tell 'em I won't come.—let 'em snivel and cry their hearts out.

FAINALL. You are very cruel, Petulant.

PETULANT. All's one, let it pass—I have a humour to be cruel.

MIRABELL. I hope they are not persons of condition that you use at this rate.

PETULANT. Condition, condition's a dried fig, if I am not in humour. By this hand, if they were your—a—a—your what-d'ye-call-'ems themselves, they must wait or rub off, if I want appetite.

MIRABELL. What-d'ye-call-'ems! What are they, Witwoud?

WITWOUD. Empresses, my Dear—By your What-d'ye-call-'ems he means sultana queens.

PETULANT. Ay, Roxolanas.[16]

MIRABELL. Cry you mercy.

FAINALL. Witwoud says they are—

PETULANT. What does he say th' are?

WITWOUD. Aye; fine ladies I say.

PETULANT. Pass on, Witwoud—Hark'ee, by this light his relations—two co-heiresses his cousins, and an old aunt, that loves caterwauling better than a conventicle.[17]

WITWOUD. Ha, ha, ha; I had a mind to see how the rogue would come off—Ha, ha, ha; gad I can't be angry with him; if he said they were my mother and my sisters.

MIRABELL. No?

WITWOUD. No; the rogue's wit and readiness of invention charm me, dear Petulant.

BETTY. They are gone sir, in great anger.

PETULANT. Enough, let 'em trundle. Anger helps complexion, saves paint.

FAINALL. This continence is all dissembled; this is in order to have something to brag of the next time he makes court to Millamant, and swear he has abandoned the whole sex for her sake.

MIRABELL. Have you not left off your impudent pretensions there yet? I shall cut your throat, sometime or other, Petulant, about that business.

PETULANT. Ay, ay, let that pass—there are other throats to be cut—

MIRABELL. Meaning mine, sir?

PETULANT. Not I—I mean nobody—I know nothing. But there are uncles and nephews in the world—and they may be rivals—what then? All's one for that.

MIRABELL. How! hark'ee Petulant, come hither—explain, or I shall call your interpreter.

PETULANT. Explain, I know nothing. Why, you have an uncle, have you not, lately come to town, and lodges by my Lady Wishfort's?

MIRABELL. True.

PETULANT. Why that's enough—you and he are not friends; and if he should marry and have a child, you may be disinherited, ha?

16 *Roxolanas,* exotic role in Davenant's *Siege of Rhodes.*
17 *conventicle,* religious meeting.

MIRABELL. Where hast thou stumbled upon all this truth?

PETULANT. All's one for that; why then, say I know something.

MIRABELL. Come, thou art an honest fellow, Petulant, and shalt make love to my mistress, thou sha't, faith. What thou heard of my uncle?

PETULANT. I, nothing I. If throats are to be cut, let swords clash; snug's the word, I shrug and am silent.

MIRABELL. O raillery, raillery. Come, I know thou art in the women's secrets. What, you're a cabalist, I know you staid at Millamant's last night, after I went. Was there any mention made of my uncle, or me? Tell me; if thou hadst but good nature equal to thy wit Petulant, Tony Witwoud, who is now thy competitor in fame, would show as dim by thee as a dead whiting's eye by a pearl of orient; he would no more be seen by thee, then Mercury is by the sun: come, I'm sure thou wo't tell me.

PETULANT. If I do, will you grant me common sense then, for the future?

MIRABELL. Faith I'll do what I can for thee; and I'll pray that Heaven may grant it thee in the meantime.

PETULANT. Well, hark'ee.

FAINALL. Petulant and you both will find Mirabell as warm a rival as a lover.

WITWOUD. Pshaw, pshaw, that she laughs at Petulant is plain. And for my part, but that it is almost a fashion to admire her, I should—hark'ee—to tell you a secret, but let it go no further—between friends, I shall never break my heart for her.

FAINALL. How!

WITWOUD. She's handsome; but she's a sort of an uncertain woman.

FAINALL. I thought you had died for her.

WITWOUD. Umh—No—

FAINALL. She has wit.

WITWOUD. 'Tis what she will hardly allow anybody else;—now, demme! I should hate that, if she were as handsome as Cleopatra. Mirabell is not so sure of her as he thinks for.

FAINALL. Why do you think so?

WITWOUD. We stayed pretty late there last night, and heard something of an uncle to Mirabell, who is lately come to town,—and is between him and the best part of his estate; Mirabell and he are at some distance, as my Lady Wishfort has been told; and you know she hates Mirabell, worse than a Quaker hates a parrot, or than a fishmonger hates a hard frost. Whether this uncle has seen Mrs. Millamant or not, I cannot say; but there were items of such a treaty being in embryo; and if it should come to life, poor Mirabell would be in some sort unfortunately fobbed, i'faith.

FAINALL. 'Tis impossible Millamant should hearken to it.

WITWOUD. Faith, my dear, I can't tell; she's a woman and a kind of a humorist.[18]

MIRABELL. And this is the sum of what you could collect last night?

PETULANT. The quintessence. Maybe Witwoud knows more, he stayed longer. Besides they never mind him; they say anything before him.

MIRABELL. I thought you had been the greatest favourite.

PETULANT. Aye *tête a tête;* But not in public, because I make remarks.

MIRABELL. Do you.

PETULANT. Aye, aye, pox I'm malicious, man. Now he's soft, you know; they are not in awe of him—the fellow's well-bred, he's what you call a—what-d'ye-call-'em, a fine gentleman. But he's silly withal.

MIRABELL. I thank you, I know as much as my curiosity requires. Fainall, are you for the Mall?

FAINALL. Aye, I'll take a turn before dinner.

WITWOUD. Aye, we'll all walk in the Park, the ladies talked of being there.

MIRABELL. I thought you were obliged to watch for your brother Sir Wilfull's arrival.

WITWOUD. No, no, he comes to his aunt's, my Lady Wishfort; pox on him, I shall be troubled with him too; what shall I do with the fool?

PETULANT. Beg him for his estate; that I may beg you afterwards; and so have but one trouble with you both.

WITWOUD. O rare Petulant; thou art as quick as a fire in a frosty morning. Thou shalt to the Mall with us; and we'll be very severe.

PETULANT. Enough! I'm in a humour to be severe.

MIRABELL. Are you? Pray then walk by yourselves,—let not us be accessory to your putting the ladies out of countenance with your senseless ribaldry; which you roar out aloud as often as they pass by you; and when you have made

18 *a kind of a humorist,* fanciful.

a handsome woman blush, then you think you have been
severe.

PETULANT. What, what? Then let 'em either show their innocence by not understanding what they hear, or else show
their discretion by not hearing what they would not be
thought to understand.

MIRABELL. But hast not thou then sense enough to know that
thou ought'st to be most ashamed thyself, when thou hast
put another out of countenance?

PETULANT. Not I, by this hand!—I always take blushing either
for a sign of guilt or ill breeding.

MIRABELL. I confess you ought to think so. You are in the
right, that you may plead the error of your judgment in
defence of your practice.

> Where modesty's ill manners, 'tis but fit
> That impudence and malice pass for wit.

(*Exeunt.*)

ACT II

[SCENE I.] *St. James's Park*

(*Enter* MRS. FAINALL *and* MRS. MARWOOD.)

MRS. FAINALL. Aye, aye, dear Marwood, if we will be happy,
we must find the means in ourselves, and among ourselves. Men are ever in extremes: either doting or averse.
While they are lovers, if they have fire and sense, their
jealousies are insupportable; and when they cease to love
(we ought to think at least) they loathe; they look upon
us with horror and distaste; they meet us like the ghosts
of what we were, and as such fly from us.

MRS. MARWOOD. True, 'tis an unhappy circumstance of life
that love should ever die before us; and that the man so
often should outlive the lover. But say what you will,
'tis better to be left, than never to have been loved. To
pass out youth in dull indifference, to refuse the sweets
of life because they once must leave us, is as preposterous,
as to wish to have been born old, because we one day
must be old. For my part, my youth may wear and waste,
but it shall never rust in my possession.

MRS. FAINALL. Then it seems you dissemble an aversion to mankind only in compliance with my mother's humour.

MRS. MARWOOD. Certainly. To be free; I have no taste of those insipid dry discourses, with which our sex of force must entertain themselves apart from men. We may affect endearments to each other, profess eternal friendships, and seem to dote like lovers; but 'tis not in our natures long to persevere. Love will resume his empire in. our breasts, and every heart, or soon or late, receive and readmit him as its lawful tyrant.

MRS. FAINALL. Bless me, how have I been deceived! Why you profess a libertine.[19]

MRS. MARWOOD. You see my friendship by my freedom. Come, be as sincere, acknowledge that your sentiments agree with mine.

MRS. FAINALL. Never.

MRS. MARWOOD. You hate mankind?

MRS. FAINALL. Heartily, inveterately.

MRS. MARWOOD. Your husband?

MRS. FAINALL. Most transcendantly; aye, tho' I say it, meritoriously.

MRS. MARWOOD. Give me your hand upon it.

MRS. FAINALL. There.

MRS. MARWOOD. I join with you; what I have said has been to try you.

MRS. FAINALL. Is it possible? Dost thou hate those vipers, men?

MRS. MARWOOD. I have done hating 'em; and am now come to despise 'em; the next thing I have to do is eternally to forget 'em.

MRS. FAINALL. There spoke the spirit of an Amazon, a Penthesilea.[20]

MRS. MARWOOD. And yet I am thinking sometimes to carry my aversion further.

MRS. FAINALL. How?

MRS. MARWOOD. Faith by marrying; if I could but find one that loved me very well, and would be thoroughly sensible of ill usage; I think I should do myself the violence of undergoing the ceremony.

MRS. FAINALL. You would not make him a cuckold?

MRS. MARWOOD. No; but I'd make him believe I did, and that's as bad.

---

[19] *libertine,* i.e., without sexual morality.
[20] *Penthesilea,* an Amazon queen.

MRS. FAINALL. Why had not you as good do it?

MRS. MARWOOD. Oh, if he should ever discover it, he would then know the worst and be out of his pain; but I would have him ever to continue upon the rack of fear and jealousy.

MRS. FAINALL. Ingenious mischief! Would thou wert married to Mirabell.

MRS. MARWOOD. Would I were.

MRS. FAINALL. You change colour.

MRS. MARWOOD. Because I hate him.

MRS. FAINALL. So do I; but I can hear him named. But what reason have you to hate him in particular?

MRS. MARWOOD. I never loved him; he is, and always was insufferably proud.

MRS. FAINALL. By the reason you give for your aversion, one would think it dissembled; for you have laid a fault to his charge, of which his enemies must acquit him.

MRS. MARWOOD. Oh, then it seems you are one of his favourable enemies! Methinks you look a little pale, and now you flush again.

MRS. FAINALL. Do I? I think I am a little sick o' the sudden.

MRS. MARWOOD. What ails you?

MRS. FAINALL. My husband. Don't you see him? He turned short upon me unawares, and has almost overcome me.

(*Enter* FAINALL *and* MIRABELL.)

MRS. MARWOOD. Ha, ha, ha; he comes opportunely for you.

MRS. FAINALL. For you, for he has brought Mirabell with him.

FAINALL. My dear.

MRS. FAINALL. My soul.

FAINALL. You don't look well today, child.

MRS. FAINALL. D'ye think so?

MIRABELL. He is the only man that does, madam.

MRS. FAINALL. The only man that would tell me so at least; and the only man from whom I could hear it without mortification.

FAINALL. Oh, my dear, I am satisfied of your tenderness; I know you cannot resent anything from me; especially what is an effect of my concern.

MRS. FAINALL. Mr. Mirabell; my mother interrupted you in a pleasant relation last night: I would fain hear it out.

MIRABELL. The persons concerned in that affair have yet a tolerable reputation. I am afraid Mr. Fainall will be censorious.

MRS. FAINALL. He has a humour more prevailing than his curiosity, and will willingly dispense with the hearing of one scandalous story, to avoid giving an occasion to make another by being seen to walk with his wife. This way, Mr. Mirabell, and I dare promise you will oblige us both.

(*Exeunt* MRS. FAINALL *and* MIRABELL.)

FAINALL. Excellent creature! Well sure if I should live to be rid of my wife, I should be a miserable man.

MRS. MARWOOD. Aye?

FAINALL. For having only that one hope, the accomplishment of it, of consequence must put an end to all my hopes; and what a wretch is he who must survive his hopes! Nothing remains when that day comes, but to sit down and weep like Alexander when he wanted other worlds to conquer.

MRS. MARWOOD. Will you not follow 'em?

FAINALL. Faith, I think not.

MRS. MARWOOD. Pray let us; I have a reason.

FAINALL. You are not jealous?

MRS. MARWOOD. Of whom?

FAINALL. Of Mirabell.

MRS. MARWOOD. If I am, is it inconsistent with my love to you that I am tender of your honour?

FAINALL. You would intimate then, as if there were a fellow-feeling between my wife and him?

MRS. MARWOOD. I think she does not hate him to that degree she would be thought.

FAINALL. But he, I fear, is too insensible.

MRS. MARWOOD. It may be you are deceived.

FAINALL. It may be so. I do now begin to apprehend it.

MRS. MARWOOD. What?

FAINALL. That I have been deceived madam, and you are false.

MRS. MARWOOD. That I am false! What mean you?

FAINALL. To let you know I see through all your little arts. Come, you both love him; and both have equally dissembled your aversion. Your mutual jealousies of one another, have made you clash till you have both struck fire. I have seen the warm confession reddening on your cheeks and sparkling from your eyes.

MRS. MARWOOD. You do me wrong.

FAINALL. I do not. 'Twas for my ease to oversee and wilfully neglect the gross advances made him by my wife; that by permitting her to be engaged, I might continue unsuspected in my pleasures; and take you oftener to my arms in full security. But could you think because the nodding husband would not wake, that e'er the watchful lover slept?

MRS. MARWOOD. And wherewithal can you reproach me?

FAINALL. With infidelity, with loving of another, with love of Mirabell.

MRS. MARWOOD. 'Tis false. I challenge you to show an instance that can confirm your groundless accusation. I hate him.

FAINALL. And wherefore do you hate him? He is insensible, and your resentment follows his neglect. An instance? The injuries you have done him are a proof: your interposing in his love. What cause had you to make discoveries of his pretended passion? To undeceive the credulous aunt, and be the officious obstacle of his match with Millamant?

MRS. MARWOOD. My obligations to my lady urged me: I had professed a friendship to her; and could not see her easy nature so abused by that dissembler.

FAINALL. What, was it conscience then? professed a friendship! Oh, the pious friendships of the female sex!

MRS. MARWOOD. More tender, more sincere, and more enduring, than all the vain and empty vows of men, whether professing love to us, or mutual faith to one another.

FAINALL. Ha, ha, ha; you are my wife's friend too.

MRS. MARWOOD. Shame and ingratitude! Do you reproach me? You, you upbraid me! Have I been false to her, thro' strict fidelity to you, and sacrificed my friendship to keep my love inviolate? And have you the baseness to charge me with the guilt, unmindful of the merit? To you it should be meritorious, that I have been vicious. And do you reflect that guilt upon me, which should lie buried in your bosom?

FAINALL. You misinterpret my reproof. I meant but to remind you of the slight account you once could make of strictest ties, when set in competition with your love to me.

MRS. MARWOOD. 'Tis false, you urged it with deliberate malice —'Twas spoke in scorn, and I never will forgive it.

FAINALL. Your guilt, not your resentment, begets your rage. If yet you loved, you could forgive a jealousy: but you are stung to find you are discovered.

MRS. MARWOOD. It shall be all discovered. You too shall be discovered; be sure you shall. I can but be exposed. If I do it myself I shall prevent your baseness.

FAINALL. Why, what will you do?

MRS. MARWOOD. Disclose it to your wife; own what has passed between us.

FAINALL. Frenzy!

MRS. MARWOOD. By all my wrongs I'll do't! I'll publish to the world the injuries you have done me, both in my fame and fortune! With both I trusted you, you bankrupt in honour, as indigent of wealth.

FAINALL. Your fame I have preserved. Your fortune has been bestowed as the prodigality of your love would have it, in pleasures which we both have shared. Yet had not you been false, I had ere this repaid it. 'Tis true—had you permitted Mirabell with Millamant to have stolen their marriage, my lady had been incensed beyond all means of reconcilement: Millamant had forfeited the moiety of her fortune, which then would have descended to my wife— and wherefore did I marry but to make lawful prize of a rich widow's wealth, and squander it on love and you?

MRS. MARWOOD. Deceit and frivolous pretence.

FAINALL. Death, am I not married? What's pretence? Am I not imprisoned, fettered? Have I not a wife? Nay a wife that was a widow, a young widow, a handsome widow; and would be again a widow, but that I have a heart of proof,[21] and something of a constitution to bustle thro' the ways of wedlock and this world! Will you yet be reconciled to truth and me?

MRS. MARWOOD. Impossible. Truth and you are inconsistent— I hate you, and shall forever.

FAINALL. For loving you?

MRS. MARWOOD. I loathe the name of love after such usage; and next to the guilt with which you would asperse[22] me, I scorn you most. Farewell!

FAINALL. Nay, we must not part thus.

MRS. MARWOOD. Let me go.

FAINALL. Come, I'm sorry.

MRS. MARWOOD. I care not—let me go—break my hands, do— I'd leave 'em to get loose.

FAINALL. I would not hurt you for the world. Have I no other hold to keep you here?

MRS. MARWOOD. Well, I have deserved it all.

FAINALL. You know I love you.

MRS. MARWOOD. Poor dissembling! O that—well, it is not yet—

---

21 *of proof,* ironclad or bulletproof.
22 *asperse,* charge.

FAINALL. What? what is it not? What is it not yet? It is not yet too late—

MRS. MARWOOD. No, it is not yet too late—I have that comfort.

FAINALL. It is to love another.

MRS. MARWOOD. But not to loathe, detest, abhor mankind, myself and the whole treacherous world.

FAINALL. Nay, this is extravagance! Come I ask your pardon—no tears—I was to blame, I could not love you and be easy in my doubts. Pray, forbear—I believe you; I'm convinced I've done you wrong; and anyway, every way will make amends. I'll hate my wife yet more, damn her! I'll part with her, rob her of all she's worth, and we'll retire somewhere, anywhere, to another world. I'll marry thee—be pacified—'Sdeath they come! Hide your face, your tears—You have a mask, wear it a moment. This way, this way, be persuaded.

(*Exeunt.*)

(*Enter* MIRABELL *and* MRS. FAINALL.)

MRS. FAINALL. They are here yet.

MIRABELL. They are turning into the other walk.

MRS. FAINALL. While I only hated my husband, I could bear to see him; but since I have despised him, he's too offensive.

MIRABELL. O you should hate with prudence.

MRS. FAINALL. Yes, for I have loved with indiscretion.

MIRABELL. You should have just so much disgust for your husband, as may be sufficient to make you relish your lover.

MRS. FAINALL. You have been the cause that I have loved without bounds, and would you set limits to that aversion of which you have been the occasion? Why did you make me marry this man?

MIRABELL. Why do we daily commit disagreeable and dangerous actions? To save that idol reputation. If the familiarities of our loves had produced that consequence, of which you were apprehensive, where could you have fixed a father's name with credit but on a husband? I knew Fainall to be a man lavish of his morals, an interested and professing friend, a false and a designing lover; yet one whose wit and outward fair behaviour have gained a reputation with the town enough to make that woman stand excused, who has suffered herself to be won by his addresses. A better man ought not to have been sacrificed to the occasion; a worse had not answered to the purpose. When you are weary of him, you know your remedy.

MRS. FAINALL. I ought to stand in some degree of credit with you, Mirabell.

MIRABELL. In justice to you, I have made you privy to my whole design, and put it in your power to ruin or advance my fortune.

MRS. FAINALL. Whom have you instructed to represent your pretended uncle?

MIRABELL. Waitwell, my servant.

MRS. FAINALL. He is an humble servant[23] to Foible, my mother's woman; and may win her to your interest.

MIRABELL. Care is taken for that—she is won and worn by this time. They were married this morning.

MRS. FAINALL. Who?

MIRABELL. Waitwell and Foible. I would not tempt my servant to betray me by trusting him too far. If your mother, in hopes to ruin me, should consent to marry my pretended uncle, he might like Mosca in *The Fox*,[24] stand upon terms; so I made him sure beforehand.

MRS. FAINALL. So, if my poor mother is caught in a contract, you will discover the imposture betimes; and release her by producing a certificate of her gallant's former marriage.

MIRABELL. Yes, upon condition she consent to my marriage with her niece, and surrender the moiety[25] of her fortune in her possession.

MRS. FAINALL. She talked last night of endeavouring at a match between Millamant and your uncle.

MIRABELL. That was by Foible's direction and my instruction, that she might seem to carry it more privately.

MRS. FAINALL. Well, I have an opinion of your success; for I believe my lady will do anything to get a husband; and when she has this, which you have provided for her, I suppose she will submit to anything to get rid of him.

MIRABELL. Yes, I think the good lady would marry anything that resembled a man, tho' 'twere no more than what a butler could pinch out of a napkin.

MRS. FAINALL. Female frailty! We must all come to it, if we

---

23 *an humble Servant*, suitor.
24 *Mosca* in *The Fox*, tricky servant in Ben Jonson's *Volpone*.
25 *moiety*, part.

live to be old and feel the craving of a false appetite when the true is decayed.

MIRABELL. An old woman's appetite is depraved like that of a girl—'tis the green sickness of a second childhood, and like the faint offer of a latter spring, serves but to usher in the fall, and withers in an affected bloom.

MRS. FAINALL. Here's your mistress.

(*Enter* MRS. MILLAMANT, WITWOUD, *and* MINCING.)

MIRABELL. Here she comes i'faith full sail, with her fan spread and her streamers out, and a shoal of fools for tenders. Ha, no, I cry her mercy!

MRS. FAINALL. I see but one poor empty sculler, and he tows her woman after him.

MIRABELL. You seem to be unattended, madam. You used to have the *beau-monde* throng after you, and a flock of gay fine perukes[26] hovering round you.

WITWOUD. Like moths about a candle. I had like to have lost my comparison for want of breath.

MILLIMANT. O I have denied myself airs today. I have walked as fast through the crowd—

WITWOUD. As a favourite in disgrace, and with as few followers.

MILLAMANT. Dear Mr. Witwoud, truce with your similitudes: For I am as sick of 'em—

WITWOUD. As a physician of a good air. I cannot help it madam, tho' 'tis against myself.

MILLAMANT. Yet again! Mincing, stand between me and his wit.

WITWOUD. Do Mrs. Mincing, like a screen before a great fire. I confess I do blaze today; I am too bright.

MRS. FAINALL. But dear Millamant, why were you so long?

MILLAMANT. Long! Lord, have I not made violent haste? I have asked every living thing I met for you; I have enquired after you as after a new fashion.

WITWOUD. Madam, truce with your similitudes. No, you met her husband and did not ask him for her.

MIRABELL. By your leave Witwoud, that were like enquiring after an old fashion, to ask a husband for his wife.

WITWOUD. Hum, a hit! a hit! a palpable hit! I confess it.

MRS. FAINALL. You were dressed before I came abroad.

26 *perukes*, wigs; i.e., gentlemen.

MILLAMANT. Ay, that's true. Oh, but then I had—Mincing what had I? Why was I so long?

MINCING. O mem, your la'ship stayed to peruse a pecquet of letters.

MILLAMANT. O aye, letters—I had letters—I am persecuted with letters—I hate letters. Nobody knows how to write letters; and yet one has 'em, one does not know why. They serve one to pin up one's hair.

WITWOUD. Is that the way? Pray, madam, do you pin up your hair with all your letters? I find I must keep copies.

MILLAMANT. Only with those in verse, Mr. Witwoud. I never pin up my hair with prose. I fancy one's hair would not curl if it were pinned up with prose. I think I tried once, Mincing.

MINCING. O mem, I shall never forget it.

MILLAMANT. Aye, poor Mincing tift[27] and tift all the morning.

MINCING. 'Till I had the cremp in my fingers I'll vow, mem. And all to no purpose. But when your la'ship pins it up with poetry, it sits so pleasant the next day as anything, and is so pure and so crips.

WITWOUD. Indeed, so crips?

MINCING. You're such a critic, Mr. Witwoud.

MILLAMANT. Mirabell, did not you take exceptions last night? Oh, ay, and went away. Now I think on't I'm angry—no, now I think on't I'm pleased—for I believe I gave you some pain.

MIRABELL. Does that please you?

MILLAMANT. Infinitely; I love to give pain.

MIRABELL. You would affect a cruelty which is not in your nature; your true vanity is in the power of pleasing.

MILLAMANT. O I ask your pardon for that—one's cruelty is one's power; and when one parts with one's cruelty, one parts with one's power; and when one has parted with that, I fancy one's old and ugly.

MIRABELL. Aye, aye, suffer your cruelty to ruin the object of your power, to destroy your lover—and then how vain, how lost a thing you'll be! Nay, 'tis true: you are no longer handsome when you've lost your lover; your beauty dies upon the instant, for beauty is the lover's gift. 'Tis he bestows your charms—your glass is all a cheat. The ugly and the old, whom the looking-glass

27 *tift*, i.e., tried to set Millamant's hair.

mortifies, yet after commendation can be flattered by it, and discover beauties in it; for that reflects our praises, rather than your face.

MILLAMANT. O the vanity of these men! Fainall, d'ye hear him? If they did not commend us, we were not handsome! Now you must know they could not commend one, if one was not handsome. Beauty the lover's gift! Lord, what is a lover, that it can give? Why one makes lovers as fast as one pleases, and they live as long as one pleases, and they die as soon as one pleases: and then if one pleases, one makes more.

WITWOUD. Very pretty. Why you make no more of making of lovers, madam, than of making so many card-matches.

MILLAMANT. One no more owes one's beauty to a lover, than one's wit to an echo. They can but reflect what we look and say; vain empty things if we are silent or unseen, and want a being.

MIRABELL. Yet to those two vain empty things, you owe two of the greatest pleasures of your life.

MILLAMANT. How so?

MIRABELL. To your lover you owe the pleasure of hearing yourselves praised; and to an echo the pleasure of hearing yourselves talk.

WITWOUD. But I know a lady that loves talking so incessantly, she won't give an echo fair play; she has that everlasting rotation of tongue, that an echo must wait till she dies, before it can catch her last words.

MILLAMANT. Oh, fiction! Fainall, let us leave these men.

MIRABELL. (*aside to* MRS. FAINALL). Draw off Witwoud.

MRS. FAINALL. Immediately; I have a word or two for Mr. Witwoud.

MIRABELL. I would beg a little private audience too—

(*Exit* WITWOUD *and* MRS. FAINALL.)

You had the tyranny to deny me last night; tho' you knew I came to impart a secret to you, that concerned my love.

MILLAMANT. You saw I was engaged.

MIRABELL. Unkind! You had the leisure to entertain a herd of fools; things who visit you from their excessive idleness; bestowing on your easiness that time, which is the incumbrance of their lives. How can you find delight in such society? It is impossible they should admire you; they are not capable: Or if they were, it should be to you as a mortification; for sure, to please a fool is some degree of folly.

MILLAMANT. I please myself. Besides, sometimes to converse with fools is for my health.

MIRABELL. Your health! Is there a worse disease than the conversation of fools?

MILLAMANT. Yes, the vapours; fools are physic for it, next to asafoetida.[28]

MIRABELL. You are not in a course[29] of fools?

MILLAMANT. Mirabell, If you persist in this offensive freedom you'll displease me. I think I must resolve after all, not to have you. We shan't agree.

MIRABELL. Not in our physic[30] it may be.

MILLAMANT. And yet our distemper in all likelihood will be the same; for we shall be sick of one another. I shan't endure to be reprimanded, nor instructed; 'tis so dull to act always by advice, and so tedious to be told of one's faults—I can't bear it. Well, I won't have you, Mirabell, —I'm resolv'd—I think—you may go. Ha, ha, ha. What would you give, that you could help loving me?

MIRABELL. I would give something that you did not know I could not help it.

MILLAMANT. Come, don't look grave then. Well, what do you say to me?

MIRABELL. I say that a man may as soon make a friend by his wit, or a fortune by his honesty, as win a woman with plain dealing and sincerity.

MILLAMANT. Sententious Mirabell! Prithee, don't look with that violent and inflexible wise face, like Solomon at the dividing of the child in an old tapestry-hanging.

MIRABELL. You are merry, madam, but I would persuade you for one moment to be serious.

MILLAMANT. What, with that face? No, if you keep your countenance, 'tis impossible I should hold mine. Well, after all, there is something very moving in a love-sick face. Ha, ha, ha! Well I won't laugh, don't be peevish— Heigho! Now I'll be melancholy, as melancholy as a watch-light. Well Mirabell, If ever you will win me, woo me now. Nay, if you are so tedious, fare you well;—I see they are walking away.

---

[28] *asafoetida*, medicine.
[29] *course*, prescription.
[30] *physic*, treatment.

MIRABELL. Can you not find in the variety of your disposition
one moment—

MILLAMANT. To hear you tell me that Foible's married, and
your plot like to speed? No.

MIRABELL. But how you came to know it—

MILLAMANT. Unless by the help of the Devil you can't imagine;
unless she should tell me herself. Which of the two it
may have been I will leave you to consider; and when
you have done thinking of that, think of me.

(Exit.)

MIRABELL. I have something more—gone! Think of you? To
think of a whirlwind, tho' 'twere in a whirlwind, were
a case of more steady contemplation; a very tranquility
of mind and mansion. A fellow that lives in a windmill
has not a more whimsical dwelling than the heart of a
man that is lodged in a woman. There is no point of the
compass to which they cannot turn, and by which they
are not turned; and by one as well as another; for motion, not method, is their occupation. To know this, and
yet continue to be in love, is to be made wise from the
dictates of reason, and yet persevere to play the fool by
the force of instinct—Oh, here come my pair of turtles!
What, billing so sweetly? Is not Valentine's day over with
you yet?

(Enter WAITWELL and FOIBLE.)

Sirrah, Waitwell, why, sure you think you were married
for your own recreation, and not for my conveniency.

WAITWELL. Your pardon, sir. With submission, we have indeed been solacing in lawful delights; but still with an eye
to business, sir. I have instructed her as well as I could. If
she can take your directions as readily as my instructions,
sir, your affairs are in a prosperous way.

MIRABELL. Give you joy, Mrs. Foible.

FOIBLE. Oh, 'las sir, I'm so ashamed! I'm afraid my lady has
been in a thousand inquietudes for me. But I protest,
sir, I made as much haste as I could.

WAITWELL. That she did indeed, sir. It was my fault that she
did not make more.

MIRABELL. That I believe.

FOIBLE. But I told my lady as you instructed me, sir, that I
had a prospect of seeing Sir Rowland, your uncle; and
that I would put her ladyship's picture in my pocket to

show him which I'll be sure to say has made him so enamoured of her beauty, that he burns with impatience to lie at her ladyship's feet and worship the original.

MIRABELL. Excellent, Foible! matrimony has made you eloquent in love.

WAITWELL. I think she has profited, sir. I think so.

FOIBLE. You have seen Madam Millamant, sir?

MIRABELL. Yes.

FOIBLE. I told her sir, because I did not know that you might find an opportunity; she had so much company last night.

MIRABELL. Your diligence will merit more—in the meantime—

(Gives her money)

FOIBLE. O dear sir, your humble servant.

WAITWELL. Spouse.

MIRABELL. Stand off sir, not a penny! Go on and prosper, Foible. The lease shall be made good and the farm stocked, if we succeed.

FOIBLE. I don't question your generosity, sir, and you need not doubt of success. If you have no more commands, sir, I'll be gone; I'm sure my lady is at her toilet, and can't dress till I come—(*Looking out.*) Oh, dear, I'm sure that was Mrs. Marwood that went by in a mask! If she has seen me with you I'm sure she'll tell my lady. I'll make haste home and prevent her. Your servant sir. B'w'y Waitwell.

(Exit FOIBLE.)

WAITWELL. Sir Rowland, if you please. The jade's so pert upon her preferment she forgets herself.

MIRABELL. Come sir, will you endeavour to forget yourself, and transform into Sir Rowland.

WAITWELL. Why, sir, it will be impossible I should remember myself: married, knighted and attended all in one day! 'Tis enough to make any man forget himself. The difficulty will be how to recover my acquaintance and familiarity with my former self, and fall from my transformation to a reformation into Waitwell. Nay, I shan't be quite the same Waitwell neither—for now I remember me, I am married, and can't be my own man again.

    Ay there's the grief; that's the sad change of life;
    To lose my title, and yet keep my wife.

(Exeunt.)

ACT III

[SCENE I.] *A room in* LADY WISHFORT'*s house*

(LADY WISHFORT *at her toilet,* PEG *waiting.*)

LADY WISHFORT. Merciful, no news of Foible yet?

PEG. No, madam.

LADY WISHFORT. I have no more patience. If I have not fretted myself till I am pale again, there's no veracity in me. Fetch me the red—the red, do you hear, sweetheart? An errant ash colour, as I'm a person. Look you how this wench stirs! Why dost thou not fetch me a little red? Did'st thou not hear me, Mopus?[31]

PEG. The red Ratifia does your ladyship mean, or the cherry-brandy?

LADY WISHFORT. Ratifia, fool? No, fool. Not the Ratifia, fool—Grant me patience! I mean the Spanish paper,[32] idiot, complexion, darling: paint, paint, paint! Dost thou understand that, changeling, dangling thy hands like bobbins before thee? Why dost thou not stir, puppet? Thou wooden thing upon wires!

PEG. Lord, madam, your ladyship is so impatient! I cannot come at the paint, madam; Mrs. Foible has locked it up, and carried the key with her.

LADY WISHFORT. A pox take you both! Fetch me the cherry-brandy then. (*Exit* PEG.) I'm as pale and as faint, I look like Mrs. Qualmsick, the curate's wife, that's always breeding. Wench! Come, come, wench, what art thou doing? Sipping? Tasting? Save thee, dost thou not know the bottle?

(*Enter* PEG *with a bottle and* china *cup.*)

PEG. Madam, I was looking for a cup.

LADY WISHFORT. A cup, save thee, and what a cup hast thou brought! Dost thou take me for a fairy, to drink out of an acorn? Why didst thou not bring thy thimble? Hast thou ne'er a brass thimble clinking in thy pocket with a bit of nutmeg? I warrant thee. Come, fill, fill!—So—again. (*One knocks.*) See who that is. Set down the

---

31 *Mopus,* mope, fool.
32 *Spanish paper,* paper used to apply rouge.

bottle first. Here, here, under the table. What, wouldst thou go with the bottle in thy hand like a tapster? As I'm a person, this wench has lived in an inn upon the road before she came to me, like Maritornes[33] the Asturian in *Don Quixote*. No Foible yet?

PEG. No Madam, Mrs. Marwood.

LADY WISHFORT. O Marwood; let her come in. Come in, good Marwood.

(*Enter* MRS. MARWOOD.)

MRS. MARWOOD. I'm surprised to find your ladyship in dishabille at this time of day.

LADY WISHFORT. Foible's a lost thing—has been abroad since morning, and never heard of since.

MRS. MARWOOD. I saw her but now, as I came masked through the park, in conference with Mirabell.

LADY WISHFORT. With Mirabell! You call my blood into my face, with mentioning that traitor. She durst not have the confidence. I sent her to negotiate an affair, in which if I'm detected, I'm undone. If that wheedling villain has wrought upon Foible to detect me, I'm ruined. Oh my dear friend, I'm a wretch of wretches if I'm detected.

MRS. MARWOOD. O madam, you cannot suspect Mrs. Foible's integrity.

LADY WISHFORT. O, he carries poison in his tongue that would corrupt integrity itself. If she has given him an opportunity, she has as good as put her integrity into his hands. Ah dear Marwood, what's integrity to an opportunity? Hark! I hear her—go, you thing, and send her in. (*Exit* PEG.) Dear friend retire into my closet, that I may examine her with more freedom. You'll pardon me dear friend, I can make bold with you—there are books over the chimney—Quarles and Prynne, and the *Short View of the Stage,* with Bunyan's works to entertain you.[34]

(*Exit* MARWOOD.)

(*Enter* FOIBLE.)

Oh, Foible, where hast thou been? What hast thou been doing?

---

[33] *Maritornes,* heroically ugly and stupid innkeeper's daughter in *Don Quixote.*

[34] *Quarles . . . Bunyan's works,* these are all Puritan books, evidently chosen by Lady Wishfort to decorate her room, and used only for moral appearance.

FOIBLE. Madam, I have seen the party.

LADY WISHFORT. But what hast thou done?

FOIBLE. Nay, 'tis your ladyship has done, and are to do; I have only promised. But a man so enamoured—so transported! Well, here it is, all that is left; all that is not kissed away! Well, if worshipping of pictures be a sin —poor sir Rowland, I say.

LADY WISHFORT. The miniature has been counted like—but hast thou not betrayed me, Foible? Hast thou not detected me to that faithless Mirabell? What had'st thou to do with him in the park? Answer me, has he got nothing out of thee?

FOIBLE (aside). So, the devil has been beforehand with me. What shall I say? Alas, madam, could I help it, if I met that confident thing? Was I in fault? If you had heard how he used me, and all upon your ladyship's account, I'm sure you would not suspect my fidelity. Nay, if that had been the worst I could have borne: but he had a fling at your ladyship too; and then I could not hold; but i'faith I gave him his own.

LADY WISHFORT. Me? What did the filthy fellow say?

FOIBLE. O Madam; 'tis a shame to say what he said—with his taunts and his fleers, tossing up his nose. Humh! (says he), what, you are a hatching some plot (says he), you are so early abroad, or catering (says he), ferreting for some disbanded officer, I warrant. Half-pay is but thin subsistence (says he)—well, what pension does your lady propose? Let me see (says he), what, she must come down pretty deep now, she's superannuated (says he) and—

LADY WISHFORT. Ods my life, I'll have him—I'll have him murdered! I'll have him poisoned! Where does he eat? I'll marry a drawer to have him poisoned in his wine. I'll send for Robin from Lockets[35]—immediately.

FOIBLE. Poison him? Poisoning's too good for him. Starve him, madam, starve him, marry Sir Rowland and get him disinherited. O you would bless yourself, to hear what he said.

LADY WISHFORT. A villain! Superannuated!

FOIBLE. Humh (says he) I hear you are laying designs against me too (says he), and Mrs. Millamant is to marry my uncle (he does not suspect a word of your ladyship);

---

[35] Robin from Locket's, a waiter in a fashionable tavern.

but (says he) I'll fit you for that, I warrant you (says he), I'll hamper you for that (says he) you and your old frippery[36] too (says he). I'll handle you—

LADY WISHFORT. Audacious villain! Handle me, would he durst! Frippery? old frippery! Was there ever such a foul-mouthed fellow? I'll be married tomorrow; I'll be contracted tonight.

FOIBLE. The sooner the better, madam.

LADY WISHFORT. Will Sir Rowland be here, say'st thou? when, Foible?

FOIBLE. Incontinently, madam. No new sheriff's wife expects the return of her husband after knighthood with that impatience in which Sir Rowland burns for the dear hour of kissing your ladyship's hands after dinner.

LADY WISHFORT. Frippery? Superannuated frippery? I'll frippery the villain; I'll reduce him to frippery and rags! A tatterdemallion! I hope to see him hung with tatters, like a Long Lane penthouse,[37] or a gibbet-thief. A slander-mouthed railer! I warrant the spendthrift prodigal's in debt as much as the million lottery,[38] or the whole court upon a birthday. I'll spoil his credit with his tailor. Yes, he shall have my niece with her fortune, he shall.

FOIBLE. He! I hope to see him lodge in Ludgate[39] first, and angle into Blackfriars for brass farthings with an old mitten.[40]

LADY WISHFORT. Aye, dear Foible; thank thee for that, dear Foible. He has put me out of all patience. I shall never recompose my features to receive Sir Rowland with any economy of face. This wretch has fretted me that I am absolutely decayed. Look, Foible.

FOIBLE. Your ladyship has frowned a little too rashly, indeed madam. There are some cracks discernible in the white varnish.

LADY WISHFORT. Let me see the glass. Cracks, say'st thou? Why I am arrantly flea'd[41]—I look like an old peeled wall. Thou must repair me Foible, before Sir Rowland comes; or I shall never keep up to my picture.

---

36 *old frippery,* worn-out clothes-horse.
37 *Long Lane penthouse,* used-clothing stall in Smithfield.
38 *the million lottery,* lottery of 1694.
39 *Ludgate,* debtor's prison.
40 *angle . . . old mitten,* beg for coins from his cell window.
41 *flea'd,* flayed, skinned.

FOIBLE. I warrant you, madam, a little art once made your picture like you, and now a little of the same art must make you like your picture. Your picture must sit for you, madam.

LADY WISHFORT. But art thou sure Sir Rowland will not fail to come? Or will a' not fail when he does come? Will he be importunate, Foible, and push? For if he should not be importunate, I shall never break decorums. I shall die with confusion, if I am forced to advance. Oh, no, I can never advance! I shall swoon if he should expect advances. No, I hope Sir Rowland is better bred than to put a lady to the necessity of breaking her forms. I won't be too coy neither. I won't give his despair—but a little disdain is not amiss; a little scorn is alluring.

FOIBLE. A little scorn becomes your ladyship.

LADY WISHFORT. Yes, but tenderness becomes me best—a sort of a dyingness—you see that picture has a sort of a—ha, Foible? A swimmingness in the eyes—yes, I'll look so. My niece affects it, but she wants features. Is Sir Rowland handsome? Let my toilet be removed—I'll dress above. I'll receive Sir Rowland here. Is he handsome? Don't answer me! I won't know: I'll be surprised. I'll be taken by surprise.

FOIBLE. By storm, madam. Sir Rowland's a brisk man.

LADY WISHFORT. Is he? Oh, then he'll importune, if he's a brisk man. I shall save decorums if Sir Rowland importunes. I have a mortal terror at the apprehension of offending against decorums. Nothing but importunity can surmount decorums. Oh I'm glad he's a brisk man. Let my things be removed, good Foible.   (*Exit.*)

(*Enter* MRS. FAINALL.)

MRS. FAINALL. O Foible, I have been in a fright lest I should come too late! That devil Marwood saw you in the park with Mirabell, and I'm afraid will discover it to my lady.

FOIBLE. Discover what, madam?

MRS. FAINALL. Nay, nay, put not on this strange face. I am privy to the whole design, and know that Waitwell, to whom thou wert this morning married, is to personate Mirabell's uncle, and, as such, winning my lady, to involve her in those difficulties, from which Mirabell only must release her, by his making his conditions to have my cousin and her fortune left to her own disposal.

FOIBLE. O dear madam, I beg your pardon. It was not my confidence in your ladyship that was deficient; but I thought the former good correspondence between your ladyship and Mr. Mirabell, might have hindered his communicating this secret.

MRS. FAINALL. Dear Foible forget that.

FOIBLE. O dear madam, Mr. Mirabell is such a sweet, winning gentleman—but your ladyship is the pattern of generosity. Sweet lady, to be so good! Mr. Mirabell cannot choose but be grateful. I find your ladyship has his heart still. Now, madam, I can safely tell your ladyship our success: Mrs. Marwood had told my lady; but I warrant I managed myself. I turned it all for the better. I told my lady that Mr. Mirabell railed at her. I laid horrid things to his charge, I'll vow; and my lady is so incensed, that she'll be contracted to Sir Rowland to-night, she says; I warrant I worked her up, that he may have her for asking for, as they say of a Welsh maidenhead.

MRS. FAINALL. O rare Foible!

FOIBLE. Madam, I beg your ladyship to acquaint Mr. Mirabell of his success. I would be seen as little as possible to speak to him; besides, I believe Madam Marwood watches me. She has a months's mind,[42] but I know Mr. Mirabell can't abide her. (*Enter Footman.*) John—remove my lady's toilet. Madam, your servant. My lady is so impatient, I fear she'll come for me, if I stay.

MRS. FAINALL. I'll go with you up the back stairs, lest I should meet her. (*Exeunt.*)

(*Enter* MRS. MARWOOD.)

MRS. MARWOOD. Indeed Mrs. Engine,[43] is it thus with you? Are you become a go-between of this importance? Yes, I shall watch you. Why this wench is the *passe-par-tout*, a very master-key to everybody's strong-box. My friend Fainall, have you carried it so swimmingly? I thought there was something in it; but it seems it's over with you. Your loathing is not from a want of appetite then, but from a surfeit. Else you could never be so cool to fall from a principal to be an assistant; to procure for him! A pattern of generosity, that I confess. Well, Mr. Fainall,

---

42 *a month's mind,* i.e., an eager desire for Mirabell.
43 *Engine,* artful dodger.

you have met with your match. O man, man! Woman,
woman! The Devil's an ass: if I were a painter, I would
draw him like an idiot, a driveler, with a bib and bells.
Man should have his head and horns, and woman the
rest of him. Poor simple fiend! "Madam Marwood has a
month's mind, but he can't abide her." 'Twere better for
him you had not been his confessor in that affair, without
you could have kept his counsel closer. I shall not prove
another pattern of generosity and stalk for him till he
takes his stand to aim at a fortune. He has not obliged
me to that with those excesses of himself! And now I'll
have none of him. Here comes the good lady, panting
ripe; with a heart full of hope, and a head full of care,
like any chemist upon the day of projection.[44]

(*Enter* LADY WISHFORT.)

LADY WISHFORT. O dear Marwood what shall I say, for this
rude forgetfulness? But my dear friend is all goodness.

MRS. MARWOOD. No apologies, dear madam. I have been very
well entertained.

LADY WISHFORT. As I'm a person I am in a very chaos to think
I should so forget myself—but I have such an olio[45] of
affairs really, I know not what to do. (*Calls*) Foible! I
expect my nephew Sir Wilfull every moment too.
(*Calls again*) Why, Foible!—He means to travel for improvement.

MRS. MARWOOD. Methinks Sir Wilfull should rather think of
marrying than travelling at his years. I hear he is turned
of forty.

LADY WISHFORT. O he's in less danger of being spoiled by his
travels. I am against my nephew's marrying too young.
It will be time enough when he comes back, and has
acquired discretion to choose for himself.

MRS. MARWOOD. Methinks Mrs. Millamant and he would
make a very fit match. He may travel afterwards. 'Tis a
thing very usual with young gentlemen.

LADY WISHFORT. I promise you I have thought on't—and since
'tis your judgment, I'll think on't again. I assure you I
will; I value your judgment extremely. On my word,
I'll propose it.

(*Enter* FOIBLE.)

[44] *projection*, process of turning lead into gold.
[45] *olio*, stew.

Come, come Foible—I had forgot my nephew will be here before dinner. I must make haste.

FOIBLE. Mr. Witwoud and Mr. Petulant, are come to dine with your ladyship.

LADY WISHFORT. Oh, dear, I can't appear till I'm dressed. Dear Marwood shall I be free with you again, and beg you to entertain 'em? I'll make all imaginable haste. Dear friend, excuse me.   (*Exit* LADY WISHFORT *and* FOIBLE.)

(*Enter* MRS. MILLAMANT *and* MINCING.)

MILLAMANT. Sure never anything was so unbred as that odious man—Marwood, your servant.

MRS. MARWOOD. You have a colour, what's the matter?

MILLAMANT. That horrid fellow, Petulant, has provoked me into a flame. I have broke my fan. Mincing, lend me yours;—Is not all the powder out of my hair?

MRS. MARWOOD. No, what has he done?

MILLAMANT. Nay, he has done nothing; he has only talked— Nay, he has said nothing neither; but he has contradicted everything that has been said. For my part, I thought Witwoud and he would have quarrelled.

MINCING. I vow Mem, I thought once they would have fit.

MILLAMANT. Well, 'tis a lamentable thing, I'll swear, that one has not the liberty of choosing one's acquaintance, as one does one's clothes.

MRS. MARWOOD. If we had the liberty, we should be as weary of one set of acquaintance, tho' never so good, as we are of one suit, tho' never so fine. A fool and a doily stuff[46] would now and then find days of grace, and be worn for variety.

MILLAMANT. I could consent to wear 'em, if they would wear alike; but fools never wear out—they are such *drap-du-Berry*[47] things! Without one could give 'em to one's chambermaid after a day or two!

MRS. MARWOOD. 'Twere better so indeed. Or what think you of the playhouse? A fine, gay, glossy fool should be given there, like a new masking habit, after the masquerade is over and we have done with the disguise. For a fool's visit is always a disguise, and never admitted by a woman of wit but to blind her affair with a lover of sense. If you would but appear bare faced now, and own Mirabell,

46 *doily stuff*, cheap cloth.
47 *drap-du-Berry*, heavy woolens.

you might as easily put off Petulant and Witwoud as
your hood and scarf. And indeed 'tis time, for the town
has found it; the secret is grown too big for the pretence. 'Tis like Mrs. Primly's great belly; she may lace it
down before, but it burnishes[48] on her hips. Indeed,
Millimant, you can no more conceal it than my Lady
Strammel can her face, that goodly face, which, in
defiance of her Rhenish-wine tea,[49] will not be compre-
hended in a mask.

MILLAMANT. I'll take my death, Marwood, you are more censorious than a decayed beauty, or a discarded toast.
Mincing, tell the men they may come up. My aunt is not
dressing here; their folly is less provoking than your
malice. "The town has found it." (*Exit* MINCING.) What
has it found? That Mirabell loves me is no more a secret
than it is a secret that you discovered it to my aunt, or
than the reason why you discovered it is a secret.

MRS. MARWOOD. You are nettled.

MILLAMANT. You're mistaken. Ridiculous!

MRS. MARWOOD. Indeed my dear, you'll tear another fan, if
you don't mitigate those violent airs.

MILLAMANT. Oh, silly! Ha, ha, ha! I could laugh immoderately.
Poor Mirabell! his constancy to me has quite destroyed
his complaisance for all the world beside. I swear, I never
enjoined it him, to be so coy. If I had the vanity to think
he would obey me; I would command him to show more
gallantry 'tis hardly well bred to be so particular on one
hand, and so insensible on the other. But I despair to
prevail, and so let him follow his own way. Ha, ha, ha!
Pardon me, dear creature, I must laugh, ha, ha, ha!
tho' I grant you 'tis a little barbarous, Ha, ha, ha!

MRS. MARWOOD. What pity 'tis, so much fine Raillery and
delivered with so significant gesture, should be so un-
happily directed to miscarry.

MILLAMANT. Ha? Dear creature, I ask your pardon—I swear
I did not mind you.

MRS. MARWOOD. Mr. Mirabell and you both may think it a
thing impossible, when I shall tell him by telling you—

MILLAMANT. Oh dear, what? for it is the same thing, if I
hear it—Ha, ha, ha!

---

48 *burnishes,* spreads out.
49 *Rhenish-wine tea,* possibly a mixture of white wine and tea, or
thin tea.

MRS. MARWOOD. That I detest him, hate him, madam.

MILLAMANT. Oh madam, why so do I—and yet the creature loves me, ha, ha, ha! How can one forbear laughing to think of it? I am a sybil if I am not amazed to think what he can see in me. I'll take my death, I think you are handsomer—and within a year or two as young. If you could but stay for me, I should overtake you—but that cannot be.—Well, that thought makes me melancholy. Now I'll be sad.

MRS. MARWOOD. Your merry note may be changed sooner than you think.

MILLAMANT. D'ye say so? Then I'm resolved I'll have a song to keep up my spirits.

(*Enter* MINCING.)

MINCING. The gentlemen stay but to comb, madam, and will wait on you.

MILLAMANT. Desire Mrs.—that is in the next room to sing the song I would have learned yesterday. You shall hear it, madam—not that there's any great matter in it, but 'tis agreeable to my humour.

SONG.

Set by MR. JOHN ECCLES *and sung by* MRS. HODGSON

I.

Love's but the frailty of the mind,
   When 'tis not with ambition joined;
A sickly flame, which if not fed, expires;
And feeding, wastes in self-consuming fires.

II.

'Tis not to wound a wanton boy
   Or amorous youth, that gives the joy;
But 'tis the glory to have pierced a swain,
For whom inferiour beauties sighed in vain.

III.

Then I alone the conquest prize
   When I insult a rival's eyes:
If there's delight in love, 'tis when I see
That heart which others bleed for, bleed for me.

(*Enter* PETULANT *and* WITWOUD.)

MILLAMANT. Is your animosity composed, gentlemen?

WITWOUD. Raillery, raillery, madam, we have no animosity—
we hit off a little wit now and then, but no animosity.
The falling out of wits is like the falling out of lovers.
We agree in the main, like treble and bass. Ha, Petulant?

PETULANT. Ay in the main—but when I have a humour to
contradict.—

WITWOUD. Aye, when he has a humour to contradict, then I
contradict too. What! I know my cue. Then we contradict one another like two battledoers; for contradictions
beget one another like Jews.

PETULANT. If he says black's black—if I have a humour to
say 'tis blue—let that pass—all's one for that. If I have
a humour to prove it, it must be granted.

WITWOUD. Not positively must—but it may—it may.

PETULANT. Yes, it positively must, upon proof positive.

WITWOUD. Ay, upon proof positive it must; but upon proof
presumptive it only may. That's a logical distinction now,
madam.

MRS. MARWOOD. I perceive your debates are of importance and
very learnedly handled.

PETULANT. Importance is one thing, and learning's another.
But a debate's a debate, that I assert.

WITWOUD. Petulant's an enemy to learning; he relies altogether on his parts.

PETULANT. No, I'm no enemy to learning; it hurts not me.

MRS. MARWOOD. That's a sign indeed it's no enemy to you.

PETULANT. No, no, it's no enemy to anybody but them that
have it.

MILLAMANT. Well, an illiterate man's my aversion. I wonder
at the impudence of any illiterate man to offer to make
love.

WITWOUD. That I confess I wonder at too.

MILLAMANT. Ah! to marry an ignorant that can hardly read
or write.

PETULANT. Why should a man be ever the further from being
married tho' he can't read, any more than he is from
being hanged? The ordinary's paid for setting the
psalm,[50] and the parish priest for reading the ceremony.
And for the rest which is to follow in both cases, a man
may do it without book—so all's one for that.

---

[50] The . . . psalm, i.e., the prison chaplain at an execution.

MILLAMANT. D'ye hear the creature? Lord, here's company, I'll be gone.   (*Exeunt* MILLAMANT *and* MINCING.)

WITWOUD. In the name of Bartlemew and his fair,[51] what have we here?

MRS. MARWOOD. 'Tis your brother, I fancy. Don't you know him?

WITWOUD. Not I. Yes, I think it is he. I've almost forgot him; I have not seen him since the Revolution.[52]

(*Enter* SIR WILFULL WITWOUD *in a country riding habit, and Servant to* LADY WISHFORT.)

SERVANT. Sir, my lady's dressing. Here's company; if you please to walk in, in the mean time.

SIR WILFULL. Dressing! What, it's but morning here I warrant with you in London; we should count it towards afternoon in our parts, down in Shropshire. Why, then, belike my aunt han't dined yet,—ha, friend?

SERVANT. Your aunt, sir?

SIR WILFULL. My aunt sir, yes my aunt sir, and your lady sir; your lady is my aunt, sir. Why, what! do'st thou not know me, friend? Why then send somebody here that does. How long has thou lived with thy lady, fellow, ha?

SERVANT. A week, sir; longer than anybody in the house, except my lady's woman.

SIR WILFULL. Why then belike thou dost not know thy lady, if thou see'st her, ha friend?

SERVANT. Why truly sir, I cannot safely swear to her face in a morning, before she is dressed. 'Tis like I may give a shrewd guess at her by this time.

SIR WILFULL. Well prithee try what thou can'st do; if thou can'st not guess, enquire her out, do'st hear, fellow? And tell her, her nephew, Sir Wilfull Witwoud is in the house.

SERVANT. I shall, sir.

SIR WILFULL. Hold ye, hear me friend; a word with you in your ear. Prithee, who are these gallants?

SERVANT. Really sir, I can't tell; here come so many here, 'tis hard to know 'em all.   (*Exit Servant.*)

---

51 *fair*, the famous Smithfield event best described by Ben Jonson in his *Bartholomew Fair*.
52 *the Revolution*, of 1688, when the Stuart James II was dethroned.

SIR WILFULL. Oons[53] this fellow knows less than a starling; I don't think a' knows his own name.

MRS. MARWOOD. Mr. Witwoud, your brother is not behind hand in forgetfulness—I fancy he has forgot you too.

WITWOUD. I hope so—the devil take him that remembers first, I say.

SIR WILFULL. Save you gentlemen and lady.

MRS. MARWOOD. For shame Mr. Witwoud; why won't you speak to him? And you, sir.

WITWOUD. Petulant, speak.

PETULANT. And you, sir.

SIR WILFULL. No offence, I hope.   (*Salutes*[54] MRS. MARWOOD.)

MRS. MARWOOD. No, sure, sir.

WITWOUD. This is a vile dog, I see that already. No offence! Ha, ha, ha, to him; to him Petulant, smoke him.[55]

PETULANT. It seems as if you had come a journey, sir; hem, hem.   (*Surveying him round*.)

SIR WILFULL. Very likely, sir, that it may seem so.

PETULANT. No offence, I hope, sir.

WITWOUD. Smoke[56] the boots, the boots; Petulant, the boots; Ha, ha, ha.

SIR WILFULL. May be not, sir; thereafter as 'tis meant, sir.

PETULANT. Sir, I presume upon the information of your boots.

SIR WILFULL. Why, 'tis like you may, sir: If you are not satisfied with the information of my boots, sir, if you will step to the stable, you may enquire further of my horse, sir.

PETULANT. Your horse, sir! Your horse is an ass, sir!

SIR WILFULL. Do you speak by way of offence, sir?

MRS. MARWOOD. The gentleman's merry, that's all, sir— 'slife, we shall have a quarrel betwixt an horse and an ass, before they find one another out. You must not take any thing amiss from your friends, sir. You are among your friends here, tho' it may be you don't know it—If I am not mistaken, you are Sir Wilfull Witwoud.

SIR WILFULL. Right, lady; I am Sir Wilfull Witwoud, so I write myself; no offence to anybody, I hope; and nephew to the Lady Wishfort, of this mansion.

MRS. MARWOOD. Don't you know this gentleman, sir?

---

[53] *Oons, oath*, "by God's wounds."
[54] *Salutes*, kisses, a customary way of greeting at that time.
[55] *smoke him*, put him down.
[56] *Smoke*, take a gander at.

SIR WILFULL. Hum! What, sure 'tis not—yea, by'r Lady, but 'tis—'sheart, I know not whether 'tis or no—yea but 'tis, by the Rekin[57] brother Anthony! What, Tony, i'faith! What, dost thou not know me? By'r Lady, nor I thee, thou art so be-cravated, and be-periwigged—'sheart why dost not speak? Art thou o'er-joyed?

WITWOUD. Odso, brother, is it you? Your servant, brother.

SIR WILFULL. Your servant! Why, yours, sir. Your servant again—'sheart, and your friend and servant to that— And a—(puff) and a flap-dragon[58] for your service, sir: And a hare's foot, and a hare's scut[59] for your service, sir; an you be so cold and so courtly!

WITWOUD. No offence, I hope, brother.

SIR WILFULL. 'Sheart sir, but there is, and much offence!— A pox, is this your Inns o' Court breeding, not to know your friends and your relations, your elders, and your betters?

WITWOUD. Why, brother Wilfull of Salop,[60] you may be as short as a Shrewsbury cake, if you please. But I tell you, 'tis not modish to know relations in town. You think you're in the country, where great lubberly brothers slabber and kiss one another when they meet, like a call of serjeants[61]—'tis not the fashion here; 'tis not indeed, dear brother.

SIR WILFULL. The fashion's a fool; and you're a fop, dear brother. 'Sheart, I've suspected this—by'r Lady I conjectured you were a fop, since you began to change the style of your letters, and write in a scrap of paper gilt round the edges, no broader than a subpoena. I might expect this, when you left off "Honoured Brother," and "hoping you are in good health," and so forth—to begin with a "Rat me, knight, I'm so sick of a last night's debauch—Oods heart," and then tell a familiar tale of a cock and a bull, and a whore and a bottle, and so conclude. You could write news before you were out of your time, when you lived with honest Pumple Nose the attorney of Furnival's Inn—You could intreat to be remembered then to your friends round the Rekin. We

57 *Rekin*, a hill in Shropshire.
58 *flap-Dragon*, raisin, i.e., something without much value.
59 *scut*, tail.
60 *Salop*, Shropshire.
61 *a call of serjeants*, group of newly appointed sergeants-at-law.

could have gazettes then, and Dawk's letter,[62] and the
Weekly Bill,[63] 'till of late days.

PETULANT. 'Slife, Witwoud, were you ever an attorney's clerk?
Of the family of the Furnivals. Ha, ha, ha!

WITWOUD. Ay, ay, but that was for a while—not long, not
long. Pshaw! I was not in my own power then. An orphan,
and this fellow was my guardian. Ay, ay, I was glad to
consent to that man to come to London. He had the
disposal of me then. If I had not agreed to that, I might
have been bound prentice to a felt-maker in Shrewsbury;
this fellow would have bound me to a maker of felts.

SIR WILFULL. 'Sheart, and better than to be bound to a maker
of fops; where, I suppose, you have served your time,
and now you may set up for yourself.

MRS. MARWOOD. You intend to travel, sir, as I'm informed.

SIR WILFULL. Belike I may Madam. I may chance to sail upon
the salt seas, if my mind hold.

PETULANT. And the wind serve.

SIR WILFULL. Serve or not serve, I shan't ask license of you,
sir; nor the weathercock your companion. I direct my
discourse to the lady, sir: 'Tis like my aunt may have
told you, madam—Yes, I have settled my concerns, I may
say now, and am minded to see foreign parts. If an' how
that the peace holds, whereby, that is, taxes abate.

MRS. MARWOOD. I thought you had designed for France at all
adventures.

SIR WILFULL. I can't tell that; 'tis like I may, and 'tis like I
may not. I am somewhat dainty in making a resolution,
because when I make it I keep it. I don't stand shill I,
shall I, then; if I say't, I'll do't: but I have thoughts to
tarry a small matter in town, to learn somewhat of your
lingo first, before I cross the seas. I'd gladly have a
spice of your French as they say, whereby to hold discourse in foreign countries.

MRS. MARWOOD. Here is an academy in town for that use.

SIR WILFULL. There is? 'Tis like there may.

MRS. MARWOOD. No doubt you will return very much improved.

WITWOUD. Yes, refined, like a Dutch skipper from a whale-
fishing.

---

[62] *Dawk's Letter,* a weekly news summary.
[63] *the Weekly Bill,* list of deaths in London, best known to us from the
plague years.

(*Enter* LADY WISHFORT *and* FAINALL.)

LADY WISHFORT. Nephew, you are welcome.

SIR WILFULL. Aunt, your servant.

FAINALL. Sir Wilfull, your most faithful servant.

SIR WILFULL. Cousin Fainall, give me your hand.

LADY WISHFORT. Cousin Witwoud, your servant; Mr. Petulant, your servant. Nephew, you are welcome again. Will you drink anything after your journey, nephew, before you eat? Dinner's almost ready.

SIR WILFULL. I'm very well I thank you aunt—however, I thank you for your courteous offer. 'Sheart, I was afraid you would have been in the fashion too, and have remembered to have forgot your relations. Here's your cousin Tony, belike, I mayn't call him brother for fear of offence.

LADY WISHFORT. O he's a railler, nephew—my cousin's a wit. And your great wits always rally their best friends to choose. When you have been abroad, nephew, you'll understand raillery better.

(FAINALL *and* MRS. MARWOOD *talk apart.*)

SIR WILFULL. Why then let him hold his tongue in the meantime; and rail when that day comes.

(*Enter* MINCING.)

MINCING. Mem, I come to acquaint your layship that dinner is impatient.

SIR WILFULL. Impatient? Why then belike it won't stay, 'till I pull off my boots. Sweetheart, can you help me to a pair of slippers? My man's with his horses. I warrant.

LADY WISHFORT. Fie, fie, nephew, you would not pull off your boots here! Go down into the hall—dinner shall stay for you. My nephew's a little unbred, you'll pardon him, madam. Gentlemen will you walk? Marwood—

MRS. MARWOOD. I'll follow you, madam—Before Sir Wilfull is ready.

(*Manent* MRS. MARWOOD *and* FAINALL.)

FAINALL. Why then Foible's a bawd, an arrant, rank, matchmaking bawd, and I, it seems, am a husband, a rankhusband; and my wife a very arrant, rank wife—all in the way of the world. 'Sdeath to be an anticipated cuckold, a cuckold in embryo! Sure, I was born with budding antlers like a young satyr, or a citizen's child.[64] 'Sdeath! to be outwitted, to be out-jilted—out-matrimony'd! If I had kept my speed like a stag, 'twere somewhat—but to crawl after with my horns like a snail, and out-stripped by my wife—'tis scurvy wedlock.

MRS. MARWOOD. Then shake it off. You have often wished for an opportunity to part, and now you have it. But first prevent their plot—the half of Millamant's fortune is too considerable to be parted with to a foe, to Mirabell.

FAINALL. Damn him! that had been mine had you not made that fond discovery. That had been forfeited, had they been married. My wife had added lustre to my horns by that increase of fortune; I could have worn 'em tipped with gold, tho' my forehead had been furnished like a deputy-lieutenant's hall.[65]

MRS. MARWOOD. They may prove a cap of maintenance[66] to you still, if you can away with your wife. And she's no worse than when you had her—I dare swear she had given up her game before she was married.

FAINALL. Hum! That may be—she might throw up her cards; but I'll be hanged if she did not put Pam[67] in her pocket.

MRS. MARWOOD. You married her to keep you; and if you can contrive to have her keep you better than you expected; why should you not keep her longer than you intended?

FAINALL. The means, the means.

MRS. MARWOOD. Discover to my lady your wife's conduct; threaten to part with her. My lady loves her, and will come to any composition to save her reputation. Take the opportunity of breaking it, just upon the discovery of this imposture. My lady will be enraged beyond bounds, and sacrifice niece, and fortune, and all, at that conjuncture. And let me alone to keep her warm; if she should flag in her part, I will not fail to prompt her.

FAINALL. Faith, this has an appearance.

MRS. MARWOOD. I'm sorry I hinted to my lady to endeavour a match between Millamant and Sir Wilfull; that may be an obstacle.

---

[64] *a citizen's child,* i.e., a London merchant.
[65] *like a deputy-lieutenant's hall,* i.e., covered with antlers.
[66] *cap of maintenance,* heraldic cap, with horns on it but symbolizing dignity.
[67] *Pam,* the knave of clubs.

FAINALL. Oh, for that matter, leave me to manage him; I'll disable him for that, he will drink like a Dane: after dinner, I'll set his hand in.

MRS. MARWOOD. Well, how do you stand affected towards your lady?

FAINALL. Why faith I'm thinking of it. Let me see—I am married already; so that's over. My wife had played the jade with me—well, that's over too. I never loved her, or if I had, why that would have been over too by this time. Jealous of her I cannot be, for I am certain; so there's an end of jealousy. Weary of her, I am, and shall be—No, there's no end of that; no, no, that were too much to hope. Thus far concerning my repose; now for my reputation. As to my own, I married not for it; so that's out of the question; and as to my part in my wife's—why she had parted with hers before; so bringing none to me, she can take none from me, 'tis against all rule of play that I should lose to one who has not wherewithal to stake.

MRS. MARWOOD. Besides, you forget, marriage is honourable.

FAINALL. Hum! Faith, and that's well thought on; marriage is honourable as you say; and if so, wherefore should cuckoldom be a discredit, being derived from so honourable a root?

MRS. MARWOOD. Nay I know not; if the root be honourable, why not the branches?

FAINALL. So, so; why this point's clear. Well how do we proceed?

MRS. MARWOOD. I will contrive a letter which shall be delivered to my lady at the time when that rascal who is to act Sir Rowland is with her. It shall come as from an unknown hand—for the less I appear to know of the truth the better I can play the incendiary. Besides, I would not have Foible provoked if I could help it,—because you know she knows some passages—nay I expect all will come out. But let the mine[68] be sprung first, and then I care not if I'm discovered.

FAINALL. If the worst come to the worst, I'll turn my wife to grass. I have already a deed of settlement of the best part of her estate which I wheedled out of her and that you shall partake at least.

68 *mine*, explosive.

MRS. MARWOOD. I hope you are convinced that I hate Mirabell,
    now you'll be no more jealous.

FAINALL. Jealous! No, by this kiss. Let husbands be jealous,
    but let the lover still believe. Or if he doubt, let it be only
    to endear his pleasure, and prepare the joy that follows
    when he proves his mistress true. But let husbands' doubts
    convert to endless jealousy; or, if they have belief, let it
    corrupt to superstition and blind credulity. I am single;
    and will herd no more with 'em. True, I wear the badge;
    but I'll disown the order. And since I take my leave of
    'em, I care not if I leave 'em a common motto to their
    common crest.

>   All husbands must, or pain, or shame, endure;
>   The wise too jealous are, fools too secure.

                                                    (*Exeunt.*)

ACT IV

[SCENE I.] *Scene continues.*

(*Enter* LADY WISHFORT *and* FOIBLE.)

LADY WISHFORT. Is Sir Rowland coming, sayest thou, Foible?
    and are things in order?

FOIBLE. Yes, madam. I have put wax lights in the sconces;
    and placed the footmen in a row in the hall, in their
    best liveries, with the coachman and postilion to fill up
    the equipage.

LADY WISHFORT. Have you pullvilled[69] the coachman and
    postilion, that they may not stink of the stable when Sir
    Rowland comes by?

FOIBLE. Yes, madam.

LADY WISHFORT. And are the dancers and the music ready,
    that he may be entertained in all points with correspon-
    dence to his passion?

FOIBLE. All is ready, madam.

LADY WISHFORT. And—well—and how do I look, Foible?

FOIBLE. Most killing well, madam.

---

69 *pullvilled,* applied aromatic powder or pulvilio.

LADY WISHFORT. Well, and how shall I receive him? In what figure shall I give his heart the first impression? There is a great deal in the first impression. Shall I sit?—no, I won't sit—I'll walk—aye, I'll walk from the door upon his entrance, and then turn full upon him—no, that will be too sudden. I'll lie—aye, I'll lie down—I'll receive him in my little dressing-room; there's a couch—Yes, yes, I'll give the first impression on a couch. I won't lie neither but loll and lean upon one elbow, with one foot a little dangling off, jogging in a thoughtful way—yes—and then as soon as he appears, start, aye, start and be surprised, and rise to meet him in a pretty disorder—Yes. Oh, nothing is more alluring than a levee from a couch in some confusion—it shows the foot to advantage, and furnishes with blushes, and recomposing airs beyond comparison. Hark! There's a coach.

FOIBLE. 'Tis he, madam.

LADY WISHFORT. Oh, dear, has my nephew made his addresses to Millamant? I ordered him.

FOIBLE. Sir Wilfull is set in to drinking, madam, in the parlour.

LADY WISHFORT. Ods my life, I'll send him to her. Call her down, Foible; bring her hither. I'll send him as I go—when they are together, then come to me, Foible, that I may not be too long alone with Sir Rowland.

(*Enter* MRS. MILLAMANT, *and* MRS. FAINALL.)

FOIBLE. Madam, I stayed here, to tell your ladyship that Mr. Mirabell has waited this half-hour for an opportunity to talk with you, tho' my lady's orders were to leave you and Sir Wilfull together. Shall I tell Mr. Mirabell that you are at leisure?

MILLAMANT. No. What would the dear man have? I am thoughtful and would amuse myself. Bid him come another time.

(*Repeating and walking about.*)

There never yet was woman made,
   Nor shall but to be cursed.[70]

That's hard!

MRS. FAINALL. You are very fond of Sir John Suckling today, Millamant, and the Poets.

[70] From a lyric of Sir John Suckling.

MILLAMANT. He? Aye, and filthy verses—So I am.

FOIBLE. Sir Wilfull is coming, madam. Shall I send Mr. Mirabell away?

MILLAMANT. Ay, if you please, Foible, send him away, Or send him hither,—just as you will, dear Foible. I think I'll see him—Shall I? Aye, let the wretch come.

(*Repeating.*) Thyrsis a youth of the inspired train—[71]

Dear Fainall, entertain Sir Wilfull—thou hast philosophy to undergo a fool, thou art married and hast patience—I would confer with my own thoughts.

MRS. FAINALL. I am obliged to you, that you would make me your proxy in this affair; but I have business of my own.

(*Enter* SIR WILFULL.)

O Sir Wilfull; you are come at the critical instant. There's your mistress up to the ears in love and contemplation, pursue your point, now or never.

SIR WILFULL. Yes; my aunt would have it so. I would gladly have been encouraged with a bottle or two, because I'm somewhat wary at first, before I am acquainted. But I hope after a time, I shall break my mind—that is upon further acquaintance. So for the present, cousin, I'll take my leave—If so be you'll be so kind to make my excuse, I'll return to my company—

(*This while* MILLAMANT *walks about repeating to herself.*)

MRS. FAINALL. O fie Sir Wilfull! What, you must not be daunted.

SIR WILFULL. Daunted! No, that's not it, it is not so much for that—for if so be that I set on't, I'll do't. But only for the present, 'tis sufficient till further acquaintance, that's all— your servant.

MRS. FAINALL. Nay, I'll swear you shall never lose so favourable an opportunity, if I can help it. I'll leave you together and lock the door.

(*Exit.*)

SIR WILFULL. Nay, nay, cousin,—I have forgot my gloves— What d'ye do? 'Sheart, a'has locked the door indeed, I think—Nay, cousin Fainall, open the door! Pshaw, what a vixen trick is this?—Nay, now a'has seen me too.

---

[71] From a lyric of Edmund Waller.

Cousin, I made bold to pass thro' as it were,—I think this door's enchanted—.

MILLAMANT (*Repeating*)

> I prithee spare me, gentle boy,
> Press me no more for that slight toy.

SIR WILFULL. Anan?[72] Cousin, your servant.

MILLAMANT.—That foolish trifle of a heart—Sir Wilfull!

SIR WILFULL. Yes,—your servant. No offence I hope, cousin.

MILLAMANT (*Repeating*)

> I swear it will not do its part,
> Tho' thou do'st thine, employ'st thy power and art.

Natural, easy suckling!

SIR WILFULL. Anan? Suckling? No such suckling neither, cousin, nor stripling: I thank Heaven, I'm no minor.

MILLAMANT. Ah rustic! ruder than Gothic.

SIR WILFULL. Well, well, I shall understand your lingo one of these days, cousin, in the meanwhile, I must answer in plain English.

MILLAMANT. Have you any business with me, Sir Wilfull?

SIR WILFULL. Not at present, cousin. Yes, I made bold to see, to come and know if that how you were disposed to fetch a walk this evening, if so be that I might not be troublesome, I would have sought a walk with you.

MILLAMANT. A walk? What then?

SIR WILFULL. Nay, nothing—only for the walk's sake, that's all—

MILLAMANT. I nauseate walking; 'tis a country diversion, I loath the country and everything that relates to it.

SIR WILFULL. Indeed! Hah! Look ye, look ye, you do? Nay, 'tis like you may—here are choice of pastimes here in town as plays and the like that must be confessed indeed.

MILLAMANT. Ah l' etourdie![73] I hate the town too.

SIR WILFULL. Dear heart, that's much—Hah! that you should hate 'em both! Hah, 'tis like you may; there are some can't relish the town, and others can't away with the country—'tis like you may be one of those, cousin.

MILLAMANT. Ha, ha, ha! Yes, 'tis like I may. You have nothing further to say to me?

---

[72] *Anan?*, What?
[73] *Ah l' etourdie*, what a blunder.

SIR WILFULL. Not at present, cousin. 'Tis like when I have an opportunity to be more private, I may break my mind in some measure—I conjecture you partly guess—however that's as time shall try—but spare to speak and spare to speed, as they say.

MILLAMANT. If it is of no great importance, Sir Wilfull, you will oblige me to leave me: I have just now a little business.—

SIR WILFULL. Enough, enough, cousin, Yes, yes, all a case—When you're disposed, when you're disposed. Now's as well as another time; and another time as well as now. All's one for that,—yes, yes, if your concerns call you, there's no haste; it will keep cold as they say,—cousin, your servant—I think this door's locked.

MILLAMANT. You may go this way, sir.

SIR WILFULL. Your servant, then with your leave I'll return to my company.

(*Exit.*)

MILLAMANT. Aye, aye, ha, ha, ha!

Like Phœbus sung the no less am'rous boy.[74]

MIRABELL. Like Daphne she as lovely and as coy.[75] Do you lock yourself up from me, to make my search more curious? Or is this pretty artifice contrived to signify that here the chase must end, and my pursuit be crowned? For you can fly no further.—

MILLAMANT. Vanity! No—I'll fly and be followed to the last moment. Tho' I am upon the very verge of matrimony, I expect you should solicit me as much as if I were wavering at the gate of a monastery, with one foot over the threshold. I'll be solicited to the very last,—nay, and afterwards.

MIRABELL. What, after the last?

MILLAMANT. O, I should think I was poor and had nothing to bestow, if I were reduced to an inglorious ease and freed from the agreeable fatigues of solicitation.

MIRABELL. But do not you know that when favours are conferred upon instant and tedious solicitation, that they diminish in their value, and that both the giver loses the grace, and the receiver lessens his pleasure?

MILLAMANT. It may be in things of common application; but

---

[74] See note 71.
[75] Mirabell caps the quotation from Waller, completing the couplet.

never sure in love. Oh, I hate a lover that can dare to think he draws a moment's air, independent of the bounty of his mistress. There is not so impudent a thing in nature as the saucy look of an assured man, confident of success. The pedantic arrogance of a very husband has not so pragmatical an air. Ah! I'll never marry, unless I am first made sure of my will and pleasure.

MIRABELL. Would you have 'em both before marriage? Or will you be contented with the first now, and stay for the other till after grace?

MILLAMANT. Ah don't be impertinent—my dear liberty, shall I leave thee? My faithful solitude, my darling contemplation, must I bid you then adieu? Ay-h adieu—my morning thoughts, agreeable wakings, indolent slumbers, all ye *douceurs*, ye *someils du matin*,[76] adieu. I can't do't, 'tis more than impossible. Positively, Mirabell, I'll lie abed in a morning as long as I please.

MIRABELL. Then I'll get up in a morning as early as I please.

MILLAMANT. Ah! Idle creature, get up when you will—and d'ye hear, I won't be call'd names after I'm married; positively I won't be call'd names.

MIRABELL. Names!

MILLAMANT. Ay as wife, spouse, my dear, joy, jewel, love, sweetheart and the rest of that nauseous cant, in which men and their wives are so fulsomely familiar—I shall never bear that. Good Mirabell, don't let us be familiar or fond, nor kiss before folks, like my Lady Fadler and Sir Francis; nor go to Hyde Park together the first Sunday in a new chariot, to provoke eyes and whispers; and then never to be seen there together again; as if we were proud of one another the first week, and ashamed of one another forever after. Let us never visit together, nor go to a play together; but let us be very strange and well-bred: let us be as strange as if we had been married a great while; and as well-bred as if we were not married at all.

MIRABELL. Have you any more conditions to offer? Hitherto your demands are pretty reasonable.

MILLAMANT. Trifles,—as liberty to pay and receive visits to and from whom I please; to write and receive letters, without interrogatories or wry faces on your part. To wear what I please; and choose conversation with regard only to my own taste; to have no obligation upon me to

---

[76] *douceurs ... someils du matin*, idle pleasures.

converse with wits that I don't like, because they are your
acquaintance; or to be intimate with fools, because they
may be your relations. Come to dinner when I please,
dine in my dressing-room when I'm out of humour, without giving a reason. To have my closet inviolate; to be
sole empress of my tea-table, which you must never
presume to approach without first asking leave. And
lastly, wherever I am, you shall always knock at the door
before you come in. These articles subscribed, if I continue to endure you a little longer, I may by degrees
dwindle into a wife.

MIRABELL. Your bill of fare is something advanced in this
latter account. Well, have I liberty to offer conditions—
that when you are dwindled into a wife, I may not be
beyond measure enlarged into a husband?

MILLAMANT. You have free leave; propose your utmost, speak
and spare not.

MIRABELL. I thank you. *Imprimis* then, I covenant that your
acquaintance be general; that you admit no sworn confidence, or intimate of your own sex, no she-friend to screen
her affairs under your countenance and tempt you to
make trial of a mutual secrecy. No decoy-duck to wheedle you a fop—scrambling to the play in a mask—then
bring you home in a pretended fright, when you think
you shall be found out, and rail at me for missing the
play, and disappointing the frolic which you had, to pick
me up and prove my constancy.

MILLAMANT. Detestable *Imprimis!* I go to the play in a mask!

MIRABELL. *Item,* I article that you continue to like your own
face as long as I shall; and while it passes current with
me, that you endeavour not to new-coin it. To which end,
together with all vizards for the day, I prohibit all masks
for the night, made of oiled skins and I know not what—
hog's-bones, hare's-gall, pig-water, and the marrow of a
roasted cat. In short, I forbid all commerce with the
gentlewoman in what-d'ye-call-it-Court. *Item,* I shut my
doors against all bawds with baskets and penny-worths of
*muslin, china, fans, atlases,*⁷⁷—*Item,* when you shall be
breeding—

MILLAMANT. Ah! name it not.

MIRABELL. Which may be presumed, with a blessing on our
endeavours—

MILLAMANT. Odious endeavours!

MIRABELL. I denounce against all strait-lacing, squeezing for a shape, till you mold my boy's head like a sugar-loaf; and instead of a man-child, make me the father to a crooked-billet. Lastly to the dominion of the tea-table, I submit. But with proviso, that you exceed not in your province; but restrain your self to native and simple tea-table drinks, as tea, chocolate and coffee. As likewise to genuine and authorized tea-table talk,—such as mending of fashions, spoiling reputations, railing at absent friends, and so forth—but that on no account you encroach upon the men's prerogative, and presume to drink healths, or toast fellows; for prevention of which; I banish all foreign forces, all auxiliaries to the tea-table, as orange-brandy, all aniseed, cinnamon, citron and barbados-waters, together with ratifia and the most noble spirit of clary,[78]—but for cowslip-wine, poppy-water and all dormitives,[79] those I allow. These provisos admitted, in other thing I may prove a tractable and complying husband.

MILLAMANT. O horrid provisos! filthy strong waters! I toast fellow! Odious men! I hate your odious provisos.

MIRABELL. Then we're agreed. Shall I kiss your hand upon the contract? And here comes one to be a witness to the sealing of the deed.

(*Enter* MRS. FAINALL.)

MILLAMANT. Fainall, what shall I do? shall I have him? I think I must have him.

MRS. FAINALL. Aye, aye, take him, take him, what should you do?

MILLAMANT. Well then—I'll take my death I'm in a horrid fright—Fainall, I shall never say it—well—I think—I'll endure you.

MRS. FAINALL. Fie, fie, have him, have him, and tell him so in plain terms: for I am sure you have a mind to him.

MILLAMANT. Are you? I think I have—and the horrid man looks as if he thought so too—Well, you ridiculous thing you, I'll have you—I won't be kissed, nor I won't be thanked—here kiss my hand tho'—so hold your tongue now, and don't say a word.

MRS. FAINALL. Mirabell, there's a necessity for your obedience;

---

[78] *orange-brandy . . . spirit of clary,* i.e., flavored alcoholic drinks.
[79] *dormitives,* sleeping potions.

you have neither time to talk nor stay. My mother is coming, and in my conscience if she should see you, would fall into fits, and maybe not recover time enough to return to Sir Rowland, who as Foible tells me is in a fair way to succeed. Therefore spare your ectasies for another occasion, and slip down the back-stairs, where Foible waits to consult you.

MILLAMANT. Aye, go, go. In the meantime I suppose you have said something to please me.

MIRABELL. I am all obedience.

(*Exit* MIRABELL.)

MRS. FAINALL. Yonder Sir Wilfull's drunk; and so noisy that my mother has been forced to leave Sir Rowland to appease him; but he answers her only with singing and drinking. What they have done by this time I know not. But Petulant and he were upon quarrelling as I came by.

MILLAMANT. Well, If Mirabell should not make a good husband, I am a lost thing, for I find I love him violently.

MRS. FAINALL. So it seems, when you mind not what's said to you. If you doubt him, you had best take up with Sir Wilfull.

MILLAMANT. How can you name that superannuated lubber, foh!

(*Enter* WITWOUD *from drinking.*)

MRS. FAINALL. So, Is the fray made up, that you have left 'em?

WITWOUD. Left 'em? I could stay no longer—I have laughed like ten christenings—I am tipsy with laughing—If I had stayed any longer I should have burst,—I must have been let out and pieced in the sides like an unsized camlet.[80] Yes, yes, the fray is composed; my lady came in like a *noli prosequi*[81] and stopped their proceedings.

MILLAMANT. What was the dispute?

WITWOUD. That's the jest, there was no dispute. They could neither of 'em speak for rage, and so fell a sputtering at one another like two roasting apples.

(*Enter* PETULANT, *drunk.*)

Now Petulant, all's over, all's well. Gad, my head begins to whim it about—Why dost thou not speak? thou art both as drunk and as mute as a fish.

---

[80] *camlet,* imitation of expensive cloth.
[81] *noli prosequi,* order to stop prosecution.

PETULANT. Look you, Mrs. Millamant,—If you can love me, dear nymph—say it—and that's the conclusion. Pass on, or pass off—that's all.

WITWOUD. Thou hast uttered volumes, folios, in less than *decimo sexto*,[82] my dear Lacedemonian,[83] Sirrah Petulant, thou art an epitomizer of words.

PETULANT. Witwoud—you are an annihilator of sense.

WITWOUD. Thou art a retailer of phrases; and dost deal in remnants of remnants, like a maker of pincushions—thou art in truth (metaphorically speaking) a speaker of shorthand.

PETULANT. Thou art (without a figure) just one-half of an ass; and Baldwin[84] yonder, thy half-brother, is the rest—A Gemini[85] of asses split would make just four of you.

WITWOUD. Thou dost bite, my dear mustard-seed; kiss me for that.

PETULANT. Stand off—I'll kiss no more males,—I have kissed your twin yonder in a humour of reconciliation, till he (hiccup) rises upon my stomach like a radish.

MILLAMANT. Eh! filthy creature—what was the quarrel?

PETULANT. There was no quarrel—there might have been a quarrel.

WITWOUD. If there had been words enow between 'em to have express'd provocation, they had gone together by the ears like a pair of castanets.

PETULANT. You were the quarrel.

MILLAMANT. Me!

PETULANT. If I have a humour to quarrel, I can make less matters conclude premises. If you are not handsome, what then, if I have a humour to prove it? If I shall have my reward, say so; if not, fight for your face the next time yourself—I'll go sleep.

WITWOUD. Do, rap thyself up like a wood-louse and dream revenge—and hear me, if thou canst learn to write by tomorrow morning, pen me a challenge—I'll carry it for thee.

PETULANT. Carry your mistress's monkey a spider,—go flea dogs, and read romances—I'll go to bed to my maid.

(*Exit.*)

---

82 *decimo sexto*, very small book.
83 *Lacedemonian*, Spartan, or one given to few words.
84 *Baldwin*, the ass in the fable of *Reynard the Fox*.
85 *Gemini*, twins.

MRS. FAINALL. He's horridly drunk—how came you all in this pickle?—

WITWOUD. A plot, a plot, to get rid of the knight,—your husband's advice; but he sneaked off.

(*Enter* LADY WISHFORT, *and* SIR WILFULL *drunk.*)

LADY WISHFORT. Out upon't, out upon't, at years of discretion, and comport yourself at this rantipole[86] rate!

SIR WILFULL. No offence, aunt.

LADY WISHFORT. Offence? As I'm a person, I'm ashamed of you.—Fogh! how you stink of Wine! D'ye think my niece will ever endure such a borachio[87]? You're an absolute borachio.

SIR WILFULL. Borachio!

LADY WISHFORT. At a time when you should commence an amour and put your best foot foremost—

SIR WILFULL. 'Sheart, an you grutch me your liquor, make a bill—Give me more drink and take my purse.

(*Sings,*)

> Prithee fill me the glass
> Till it laugh in my face,
> With ale that is potent and mellow;
> He that whines for a lass,
> Is an ignorant ass,
> For a bumper has not its fellow.

But if you would have me marry my cousin,—say the word, and I'll do't—Wilfull will do't, that's the word—Wilfull will do't, that's my crest—my motto I have forgot.

LADY WISHFORT. My nephew's a little overtaken, Cousin—but 'tis with drinking your health—O' my word, you are obliged to him.

SIR WILFULL. *In vino veritas*, aunt. If I drunk your health to-day cousin, I am a borachio. But if you have a mind to be married, say the word, and send for the piper, Wilfull will do't. If not, dust it away, and let's have tother round. Tony, 'Ods heart where's Tony? Tony's an honest fellow, but he spits after a bumper, and that's a fault.

(*Sings,*)

---

86 *rantipole*, disorderly.
87 *borachio*, winebag or drunkard (Spanish).

We'll drink and we'll never ha' done boys
Put the glass then around with the sun boys;
Let Apollo's example invite us;
For he's drunk every night,
And that makes him so bright,
That he's able next morning to light us.

The Sun's a good pimple,[88] an honest soaker; he has a cellar at your Antipodes.[89] If I travel, aunt, I touch at your Antipodes. Your Antipodes are a good rascally sort of topsy-turvy fellow. If I had a bumper I'd stand upon my head and drink a health to 'em—A match or no match, cousin, with the hard name—aunt, Wilfull will do't, If she has her maidenhead let her look to't,—if she has not, let her keep her own counsel in the meantime, and cry out at the nine month's end.

MILLAMANT. Your pardon, madam, I can stay no longer—Sir Wilfull grows very powerful, Eh! how he smells! I shall be overcome if I stay.

(*Exeunt* MILLAMANT *and* MRS. FAINALL.)

Come, cousin.

LADY WISHFORT. Smells! he would poison a tallow-chandler and his family. Beastly creature, I know not what to do with him! Travel, quoth' a! Aye, travel, travel, get thee gone, get thee but far enough, to the Saracens or the Tartars, or the Turks—for thou art not fit to live in a Christian commonwealth, thou beastly pagan.

SIR WILFULL. Turks? no; no Turks, aunt: Your Turks are infidels, and believe not in the grape. Your Mahometan, your Mussulman is a dry stinkard—No offence, aunt. My map says that your Turk is not so honest a man as your Christian. I cannot find by the map that your Mufti is orthodox—whereby it is a plain case, that orthodox is a hard word, aunt, and (*hiccup*), Greek for claret.

(*Sings.*)

To drink is a Christian diversion,
Unknown to the Turk and the Persian:
Let Mahometan fools
Live by heathenish rules,

---

88 *pimple*, pal.
89 *Antipodes*, ends of the earth.

And be damned over tea-cups and coffee.
But let British lads sing,
Crown a health to the king,
And a fig for your Sultan and Sophy![90]
Ah, Tony!

(*Enter* FOIBLE, *and whispers* LADY WISHFORT.)

LADY WISHFORT. Sir Rowland impatient? Good lack! what shall
I do with this beastly tumbril?[91]—Go lie down and
sleep, you sot!—or, as I'm a person, I'll have you
bastinadoed[92] with broomsticks. Call up the wenches.

(*Exit* FOIBLE.)

SIR WILFULL. Ahey! wenches, where are the wenches?

LADY WISHFORT. Dear Cousin Witwoud, get him away, and
you will bind me to you inviolably. I have an affair of
moment that invades me with some precipitation. You
will oblige me to all futurity.

WITWOUD. Come, knight—pox on him, I don't know what to
say to him—will you go to a cock-match?

SIR WILFULL. With a wench, Tony? Is she a shakebag,[93] sirrah?
let me bite your cheek for that.

WITWOUD. Horrible! He has a breath like a bagpipe—aye, aye,
come, will you march, my Salopian?

SIR WILFULL. Lead on little Tony—I'll follow thee my
Anthony,[94] my Tantony. Sirrah, thou sha't be my
Tan'tony; and I'll be thy pig.
—and a fig for your Sultan and Sophy.

(*Exit singing with* WITWOUD.)

LADY WISHFORT. This will never do. It will never make a match
—at least before he has been abroad.

(*Enter* WAITWELL, *disguised as* SIR ROWLAND.)

Dear Sir Rowland, I am confounded with confusion at
the retrospection of my own rudeness,—I have more
pardons to ask than the Pope distributes in the year of

---

[90] *Sophy*, Emperor of Persia.
[91] *tumbril*, dung-cart.
[92] *bastinadoed*, beaten across the soles of the feet.
[93] *shakebag*, game.
[94] *Anthony*, patron saint of swineherds.

jubilee. But I hope where there is likely to be so near an alliance, we may unbend the severity of decorum and dispense with a little ceremony.

WAITWELL. My impatience, madam, is the effect of my transport; and till I have the possession of your adorable person, I am tantalized on a rack; and do but hang, madam, on the tenter of expectation.

LADY WISHFORT. You have excess of gallantry, Sir Rowland, and press things to a conclusion with a most prevailing vehemence. But a day or two for decency of marriage—

WAITWELL. For decency of funeral, madam. The delay will break my heart—or, if that should fail, I shall be poisoned. My nephew will get an inkling of my designs and poison me; and I would willingly starve him before I die—I would gladly go out of the world with that satisfaction. That would be some comfort to me, if I could but live so long as to be revenged on that unnatural viper!

LADY WISHFORT. Is he so unnatural, say you? truly I would contribute much both to the saving of your life and the accomplishment of your revenge—not that I respect myself; tho' he has been a perfidious wretch to me.

WAITWELL. Perfidious to you!

LADY WISHFORT. Oh, Sir Rowland, the hours that he has died away at my feet, the tears that he has shed, the oaths that he has sworn, the palpitations that he has felt, the trances, and the tremblings, the ardors and the ecstasies, the kneelings and the risings, the heart-heavings and the hand-grippings, the pangs and the pathetic regards of his protesting eyes! Oh, no memory can register!

WAITWELL. What, my rival! is the rebel my rival? a'dies!

LADY WISHFORT. No, don't kill him at once Sir Rowland, starve him gradually, inch by inch.

WAITWELL. I'll do't. In three weeks he shall be barefoot; in a month out at knees with begging an alms. He shall starve upward and upward, till he has nothing living but his head, and then go out in a stink like a candle's end upon a save-all.[95]

LADY WISHFORT. Well, Sir Rowland, you have the way—you are no novice in the labyrinth of love; you have the clue. But as I am a person, Sir Rowland, you must not attribute my yielding to any sinister appetite, or indigestion

---

[95] *save-all,* candle end holder.

of widowhood; nor impute my complacency to any lethargy of continence. I hope you do not think me prone to any iteration of nuptials.

WAITWELL. Far be it from me—

LADY WISHFORT. If you do, I protest I must recede—or think that I have made a prostitution of decorums, but in the vehemence of compassion, and to save the life of a person of so much importance—

WAITWELL. I esteem it so—

LADY WISHFORT. Or else you wrong my condescension—

WAITWELL. I do not, I do not—

LADY WISHFORT. Indeed you do.

WAITWELL. I do not, fair shrine of virtue.

LADY WISHFORT. If you think the least scruple of carnality was an ingredient—

WAITWELL. Dear madam, no. You are all camphire and frankincense, all chastity and odour.

LADY WISHFORT. Or that—

(*Enter* FOIBLE.)

FOIBLE. Madam, the dancers are ready, and there's one with a letter who must deliver it into your own hands.

LADY WISHFORT. Sir Rowland, will you give me leave? think favourably, judge candidly and conclude you have found a person who would suffer racks in honour's cause, dear Sir Rowland, and will wait on you incessantly.　　(*Exit.*)

WAITWELL. Fie, fie!—What a slavery have I undergone; spouse, hast thou any cordial? I want spirits.

FOIBLE. What a washy rogue art thou, to pant thus for a quarter of an hour's lying and swearing to a fine lady!

WAITWELL. O, she is the antidote to desire. Spouse, thou wilt fare the worse for't—I shall have no appetite to iteration of nuptials this eight-and-forty hours. By this hand I'd rather be a chairman in the dogdays than act Sir Rowland, till this time tomorrow.

(*Enter* LADY WISHFORT *with a letter.*)

LADY WISHFORT. Call in the dancers. Sir Rowland, we'll sit if you please, and see the entertainment.　　(*Dance.*)

　　Now, with your permission, Sir Rowland, I will peruse my letter. I would open it in your presence because I would not make you uneasy. If it should make you uneasy, I would burn it. Speak if it does—but you may see by the superscription it is like a woman's hand.

FOIBLE (*to him*). By Heaven! Marwood's, I know it. My heart aches—get it from her—.

WAITWELL. A woman's hand? No, madam, that's no woman's hand; I see that already. That's somebody whose throat must be cut.

LADY WISHFORT. Nay Sir Rowland, since you give me a proof of your passion by your jealousy, I promise you I'll make you a return by a frank communication—you shall see it —we'll open it together—look you here.

Reads—"Madam, tho' unknown to you" (Look you there 'tis from nobody that I know)—"I have that honour for your character that I think myself obliged to let you know you are abused. He who pretends to be Sir Rowland is a cheat and a rascal."— Oh, Heavens! what's this?

FOIBLE. Unfortunate, all's ruined.

WAITWELL. How, how, Let me see, let me see—(*reading*) "A rascal and disguised and suborned for that imposture,"— O villainy, O villainy!—by the contrivance of—

LADY WISHFORT. I shall faint, I shall die, I shall die, oh!

FOIBLE (*to him*). Say 'tis your nephew's hand—quickly, his plot,—swear, swear it!

WAITWELL. Here's a villain! Madam, don't you perceive it, don't you see it?

LADY WISHFORT. Too well, too well. I have seen too much.

WAITWELL. I told you at first I knew the hand. A woman's hand? the rascal writes a sort of a large hand; your Roman hand—I saw there was a throat to be cut presently. If he were my son as he is my nephew I'd pistol him—

FOIBLE. O treachery! But are you sure, Sir Rowland, it is his writing?

WAITWELL. Sure? am I here? do I live? do I love this pearl of India? I have twenty letters in my pocket from him, in the same character.

LADY WISHFORT. How!

FOIBLE. O what luck it is, Sir Rowland, that you were present at this juncture! this was the business that brought Mr. Mirabell disguised to Madam Millamant this afternoon. I thought something was contriving, when he stole by me and would have hid his face.

LADY WISHFORT. How, how!—I heard the villain was in the house indeed, and now I remember, my niece went away

abruptly, when Sir Wilfull was to have made his
addresses.

FOIBLE. Then, then madam, Mr. Mirabell waited for her in
her chamber, but I would not tell your ladyship to discompose you when you were to receive Sir Rowland.

WAITWELL. Enough, his date is short.

FOIBLE. No, good Sir Rowland, don't incur the law.

WAITWELL. Law? I care not for law. I can but die, and 'tis in
a good cause—my lady shall be satisfied of my truth
and innocence, tho' it cost me my life.

LADY WISHFORT. No, dear Sir Rowland, don't fight, if you
should be killed I must never show my face; or hanged,
—Oh, consider my reputation, Sir Rowland!—No, you
shan't fight. I'll go in and examine my niece; I'll make
her confess. I conjure you Sir Rowland by all your love
not to fight.

WAITWELL. I am charmed madam! I obey. But some proof
you must let me give you; I'll go for a black box which
contains the writings of my whole estate, and deliver
that into your hands.

LADY WISHFORT. Aye, dear Sir Rowland, that will be some
comfort; bring the black box.

WAITWELL. And may I presume to bring a contract to be
signed this night? May I hope so far?

LADY WISHFORT. Bring what you will; but come alive, pray
come alive. O this is a happy discovery!

WAITWELL. Dead or alive I'll come—and married we will be
in spite of treachery; Aye and get an heir that shall defeat
the last remaining glimpse of hope in my abandoned
nephew. Come, my buxom widow.

> Ere long you shall substantial proof receive
> That I'm an arrant knight—

FOIBLE. Or arrant knave. (*aside*)

(*Exeunt.*)

ACT V

[SCENE I.] *Scene continues*

(LADY WISHFORT *and* FOIBLE.)

LADY WISHFORT. Out of my house, out of my house, thou
viper, thou serpent, that I have fostered, thou bosom
traitoress, that I raised from nothing!—Begone, begone,

begone, go! go!—That I took from washing of old gauze and weaving of dead hair, with a bleak blue nose over a chafing-dish of starved embers and dining behind a traverse rag, in a shop no bigger than a bird-cage! Go, go, starve again, do! do! ·

FOIBLE. Dear madam, I'll beg pardon on my knees.

LADY WISHFORT. Away! out, out! Go, set up for yourself again! Do, drive a trade, do, with your three penny-worth of small ware, flaunting upon a packthread under a brandy-seller's bulk,[96] or against a dead wall by a ballad-monger. Go hang out an old frisoneer-gorget,[97] with a yard of yellow Colberteen again; do! An old gnawed mask, two rows of pins and a child's fiddle; a glass necklace with the beads broken, and a quilted night-cap with one ear. Go, go, drive a trade! These were your commodities, you treacherous trull,[98] this was your merchandise you dealt in when I took you into my house, placed you next myself, and made you governante[99] of my whole family. You have forgot this, have you, now you have feathered your nest?

FOIBLE. No, no, dear madam. Do but hear me, have but a moment's patience—I'll confess all. Mr. Mirabell seduced me; I am not the first that he has wheedled with his dissembling tongue; Your ladyship's own wisdom has been deluded by him, then how should I a poor ignorant, defend myself? O Madam, if you knew but what he promised me, and how he assured me your ladyship should come to no damage! Or else the wealth of the Indies shou'd not have bribed me to conspire against so good, so sweet, so kind a lady as you have been to me.

LADY WISHFORT. No damage? What, to betray me, to marry me to a cast serving-man; to make me a receptacle, an hospital for a decayed pimp? No damage? O thou frontless impudence, more than a big-bellied actress!

FOIBLE. Pray, do but hear me madam, he could not marry your ladyship, madam—No, indeed, his marriage was to have been void in law, for he was married to me first, to secure your ladyship. He could not have bedded your ladyship: for if he had consummated with your ladyship,

---

[96] *bulk*, stall.
[97] *frisoneer-gorget*, neckpiece of cheap Dutch cloth.
[98] *trull*, whore.
[99] *governante*, housekeeper.

he must have run the risk of the law, and been put upon his clergy.[100] Yes, indeed, I enquired of the law in that case before I would meddle or make.

LADY WISHFORT. What, then I have been your property, have I? I have been convenient to you it seems! While you were catering for Mirabell, I have been broker for you? What, have you made a passive bawd of me? This exceeds all precedent! I am brought to fine uses, to become a botcher of second-hand marriages between Abigails and Andrews![101] I'll couple you, yes, I'll baste you together, you and your Philander. I'll Dukes-Place you, as I'm a person. Your turtle is in custody already; you shall coo in the same cage if there be constable or warrant in the parish.

(*Exit.*)

FOIBLE. O that ever I was born, O that I was ever married, —a Bride, aye I shall be a Bridewell-bride.[102] Oh!

(*Enter* MRS. FAINALL.)

MRS. FAINALL. Poor Foible, what's the matter?

FOIBLE. O madam, my lady's gone for a constable; I shall be had to a justice and put to Bridewell to beat hemp; poor Waitwell's gone to prison already.

MRS. FAINALL. Have a good heart Foible, Mirabell's gone to give security for him. This is all Marwood's and my husband's doing.

FOIBLE. Yes, yes; I know it, madam; she was in my lady's closet, and overheard all that you said to me before dinner. She sent the letter to my lady, and that missing effect, Mr. Fainall laid this plot to arrest Waitwell, when he pretended to go for the papers, and in the meantime Mrs. Marwood declared all to my lady.

MRS. FAINALL. Was there no mention made of me in the letter? My mother does not suspect my being in the confederacy? I fancy Marwood has not told her, tho' she has told my husband.

FOIBLE. Yes, madam; but my lady did not see that part; we

---

[100] *put upon his clergy,* the benefit of clergy, or ability to read, prevented certain punishments of civil law.
[101] *Abigails and Andrews,* servants.
[102] *Bridewell-bride,* prisoner in London's house of correction for women.

stifled the letter before she read so far. Has that mischievous devil told Mr. Fainall of your ladyship then?

MRS. FAINALL. Aye, all's out, My affair with Mirabell, everything discovered. This is the last day of our living together, that's my comfort.

FOIBLE. Indeed, madam, and so 'tis a comfort if you knew all, —he has been even with your ladyship; which I could have told you long enough since, but I love to keep peace and quietness by my good will: I had rather bring friends together, than set 'em at distance. But Mrs. Marwood and he are nearer related than ever their parents thought for.

MRS. FAINALL. Sayest thou so Foible? Canst thou prove this?

FOIBLE. I can take my oath of it madam, so can Mrs. Mincing; we have had many a fair word from Madam Marwood to conceal something that passed in our chamber one evening when you were at Hyde Park and we were thought to have gone a walking: but we went up unawares—tho' we were sworn to secrecy too; Madam Marwood took a book and swore us upon it, but it was but a book of verses and poems. So as long as it was not a Bible oath, we may break it with a safe conscience.

MRS. FAINALL. This discovery is the most opportune thing I could wish. Now, Mincing?

(*Enter* MINCING.)

MINCING. My lady would speak with Mrs. Foible, mem. Mr. Mirabell is with her, he has set your spouse at liberty, Mrs. Foible, and would have you hide yourself in my lady's closet, till my old lady's anger is abated. Oh, my old lady is in a perilous passion at something Mr. Fainall has said. He swears, and my old lady cries. There's a fearful hurricane, I vow. He says, mem, how that he'll have my lady's fortune made over to him, or he'll be divorced.

MRS. FAINALL. Does your lady and Mirabell know that?

MINCING. Yes, mem, they have sent me to see if Sir Wilfull be sober, and to bring him to them. My lady is resolved to have him, I think, rather than lose such a vast sum as six thousand pound. Oh, come Mrs. Foible, I hear my old lady.

MRS. FAINALL. Foible, you must tell Mincing, that she must prepare to vouch when I call her.

FOIBLE. Yes, yes, madam.

MINCING. Oh, yes, mem, I'll vouch any thing for your ladyship's service, be what it will.

(*Exeunt* MINCING *and* FOIBLE.)

(*Enter* LADY WISHFORT *and* MARWOOD.)

LADY WISHFORT. O my dear friend, how can I enumerate the
benefits that I have received from your goodness? To you
I owe the timely discovery of the false vows of Mirabell;
to you the detection of the imposter Sir Rowland. And
now you are become an intercessor with my son-in-law, to
save the honour of my house, and compound for the
frailties of my daughter. Well, friend, you are enough to
reconcile me to the bad world, or else I would retire to
deserts and solitudes; and feed harmless sheep by groves
and purling streams. Dear Marwood, let us leave the
world, and retire by ourselves, and be shepherdesses.

MRS. MARWOOD. Let us first dispatch the affair in hand,
madam; we shall have leisure to think of retirement afterwards. Here is one who is concerned in the treaty.

LADY WISHFORT. Oh, daughter, daughter, is it possible thou
shoudst be my child, bone of my bone, and flesh of my
flesh, and as I may say, another me, and yet transgress
the most minute particle of severe virtue? Is it possible
you should lean aside to iniquity who have been cast in
the direct mold of virtue? I have not only been a mold
but a pattern for you, and a model for you after you were
brought into the world.

MRS. FAINALL. I don't understand your ladyship.

LADY WISHFORT. Not understand? Why have you not been
naught? Have you not been sophisticated? Not understand? Here I am ruined to compound for your caprices
and your cuckoldoms. I must pawn my plate, and my
jewels, and ruin my niece, and all little enough—

MRS. FAINALL. I am wronged and abused, and so are you. 'Tis
a false accusation, as false as Hell, as false as your friend
there, aye, or your friend's friend, my false husband.

MRS. MARWOOD. My friend, Mrs. Fainall? Your husband my
friend? What do you mean?

MRS. FAINALL. I know what I mean madam, and so do you;
and so shall the world at a time convenient.

MRS. MARWOOD. I am sorry to see you so passionate, madam.
More temper would look more like innocence. But I have
done. I am sorry my zeal to serve your ladyship and

family should admit of misconstruction, or make me liable to affronts. You will pardon me, madam, if I meddle no more with an affair in which I am not personally concerned.

LADY WISHFORT. Oh, dear friend; I am so ashamed that you should meet with such returns. You ought to ask pardon on your knees, ungrateful (*to* MRS. FAINALL) creature; she deserves more from you than all your life can accomplish (*to* MRS. MARWOOD) Oh, don't leave me destitute in this perplexity! No, stick to me, my good genius.

MRS. FAINALL. I tell you madam you're abused—stick to you? aye, like a leech, to suck your best blood—she'll drop off when she's full. Madam, you shan't pawn a bodkin[103] nor part with a brass counter in composition for me. I defy 'em all. Let 'em prove their aspersions: I know my own innocence, and dare stand a trial.

(*Exit.*)

LADY WISHFORT. Why, If she should be innocent, if she should be wronged after all, ha? I don't know what to think—and I promise you, her education has been unexceptionable—I may say it; for I chiefly made it my own care to initiate her very infancy in the rudiments of virtue, and to impress upon her tender years a young odium and aversion to the very sight of men. Aye, friend, she would ha' shrieked if she had but seen a man, till she was in her teens. As I'm a person 'tis true—she was never suffered to play with a male child, tho' but in coats; nay, her very babies[104] were of the feminine gender. Oh, she never looked a man in the face but her own father or the chaplain, and him we made a shift to put upon her for a woman, by the help of his long garments and his sleek face, till she was going in her fifteen.

MRS. MARWOOD. Twas much she should be deceived so long.

LADY WISHFORT. I warrant you, or she would never have born to have been catechised by him; and have heard his long lectures against singing and dancing and such debaucheries; and going to filthy plays; and profane music-meetings, where the lewd trebles squeak nothing but bawdy, and the basses roar blasphemy. Oh, she would have swooned at the sight or name of an obscene play-

---

103 *bodkin,* pin.
104 *babies,* dolls.

book! And can I think, after all this, that my daughter can be naught? What, a whore? And thought it excommunication to set her foot within the door of a playhouse? Oh, my dear friend, I can't believe it. No, no! As she says, let him prove it, let him prove it.

MRS. MARWOOD. Prove it, madam? What, and have your name prostituted in a public court? Yours and your daughter's reputation worried at the bar by a pack of bawling lawyers? To be ushered in with an "O Yez" of scandal; and have your case opened by an old fumbling lecher in a quoif[105] like a man midwife; to bring your daughter's infamy to light; to be a theme for legal punsters and quibblers by the statute; and become a jest against a rule of court, where there is no precedent for a jest in any record; not even in Domesday Book: to discompose the gravity of the bench, and provoke naughty interrogatories in more naughty law Latin; while the good judge, tickled with the proceeding, simpers under a grey beard, and fidges off and on his cushion as if he had swallowed cantharides,[106] or sat upon cow itch.[107]

LADY WISHFORT. Oh, 'tis very hard!

MRS. MARWOOD. And then to have my young revellers of the Temple take notes like 'prentices at a conventicle; and after, talk it all over again in commons, or before drawers in an eating-house.

LADY WISHFORT. Worse and worse.

MRS. MARWOOD. Nay, this is nothing; if it would end here, 'twere well. But it must after this be consigned by the shorthand writers to the public press; and from thence be transferred to the hands, nay into the throats and lungs of hawkers, with voices more licentious than the loud flounder-man's or the woman that cries grey-pease; and this you must hear till you are stunned; nay, you must hear nothing else for some days.

LADY WISHFORT. Oh, 'tis insupportable! No, no, dear friend make it up, make it up; ay, ay, I'll compound. I'll give up all, myself and my all, my niece and her all—anything, everything for composition.

MRS. MARWOOD. Nay, madam, I advise nothing, I only lay before you as a friend the inconveniences which perhaps

---

105 *quoif,* white wig.
106 *cantharides,* a diuretic.
107 *cow-itch,* bristled plant.

you have overseen. Here comes Mr. Fainall. If he will be satisfied to huddle up all in silence, I shall be glad. You must think I would rather congratulate than condole with you.

(*Enter* FAINALL.)

LADY WISHFORT. Aye, aye, I do not doubt it, dear Marwood; No, no, I do not doubt it.

FAINALL. Well madam; I have suffered myself to be overcome by the importunity of this lady, your friend; and am content you shall enjoy your own proper estate during life; on condition you oblige yourself never to marry, under such penalty as I think convenient.

LADY WISHFORT. Never to marry?

FAINALL. No more Sir Rowlands—the next imposture may not be so timely detected.

MRS. MARWOOD. That condition I dare answer, my lady will consent to without difficulty; she has already but too much experienced the perfidiousness of men. Besides, madam, when we retire to our pastoral solitude we shall bid adieu to all other thoughts.

LADY WISHFORT. Aye that's true; but in case of necessity; as of health, or some such emergency—

FAINALL. O, if you are prescribed marriage, you shall be considered; I will only reserve to myself the power to choose for you. If your physic be wholesome, it matters not who is your apothecary. Next, my wife shall settle on me the remainder of her fortune not made over already, and for her maintenance depend entirely on my discretion.

LADY WISHFORT. This is most inhumanly savage, exceeding the barbarity of a Muscovite husband.

FAINALL. I learned it from his Czarish majesty's retinue,[108] in a winter evening's conference over brandy and pepper, amongst other secrets of matrimony and policy as they are at present practised in the northern hemisphere. But this must be agreed unto, and that positively. Lastly, I will be endowed in right of my wife with that six thousand pound which is the moiety of Mrs. Millamant's fortune in your possession: and which she has forfeited (as will appear by the last will and testament of your deceased husband, Sir Jonathan Wishfort) by her dis-

---

[108] *his Czarish majesty's retinue,* the followers of Peter the Great who visited London in 1697.

obedience in contracting herself against your consent or
knowledge and by refusing the offered match with Sir
Wilfull Witwoud, which you, like a careful aunt, had
provided for her.

LADY WISHFORT. My nephew was *non compos* and could not
make his addresses.

FAINALL. I come to make demands—I'll hear no objections.

LADY WISHFORT. You will grant me time to consider.

FAINALL. Yes, while the instrument is drawing, to which you
must set your hand till more sufficient deeds can be
perfected; which I will take care shall be done with all
possible speed. In the meanwhile, I will go for the said
instrument, and till my return you may balance this matter in your own discretion.

(*Exit* FAINALL.)

LADY WISHFORT. This insolence is beyond all precedent, all
parallel! Must I be subject to this merciless villain?

MRS. MARWOOD. 'Tis severe indeed madam, that you should
smart for your daughter's wantonness.

LADY WISHFORT. 'Twas against my consent that she married
this barbarian, But she would have him, tho' her year was
not out. Ah! her first husband, my son Languish, would
not have carried it thus. Well, that was my choice, this
is hers; she is matched now with a witness—I shall be
mad, dear friend, is there no comfort for me? Must I
live to be confiscated at this rebel-rate?[109] Here come
two more of my Egyptian plagues too.

(*Enter* MILLAMANT *and* SIR WILFULL.)

SIR WILFULL. Aunt, your servant.

LADY WISHFORT. Out, caterpillar, Call not me aunt, I know thee
not.

SIR WILFULL. I confess I have been a little in disguise as they
say,—'Sheart! and I'm sorry for't. What would you have?
I hope I committed no offence, aunt—and if I did I am
willing to make satisfaction; and what can a man say
fairer? If I have broke anything, I'll pay for't, an it cost a
pound. And so let that content for what's past, and make
no more words. For what's to come to pleasure you I'm

[109] *at this rebel-rate*, in the way that the property of traitors is
confiscated.

willing to marry my cousin. So pray let's all be friends, she and I are agreed upon the matter, before a witness.

LADY WISHFORT. How's this, dear niece? Have I any comfort? Can this be true?

MILLAMANT. I am content to be a sacrifice to your repose, madam, and to convince you that I had no hand in the plot, as you were misinformed. I have laid my commands on Mirabell to come in person and be a witness that I give my hand to this flower of knighthood; and for the contract that past between Mirabell and me, I have obliged him to make a resignation of it in your ladyship's presence. He is without and waits your leave for admittance.

LADY WISHFORT. Well, I'll swear I am something revived at this testimony of your obedience; but I cannot admit that traitor—I fear I cannot fortify myself to support his appearance. He is as terrible to me as a gorgon; if I see him, I fear I shall turn to stone, petrify incessantly.

MILLAMANT. If you disoblige him he may resent your refusal and insist upon the contract still. Then 'tis the last time he will be offensive to you.

LADY WISHFORT. Are you sure it will be the last time? If I were sure of that—shall I never see him again?

MILLAMANT. Sir Wilfull, you and he are to travel together, are you not?

SIR WILFULL. 'Sheart the gentleman's a civil gentleman, aunt, let him come in; why we are sworn brothers and fellow travellers. We are to be Pylades and Orestes,[110] he and I—he is to be my interpreter in foreign parts. He has been overseas once already; and with proviso that I marry my cousin, will cross 'em once again only to bear me company. 'Sheart, I'll call him in. An I set on't once, he shall come in; and see who'll hinder him.

(*Exit.*)

MRS. MARWOOD. This is precious fooling, if it would pass, but I'll know the bottom of it.

LADY WISHFORT. O dear Marwood, you are not going?

MARWOOD. Not far, madam; I'll return immediately.

(*Exit.*)

(*Re-enter* SIR WILFULL *and* MIRABELL.)

110 *Pylades and Orestes,* friends in Greek mythology.

SIR WILFULL. Look up, man, I'll stand by you, 'sbud an she do
frown, she can't kill you;—besides—harkee, she dare not
frown desperately, because her face is none of her own;
'Sheart an she should, her forehead would wrinkle like
the coat of a cream-cheese; but mum for that, fellow-
traveller.

MIRABELL. If a deep sense of the many injuries I have offered
to so good a lady, with a sincere remorse, and a hearty
contrition can but obtain the least glance of compassion
I am too happy. Ah, madam, there was a time—but let
it be forgotten—I confess I have deservedly forfeited the
high place I once held, of sighing at your feet; nay kill
me not, by turning from me in disdain,—I come not to
plead for favour—nay not for pardon; I am a suppliant
only for your pity. I am going where I never shall behold
you more—

SIR WILFULL. How, fellow-traveller! You shall go by yourself
then.

MIRABELL. Let me be pitied first; and afterwards forgotten,
—I ask no more.

SIR WILFULL. By'r Lady, a very reasonable request; and will
cost you nothing, aunt—Come, come, forgive and forget,
aunt, why you must, an you are a Christian.

MIRABELL. Consider madam, in reality; You could not receive
much prejudice; it was an innocent device; tho' I confess
it had a face of guiltiness, it was at most an artifice which
love contrived—and errors which love produces have
ever been accounted venial. At least think it is punishment
enough that I have lost what in my heart I hold most dear,
that to your cruel indignation, I have offered up this
beauty, and with her my peace and quiet; nay all my
hopes of future comfort.

SIR WILFULL. An he does not move me, would I might never
be o' the Quorum[111]—an it were not as good a deed as to
drink, to give her to him again, I would I might never
take shipping! Aunt, if you don't forgive quickly; I shall
melt, I can tell you that. My contract went no further
than a little mouth glue, and that's hardly dry—one
doleful sigh more from my fellow-traveller and 'tis
dissolved.

LADY WISHFORT. Well, nephew, upon your account—ah, he has
a false, insinuating tongue! Well, sir, I will stifle my

111 o' the Quorum, justice of the peace.

just resentment at my nephew's request. I will endeavour what I can to forget, but on proviso that you resign the contract with my niece immediately.

MIRABELL. It is in writing and with papers of concern; but I have sent my servant for it, and will deliver it to you, with all acknowledgments for your transcendent goodness.

LADY WISHFORT. (*apart*). Oh, he has witchcraft in his eyes and tongue! When I did not see him I could have bribed a villain to his assassination; but his appearance rakes the embers which have so long lain smothered in my breast.—

(*Enter* FAINALL *and* MRS. MARWOOD.)

FAINALL. Your date of deliberation madam, is expired. Here is the instrument, are you prepared to sign?

LADY WISHFORT. If I were prepared; I am not impowered. My niece exerts a lawful claim, having matched herself by my direction to Sir Wilfull.

FAINALL. That sham is too gross to pass on me—tho 'tis impos'd on you, madam.

MILLAMANT. Sir, I have given my consent.

MIRABELL. And, sir, I have resigned my pretensions.

SIR WILFULL. And, sir, I assert my right; and will maintain it in defiance of you, sir, and of your instrument. 'Sheart an you talk of an instrument, sir, I have an old fox[112] by my thigh shall hack your instrument of ram vellum[113] to shreds, sir. It shall not be sufficient for a mittimus[114] or a tailor's measure. Therefore, withdraw your instrument, sir or by'r Lady I shall draw mine.

LADY WISHFORT. Hold, nephew, hold.

MILLAMANT. Goor Sir Wilfull, respite your valour.

FAINALL. Indeed? are you provided of a guard, with your single beef-eater there? But I'm prepared for you, and insist upon my first proposal. You shall submit your own estate to my management, and absolutely make over my wife's to my sole use, as pursuant to the purport and tenor of this other covenant. I suppose, Madam, your consent is not requisite in this case; nor Mr. Mirabell, your resignation; nor Sir Wilfull, your right. You may draw your fox if you please, sir, and make a bear-garden flourish somewhere else, for here it will not avail.

112 *Fox*, sword.
113 *ram vellum*, sheepskin.
114 *mittimus*, warrant.

reputation is all
in this
body

This, my lady Wishfort, must be subscribed, or your darling daughter's turned adrift like a leaky hulk to sink or swim as she and the current of this lewd town can agree.

LADY WISHFORT. Is there no means, no remedy, to stop my ruin? Ungrateful wretch! dost thou not owe thy being, thy subsistence to my daughter's fortune?

FAINALL. I'll answer you when I have the rest of it in my possession.

MIRABELL. But that you would not accept of a remedy from my hands—I own I have not deserved you should owe any obligation to me; or else perhaps I could advise.

LADY WISHFORT. Oh, what? what? to save me and my child from ruin, from want, I'll forgive all that's past; nay I'll consent to anything to come, to be delivered from this tyranny.

MIRABELL. Aye madam; but that is too late, my reward is intercepted. You have disposed of her, who only could have made me a compensation for all my services. But be it as it may, I am resolved I'll serve you; you shall not be wronged in this savage manner!

LADY WISHFORT. How! dear Mr. Mirabell, can you be so generous at last? But it is not possible. Harkee, I'll break my nephew's match; you shall have my niece yet, and all her fortune; if you can but save me from this imminent danger.

MIRABELL. Will you? I take you at your word. I ask no more. I must have leave for two criminals to appear.

LADY WISHFORT. Aye, aye, anybody, anybody.

MIRABELL. Foible is one, and a penitent.

(*Enter* MRS. FAINALL, FOIBLE, *and* MINCING.)

MRS. MARWOOD. (*to* Fainall) Oh, my shame! (Mirabell *and* Lady Wishfort *go to* Mrs. Fainall *and* Foible). These corrupt things are bought and brought hither to expose me—

FAINALL. If it must all come out, why let 'em know it, 'tis but the way of the world. That shall not urge me to relinquish or abate one title of my terms; no, I will insist the more.

FOIBLE. Yes, indeed, madam; I'll take my Bible oath of it.

MINCING. And so will I, mem.

LADY WISHFORT. O Marwood, Marwood, art thou false? My friend deceive me? Hast thou been a wicked accomplice with that profligate man?

MRS. MARWOOD. Have you so much ingratitude and injustice to give credit against your friend to the aspersions of two such mercenary trulls?

MINCING. Mercenary, mem? I scorn your words. 'Tis true we found you and Mr. Fainall in the blue garret; by the same token, you swore us to secrecy upon Messalinas's poems.[115] Mercenary? No, if we would have been mercenary, we should have held our tongues; you would have bribed us sufficiently.

FAINALL. Go, you are an insignificant thing! Well, what are you the better for this? Is this Mr. Mirabell's expedient? I'll be put off no longer. You thing that was a wife shall smart for this. I will not leave thee wherewithal to hide thy shame; your body shall be naked as your reputation.

MRS. FAINALL. I despise you and defy your malice! You have aspersed me wrongfully—I have proved your falsehood! Go, you and your treacherous—I will not name it, but, starve together—perish.

FAINALL. Not while you are worth a groat, indeed, my dear. Madam, I'll be fooled no longer.

LADY WISHFORT. Ah, Mr. Mirabell, this is small comfort, the detection of this affair.

MIRABELL. Oh, in good time—your leave for the other offender and penitent to appear, madam.

(*Enter* WAITWELL *with a box of writings.*)

LADY WISHFORT. O Sir Rowland—well, rascal.

WAITWELL. What your ladyship pleases. I have brought the black box at last, madam.

MIRABELL. Give it me. Madam, you remember your promise?

LADY WISHFORT. Aye, dear sir.

MIRABELL. Where are the gentlemen?

WAITWELL. At hand sir, rubbing their eyes—just risen from sleep.

FAINALL. 'Sdeath what's this to me? I'll not wait your private concerns.

(*Enter* PETULANT *and* WITWOUD.)

PETULANT. How now? What's the matter? Whose hand's out?

WITWOUD. Heyday! What are you all got together like players at the end of the last act?

---

[115] *Messalina's poems,* mispronunciation of a common title, *Miscellany.*

MIRABELL. You may remember, gentlemen, I once requested your hands as witness to a certain parchment.

WITWOUD. Aye I do, my hand I remember—Petulant set his mark.

MIRABELL. You wrong him, his name is fairly written as shall appear. You do not remember, gentlemen, anything of what that parchment contained—(*undoing the box.*)

WITWOUD. No.

PETULANT. Not I. I writ, I read nothing.

MIRABELL. Very well, now you shall know—madam, your promise.

LADY WISHFORT. Ay, ay, sir, upon my honour.

MIRABELL. Mr. Fainall, it is now time that you should know that your lady, while she was at her own disposal, and before you had by your insinuations wheedled her out of a pretended settlement of the greatest part of her fortune—

FAINALL. Sir! pretended!

MIRABELL. Yes, Sir. I say that this lady while a widow, having it seems received some cautions respecting your inconstancy and tyranny of temper, which from her own partial opinion and fondness of you she could never have suspected—she did, I say, by the wholesome advice of friends and of sages learned in the laws of this land, deliver this same as her act and deed to me in trust, and to the uses within mentioned. You may read if you please —(*holding out the parchment.*) tho' perhaps what is inscribed on the back may serve your occasions.

FAINALL. Very likely, sir! What's here? Damnation! (*Reads.*) "A deed of conveyance of the whole estate real of Arabella Languish widow in trust to Edward Mirabell." Confusion!

MIRABELL. Even so sir, 'tis the way of the world, sir: of the widows of the world. I suppose this deed may bear an elder date than what you have obtained from your lady.

FAINALL. Perfidious fiend! then thus I'll be revenged.—(*offers to run at* MRS. FAINALL.)

SIR WILFULL. Hold sir, now you may make your bear-garden flourish somewhere else, sir.

FAINALL. Mirabell, you shall hear of this sir, be sure you shall. Let me pass, oaf.

(*Exit.*)

MRS. FAINALL. Madam, you seem to stifle your resentment: You had better give it vent.

MRS. MARWOOD. Yes it shall have vent—and to your confusion, or I'll perish in the attempt.

(*Exit.*)

LADY WISHFORT. Oh, daughter; daughter, 'tis plain thou hast inherited thy mother's prudence.

MRS. FAINALL. Thank Mr. Mirabell, a cautious friend, to whose advice all is owing.

LADY WISHFORT. Well, Mr. Mirabell, you have kept your promise, and I must perform mine. First, I pardon for your sake, Sir Rowland there and Foible. The next thing is to break the matter to my nephew—and how to do that—

MIRABELL. For that madam, give yourself no trouble—let me have your consent. Sir Wilfull is my friend; he has had compassion upon lovers and generously engaged a volunteer in this action for our service, and now designs to prosecute his travels.

SIR WILFULL. 'Sheart, aunt, I have no mind to marry. My cousin's a fine lady, and the gentleman loves her, and she loves him, and they deserve one another. My resolution is to see foreign parts—I have set on't—and when I'm set on't, I must do't. And if these two gentlemen would travel too, I think they may be spared.

PETULANT. For my part, I say little—I think things are best off or on.

WITWOUD. Gad, I understand nothing of the matter; I'm in a maze yet, like a dog in a dancing-school.

LADY WISHFORT. Well sir, take her, and with her all the joy I can give you.

MILLAMANT. Why does not the man take me? Would you have me give myself to you over again.

MIRABELL. Aye, and over and over again; for I would have you as often as possibly I can. (*Kisses her hand*). Well, Heaven grant I love you not too well; that's all my fear.

SIR WILFULL. 'Sheart you'll have him time enough to toy after you're married. Or if you will toy now let us have a dance in thē meantime, that we who are not lovers may have some other employment besides looking on.

MIRABELL. With all my heart dear Sir Wilfull. What shall we do for music?

FOIBLE. Oh, sir, some that were provided for Sir Rowland's entertainment are yet within call.

(*A Dance.*)

LADY WISHFORT. As I am a person, I can hold out no longer.— I have wasted my spirits so today already that I am ready to sink under the fatigue; and I cannot but have some fears upon me yet that my son Fainall will pursue some desperate course.

MIRABELL. Madam, disquiet not yourself on that account; to my knowledge his circumstances are such he must of force comply. For my part, I will contribute all that in me lies to a reunion; (*To* MRS. FAINALL) in the meantime, madam, let me before these witnesses restore to you this deed of trust. It may be a means well managed to make you live easily together.

From hence let those be warned, who mean to wed;
Lest mutual falsehood stain the bridal bed:
For each deceiver to his cost may find,
That marriage frauds too oft are paid in kind.

(*Exeunt Omnes.*)

EPILOGUE

After our epilogue this crowd dismisses,
I'm thinking how this play'll be pulled to pieces.
But pray consider, ere you doom its fall,
How hard a thing 'twould be, to please you all.
There are some critics so with spleen diseased,[116]
They scarcely come inclining to be pleased:
And sure he must have more than mortal skill,
Who pleases any one against his will.
Then, all bad poets we are sure are foes,
And how their number's swell'd the town well knows:
In shoals I've marked 'em judging in the pit;
Tho' they're on no pretence for judgment fit
But that they have been damned for want of wit.
Since when, they by their own offences taught
Set up for spies on plays, and finding fault.
Others there are whose malice we'd prevent;
Such who watch plays with scurrilous intent
To mark out who by characters are meant.
And tho' no perfect likeness they can trace,
Yet each pretends to know the copied face.
These with false glosses feed their own ill nature,
And turn to libel what was meant a satire.
May such malicious fops this fortune find,
To think themselves alone the fools designed:
If any are so arrogantly vain,
To think they singly can support a scene,
And furnish fool enough to entertain.
For well the learned and the judicious know,
That satire scorns to stoop so meanly low,
As any one abstracted fop to show.

116 *with spleen diseased,* irritable.

For, as when painters form a matchless face,
They from each fair one catch some different grace,
And shining features in one portrait blend,
To which no single beauty must pretend:
So poets oft do in one piece expose
Whole *belles assemblées*[117] of Coquettes and beaux.

(*Finis*)

---

[117] *belles assemblées*, parties.

SIGNET CLASSICS and MENTOR Drama Anthologies

☐ **THE SIGNET CLASSIC BOOK OF 18TH- AND 19TH-CENTURY BRITISH DRAMA edited and with an Introduction by Katharine Rogers.** A collection of eight milestones in British drama: *The Beaux' Stratagem, The Conscious Lovers, The Beggar's Opera, The London Merchant, School for Scandal, The Octoroon, Ruddigore,* and *The Importance of Being Earnest.*
(#CE1265—$2.95)

☐ **THE GENIUS OF THE EARLY ENGLISH THEATER edited by Barnet, Berman, and Burto.** Complete plays including three anonymous plays—*Abraham and Isaac, The Second Shepherd's Play,* and *Everyman,* and Marlowe's *Doctor Faustus,* Shakespeare's *Macbeth,* Jonson's *Volpone,* and Milton's *Samson Agonistes.* Also includes critical essays. (#ME1889—$2.50)

☐ **EIGHT GREAT COMEDIES edited by Barnet, Berman, and Burto.** Complete English texts of *The Clouds,* Machiavelli's *Mandragola, Twelfth Night, The Miser, The Beggar's Opera, Importance of Being Earnest, Uncle Vanya,* and *Arms and the Man.* With essays on the comic view. (#ME1840—$2.50)

☐ **EIGHT GREAT TRAGEDIES edited by Barnet, Berman, and Burto.** Complete English texts of *Prometheus Bound, Oedipus the King, Hippolytus, King Lear, Ghosts, Miss Julie, On Baile's Strand,* and *Desire Under the Elms.* With essays on the tragic view. (#ME1911—$2.50)

☐ **THE MENTOR BOOK OF SHORT PLAYS edited by Richard H. Goldstone and Abraham H. Lass.** A treasury of drama by some of the finest playwrights of the century. Includes plays by Anton Chekov, Tennessee Williams, Thornton Wilder, and others. (#ME1730—$2.25)

Buy them at your local

bookstore or use coupon

on next page for ordering.

Recommended Reading in SIGNET Classic and MENTOR Editions

- [ ] **THREE BY BEN JONSON: VOLPONE, THE ALCHEMIST, AND MERCURY VINDICATED (A Masque) with an Introduction and Notes by Jonathan Price.** The mercilessly barbed comic genius that places Ben Jonson second only to Shakespeare among Elizabethan dramatists shines forth in these, his masterpieces. (#CE1368—$2.95)

- [ ] **PLAYS by George Bernard Shaw, Introduction by Eric Bentley.** *Men and Superman, Candida, Arms and the Man,* and *Mrs. Warren's Profession.* (#CE1480—$2.95)*

- [ ] **FOUR PLAYS BY TENNESSEE WILLIAMS: SUMMER AND SMOKE, ORPHEUS DESCENDING, SUDDENLY LAST SUMMER AND PERIOD OF ADJUSTMENT.** Love, hate, comedy, tragedy, joy, sorrow, passion, violence—all come alive in these four magnificent plays. (#CE1438—$2.95)

- [ ] **THREE BY TENNESSEE WILLIAMS: SWEET BIRD OF YOUTH, THE ROSE TATTOO AND THE NIGHT OF THE IGUANA.** Three of the Pulitzer Prize-winning author's most brilliant plays. (#CE1328—$2.50)

- [ ] **CLASSIC SCENES edited and translated by Jonathan Price.** In this single volume are 48 outstanding examples of playwriting genius—all of them enticing invitations to both amateur and professional performers. Each scene is accompanied by commentary that sets the scene in historical perspective, places it within the body of the play, and explores the key aspects involved in bringing the characters and actors vividly alive. (#ME1779—$2.75)

*Not available in Canada